THE IDEA OF RAJASTHAN

EXPLORATIONS IN REGIONAL IDENTITY

Vol. I
CONSTRUCTIONS

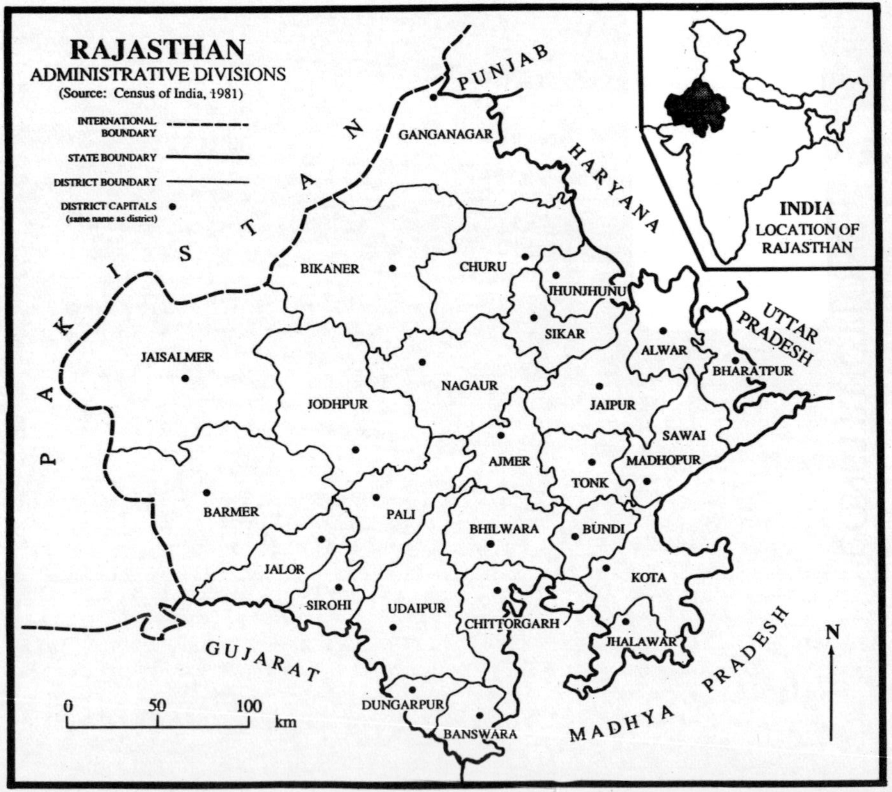
RAJASTHAN
ADMINISTRATIVE DIVISIONS
(Source: Census of India, 1981)
INTERNATIONAL BOUNDARY
STATE BOUNDARY
DISTRICT BOUNDARY
DISTRICT CAPITALS (same name as district)
PAKISTAN
PUNJAB
HARYANA
UTTAR PRADESH
MADHYA PRADESH
GUJARAT
GANGANAGAR
BIKANER
CHURU
JHUNJHUNU
SIKAR
ALWAR
BHARATPUR
JAISALMER
NAGAUR
JAIPUR
JODHPUR
SAWAI MADHOPUR
AJMER
TONK
BARMER
PALI
BHILWARA
BUNDI
JALOR
KOTA
SIROHI
UDAIPUR
CHITTORGARH
JHALAWAR
DUNGARPUR
BANSWARA
0 50 100 km
N
INDIA
LOCATION OF RAJASTHAN

THE IDEA OF RAJASTHAN

Explorations in Regional Identity

Volume I: CONSTRUCTIONS

Edited by

KARINE SCHOMER
JOAN L. ERDMAN
DERYCK O. LODRICK
LLOYD I. RUDOLPH

MANOHAR
American Institute of Indian Studies
2001

First published 1994
Paperback edition 2001

ISBN 81-7304-304-3

Published by
Ajay Kumar Jain for
Manohar Publishers & Distributors
4753/23 Ansari Road, Daryaganj
New Delhi 110 002

Printed at
Rajkamal Electric Press
B 35/9 G T Karnal Road Indl Area
Delhi 110 033

To the People of Rajasthan

CONTENTS

ART AS COMMUNICATION

INTRODUCTION

Despite the rapidly spreading cosmopolitanism of the late twentieth century, regional identities are assuming increased significance in many parts of the world, and the study of regions is becoming more, not less, important. In India, with its exceptional cultural diversity and range of physical environments, regional traditions and the implications of strong regional identities are central issues and contemporary concerns. Over the past thirty years, scholarship on India has shown a marked shift away from the all-India perspectives of classical Indology, with their emphasis on Sanskrit texts and Brahmanical culture. Historical studies have moved away from the external perspectives of the British Raj and the Mughal Empire. At the same time, anthropological study has turned from a focus on isolated "little communities" such as villages, castes and tribes to the examination of supra-local patterns and networks. Conceptualizations of Indic civilization as a whole increasingly stress the significance of regional and areal components, as evidenced by Maureen L.P. Patterson's unique bibliographic synthesis, *South Asian Civilizations* (1981), which is organized as a complex architectonic scheme of geo-cultural areas, cultural-linguistic regions, and sub-regional areal units.

Both Indian and non-Indian scholars have turned their attention to regions of the subcontinent. The focus of their research, however, has been largely on specific topics in the humanities and social sciences rather than on questions of regional distinctiveness and regional identity. On the other hand, scholarship addressing questions of regions and regionalism, which has been mostly in the social sciences, has been primarily concerned with definitions, typologies, models, problems of region versus center in the modern nation-state, and broad theoretical formulations about regional patterns in Indic civilization.

Among the early landmark works on the issue of regions are Selig Harrison's *India: The Most Dangerous Decades* (1962), which saw India's regional diversity as a threat to national unity, and Robert S.

Crane's *Regions and Regionalism in South Asian Studies* (1967). An edited volume, the latter work grew out of a symposium held at Duke University to examine methodological questions in the study of regions and the role of regions in South Asian political, social and economic affairs. More recent works include the history symposium *Region and Realm in Traditional India* (1977) edited by Richard G. Fox, geographer David E. Sopher's *An Exploration of India* (1982), a comparative work on South and Southeast Asia by scholars in Holland entitled *Focus on the Region in Asia* (1982), Akhtar Majeed's *Regionalism: Developmental Tensions in India* (1984), and *Region and Nation in India* (1985), edited by Paul Wallace.

We acknowledge these works for the concerns they have raised, their clear definitions of concepts, and their subcontinental, comparative and disciplinary perspectives on the subject of Indian regions. Our aim, however, is not so much to enter and further the theoretical debate about regions as parts of a whole, but to consider in depth a particular regional identity. This collection thus bears closer kinship to works such as *The Cult of Jagannath and the Regional Tradition of Orissa* (1978) or the older work on Maharashtra by G.A. Deleury, *The Cult of Vithoba* (1960), both interdisciplinary studies of the role of cults and pilgrimage centers in the formation of particular regional cultures of India.

Every human collectivity has a sense of place, a subjective connection to its natural and man-made environment, with its physical features, institutional and social patterns, historical traditions and cultural landscapes. While regions are grounded in objective realities, they are also subjective constructs, for both outsiders and insiders. To explore a regional identity is thus to explore an idea. At the heart of our approach is such an exploration, the attempt to discover and understand more deeply what is distinctive about the region of northwestern India known as Rajasthan.

Accordingly, while the writers here consider theoretical issues in their own disciplines, each paper also addresses the subject of Rajasthan's regional identity. Thus the work as a whole provides a composite, interdisciplinary, multi-faceted picture of Rajasthan. Not intended to be all-inclusive, its aim is to stimulate further thinking about this particular region's identity. Our theoretical contribution is to suggest that the study of regions is incomplete if it does not go beyond the analysis of generic variables determined by *a priori* definitions. To understand a regional identity in all its uniqueness requires informed and sensitive insight into the complex and subtle characteristics of the particular geographical area, its inhabitants, and the cultures they have created. Environmental influences and limitations, remembered histories, language, literary styles, cultural traditions, common institutions, mutually recognized social structures, shared symbols – all need to be carefully considered, in their interrelations, with plural perspectives, and in comparison with other regions.

The Idea of Rajasthan originated on a beautiful afternoon in November 1981, when a group of seventeen scholars attending the West Coast regional meetings of the Association for Asian Studies convened in Karine Schomer's home at 1 My Way, high above Berkeley, California. Through large picture windows, we could see the dry hills on the far side of Wildcat Canyon, a landscape uncannily reminiscent of the hills of Rajasthan. Our purpose was to discuss current directions in research on Rajathan, to test interest in developing a network of scholars working on the region, and to enlist participation in a project to explore the nature of Rajasthan's regional identity. We represented a number of disciplines – anthropology, art history, ethnomusicology, folklore, geography, history, language studies, literature, and political science. Though we all shared an interest in Rajasthan, many of us were strangers to one another. None imagined then that this gathering would result in a decade of scholarly collaboration and the present two-volume work.

At that time, there were individual scholars working on Rajasthan in several American universities, especially the University of Chicago, but a number of special initiatives were taking place at the University of California at Berkeley. Komal Kothari, Director of the Rajasthan Institute of Folklore (Rupayan Sansthan) had spent a semester on the campus as a Fulbright Scholar-in-Residence. In collaboration with Leela Mathur of the Rajasthan Association of North America, Karine Schomer had initiated Rajasthani language instruction in the Department of South and Southeast Asian Studies. Faculty members and graduate students in other disciplines were turning their attention towards Rajasthan as well. Karine Schomer had just been awarded a three-year grant from the U.S. Department of Education to produce a language primer for the major Rajasthani dialects and an edited volume of essays on Rajasthan. Just before our meeting several of us had presented a panel entitled "Performing Rajasthan's Culture," which embodied in embryonic form the project we were gathering to discuss.

It was the recognition of Rajasthan as a distinctive cultural region of India that had inspired our meeting. Deeply involved with our own research, we had been working in relative isolation, generally unconnected to the work of scholars outside our particular disciplines. We therefore lacked a sense of our scholarship's relevance to an overall understanding of Rajasthan. As we discussed the project, a consensus emerged that a descriptive survey or commissioned essays on particular topics was not our goal. Instead, we would seek to provide a focus and a broader context for current research by asking scholars to consider what their work could contribute to the exploration of Rajasthan's distinctive regional identity. Contributions would be sought from a wide spectrum of disciplines, ranging from sciences concerned with the natural environment to the humanities and social sciences. Each scholar would be asked to work from individual research towards statements about Rajasthan as a region and comparative issues raised by the study of Rajasthan. We envisioned a work that would explore facets of Rajasthan's distinctive regional identity, place specialized research within a broader context of inquiry, and provide a model for the interdisciplinary study of regions.

The story of *The Idea of Rajasthan* is inseparable from that of the scholarly community of which it is a product and which it helped create. At our 1981 gathering, we had agreed on the need for networking. We decided to revive a scholarly association started by Lloyd and Susanne Rudolph at the University of Chicago in the late 1960s, which had been dormant for many years. At the 1982 Association for Asian Studies (AAS) meetings in Chicago, the Rajasthan Studies Group-AAS was formally constituted, and an executive committee elected. Plans were laid for gathering and disseminating information, encouraging scholarly contacts, promoting research, and formulating panels and seminars.

In 1983, Joan Erdman and Ann Gold conducted a survey and prepared a report entitled "Current Directions in Rajasthan Studies." In the same year, a panel entitled "Rajasthani Regionalism: Natural and Cultural Signs of Distinctiveness" was presented at the Association for Asian Studies meetings in San Francisco. Papers from this session, like those of the earlier Berkeley panel, eventually found their way into *The Idea of*

Rajasthan. Other panel presentations followed, and a bibliography of recent work on Rajasthan by scholars in North America and Europe was prepared and distributed.

The Rajasthan Studies Group-AAS gradually expanded to include an international membership. Following networking efforts by the Rudolphs and Karine Schomer in India in 1983-84, the group entered into a collaborative relationship with a new Jaipur-based Rajasthan Studies Group-India, led by Prof. Satish Chandra and Dr. Rajendra Joshi. This led to our participation in two international seminars focusing on conservation of the environment and culture in Rajasthan, the first held in Jaipur in 1987, the second in Udaipur in 1991. Through these seminars and panels, collaborative work on *The Idea of Rajasthan,* and the organizational efforts of both Rajasthan Studies groups, a vital international community of scholars interested in Rajasthan has developed.

To ensure that *The Idea of Rajasthan* would benefit from breadth of vision and the advantage of multiple disciplinary critiques for each contribution, the Rajasthan Studies Group-AAS appointed a panel of four editors to oversee the project. Each editor offered particular expertise: Karine Schomer (language, literature, folklore and cultural history) as editor-in-chief, Joan Erdman (anthropology, cultural performance and cultural policy), Deryck Lodrick (geography and cultural ecology), and Lloyd Rudolph (political science and intellectual history).

In the spring of 1983, the call for contributions went out to an international list of scholars, followed over the next few years by additional solicitations as more scholars working on Rajasthan came to our attention through the expanding Rajasthan Studies Group network. Every paper received was critiqued by each editor, was discussed by the editorial panel as a whole, and became the subject of extensive scholarly dialogue with the author. As papers and comments travelled back and forth between editors and contributors, *The Idea of Rajasthan* grew from one to two volumes, at the same time developing more precisely its focus and structure.

Thus *The Idea of Rajasthan* is the product of extensive and intense scholarly exchanges over a decade. We have had ongoing dialogues about Rajasthan as a geographical entity and way of life, shaped by its physical, historical and cultural environments, their interactions, and how they have been constructed and institutionalized. With two editors in Chicago, two in the San Francisco area, and contributors dispersed over several continents, our dialogues have been conducted through letters, long-distance telephone calls and face-to-face sessions at conferences and other meetings. We often disagreed, but we remained convinced that there was wisdom in our original idea, and that, out of the diversity of our scholarship, we were forging an integrated perspective on Rajasthan and breaking new ground in the study of regions and regional identity.

Our papers, grouped into two volumes and four thematic sections, offer interrelated perspectives on various aspects of Rajasthan's regional identity. The volume subtitled *Constructions* looks at how Rajasthanis and outsiders have created and defined Rajasthan, and examines the processes through which a Rajasthani regional identity has evolved and is performed. The volume subtitled *Institutions* analyzes enduring structures, adaptations, arrangements, and ways of life and thought that have characterized and shaped the lives of Rajasthanis in their region. The numbering of the volumes does not indicate a logical sequence but a complementarity.

"Identity as Process" opens the *Constructions* volume with a group of papers which consider how a sense of regional identity is created and reinforced. In the opening paper by Deryck Lodrick, definitions of Rajasthan as a bounded geographical area by outside observers and administrative authorities are contrasted with subjective awareness of regional and sub-regional identities. Taking the perspective from within Rajasthan, Joan Erdman shows how a modern multi-media production, "*Dhartī Dhorāṅ Rī*" (Land of Shifting Sands), seeks to develop a regional identity for all Rajasthanis through a program incorporating the stories and symbols of sub-regions and distinctive communities into a pluralistic whole.

The reinforcement of regional identity through shared religious performance is the subject of Ann Gold's study, which shows that Rajasthanis make clear distinctions between the quality of pilgrimage to regional shrines and pilgrimage to pan-Indian sacred places. The role of cultural performances in encapsulating and enacting a regional way of life is examined in Karine Schomer's paper on the Rajput wedding custom of riddling the bridegroom and the content of Rajasthani riddle repertoires.

The evidence historical monuments provide about the formation of a Rajasthani regional identity is considered by Michael Meister. Focusing on the evolution of architectural styles under the patronage of Rajput rulers, he sees an ongoing alternation between sub-regional differentiation and regional unification which has led to a gradual integration of styles. Finally, on the basis of archaeological site analysis, Henri-Paul Francfort shows that ancient Ḥarappan civilization did not penetrate the natural frontiers separating the arid and mountainous area of present-day Rajasthan from the surrounding alluvial plains, thus suggesting that Rajasthan's regional distinctiveness has roots in prehistory.

How the arts represent and reflect regional cultural identity is addressed in the section on "Art as Communication." Rajasthan's musical traditions are deeply embedded in the society through hereditary patronage arrangements. Komal Kothari reports on the Manganiyars of western Rajasthan, folk professionals who perform at life-cycle ceremonies of their village patrons and carry forward a sophisticated musical tradition that differs significantly from the classical "Hindustani" music patronized by the more cosmopolitan royal courts. The musical tradition associated with temples in the regional cult center of Nathdvara is the subject of Anne-Marie Gaston's paper. Showing that the music derives its meaning and continued appeal from the ritual context, she argues that without this context, it could not survive.

Artistic representations reveal the Rajasthani predilection for archetypes and timeless ideals. The art and role of the now vanishing street performers known as *bahurūpiyās,* whose satirical portrayals of familiar castes, occupations and character types hold up a mirror to the society, is the focus of John Emigh's contribution. In the court tradition of royal portraiture, Vishakha Desai finds a persistent preference for timeless, iconographic representation of idealized kingship rather than depiction of the observed physiognomy of individual rulers. The final paper of the *Constructions* volume, by William Noble and Ad Ram Sankhyan, seeks to interpret the religious meaning, symbolism and sub-regional stylistic variation of the *satī* memorials that are such a poignant part of the visual landscape of Rajasthan.

The *Institutions* volume opens with a section on "Locales and Social Structures," which examines grass-roots economic, social and political adaptations to Rajasthan's limited-resource environment and the legacy of its traditional feudal polity. The adaptive strategies employed by villagers in western Rajasthan to survive the severe droughts endemic to the region, and the dynamics of a Rajasthani village under drought conditions, are the subject of Carol Henderson's paper. Thomas Rosin looks at long-term adaptive trends among rural peoples in the Aravalli hills of central Rajasthan, analyzing both local agrarian management strategies and the historical significance of migration. Demographic and ethnographic data are correlated with ecology by Pauline Kolenda to explain the high proportion of joint-family households found in Rajasthan, particularly in the state's semi-arid zone. In the last paper of this section, James Björkman and the late Het Ram Chaturvedi trace the history of Rajasthan's experiment with local self-government after India's independence. Their thesis is that it succeeded initially because the old princely order had been discredited, but was gradually undermined by competing interests of state-level politicians and administrative agencies.

"Power and Hegemony" examines dimensions of the Rajputs' historic dominance in the area which is now Rajasthan. The political, economic and social processes whereby Rajputs rose to prominence in the early medieval period, and the stages by which their distinctive clan structure evolved are examined by B.D. Chattopadhyaya. Using local primary sources, Norman Ziegler traces the emergence of Rajput state systems in the 15th and early 16th centuries, and demonstrates a close connection between increased availability and use of horses, campaigns of conquest, and the evolution of centralized rule. Mughal-Rajput marriage alliances, still a controversial subject, are considered by Frances Taft, who analyzes their origins, their recently documented extensiveness, and their political role as seen from both Mughal and Rajput perspectives.

The influence of Rajput ideals and institutions on religion and the arts is the subject of the last two papers of the *Institutions* volume. The history and institutional structures of a regional sect, the Dadu-*panth,* are shown by Daniel Gold to have been significantly shaped by Rajput values and the environment of Jaipur court patronage. Finally, Edward Haynes considers the traditional expectation that Rajput rulers should be patrons of the arts, and examines the use of arts patronage by the rulers of Alwar state to enhance their status and legitimacy.

Our papers thus include topics ranging from prehistory to the present, and examine issues as varied as ecological adaptation, cultural continuity and political legitimacy. Individually and in mutually reinforcing ways, they touch upon many interweaving themes of Rajasthani life. Ultimately, however, they are concerned with a common underlying purpose: exploring the multiple dimensions of Rajsthan's enduring regional identity. While establishing certain fundamental characteristics of the region as both objective realities and subjective constructs, they raise as many questions as they answer – not only for Rajasthan, but for the comparative study of regions and regional identity as well.

ACKNOWLEDGEMENTS

As a long project comes to fruition, there is a sense of accomplishment, but also a sense of loss. During its ten-year gestation period, *The Idea of Rajasthan* sustained strong scholarly interaction over time and across continents, in which all involved gained susbtantial breadth and depth in their understanding of Rajasthan and of regions in general. Because the interaction was so strong, and editorial involvement with each contribution so thoroughgoing, shared perspectives have permeated the final product and given it a unity uncommon in collections of scholarly papers. Without this mode of engaged collegiality, the outcome would have been very different.

The position of editor-in-chief suggests a sense of grand orchestration, but conceals the reality of large quantities of midnight oil and strong tea, tightrope diplomacy, and the burden of ultimate responsibility for the most minute of details. The list of people who have made this project possible is long. My first thanks go to my indefatigable co-editors, who persisted with me in this time-consuming labor of love. Without Lloyd Rudolph's breadth of knowledge and keen critical insights, Joan Erdman's sharp mind for conceptual constructs, Deryck Lodrick's meticulous scholarly precision, and the painstaking care each of them expended on every contribution submitted, the editorial task would have been overwhelming. They join me in thanking the contributors, whose patience with the constantly evolving editorial vision and willingness to accept our demanding requirements represents collegial forbearance at its best. We are also grateful for the continued interest and support of the Rajasthan Studies Group-AAS membership as a whole, whose repeated question, "When will the book come out?" urged us to presevere.

We acknowlege with appreciation the financial support of the U.S. Department of Education's International Research and Studies Program, whose initial grant made possible the launching of the project. Our thanks go to the University of California's

Center for South and Southeast Asia Studies, which administered the grant. We are grateful to the American Institute of Indian Studies for inclusion of this work in their publications series. Our publishers, patient in working with our complex production needs and unexpected delays, deserve our thanks as well. Permission to use illustrations was generously granted by the National Museum (New Delhi), the National Gallery of Victoria (Melbourne), the American Institute of Indian Studies Centre for Art and Archeaology (Varanasi), the Boston Museum of Fine Arts, the Brooklyn Museum, and the private collections of Catherine and Ralph Benkaim, Guru Purushottam Das, and Shri Krishna Deva. With a few exceptions, the supporting maps were conceptualized and developed by Deryck Lodrick, and produced by Shelby Hall, Molly Block and Mary Cunha. Clerical and logistical support was ably provided by Maria Firmacion.

Among the many scholars whose encouragement, interest and advice sustained our collective effort are Professors N. Gerald Barrier, Frank F. Conlon, John S. Hawley, Maureen L.P. Patterson, Joseph E. Schwartzberg, and Joanna G. Williams in the United States, and our Indian colleagues Professor Satish Chandra, Dr. Rajendra Joshi, and Padmashri Komal Kothari. The list of all the other people each editor and contributor would like to acknowledge individually is far too long to include here. My own most heartfelt thanks go to my husband, photographer-writer Raphael Shevelev, who not only gave me steady personal and intellectual support in the final years of the project, but became passionately involved in the exploration of Rajasthan's distinctive visual identity.

KARINE SCHOMER

El Cerrito, California
December 10, 1992

NOTE ON TRANSLITERATION

The scheme of transliteration followed in this work is the standard system internationally used for Indic and Perso-Arabic languages, with a few modifications designed to make the text less forbidding to non-specialists and to reflect Hindi and Rajasthani pronunciation. To bring the transliteration closer to pronunciation, the palatal consonant *c* and its aspirate *ch* are rendered, respectively, as *ch* and *chh*. A nasal before a consonant (*anusvara*) is rendered by *n* for all classes of consonants except the retroflexes (*ṭ*, *ṭh*, *ḍ*, *ḍh*) and the labials (*p*, *ph*, *b*, *bh*); before these, it is represented by *ṇ* and *m*, respectively. Nazalization of vowels is rendered by *ṅ*. In transliterating Hindi and Rajasthani words, latitude has been exercised in omitting the inherent *a* in both word-final and medial syllables. A few words (e.g. *purdah, zenana*) appear in their commonly accepted transliteration. Finally, when italicized words embedded in the English text are pluralized, the English plural *s* is also italicized. All proper names appearing as part of the English text are given in their generally accepted anglicized form, as are Indian words that have come into general English usage (e.g., raja, guru). Only italicized words in Indian languages are formally transliterated.

IDENTITY AS PROCESS

RAJASTHAN AS A REGION: MYTH OR REALITY?

DERYCK O. LODRICK

The country of the Rajputs (Rajputana), the land of kings (Rajwara, Raethana), the region of death (Marusthali, Marwar) – such names have all been used to refer to the arid and semi-arid areas of northwestern India in which the state of Rajasthan is situated. For many, Rajasthan is a land of sweeping desert vistas and brilliant sunsets, colorful villagers, Rajput chivalry and tawny hills crowned by forts and battlements. Such perceptions, however, are mental images of an often distant land that seek the essence of place in a few fleeting cameos. In reality, these images are far from complete and highly selective. The desert provides an extremely hostile environment for its inhabitants, the sunsets are often appreciated less for their aesthetic value than for the relief they afford from the blistering heat of the day, and Rajputs no longer rule in Rajasthan. Yet, in a sense, this highly romanticized view of Rajasthan contains more than a kernel of truth. The desert evokes a response to the environment that is reflected in a distinctive human ecology, and multi-hued turbans and brightly colored clothes are an integral part of Rajasthan's rural landscape. The persistent identification of Rajasthan with Rajputs, moreover, bears eloquent testimony to the historical importance of the Rajput presence in this part of India.

The desert, the dress of the people, and the Rajput clans have not only helped create an image of Rajasthan, they are also elements of a specific environmental setting, cultural tradition and social structure that have all played a significant role in shaping the character of modern Rajasthan. This paper seeks to examine whether these elements, along with other aspects of land, life and people in the area, are pervasive enough and powerful enough to differentiate Rajasthan from neighboring areas of the Indian subcontinent, or whether they serve only to perpetuate a myth with little basis in reality. Is Rajasthan a region, possessed of unique and distinctive qualities, or is it merely an administrative convenience – territory outlined on a map, enclosed by boundary lines, and designated by a suggestive label? Furthermore, if Rajasthan *is* held to be a region, what is the basis of its recognition as such? Is Rajasthan's distinctiveness reflected in a sense of regional identity recognized and shared by the state's inhabitants? If so, what are the implications of this in a country like India, in which strong commitment to a regional identity may find expression in regionalism and even, in extreme cases, in separatism?

These questions are examined in the following pages, although definitive answers to many of them extend far beyond the scope of this study. The paper first reviews some theoretical aspects of the regional concept, considers ways in which Rajasthan has been viewed as a region, and finally evaluates the nature and strength of the regional character of Rajasthan itself. By examining Rajasthan within the conceptual framework of the region, this paper sets out a foundation from which more general questions of regional identity and regionalism in Rajasthan might be explored.

The Concept of the Region

Few concepts in the social sciences have received as much attention yet at the same time generated so little consensus as that of the region. For some scholars, *a priori* and self-evident regions simply exist, and debate on the subject is meaningless (Fleming 1973:206*n*5). Others, by contrast, see the region as a myth, embodying a concept so vague and used in so many different contexts as to have little value. Jacqueline Beaujeu-Garnier, for example, after examining over 40 definitions of the region collected by Odum and Moore (1938), was able to identify only one point of unanimity – that of the region as a spatial unit distinct from the space that surrounds it. Beyond this, she concludes "It [the region] means all things to all men" (1976:79, 81).

Despite this view, other points of consensus emerge from the extensive literature in the social sciences devoted to the concept of the region. Geographers, for example, hold that the region "is not an object, either self-determined or nature-given. It is an intellectual concept, an entity for the purpose of thought created by the selection of certain features that are relevant to an areal interest or problem" (Whittlesey 1954:30).[1] This view of the region as a mental construct, an intellectual device for the analysis of phenomena on the earth's surface, is responsible for much of the confusion that surrounds the concept itself. It leads, in particular, to formulation of several distinct typologies of region. The situation becomes even more complicated, because categories of regions generated by different typologies are not mutually exclusive. Thus, although each typology is based on its own criteria and develops a unique system of regional classification, typologies may overlap, creating identical regions on disparate conceptual bases, and may even influence each other's development.

Geographers commonly recognize that, in terms of the basis for their recognition, all regions may be classified as *instituted, denoted*, or *naively given. Instituted* regions are "instituted by human agency as distinctive and discrete units limiting the areal extent of operation of certain functions" (Hartshorne 1965:619), and are generally administrative in nature. *Denoted* regions are created primarily for the purpose of organizing and analyzing information, while the *naively given* region is "recognized as a meaningful territorial entity by the people who live there and/or by other people to whom it is of some concern" (Schwartzberg 1967:89-90). These same categories of regions, however, can be arrayed in a different manner. Regions such as instituted regions, over which there can be little disagreement, have been labeled *objective*, whereas denoted and naively given regions, which have their origins in people's perceptions, in their mental ordering of the world around them, may be considered *subjective*.[2] Numerous other typologies of varying value have been developed by scholars for the purpose of studying regions.[3]

All the categories of region noted above share certain attributes (e.g. areal extent, defining criteria, boundaries), yet they also encompass a distinction that is crucial to understanding the regional character of Rajasthan. The perspective from which some regions are viewed is fundamentally different from that of others. Both instituted and denoted regions, for example, are conscious creations, designed for a particular purpose at a particular point in time, and subsequently proferred to the world as *de facto* regions. Thus the designation of much of the area of modern Rajasthan as a *subah* by the Mughals in 1594, or the grouping of princely states in the same area into the Rajputana Agency by the British over two centuries later, imposed instituted regions on the space of northwestern India. *Subah* and Agency were created with the stroke of the pen, and the area's inhabitants as well as the world at large were presented with a region. Similarly, scholarly studies have generated conceptions of Rajasthan as a denoted region, as in the case of Grierson's Rajasthani language area (1908:1) or Spate's view of Rajasthan as a refuge area (1954:149). Whether or not one accepts the underlying rationale of such efforts, the end result is still regions which are the products of the minds of their creators, superimposed on the land and peoples of northwestern India.

Denoted regions most certainly, and often instituted regions as well, are invariably perceived and formally defined by observers looking on from the *outside*. Perceptually, when boundaries are drawn around these regions, the enclosed segment of space is seen as external to the self; boundaries are not drawn with oneself inside them. In this sense, even though the reasons for doing so might be perfectly acceptable, both the idea of a region and its delineation are *imposed* on a particular geographic area and its inhabitants. Such regions might be termed "observed" in that they involve an external perspective, are often purpose-oriented, and find general acceptance for their defining criteria.

The naively given region embodies a totally different perspective. It lacks the underlying purpose of instituted and denoted regions, and involves little conscious definition by those who recognize it. As subjective space, the naively given region is perceived space, but even here an important distinction must be drawn. To Europeans in classical times, for example, India was a distant land along and beyond the Indus, a part of the world seen from afar and familiar essentially on a locational basis (Schwartzberg 1967:90). Of far greater significance to this discussion, however, is what is termed here the "experienced" region, the naively given region that is rooted in people's perceptions of the space they occupy. The experienced region involves an internal perspective, and is based on an implicit consensus among the inhabitants of a particular area of the world as to its existence. This acceptance might not be universal and even the participants themselves might be hard put to isolate precisely the distinctive character of their region, yet this in no way detracts from the reality of the region's existence. In a sense, the experienced region represents a people's shared reaction to their particular segment of space, or specific features associated with that space, that leads to an awareness of its distinctiveness.

The observed/experienced conceptualization outlined here departs from other typologies of region, but it nonetheless has relevance for understanding two further concepts associated with the region. Observed regions are usually defined by criteria that are non-specific, i.e. they have a wide distribution over the earth's surface. Much of Rajasthan is a desert, for example, but deserts defined by the same climatic parameters exist in other parts of the world as well. Consequently, the Rajasthan desert, when defined by objective criteria (even though these might be subjectively determined), forms part of a broader system of regions all sharing a common basis of identification. The process of conceptualizing such regional systems, what geographers term "regionalization," involves the same problems faced in conceptualizing and delineating individual regions, and in effect extends the concept of the region over large areas of the earth. Regionalization is thus a logical adjunct to the concept of the region, and no consideration of a region that goes beyond mere description would be complete without some reference to it.

Experienced regions, however, are defined according to criteria that are specific in place and time. Deserts exist elsewhere, but in no other region of the world does precisely the same mix of peoples live in quite the same environment, subject to the same geographical and historical relationships, as in Rajasthan. From this point of view Rajasthan is unique, and so too are its inhabitants' perceptions of Rajasthan as a region. This conception of Rajasthan is determined by insiders, by people who experience and share in the characteristics of a unique segment of space, and embodies an element of participation that is completely lacking from all other types of regions. Such involvement may lead to an awareness of a distinctive regional identity. Sometimes the nature and strength of ties between the region and its inhabitants develop to the point where they find expression in social or political action. It is thus the experienced region that underlies both the concept and phenomenon of regionalism, corollaries of the regional concept that are of great concern not only to academic social scientists but also to politicians, planners, and administrators who often face the task of welding diverse regional entities into some sort of viable, functioning whole.[4]

Observed and experienced regions, or, for that matter, any other conceptualization of region, are indeed neither "self-determined or nature-given." As intellectual constructs, they represent abstractions of the same reality from differing points of view. They involve few absolutes, may differ considerably in their nature, and vary in relative importance or even in their very existence over time. They are, nonetheless, useful heuristic devices for examining the ways in which, and the processes through which, Rajasthan has come to be seen as a region.

Rajasthan as Political Space

Many features commonly identified with Rajasthan today are present over more extensive areas of northern and western India. For example, although it was in Rajasthan that Rajputs first appeared on the Indian scene during the early medieval period (the Gurjaras[5] were present there by the end of the 6th century A.D.),[6] they rapidly extended their political control over much of India in the following centuries. Under Bhoja I (836-885), the empire of the Gurjara-Pratihara Rajputs extended from Sind to the lower Ganges valley, and from the Himalayan foothills to the Narmada River. Although rival clans such as the Chauhans, Pariharas and Guhilas rose to prominence in Rajasthan following the disintegration of the Gurjara-Pratihara empire around the middle of the 10th century, major centers of Rajput power continued to exist throughout northern India. The Solanki clan ruled much of Gujarat, for instance, while the Paramaras held sway in Malwa and the Chandellas controlled Bundelkhand. Even today, in terms of both absolute numbers of Rajputs as well as of percentages of Rajputs in the population, Rajasthan is outranked by several states in northern India.[7] Yet it is Rajasthan that is consistently identified with Rajputs and the Rajput ethos.

One of the reasons for this lies in early conceptions of Rajasthan as a region and the role of Rajputs in these conceptions. In its areal extent, modern Rajasthan coincides closely with space first conceived of as a region and formally defined as such during the 16th century. The recognition accorded at this point in time suggests the involvement of specific historical forces in bringing Rajasthan's regional character to the fore. During the 16th century, such forces clearly included the existence of Rajput states in northwestern India, the Muslim presence in the Indian subcontinent, and the nature of Rajput relations with the central Mughal power.

By the 12th century, a belt of Rajput kingdoms, many of them built on the ruins of the older Gurjara-Pratihara empire, stretched across India from the Arabian Sea to the central Ganges valley. There was little to distinguish the Rajput states of what is now Rajasthan from any of the other Rajput states of northern India. Events at the end of the 12th century, however, drastically altered this situation. The Muslim conquest of India followed a classic pattern: penetration of the Punjab plains, a critical battle for the control of Delhi fought to the west of the Delhi gap (in this case, the second battle of Tarain in 1192), and subsequent expansion southeast along the Ganges valley and southwestwards to the Gujarat ports. Muhammad Ghuri's defeat of the Rajputs under Prithviraj Chauhan at Tarain firmly established Muslim power in the heartland of India, but it also had more immediate consequences for the Rajput states of northern India. Chauhan power came to an end in Rajasthan, the subsequent destruction of the Rajput kingdoms of the Ganges plains virtually eliminated the Rajput political presence from this area and, as Muslim forces moved south and west through Malwa along the traditional route to Gujarat, they encircled the Rajput states in the northwest (Banerjee 1983:68-72).

A pattern had thus been set by the early decades of the 13th century. The lands of the conquered Chauhans had been incorporated into the Delhi Sultanate, and from this base Qutub-ud-din-Aibak, who succeeded Muhammad Ghuri in 1206, made repeated but unsuccessful attempts to subdue the Rajput clans of Rajasthan (Thapar 1966:238). For some four centuries, in addition to the internecine conflicts within Rajasthan that pitted Rajput princes against each other, a series of inconclusive campaigns were fought between the rulers in Delhi and the Rajputs in Rajasthan. The Rajputs, using guerrilla tactics, harassed the imperial forces from their strongholds in the hills, but never united to inflict a major defeat on them. On the other hand, the central power in Delhi was never able to complete the military subjugation of the Rajput states of Rajasthan, especially those in the desert wastes of the Thar or in the extreme south. Marwar and Mewar, for example, not only were able to preserve their independence, but at times posed a threat to Delhi itself.[8] The popular conception of the Rajput as a chivalrous warrior, defending honor and religion against the Muslim invader in the hills and deserts of Rajasthan is drawn from this period of Indian history.

Armed resistance, however, is only one facet of the complex relations that were evolving between the Rajput clans of Rajasthan and the ruling powers in North India during this time. What the Turks, Afghans and early Mughals failed to bring about by force was, to a large extent, achieved by Akbar through a combination of military action and diplomacy. Mughal troops still faced Rajputs in the field, as at Chittor and Ranthambore in 1568-69, but by 1570 Akbar had succeeded in enlisting many of the prominent Rajput chiefs into his service, often cementing alliances through marriages with ruling Rajput houses. Indeed, much of the success and stability of the Mughal empire under Akbar and his successors depended on Rajput support, and Rajputs served with distinction as military leaders, provincial governors and imperial advisors. Man Singh of Amber, for example, held appointments as governor of Kabul and Bihar, and was responsible for extending Mughal power over much of eastern India. He even led the imperial army that defeated Rana Pratap Singh of Mewar at the battle of Haldighati in 1576 (Srivastava 1962:206-211, 337ff.). Moreover, if the Mughals benefited from Rajput support, Rajputs gained from their involvement with the Mughals. Imperial service enabled individual Rajput rulers, such as Man Singh of Amber and Jaswant Singh of Marwar, to strengthen their internal power base against potential clan rivals and to extend their state's influence at the expense of other Rajput states.

Cooperation with the Mughals, therefore, is as much a part of Rajput history as opposition to Mughal rule. This inability to unite against a common external threat underscores the lack of any sense of political cohesiveness amongst the Rajputs at the time. The most significant element in the Rajput political system was the clan, and clan loyalties far outweighed concerns for caste interests (Hallissey 1977:10-13). Thus, despite the distinctiveness of their political and military systems, despite a common cultural heritage and the sense of broader community inherent in social customs such as clan exogamy and related marriage ties, the Rajput states of Rajasthan remained an assemblage of individual, often warring kingdoms, each pursuing its own interests, and each displaying varying degrees of hostility or dependence in its relations with the central power.

Nonetheless, during this period, i.e. from the 13th to the 16th centuries, the fluctuating and often blurred outlines of Rajasthan as discrete political space occasionally came into focus. There existed a core of Rajput states in Rajasthan, protected by the desert to the west and hemmed in by Muslim-ruled states on the north, east and south, that kept their independence for several centuries after Rajput kingdoms elsewhere had fallen. During 400 years of resistance to, and accommodation with, expansionist alien powers at the center, the Rajput states of Rajasthan remained bearers and guardians of cultural traditions and a way of life that had been evolving since the 7th and 8th centuries. Even after their integration into the Mughal empire by Akbar toward the close of the 16th century, these states managed to maintain a discrete, albeit subordinate, political existence.[9] In doing so, they preserved much of their Rajput heritage, elements of which survived relatively unaltered until the middle of the 20th century.

If the Rajput states in the area shared a common history and culture, it was the Mughals who first drew a boundary around the region approximating the modern state of Rajasthan. Administratively, the Mughal empire was divided into 12 (later 15) provinces or *subahs*, and in 1594 the Rajput states newly subdued by Akbar were grouped together to form the *subah* of Ajmer. Although it is doubtful that the Rajputs or any other inhabitants of the area at that time shared any sense of belonging to a regional entity, the *subah* of Ajmer was instituted as a region, and represented the first formal delineation of Rajasthan as political space. This recognition of the region, although from an external perspective, was not merely an arbitrary decision. Stern (1977) has argued, for example, that the Rajput states of the area showed enough similarities in their internal organization, especially in terms of the role of caste and kinship in maintaining power, to be considered a coherent political unit. That the Mughal conception of Rajasthan as a region was based on cultural and historical realities is clearly seen in the persistence of the region's boundaries since the 16th century.

The *subah* of Ajmer reappeared under a different guise during the British period. Entering the subcontinent from the sea rather than along the traditional invasion routes from the northwest, the

British avoided immediate military confrontations with the Rajput states of northwestern India. However, though they remained outside direct British rule, the princely states of Rajasthan were eventually brought under British hegemony in the aftermath of the Maratha Wars. And once again, a foreign central power perceived enough similarities among these states to group them into an informal administrative unit. Many so-called States Agencies existed in western and central India, but it is no coincidence that the largest and most powerful Rajput states of western India should have been grouped under the Rajputana Agency (Vashishtha 1978: 40-41), later renamed Rajputana Province (See Map 1).

Once this separate political and administrative indentity had been established, it was perpetuated by divergence in the historical development of Rajputana and the surrounding British territories in the following centuries. Local polities, methods of administering justice, land tenure systems, caste relations – virtually all the trappings of Rajput feudal society – were preserved more or less intact in the region while much of the rest of India came under direct rule of the British colonial government. Moreover, although its survival was in part contingent on existing British conceptions of Rajputana's distinctiveness, Rajput society itself influenced later British perceptions of the region. It was the romantic picture of a noble, feudal aristocracy presented in Tod's *Annals and Antiquities of Rajasthan* (published in 1829-32) that became part of the British consciousness, and subsequently came to dominate British views of Rajputs and of Rajasthan.[10]

The boundaries of the modern state of Rajasthan approximate those of the British province of Rajputana. It was, however, by no means inevitable that the successor state to Rajputana should assume the form it did. During the integration of the princely states into an independent India, there was discussion that some, such as Kota, Dungarpur and Jhalawar, be joined with the central Indian states. In Bharatpur and Dholpur, sentiment existed for a merger with the United Provinces. Many of the Rajputana states were formed into several smaller Unions, such as the Matsya Union and the Rajasthan Union, before the creation of the state of Rajasthan (Menon 1985:250-273). This process of state formation involved many of the same forces at play during Mughal and British times, e.g. power relations between individual Rajput states and the center, rivalry between states, and questions of precedence among

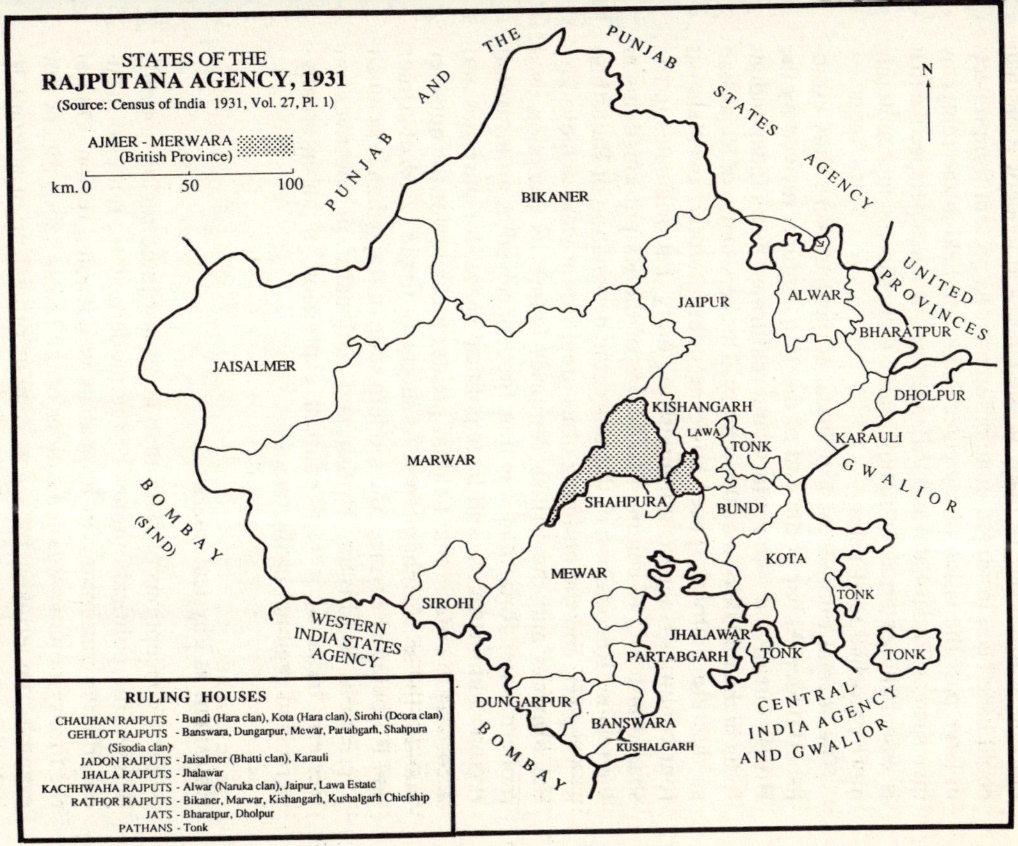

Map 1: **States of the Rajputana Agency, 1931**

the various rulers of the Rajput states.[11] As in earlier times, the outcome was but one of many possibilities, and modern Rajasthan could have been instituted quite differently. Its present form reflects in large part the vision of a greater Rajasthan held at the center by men such as Sardar Patel and V.P. Menon – again, a perspective that is essentially external in nature – and their success in countering more parochial tendencies.

The formal outlines of a political Rajasthan were thus established under Akbar at the end of the 16th century, revived by the British during the 19th century, and reaffirmed by an independent India in the middle of the 20th century. This persistence of Rajasthan as discrete political space, however intermittently, over almost four centuries, suggests an underlying unity that originates in the shared history and common traditions of the Rajput kingdoms in the region. Recognition of this unity, the designation of Rajasthan as a region, and the outlining of its areal extent were achieved by the Mughals and the British centuries before its inception as a modern state. Rajasthan was thus first conceived as an instituted region, administrative and later political space, for purposes and according to criteria that held far greater meaning for the outsider than for the area's inhabitants. As successor to the *subah* of Ajmer and Rajputana Province, the modern state of Rajasthan is as much a creation of Muslim, British and nationalist perspectives on western India as it is a political expression of an internally-perceived regional distinctiveness.

Rajasthan as Physical Space

Early conceptions of Rajasthan as an instituted region not only defined the political outlines of the modern state, but also influenced later conceptions of Rajasthan as a denoted region. One of the first systematic regionalizations of the Indian subcontinent, for example, undertaken by a government official in an attempt to indentify rainfall regions, defined these regions essentially along the lines of existing administrative boundaries.[12] In this scheme, Rajputana the instituted region became Rajputana the rainfall province, a denoted region. The disadvantages of using administrative boundaries to define physical regions as well as the problems of scale inherent in provincial boundaries were recognized (H.F. Blanford 1886:9), but administrative boundaries continued to be used in various schemes of physical regions that appeared during the next several decades.

Whatever the shortcomings of these early attempts to define physical regions in India, they clearly belie the popular conception of a unity imposed on Rajasthan by a desert climate. H.F. Blanford, for example, identified 25 rainfall provinces in British India, yet only the Rajputana rainfall province was divided into an eastern and western division, roughly along the line of the Aravalli mountain system (1886: Plate I). This internal distinction was acknowledged by John Eliot in a later work that saw eastern and western Rajputana as climatic regions in their own right (India. Meteorological Department 1906:xxiv, Plate 6 Upper). Some schemes of natural divisions even placed the two halves of Rajasthan in two quite separate regions of northern India (*ibid.*, Plate 5 Lower, Plate 6 Lower).[13] Thus even regionalizations of the subcontinent undertaken at the grossest scale distinguish eastern Rajasthan from western Rasjasthan on climatic grounds, and this distinction becomes even more pronounced when other aspects of the physical environment are taken into account. From the pioneering studies of Baker (1928) and Stamp (1928) to more recent regionalizations of India that place emphasis on physical criteria (e.g. Pithawalla 1939a, 1939b, Ahmad 1941, Spate 1954, Singh 1971), one significant idea emerges: Rajasthan lacks the physical homogeneity to be considered a physical or natural region (see Map 2).

The most prominent relief feature in Rajasthan is the Aravalli Range, running northeast-southwest through the center of the state for over 600 km. For much of their length the Aravallis form a narrow belt of low, though often precipitous, parallel ridges rather than a continuous mountain system. In the north they rarely exceed a height of 1000 m and average considerably less, but in the south they increase in width, complexity, and elevation, reaching a maximum of 1,722 m at Mount Abu. Although a physical region in its own right, the Aravallis are more often seen as a boundary separating the Thar Desert from the plains and plateaus of eastern Rajasthan. Southeast from the Aravallis, low-lying plains alternate with narrow escarpments as the land rises toward the Harauti Plateau, an extension into Rajasthan of the Malwa uplands. The region is drained by the Banas and Chambal rivers, the well-

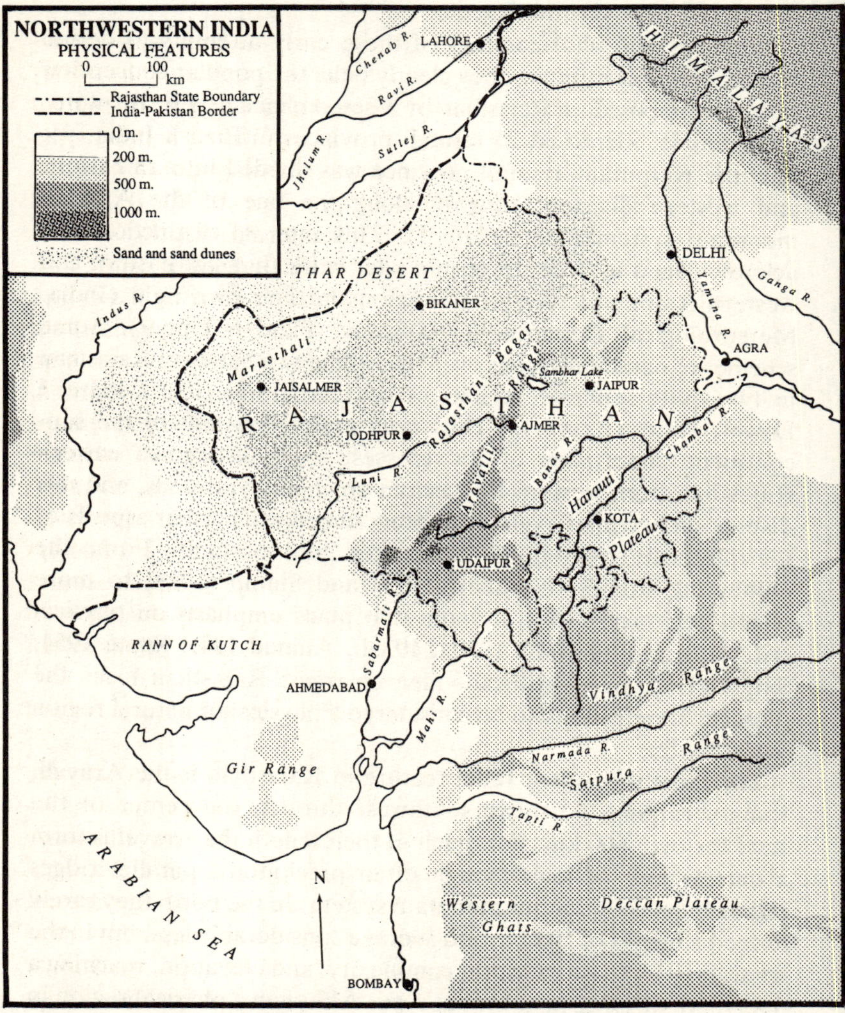

Map 2: **Northwestern India: Physical Features**

watered alluvial lowlands of the latter forming one of the more productive environmental settings in all Rajasthan.

This area starkly contrasts with the barren plains that extend north and west from the base of the Aravallis as far as the Sutlej and Indus rivers. A transitional zone, known as the Rajasthan Bagar, parallels the Aravallis from Gujarat in the south to the Punjab border in the north. Receiving slightly higher rainfall than the true desert to the west, the southern areas of the Bagar are drained by the River Luni. North of the Luni Basin is the Shekhawati tract, an area of internal drainage characterized by saline soils and salt lakes such as Lake Sambhar, and with much of its surface covered by sand dunes. The heart of the desert in Rajasthan, however, lies to the west of the Bagar.[14] Here is the true Marusthali – a region of barren wastelands, bare rocky surfaces, and sand dunes. Mean maximum temperatures over much of the area average around 45 degrees C (113 degrees F) in summer, yet the thermometer can drop below freezing in winter. Annual rainfall amounts to considerably less than 254 mm (10") through much of the region, and exhibits the high variability so typical of desert climates. With the exception of relatively dune-free areas around Jaisalmer and Bikaner, virtually the entire land surface is covered by sand, the dunes rising as high as 150 m, shaped by and often shifting before the wind.[15]

The Marusthali is but one example of the physical complexity of Rajasthan, whose environmental diversity undercuts any notion of Rajasthan as a discrete physical region. Even at a scale that picks out macro-regions over the subcontinent, Rajasthan straddles two major physiographic divisions, with their common boundary running through the center of the state along the Aravalli mountain system. Similarly, though much of the region experiences an arid and semi-arid climate, popular conceptions of Rajasthan as a desert land take little account of internal climatic variations. Rajasthan's western districts, for example, characterized by minimal rainfall and all that this implies for landforms and soil development, vegetation, and human occupance, show greater physical affinities with neighboring areas of Pakistan than with the more humid districts in the east and southeast of the state. The western boundary of Rajasthan bisects rather than circumscribes a physical region, and this is true of virtually all of the state's boundaries. If Rajasthan is to be considered a region in a sense other than an administrative one, its uniqueness must be sought in cultural and historical factors rather than in its physical environment.

Rajasthan as Cultural Space

A sense of Rajasthan as distinct cultural space existed in the minds of administrators prior to the first appearance of modern writings on Indian society and culture. Both the *subah* of Ajmer and the Rajputana Agency, for example, involved recognition – albeit by outsiders – of an underlying unity based on cultural and historical attributes. Similarly, much the same sense of cultural distinctiveness runs through Tod's classic account of Rajputana. However, although the significance of cultural variation over the Indian subcontinent was recognized during the 19th century, interest in cultural regions tended to be subordinated to a concern for physical types and racial classification (Cohn 1967:17-18). It was not until the early decades of the 20th century that the geographic outlines of Rajasthan as distinctive cultural space, identified on the basis of a systematic examination of cultural patterns, began to emerge. Even as late as 1929, Rajasthan was seen by some as merely a part of the broader belt of Rajput states that extended across central and western India (Richards 1929:25-26).

Delineation of Rajasthan as a cultural region in the early 20th century was an outgrowth of the massive accumulation of information on India's peoples and cultures undertaken by the British colonial administration. Initiated at the beginning of the 19th century by the East India Company, this effort culminated in the late 19th and early 20th centuries with publications such as Risley's *The Tribes and Castes of Bengal* (1891-92), Grierson's *Linguistic Survey of India* (1903-22), Thurston's seven-volume *Castes and Tribes of Southern India* (1909), and establishment of the decennial Census of India in 1871. The political status of the princely states, however, excluded them from the early stages of this information gathering. With the notable exception of Tod's *Annals and Antiquities of Rajasthan* (1829-32), it was not until the end of the 1870s that accounts in English of individual states in Rajputana began to appear.[16] By 1901 ethnographic data were reported in the Census of India and census operations covered all of India, including the princely states of Rajputana. Although cultural data in census returns were recorded by administrative units (the instituted region again influencing conceptions of the denoted region), availability of such information made possible the systematic analysis of cultural patterns in India. This information also determined, to a considerable extent, the criteria by which cultural regions were identified. Much impetus for information-gathering in India during the 19th and early 20th centuries came from official sources, and this effort focused on data of primary interest to colonial administrators. Thus religious, linguistic, caste, and other ethnic patterns were documented for the entire subcontinent and became the principal basis for systems of cultural regionalization, while other aspects of regional culture such as literature, art, and music received less attention.[17]

It was Grierson's work with language at the beginning of the 20th century that essentially defined Rajasthan as a cultural region. Earlier scholars had classified the languages spoken in Rajasthan as dialects belonging to Western Hindi (Kellogg 1875:68-69), which forms part of the Hindi language belt stretching from Rajasthan to Bihar and from the Himalayan foothills to the Narmada River. Grierson, on the other hand, saw the dialects of Rajasthan as distinct from Western Hindi and worthy of being considered a separate language. He used the term Rajasthani, "literally the language of Rajasthan, or Rajwara, the country of the Rajputs" (1908:1), to identify the five major dialects and their numerous variations spoken over much of Rajputana Province.

More recent linguistic scholarship, however, suggests that the Rajasthani language is not so easily defined. Although the dialects in the northwest and southeast of Rajasthan are clearly distinguishable from the neighboring Punjabi and Marathi tongues, the boundaries of the Rajasthani language are not so clear elsewhere. The westernmost dialects of Rajasthan show close affinities with Sindhi and Lahnda, in the southwest they are virtually indistinguishable from Gujarati, and to the northeast Rajasthani dialects merge imperceptibly into those of Western Hindi (Magier 1983:7-8). Even today, Rajasthani has no standing as an official language, although it is recognized by the Sahitya Akademi as a literary language (Maheshwari 1980:244).[18] Rajasthani was, in effect, declared a language by Grierson, and one wonders to what extent existing conceptions of Rajasthan as a political region played a role in this definition. Nonetheless, once established, the concept of a Rajasthani language area (See Map 3) strongly influenced subsequent conceptions of Rajasthan as a cultural region. Schwartzberg's recent classification of culture realms, culture regions, and culture areas in the Indian subcontinent, for example, isolates a Rajasthan Culture Area that appears to be defined by the area in which the Rajasthani "dialect group" is spoken (1978:100, 109).

Though language effectively defines the spatial extent of Rajasthan as a cultural region, any scheme of cultural regionalization based on individual elements of culture can provide, at best, only an incomplete picture of the culture found within its boundaries. This is a result of more than just the selective nature of the "culture" it depicts. It involves the scale and perspective inherent in the process of regionalization, the isochronic nature of such regional models, and most of all the inability of such models to show relationships among various elements of culture. For example, this paper argues that the historical presence of Rajputs has contributed significantly to the distinctiveness of modern Rajasthan, yet their importance is hardly discernible from numerical measures of their strength in the state. In total numbers, Rajputs rank fifth in Rajasthan (5.6% of the population) after Jats (9.3%), Brahmans (7.6%), Chamars (6.8%) and Bhils (5.8%).[19]

Mere numbers, moreover, reveal little about interaction among castes or the unique contributions of particular groups to the distinctiveness of Rajasthani culture. Charans and Bhats, for example, each account for only some 0.3% of Rajasthan's population, yet their functions as hereditary bards and genealogists for the Rajputs assign them a role in the region's culture out of proportion to their numbers. Similarly, Lohars (0.7%) numerically rank 27th among the castes of Rajasthan, yet no one who has travelled in the area can fail to associate these colorful blacksmiths with the rural landscape of Rajasthan. Another distinctive element in Rajasthan is the tribal peoples. In 1981, 12.2% of the state's population belonged to "Scheduled Tribes", with regional concentrations (mainly Bhils) in the southern districts of Dungarpur and Banswara rising as high as 64.4% and 72.6% respectively.[20] Although these districts lie outside the Rajasthan Culture Area as defined by Schwartzberg, the presence in Rajasthan of Bhils, Minas, and other tribals and the relations of the tribal populations

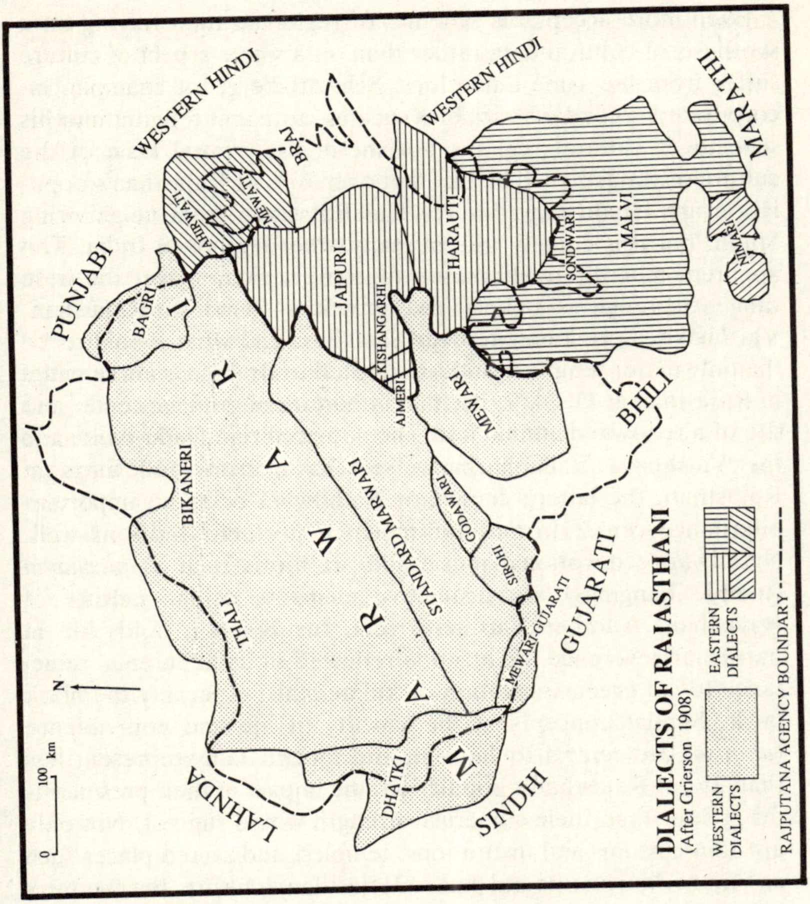

Map 3: **Dialects of Rajasthani**

with caste society are as much a part of Rajasthan's cultural distinctiveness as are traditions of Rajput chivalry.

Even more acceptable schemes of regionalization relying on a synthesis of cultural data rather than on a single aspect of culture suffer from the same limitations. Schwartzberg, for example, incorporated secondary variables such as caste and religion into his scheme of cultural regions, but these, too, reveal little of the culture of Rajasthan. The fact that over 90% of Rajasthan's population are Hindu may differentiate Rajasthan from neighboring Sindh, but it is equally true of many other regions of India. This apparent monolithic Hinduism, moreover, glosses over the wide range of religious beliefs and practices found in Rajasthan. Vaishnavites predominate over Shaivites, and what is said to be the only major temple in India dedicated to Brahma is also located in Rajasthan at Pushkar, itself an important pilgrimage center and site of a renowned annual fair. The non-sectarian Dadu-*panth* and the Vaishnava Vallabhacharya sect have strong followings in Rajasthan, the latter's temple at Nathdwara being an important pilgrimage center (*tīrtha*) for much of northern India as well. Nathdwara's devotional music and art forms such as *picchavāī* (temple hangings) are distinctive elements of the culture of Rajasthan. Another Vaishnava sect, the Bishnoi, holds life in particular reverence, an attitude reflected in its adherents' reluctance to cut green vegetation or kill animals, especially the black buck. Similar concepts of the sanctity of life and non-violence (*ahiṃsā*) are central to Jainism, and though Jains represent less than 2% of Rajasthan's population, the impact of their presence is far greater than their numerical strength would suggest. Not only are Jain customs and institutions, temples, and sacred places such as Mount Abu an integral part of Rajasthan's culture, but the Jains of Rajasthan have achieved a position of economic prominence in the state – as indeed they have over much of India – unsurpassed by any other community of similar size. Muslims, the largest religious minority in the state (6.5%), Christians, Sikhs and Buddhists also contribute to the diversity of religions in Rajasthan.

Few of these aspects of Rajasthan's culture could, by themselves, define a Rajasthani culture area. Jains are prominent in Gujarat to the southwest as well as in Rajasthan. Concentrations of tribal peoples are typical of the "tribal belt" that stretches across central India from Rajasthan and Gujarat, through Madhya

Pradesh, to Bihar and Orissa. Even in terms of caste distribution, Rajasthan reflects patterns characteristic of much of the northern plains (Schwartzberg 1965, 1968). Yet each aspect forms part of the specific complex of castes and religions, customs and material culture, social relations and economic systems found in Rajasthan that may be charcterized as uniquely Rajasthani.

Furthermore, efforts to define a Rajasthan culture area on the basis of variables such as language, caste or religion – singly or together – hardly touch the surface of what might be considered a distinctively Rajasthani culture. The contributions of Rajputs to Rajasthani life, for example, extends beyond their political and social histories.[21] Rajput courts were important centers for literature and the arts. Schools of painting developed in smaller states such as Kishangarh and Sirohi, as well in centers such as Jaipur, Jodhpur and Udaipur (Mewar). Painting, music, a vernacular literature often extolling the exploits of Rajput heroes – all flourished under the patronage of Rajput rulers. In addition, Rajputs were great builders, undertaking construction of Hindu and Jain temples, palaces, forts, reservoirs, and irrigation systems.[22] Indeed, much of what is today considered typically Rajasthani reflects the past activities of Rajput rulers in Rajasthan.

If Rajputs form a dominating influence in Rajasthan's history and society, however, Rajasthani culture is not only that of the former ruling elite (Qanungo 1960:38). The literary heritage of Rajasthan embraces the devotional outpourings of poet-saints such as Mirabai, Dadu Dayal and Jambhoji as well as popular ballads and epics. And even though folk heroes such as Ramdeoji, Gogaji and Pabuji might be of the Rajput castes, they are revered by the community at large (Ahuja 1980:91-96, 137). What could be more representative of Rajasthani folk culture than the ballad of Pabuji, sung before a painted scroll *paḍ* – itself an elaborate work of folk art – and depicting incidents from his life, accompanied by music and dancing, and performed by traveling minstrel *bhopās* for traditional village audiences? Ballads and folk-songs, *mehndī* and *mandaṇā*, popular dramas (*khyāls*), festivals such as Gangaur, musician castes and puppeteers – all evoke a sense of a culture that is uniquely Rajasthani.

Yet to what extent and in what manner do these elements combine to form a cohesive and distinctive Rajasthani culture? Many traits that are commonly viewed as "Rajasthani" are in fact associated with specific communities and locales within Rajasthan, and identified as such by the region's inhabitants. From this perspective, the idea of Rajasthan as a cohesive cultural entity has little meaning. Nonetheless, at a more general level of observation and viewed from an external perspective, conceptions of Rajasthan as unique cultural (and political) space persist in recent scholarship. Spate (1954:145-146) postulates the existence in India of perennial nuclear regions, centers of power generally located in favorable agricultural areas that persist through Indian history. His map showing the relative permanence of boundaries over the Indian subcontinent picks out Rajputana as a spatial entity, along with Gujarat, Malwa and other regions, but Rajputana stands out as a refuge area rather than a nuclear region. Subbarao (1958:11-12) argues that in addition to areas of attraction (nuclear regions) two further categories – areas of relative isolation and *cul de sacs* – can be identified. Areas of relative isolation "can ultimately be linked with the system of trans-continental communication . . . [they] are characterized by their distance from the main highways for the movement of peoples and cultures [and] display a different and complicated culture pattern." *Cul de sacs* are refuge zones in which inhabitants isolate themselves from broader trends and events, and preserve elements of earlier cultural patterns. Subbarao sees the Aravallis as a *cul de sac*, the desert to the west as an area of relative isolation, and Mewar as bordering the Malwa nuclear region. Spate's concept of nuclear regions reappears in the form of cultural-political core areas (Sopher 1962:121ff; 1980:291; Malik 1968). Once again Rajasthan stands out prominently as *not* a core area but surrounded by them. Gujarat and Malwa to the southeast, the Ganga-Yamuna Doab, the Punjab to the north and Sindh to the west have all been persistent centers of power in India (see Map 4). As Sopher points out, Rajasthan's cultural distinctiveness stems in large part from having effectively remained outside the sphere of dominance of any of the political and cultural cores (1962:122).

Rajasthan is thus seen as a cultural and historical region[23] as well as a political one. Yet these concepts of region all reflect the perspective of the outside observer, whether Mughal official, British administrator, modern scholar, nationalist politician, or even of most educated Indians. To examine Rajasthan from the perspective of the subjective, experienced region, we must consider

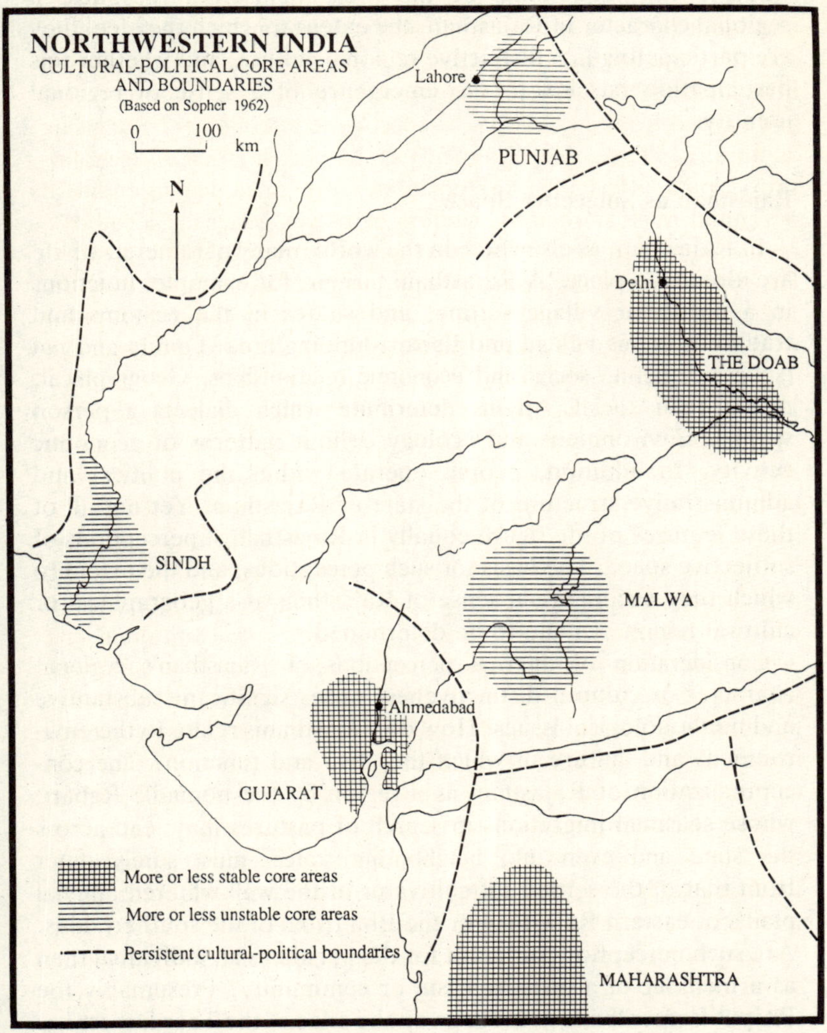

Map 4: **Northwestern India: Cultural-Political Core Areas and Boundaries**

whether the inhabitants of the area themselves recognize a regional character in Rajasthan, the extent to which they feel they are participating in a distinctive regional culture, and whether this participation has led to the emergence of a sense of regional identity.

Rajasthan as Subjective Space

In Rajasthan, as elsewhere in the world, many parameters of life are already in place. A Rajasthani farmer, for example, functions in a particular village setting, and shares in the customs and traditions of his village and its surrounding area. Family and *jāti* (subcaste) define social and economic relationships. Geographical, rather than social, origins determine which dialects a person speaks. Environment and ecology delimit patterns of economic activity. In addition, people operate within the political and administrative structure of the state of Rajasthan. Yet not all of these features of life figure equally in Rajasthanis' perceptions of subjective space. The basis for such perceptions, and the extent to which they encompass a sense of Rajasthan as a geographical or cultural region, remain to be determined.

Consideration of internal perceptions of Rajasthan's regional character or cultural distinctiveness raises significant substantive and methodological issues. How do Rajasthanis relate to the environment and culture in which they live and function? The conceptualization of Rajasthan as a region by the nomadic Rebari, whose seasonal migrations in search of pastures may lead across the state and even into neighboring states, must surely differ from that of the settled Jat cultivator of the well-watered alluvial plains of eastern Rajasthan or the Bhil tribal of the southern hills. Are such perceptions different for the person as an individual than as a member of a broader caste or community? Presumably the Rajput farmer living in a village on the edge of the Thar Desert has a somewhat different view of his Rajput heritage than the former raja or *ṭhākur* with a tradition of centuries of rule behind him. Rajput perceptions of a regional culture, moreover, might be expected to differ considerably from those of Brahmans, Jats, Banias, Rawats or any of the other communities living in Rajasthan. What, therefore, determines the relative strength of the elements shaping subjective perceptions of Rajasthan's distinctiveness, and how can these be identified?

Some preliminary answers to such questions, from both the substantive and methodological perspectives, are to be found in a recent study of folk regions by Joseph Schwartzberg (1985). Studies of traditional and folk regions have been undertaken elsewhere in India, for example in Malwa (Mayer 1960), Tamil Nadu (Beck 1972), Bundelkhand (Jain 1975), Rohilkhand and Oudh (Sopher 1977), and Gujarat (Bhatt 1980). Rajasthan, however, has received relatively little attention and Schwartzberg's work, though not focused exclusively on Rajasthan, breaks new ground in examining subjective regions in the area. Primarily a methodological experiment, the study also set out to discern factors according to which "people perceive, relate to and mentally compartmentalize their surroundings" (1985:206). Schwartzberg identified and mapped several regions (*ilāqā*)[24] and even subregions perceived as such by the inhabitants of northeastern Rajasthan and neighboring areas of Haryana, Uttar Pradesh and Delhi (See Map 5). In his ranking of factors on which the recognition of these "folk regions" was based, caste was the most important. Thus the dominance of Ahirs, Gujars, Jats and Meos was acknowledged in regional names such as Ahirwal, Gujrot, Jattot and Mewat. Next in importance came the former landholders and/or methods of revenue collection of the area. Shekhawati and Torawati, for example, were the former princely estates of the Shekhawat clan of Rajputs, while subregions referred to by numerical designations (Sataisa, for example, translates as 27) supposedly derive their names from the grouping of villages for administrative purposes.[25] Only one region (Chhind) was distinguished on the basis of dialect, even though significant dialect differences existed in the area studied.[26] Other categories of folk region identified by Schwartzberg included historic regions (e.g. Rath, Braj) and those associated with landforms (Wal, Naida) and other physical elements of the landscape.[27]

Schwartzberg's study reveals interesting differences between Rajasthan and the adjacent states (See Table 1). Caste is a significant element underlying folk regions in Haryana, but it appears to play a secondary role in defining subjective space in northeastern Rajasthan.[28] Of the caste regions found in Rajasthan,

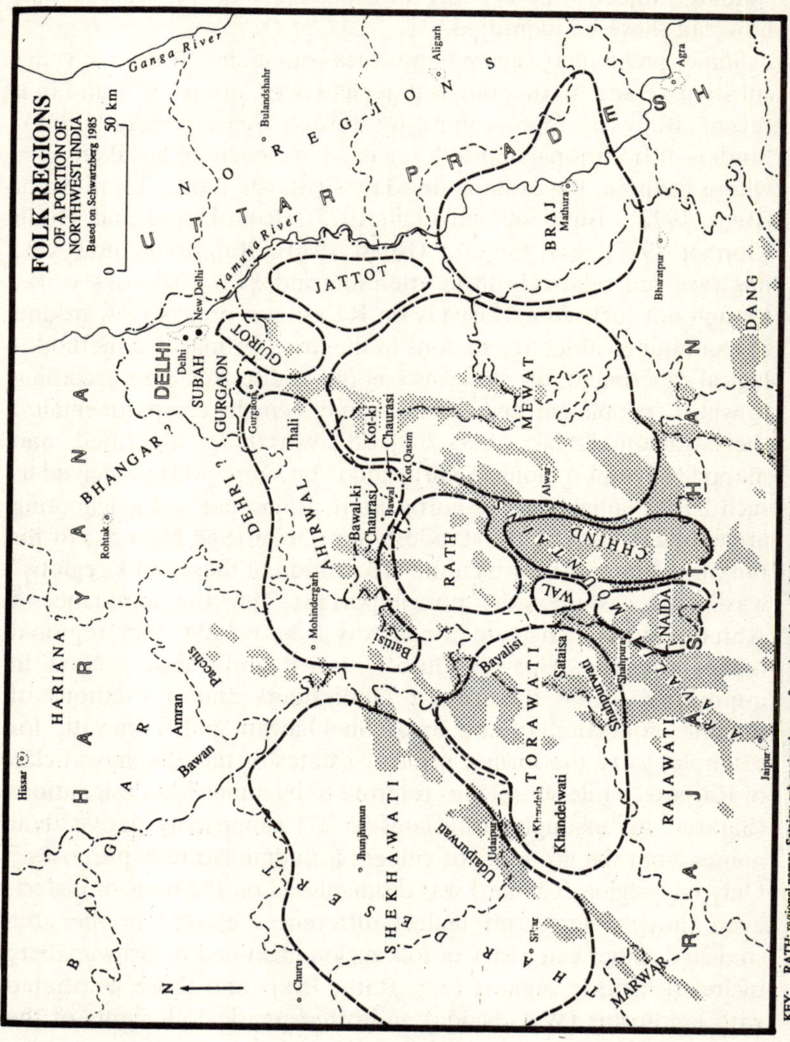

KEY: RATH: regional name; Sataisa: sub-regional name; ? : region with particularly vague limits; ——: approximate limits of areas clearly within the region named;

Ahirwal barely extends into the state from Haryana and Mewat straddles the border with Haryana as well. Close to half of the regions and subregions identified by Schwartzberg in Rajasthan, however, are perceived on the basis of former landholders and/or methods of revenue collection. Territorial associations with former Rajput ruling clans are apparently of greater importance in Rajasthani perceptions of subjective space, at least in the northeast of the state, than in those of neighboring peoples.

Although they have yet to be fully documented and mapped, subjective regions – whether classed as folk, traditional, or geographical regions – may be identified elsewhere in Rajasthan. According to Komal Kothari (personal communication), an area west of Jaisalmer is known by the local population as Dhat, after a grass that grows in the region. Khadal, the name of a breed of camel, designates another part of Jaisalmer District. Similarly, inhabitants of the Godwar tract, an area lying to the west of the Aravallis, recognize several regions on the basis of vegetation, agricultural practices, and physiography. Khuni, literally "elbow", is characterized by a particular kind of grass and a single annual harvest, the crops grown being other than corn; Jhaura is an area which supports two harvests a year, with the winter crop cultivated without irrigation; and Rohi is mountainous, highly subject to erosion, and once again associated with varieties of grasses not found in adjacent regions.

In Rajasthan, therefore, people mentally order subjective space according to criteria that include caste, former landholders, dialect, history, the physical environment and economic patterns. The subjective regions identified by Schwartzberg and Kothari, however, contribute more to a sense of Rajasthan's physical and cultural diversity than to any conception of the region as a geographic, cultural or even political entity. Folk regions such as Wal or Naida distinguished on the basis of landforms or physical features, for example, tend to be limited in size. Even where such regions cover more extensive geographical areas, as with *marusthalī*, *mārwāṛ*, and *bāgar*, these still remain subregions of Rajasthan rather than define Rajasthan itself. Similarly, such caste and tribal concentrations as exist in Rajasthan also give rise to localized regions, serving as much to emphasize the ethnic and social complexity of the state's population as to outline its particular characteristics. And, while historic associations with Rajput clans

Table 1

Folk Regions of a Portion of Northwest India (Based on Schwartzberg 1985)

State	*Caste*	*Dialect*	*Former Land-holders/Revenue Collection*	*Historic*	*Landforms*	*Vegetation Soils*
Rajasthan	MEWAT	CHHIND	SHEKHAWATI	RATH	NADIA	MARWAR
	(AHIRWAL)		TORAWATI	(BRAJ)	WAL	BAGAR?
			RAJAWATI		DANG	
			Bayalisi			
			Khandelwati			
			Kot-ki-Chaurasi			
			Sataisa			
			Shahpurwati			
			Udaipurwati			
Haryana	AHIRWAL		Battisi	GURGAON		(BAGAR?)
	(MEWAT)		Bawal-ki-Chaurasi	Amran		BHANGAR?
	JATTOT		Pacchis	Bawan		DEHRI?
	GUJROT					HARIANA?
						Thali
Uttar Pradesh				BRAJ		
				Banausa		
Delhi	(GUJROT)			SUBAH		

Key: MEWAT, regional name; (MEWAT), smaller part of a region lying in two state Sataisa, subregional name; ? identifies regions with particularly vague limit Regions in each category are arranged in descending order of size (where known and clearly defined regions precede those with vague limits. Subregions are arrange alphabetically.

Note: This information is derived from the detailed map of folk regions that was submitte by Schwartzberg for publication with his article in Mukerji and Ahmad, eds. *Indi Culture, Society and Economy. Geographical Essays in Honour of Prof. Asok Mitr (1985)*, but that was omitted from that volume. Map 5 in this paper is based, wit Schwartzberg's permission, on the original map. Copies of the map may be obtain from Prof. Schwartzberg by writing to him at: Department of Geography, University of Minnesota, Minneapolis, MN 55455, U.S.A.

provide links to broader Rajasthani cultural traditions, they also act as reminders of the political fragmentation of the past.

This historical fragmentation of political space is echoed to some extent in the cultural sphere. As political regions, the former princely states of Rajasthan were instituted regions, and even today may survive as such in the internal administrative structure of the modern state of Rajasthan.[29] However, there is evidence to suggest some states (or groupings of states) are important subjective regions as well. In Rajasthan, dialect is often closely related in its development with internal political, historical and even physical regions. Marwari, for instance, is the dialect of the former Rajput state of Marwar, a name reflecting the severe physical environment of the Thar Desert and still used to designate a folk region today. Such associations of language, political space, and elements of the physical environment reflect evolutionary relationships of long historical standing that in some instances have been accompanied by the development of distinctive cultural traditions. As a result, strongly defined subregional cultures have emerged in Rajasthan, based on specific dialects, regional literary traditions, local histories and customs, and identified with specific political entities or even clan lineages. Terms such as Marwari, Mewari and Harauti define meaningful subjective space for Rajasthanis, carrying connotations of internally perceived cultural regions as well as of denoted language regions or instituted political space. The extent to which princely states in Rajasthan were subjective regions and the complex processes by which their inception and existence as instituted, objective regions influenced their development as experienced, subjective regions and vice versa remain to be explored. But it can be argued that, historically, the most persistent, the most readily defined and, in many ways the most significant, regional entity in Rajasthan has been the former princely state. This may be true in terms of subjective space as well.

This is not to say that a sense of a greater Rajasthan does not exist in Rajasthani perceptions. The creation in the past of an instituted Rajasthan – whether *subah*, province, or state – reflected cultural and historical realities in which at least some of the region's inhabitants shared. Despite their individual clan loyalties, segmented polities and internecine conflicts, for example, Rajputs in Rajasthan shared bonds of culture and history that subsumed more local identities. Traditions of descent from ancient Kshatriya dynasties of India, the legitimization of Kshatriya status afforded by bardic and genealogical castes, the importance of clan and family, clan exogamy, the military and political organization of states, the role of bureaucratic lineages in state administration, the Rajput ethic – all linked Rajputs to a cultural tradition that encompassed all of Rajasthan, and even more extensive areas of northwestern India. Prior to the Maratha conquest, Rajputana (interpreted literally as the land of Rajputs) would have extended from the Sutlej to Agra and Gwalior (Bahadur 1978:iii).

Yet it was the more restricted area approximating modern Rajasthan that came to be identified with Rajput culture, and this sense of Rajasthan as something special has entered subjective perceptions as well. The Rajput ethic and Kshatriya caste culture remained more central to Rajput identity in Rajasthan than in other parts of India and "Rajputs in Rajasthan more than Rajputs elsewhere were reared to cherish the virtues of valour and honour of a warrior ruling aristocracy" (Rudolph and Rudolph 1984:41). Clans of the area such as the Gehlots and Rathors were accorded high status by the Rajput community, and their daughters were highly sought after in marriage. And it was the "Mewar" tradition of opposition to the Mughals that came to be accepted as standard Rajput history, a perspective on the past encouraged by nationalists during their struggle for independence from yet another alien central power during the 19th and 20th centuries. Centuries of Rajput rule and traditions of Rajput culture have thus set their imprint firmly on the minds of Rajasthanis, non-Rajputs as well as Rajputs, representing what has been called the Nostalgic-Romantic tradition in modern Rajasthani culture (Erdman 1985:14).

Conceptions of Rajasthan as subjective, cultural space do not necessarily accord with the instituted Rajasthan. The greater Rajasthan of the Rajputs, for instance, has parallels in other areas. Komal Kothari (personal communication) notes that for some Rajasthan may be defined as the area in which tie-and-dye textiles (*chuṅdaṛī*) are used for ritual purposes. In this sense, "Rajasthan" extends over much of western India, including extensive areas of Gujarat and Malwa, but excluding areas of the modern state of Rajasthan such as Bharatpur and part of Alwar. Despite this, Rajasthani perceptions reflect a sense of overarching structures that define an area more closely approximating modern Rajasthan. Local proverbs, for example, often refer to geographic locales in a manner suggesting they are seen as belonging to a distinct geographical or cultural entity.[30] The physical diversity of the region is countered to some extent by the complementarity of the wet and the dry zones, and the resulting economic interaction. Marriage ties have forged long-lasting relationships between the clans of the region. Some awareness of this sense of Rajasthan as a regional entity is seen in the use of names such as Rajwara and Rae'thana (leading to the later forms of Rajputana and Rajasthan) for the area in local dialects (Tod 1978:I, 1).

It is language, however, that does most to define Rajasthan as a subjective region in which perceived cultural space and instituted political space coincide. Language, as the vehicle of culture, is often seen as an underlying cohesive force that welds people into a distinct cultural entity. Beyond mere communication, language provides access to the history, traditions, myths, and symbols of a particular group, and in certain situations may itself become a symbol of that group. Where diverse ethnic or cultural groups are subsumed by political boundaries, for instance, language may become the standard of a regional culture. Adherence to regional tongues and related literary forms often assumes the role of a cultural statement of independence from a larger political whole. In India, for example, Bengali, Gujarati, and Tamil provide the foundation of strong regional cultures that are perceived as such by the people for whom these are mother tongues. In many instances, the sense of identity forged by regional language and cultures has been so strong as to generate popular agitation for the realignment of state political boundaries, as occurred in India in the early years of Independence. Today, this sense of regional identity underlies, in part, the secessionist demands of the Sikhs in the Punjab and the Tamils of Sri Lanka.

In Rajasthan the situation is somewhat different. Many Rajasthanis speak Hindi, the language of government, education and business, and the intelligentsia. As a cultural region, however, Rajasthan is defined essentially by the extent over which a Rajasthani language (as construed by Grierson) or a Rajasthani dialect group is spoken. Rajasthanis may speak several local dialects, but they often identify most closely with one – usually that of the area of Rajasthan from which they originate. It is this dialect that figures prominently in Rajasthanis' awareness of regional identity. One speaks Marwari, Dhundhari or Harauti, and it is through this primary tongue that one interacts with the world around one and gains access to local culture and cultural traditions. Linguistically, for many Rajasthanis, the dialect region is of more significance as subjective space than some broader area defined by a putative Rajasthani language.

Despite Rajasthanis' identification with language at the dialect rather than the broader regional level, the Rajasthani culture area does display linguistic traits normally associated with more clearly established regional cultures. From the 13th century onwards, there evolved a series of literary languages (e.g. Old Western Rajasthani, Dingal, Middle Marwari) in which an extensive literature was created (Magier 1983:17-19). These languages gained acceptance over areas more widespread than the dialect regions of Rajasthan, and may be regarded as truly Rajasthani in character. Middle Marwari was first used extensively at the Marwar court in the late 16th century, but it soon evolved into the major prose language for Rajasthan, and for over 200 years "all letters, historical tales and folk-stories, all learned prose and all the prose chronicles to appear in the vernacular in Rajasthan were written in this language" (Smith 1975:435). Thus there exists in Rajasthan a literary tradition embracing a corpus of what has come to be seen as a distinctly Rajasthani literature, and an awareness of this regional literary heritage is one factor behind recent attempts by some intelligentsia in Rajasthan to gain recognition for Rajasthani as an official language.[31] If Rajasthan is defined as a culture area on the basis of language, language – in its own way – underlies and reinforces perceptions of Rajasthan as a subjective, experienced region as well.

This conceptualization of Rajasthan as a cultural entity, however, is by no means held equally by all Rajasthanis. Rajasthani perceptions of subjective space are based on a variety of cultural, historical and environmental factors.[32] The resulting subjective regions range from relatively restricted areas within Rajasthan to a greater Rajasthan that might extend far beyond the geographic limits of the modern state. Rajasthanis recognize and identify with several kinds of subjective space at the same time. The nature and strength of this identification, moreover, vary according to time, circumstance and context. Without much more extensive research into Rajasthani viewpoints – especially in Rajasthani sources – than can be undertaken here, it is difficult to assess accurately the strength of Rajasthanis' sense of identity with one category of subjective space rather than another. Historically, however, delineation of Rajasthan as distinct geographic space was achieved by outsiders, and then from the external perspective. Identification of the peoples within the area with this regional entity must have been minimal at best. There existed, and still exists, a sense of things Rajasthani – of the character of Rajput society, the desert environment, the distinctiveness of cultural and historical traditions in the region, etc. – that can be regarded perhaps as an awareness of regional identity. But, historically, this certainly lacked the strong sense of unity and the ties of language and culture to well-defined geographic space that is normally associated with regionalism. In Rajasthanis' perceptions of subjective space, community, dialect, historical region or subregional culture have often been as significant as any concept of a greater Rajasthan.

Conclusions

In northwestern India, a distinctive way of life involving specific peoples, cultures and environments has been evolving for perhaps a thousand years. Defined in the broadest of terms by the dominating influence of Rajput polity and society, this way of life over time has come to be closely identified with the arid and semi-arid lands encompassed by modern Rajasthan. The general outlines of this region first emerged during the Muslim expansion into northwestern India in medieval times, and its underlying historical and cultural unity was recognized in its subsequent organization as a political region under the Mughals. The continued survival of the region (as *subah*, province and state) and the persistence of its political boundaries from the late 16th century to the present are measures of the strength of Rajasthan's regional character – at least, as perceived by Mughal administrators, British colonial officials, and the nationalist politicians responsible for the integration of the princely states into the Union of India.

A sense of Rajasthan's regional character has also long been shared by many of the area's inhabitants. This has not, however, led to the emergence of regionalism as a political force in Rajasthan, or even resulted in a chauvinstic identification with a regional culture. Although Rajasthani culture is often perceived in holistic terms, it is as much an assemblage of disparate, localized traditions that are Rajasthani in character as a cohesive cultural entity. For many Rajasthanis, a poorly developed sense of Rajasthan as a region and, perhaps, the greater hold on their loyalties of other kinds of socio-cultural and geographic space have inhibited development of a well-defined regional consciousness or regional identity.

Conceptualization of regions and the emergence of regional identities reflect processes involving complex historical, cultural and social forces working in a particular geographic setting over lengthy periods of time. Such processes have acted in the past to define Rajasthan as a cultural, historical and even political region, while at the same time subordinating the development of a strongly-defined regional identity to other loyalties. These processes continue at work today. With the outlines of a political Rajasthan firmly established, however, they may be expected to assume differing roles than in the past. Beyond merely encouraging identification with a political and administrative unit, they now serve to promote a regional awareness, emphasizing and reinforcing existing perceptions of Rajasthan as a cultural and historical region over lesser and more parochial ones. A Rajasthani regional identity appears to be emerging today that is based, at least in part, on an increasing awareness among the region's inhabitants of a common heritage originating in Rajasthan's broader cultural, historical and political traditions.

ENDNOTES

1. Although the concept of the region is shared by many of the social sciences (and is also utilized by some of the life sciences), it has traditionally played a central, and sometimes dominating, role in defining both the objectives and the methodology of geography as an academic discipline. The standard work on the place of the regional concept in geographic thought is Richard Hartshorne's *The Nature of Geography:A Crtical Survey of Current Thought in the Light of the Past* (1939), along with his later *Perspective on the Nature of Geography* (1959). The region is the specific focus of Whittlesey (1954). A critique of prevailing views on the concept of the region is found in Kimble (1951). Further discussion of the region and regional systems can be found in Amadeo and Golledge (1975), Entrikin (1981) and Grigg (1965). Additional bibliographic references are to be found in Larkin and Peters (1983). A broad treatment of the regional concept in the social sciences is provided in Vance (1968).

2. See Cohn (1967) for a discussion of the concept of objective and subjective regions, and Stein (1967) for a critique of these concepts.
3. In addition to the regional typologies discussed in the text, two others deserve mention. Regions can be categorized according to the nature of their delimiting criteria rather than their mode of recognition, resulting in the "formal" (uniform) and "functional" (nodal) region. In formal regions, the distinguishing criteria are distributed uniformly throughout the area in question, whereas the functional region is characterized by internal organization and circulation around a central node, with the dominating influence of the node diminishing toward the periphery of the region. A further basis for identifying regions is the complexity rather than the nature of their delimiting criteria, leading to the recognition of single-feature regions and multiple-feature regions.
4. For a discussion of regionalism, see Hintze (1934). Although the United States is the main focus, historical and theoretical aspects of both regionalism and the region are examined in Odum and Moore (1938) and Jensen (1952). Two important works dealing specifically with South Asia are Crane (1967) and Fox (1977). More recently, the question of regions in India has been addressed in Wallace (1985).
5. Known also as Pratiharas, and Gurjara-Pratiharas, the Gurjaras were a prominent clan of *agnikula* Rajputs who were later to rule the extensive Gurjara-Pratihara empire from their base at Kanauj (now in Uttar Pradesh). While many Rajput clans claim descent from solar and lunar Kshatriya dynasties of ancient India, the *agnikula* ("fire-race") Rajputs assert a different origin. According to legend, they sprang from the fire-pit of the sage Vashishtha on Mount Abu (in southern Rajasthan), created by the gods to aid the Brahmans in their struggle with Buddhists and foreigners. Other *agnikula* clans include the Paramaras, Chauhans and Solankis (Walker 1968:II, 274-275).
6. The question of Rajput origins remains a controversial issue today. For a discussion of this topic, see Chattopadhyaya (1976).
7. According to the 1931 Census of India, which provides the most recent data on caste in India, the numbers of Rajputs in the United Provinces, Punjab and Bihar far exceeded those in Rajputana. In terms of percentage of Rajputs in the population, Rajputana was surpassed by Kashmir, Punjab, United Provinces, Central India, and the Bihar sub-province of Bengal.
8. The last major effort to establish Hindu control of the critical Doab area, the plains between the Ganga and Yamuna rivers, was led by Rana Sangram Singh (Rana Sanga) of Mewar. This attempt ended with the defeat of the Rajput forces at Kanua (1527).
9. Akbar followed the policy of acknowledging the authority of the Rajput chieftains in their own kingdoms, once they had accepted Mughal suzerainty. Although the Mughal emperor was involved in matters of succession, a raja had a free hand in internal affairs as long as his policies did not impinge on imperial affairs (Hallissey 1977:22-24).
10. Captain (later Lieutenant-Colonel) James Tod was Political Agent at Mewar from 1818 to 1822, and his account of Rajasthan was obviously influenced by the Mewar view of Rajput history as one of valiant resistance to the invading Muslims. Tod's strong pro-Rajput sentiments and his views on non-interference brought him afoul of superiors such as Major-General Sir David Ochterlony,

who favored greater British involvement in Rajput affairs. Ochterlony, who held the appointments of Resident at Delhi and later Resident in Malwa and Rajputana, succeeded in greatly limiting the extent of Tod's political jurisdiction until eventually Tod resigned from his Mewar post in 1822.

11. In early 1949, when the rulers of Jaipur, Jodhpur, Bikaner and Jaisalmer agreed to integrate their states with the existing Rajasthan Union, the first question that arose was who should head the new state. The popular leaders of Rajasthan endorsed Maharaja Sawai Man Singh of Jaipur for the position of Rajpramukh. However, the Maharana of Udaipur has traditionally been viewed as the most senior of the Rajputana rulers, and Bhupal Singh of Udaipur also pressed for the appointment. This dilemma was solved by creating the title of Maharajpramukh for Bhupal Singh, who took ceremonial precedence over the Rajpramukh, but otherwise played little role in the administration of the Union (Menon 1985:264).
12. The origins of the region as an intellectual concept in modern scholarship are traced by Hartshorne to the late 18th century when, unhappy with conventional regionalizations of the world along political lines, scholars in Germany and France sought to define regions according to natural boundaries (1939:37-38, 250). This concern with natural, i.e. physical, regions inevitably led to the first attempt to develop regional systems in India being based on physical criteria. Although a few weather stations had been established by the East India Company as early as the late 18th Century, meteorological records in India were haphazard and of dubious quality. In 1875, however, an imperial system was set up to collect meteorological data and H.F. Blanford appointed to oversee the operation. Over the next decade, Blanford collected rainfall records from all over the subcontinent, collated and evaluated the information at his disposal, and published a lengthy monograph in which he developed his scheme of rainfall regions in India (1886).
13. W. T. Blanford divided British India into 19 physical "tracts" grouped into five major regions. He placed Rajputana in two of the latter. The desert areas west of the Aravallis were included in the Punjab tract of the Indo-Gangetic Plain Region that extended as far as the hills of Baluchistan, while the eastern areas fell within the Rajputana or Central India tract of the Peninsula Region (1901:343-345). In the same year, the Government of India adopted a system of natural divisions for purposes ranging from the India Daily Weather Reports to the reporting of statistics in the 1901 Census of India that again split Rajputana between two regions, the North West Dry Area and the Central India Plateau (India. Meteorological Department 1906:Plate 6 Lower). A similar division is seen in the medical provinces (the Indus Valley and North-West Rajputana Province and the East Rajputana, Central India and Gujarat Province) drawn up by the India Medical Department (*ibid*., xxiii, Plate 5 Lower).
14. The desert occupies all of Jaisalmer and Bikaner Districts, and extensive areas of Barmer, Jodhpur and Churu Districts.
15. The preceding discussion is based on Spate (1954), Alsdorf (1955), Mishra (1967) and Singh (1971).
16. An early description of Ajmer-Merwara is found in Dixon's *Sketch of Mairwara* (1850). Ajmer, however, was ceded to the British by the Marathas in

1818, and came under direct British rule. Being part of the North West Provinces at the time, Ajmer-Merwara (the two districts were joined administratively in 1842) was included in the census carried out there in 1865. Later, as a Commissioner's Province, Ajmer-Merwara was included in the first Census of India (1871-72), which excluded the feudatory states of Rajputana. Although census reports on the princely states of Rajputana appeared in 1881 and 1891, these states were completely enumerated in the Census for the first time only in 1901. Similarly, prior to the three-volume *Rajputana Gazetteer* that appeared in 1879-80, accounts existed for only a few states in Rajputana, e.g Brooke's histories of Mewar (1859) and Jaipur (1868) and Powlett's Gazetteers of Bikaner (1874a) and Karauli (1874b). Complete state-wide coverage of the District Gazetteers was undertaken by the Government of Rajasthan only in the decades after Independence.

17. Bose (1956) has suggested that even aspects of culture such as the traditional manner in which food is prepared, the ritual use of food, dress or funerary customs can be used to identify culture zones in India.
18. The Eighth Schedule of the Constitution of India recognized 14 official languages, to which a 15th, Sindhi, was added in 1967 (Chitaley and Rao 1974:V, 846). Rajasthani was not included in this list, and in the view of some this has been detrimental to its development. Rajasthani has received recognition as a literary language by the national Sahitya Akademi, and a Rajasthan Sahitya Akademi has been established to support and promote Rajasthani literature (Kothari 1973).
19. The data on caste presented here are taken from the 1931 Census of India (India, Census Commissioner 1932, 1933). While these figures might be expected to have changed in the flux of the post-Independence years, this was the last census that published comprehensive data on caste. In 1941, World War II drastically curtailed census operations, and in subsequent censuses questions on caste – with the exception of those directed toward Scheduled Castes and Tribes – were avoided out of concern for their potential social divisiveness.
20. The Indian Constitution recognized the existence of socially and economically backward classes in India, and undertook to protect them from social injustice and to promote their welfare (Articles 338, 366 (24), (25)). These communities were listed in a Schedule appended to the Constitution and came to be known as Scheduled Castes and Scheduled Tribes (Chitaley and Rao 1974). The Scheduled Castes and Tribes Lists (Modification) Order, 1956, issued by the President of India, lists Bhils, Bhil Minas, Damars (Damorias), Garasias (excluding Rajput Garasias), Minas and Sehrias (Sahariyas) as Scheduled Tribes throughout most of Rajasthan. (Ajmer District and two other areas in the state have different communities on their list of Scheduled Tribes.) In addition, some 80 communities in Rajasthan, accounting for 17% of the population, are classed as Scheduled Castes. The largest of these groups include Chamars, Balais, Bairwas and Bhangis. In 1981, Scheduled Castes and Tribes made up 29.25% of Rajasthan's population (*Census of India, 1981. Ser. 18. Pt. 2-B*, p.11).
21. Rajput society and culture in Rajasthan forms a major focus of scholarly interest for political scientists Susanne Hoeber Rudolph and Lloyd Rudolph. A

selection of their writings covering some three decades of research on Rajasthan is to be found in their *Essays on Rajputana* (1984).

22. There are no natural fresh-water lakes in Rajasthan, and many of the extensive bodies of water found in the state today are artifical lakes constructed by past rulers. For example, Raj Samand, near the town of Kankroli in Udaipur District was dammed in 1661 by Rana Raj Singh of Mewar and Jai Samand, south east of Udaipur, was built in 1681 by Rana Jai Singh of Mewar (*Rajputana Gazetteer* 1:36). Even some of Rajasthan's modern irrigation projects were foreshadowed during the period of princely rule, though often such construction undertaken in princely states reflected the influence of British advisers. Although they never materialized, plans were developed by Kota and Mewar for use of the Chambal River, which now provides power and irrigation through the Chambal Project (Mishra 1967:83-84). Similarly, the Rajasthan Canal – renamed the Indira Gandhi Canal in honor of the late Prime Minister – has a precedent in the Gang Canal, constructed by Ganga Singh of Bikaner in 1922-27. The ambitious Rajasthan Canal Project brings water over 600 km from the River Sutlej to Ganganagar, Bikaner and Jaisalmer Districts in the heart of the Thar Desert.
23. For a discussion of the concept of historical regions, its application to the Indian subcontinent, and a critique of the concept, see Barun De, Bernard S. Cohn, and Burton Stein in Crane (1967).
24. *Ilāqā*, having the connotation of region in Persian and derived ultimately from the Arabic word for flag, was selected by Schwartzberg after discussion with knowledgeable people in the area as coming closest to the concept he was investigating. Where this was not understood, alternatives such as *kṣetra* and *deś* were mentioned, although in some instances none of these terms appeared to have meaning for informants (1985:223*n*7).
25. Schwartzberg, however, suggests that the names for these subregions reflect auspicious numbers in Indian numerology rather than the actual number of villages – past or present – in the area (1985:217).
26. The region designated Chhind by its inhabitants is apparently recognized on the basis of its distinctive dialect. Informants in neighboring areas somewhat derisively refer to the region as "Chaikada," the region where people say *chai* rather than *hai* for the present indicative, third person singular case of the verb "to be" (Schwartzberg 1985:218).
27. Wal derives its name from a topographic term meaning small, hill-girt basin, while Naida, also called Durgarwada (rough country) is a hilly tract of land. Folk regions outside present-day Rajasthan recognized on the basis of the physical environment include Bagar (a dry dusty tract), Hariana (a relatively green well-watered country), Dehri (a region prone to water-logging by brackish water), Thali (a sandy tract), and Bhangar – a local generic term for elevated alluvial tracts found over much of the Indo-Gangetic Plain (Schwartzberg 1985:218).
28. This reflects, in part, the absence of any major regional concentrations of castes or communities in northeastern Rajasthan. Where these do occur elsewhere in Rajasthan, they may find expression in regional nomenclature. Thus Bhilwara and Merwara refer to areas populated by Bhils and Mers, tribal peoples of south-central Rajasthan.
29. Despite boundary adjustments, many of Rajasthan's present-day districts

(e.g. Alwar, Bundi, Sirohi) approximate the territories of the former princely states.

30. For example: *Marwar nar neepaje, nari Jaisalmer,*
Turi to Sindhan santra, kashal Bikanir.

"The finest men are born in Marwar, while the loveliest women hail from Jaisalmer; the horses of Sind and the camels of Bikanir are the best" (Ahuja 1980:113).

31. Because of the number of its speakers as well as its prominence as a literary language, Marwari is suggested by many as the most suitable of the state's dialects to be officially recognized as "Rajasthani."
32. Bhatt (1980:55-57) proposes a model demonstrating how the traditional Indian social system functions in space, incorporating elements such as territorial units, productivity base, social and political organization, and language and dialects. His hierarchy of sociocultural space commences with households, and progresses through hamlets/wards, villages, folk regions and subcultural regions to cultural-linguistic regions and the broader division of India into Aryan and Dravidian cultural realms. The present discussion of the regional character of Rajasthan has been undertaken primarily at the levels of the folk region (e.g. Shekhawati or Torawati), the sub-cultural region (Marwar or Mewar) and the cultural-linguistic region (Rajasthan).

REFERENCES CITED

Ahmad, Kazi S.
1941 "Physiographic Divisions of India." *The Indian Geographical Journal* 16:257-267.

Ahuja, D.R.
1980 *Folklore of Rajasthan*. New Delhi: National Book Trust.

Alsdorf, Ludwig
1955 *Vorderindien: Bharat, Pakistan, Ceylon, Ein Landes- und Kulturkunde*. Braunschweig: Georg Westermann Verlag.

Amadeo, Douglas and Reginald G. Golledge
1975 *An Introduction to Scientific Reasoning in Geography*. New York: John Wiley.

Bahadur, K.P., ed.
1978 *Caste, Tribes and Culture of Rajputs*. Delhi: Ess Ess Publications.

Baker, J.N.L.
1928 "Notes on the Natural Regions of India." *Geography* 14:447-455.

Banerjee, A.C.
1983 "Rajput Resistance to Muslim Invasions." In his *Aspects of Rajput State and Society*. New Delhi: Rajesh Publications.

Beaujeu-Garnier, Jacqueline
1976 *Methods and Perspectives in Geography*. Jennifer Bray, transl. London and New York: Longman.

Beck, Brenda E.F.
1972 *Peasant Society in Konku: A Study of Right and Left Subcastes in South India*. Vancouver: University of British Columbia Press.

Bhatt, Bharat L.
1980 "India and Indian Regions: A Critical Overview." In *An Exploration of India: Geographical Perspectives on Society and Culture*. David E.Sopher, ed. pp. 35-61. Ithaca, N.Y.: Cornell University Press.

Blanford, H.F.
1886 "On the Rainfall of India." Part 1. *Indian Meteorological Memoirs* 3(1):1-116.

Blanford, W.T.
1901 "The Distribution of Vertebrate Animals in India, Ceylon, and Burma." *Philosophical Transactions of the Royal Society of London*. Series B. 194:335-436.

Bose, N.K.
1956 "Culture Zones of India." *Geographical Review of India* 18(4): 1-12.

Brooke, J.C.
1859 *History of Meywar*. Calcutta.
1868 *Political History of the State of Jeypore*. Selections from the Records of the Government of India. Series 150. No. 65.

Chattopadhyaya, B.D.
1976 "Origin of the Rajputs: The Political, Economic and Social Processes in Early Medieval Rajasthan." *The Indian Historical Review* 3(1): 59-82.

Chitaley, D.V. and S. Appu Rao.
1974 *The Constitution of India*. 5 vols. 2nd ed. Bombay: All India Reporter.

Cohn, Bernard S.
1967 "Regions Subjective and Objective: Their Relation to the Study of Modern Indian History and Society." In *Regions and Regionalism in South Asian Studies*. Robert I. Crane, ed. pp. 5-37. Durham, N.C.: Duke University, Program in Comparative Studies on Southern Asia.

Crane, Robert I., ed.
1967 *Regions and Regionalism in South Asian Studies: An Exploratory Study*. Durham, N.C.: Duke University, Program in Comparative Studies on Southern Asia.

De, Barun
1967 "A Historical Perspective on Theories of Regionalization in India." In *Regions and Regionalism in South Asian Studies*. Robert I. Crane, ed. pp. 48-88. Durham, N.C.: Duke University, Program in Comparative Studies on Southern Asia.

Dixon, C.J.
1850 *Sketch of Mairwara*. London: Smith, Elder.

Entrikin, J. Nicholas.
1981 "Philosophical Issues in the Scientific Study of Regions." In *Geography and the Urban Environment: Progress in Research and Applications. Vol. IV*. D.T. Herbert and R.J. Johnston, eds. pp. 1-27. New York: John Wiley.

Erdman, Joan L.
1985 *Patrons and Performers in Rajasthan: The Subtle Tradition*. Delhi: Chanakya Publications.

Fleming, Douglas K.
1973 "The Regionalizing Ritual." *The Scottish Geographical Magazine* 89:196-207.

Fox, Richard G., ed.
1977 *Region and Realm in Traditional India*. Durham, N.C: Duke University, Program in Comparative Studies on Southern Asia.

Grierson, George A.
1903-22 *Linguistic Survey of India*. 19 vols. Calcutta: Superintendent of Government Printing.
1908 *Linguistic Survey of India. Vol. IX. Indo-Aryan Family. Central Group. Part II. Specimens of Rajasthani and Gujarati*. Calcutta: Superintendent of Government Printing.

Grigg, David
1965 "The Logic of Regional Systems." *Annals of the Association of American Geographers* 55:465-491.

Hallissey, Robert C.
1977 *The Rajput Rebellion Against Aurangzeb: A Study of the Mughal Empire In Seventeenth-Century India*. Columbia and London: University of Missouri Press.

Hartshorne, Richard
1939 *The Nature of Geography: A Critical Survey of Current Thought in the Light of the Past*. Lancaster, Pa.: Association of American Geographers.
1959 *Perspective on the Nature of Geography*. Chicago: Rand McNally.
1965 "Practical and Academic Regions." *Annals of the Association of American Geographers* 55:619.

Hintze, Hedwig
1934 "Regionalism." *Encyclopedia of the Social Sciences* 13:208-218.

India. Census Commissioner
1932 *Census of India, 1931. Volume 12. Central Provinces and Berar*. Nagpur: Government Printing.
Census of India, 1931. Volume 20. Central India Agency. Delhi: Manager of Publications.
Census of India, 1931. Volume 27. Rajputana Agency. Meerut: Saraswati Press.
1933 *Census of India, 1931. Volume 1. India. Pt. 2. Imperial Tables*. Delhi: Manager of Publications.
Census of India, 1931. Volume 8. Bombay Presidency. Bombay: Government Central Press.
Census of India, 1931. Volume 10. Western India States Agency. Bombay: Government Central Press.
Census of India, 1931. Volume 17. Punjab. Lahore: Civil and Military Gazette Press.
Census of India, 1931. Volume 18. United Provinces. Allahabad: Superintendent, Printing and Stationery.

India. Meteorological Department
1906 *Climatological Atlas of India*. Edinburgh: J. Bartholomew.

India (Republic). Office of the Registrar General
1984 *Census of India, 1981. Series 18. Rajasthan. Pt. 2-B. Primary Census Abstract*. Delhi: Controller of Publications.

Jain, Ravindra K.
1975 "Bundela Genealogy and Legends: The Past of an Indigenous Ruling Group of Central India." In *Studies in Social Anthropology: Essays in Memory of E.E. Evans-Pritchard by His Former Colleagues*. J.H.M. Beattie and R.G. Lienhardt, eds. pp. 238-272. London: Oxford University Press.

Jensen, Merrill, ed.
1952 *Regionalism in America*. Madison, Wisc.: University of Wisconsin Press.

Kellogg, S.H.
1875 *A Grammar of the Hindi Language*. New Delhi: Oriental Books Reprint Corporation.

Kimble, George H.T.
1951 "The Inadequacy of the Regional Concept." In *London Essays in Geography*. L.D. Stamp and S.W. Wooldridge, eds. pp. 151-174. London: Longman.

Kothari, Komal
1973 "Rajasthani." In *Indian Literature Since Independence*. K.R. Srinivasa Iyengar, ed. pp. 252-265. New Delhi: Sahitya Akademi.

Larkin, Robert P. and Gary L. Peters
1983 "Region." In their *Dictionary of Concepts in Human Geography*. pp. 199-205. Westport, Conn. and London: Greenwood Press.

Magier, David
1983 "Topics in the Grammar of Marwari." Ph.D. Dissertation, Department of Linguistics, University of California, Berkeley.

Maheshwari, Hiralal
1980 *History of Rajasthani Literature*. New Delhi: Sahitya Akademi.

Malik, S.C.
1968 *Indian Civilization: The Formative Period*. Simla: Indian Institute of Advanced Study.

Mayer, Adrian C.
1960 *Caste and Kinship in Central India: A Village and Its Region*. Berkeley: University of California Press.

Menon, V.P.
1985 *Integration of the Indian States*. Hyderabad, A.P.: Orient Longman.

Mishra, V.C.
1967 *Geography of Rajasthan*. New Delhi: National Book Trust.

Mukerji, A.B. and Aijazudin Ahmad, eds.
1985 *India, Culture, Society and Economy. Geographical Essays in Honor of Professor Asok Mitra*, New Delhi: Inter-India Publications.

Odum, Howard W. and Harry E. Moore, eds.
1938 *American Regionalism: A Cultural-Historical Approach to National Integration*. New York: Henry Holt.

Pithawalla, Maneck B.
1939a "The Need of Uniformity in the Physiographic Divisions of India." *Journal of the Madras Geographical Association* 14:213-228.
1939b Physiographic Divisions of India." *Journal of the Madras Geographical Association* 14:423-434.

Powlett, P.W.
1874a *Gazetteer of Bikaner*. Calcutta: Superintendent of Government Printing.
1874b *Gazetteer of the Karauli State*. Calcutta: Superintendent of Government Printing.

Qanungo, K.R.
1960 "The Role of Non-Rajputs in the History of Rajputana." In his *Studies in Rajput History*. pp. 38-67. Delhi: S. Chand.

Rajputana Gazetteer
1879-80 *The Rajputana Gazetteer*. 3 vols. Calcutta: Superintendent of Government Printing.

Richards, F.J.
1929 "Cultural Regions of India." *Geography* 15:20-29.

Risley, Herbert H.
1891-92 *The Tribes and Castes of Bengal*. 2 vols. Calcutta: Bengal Secretariat Press.

Rudolph, Susanne Hoeber and Lloyd I. Rudolph
1984 *Essays on Rajputana: Reflections on History, Culture and Administration*. New Delhi: Concept.

Schwartzberg, Joseph E.
1965 "The Distribution of Selected Castes in the North Indian Plain." *Geographical Review* 55:477-495.
1967 "Prolegomena to the Study of South Asian Regions and Regionalism." In *Regions and Regionalism in South Asian Studies*. Robert I. Crane, ed. pp. 89-111. Durham, N.C.: Duke University, Program in Comparative Studies on Southern Asia.
1968 "Caste Regions of the North Indian Plain." In *Structure and Change in Indian Society*. Milton B. Singer and Bernard S. Cohn, eds. pp. 81-114. Chicago: Aldine.
1985 "Folk Regions in Northwestern India." In *India: Culture, Society and Economy. Geographical Essays in Honor of Professor Asok Mitra*. A.B. Mukerji and Aijazudin Ahmad, eds. pp. 205-235. New Delhi: Inter-India Publications.

Schwartzberg, Joseph E., ed.
1978 *A Historical Atlas of South Asia*. Chicago and London: University of Chicago Press.

Singh, R.L., ed.
1971 *India: A Regional Geography*. Varanaṣi: National Geographical Society of India.

Smith, John D.
1975 "An Introduction to the Language of the Historical Documents from Rajasthan." *Modern Asian Studies* 9:433-464.

Sopher, David E.
1962 "Indian Peoples and Their History." In *India: A Compendium*. Raye R. Platt, ed. pp. 46-128. New York: American Geographical Society.
1977 "Rohilkhand and Oudh: An Exploration of Social Gradients Across a Political Frontier." In *Region and Realm in Traditional India*. Richard G. Fox, ed. pp. 281-307. Durham, N.C.: Duke University, Program in Comparative Studies on Southern Asia.

Sopher, David E., ed.
1980 *An Exploration of India: Geographical Perspectives on Society and Culture*. Ithaca, N.Y.: Cornell University Press.

Spate, O.H.K.
1954 *India and Pakistan: Land, People and Economy*. London: Methuen.

Srivastava, A.L.
1962 *Akbar the Great. Vol. 1. Political History, 1542-1605 AD*. Agra: Shiva Lal Agarwala.

Stamp, Dudley L.
1928 "The Natural Regions of India." *Geography* 14:502-506.

Stein, Burton
1967 "Comment on Regions Subjective and Objective: Their Relation to the Study of Modern Indian History and Society, by Bernard S. Cohn." In *Regions and Regionalism in South Asian Studies*. Robert I. Crane, ed. pp. 41-47. Durham, N.C.: Duke University, Program in Comparative Studies on Southern Asia.

Stern, Henri
1977 "Power in Traditional India: Territory, Caste, and Kinship in Rajasthan." In *Realm and Region in Traditional India*. Richard G. Fox, ed. pp. 52-78. Durham, N.C.: Duke University, Program in Comparative Studies on Southern Asia.

Subbarao, Bendapudi
1958 *The Personality of India: Pre- and Proto-Historic Foundation of India and Pakistan*. Baroda: M. S. University Archaeology Series No. 3.

Thapar, Romila
1966 *A History of India*. Vol. I. Harmondsworth, Middlesex, England: Penguin Books.

Thurston, Edgar
1909 *Castes and Tribes of Southern India*. 7 vols. Madras: Madras Government Press.

Tod, James
1978 *Annals and Antiquities of Rajasthan, or The Central and Western Rajput States of India*. Reprinted in 2 Vols. New Delhi: M. N. Publishers. (1st ed. 1829-32)

Vance, Rupert B.
1968 "Region." *International Encyclopedia of the Social Sciences* 13:377-382.

Vashishtha, Vijay Kumar
1978 *Rajputana Agency 1832-1858: A Study of British Relations with the States of Rajputana during the Period with Special Emphasis on the Role of Rajputana Agency*. Jaipur: Aalekh Publishers.

Walker, Benjamin
1968 *Hindu World: An Encyclopedic Survey of Hinduism*. 2 vols. London: George Allen and Unwin.

Wallace, Paul, ed.
1985 *Region and Nation in India*. New Delhi: Oxford and IBH Publishing House.

Whittlesey, Derwent
1954 "The Regional Concept and the Regional Method." In *American Geography: Inventory and Prospect*. Preston E. James and Clarence F. Jones, eds. pp. 19-68. Syracuse, N.Y.: Syracuse University Press.

BECOMING RAJASTHANI: PLURALISM AND THE PRODUCTION OF *DHARTĪ DHORĀṄ RĪ*

JOAN L. ERDMAN

After the formation of the state of Rajasthan in 1949, many people were attracted to its new capital, Jaipur. Those who came from other towns and villages of Rajasthan identified themselves with their new state, while those who immigrated from outside Rajasthan and decided to stay sought ways to establish themselves as Rajasthani. Looking forward rather than backward, invigorated by the new powers of the people in India's democratic republic, the newcomers educated their children in the schools for social and economic advancement, and tried to enculturate them with an identity of individualism and belonging to their new state. While the new Jaipuris were mainly Hindus, they were nationalist in their cultural outlook. The meeting of non-Rajasthanis with Rajasthan immigrants to Jaipur led to a new amalgam for Jaipur as a cultural center. Embracing differences, the immigrants sought to redefine Jaipur as a modern cultural capital, Rajasthan as a state rich in folk and classical traditions, and India's democratic pluralism as the touchstone for their ideas of modernity.

The end of princely rule in Rajasthan has been less studied than its previous glories and decline, and continuities have been given priority in historical studies. Yet for Rajasthan's people, the change from princely states, however interdependent and superordinated, to a single, egalitarian, and democratic state affected their lives as directly as the continuities. For the generations born during princely rule, loyalties to their natal states and traditional advantages of education and position persisted well into the post-independence period. But, for many Rajasthanis, access to educational opportunities, recognition of their rights as citizens, and consideration of themselves as makers of their own destinies was a leap into a newly constructed actuality. Acceptance of the new situation took place within circumstances where, for many Rajput families, enduring village power structures, lingering loyalties to former rulers, and the end of patronage owed to hereditary retainers made transformations less noticeable, at least until the post-princely state generation grew into adulthood.

For newcomers to the state, Rajasthan's traditions were unknown, while for peoples of Rajasthan, loyalties were traditionally multi-layered and particularized. Historic events, festivals and cultural performances, heroes and devotees, and even certain places in Rajasthan, were perceived as belonging to certain local groups or regions, rather than representing a cultural entirety. The idea of Rajputana, conceived during British rule in India and indirect rule in the Aravalli and Thar Desert areas, was a designation by outsiders, not by the peoples of the demarcated areas. A Rajput lady visiting in Jaipur one evening told me that she "admires foreigners who come and travel all over India and see it as a whole, while we see it in terms of its regions and communities."[1] Just as immigrants who considered themselves Gujaratis or Bengalis or Maharashtrians are surprised to be known as "Indians" or "Asian Indians" in America, peoples inside Rajasthan knew themselves as distinct communities, and it was outsiders who, assigning predominance to Rajput power, coined the names "Rajputana" and "Rajasthan." Pluralism is an insiders' view of differences and distinctiveness.

The peoples of the Aravallis, the Thar Desert and the Banas River areas think of themselves as Meenas, Meos, Gujars, Jats, Dholis, Manganiyars, Langas, Karbelias or Charans, as Shekhawats, Rathores, Kachhwahas or Chauhans, or as Bhils, Grassias, Kalavants or Kaum Khanis. For Rajasthanis, externally imposed analytic distinctions between tribe, clan, community and caste are less important than relationships among them: everyone *knows* who the others are, and social and political structures are dependent on complementarity and cooperation as well as differences through names and labels.

For any of the members of these groups to consider themselves Rajasthanis with all the rest of the peoples within the political boundaries of the state, a great leap of conceptualization was called for. Except when travelling outside the state, which led to identification as "Rajasthanis,"[2] there was no need to characterize the obvious: if one was living in Rajasthan, the main identity was community and *desh* (place of birth or ancestral home).

According to folklorist Komal Kothari,[3] groups or communities (*kaum*) often have two or three names, used in circumstances which depend on who is naming them—themselves or others—and whether they are being praised or denigrated by the outside name-giver. A musician may be known generically to urbanite professionals as a Mirasi, but will be called Dholi by his traditional patron and may even have a third name, which is used by others to suggest his status or relationship in a particular context.[4] What is germane is determined by who is using the name and in what specific context and relationship. Just as an African-American can use the word "nigger" for a fellow African-American as a brotherly appellation while a non-African-American using the term is perceived as debasing the same person, so who identifies a Rajasthani as something accrues and bestows status in a particular situation and context. In modern Rajasthan, performing stage artists are admired and high status guests, while Mirasis, or traditional musicians, continue to have low status. For contemporary musicians, making the transition from traditional Mirasi to admired stage artist is a delicate (and often difficult) process, since they are perceived as heirs to customary patronage and the status which was its corollary.

Efforts from within the newly-formed state of Rajasthan to build a common identity among its peoples stems from the formation of the state and designation of Jaipur as capital after independence. The transformation of a patchwork of princely domains into a single unitary state was not a foregone conclusion. Nor was the significance of Jaipur as a cultural center assured. Resettled Indians from the south and elsewhere were obviously outsiders to Rajasthan. They were not heir to any community of Rajasthan traditions, and were unaware of the state's folk and classical heritage. However, some immigrants to Jaipur who came from former princely realms within Rajputana had absorbed India's classical arts in their youth, and sought this "high culture" in their new surroundings.

Young men and women who grew to maturity during the independence struggle, and embraced the values of the nationalist Congress Party, or the Communist Party, or organizations that promoted religious or rightist values, found themselves after 1947 in need of vocations which would carry their commitments forward. In Rajasthan, the founders of the Jaipur-based *Rajasthan Patrika* (the state's major newspaper), the creator of the Bharatiya Lok Kala Mandal (a folk museum in Udaipur), the designer of the Rajasthan State Archives in Bikaner, and many others, sought to develop cultural voices and historical significance for the future of their new state. Connecting the past to the desired future meant both preservation and assertion of a pluralism which had been hidden in traditional hierarchies or submerged in an outsiders' view of Rajputana and Rajput preeminence, while at the same time not denying the history of Rajasthan's heroic past. This agenda for the new state, designed to foster integration and acceptance of a pluralist blending of communities, was a cultural formulation championed more creatively by private institutions than official ones.

In the early 1960s, when I first lived in Jaipur,[5] traditional musical evenings still took place within the contexts of princely patronage, albeit partly sponsored by wealthy businessmen. Singers and dancers were brought from western Rajasthan – places such as Pokaran (near Phalodi) or Bikaner – and the functions were attended by men and important foreign dignitaries or scholarly guests.[6] The song texts were part of the living tradition, usually sung in the regional *māṅdh*,[7] and related tales of heroism, unrequited love, decorative beauty and erotic unions. A musical evening was a party, which combined drinking and talk with performance in an atmosphere of mutual communication and understanding. The listeners were not so much an audience as parts of a plural community, which included patrons, artists, servants, and foreigners, all in their appropriate and relative statuses. The musicians warmed up on a stairway outside the music hall, and were given dinner apart from the invited guests, according to traditional status positionings.

By the mid-1970s when I returned for a prolonged stay, Jaipur's traditional patrons had been replaced by private organizations and official government institutions. Ravindra Manch (Fig. 1), a theater built to celebrate the Tagore centenary in 1964 in Ram Niwas Bagh, the town's major garden and park,[8] was the site for exhibitions and stage programs of music and dance. The large *havelīs* (mansions) of Rajput nobility had become (or were becoming) hotels and guest houses. Rajasthan's Lalit Kala Akademi based in Jaipur,

Fig. 1: **Ravindra Manch in the Ram Niwas Bagh, Jaipur's first modern theatre. (Photograph by the author)**

Sangeet Natak Akademi based in Jodhpur, Department of Tourism, and Ministry for Education were all absorbed in recreating Jaipur as a cultural center, according to their varied purposes.

When I asked friends in the university and in town whom I should meet with to talk about current cultural performances, they all recommended Shri Kaushal Bhargava. Our meeting proved fortuitous, and I was soon engaged in the ethnography of a Jaipur-based contemporary cultural organization, Rajasthan Tarun Kalakar Parishad (Rajasthan Young Artists Society). The Parishad had evolved in Rajasthan during the past two decades into a promoter of culture among youth, a presenter of famed performing artists from all over India, and the producer of a travelling multi-media program, *Dhartī Dhorāṅ Rī* (Land of Shifting Sands), which invoked the idea of belonging to Rajasthan. This paper analyzes the goals and impact of that organization through a history of its development, the dedication of its organizational secretary, and the symbolic impact of its productions and programs. The Parishad's production of *Dhartī Dhorāṅ Rī* is seen as the culmination of goals generated and established during its formative period.

A Private Cultural Institution for Post-Independence Rajasthan

> "It is easy to get a child out of a woman after nine months, but difficult to get a file from the Secretariat after nine years!"
>
> – Kaushal Bhargava, on the formation of an autonomous committee to manage Ravindra Manch

During the period of the princely states, Rajasthan's cultural institutions were dependent on royal support and aristocratic pastimes. In 1942, Jaipur State dissolved its *Guṅījankhānā* (Department of Virtuosos)[9]. Other states, too, had institutionalized support for performing artists, which ended shortly before or at the time of their integration into the Indian union. On the assumption that the new state of Rajasthan would assume the responsibilities of its predecessors, the Ministry of Education was mandated to form institutions and regulations for the promotion of learning and culture. In 1953 the Sangeet Natak Akademi was founded at the national level as a regional and national institution, but by the 1960s the national Akademi had divested itself of responsibility for state branches, and each state had to develop its own program and support for the performing arts.[10] During Rajasthan's formation, in order to settle rival claims for preeminence, state offices and institutions had been distributed among four former princely seats in the state, with the new state capital at Jaipur. Rajasthan's Sangeet Natak Akademi was based in Jodhpur,[11] yet this agency was selected as the first manager of Jaipur's major hall, Ravindra Manch, from its inception in 1963 until 1972.[12] As the only auditorium in Jaipur available to all groups,[13] it provided the first opportunity for cultural organizations to plan professional seasons of music, dance and drama.

In western Rajasthan, Sangeet Natak Akademi officers devoted their efforts primarily to researching, cataloguing and preserving the folklore of the state. Neither classical music, nor the development of an interest in music and dance among Rajasthan's youth, attracted its attention. Seeing that there was a gap between the Akademi's program and the desire of many people to hear and see the finest of India's classical artists, a group in Jaipur gradually evolved which turned towards promotion of classical music and dance among local residents, especially the growing middle classes, and the encouragement of performing arts among youth.

In 1955 an advocate, Rajasthan Minister of Finance Brij Sunder Sharma, joined with other Jaipur-based devotees of Indian classical music to form the Rajasthan Tarun Kalakar Parishad (Rajasthan Young Artists Society), and held a first performance at the home of Rajasthan Prime Minister Shri Mohan Mukerjee.[14] Sharma became president of the Parishad in 1957 and Kaushal Bhargava, another founder, became organizing secretary. After further performances at the Government Hostel, the Parishad held a competition in music, dance and drama, funded by a grant from the Rajasthan Sangeet Natak Akademi, of which Sharma was then chairman. Continuing to hold competitions and conferences in Jaipur, the Parishad officers saw a new possibility in the opening of Ravindra Manch in 1964. Planning to use the facility on a regular basis, the Parishad's leaders founded Shruti Mandal[15] to develop an interest in classical music and dance among a wider audience. Their intent was to hold six programs with major artists each year, and to cultivate a disciplined, knowledgeable, paying audience who could appreciate classical performing arts. The opening concert, a recital by sitarist Pandit Ravi Shankar, took place on August 17, 1964 at Ravindra Manch, and brought significant public attention to the group. Initially, members treated the organization like a club, coming and going as it suited them. But by encouraging listening sessions, providing excellent programs, and supporting a full-time organizing secretary, Shruti Mandal became a stable and successful producer of classical arts in Jaipur, and attracted the attention of India's finest artists and a major private patron.

In the spring of 1965, the Parishad initiated a camp for teaching and learning dance which was extended into the Nupur School of Dance.[16] But these dance classes had to be discontinued when the cost of renting a teaching space at Ravindra Manch was increased tenfold, dance guru Kundan Lal left for Delhi, and internal disagreements were abetted by competing schools and organizers.[17] Kaushal Bhargava decided to concentrate on his vocation of recording and his photographic art, and opportunities for holding international festivals in Jaipur became a new direction for the Parishad.

In 1967 the Jaipur Festival was inaugurated in a collaboration between the Parishad and Max Mueller Bhavan,[18] based in New Delhi. The team produced their first festival in 1968, at Jaipur's ancient capital of Amber, which drew an audience of about 4000 people, including five ambassadors from Delhi, delegates from an international economic conference, and Jaipur aristocrats. One evening was devoted to Rajasthani artists, who were brought from their villages and presented without any contrived staging or make-up. Some European viewers were so enticed by the joyousness of these folk performances that they prevailed upon the organizer to present them again the next morning, which resulted in a four-hour performance on the lawns of Ravindra Manch. Based on this success, some of the folk artists were invited for a festival in Sweden, where they were escorted by Kaushal Bhargava. The 1969 festival, at the newly refurbished Jal Mahal between Jaipur and Amber, drew a record gathering of nearly 7000, with the cooperation of the Public Works Department and the police, who arranged special buses from Bari Chauper in Jaipur to the performance site. The program ranged from folk to classical, including Langa musicians, court singers Gauribai and Alajulai, folk dances by the Rajasthan Tarun Kalakar Parishad students, *dhrupad* (vocal) and *khayāl* (on *sitār*) performances and a finale by all-India artist Sonal Mansingh in an Odissi dance recital. Government officials allocated funds and the artists were paid modestly for their participation.

By the 1970s the Rajasthan Tarun Kalakar Parishad had set up a regular production team for dances and ballets, and Shruti Mandal, with the support of a key Jaipur patron, was thriving as a producer of concerts. A plan was devised to collect funds to support Parishad programs by touring a multi-media production on Rajasthan to all districts of the state. By establishing relationships with patrons, organizers, audiences and officials in government, police and railways, the Parishad network grew to include dozens of towns and large villages in Rajasthan. Through private initiative this cultural organization played a central role in reinventing Jaipur as a cultural center. During its growth the Parishad had become an agency for cultural change in Rajasthan by engaging the youth in arts and contests, producing public concerts and international festivals, and developing the components for its production of *Dhartī Dhorāṅ Rī*.

Dedicated to Rajasthan's People and Culture: Shri Kaushal Bhargava

> "The difference is in the seeing. If I want to see beauty, I can see it anywhere. If I want to see dirt I can. I have my eye trained to see beauty only, and that's why my eye will [see it]. To me the human being is all the same. Once you start thinking in terms of creativity, you have to forget anything that binds you, that restricts your freedom."
>
> – Kaushal Bhargava

When I first met him in the 1970s, Kaushal Bhargava was an acknowledged leader in Jaipur's cultural renaissance. He had founded and developed durable institutions. He had outlasted several of his critics and competitors. He had gained the acknowledgement and support of leading scholars, artists, officials and patrons. He continued to find new projects to sustain and engage his photographic eye and convey his symbolic messages. Without Kaushal Bhargava the production of *Dhartī Dhorāṅ Rī* would never have been conceived and carried out. Since his invention of its multi-media format, there have been imitators and clones, but none have matched his scope or artistry. And no other artist has communicated the message of belonging to Rajasthan so ardently. By the time he created *Dhartī Dhorāṅ Rī* Kaushal was already a mature artist, though it is difficult to measure his progress since there are no typical career patterns for artists who bridge pre- and post-independence India (nor, perhaps, for any artist). His background before reaching Jaipur is sketchy, despite efforts to elicit sequences and dates. There are events and involvements he would prefer to leave vague or unspoken. Being optimistically oriented towards the future, he sees his past not as a blueprint for building, but as source material for his work and commitment. At times he recalls key events anecdotally to illuminate values and to convey the seasoning that comes from sharp experiences, reinforcing the choice he made in 1962 to dedicate his life to producing and organizing the arts.

Shri Kaushal Bhargava was born in Alwar State at Kishengarh Fort near the village where his parents lived until 1914. He was raised in an atmosphere of Brahman devotion and aesthetic connoisseurship. His father, an excellent horseman, had also studied the Persian language, and thus succeeded memorably as a Nazim (Collector) in the employ of Alwar State, from which he retired in the 1930s. He died in 1948. The family owned lands in village Bahadurpur, ten miles outside Alwar, but lived in Alwar City, where Kaushal was raised with four brothers and three sisters. All were educated and entered government service or other professions, but Kaushal, the youngest son and especially devoted to his strong and religious mother, had an artistic nature. Alwar State's Maharaja Jai Singh, before he was removed to Paris (where he died in 1937), was a patron of the arts, and his court attracted major performing artists—Allah Bande Khan of the Dagar Bani, Inayat Khan, Nasiruddin Khan, Abdul Wahab, *bīn* player Sadiq Ali (father of Delhi's Asad Ali Khan), Mashuk Ali who went to Pakistan, and others. Kaushal began studying *tablā* in 1941 with a *gharānā*[19] teacher, Din Mohamed, the son of the late court artist Abdul Wahab. Leaving his Alwar college, he travelled to Calcutta, Lucknow and eventually Delhi, where he lived with a master ivory carver and learned this art before leaving in 1945 as the craft became commercialized. From his mother's example, Kaushal Bhargava saw the arts as incompatible with business, since their goals were reached through paths with diverging values. The arts were for *rasikas*, those who could feel and be touched by aesthetic delight; business encouraged a contractual relationship between provider and consumer, based on materialistic needs and desires. In each of his attempts to find a professional vocation, Bhargava was more interested in issues of design and charm than in profit and expansion.

In 1951, when he came to Jaipur and set up a tailoring business in the main bazar, his wizardry in designing stylish and well-fitting suits quickly attracted a demanding and high class clientele. Eventually a distaste for collecting outstanding bills led him to close the business, and he agreed to manage the founding of Jaipur's Khadi Ghar (Handloom House) – a job in closer conformity with his desire to leave profit-seeking business behind. Offered government service, he sensed it would interfere with his freedom and refused. Finally, in 1962, having reduced all his expenses to a minimum, and moving in the same building from several rooms to a single one, Kaushal left all business for the arts. In the ten years he had been in Jaipur, he had become friends with others interested in classical music, formed a performing ensemble in which he played flute, established links with government officials and artists, and, as one of the initial founders of Rajasthan Tarun Kalakar Parishad, had become its organizing secretary.

While Kaushal Bhargava remained close to his sisters and two surviving brothers, he lived alone. In the 1940s he was romantically attached to a girl in Alwar, but their liaison was socially impossible, so they could not plan to marry. Eventually she developed tuberculosis and died, and Kaushal felt he had made a mistake in listening to society's conventions instead of his own heart. As an unmarried man in Jaipur society, Kaushal had a position in many families – as guide and counsel, as "uncle" and friend, as a guest and extended family member. While involvement with a wife and perhaps children would have made him socially similar to his cultural constituents, his singleness provided a platform for choices about engagement and disengagement unique in the world of the arts. It also gave Kaushalji a rare status – separate and independent yet connected to many.

Kaushal Bhargava's capacity to make personal connections with people from varied communities and vocations was essential to his success. Like many of his friends, he was an outsider to Jaipur who was attracted to the new capital after independence. Confidant

Shesh Narayan, employed in the postal service, said that Kaushal Bhargava and his group were the reason he stayed in Jaipur rather than returning to his South Indian home. Kaushal understood that reaching out to people's needs for recognition and significance in a tumultous period of cultural disarray could give them pride and confidence. For those who were immigrants to Rajasthan, identification with its culture and through it to an all-India culture made them feel that they belonged in their adopted home. For many whose occupations were boringly repetitive or unwelcome (such as collecting taxes), or secularly dispassionate, the arts provided a relief and access to felt emotions and civilizing pleasures. Creating opportunities for youth to carry their adopted or the next generation's culture forward pleased parents who were raising children in a world different from their own times and experiences. In Tarun Kalakar Parishad there was a chance to prove through competition a student's success in music and dance. Membership in Shruti Mandal would bring India's best artists to the city which they now claimed as their own. Bhargava, in dedicating himself full-time to promoting and producing the arts, even before having steady patronage, was a beacon for concerned and adoptive Rajasthanis.

Kaushal Bhargava's life-style and domestic arrangement were a signal of his dedication. Living in a single room, surrounded by cupboards filled with his tapes and slides, his typewriter propped on a wooden box containing addresses, pens and papers, the projector atop a tall stool and focused on a wall left blank for slide showings, Kaushalji kept in constant touch with his comrades and constituents by telephone. A closet with a drawing of his mother above its doors served as combination kitchen, storage space, and dressing room. Two chairs and a large platform bed with bolsters were the only furnishings. Outside the room on the verandah were more chairs and a table, pleasant in the in-between times and seasons when it was neither too hot nor too cold to sit there. Through all the seasons the *tulsī* plant flourished, sometimes with a cloth hanging from its branches to dry in the afternoon sun. Every corner and shelf was occupied by musical instruments, books and speakers. Each morning a peon who slept in a passageway near the huge wooden door to the building hauled pots of water to the third floor verandah where tiny rooms for bath and toilet were placed. The open verandah at the front of the building provided a view south over New Gate to the Ram Lila Ground and the Ram Niwas Bagh gardens with Ravindra Manch. Looking northwards along the broad Jaipur street Chaura Rasta, one could sometimes see Tripolia, the main gate to the City Palace, through the haze and trees. Poised just inside the old city's newest gate, with a clear view of the growing city outside, Kaushal's symbolic position was not lost on him or his visitors. Clearly Bhargava belonged to both Jaipur's past and its present. Though his abode was modest, his aspirations for Jaipur's cultural growth were not.

Gradually an assortment of seekers had been drawn to Kaushal Bhargava's door: folk artists from western Rajasthan, connoisseurs needing tickets to programs, officials soliciting performances for tourists and other occasions, parents wanting advice on teaching their children dance and music, out-of-towners trying to bring a Rajasthan show to their city or town, assistants planning tours and rehearsals, confidants and friends discussing next projects and artists, potential patrons viewing Bhargava's slide stories, and others. Especially engaging were the professional photographers who came to meet one of their own, and see his current work. Although Kaushalji has never published books of his photographs, his works have been used (and sometimes credited) in a number of Rajasthan publications. But selling his photographs seemed less interesting to Kaushal than taking them and placing them in his slide stories. He photographed only in Rajasthan. "Kashmir is beautiful," he says, "but what's the use? I must be in Rajasthan."

After the demise of the Nupur School of Dance, some students who had reached a level of proficiency were invited to join a production team, and practice their *ghūmar* and *gaṇgaur* dances to be presented on special occasions. It's not clear when the idea arose to combine the dances with Kaushalji's slides, but the development of a script was a piecemeal process of additions and refinement. Opportunities to travel in Rajasthan were found in escorting various officials and guests on tours; historical data was gleaned from books, tours and conversations with knowledgeable participants; a dance master who had trained with Uday Shankar at his famed Almora India Culture Center was hired; and experiments were made in finding a format to combine the new technology with the revitalized folk dances performed by Jaipur students.

The Symbolic Impact of *Dhartī Dhoṛaṅ Rī*

"My attempt is to use photography as a simile for language. The slides are special; they are replacing film which is only plastic images passing by. But if you see a real human being weeping you can't help but be moved. So humans as well as slides are brought on stage. You need to have real things to explain abstractions, which not all can understand."

– Kaushal Bhargava

By the late 1970s, 30 years after integration of the princely states into the Indian union and the creation of modern Rajasthan, the once youthful generations who remembered the days of the princes were at the peak of their professions, in government and politics, in business and trade, in education and culture. These men and women were concerned that Rajasthan's new generations remember their heritage and remain loyal to the state, while at the same time espousing modern values of responsibility, advancement and self-respect. Seeing the past as the "good old days,"[20] many among the aging elites of Rajasthan recalled a period when loyalty to one's *kaum* or community was not racist or regionalist, but a dedication to identifying the self by connection with one's own kind. Communities, in their opinion, were not then ranged against each other, but integrated into a pluralistic pattern of cooperation and coordination, dependent of course on the primacy of an all-powerful ruler or rule and the inferiorities concordant with the acceptance of Rajput and British hegemony. Two different patterns of relationship – the democratic egalitarian, and the power-based hierarchic – coexist in modern Rajasthan, and are the source for partisan cultural statements, as well as political tensions.

What those who proposed a pluralistic Rajasthan sought was a cultural conception which would connect the sub-regions and their peoples, stressing the common and shared components of their lives. One route to unity was a kind of "melting pot" – blending all components into a singular whole (as perhaps with the arguments for a single language called "Rajasthani"). Another path was to gather together the diverse pieces into an account which had continuity and a direction. This narrative process could incorporate the stories of distinctive groups and peoples and places who would, through time, see themselves as a pluralistic whole. The latter vision was the basis for the production of the multi-media production, *Dhartī Dhorāṅ Rī*.

Cultivating a Regional Identity

The process of developing regional identity in Rajasthan, loyalty to a state as well as to family and *desh* (by which is usually meant a village), is a gradual one, marked by celebrations, public ceremonies, political speeches and participation, as well as consolidation in social and economic spheres. In India, the celebrations of 26th January (Republic Day) and 15th August (Independence Day), all-India elections and other national events renew and continue the process of developing national identity, while regional parallels encourage local loyalties. Nehru's *Discovery of India*, and the musical show created after independence with the same name, are cultural contributions to a process of creating national identity.[21]

The idea of Kaushal Bhargava in his production of *Dhartī Dhorāṅ Rī* was to develop a program which *all* Rajasthanis could feel was their own, and which would represent their social bonding in a sequence of images and statements. The perspective of *Dhartī Dhorāṅ Rī* was not partial or segmentary, but inclusionary, giving each group which saw it the chance to suggest further views to be incorporated as part of the whole, Rajasthan. Bhargava's sophistication in provoking this kind of thinking should not be overlooked in understanding the goals of his production.

This multi-media show, incorporating slides and taped narrative, live music and folk dances, has played in villages in almost all the districts of Rajasthan (as well as outside the state and outside India). It has been seen in Karauli and Hindoun, in Ganganagar and Jodhpur, in Khetri and Pilani, by fairgoers and millowners, by members of Parliament and state legislatures, by tourist groups and teachers. But its largest and most significant audience has been the villagers of Rajasthan, who come in throngs as large as 10,000 for one program, to see and hear the presentation of their own place. While their initial intent may be to observe the live dancers or the miracles of audio-visual screenings and sound, they are immediately drawn into the process of witnessing their own heroes and places, themselves in fact, in the images before their eyes. It is a *darśan* (viewing) of Rajasthan itself, the new state of an independent India, shown not only in magnificent photographs on a huge screen, depicted not only in the booming voice of the narrator and lyrical music of its artists, but also in the youth, creating their own music and dances onstage. For viewers from Rajasthan, the program is a lesson in feeling proud of the heritage and traditions of the state as a whole, and identifying with them. The challenge of the program's creator was to make all the distinctive peoples feel that the production was about them, and that they, the audience, were one with earlier and future viewers in Rajasthan.

Kaushal Bhargava's artistic vision is revealed in the choices he made in bringing the production together. His medium could be called "folk-modern." He used the familiar format of *paḍ*,[22] showing scenes of events being talked or sung about, but shifted from all the scenes being present at the same time on a huge painted scroll to presenting each scene separately as a single slide projected on a large screen. Usually, he projects the slides and plays the taped voice-and-music accompaniment from behind the opaque screen, so that no apparatus is visible to the audience. This technique creates the same mystery and delight as a traditional Indian shadow puppet show, with voice and views coming from an unseen source. Rather than depending entirely on this modern media display, he also brings the vitality of live performance into the program, by interspersing sections of the slide-and-tape narrative with lively dancers and musicians who appear onstage. The dances are performed by teenage girls and boys from Jaipur, school and college students who have been trained in Rajasthani movements and songs, and in staged presentation of them. The musicians, youthful singers and instrumentalists from Jaipur and nearby areas, adapt their voices and instruments, which at various times have included *ḍholak* (double-headed folk drum), *sitār*, flute, *tālī* (small cymbals) and *tablā*, to songs heard while travelling through the different districts of Rajasthan.

During the program there is a complementarity of image and movement, with neither the dances nor the slides being secondary in importance and impact. The well-paced show allows no separation between the two media types, each segment following immediately on the other or even overlapping, creating a continuing energy of performance. Subtle structural connections between image, taped and live sounds, and live presentation give the program a visual and auditory narrative in addition to the conceptual geographic and historical progression. The description of the program as "like *paḍ*" was made by its producer on several occasions. For Rajasthani audiences, townspeople and villagers alike, the *Dhartī Dhorāṅ Rī* media was new but familiar, and in the pre-television period,[23] transitional in modern India, it was sufficiently innovative to bring crowds, but familiar enough to evoke identification with its songs and messages.[24]

The production has a further educational purpose. By participating in it and touring around Rajasthan, the young people who perform are themselves learning about their culture and state (Fig. 2) Their parents were delighted with the unusual opportunity given their sons and daughters for chaperoned travel in Rajasthan, involvement in the performances, and the small stipends earned by each youth for participation in the touring troupe. In each place where the program is given, Bhargava arranges for a tour of a nearby fort or palace, wildlife sanctuary or industrial site, temple or mosque. It's an experiential course in the Rajasthani heritage, and parents of the participants recognize its educational value. For Bhargava, it is a chance to photograph new places and peoples; for the musicians it is an opportunity to hear local songs and instruments. Occasionally, when a new dance is found, in a temple or at a festival, the dancers watch it carefully and their teacher uses it as the basis for new choreography. Bhargava meets many people at each performance, and they offer their expertise on the local surroundings—what should be included because it is wonderful or important. Audiences see it as *their* program and feel free to offer suggestions and additions, giving Bhargava crucial feedback on what is seen and understood, and what can be added or deleted. He changes the slides for each show, rearranging them or replacing some, depending on what has been recently photographed or where the program is to be held. The taped narration and music is the same, but the length of the program can be manipulated to fit the organizer's schedule by adding or deleting dance numbers. (Fig. 3) Thus the program can last from 30 minutes (taped narration and slides only) to two hours.

There is a romance to the *Dhartī Dhorāṅ Rī* tours which can be illustrated only through a description of its progress from Jaipur to another town, and a recognition that from the viewpoint of the troupe members the entire process of rehearsing and presenting

Fig. 2: The *Dhartī Dhorāṅ Rī* troupe on tour in Ranthambore near Sawai Madhopur, November 3, 1976. Dance Master Ranjit Shikari, is at upper left, the author sitting on the steps below him. (Photograph by Kaushal Bhargava)

Fig. 3: Rehearsal of *Dhartī Dhorāṅ Rı* dance in the courtyard of the Sati Mata temple's *dharamśālā* (travellers' guest house), Jhunjhunu, January 5, 1977 (Photograph by the author)

shows all over Rajasthan is a unique experience. A sample from a 1976 tour can convey the multiple opportunities for learning about Rajasthan, Rajasthani peoples, artistic discipline, flexibility, different ways of life, and even how to learn. Not surprisingly, the touring troupe gathers guests who travel with the group and are solicited as helpers along the way. Thus my travel with the troupe was not a particularly unusual event.

> After midnight we gather at the Jaipur Railway Station, joining sleeping bodies stretched on boxes and bedsheets, waiting for the train to Sawai Madhopur. The troupe's teenage girls group tightly together in the cool February evening, wrapped in their shawls, softly gossiping and occasionally tossing a glance to one of the boys or the musicians. I sit with management, and we are mostly silent, keeping thoughts to ourselves and watching to make sure no one wanders off at a crucial moment. There is a great deal of baggage – the troupe travels with all its lighting, instruments, costumes and props, as well as a small case for each artist, assistant and manager, and a slide projector and huge sheet for a screen. Tomorrow night the show will be in a small town south of Jaipur, arranged by the local Superintendent of Police, who is a friend of the troupe's creator and director, Shri Kaushal Bhargava.
>
> Reaching the town at dawn we sleepily disgorge ourselves from the train without even tea to warm us against the still chill February morning. A *dharamśālā*[25] almost on the train tracks is indicated, and we are promised some breakfast soon. Kaushalji assigns an assistant to oversee settling the troupe, then heads for the "theater" with the local in-charge, taking the troupe's technical staff and all the equipment with him. The show will be outdoors, in a Ramlila ground on which a stage is being built of bricks and sand, with a huge canvas thrown over it. The first problem is a three-stage electricity connection which is essential for the powerful lights, the tape recorder and projector, then some 'green rooms' for the dancers made from tents, and other canvas barriers for stage wings and crowd control. In such small towns mostly men attend the show. Unaccustomed to seeing young women on stage, they sometimes rush to the stage at the end or peer into the dressing rooms during changes. A recent program at Kishangarh attended by more than 10,000 ended in an urgent forward crush so forceful that I escaped only by

grapping the shoulder of an accompanying Jaipur journalist who had warned earlier of the risk.

Before the Sawai Madhopur program began, I had asked Kaushalji how he maintained his calm and serious demeanor even when preparations for the show were far from complete when the troupe arrived, and the situation seemed hopeless. "I always assume that the [local organizers] have done as much as they could," he said. "Then I go on from there." The tech (technical arrangement) for the show is complex, yet it usually comes off without any major problems, except in unusual circumstances.

This time, the state, with its durrie-over-blocks[26] construction, is exceptionally uneven, and in the Chiromini dance where the young women carry burning firepots on their heads – a spectacular sight in the darkness of the open air theater – one pot falls to the stage and the cotton tarpaulin starts to burn. Like troupers everywhere, the artists continue to dance, while the embarrassed victim runs off the stage with a slightly burned foot. Someone sitting with the musicians takes their pitcher of water to the burning spot and unceremoniously dumps it, extinguishing the fire. In a later show for an army general in Khetri north of Jaipur even the three-stage [electrical] connection fails, and the show is continued with burning open lanterns along the front of the stage, increasing the tension of each dance as skirts whirl over dangerous flames. When 'the show must go on' in India, circumstances can be precarious.[27]

Ranjit Shikari, the *Dhartī Dhorāṅ Rī* dance master, was raised in Ahmedabad in Gujarat, which is culturally a contiguous region with southern Rajasthan.[28] His father worked in the textile mills, and Shikari was educated up to the sixth class in Gujarati and English. When he was 16 Uday Shankar and his company of musicians and dancers visited Ahmedabad, and the troupe manager agreed to take the youth back to the Uday Shankar Culture Centre in Almora. Shikari had already been initiated into dance and music by the guru in his local *mohallā* (inner-city neighborhood). At Almora he learned in Shankar's special creative dance classes, as well as from Sachin Shankar, Shanti Bardhan and Narendra Sharma, each of whom became modern choreographers of Indian dance.[29] The genius of Uday Shankar was in training not only dancers but choreographers, and when Shikari left Almora he began working independently, composing ballets with modern themes. His 1942 ballet, "Bharat Choro" (Quit India) led to his arrest but he was paroled since he was "only an artist, a dancer".[30] He rechoreographed the ballet as "Sarvodaya Ka Marg" (Path of Sarvodaya),[31] and then joined Shanti Bardhan's Little Ballet Troupe as an artist, later moving to Sachin Shankar's Ballet Unit. Another former Uday Shankar student, Devilal Samar, founder of the Bharatiya Lok Kala Mandal (a folk museum) in Udaipur, brought Shikari to the museum, where he composed ballets based on desert themes and valiant heroines. In 1971 Shikari was invited to Jaipur by dramatist Pramod Bhasin for his Trimurthi organization,[32] and he composed a "Rajasthan Darshan" ballet, as well as choreographing ballets for Mahavir School and Kanoria College. Later, he joined a cultural organization in Alwar called Kala Bharati, and from there came to Rajasthan Tarun Kalakar Parishad to choreograph and direct the dances for *Dhartī Dhorāṅ Rī*.

Shikari's authenticity, derived from his *mohallā* childhood beginnings, his training at Uday Shankar's Almora Culture Centre and his experience in Indian dance troupes and ballet choreography, brought a unique talent to the Parishad's program. Transforming tribal and traditional dances into staged performances required comprehension of their structural integrity as well as their characteristic movements and postures. Training urban school students to convey the typical communicative gestures of these dances demanded patience and subtlety. And working within the context of a multi-media production meant cultivating an awareness of and accommodation to the narrative line of the audio-visual sections. Ranjit Shikari's mastery of all facets of choreography and dance training were evident in the enthusiastic performances of his young student dancers. In addition, he provided a legitimation for the modern goals of the *Dhartī Dhorāṅ Rī* program. Honored by the Gujarati government for his achievements, Shikari had danced for world notables, including Eisenhower, Khrushchev, Bulganin, Chou En Lai, Queen Elizabeth II, Marshall Tito, Nasser, Radhakrishnan, Rajendra Prasad, C. Rajagopalachari, Pandit Nehru, Lal Bahadur Shastri and Mrs. Indira Gandhi. His choreography affirmed the significance of dance as part of the regional and national wealth of an independent India.

Dhartī Dhorāṅ Rī tours are opportunities for extending the inclusiveness of the production, and expanding the knowledge of Rajasthan for troupe members. In Karauli the troupe visits the Madan Mohan temple next to the palace of Rajkumar Brijendra Pal, who hosts the visit. Before taking *darśan* of the deity, the Parishad musicians bring their harmonium, *tablā* and cymbals, and sing *bhajans* (devotional songs) in the temple. Later, after exclaiming over the palace's fine portraits and decaying splendors, they move on to Kaila Devi temple, 27 kilometres from Karauli. Built in 1789, it contains portraits of Karauli's royal family, including a childhood painting of their host. The group sings and dances in front of the deity, and then a local man dances and sings. The group's sitarist, Shyam, is assigned to write the words and song dictated by this man, and it is learned by the musicians and performed the next evening in Hindoun, an immediate addition to *Dhartī Dhorāṅ Rī*, and a gesture of significance to the local audience.

What is *Dhartī Dhorāṅ Rī* all about? Basically, it evokes, illuminates and praises Rajasthan's land and peoples and their traditions. The photographs show places and communities in ways that Rajasthanis themselves recognize but do not usually notice. Bhargava's camera is an education in seeing Rajasthan, his special art that of showing what has always been there, but has not been fully appreciated in an aesthetic sense before. The narration in modern standard Hindi uses a highly Sanskritized vocabulary, which often leads to queries after the program about the meaning and intent of several words and phrases. This choice of a supra-regional language, that of national broadcasting and modern Hindi literature, is purposeful, a complement to the specifically Rajasthani slides, placing Rajasthan within the national discourse and reaching beyond Rajasthan to broader Indian audiences.

Content as Touchstone

A ringing proclamation of the heroic character of Rajasthan's men and women opens the narrative of *Dhartī Dhorāṅ Rī*. The taped voice uses a lexicon which is highly Sanskritized and difficult to translate into colloquial English. Its form and content strongly evoke deep cultural memories and emotional attachments for Rajasthanis – whose enculturation is different from that of outside listeners. It begins with a dramatic booming announcement.

> This land of heroes, Rajasthan!
>
> In each particle of this land is written a tale of bravery, courage, surrender, and sacrifice. For centuries, the blue sky of this land has reverberated with the sounds of battles. Here generations of strong-willed Rajputs have donned the sacrificial orange (*kesariyā*).[33]
>
> Strong and handsomely built, with an elegant turban and a well-groomed mustache, this is the Rajput before whom the lion's tail falls in fear, and elephants give way.
>
> It was here in Rajasthan that Queen Hadi cut off her head and sent it to her husband leaving for the battlefield.[34] Slim bodied, beautifully formed, wearing a tightly-fitting bodice, *ṭīkā*[35] on her forehead – if you bow to her, tears of emotion will fall on her clothes, if you tease her she can roar like a lioness. Pure as the goddess Uma, the secret of Rajput honor, these are Rajput women.[36]

The Hindi words have a resonance, cadence and alliteration which is impossible to reproduce in English. The sound of the narration, with its deep resonating voice and musical background, cannot be experienced from the printed page. Yet it is clear that this is a beginning designed to capture the audience's attention, engage them with the content, and suggest that what they are viewing and hearing is something splendid which can give them energy and pride.

In the first lines Bhargava evokes the state's Rajput legacy, the heroism of its men and women, their qualities of courage and grace, and the deeply felt emotions of a warrior culture. While this narration proceeds, he shows on the screen landscapes, dunes and forts, temples and peoples, bringing all together into an on-going participatory play which gives audience and players a sense of commonality and collective goals and vision.

For Rajasthanis mention of *pagṛī* (turban), *kesariyā*, *ṭīkā* and *tyāg* (in the sense of surrender to one's destiny) makes the semantics colloquial, attached to known symbols of their own cultural heritage. Whatever the meanings for all of India, here the associations are direct, particular, and heartfelt. In this program the effort is to bring together sets of attachments which together will generate a Rajasthanī loyalty and responsiveness.

Performance as an Integrative Process

What *Dhartī Dhorāṅ Rī* represents is a conscious development of symbols for all of Rajasthan, which is intended as a call to *cultural* action, namely the development of a Rajasthani identity. For Rajasthani people, their lands have always been subjective territories known through their chronicles, communities, heroes and forts, pilgrimage sites and temples, colors and seasons, songs and dances. The contents were more important than the boundaries. To reinvent Rajasthan as a cultural entity required the vision of a believer, the technique of an enlightened organizer, and a modern awareness of symbolic design. "My slides have a message," says Bhargava, who photographs to construct particular images and uses the photographs in his show to forge meanings.

Bhargava's slides present Rajasthan's people and places hugely, bigger than life: the elaborate silver waist decoration of a nomadic girl, the neatly curled mustache and intricately wound turban of a Rajput man, the dusty and visibly poignant place where Rajput princesses committed *jauhar*,[37] immolating themselves on a pyre so their men could fight valiantly to the death. As Bhargava himself says, "The difference is in the seeing." He has trained himself to see the beauty of Rajasthan and its peoples, and so he sees it everywhere. His slides are striking images which do what all artists propose: make us see anew what has been taken for granted or not even noticed before.

Clear about his purposes and limits, Bhargava points out that his goal is not to make a documentary, but "to give a feeling of emotion through slides. Slides don't have to show what is said, and often don't." A photograph is a still image – one that lingers in the mind, unlike a moving image which is enveloped in the complexity of on-going time. "When you see a film, one sequence overlaps the other so quickly that you lose them. But if you see a thing still on a screen, it can be remembered even after 50 years. If you see a picture and I say something, then it remains with you for a long time."

Kaushal Bhargava recognizes that the potential for shaping people's viewpoints is embedded in his combination of visual and audio media. He would probably agree with Gombrich's statement that the "mutual support of language and image facilitates memorizing. The use of two independent channels, as it were, guarantees the ease of reconstruction."[38] Like film makers, Bhargava also has a musical score, but for *Dhartī Dhorāṅ Rī* it is composed from his recordings of classical and folk artists, and from sound effects created in his own room in the early hours of the morning when no external sounds intrude. Although the narrative of *Dhartī Dhorāṅ Rī* is sometimes difficult for colloquial audiences, the *dohā* (couplet) of Rana Pratap, and the lines of the poet Bihari are easily apprehended by most Rajasthanis, who remember the poetic images as well as the visual ones.[39]

The sequences of slides with taped narrative and music focus the mind and encourage concentration on images and sounds. During the slides and their accompanying taped narration, there is no distraction created by live dancing girls onstage, or musicians playing to the audience or other artists. Only the technically surprising miracle of projected visions and disembodied sound emanating from speakers engages the audience's attention. The content urges each audience member to recognize his and her own place in Rajasthan among those pictured so pleasingly, to see his and her own community or places of devotion. The viewers are placed within Rajasthan's history and its modernity, and the plurality of Rajasthani peoples is depicted as an asset, not an imperfection or potential source of conflict.

Dhartī Dhorāṅ Rī is a Rajasthani rather than a Hindi phrase. It is the title of a post-independence song heard on the radio, but that is not the key to Bhargava's usage, which preceded the song. The phrase speaks of what is old and enduring, namely the earth, ground or land (*dhartī*), and the sand dunes or moving hills of the desert (*dhorā*). The earth remains solid while the sand dunes are always shifting.[40] While *dhartī* is a word in Sanskrit, Hindi and Rajasthani, the latter word, *dhorā* is pure Rajasthani, as is the grammatical construction of the phrase. The title of Bhargava's program suggests therefore both the stability of the sustaining and supporting earth or land, and also the peculiar Rajasthani geomorphic feature of shifting sand dunes. Though confined to the western desert area of Rajasthan, this is the image outsiders have of Rajasthan as a whole. By showing slides of the immovable Aravalli mountains as well as the shifting sand dunes, Bhargava enlarges outsiders' views of the state, while satisfying the local knowledge of insiders.

The finale of the production is the entire live cast singing a song entitled "*Dhartī Dhorāṅ Rī*"– not the popular song, but a folk song created especially for the show. Thus the words announce both an on-going process and a statement of vitally and conceptually important features of the land. Rajasthan, it says, is a land of shifting, moving sands. (Note the relationship to the "particles" of sand mentioned in the first paragraph of the opening narrative.)

> Land of the brave [*vīr*],
> *Dhorāṅ rī dhartī.*
> Its legends will go on forever.
> Future generations will go on singing,
> *Dhartī dhorāṅ rī.*

And the song's refrain says:

> *Dhartī dhorāṅ rī, dhartī dhorāṅ rī,*
> Come, *dhartī dhorāṅ rī.*
> Shy of going to heaven,
> The gods come to *dhartī* to play.
> Men and women sing its praises:
> *Dhartī dhorāṅ rī.*[41]

The verses describe poetically the attributes of this land, Rajasthan: sweet-singing birds whose songs come like waves of water from on high, fearsome lightning that flashes intermittently, lion-like Bikaner, the pomp and show of Ajmer, the spider-web of Chittor Fort, and the fame of Amer, Abu, Jaisalmer, and Jodhpur.

Various sections in the production speak of the temples of the Aravalli hills, famed devotional poets, teachers and holy men, the environment and its relationship to Rajasthan's strong inhabitants, the use of Rajasthan as a refuge from strife, the forts and chronicles of bravery and patronage, the battles and sacrifices, the chastity of beautiful Padmini, the fleet-footed horse Chetak and its rider Maharana Pratap, the elegance of the carved temples at Ranakpur and the classic design of Jaipur, Rajasthan's art and beauty, the *līlā* (divine play) of Krishna, the coming of freedom and singing of the anthem "*Bande Mātaram*" (Hail to the Mother), and the opening of Rajasthan's treasures[42] to its peoples.[43]

The dances are derived from multiple sources: tribal dances, women's and men's folk dances, seasonal dances, community and religious dances, and classical *kathak*. They include a choreographed representation of the dance of peacocks, a display of firepots balanced on dancers' heads, the giving of praise to a raja, the clash of sticks and cymbals, celebration of the festival of Gangaur,[44] and a version of *ghūmar*, a traditional dance of Rajput women. In some dances the words of the accompanying song are mimed; for others the dance movements are characteristic of the occasion the song describes. Inclusion of all this variety of place, people, and cultural performance gives each person in every audience something to call their own, which is seen in this amazing and entertaining collection of Rajasthani symbols and artistic forms.

Envisioning Rajasthan as a Cultural Resource

The performance of Rajasthan's culture in *Dhartī Dhorāṅ Rī* is a way of identifying Rajasthan's symbols, acknowledging its history, giving voice to all its peoples, and presenting the panorama of its landscapes. The production is intended to show Rajasthan's cultural wealth as contributing to the process of creating an Indian nation, one which is composed of various parts. Decades ago, when the Soviet Union decided to project its performance culture abroad, it was to regional dances and troupes that the government turned. India has done likewise in its Festivals of India presented abroad. Cultural creativity is often attached to symbols and events which are local and regional,[45] and must be viewed narratively, or sequentially, in order to give each its appropriate voice. While, at their best, such arts are accessible to outsiders, they have special and subtle meaning to those whose culture they represent, for "insiders" recognize the symbols and places emotionally and viscerally – they feel an attachment to the art itself because it is also in them as part of their cultural heritage.

Perhaps is it necessary to be in Rajasthan to appreciate the meaning of *Dhartī Dhorāṅ Rī*, or to be Rajasthani. Seeing the slides alone and listening to the recorded narrative in Delhi or New York or Chicago produces an irritation with the juxtaposition of slide and audio, a superiority towards the emotionalism, and an impatience with the simplicity. Yet in Rajasthan the commitment of the young artists to the program, the acclaim of huge audiences in towns and villages, and the elation of organizers presenting the show cannot be denied. Even foreigners travelling in the state can find its essence in *Dhartī Dhorāṅ Rī*, as this note from my 1976 diary suggests.

> Later, after the show, two student visitors from London and New Zealand on educational fellowships question Kaushalji while he reclines on a *charpoy* [wooden cot with woven center] at the *dharamśālā*. I realize that they are stunned by the quality and excitement of *Dhartī Dhorāṅ Rī*. They say the show has taught them more about Rajasthan than they have learned in two weeks touring the state.

In *Dhartī Dhorāṅ Rī*, the turning point in the narrative is not the creation of the state of Rajasthan, but the raising of India's national flag at independence. The artists heard on the taped sound track are not only Rajasthani performers, but also Bombay-based Shiv Kumar Sharma (santoor) and Hari Prasad Chaurasia (flute), nationally and internationally known and praised instrumentalists of India's classical (Hindustani) music. Rajasthan is, for Kaushal Bhargava, and in his message to all his audiences within Rajasthan and outside, an integral part of India, and of the world, and its culture can speak of values local, regional, national, and human so that audiences can find within its performance values and symbols with which they are associated and identify.

Dhartī Dhorāṅ Rī deserves special attention and viewing because of its effort to integrate Rajasthan's cultural components into a regional identity, and its success in working towards that goal. But *caveat emptor*. This is not merely an entertaining program, intended to divert the audience from its mundane cares, nor is it a travelogue designed to introduce tourists to this Indian state. In order to see what is being shown, one must accept the premise of Bhargava's production: to know Rajasthan one must be of it, to learn about Rajasthan one must live in it, to understand Rajasthan one must educate oneself about its history, people, cultures, lands, and seasons. The movement of artists in and out of Rajasthan, the presentation of Rajasthan's cultural performances to audiences within the state and outside of it now provide access to arts previously confined to private *gharānās* in princely houses or to the communities who patronized particular performance styles. For viewers outside Rajasthan, anything which comes from the state is Rajasthani. *Dhartī Dhorāṅ Rī* has established that whatever comes from the state and is viewed inside the state is not only a representation of a particular community or sub-region, but also Rajasthani.

Creating the image of a state, a nation, a president or a culture is a substantial task, one which requires the use and manipulation of symbols, signs and other indices of value and meaning. It is a sign of Kaushal Bhargava's vision in *Dhartī Dhorāṅ Rī* that the production has been successful within the state, and that the people within the state who see it understand and identify with its message that Rajasthan is for *all* Rajasthanis, not only for particular elites or powerful personages. This democratic message is inspiring for communities striving to take part in modern India, and provocative for those who would recreate the aristocratic hegemony cast off at independence with the promulgation of constitutional rights for all Indians. So there is a social, political, and economic message in this production, not of boundaries and separateness, but of cooperation and embeddedness. Such cultural performances are sometimes too optimistic to accrue critical acclaim from persons with cynical or myopic viewpoints, but encouraging messages are needed, according to Bhargava as well as the hundreds of thousands of viewers who have appreciated the show. Many who attend say they have never before realized that Rajasthan is so beautiful, and they are newly eager to claim it as their homeland. Supporters and critics of *Dhartī Dhorāṅ Rī* are united in their concern to make the program widely available to all Rajasthanis and Indians outside the state.

The balance between Rajasthani identity-building, as expressed in the production of *Dhartī Dhorāṅ Rī*, and the efforts to export this production and to bring in artists from outside Rajasthan to perform for Rajasthanis, is the key to understanding its invocation of a traditional philosophy of inclusion. Rajasthanis are to bring their culture to other regions, and invite artists from other parts of India so that they can enjoy their cultural performances as well. Becoming Rajasthani means establishing overlapping identities which can then speak to each other as complements. The Rajasthan Tarun Kalakar Parishad has brought troupes from other parts of India to perform in Rajasthan. Artists are invited to perform in Jaipur and also to tour in other cities of Rajasthan, such as Ajmer, Alwar, Jodhpur and Udaipur, which also have audiences of all-India tastes. Thus the performing arts within India, as across national boundaries, become the transmitters of an integrative and mutually appreciative philosophy of pluralism, which introduces peoples to their neighbors far and near through their symbols and songs, emblems and rhetoric.

ENDNOTES

This paper was originally presented at the Western Association for Asian Studies meeting, University of California-Berkeley, in November 1981, as "Rajasthani Regionalism: The Production of *Dhartī Dhorāṅ Rī*," in a panel entitled "Actors and Audiences: Performing Rajasthan's Culture."

1. Discussion on January 1, 1977. Mrs. S. Singh was talking about Veronica Ion's book, *Indian Mythology* (1976) which she had recently seen.
2. See, for instance, Gold 1988:22-26, where she discusses the identification of Rajasthani pilgrims from village Ghatiyali when travelling outside their state.
3. Co-founder with writer Vijay Dan Detha of Rupayan Sansthan (Rajasthan Institute of Folklore) in village Borunda near Jodhpur, Padma Shri Komal Kothari has explored the traditions of peoples in all parts of Rajasthan. Numerous discussions with Komal Kothari have furthered my understanding of Rajasthani peoples and their categories.
4. Such a name might be *tabalchī*, indicating that the musician plays the drum pair *tablā*, but is from a low status community not assigned artist or *kalākār* status.
5. I resided as a paying guest at Bissau House, and my host for the musical evenings was a *ṭhākur* (a Rajput nobleman), Raghubir Singh of Bissau, who later became the first president of Shruti Mandal.
6. An advantage of being a foreigner was inclusion in events traditionally segregated by sex. Although female, I was invited to the men-only musical evenings since I was a foreign guest; Rajput men attended without female members of their families. The singers were the only other women present, except on two occasions when the Thakur Rani of Bissau honored me by her presence for a short time. Later, when I was given permission to visit the *zenānā* (women's quarters) of the City Palace to observe Gangaur festivities, being a woman made access feasible and acceptable. Thus as ethnographer I have been able in Rajasthan to use my identities strategically to attain access.
7. Though classical *rāga* Mandh is based on Rajasthani *māṅdh*, it should not be conflated with it. As vocalist Lakshmi Shankar explained to me, Rajasthani *māṅdh* is a tonal composition, presented in various forms ranging from songs to professional instrumental folk music. The *māṅdh* presented at the Thakur of Bissau's soirees and supported by a nostalgic Marwari businessman settled outside Rajasthan, in the industrial city of Kanpur, was usually from Pokaran, near Jodhpur, said to be the source for the best singers at that time.
8. The addition of a theater to the Ram Niwas Bagh landscape of park, zoo, and museum finally completed the cultural complex begun in 1867 by Maharaja Ram Singh II of Jaipur with the collaboration of Lt. Swinton Jacob, an engineer who served at Jaipur until 1911 (Metcalf 1989:132).
9. See Erdman 1985 for the history of this department of performing artists in Jaipur State.
10. For a discussion of the national *akademis* and their policies, see Erdman 1984.
11. An early secretary of Rajasthan Sangeet Natak Akademi was Shri Komal Kothari, who later became co-founder with Vijay Dan Detha of Rupayan Sansthan.
12. From 1972 to 1975, Ravindra Manch was managed by the Rajasthan Lalit Kala Akademi, then was taken under the Education Department of the Govern-

ment of Rajasthan, purportedly to make its running more efficient and controlled. Ram Kalyan, the manager of the theater in 1976, was a government official (Deputy District Education Director), as was his predecessor, H.C. Mehta. In 1977 the government was planning to form an autonomous body (with the Education Commissioner as president) to facilitate management of Ravindra Manch, as government financial rules were so stringent that it was difficult to maintain flexibility for program needs. Despite a long period of planning the change had not yet taken place. "The conception has taken place, but when the body will be formed we don't know," says Kaushal Bhargava (Interview with Ram Kalyan, December 3, 1976).

13. Other halls are in the colleges, the university, and schools, and are used for their functions only. Jaipur's first public hall, built in 1882 and named Albert Hall, is now part of the Rajasthan State Museum in the Ram Bagh gardens. It has no permanent stage or technical facilities and is closed, except for an occasional exhibition.
14. Interview with Brij Sunder Sharma, December 12, 1976. Brij Sunder Sharma came to Jaipur from Bundi in 1949, and built his house there in 1953, where he hosted private musical evenings. By 1955 he had become Minister of Finance, Labor and Forests in the Rajasthan government. Speaking of his qualities on a separate occasion, an associate of the Parishad said, "We think our president is too nice a man to succeed in politics, but he was a very good Finance Minister."
15. Shruti Mandal was intended to mean "Listeners' Circle," but as several experts in Jaipur have pointed out, it is neither good Sanskrit nor Hindi. However, the name seems to serve its purpose.
16. *Nupūr* means an anklet, specifically the anklet of bells traditionally used by dancers in both folk and classical Rajasthani styles.
17. Interview with Kaushal Bhargava, December 19, 1976. The formation and dissolution of Nupur is a separate chapter in Jaipur's history of dance teaching and organizations. One dancer from Nupur, Prerna Shrimali, has become a leading dancer at Sangeet Natak Akademi's Kathak Kendra in New Delhi, where she went for further training with Pandit Birju Maharaj and her former guru from the Jaipur dance school.
18. Max Mueller Bhavan is a German government institution devoted to presenting educational and cultural events, teaching German language, and cooperating with local cultural organizations for special occasions.
19. A *gharānā* is a hereditary line of musicians, whose style and repertoire are passed on from masters to disciples through many generations.
20. See Erdman 1985, Preface, for a discussion of "the good old days" as seen by performing artists in post-independence Rajasthan.
21. In the 1980s the popular *Rāmāyaṇa* and *Mahābhārata* television series offered a sense of national identity for Hindus and those who value Hindu traditions. Although nationally broadcast, they did not provide a vision of a common identity for Indians of all religions. They were thus received by some viewers as a message of separateness, including Indians who felt excluded or unhappy because not represented by this series which was given national coverage and prime time television showings.
22. *Paḍ* is a performance by touring folk professional artists called *bhopās* in Rajasthan who chant, sing, dance and play narrative legends in front of a long

wide scroll painting. The painting depicts events in the story of the hero, and each section is lighted with a lantern as that event is described. Narrative recitative is interspersed with light songs from local traditions or films. The male singer plays a stringed instrument such as *ravaṇhatta* or *bīn*, and the other singer, his wife, holds the lantern and sometimes dances. Two favorite *paḍs* of Rajasthan are *Pābūjī* and *Devnārāyaṇ*.

23. The first television station came to Rajasthan in 1977, at Jaipur, and the touring of *Dhartī Dhorāṅ Rī* has been gradually reduced since then. While television is certainly not the only reason for this – Bhargava has turned to other projects and programs and television still reaches only a few sites in Rajasthan – it is certainly a media replacement for many previously public gatherings at cultural programs.
24. There have been occasional problems with villagers and officials who saw the presence of young women onstage as invitations to court them. Bhargava has provided chaperones for his dancers, and observed all proprieties for these school-going teenagers, for whom the dancing and touring are part of their education about Rajasthan as well.
25. A *dharamśālā* is a simple house which gains its donor merit for offering shelter to strangers. It contains rooms for travellers, who must supply their own bedding and meals.
26. A *durrie* is a woven cotton carpet.
27. This description is based in my diaries for November 1976.
28. The cultural continuity between northern Gujarat and southern Rajasthan is exemplified in architecture, in crafts, in the free movement of nomadic and tribal groups across the borders, in historical ties and trade. While some arguments have been made that Gujarat and Rajasthan should be considered a single cultural region, the interchange across borders with Madhya Pradesh, Haryana and Uttar Pradesh makes each of Rajasthan's boundaries politically determinate but culturally permeable.
29. For a history of the modern dance movement in India and Uday Shankar's role in it, see Khokar 1983 and Erdman 1987. I am currently working on a full-length book about the modern renaissance in Indian dance and Uday Shankar's role in creating choreography for the stage and his film, *Kalpana*..
30. Interview with Ranjit Shikari, January 2, 1977 in Jaipur.
31. *Sarvodaya*, meaning "the welfare of all," was the title Mahatma Gandhi used for his translation of Ruskin's *Unto the Last*. This book, as well as his *Hind Swaraj*, was proscribed by the government. Both were reprinted and sold as an act of civil disobedience during the freedom struggle (Gandhi 1957:299, 462).
32. Trimurthi produces dramas and dance-dramas in Jaipur, on an occasional basis, using often talented but amateur actors who had no path to professionalism in post-independence Jaipur.
33. Wearing *kesariyā* is a symbol of the warriors' intention to "do or die," i.e., fight to the death. Such an occasion arises when there is no hope of victory, but surrender is unthinkable.
34. This story, known to most Rajasthanis, tells of a beautiful new queen very much in love with her husband, as he was with her. In order to assure that he would fight bravely to the death in the coming battle, she sent her head to him on a platter as he was leaving, so that he would fulfil his duty as a Rajput

warrior and fight to the death, rather than longing to return to his adored wife. The tale is intended to show the courage of Rajput women, matching the bravery of their men.

35. This spot of color on the forehead between the eyes symbolizes the status of a wife, usually accompanied by red powder in the center parting of the hair. A *ṭīkā* can also mean that its wearer has taken recently the *darśan* of a deity; or it may be a part of a woman's makeup, like lipstick or mascara elsewhere.
36. My translation is based on a script written by Kaushal Bhargava with the assistance of Brijesh Kulshrestha. My thanks for M. L. Sharma for help with original translation, and to Karine Schomer for further suggestions. Bhargava tried many times to write or commission a successful English translation of the program, but was always dissatisfied with the results. He said that the language of the Hindi original had a flavor and sound which was untranslatable and contextual. I am inclined to agree with him, and the translation provided here is only a diluted rendering of the original, lacking in indigenous polysemy as well as the ringing importance of the spoken words.
37. *Jauhar* is the self-sacrifice of Rajput women, when their men go into battle to fight to the death. By their own deaths, the women free their husbands and sons from concern about the possibility of an enemy dishonoring their women.
38. Gombrich 1972. He goes on to point out that "This is the basis of the ancient 'art of memory'. . . that advises the practitioner to translate any verbal message into visual form." Gombrich's insight and Bhargava's practice are manifestations of the same philosophy of art.
39. See Erdman 1985:188-189.
40. I am reminded of a trip to a western Rajasthan village near Jodhpur during the summer of 1987, which took a surprisingly long time, given the indication of distance and roads on my map. When I asked about our route, I was told that the dune had moved, and now we had to "go around" to get there.
41. From Erdman 1985:192, 197.
42. What Bhargava appears to be referring to are the art works hidden in palace storage rooms, the artists kept for private royal use, and the wealth of jewels and costumes maintained for the private use of princely families. But he also is referring metaphorically to education, access to government service, and other opportunities previously allocated only to those of appropriate or hereditary status.
43. For a complete translation of the script, and a charting of the coordination of slides, dances and songs, see Erdman 1985: 185-203.
44. This festival, celebrated in Rajput states and *ṭhikānās* before and after independence, is described in Erdman 1985:165-174.
45. The significance of the landscape for the poetic voice can be seen, for instance, in the poems and explanations of A.K. Ramanujan's *The Interior Landscape* (1970), in regard to references and symbols in classical Tamil poetry.

REFERENCES CITED

Erdman, Joan L.
1984 "Who Should Speak for the Performing Arts? The Case of the Delhi Dancers." In *Cultural Policy in India*: Lloyd I. Rudolph, ed. Pp. 77-104. New Delhi: Chanakya Publications.
1985 *Patrons and Performers in Rajasthan: The Subtle Tradition*. New Delhi: Chanakya Publications.
1987 "Performance as Translation: Uday Shankar in the West." In *The Drama Review* 31(1):64–88.

Gandhi, Mohandas K.
1957 *An Autobiography: The Story of My Experiments with Truth*. Translated from Gujarati by Mahadev Desai [1940]. Boston: Beacon Press.

Gold, Ann Grodzins
1988 *Fruitful Journeys: The Ways of Rajasthani Pilgrims*. Berkeley: University of California Press.

Gombrich, E.H.
1972 "The Visual Image." *Scientific American 227(2):82-87.*

Ions, Veronica
1976 *Indian Mythology*. London: Hamlyn.

Khokar, Mohan
1983 *His Dance, His Life: A Portrait of Uday Shankar*. New Delhi: Himalayan Books.

Metcalf, Thomas R.
1989 *An Imperial Vision: Indian Architecture and Britain's Raj*. Berkeley: University of California Press.

Ramanujan, A.K.
1970 *The Interior Landscape*. London: Peter Owen.

JĀTRĀ, YĀTRĀ AND PRESSING DOWN PEBBLES: PILGRIMAGE WITHIN AND BEYOND RAJASTHAN

ANN GRODZINS GOLD

Rajasthani villagers seek access to special powers in many places and in many ways. A *jātrī*, in the term's broadest sense for Rajasthanis, is a traveller, but this paper will explore the desires and practices of *jātrīs* as "pilgrims" – defined as travellers to founts of power. Such sources – including deities' icons, trees, stones, caves, waters, hilltops and living saints, to mention only some – are frequently found in or near established shrines and temples. While pilgrims may travel long distances to reach locations of special power, some *jātrīs*' goals are attained after a 20 minute walk down the road, or a brief bicycle or oxcart ride.

In the course of 21 months of fieldwork on Hindu pilgrimage based in a village of Ajmer district,[1] indigenous ways of understanding all pilgrims' journeys were elicited and explored (Gold 1988). Research methods, grounded in participant observation, included in-depth open interviews and extensive collection of oral and printed folklore. The project found intraregional pilgrimage – brief journeys to familiar gods – to be associated by rural Rajasthanis with a distinctive transactional ambiance contrasting with most styles of extraregional quests.

The shrines of Rajasthan have been characterized by Komal Kothari as the rural peoples' ". . . court of justice, their hospital and mental home, their guidance clinic as well as the focus of their faith" (1982:5). In describing the functions of these shrines, Kothari uses pragmatically oriented secular service institutions as his chief metaphor, subordinating devotional aspects. Journeys to local and regional shrines are in fact most often made to obtain some kind of concrete boon or assistance; they are motivated by responses to specific problems as varied as snakebite, infertility, madness, unemployment, or domestic disharmony. But such journeys are also expressions of, and opportunities for, worship.

Informants' articulations of the qualities involved in creating the distinction between pilgrimage within and beyond their region include a developing awareness of Rajasthan as a bounded culture area. Accumulated experiences of intraregional pilgrimage may then contribute – for persons whose primary identities are with caste, village or local princedom – to a broader sense of regional unity and uniqueness.

These related propositions will be considered along several converging lines of approach. First, constituents of the contrast between intraregional and pan-Indian pilgrimage as expressed in ordinary discourse and in oral traditions are explored. Second, one shrine's particular transactional patterns are described in some detail, and generalizations applicable to the broader picture are drawn. Third, characteristic motivational concerns of pilgrims to Rajasthan's regional shrines are analyzed and one very common aim – obtaining progeny for previously childless couples – is closely examined. Fourth and finally, a motivational complex more typical of shrines with a pan-regional rather than purely local catchment area is described as diverging somewhat from the previous cases. At such places, often dedicated to regional incarnations of pan-Hindu gods, Rajasthanis may participate in a style of pilgrimage closer to the extraregional, even as they perceive themselves more clearly as belonging to one region.

The Distinction between *Jātrā* and *Yātrā*

In describing and categorizing pilgrims' journeys, most village informants held that shorter journeys to local shrines are not like those which reach more distant localities, gods and goals. Some persons enunciated the contrast with a differential usage of Rajasthani *jātrā* versus Sanskrit and Hindi *yātrā*. The transformation of Sanskrit *y* into *j* is a phonetic change common in many colloquial North Indian tongues. This change is not ordinarily accompanied by a change in meaning. A fair number among my Rajasthani-speaking informants, however, most often those school-educated in Hindi, retained both words and insisted that each carried distinct semantic content.[2] According to these informants, *yātrā* indicated pilgrimage to a *tīrtha* or 'crossing place'[3] such as the Ganges river at Hardwar or Gaya, the temple of Jagannath Puri near the Orissa coast, or the Himalayan peak of Shri Badrinath. Such journeys indeed are frequently designated with the compound *tīrthayātrā*. *Jātrā*, on the other hand, implied a trip to any of the countless shrines dedicated to 'goddesses-and-gods' (*devīdevatā*) most often of local origin and fame.[4]

Informants pointed to two factors as most significant in setting *yātrā* apart from *jātrā*. First was the "rank" of the deity or deities involved. *Yātrā* concerned places of 'the Lord' (*bhagvān*), vast and omnipotent, to be approached with 'selfless devotion' (*bhakti*). *Jātrā* took pilgrims to lesser gods and goddesses, many of whom had once been human and whose powers were more susceptible to manipulation than adoration. The second major differentiating factor was found in pilgrims' objectives. *Yātrīs*, some said, pursued 'merit' (*puṇya*), 'moral duty' (*dharma*), 'removal of sins' (*pāp dūr karbo*) and, occasionally, 'release' (*mokṣa*). Others held that *yātrīs* went only 'to take in the vision' (*darśan laibo*) of many divinities, 'to wander aimlessly' (*ghūmbo*), or 'to see-and-enjoy' (*dekhbo-chhokhbo*). Opposed to all the intangible configurations of purpose stated for *yātrā* were the solid goals of *jātrīs*, who most often had particular 'work' (*kām, karaj*) to be done, or vows to fulfil.

In keeping with these differences, *yātrā* is set above the particularities of village social life by rituals of departure and return (see Gold 1988). An auspicious time for embarking on such a journey must be determined by a Brahman; the goddess Pathvari Ma (Path Mother) must be worshipped both going and coming. When pilgrims return imbued with the qualities of crossing places, even their superiors in age or caste touch their feet. *Jātrā* is neither hedged by ritual attention nor transformative of personal identity. A decision to petition a local shrine deity may be taken at any time and accomplished without public fanfare. Illiterate informants did not always enunciate the *yātrā* versus *jātrā* distinction, but they conceptualized it in quite the same manner. They readily contrasted both the powers and fruits of crossing places with those of shrines dedicated to local deities – places generically known as *devasthān* (literally 'god-places').

One way to frame the contrast between *jātrā and yātrā* is to look at some texts of songs appropriate to each. Singing is an important part of almost every ritual and social event in rural Rajasthan, and journeys are no exception. The transactional situation of *jātrā* is aptly portrayed in the following women's song which praises the goddess, naming her only as Maiji or Mother. Sung in chorus but worded as question-and-answer dialogue, the verses are understood as an interchange between devotees and the goddess herself; they are asking about her distinguished pilgrims from afar. This version was recorded on the last day of Navaratra – Nine Nights dedicated to the goddess – when devotees in procession worship at each of her village shrines; it is also popularly sung by groups of pilgrims en route to, or worshipping at, goddess temples beyond village parameters.

Song of the Goddess

[Each line begins "O Mother" and each line is immediately repeated once.]

Where have the gentlemen come from, where have the *jātrīs* come from?
The gentlemen came from Bundi, the *jātrīs* came from Kota.[a]
How did the gentlemen come, how did the *jātrīs* come?
The gentlemen came in trains, the *jātrīs* came by bus.
Where did the gentlemen disembark, where did the *jātrīs* disembark?
The gentlemen stopped at the station, the *jātrīs* stopped at the food stall.
What did the gentlemen bring, what did the *jātrīs* bring?
The gentlemen brought grain,[b] the *jātrīs* brought sweets.
What do the gentlemen ask, what do the *jātrīs* ask?
The gentlemen ask for jobs, the *jātrīs* ask for sons.
What do the gentlemen offer, what do the *jātrīs* offer?
The gentlemen offer feasts, the *jātrīs* offer goats.

[Recorded by Joseph Miller]

[a] Bundi and Kota are two major cities near the village where the song was recorded.

[b] The word used here is not common *anāj*, but *maṭharī*, a term aplied only to grains placed as offerings on shrines.

The events schematized here represent a rather typical sequence for regional shrines. On a first visit, petitioners are likely to present a small quantity of grain which may be designated either for the priest or to be scattered as pigeon-feed. These grains are also employed in a simple divination technique: the shrine priest takes up a few from the pile and counts them to see if an auspicious number shows that the deity looks favorably on the pilgrim's enterprise.

Offerings of sweets are always appropriate and carry more prestige than simple grain. They might be expected from the high-class, city-dwelling pilgrims portrayed in the song. What do the *jātrīs* ask for? Jobs and sons are certainly high on the list. Covering a whole range of miraculous feats, the word 'proof' (*parchyo*) (see below) may also be inserted in the song here. Finally, when proofs have been received – jobs secured, sons born – then major thank-offerings are expected, particularly goats and feasts.[5]

The following song of *tīrthayātrā,* dedicated to Badrinath and recorded among a mixed-caste company on a month-long bus pilgrimage to major Hindu centers outside Rajasthan, displays strongly contrasting attitudes and aims held by pilgrims. Badrinath is a form of Vishnu whose site in the Himalayas is the northern node of the *chār dhām* or four established points of Hindu pilgrimage, each located in one of the cardinal directions and comprising in their circuit a complete subcontinental tour.

Song of Badrinath

[Refrain] Listen, Brothers, Sadhus, Saints, he is beloved;
The high mount is Badrinath's.
Master of the Poor, his ford is difficult.

[1] Praise Ram of Dwarka;[a] by the Lord's Stairs[b]
Ganga measures deep, my Lord Ram.
Atop the mountain of the three worlds expansive Badri reigns.

[2] O Ram, midway to the peak it's very steep, I cannot climb, my Ram.
Let Badrinath grab either hand and take me.

[3] Ram, whoever sings of vast Badri will not suffer birth again, my Ram.
Woman becomes man, all the company will cross over.

Dwarkanath in Gujarat is the westernmost of the *chār dhām*, and the city where Lord Krishna once reigned as a king.

[b] Har Ki Pairi ('the Lord's Stairs') is the name of the chief bathing *ghāt* at Hardwar, a *tīrtha* usually visited by pilgrims on their way to Badrinath, as it lies on the route.

The journey to Badrinath is portrayed as hard, just as classical 'lawbooks' (*dharmaśāstra*; see for example Kane 1953:IV,552-722; Salomon 1985) say journeys to crossing places should be. The weary and humble devotee struggles to reach his goal, and expresses his dependence on the Lord's help to do so. Indeed, the refrain praises Badri's place just because it is 'difficult' (*kararo*) to attain. Badrinath's pilgrim offers devotion demonstrated in the arduous effort he makes to reach the *tīrtha*. Although the singers in this case were in fact riding on a bus, they evoked foot-pilgrimage as the paradigmatic worshipful approach to Badrinath. By contrast, the goddess devotees of the previous example who were actually walking exalted the object of their devotion by describing her *jātrīs* as sophisticated and wealthy enough to come to her by train and bus. Badrinath's pilgrimage, as the journey's famed difficulty expresses, is a total sacrifice of self; the fruit sought is the ultimate Hindu goal: freedom from rebirth expressed here as 'to cross over' (*pār karbo*). Informants told me that what was crossed was the 'ocean of existence' (*bhāv sāgar*).

The contrasts both ideological and practical between *jātrā* and *yātrā* are thus established in these two songs. *Jātrīs* to the goddess offer goods, while *yātrīs* to Badrinath offer their efforts and sufferings. *Jātrīs* to the goddess bargain for boons (feasts and goats for jobs and sons), while *yātrīs* to Badrinath express faith that the high and merciful Lord will grant salvation. *Jātrīs* to the goddess ride buses and trains; *yātrīs* to Badri struggle painfully up a difficult path.

Another devotional song recorded among a group of women pilgrims during a night-long session at a shrine dedicated to the Rajasthani hero-god Dev Narayanji[6] is particularly relevant here. Its theme is the very opposition between journeys to distant crossing places and patronage of regional shrines that this paper seeks to elucidate. In the song a female devotee, addressing Dev Narayanji, claims that, had her in-laws not gone off on a *tīrtha-yātrā* to foreign parts, she would honor him with fine offerings appropriate for the deities of regional shrines.

Song of Dev Narayanji (1)

Husband's Mother and Husband's Father, O Narayan, have gone to *tīrthas*.
Had they not gone, I would sponsor your fair, O Dev.
I would sponsor your fair, I would build your shrine,
I would make fire-oblations from the pot of *ghī*, O Dev.

Husband's Elder Brother and his wife have gone to *tīrthas*.
Had they not gone, I would build your dome, O Dev.
I would build your dome, I would raise its crown,
I would make fire-oblations from the pot of *ghī*, O Dev.

Husband's Mother and Husband's Father, O Narayan, journeyed to foreign lands.
Had they not gone, I would build your eaves, O Dev.
I would sponsor night-long hymns and feast your *jātrīs*.
I would make fire-oblations from the pot of *ghī*, O Dev.

[Recorded by Joseph Miller].

Left behind, without resources, the singer implies that her own faith in a regional diety is more worthwhile than the (unspecified) motivations of her husband's family for pilgrimage in 'foreign lands' (*pardeś*). There, presumably, they are squandering the money that she, had she her way, would use to make the grand offerings to Devji suggested in the verses of the song. Architectural embellishments on a shrine or the sponsorship of a night-long sing and subsequent feast represent costly and impressive investments in a particular deity. Such major offerings are typically made at shrines only after a strongly coveted boon has been received: a dramatic cure, a financial success, or – most frequently for married women like the singers – the birth of a son. Most shrine pilgrimage involves similar transactional dynamics.

Vows and Proofs: Transactional patterns at Rajasthani Shrines

At the place of Shri Lakreshvar Mahadev, located near Bundi, several kinds of exchanges flow between pilgrims, gods and priests. Although some elements of these transactions are particular to the nature of this one place, patterns common to most of Rajasthan's regional shrines can be discerned through a close examination of what transpires within Shri Lakreshvar Mahadev's domain. The following *bhajan*, praising this manifestation of Shiva whose name translates as 'Lord of Wood', mentions several sorts of givings and receivings.

Bhajan of Shri Lakreshvar Mahadev

[Refrain] Shiva-Shankar, you are beloved,
Lord of Wood, you are beloved.
I've come wandering through your twisted brambles;
Lord of Wood, give me *darśan*.

[1] Your many pilgrims come,
Bringing bundles of wood;
Some lift up big stones.
Give me *darśan*.

[2] Bang your gong, bang your gong,
Ringing bells, conch and drum;
You are Parvati's beloved.
Give me *darśan*.

[3] I will sing your virtues only,
I will bow my head at your feet;
Whoever comes time and time again
Will receive proofs.

[4] Your server Mishri Nath Pujari[a]
Dispenses precious foot-nectar's goodness.
You are Shiva,
Simple storehouse-keeper.

[a] The closing verse of most *bhajans* contains a 'signature' (*chhāp*) revealing its "author." Here Mishri is a given name, Nath a caste name, and Pujari a title ('worship-priest').

In the *bhajan*'s refrain a pilgrim makes the effort of coming to the deity's place via a difficult, thorny route. In return he asks only for *darśan*, or a divine viewing. Badrinath's song addressed to the high god of a pan-Indian crossing place evokes in a similar vein pilgrims' hardship and their desire for intangible, subtle, transformative fruits. The first verse of Shri Lakreshvar Mahadev's *bhajan*, however, refers to a practice typical of Rajasthani shrines:

that of pilgrims giving a god their 'labor', for which the special term *begār* is used.

The original meaning of *begār* was hard labor which great 'landlords' (*ṭhākurs*) – usually of the ruling Rajput caste – conscripted from the peasants as a kind of tax. From that usage, according to the *Rājasthānī Sabad Kos* (Lalas 1962-78), the term came to refer in popular sayings to work done improperly or halfheartedly, or to any meaningless, profitless work. In the context of shrines, however, *begār* signifies labor freely given to please and honor a god. Like traversing brambles on the way to the shrine, *begār* represents a physical sacrifice. It is also a recognition of the deity as ruler, and a statement of humble surrender to that divine authority. As the Lord of Wood, Lakreshvar Mahadev is pleased to receive 'bundles of firewood' (*moḷī*), which pilgrims must gather outside the shrine's ground and carry to his temple on their heads. Circumambulations with heavy stones balanced on the head are a popular form of *begār* at numerous Rajasthani deities' shrines. Once again, in exchange for difficult effort, the worshipper asks only for *darśan*.

The next verse depicts typical shrine 'service' (*sevā*) involving the pleasing sounds of gong, bell, conch and drum. Normally the transmission of these sounds to a god is performed not by pilgrims but by the shrine-priest, at fixed times – daily or twice daily. These, then, are part of the deity's essential, everyday fare, and not any extraordinary, persuasive gift. However, should such services be neglected, a god is thought likely to withdraw his favor, and even to act punitively towards those responsible for this neglect. Regular *sevā* is thus a basic prerequisite for more ambitious negotiations with any deity.

The third verse takes us closer to the heart of shrine transactions. Pilgrims offer praise songs, full prostrations, and repeated visits. What they expect to receive in return, and the future tense is used here, are 'proofs' (*parchyo*) – that is, demonstrations of the deity's special power: boons, cures, knowledge, all kinds of wonders. Thus by giving of themselves, lowering themselves, acting out their devotion, pilgrims put themselves in a position both to extract and absorb powerful emanations from the object of their worshipful attentions.

In the signature line we learn that the source of this *bhajan* is the worship-priest himself. He defines his own role in relation to the deity as 'server' (*sevak*), and in relation to pilgrims as dispenser of the potent, healing liquid called *charaṇāmrit*. The literal meaning of *charaṇāmrit* is 'foot-nectar' – its original usage referring to water with which the feet of living saints or gurus has been bathed. In Rajasthani temples and shrines, *charaṇāmrit* – called colloquially *khoḷaṇ* or 'rinse water' – commonly designates water that has been worshipfully poured over icons in order to bathe and refresh the deities, and then collected for distribution to pilgrims. The priest identifies himself only as the dispenser of this liquid grace. It is Shiva as 'storehouse-keeper' (*bhaṇḍārī*) who owns all the well-being available at the shrine. The epithet 'simple' (*bhoḷo*), although a common one for Shiva, is striking here for its opposition to the nature of most storehouse-keepers – archetypically selfish merchants and their ilk. Unlike these people, Shiva will freely share his boundless riches.

This *bhajan* does not portray all that transpires at the Lord of Wood's shrine. The shrine's history and iconography, learned through interviews with the presiding priest and a number of pilgrims there, reveal a complex association of powers at the core of Lakreshvar's effectiveness. The chief deity of this spot is Mahadev, the name frequently given to the pan-Hindu god Shiva in Rajasthan and elsewhere. But Lakreshvar Mahadev is a particular local manifestation of the great divinity Shiva, surrounded by and also merged with less high, closer to human, more accessible beings.

The shrine of Lakreshvar Mahadev originated with a renouncer named Lakar ('Wood') Nath, a devotee of Mahadev, who performed 'ascetic feats' (*tapas*) on the site. According to legend, the original icons miraculously emerged from the ground and were first worshipped by this Lakar Nath. They are a group of small oval stones, egg-like and rather different in appearance from the usual, monolithic Shiva *linga*. According to Lakreshvar Mahadev's priest, they are nevertheless "accepted as Shiva's *lingas*."

Also present here from ancient times are Dev Narayanji's bricks.[7] Despite the fact that Devji is traditionally considered an incarnation of Vishnu, here – again according to the priest – "the work of Mahadev and Devji are one, but the chief is Mahadev." 'Chief' is a translation of the priest's *mukhyo* – a term commonly applied to a head of household or the most influential person in a particular group. The central shrine housing Shiva and Devji is said to be built upon Lakar Nath's 'ascetic hearth' (*dhūṇī*), and the bundles of wood carried by pilgrims offering *begār* to Shiva are said to be fuel for Lakar Nath's fire.

Thus there are at least three levels of power in action here: Mahadev's, Dev Narayan's and Lakar Nath's. Pilgrims and priest may claim to accept these as "one *māyā*" – a cliché implying that a variety of forms masks the monistic nature of all divinity – yet each being supplies a distinct quality to the shrine. Shiva is the supreme Lord whose mere viewing cleanses the soul. Dev Narayan is the well-loved hero of popular local legends, a descended incarnation (*avatār*) of Lord Vishnu, and the successful curing deity of many other Rajasthani shrines. Lakar Nath was a mortal man, but an ascetic whose devotion to Shiva established the high god's power at this place and made it accessible to pilgrims. Lakar Nath's concentrated self-descipline left a permanent residue here, enshrined in his hearth, a focus of worship in its own right.[8]

Although pilgrims may come to the Lord of Wood's shrine for any reason, its greatest fame in the surrounding area is for effectiveness in the 'cure of bleeding piles' (*massā bavasīr ko ilāj*). A person suffering from piles and wishing to evoke Lakreshvar Mahadev's aid should tie a 'charmed string' (*beḷ*) around his neck, taking the god's name and vowing, if he is successfully cured, to make a pilgrimage to the shrine bringing a "cartload" of eggplants. He himself foregoes eating eggplants until his vow is fulfilled. Why eggplants? The only answer provided by informants was that Shiva, being 'simple' (*bhoḷo*) is made 'happy' (*rājī*) with simple vegetables.

When the healed pilgrim comes to Lakreshvar's shrine to fulfil his vow, he brings a toy cart, constructed of leaves and twigs, containing a few small eggplants. He sets it before the icons, opens his charmed string and ties it to one of the shrine's large pillars, and usually makes a modest cash offering. Subsequently he is released from the eggplant taboo. One pilgrim encountered at the shrine was holding a costly feast to celebrate his hemorrhoids' successful cure. This man, an educated villager who held a responsible job in small bank in nearby Bundi, had undergone treatment at the town hospital for his affliction. Before initiating the medical remedy, however, he tied on a charmed string in the name of Lakreshvar Mahadev and pledged to give the usual eggplants plus this feast at the shrine in the deity's honor if the hospital cure worked.

To combine forces in this fashion is not uncommon among educated rural folk who have acquired respect for modern Western medical methods, but retain a persistent faith in the powers of shrine deities. The feast food was ritually offered to all three of the shrine's major deities before members of the thankful pilgrim's party – young businessmen in Western dress – partook of it. Their picnic-like gathering was thus a tribute to the shrine's power involving consumption of its various deities' *prasād*.

Clearly rather complex flows of substances and powers, of faith and miracles, lie at the heart of Rajasthani shrines' effectiveness. How may these be most broadly schematized? The portrayal of Lakreshvar Mahadev's place highlights several elements common to all shrines' workings, essential among which are vows and proofs.

Ordering negotiations between men and deities in the context of *jātrā* is the *bolārī* or *votano* – literally something which is spoken, but translatable as 'vow' or 'pledge'. Vows may be made at home when some sudden distress arises. Taking the chosen deity's name, a person will say something like: "If my daughter recovers from this illness, I will cause her to bow at your shrine and I will hold a feast there." Vows are also frequently made on an initial pilgrimage, with a promise to return if the boon is granted.

Especially in the case of sickness, such pledges may be marked – as in the Lord of Wood's hemorrhoids cure – by the afflicted person tying a piece of raw cotton string or a strip of cloth torn from a turban around his neck or wrist. These pledge-markers are called *beḷ* or *tāntī*.[9] When vows are fulfilled, the strings or strips, unknotted at the shrine and tied onto a convenient pillar or tree there, accumulate to become visible evidence of that particular deity's effectiveness. Many kinds of thank-offerings – from iron tridents, colored ceramic tiles and miniature silver umbrellas to one-room structures where pilgrims may sleep and ornate domes constructed above the main icons – also bear impressive testimony to pledges redeemed, implying boons granted. The pilgrim or potential pilgrim's vow is rendered void and he is accountable for nothing if his wish did not come true.

If a vow is made at the shrine, during this initial encounter both pilgrim and deity may give in unqualified fashion what they have in abundance. The pilgrim freely expresses 'faith' (*viśvās*), and physically demonstrates his surrender to the god by performing acts such as prostrations, circumambulations, and heavy labor without compensation. However he usually restricts his investment in limited valuable goods to a token coin, a handful of grain, a tiny bottle of *ghī*, a packet of cheap incense. Similarly the deity's potent but plentiful waste products – bath water, ash, food-leavings, and the flow of *darśan* – are generously forthcoming. The pilgrim states his case and contracts to offer something relatively rare and costly after the deity has accomplished the pilgrim's "work."

The word most commonly used by villagers for local deities' manifestations of power is *parchyo* or 'proof'. This is what the pilgrims 'ask' or 'demand' (*māngbo*) in the Song of the Goddess and receive in Shri Lakreshvar's *bhajan*. It is a significant term, differing from 'wonder' (*chamatkār*) in that it seems to imply not just a flash of special power but a response to human needs. The gods give proofs as pilgrims demand them. And, continuing the balanced interchange, a god who does not give proofs does not receive pleasing offerings from thankful devotees.

Deities are perceived as needing or coveting what pilgrims promise to bring; that is at least one reason why they do the difficult work of curing and otherwise helping men.[10] Unless a promise of future payment accompanies the pilgrim's prayer, the god – except by occasional caprice – is not likely to grant it. Moreover, a person who gets what he asked and does not make good his vow is inviting punishment: the loss of the boon at least, if not far greater disaster. Punishments visited on defaulting pilgrims are popularly discussed, and also classified as proofs.

Negotiations and reciprocal deals are appropriately entered into with the goddesses-and-gods of regional shrines. They would not be suitable modes of approach to the Lord in temples or crossing places, who is held above and beyond considerations of 'taking-and-giving' (*laibo-debo*). Thus vows and proofs are paradigmatically associated with *jātrā* but not with *yātrā*.[11]

The flow of substances and powers involved in shrine pilgrimage is not confined to the space of the shrine, as the practice of pre-*jātrā* vows demonstrates. All kinds of things continually move back and forth between home village and deity's place in the course of any pilgrim's interactions with a god. Many *jātrīs* will describe their trips in concrete terms of what they gave and what they brought back. To bring home and redistribute a deity's power-imbued leavings is integral if not defining to the act of shrine pilgrimage, as this humbling interview fragment instructs the naive anthropologist:

Interviewer (hereafter I): When you made a burnt offering with coconut, what did the priest return to you?
Jātrī (hereafter J): *Prasād* of coconut and ashes.

I: What did you do with the *prasād* and ash?
J: Oh, I ate some and brought some here [to her home village].

I: What did you do with that which you brought home?
J: I gave it to the children. If I did not do that, what would be the use of going there [to the deity's place]? I hardly went just to wander. If you know so little, why are you asking me?

A member of the leatherworking Regar caste, this woman forcefully declares, in describing her use of *prasād*, a focused purposefulness to her journey which she contrasts with going "just to wander" – a contrast frequently used to distinguish *jātrā* from *yātrā*. Her journey's purpose, moreover, was not merely to fetch *prasād*; rather, as with most *jātrīs*, it originated in concern for her family's well-being. Multiple motivations often underlie transactional patterns of regional pilgrimage.

From Sorrow to Contentment

People go to shrines because they are suffering from troubles and seeking physical and material attributes of happiness. One man, when asked about his constant recourse to deities' places during his son's long-term, undiagnosed, incapacitating illness, said: "Squirrels run to the *pīpal* tree" (*ṭālī kī dauṛ pīpal tak*). My assistant explained this informant's use of the local 'saying' (*kahāvat*) to me as follows: "Whenever he is in some trouble or danger, the squirrel is able to run and climb the *pīpal* tree; he can go no further than this. In just this way, when M's son became sick he came straight to the deities." As the *pīpal* tree traditionally offers shelter to a frightened animal who has no other place to go, so the gods of shrines offer relief and solutions to men under all kinds of stress; and, as the saying implies, beyond them there is no readily conceivable recourse.

When bluntly approached in the environs of a deity's place and asked the purpose of their presence, many Rajasthani pilgrims will reply expressively, 'sorrow-and-trouble' (*dukh-taklīf*). One priest of a powerful place of the goddess informed me (in standard Hindi) that by pleasing her "every single sorrow of the body is removed" (*har ek śarīr kā dukh dūr hotā hai*). These are explicitly sorrows of the perishable body (*śarīr*) not the undying, transmigrating 'soul' or 'self' (*ātmā*). The opposition posed here is not between body and soul, or physical and spiritual as such, but between the person living and coping in the 'world of flux' (*samsāra*) and the person as eternal, unchanging self.

Pilgrimage to Rajasthani shrines, *jātrā*, indeed has little if anything to do with the *ātmā*, its accumulation of 'merit' (*puṇya*) or ultimate 'release' (*mokṣa*). Largely unconcerned with future births, the work of shrines is for this life and on this body. While pilgrims answer "sorrow-and-trouble" when asked why they have come to shrines, when asked for what they pray, they most often reply by referring to one or more attributes of well-being.[12]

Well-being may be thought of as the collective opposite of the multiple sorrows and troubles from which people take refuge in the gods. The complex of well-being includes health, prosperity and progeny, which, taken together, produce a contentment – *sukh-śānti*, literally 'happiness-and-peace' – that is the highest and most diffuse goal usually claimed by *jātrīs*.[13] All components of well-being are notably "this-worldly" in the sense that they concern comforts of one's current birth, although the yearning for sons certainly has a strong soteriological component.[14]

Pilgrims recently returned from Ramdevra, the hero-god Ramdevji's[15] place northwest of Jodhpur, were asked what prayers they had made to Ramdevji while on their pilgrimage. These peasant pilgrims' replies were individually worded but homogeneously constructed:

> Interviewer (hereafter I): When you went and had *darśan* what did you think in your mind?
>
> *Jātrī* (hereafter J): Keep me 'flourishing' (*harī-bharī*) and 'happy' (*rājī-khuśī*), and I will come and offer 51 rupees.

I: While you were prostrating yourself [before the icon of Ramdevji], what were you thinking?

J: At that time I was thinking nothing, except that, if in this year I get 2000 rupees income I'll come to Ramdevji again.

I: What were you thinking when taking *darśan*? Did you make another 'vow' (*bolārī*)? [This pilgrim had just fulfilled a vow for a snakebite cured in Ramdevji's name.]

J: Yes, I thought, if I have a grandson I will send my son and his wife both to prostrate themselves here.

I: When you were in the temple looking at the icon, what were you saying in your mind?

J: Nothing, but for the first time I went I thought, "If my 'garden' (*bāṛī* – a common metaphor for family) flowers, then I will offer up 21 rupees." This time I just thought, "Give me cash and bread, keep me happy, enough!" What else could you want? Now the family has flowered; now only wealth and contentment are needed.

The pilgrimage to Ramdevji, as these responses demonstrate, is made by most *jātrīs* for specific boons, or out of allegiance generated by boons previously granted. Very evident, moreover, is the frankly transactional nature of the pilgrims' relations with the god. Each has bargained unabashedly with Ramdevji for blessings of food and cash, health and happiness, sons and sons' sons.

The getting of progeny – a flowering garden (the popular image of family fertility) – is one of the pivotal motivating forces behind *jātrā*. Not only anxious prospective parents but anxious prospective grandparents, brother, sisters, uncles and aunts will make vows and journeys on behalf of barren kinfolk. Although I conducted no statistical survey, it was clear that infertility was numerically as well as emotionally one of the most powerful rationales for shrine pilgrimage.

A common sight at many of Rajasthan's local shrines is clusters of wide straw baskets hanging from tree branches or rooftops. Some appear new while others are weathered by wind, sun and rain to various stages of disintegration. These baskets – called *pālaṇo* or 'cradles' – are placed there as thank-offerings from pilgrims who have received the boon of a living child's birth. Each basket thus stands for a child born, and a shrine with ample quantities of these baskets on display possesses indisputable testimony of its power to grant fertility.

In the following song, when Devji promises his plaintive pilgrim that he will have her "raise an immortal cradle," he is promising her a child. Although there are three separate "voices" in this song – the barren wife, the taunting father-in-law and the god Dev Narayanji – it is sung in unison by a group of women.

Song of Dev Narayanji (2)

Father-in-law taunts me, my Lord Ubi[a] in your fine place,
Father-in-law taunts me:
Daughter-in-law, they play, they play, the sons of your husband's brothers' wives.
You have remained a barren woman since your birth.
Lord, why do I bring shame to my mother and father?
Why did they feed me milk, a barren woman?
Girl-child, you come, come to my shrine!
Girl-child, come, come to the Devji of Ghatiyali![b]
I'll have you raise an immortal cradle.

[Recorded by Joseph Miller]

[a] Ubi is another name of Dev Narayanji.
[b] Ghatiyali is the name of a village near which the Devji shrine attended by the singers is located.

Inside the baskets that are offered are coconuts swaddled in cloth, and these are the same tokens used in the rite of 'pouch-filling' (*jhoḷī bharbo*) which women seeking children undergo at many shrines. The "immortal" cradle-basket remains hanging until the elements destroy it – a very slow process. It thus stands as a wish for the child born by the deity's grace to endure forever in the deity's shelter. Although details vary from place to place, the crux of pouch-filling is, as the name indicates, a magical gesture of impregnation: usually placing a coconut inside a woman's customary 'wrap' (*oṛhṇī*), which has been specially arranged to form a secure receptacle.

A woman desiring a child will wear her hair newly washed and unbraided when she goes to a shrine for pouch-filling. "Open" hair is a cultural sign of female receptivity – to both sexual and spiritual penetrations.[16] The coconut, provided by the barren woman or one of her relatives and set as an offering on the shrine, is often swaddled in red cloth evoking the blood of birth and the auspicious vigor of life. This coconut will be placed in the *jātrī*'s prearranged pouch by a priest who may or may not be possessed by a deity.

At the time of pouch-filling no major cash offering is presented to the god, but the woman and her family members speak vows to return with considerable amounts (51 or 101 rupees are typical), or to finance some construction at the shrine, should a healthy child be born. Sometimes they may specify a male child. This pledge should be fulfilled shortly after the birth. At that time, the same coconut which the pilgrim received in her pouch returns to the shrine in the cradle-basket hung as a postpartum thank-offering. When the cradle-basket is hung, the infant is made to give its first obeisance to the deity, who will now be its life-long protector.

At Ramdevji's shrine, pouch-filling has developed into an event which not only promises miracles but demonstrates them. There the candidate for pouch-filling sits by the shore of the lake on the temple grounds. The priest tosses her coconut into the lake. The coconut then, witnesses claim, bounces back of its own accord into the woman's pouch – *if* she is destined to bear a child. Sometimes it takes a couple of tries, which are interpreted as intervening miscarriages before the full-term birth of a living child.

At other shrines, on occasion, the work of giving children may be effected less dramatically. Perhaps neither priest nor coconut is required but only an inner vow. One man, himself an only son, had fathered one daughter but remained without further progeny for seven years. His elder sister, proud wife of a Brahman expert in Sanskrit ritual, heard from some lower-caste women of the great powers of a local Sagasji.[17] Mocking that deity and his devotees, she challenged him to do the impossible – to give her brother a son. Scornfully she vowed allegiance to the shrine if her wish should be fulfilled. Almost immediately following her skeptic's vow, the brother's wife conceived.

When the ensuing male child was a few months old, the women of this family went as *jātrīs* on an auspicious day to Sagasji's out-of-the-way place for the infant's first prostration. A small troop of ladies and children, they proceeded on foot to a lonely but tidy platform-shrine far away from any habitation. The shrine-priest, a busy farmer, had not been summoned for this ceremony. The Brahman women thus performed Sagasji's worship without benefit of male priestcraft, employing a young boy (aged seven or eight) to climb up on the platform in order to anoint the icon and give the burnt offerings.[18]

The baby's paternal grandmother, a widow who daily performed service in the Gujarati Brahman's Krishna temple, addressed Sagasji in fervent prayer, making a poignant and eloquent declaration of her previous want and current satisfaction and gratitude. The infant, eyes heavily daubed with protective *koyal* and dressed in bright new clothing, was briefly laid howling on top of a pile of grains offered on the platform. He was considered to have been given by the deity, and thus was now received as *prasād* by his mother and father's mother. The grains were left for the absent priest to collect, if livestock or birds did not consume them first.

In this simple rite the pouch-filling process was in a sense replicated after the fact of birth. Just as the coconut for pouch-filling is first offered and then received, so this child was surrendered on the shrine before his mother and grandmother reclaimed him. All children who are "given" by deities, and this is a large percentage, are referred to as belonging to the god rather than to their parents. Often the answer to the question "Is this your child?" is "No, it is God's (*bhagvān ko*)."

Women's devotion to local shrine deities such as Dev Narayanji, Ramdevji and Sagasji – and to their places of enshrinement – is often based on desire or gratitude for the birth of children. In women's oral traditions, this devotion may sometimes be portrayed as opposed by and opposing the authority of male in-laws, while at other times it allies itself with the same authorities. In the following song the singer's point of view is characteristic of a young woman's stereotypical estrangement from her husband's family during the early years of her marriage, when – prior to the birth of a healthy, male child – she has little status, voice or comfort.

Song of Dev Narayanji (3)

Father-in-law, don't forbid me to go and bow to Devji;
Father-in-law, those who forbid are marked with fault.
  I will go to the brave Lord.
Daughter-in-law, what is your proof of brave Devji?
Father-in-law, to one hundred barren cows he gave calves;

Father-in-law, to me he gave a god-like son.
That is my proof of brave Devji.
[The same lines are repeated, inserting "husband's elder brother" and "husband's youger brother."]

[Recorded by Joseph Miller]

The birth of a son vindicates the woman's devotion (and her practice of *jātrā*) in the eyes of her forbidding male in-laws. The child gifted to her by the god becomes not only Devji's 'proof' (*parchyo*) to her but her proof to her affines of the righteousness of her faith. In the next example, using quite a different tactic, the female devotee addresses the same deity, Dev Narayanji, as "established" by her father-in-law and her husband's brothers. The term "established" refers to the empowering of an icon. Traditionally it is five men who must join to validate this act; "established-by-one-hundred" is thus praiseful hyperbole while "established-by-father-in-law" seems to express particular respect for that personage.

Song of Dev Narayanji (4)

[1] I am wrapped in a shawl, I have come to Narayan.
Established-by-five Devji, will you hear my plea?
Worship-established Devji, will you hear my plea?

[Refrain] If you hear my request then hear me like this:
On the sloping roof a long-tailed peacock.[a]

[2] I have put on a nose-ring, I am wrapped in a shawl.
Established-by-husband's-father Devji, will you hear my plea?
Established-by-one-hundred Dev, will you hear my plea?
[3] I have put on a full set of bangles, I have put on a forehead ornament.
Established-by-husband's-elder-brother Devji, will you hear my plea?
Established-by-husband's-younger-brother Dev, will you hear my plea?

[Refrain-new] If you hear my plea, then hear me like this:
Give sons to barren women.

[Recorded by Joseph Miller]

[a] A peacock on the roof is an auspicious sign.

The second set of verses proposes explicit exchanges with the god. This set of propositions, building up to the petitioner's acknowledging the object of her plea – the birth of a son – epitomizes the transactional nature of *jātrā* in the special context of pouch-filling.

Song of Dev Narayanji (4b)

[1] Established-in-bricks-Devji, will you hear my plea?
Shadower-of-the-priest[a] Devji, will you hear my plea?
If you hear my plea I will build you a dome,
Atop the dome I'll raise up a crown.
[2] Banjyari's[b] true Devji, will you hear my plea?
Ghanti's simple Devji, will you hear my plea?
If you hear my plea, then I'll offer a throne;
After that I'll present an iron cane.
[3] Puvali's true Devji, will you hear my plea?
Ghanti's simple Devji, will you hear my plea?
If you give a son, then I'll give you a big feast;
At Puvali I'll raise up a flag pole.

[Recorded by Joseph Miller]

[a] One way to refer to possession by a deity is 'shadow' (*chhāyā*).
[b] Banjyari as well as the following place names (Ghanti, Puvali) are locations of famed Dev Narayan shrines.

In these women's songs, and in the progression from pouch-filling to the child's first prostration, both the pattern of vows and proofs, and the transition from sorrow to contentment are evident. Conception and birth, however, are only the first accomplishments of parenthood. Children must also be safely reared, and this process is fraught with danger at every stage. After they survive to maturity they should be peacefully married, gainfully employed, and themselves become the producers of male progeny. All these connected phases of the worldly cycle – components of well-being – may be enhanced by resort to shrines. A child given by a god continues to belong to that power, and thus to command its attention and partake of its 'shelter' (*śaraṇ*).

Pressing Down Pebbles

Long-term affiliations with particular shrines, including those established from birth through a deity's grace, may involve repeated visits by *jātrīs* who demand no explicit boons. Within the regional pilgrimage complex, Rajasthani villagers recognize and describe a type of journey made for diffuse reasons of dedicated devotion. The common colloquialism for such a pilgrimage is *kānkaṛī gūndhbo* or 'to press down pebbles' – that is, to place one's feet deliberately on the grounds of a deity's shrine. Although the term may be applied to a single journey, its usage more often implies periodic visits: thus, "I go every year, just to press down pebbles." The term is often used in opposition to having particular work to achieve or vows to fulfil.

One woman had made the pilgrimage to Ramdevji for twelve consecutive years. She firmly contrasted, however, the first seven years, when she was fulfilling a vow, with her current practice of an annual pilgrimage "only to press down pebbles."

> *Jātrī* (hereafter J): Now there is no necessity. We go happily; we only ask for contentment.
> Interviewer (hereafter I): This time when you went what prayer did you make?
> J: "We have come to your door; keep us in contentment."
> I: Do you ask for 'release' (*mokṣa*)?
> J: Contentment, no sickness, enough!

Her goals are thus neither specific nor soteriological. The diffuse objective of contentment is all she will allow, and she is firm and proud on this point. There is a way in which having no specific motivation elevates the act of pilgrimage. When *jātrā* is said to be for "pressing down pebbles," – that is, not precipitated by a desire for particular boons – its motivational complex more closely approaches the devotional selflessness characteristic of *yātrā*.

Although any small shrine may be placed where some *jātrīs* go "only to press down pebbles," a few major pan-regional pilgrims' centers of Rajasthan emerged most frequently in informants' statements as inspiring such journeys. Some informants also argued that these places – including Diggi in Tonk district, Ramdevra in Marwar, and Ranthambaur Ganeshji in Savai Madhopur – were *tīrthas*.

Diggi may serve as an example. It is a most unenchanting, dusty little town, quite lacking in the natural beauty associated with most pan-Hindu pilgrimage sites. Its water reservoir is so shallow and murky that hygiene-conscious pilgrims hesitate to bathe there. Yet Diggi's Shri Kalyanji temple and icon have widespread fame in the areas surrounding Jaipur and Ajmer. Fair numbers of pilgrims visit Diggi every day, and monthly on the full moon *tithi* buses and resthouses are jammed with crowds seeking access to the extra power available during that auspicious time.

Once again, praises sung by devotees serve to highlight the qualities of their pilgrimage. The following song, recorded inside the temple of Shri Kalyanji at Diggi, does not propose bargains but it does tell of wonders and cures.

Song of Shri Kalyanji

[Refrain] Grain-giver, truly look upon me,
Kalyanji, hear me wholly!
The king of Diggi in Dhundar land[a] is a great Lord.

[1] Crippled and lame your many pilgrims come.
Remove the lepers' leprosy.[b]
[2] Yes, the crested turban on your head is lovely,
rings in your ears so pleasing.
And in that beard twinkle and twinkle
the rays of diamonds.[c]
[3] Yes, thrice-daily glimpsed your temple's wondrous beauty,[d]
removes the sad folks' sorrow,
And gives eyes to the blind.
[4] My boat in the whirlpool lurches and tilts,
swirling me from the shore.
My boat is caught midstream, Kalyanji,
cross me over, Lord!

[a] Dhundar is a former name of the region ruled from Jaipur or Amber.

[b] In the temple's founding myth, Kalyanji's first miracle was to cure a king of leprosy caused by a heavenly nymph's curse.

[c] The icon of Shri Kalyanji had diamonds set into its chin.

[d] Kalyanji's *darśan* is given three times daily, and there is an extraordinary aspect to it: in the morning the icon appears as a child, at midday as a man in his prime, and in the evening as if aged.

It is immediately apparent that the attitudes of Shri Kalyanji's pilgrims combine elements of *jātrā* and *yātrā*. First, the deity is called upon to cure cripples and lepers, and lauded for giving sight to the blind – curative functions typical of regional shrines. Ultimately, however, Kalyanji is implored for help in "crossing over," just as is Badrinath, the high deity who can be reached only on a difficult *tīrthayātrā*. Moreover, the pilgrim to Kalyanji humbly expresses his own helpless inadequacy at reaching the goal, as do Badrinath's pilgrims. But Diggi is not a distant *tīrtha* and no metaphorically apt mountain need be climbed to get there. Most of Shri Kalyanji's *jātrīs* probably manage the trip in less than a day by bus.

The identity of Kalyan with Dhundar land is an important part of his appeal. In that sense, he is a localized, rooted Rajasthani deity whose scope is far narrower than Badrinath's atop "the mountain of the three worlds." But he is, at the same time, a 'form' (*rūp*), not a 'descended incarnation' (*avatār*) of the Lord.[19] He never lived as a man; he is the high god Vishnu and not a *devatā*. This was the reason many informants supplied for calling Diggi a "crossing place." As *bhagvān*, Shri Kalyanji was himself a remover of sins (as well as other troubles) and thus a pilgrimage to his feet was cleansing in the same way as a bath in the Ganges. Nonetheless, pilgrimage to Shri Kalyanji at Diggi is often made to fulfil vows or seek help in a fashion absolutely typical of *jātrā* to more localized, lesser deities. Pilgrims negotiate with the sparkling king of Diggi just as they do with any other deity of more circumscribed scope.

Villagers in fact respect Kalyanji as a particularly potent healing god. Especially when perilous diseases such as typhoid or hepatitis strike, it is common to vow a pilgrimage to Kalyan's temple. At least once a year a special bus, filled largely with persons fulfilling such vows, makes a 48-hour round-trip journey from the village where my research was conducted to Diggi and back. On this bus are also always some persons going "only for *darśan*" or "just to press down pebbles." Those who claimed less instrumental goals did so in the fashion of Ramdevji's pilgrim quoted above, with speeches indicating that they felt their non-pragmatic motives to be somehow superior.

The relationship between pilgrims and deities that underlies the "pressing down pebbles" mode of *jātrā* may be illuminated by reference to the triadic results of deliverance identified by Susan Wadley (1975:107-125) in her study of village religion in Uttar Pradesh. Wadley's three kinds of deliverance – salvation, shelter and rescue – correspond with the various goals of Rajasthani pilgrims which have been discussed here. Salvation is release – a final "crossing over" – the high goal of *yātrā*. Rescue is relief from immediately disastrous situations, and thus applies to the aims of *jātrā* associated with work and vows. Shelter (*śaraṇ*), the middle term, implies several things: protection, removal of sins and sorrows, and thus potential attainment of happiness. It is also strongly associated with an enduring, mutually satisfying relationship between deity and devotee. The configuration of meanings denoted by "shelter" fits well with that which underlies journeys made to "press down pebbles."

Rather than dichotomous, *jātrā* and *yātrā* should be understood as being on a continuum, with the "shelter" type of journey, "pressing down pebbles," at some intermediate position. There is also an apparent correlation between this intermediate kind of pilgrimage and shrines like Ramdevji's and Shri Kalyanji's – shrines of more than local, but distinctly regional, significance. Ascribed the higher rank of "crossing places," such spots still retain the effective wondrous powers wielded by deities who do pilgrims' work and accept offerings in recompense. The gods of such shrines, pan-Hindu deities in regional forms, inspire pilgrims' journeys made in order to sustain contact with these deities' general beneficent powers. Pilgrims periodically renew their connection with these sources of well-being through touch ("pressing down pebbles" with their feet), through the eyes (taking *darśan*), and through other modes of substantial incorporation (e.g., consumption or application to their bodies of food, ash, and bathwater residues).

Rural Rajasthanis, it has been shown here, characterize intra-regional pilgrimage as distinct from *tīrthayātrā* beyond Rajasthan primarily according to its concrete motivational interests and corresponding exchange relations entered into with the deities approached. However, at a few major regional shrines dedicated to Rajasthani forms of the high gods of Hinduism, this major distinction – between *jātrā* and *yātrā* – begins to dissolve. Moreover, at such shrines (pilgrimage places with pan-regional catchment areas), pilgrims do not experience the climatic and linguistic alienation they often feel at Hardwar, Gaya or Puri (Gold 1988). On the contrary, in encountering fellow-*jātrīs* from diverse parts of Rajasthan, pilgrims discover shared regional traditions of worship and folklore even as they note and relish the myriad contrasting styles of speech, dress, ornaments or food preparation. The elevation of boon-oriented *jātrā* to a more selfless devotional pilgrimage is realized, then, in the context of worshipping deities of pan-regional influence among a confluence of Rajasthanis from many localities and a wide range of caste and economic levels.

Long before its political unification as a modern Indian state, Rajasthan's chief homogeneity was located by Tod in its religion which, he said, " . . . operates to counteract that dissimilarity in manners, which would naturally be expected amidst so great a variety from situation or climate" (1978:I,100). The current and very popular religious practice of journeying to sources of special power both substantiates and stimulates awareness of regional identity for Rajasthanis. As *yātrīs* with diffuse devotional motivations for visiting pan-Indian deities, they retain a sense of their regional origins while journeying extra-regionally. Within Rajasthan, *jātrīs* understand intimate, give-and-take dealings as appropriate with local familiar deities, and seek shelter at the major shrines of gods with state-wide cults whose legendary and historical roots are deep in Rajasthani culture.

ENDNOTES

This paper is based on 21 months of field work in India (1979-81), funded by the American Institute of Indian Studies and the Social Science Research Council, and supervised by Komal Kothari, Director of the Rupayan Sansthan (Rajasthan Institute of Folklore). Many helpers in the field, but most particulary Bhoju R.Gujar and Nathu N.Nath, contributed to the gathering and interpretation of the materials. Joan L.Erdman, Bhoju R.Gujar, Mckim Marriott and Milton Singer read and commented on earlier versions of the paper. Special thanks are due to Joseph C.Miller for his generosity with his field materials, particularly those women's songs noted in the text as part of his collection of recordings.

1. Before Independence, this village fell within the boundaries of Ajmer-Merwara, a small island of British sovereignty in a sea of princely states. On Vyas's map showing the locations of various Rajasthani dialects (in Lalas 1962-78), the village appears to lie in an area where several might be encountered. Moreover, language in these parts shows strong signs of influence from Urdu, the courtly tongue of the Muslim rulers who held Ajmer for centuries before the arrival of the British. Today, villagers' speech is also increasingly affected by standard Hindi, which is not only the educational medium in schools but the language of important public performances such as the annual Ram Lila or the sermons and expositions given by itinerant religious authorities. A sense of having their own distinctive, local *bhāśā* is quite strong among the village population, however. Women whose natal homes might be a day's journey distant told laughingly how, as new brides, they had not been able to understand the speech of their husbands and in-laws. This local language does not display several common characteristics of Rajasthani dialects. For example, *ko, kī, kā* are used rather than *ro, rī, rā*; and a palatal *ś*, which Rajasthani usually merges with *s*, is present.

   The linguistic situation of my fieldwork was, moreover, complex. Some informants spoke only local Rajasthani; some spoke pure Hindi; many spoke mostly Rajasthani but threw in Hindi words and syntax to varying degrees. In this paper, I supply original terms and phrases not as I heard them (never trusting my ears), but as they were written for me by literate, village-born assistants – either taking notes or transcribing tapes. If informants spoke in Hindi, I quote Hindi; if they spoke in local Rajasthani, I give that form.
2. The *Rājasthānī Sabad Kos* (Lalas 1962-78) gives only *yātrā* for *jātrā*. McKim Marriott (personal communication) notes that a similar meaningful distinction of *jātrā* from *yātrā* occurs in Madhya Pradesh and Maharashtra as well as Rajasthan.
3. The literal meaning of *tīrtha* is a river ford. I follow Eck (1981:344) in translating it, almost consistently, as a 'crossing place'.
4. The cultural geographer Surinder Bhardwaj has described two circulation patterns for Hindu pilgrimage which he calls "merit" or "general," and "specific." These patterns correlate broadly with journeys, respectively, to pan-Hindu and to regional or local shrines (1973:168-172).
5. It should be noted that not all the local deities of Rajasthan appreciate animal sacrifice, which is largely reserved for the goddess and Bhairuji.
6. For Dev Narayanji, see Joshi (1976:29-69), Kothari (1982:18-22) and Miller (1980).
7. Although carved stone and painted icons of Dev Narayanji as a noble-looking warrior on a horse exist, all his places also have 'bricks' (*īṇṭ*) enshrined as non-anthropomorphic representations of Devji and other heroes of this epic.
8. Many Rajasthani shrines have ascetics' hearths within their domains. According to some informants, the chartering 'ascetic feats' (*tapasyā*) of a 'renouncer' (*sannyāsī*) are necessary features in any great shrine's development.
9. The terms *beḷ* and *tāntī* were used interchangeably by some informants but not by others. Both refer to cotton string or strips of cloth worn in the name of a god, usually in association with a vow or cure. Some villagers insisted that a *tāntī* had seven knots in it, was made from a strip torn from a turban, and used

most particularly in cases of snake bite or dog bite; *beḷ* then would more generally indicate any of the pledge-strings seen tied to trees and pillars at hundreds of shrines.

10. See Moreno (1984) for an elaborate discussion and illustrations of how pilgrims very physically serve the imperative needs of deities in Tamilnad.
11. Bhardwaj also mentions 'vows' (*sukhnā*) as strongly associated with his "specific" pattern (1973:158-162). *Yātrā* often begins with a 'resolution' (*sankalpa*) but this is more an inner dedication of the pilgrim to his journey than a deal with a god.
12. By 'well-being', I gloss the total implication of several adjectival and nominal phrases applied to the human condition. While each might be more poetically translated, all do, I believe, amount to the same thing. The most commonly used is *sukh-śānti* ('happiness-and-peace' or 'contentment'). Others include *rājī-khuśī* ('joyfulness-and-happiness') and *harā-bharā/harī-bharī* ('replete with greenness').
13. See Pfaffenberger (1982:79) for a similar complex of "peace, wealth, grain and sons" underlying Tamil temple-building (and Vedic sacrifice).
14. See *Garuda Purana* (1911:53) for praises of the son as agent of salvation for his father.
15. See Binford (1976) for Ramdevji's pilgrimage, and Bishnoi (1979) for Ramdevji's legend.
16. Normally women will never wear their hair unbraided in public; a woman wishing to be possessed by a deity, however, will leave her hair "open" (Gold 1988:151, 202).
17. A Sagasji is a category of deity deriving from the violent, heroic death of an unknown warrior.
18. Except in rare cases, women are forbidden to mount a shrine platform because of what is believed to be their inherent uncleanness – often explained as the possibility that they are wearing a skirt which at some time might have come into contact with menstrual blood.
19. McKim Marriott (personal communication) has pointed out that pan-Hindu gods with regional shrines and identities, like Shri Kalyanji, are found in other parts of India as well – for example, Vithoba in Maharashtra and Vyankateshvar in the Telugu–Tamil country.

REFERENCES CITED

Bhardwaj, Surinder M.

1973 *Hindu Places of Pilgrimage in India: A Study in Cultural Geography*. Berkeley: University of California Press.

Binford, Mira R.

1976 "Mixing in the Color of Rām of Rānujā." In *Hinduism: New Essays in the History of Religions*. B.L. Smith, ed. pp. 120-142. Leiden: E.J. Brill.

Bishnoi, Sonaram

1979 *Bābā Rāmdev Sambandhī Lok-Sāhitya* (Folk Literature Connected with Ramdevji). Jodhpur: Usha Publishing House.

Eck, Diana L.
1981 "India's Tīrthas: "Crossings" in Sacred Geography." *History of Religions* 20:323-344.

Garuḍa Purāṇa
1911 *Garuḍa Purāṇa* (*Saroddhara*). Ernest Wood and S.V.Subrahmanyam, transl. *The Sacred Books of the Hindus*, Vol. 9. Allahabad: The Indian Press.

Gold, Ann Grodzins
1988 *Fruitful Journeys: The Ways of Rajasthani Pilgrims*. Berkeley: University of California Press.

Joshi, Om Prakash
1976 *Painted Folklore and Folklore Painters of India*. Delhi: Concept Publishing Company.

Kane, P.V.
1953 *History of Dharmashāstra*, vol. 4. Poona: Bhandarkar Oriental Research Institute.

Kothari, Komal
1982 "The Shrine: An Expression of Social Needs." In *Gods of the Byways*, pp. 5-32. Oxford: Museum of Modern Art.

Lalas, Sitaram
1962-78 *Rājasthānī Sabad Kos*. 9 vols. Jodhpur: Rajasthani Shodh Sansthan.

Miller, Joseph C.
1980 "Current Investigations in the Genre of Rajasthānī Paṛa-Painting Recitations." In *Early Hindī Devotional Literature in Current Research*. Winand M. Callewaert, ed. pp. 116-125. New Delhi: Impex India.

Moreno Arcas, Manuel
1984 "Murugan, A God of Healing Poisons: The Physics of Worship in a South Indian Center for Pilgrimage." Ph.D. dissertation, Department of Anthropology, University of Chicago.

Pfaffenberger, Bryan
1982 *Caste in Tamil Culture: The Religious Foundations of Sudra Domination in Tamil Sri Lanka*. Syracuse, New York: Maxwell School of Citizenship and Public Affairs, South Asian Series, No. 7.

Salomon, Richard G.
1985 *The Bridge to the Three Holy Cities: The Sāmānya-Praghaṭṭaka of Nārāyana Bhaṭṭa's Tristhalīsetu*. Delhi: Motilal Banarsidass.

Tod, James
1978 *Annals and Antiquities of Rajasthan*. 2 vols. New Delhi: M.N.Publishers. (1st ed. 1829-32)

Wadley, Susan S.
1975 *Shakti: Power in the Conceptual Structure of Karimpur Religion*. Chicago: Department of Anthropology, University of Chicago Studies in Anthropology, No. 2.

Jowett, B. transl.
1944 *Plato: The Republic.* 3rd ed. New York: Heritage Press. (First published 1892).

Mathur, V.B.
1969 *Ethnographic Atlas of Rajasthan with Reference to Scheduled Castes and Scheduled Tribes.* Jaipur: Rajasthan Census Operations.

Raghavan, V.
1981 "Sanskrit Drama into Performance." In Sanskrit Drama into Performance, Rachel Van M. Baumer and James R. Brandon, eds. pp. 9-44. Honolulu: University of Hawaii.

Russell, R.V. and Rai Bahadur Hira Lal
1975 *Tribes and Castes of the Central Provinces of India. 4 vols. Delhi: Rajdhani Book Centre.* (1st ed. 1915)

Sharma, G.N.
1968 *Social Life in Medieval Rajasthan: 1500-1800 A.D.* Agra: Laxmi Narain Agarwal.

Welsford, Enid
1968 *The Fool: His Social and Literary History.* London: Faber and Faber (1st ed. 1935)

Willeford, William
1969 *The Fool and His Scepter: A Study in Clowns and Jesters and Their Audience.* Evanston, Ill.: Northwestern University Press.

TESTING THE GROOM: RIDDLING AT RAJASTHANI WEDDINGS AS CULTURAL PERFORMANCE

KARINE SCHOMER

In 1901, Amar Singh, eldest son and future heir of the Kanota *ṭhikānā* (feudal estate) in Rajputana's Jaipur state, was married to the daughter of the *ṭhākur* (feudal lord) of Satheen, a *ṭhikānā* of Jodhpur state. Twenty-three years old, Amar Singh had been educated away from home under the guardianship of Sir Pratap Singh, the modernizing regent of Jodhpur, an early follower of the reformist Arya Samaj movement and a man who disdained Hindu ceremonies and rituals. Amar Singh was first educated in an English-medium primary school, then tutored by a remarkable Jodhpur bard (*chāraṇ*), Bharat Ram Nathji Ratnu, one of the first men in Rajputana to travel to Europe and to graduate from an English-medium university in British India. Amar Singh's Victorian education and the time he spent as a young man serving in the Imperial Cadet Corps (including fighting in China during the Boxer Rebellion) broadened his knowledge of the world and exposed him to the influence of British values, ideas and customs. But is also distanced him from the culture and traditions of his native Rajputana.[1]

From 1898 to shortly before his death in 1942, Amar Singh kept an extensive personal diary in English.[2] Rich in observations of people, places and events, it is also a candid record of personal experiences, and of reflections and judgments on his noble Rajput world. The diary entries for the period from September 17 to October 1, 1901 narrate in great detail events surrounding his wedding and his reactions to them (Singh 1901). Throughout the proceedings, he seemed bewildered, forced to play a role in an unfamiliar world for which his upbringing had not prepared him.

Amar Singh's bewilderment reached its high point the morning after the wedding ceremony, when he was called by the women of his bride's family for the custom known as *kaṅvar kalevo* (breakfast for the groom) in the *zenānā* (women's quarters). His diary records the events.

> Next morning after my marriage . . . the women came singing and rejoicing to call me to their house. . . . Once inside the zenana I was conducted in a small but a nice room of the deshi fashion .... I walked straight up and sat with a reclining posture on the carpet and in a couple of minutes the room was chokeful [sic] of women. They crowded one over the other simply for the purpose of looking at my face. I soon got tired of it and wanted very much to clear them out, but simply bore up with them with the thought of not wounding and hurting their feelings. Ten minutes later my wife was conducted in supported by a couple of women on each side and as many behind. Near the foot of the carpet they stopped her and I was wanted or rather asked to get up and conduct [her] myself on the carpet. After a short deliberation I had to do it. Next the women wanted us to sit quite too closely, but try what they may, we did not do that . . .
>
> Now these ... ladies of the house began to question me on several silly questions. There were many to which I turned a deaf ear. In the very beginning, when these questions commenced, I told them that I had passed my years all through with Sarkar [Sir Pratap Singh] and had never been in the company of women and consequently knew not a single riddle of theirs. They would not hear to this objection of mine but continued to play question after question and I was obliged to turn a deaf ear by which they seemed a little annoyed . . .
>
> They had also stood against the door and asked me to open the door which was closed. In fact the door was open ajar but the woman standing in it wanted me to repeat some silly verse which is meant as the key to it. I did not know it but said simply that the doors of this house were now quite open for me since they had married me their daughter. They began to laugh and got out of the way. Then they asked many other questions but I knew none and so there was no answer from me. To show their silliness I will write a few here. How can a man understand them? I have myself now learned their meaning from my cousin Lachman Singh the other day when we all sat joking together:

– *kharvar khopo* [an energetic old bull] means 'father-in-law'.
– *kag godavani* [the sharp one who keeps you in your place] means 'mother-in-law'.
– *sirakh may ri sakhi* [the companion who is in the quilt] means 'wife'.
– *tamtami ra bij* [twinkling seeds] means 'eyes'.

Now just think of the silliness of these questions! How can a man unexperienced like me understand and give a proper answer? (Singh 1901: IX)[3]

What Amar Singh had encountered was the traditional Rajput wedding custom of the bride's female relatives and friends mock-testing the bridegroom's intelligence and knowledge of the culture through riddles and games of wit. Raised under the tutelage of Sir Pratap, away from the Kanota mansion (*havelī*) in Jaipur, with its dense multi-generational population, he was unprepared to respond, being innocent of many areas of social and cultural knowledge transmitted through the ongoing ceremonials of the extended upper-class family of Rajputana. In particular, he was unfamiliar and ill at ease with the cultural world of Rajput women. He had never before taken part in wedding ceremonies. Despite his formal education, he was unprepared for his own wedding, a rite of passage not so much uniting two individuals as linking two families and incorporating the new couple into the social and cultural universe of Rajput society.[4]

Riddling Context

The Rajasthani custom of riddling the groom is most characteristic of Rajputs and other communities (such as Charans and Jains) in which women traditionally observed rules of seclusion (*purdah*) and lived in segregated women's quarters (*zenānā*). The extent to which it occurs in other communities is a matter for further investigation, as is the degree to which it is practiced nowadays, especially in urban and expatriate settings, and the existence of comparable customs in regions adjacent to Rajasthan. These ethnographic questions, while important, are beyond the scope of this study, which focuses on the riddles themselves as verbal art and cultural performance. Nevertheless, to understand *why* the groom is riddled in certain Rajasthani communities requires seeing how this custom fits into the underlying structure of marriage alliances in the community and the construction of the wedding ceremonies that establish these alliances.

Weddings in Rajasthan consist of a series of traditional ceremonies, many of which are similar to their counterparts in other regions of India, but some of which are distinctive.[5] There are rituals, ceremonial customs, feasts, games and entertainments, on both the bride's and the groom's sides. Different events are controlled by the groom's men, the groom's women, the bride's men, or the bride's women. Among Rajasthani communities like the Rajputs, who have extended families in which women live together in *zenānās*, there tend to be more distinctive customs that are controlled by women and express their solidarity than in communities or regions where there is less seclusion of women.

Though weddings differ from community to community, and from family to family, certain structural features are present in some form or other in all weddings of the Rajput type most characteristic of Rajasthan. All such weddings represent both an alliance between two families and the taking away of a bride from her natal home and family to be incorporated into her husband's home and family. As a result, there are both ceremonies that have to do with exchange and ceremonies that have to do with "claiming" and "releasing" the bride. Furthermore, from the engagement (*sagāī*) to the ceremony months or years after the wedding when the groom takes the bride home to live with him permanently (*gaunā* or *muklāvā*), men and women on both sides play separate ceremonial roles that express the relationship between the two families and these underlying social structures. What Amar Singh failed to understand was that the "silly questions" with which the women of his bride's family plied him were an integral and necessary part of his wedding – both an ice-breaking ceremonial event, allowing them to get to know him, and a symbolic act, testing his worthiness and giving the *zenānā*'s approval to his taking the bride away.

The riddling of the groom comes at the end of a long ceremonial sequence in which the groom and the men of his family, at the invitation of and with the cooperation of the bride's men folk, symbolically conquer the bride from her natal family, while the bride's women folk both bless the event and symbolically resist it. The pageantry of conquest, common to North Indian weddings as a whole, is especially marked in Rajput and Rajput-influenced wedding customs in Rajasthan—as is the mock-resistance of the bride's women. As in the rest of North India, weddings in Rajasthan take place at the bride's home, and the wedding party (*bārāt*) arrives in procession, with the groom mounted on a caparisoned mare (or, in the case of the Rajput aristocracy, an elephant) and a hired band of male musicians playing at top volume. In Rajasthan, however, the groom is always dressed up as a Rajput warrior, with a large ornamented turban, necklaces, garlands of flowers around his neck, and a sword at his side; moreover, among Rajputs and other communities that practice *purdah*, the *bārāt* is traditionally all male, and the groom's female relatives do not attend the wedding. There is also a distinctive Rajasthani tradition known as *toraṇ māraṇo* (striking the *toraṇ*), in which the groom dramatically strikes with his sword a special fortress-shaped ornament known as *toraṇ*, which hangs in the entrance of the bride's home and represents the power of her family.

The customs surrounding the groom's arrival show clearly the separation of the men's and women's worlds, the ambivalent attitude of the bride's women toward the "conquest" of the bride, and their dual role in both blessing the groom and setting up ceremonial barriers against his entry. While the men of the family stand in the outer courtyard to receive the *bārāt*, the women remain in the verandah area, singing loud songs of welcome that compete with the male band, creating a tremendous cacophony that adds to the atmosphere of excitement and anticipation. Many of the women's songs are of the type known as *gālīs*—songs that tease, ridicule and insult the groom and his party.[6] Though *gālīs* are playful, the fact they are sung at all is an indication of the *zenānā*'s ambivalence.

Likewise, while the men of the family receive the groom's party in a straightforward way—a hierarchically structured exchange of embraces between the fathers, the uncles and the brothers on both sides, starting with the seniormost and ending with the youngest—the ceremony in which the women allow the groom and his party to enter the house expresses both welcome and resistance. First, the bride's mother honors the groom as a temporary god by performing *āratī* before him (moving an oil lamp in slow circles), putting a garland around his neck, and applying a ceremonial *ṭīkā* mark on his forehead. Then the other women perform *āratī*, and tie a new turban over the one he is wearing, as a sign of incorporating him into the family. Only then are he and his party allowed to enter, and even then, there is a gauntlet of practical jokes to be endured. The mother, while putting the *ṭīkā* on the groom's forehead, may try to smear it on his nose as well. Then some of the younger women may bring out a piece of string and pretend to measure the groom's height and the width of his shoulders. The bride may throw a rice ball at him. Sweets offered to the groom and his friends may be inedible items such as *pakoṛās* (stuffed fritters) filled with cotton, or *gulāb jāmuns* (brown ball-shaped sweets) made of mud or dung. The humor can be quite broad, including placing a *pāpaḍ* (a thin crispy cake made of chick-pea flour) under the guests' seats, so that an embarrassing noise is heard when they sit down.

The actual wedding ceremony (*byāh* or *śādī)*, consisting of elaborate Sanskritic rituals culminating in *pherā*, the circumambulations of the sacred fire that seal the marriage, is presided over by a Brahman priest. Though it is by the performance of these rituals that the daughter of the family becomes wife and daughter-in-law in the groom's family, and thereby ceases to belong to her natal *zenānā*, the women of her family play little direct role in them. The giving away of the bride (*kanyādān*) is performed by her father or an older male relative, other rituals involve the bride's brother and her maternal uncle; though the bride's mother sits next to her husband as the rituals are performed, she does little herself other than join her husband in the ritual of touching the bride's feet. The women of the groom's family (the *zenānā* to which the bride henceforth belongs) are not present at all.

It is in the context of these basic structures and structural exclusions that one needs to see two distinctive Rajasthani customs. One is the riddling of the groom, which may start informally as soon as the wedding ceremony is over, is concentrated heavily in the next morning's 'breakfast for the groom', and is an important part of the interaction between the groom and his female in-laws for several years after the wedding, every time he comes visiting, especially on the occasion of the *gaunā* or *muklāvā*. The other is the custom known as *ṭūṅṭiyo*, a mock-wedding performed at the groom's home by the women of his family at the very time the real wedding ceremony (*byāh*) is taking place at the bride's home. While the *byāh* is solemn, entails rigorously precise carrying out of prescribed rituals, and is controlled by an officiating priest and the male members of the bride's family, *ṭūṅṭiyo* is a boisterous, often bawdy affair, full of improvisation, and entirely controlled by the women of the groom's family. Different women play the roles of the groom, the bride, the father, the mother-in-law, the priest, and all the other personages involved in a wedding, with good-humored fun at the expense of all. The evening of the *ṭūṅṭiyo* is also an occasion for songs, dances and games, and is used by the women to practice *gālīs* and riddles for the next time they take part in a wedding as women on a bride's side, and it therefore becomes *their* turn to welcome and riddle a groom. In this context, riddles are often set to music and sung for easier memorization.[7]

The riddling of a groom by his female in-laws always takes place in a context where they have him surrounded and have the upper hand. Riddles are intermixed with tricks, such as hiding his shoes, games designed to embarrass him by forcing physical contact with the bride,[8] and tests of intelligence such as demanding that he recite some poetry in order to be allowed into or out of a room—a demand which Amar Singh, in his arrogant innocence of the custom and its significance, found preposterous.

Though women of all ages may be present at the 'breakfast for the groom' and other occasions when the groom is riddled, it is the women who have been married for some time and already have children who pose the riddles. Younger girls, including younger sisters of the bride, may suggest riddles, but do not ask them, in part because their content is often suggestive of sexual matters they are not supposed to know about. Older women, too, and recent brides, who are supposed to act demure, may suggest riddles, but do not normally ask them directly. The riddling is thus done principally by women whose relationship to the groom is that of older sisters-in-law, women who are both sexually mature and old enough so that it is considered appropriate for them to be testing him and "safe" for them to be teasing and taunting him.

In the context of a *zenānā* culture such as that of the Rajputs and Rajput-influenced communities of Rajasthan, riddling the groom is a custom that empowers the bride's women by giving them an active ceremonial role in "releasing" the daughter of the house to her new in-laws. It also provides, through humorous mock-confrontation, a way of both revealing and concealing their ambivalent feelings toward the conquering groom who will be taking the bride away. Finally, it gives them the opportunity to test the groom's worthiness—his poise, his intelligence, his wit, and his knowledge of the culture, including those dimensions of the culture that are of special interest to them as women.

Learning the Riddle Tradition

While the forms, thought structure, poetic imagery, subject-matter and world view of Rajasthani riddles are common to the region as a whole (and shared to varying degrees by adjoining linguistic and cultural regions),[9] every family, caste, neighborhood or village community in Rajasthan has its own repertoire. The riddle lore of any group is continuously enriched by new riddles brought in by outsiders—not only relatives and visitors, but also itinerant groups and individuals whose specialized occupations bring them to homes and villages as part of their regular rounds.

An important category of outsiders in this respect is the new brides. Along with songs and customs, they bring the riddles they learned in their childhood homes through participation in weddings and other riddling occasions. As a result, the riddle repertoire of a given family, village or community is not unique, but consists of riddles known throughout the region within which its marriage networks operate—networks which may extend throughout Rajasthan, and even beyond. Riddles heard in one locality are likely to show up elsewhere as well, creating an identifiable though fluid pan-Rajasthani body of common riddle lore. This movement of riddles is also evident in the fact that the riddles of any given locality exhibit a considerable amount of linguistic variation, ranging from the local dialect to dialects of other sub-regions of Rajasthan and, to a lesser extent, dialects of neighboring Hindi and Gujarati-speaking regions.[10]

Riddles and the art of riddling are passed on through oral tradition, during informal sessions of the kind described for western Uttar Pradesh by Dundes and Vatuk (1974: 88-92). Among Rajputs and other communities that practice ceremonial riddling of the bridegroom, weddings are also important occasions of transmission, as are the singing sessions at the *ṭūnṭiyo*, where women learn and practice riddles for use at future weddings.

Unlike Amar Singh, a traditional Rajput bridegroom would have been thoroughly prepared for the riddling assault by the women who were to become his new in-laws. As a small child, he would have sat with his mother and other women of the family while they sang songs and riddles and performed *ṭūṅṭiyo*. As a young boy, he would probably have experienced a sister's wedding in his own home or played the role of groom's escort to an older brother or cousin.[11] Later on, he might have been a member of the *bārāt* (wedding procession) for a brother, cousin or friend. As his own wedding approached, his friends and female relatives might have helped him prepare by making him memorize verses and practice answering riddles.

In rural Rajasthan, this traditional "training" of bridegrooms continues to this day. Yet, as in the case of Amar Singh nearly a century ago, urban living, modern education, employment shifts and geographical mobility tend to distance men from these informal modes of cultural education. As a result, there is a "gender gap" between women, especially rural women, whose more traditional upbringing and home-centered culture has preserved knowledge of the riddle lore, and educated young men, who approach their weddings untrained in the art of riddling and the community's repertoire of customary riddles.

Starting in the late 19th century, oral modes of riddle transmission and training began to be supplemented by printed manuals dealing with what a groom needs to know about marriage and for his wedding ceremony. Very popular in the first half of the 20th century and still published today, these manuals were an important resource for prospective bridegrooms, especially those living outside Rajasthan. The most popular of these, *Muklāvā-Bahār* (Agraval 1961) was written in the 1930s by a Marwari merchant living in the Chhattisgarh area of the Central Provinces (now Madhya Pradesh), and has been continuously published since then. While some pages are devoted to practical matters relating to married life, the major portion consists of riddles, proverbs, songs and entertainments. Nearly half of the total length is a detailed fictional account of a young man named Madanlal, who goes to get married and endures a gauntlet of riddles and tests at the hands of his bride's women relatives and friends (*ibid.*, 1-194). In the preface, the author recounts with considerable emotion his own embarrassment as a young man when he was unable to answer the riddles at his own wedding, and offers the book as an aid to other hapless bridegrooms whose intelligence and wit will be judged on the basis of their performance in these tests (*ibid.*, i-iii).

The ceremonial riddling of the groom embedded in wedding customs, women's sessions in which riddles are practiced by being sung, and the training of bridegrooms by their friends and with the help of manuals – all contribute to the preservation, cultivation and transmission of the riddling tradition of Rajasthan. The movement of people between one locality and another, especially of brides moving from their native place to their husband's village or town, contributes to its constant enrichment. Among urban Rajasthanis and those living outside Rajasthan, the tradition is no longer as strong as it once was, but its connection to the all-important religious ceremony of marriage increases the probability that the art will continue to be cultivated longer than in cultures where the performance context of riddles is unrelated to larger ritual contexts.

The Poetics of Rajasthani Riddles

Riddles, whatever their performance context or functional role in society, are first and foremost a genre of verbal art – structured play with words. Riddles entertain, challenge the mind, and express through artful devices particular ideas about reality. As a traditional oral genre, riddles everywhere are highly formulaic, dependent for their aesthetic success and solvability on the riddler and riddlee's participation in the conventions and perceptions of a shared cultural universe.

Like all verbal folklore, riddles can be analyzed from the perspectives of several academic disciplines. Anthropological approaches look to their role in validating social institutions and transmitting culture; linguistic theory examines them as structured utterances; literary criticism analyzes them as oral literature making use of poetic devices to achieve artistic ends. From the beginnings of modern folklore study, collection and "appreciation" have gone side by side with theoretical efforts to come to a satisfactory definition of the riddle as a folklore genre. Taking as their point of departure the classic definition of Taylor (1943), riddle scholars over the past several decades have been using the insights of all three disciplines to refine our understanding of what riddles are, how they are performed, what makes for a successful riddle, and how riddles function in society.[12] This study combines elements of these different approaches, but is centrally concerned with examining Rajasthani riddles as verbal art that expresses a regional aesthetic sensibility and cultural consciousness.

The elements that make up the poetics of riddles are their underlying logical structure, their formal characteristics, their fanciful metaphorical imagery, and the linguistic and literary devices they use to achieve ambiguity and wit, including the clues with which they tease the riddlee towards the answer. When Amar Singh was asked to guess the meaning of "*ṭamṭamī rā bīj*" ("twinkling seeds"), he was presented with what Georges and Dundes have classified structurally as a "non-oppositional metaphoric" riddle – one in which the riddle referent (the item to be guessed) and the descriptive element (the apparent referent and the assertion made about it) are different, and there is no opposition stated within the descriptive element (1963: 114).

The descriptive element in this riddle is a single prose phrase ("twinkling seeds"), introduced by no explicit riddle marker and interrogative only in intent, not in form, calling for a single word ("eyes") as answer. The imagery of seeds as a metaphor for eyes, in particular the elongated seeds of the sesame plant (*til*), is a familiar convention in India's literary and folk traditions. The device of adding the qualifier "twinkling" both provides a clue and adds a further associative dimension.

The following riddle, of the same structural type, has the added formal element of rhyme.

> *Q*: *ek jināvar aisā*
> *jiskī pūṅchhaṛī pai paisā*
> *A*: *mor* (*K&D: I, no. 37*)
>
> Q: An animal
> with coins on its tail.
> A: A peacock.

The metaphor here, picturing the striking irridescent "eyes" on the tip of a peacock's tail through the image of shiny, man-made coins (specifically, the large one-*paisā* coin of pre-independence days), is another one common to India's folk traditions.

A third riddle juxtaposes the animal and vegetable worlds

through visual metaphor, and involves the use of a riddle-marking formula ("Don't get it? Ask your father!").

> *Q*: *līlī ghoṛī jharmar pūṅchh*
> *na āvai tau thārā bāp nai pūchh*
> *A*: *makiyau* (*K&D: I, no. 299*)

> Q: A green horse with a wispy tail.
> Don't get it? Ask your father!
> A: Corn.

Many Rajasthani riddles use the rhyming couplet form known as *dohā*, a meter common to oral tradition in both Rajasthan and the Hindi-speaking regions of the North Indian heartland. Succinct, amenable to memorization and composition, and especially suited to singing, *dohā* has regular, clearly marked rhythmic breaks which encourage the organization of meaning into four short units, as well as patterns of parallelism or opposition (Dundes and Vatuk 1963: 124; Schomer 1987: 62-64).

> *Q*: *kākī rai doya kānaṛā*
> *kākau būḍhau bacchak*
> ***Kākī hilāyā kānaṛā***
> ***kākau paṛyau daṭak***
> *A*: *tāḷau-chābī* (*K&D: II, no. 3*)

> Q: Auntie has two ears,
> old uncle a belly-button.[13]
> Auntie wiggles her ears,
> uncle falls with a thud.
> A: Padlock and key.

The metaphor here, fresh because unconventional, is comical and mock-obscene. It involves two descriptive elements, one visual (the traditional Indian key is split-headed and the padlock pot-bellied in shape) and one functional (the action of lock and key envisioned as some kind of human sexual play).

Another riddle in *dohā* form has near rather than perfect end rhyme. It involves a metaphor based not on visual similarity but an activity perceived as common to the animal and human worlds.

> *Q*: *ek nār chatur ghaṇī*
> *lapsī karai suvād*
> *binā tavai bina kuṛacchalai*
> *bina chūlhā bina āg*
> *A*: *madhumakkī* (*MB: 42, no. 2*)

Q: Very clever woman,
makes sweet *lapsī*.
No grill, no spoon,
no stove, no fire.
A: A honeybee.

Structurally, this riddle has two descriptive elements, but the second is a seeming logical contradiction of the first: *lapsī* (a typical Rajasthani sweet dish) can't be made without grill, spoon, stove or fire. It is thus a riddle of the type Georges and Dundes call "privational contradictive" (1963: 115). The contradictive element, foregrounded by the repetitive "no" phrases, also serves as a strong clue that the answer will be in a domain other than kitchen and cooking.

In the following riddle, of the "antithetical contradictive" type (*ibid.*, 114-115), the two sets of descriptive elements seem to be mutually exclusive.

Q: *sapanī kī tarah par sāṅp nahīṅ*
mūṅh meṅ jībh par kāṭatī nahīṅ
A: *"pen"* (*K&D: I, no. 207*)
Q: Like a snake but not a snake.
Tongue in its mouth but doesn't bite.
A: A pen.

The seemingly insoluble contradiction, referred to in riddle scholarship as "the block," i.e., the element through which the riddler seeks to outwit the riddlee, is resolved through the metaphor, which juxtaposes the tongue of a snake and the nib of a pen, once again linking the natural world and the world of man-made objects.

A more difficult riddle of this type creates the "block" through exploitation of linguistic ambiguity.

Q: *śyām hai par śyām nahīṅ*
baṅśī kī guṅjār par baṅśīdhar nahīṅ
A: *bhauṅrā* (*K&D: I, no. 262*)
Q: Dark One but not the Dark One.
Flute sound but not the Flute Bearer
A: A bumblebee.

What should be a description of the god Krishna, who is dark-skinned and plays the flute, is categorically denied. But *śyām* is both one of Krishna's names (The Dark One) and the adjective for either "dark" or "black," while *guṅjār* can refer to either the sound of an instrument or the humming of insects. To "get" this riddle therefore requires grasping a metaphor rolled up within a double linguistic ambiguity.

Non-oppositional riddles (Georges and Dunds 1963: 113-114) can also be difficult to grasp, with metaphors involving a series of juxtapositions that require multiple leaps of imagination.

Q: *aṛabaṛa pān aneka phal*
jyāṅrā nyārā nāṅv
jaṛa kāṭyāṅ phal nīpajai
uṇ rūṅkh rau kāī nāṅv
A: *kumār rī chāk* (*K&D: I, no. 64*)

Q: Leaves shake, fruit grows
of many kinds.
Roots are cut, fruit drops.
What's this tree called?
A: The potter's wheel.

In this *dohā* riddle, the metaphor moves through three phases paralleling the process of making pottery: the shaking of the lump of clay as the wheel turns, pots of different kinds being shaped as if growing out of the wheel, and the separation of the pots from the wheel with a piece of potter's thread.

A common riddle throughout India is the multiple riddle, in which a series of questions are clustered together. The following *dohā* riddle, with the answer also in *dohā* form, is of this kind.

Q: *kaun sarovar pāl binā*
kaun peḍ binā ḍāl
kaun pakherū paṅkh binā
kaun maut binā kāl
A: *naiṇa sarovar pāl binā*
dharma peḍ binā ḍāḷ
jīv pakherū paṅkh binā
nīṅd maut binā kāl (*MB: 48, no. 2*)

Q: What lake is without shore,
what tree without branches?
What bird is without wings,
what dying without death?
A: Eyes are a lake without shore,
true religion a branchless tree.
The soul is a bird without wings,
sleep is dying without death.

All four of these metaphors are ancient philosophical ones that appear frequently in Indian poetry and proverbial sayings. The riddle is therefore not a "true riddle" in the sense of a puzzle to be figured out through metaphorical imagination and wit (Taylor 1943: 129), but a conventional wisdom question whose answer is to be recalled from memory and tradition. Such "riddling questions," "special knowledge" riddles, or "cathetical" riddles[14] are also part of Rajasthan's riddle traditions.

Another kind of riddle tells a story or sets forth an enigmatic situation that needs to be explained in narrative terms. Such riddles are often in the form of a dialogue, and may allow more than one answer.

Q: *maiṅ levā āī tanne*
tū pakaḍ baiṭhyo manne
tū chhoḍ de manne
maiṅ le jāūṅ tanne (*MB: 50, no. 6*)

Q: I came to take you,
you caught me.
Let go of me,
I'll take you.

A-1: *pānī levā gaī*
jad baras hona lagī

A-1: You went to get water,
it started to rain.

A-2: *bor toḍabā gaī*
jad jhaḍī meṅ phaṅs gaī

A-2: You went to pick berries,
thorns caught you.

The riddle structure here is "literal non-oppositional" (Georges and Dundes 1963: 113-114), with riddle referent and descriptive element the same thing, and no metaphor involved. Such riddles often take the form of simple prose questions.

Q: *vā kaī chīj hai jo jāy pachai nī āvau?*
A: *javānī* (*MB: 20, no. 3*)

Q: What is it that once gone never returns?
A: Youth.

Also of this structural type are conundrums, riddles which present a logical problem to be worked out.

Q: *tīn akṣar kā merā nām*
ulṭā sīdhā ek samān
jo ātā hai jāti ke nām
A: *īsāī* (*K&D: I, no. 30*)

Q: Three syllables has my name,
Forward and backward the same,
Used by a caste as its name.
A: *īsāī* (Christian)

This particular conundrum is based on the spelling of the word for 'Christian', whose three syllables (*ī-sā-ī*) read the same in either direction; others are arithmetical, or involve kinship relations and other "special knowledge" systems.

Also in the category of "literal non-oppositional" riddles is riddling repartee. In *Muklāvā-Bahār*, young Madanlal is shown at the 'breakfast for the groom', surrounded by laughing women, fielding a rapid-fire series of trick questions from his older sisters-in-law. As is characteristic of this occasion, many questions are mock-obscene, designed to embarrass him as well as test how quickly he can think on his feet.

Q: *the āyā jike rāste kuṇ-kuṇ āyā?*
A: *mhārā bhāṇ bhāī.*
Q: *the baiṭho jad dhartī par pahalī ke ṭeko?*
A: *nijar.*
Q: *the sāsare jāvo jad pailyāṅ ke māro?*
A: *toraṇ.*
Q: *thāre āge pāchhe kāī?*
A: *lugāyāṅ.*
Q: *thārī dhotī meṅ ke?*
A: *lāṅg.*
Q: *thārā bāpkī lambī ke?*
A: *pagaṛī.*
Q: *thārī māṅko chauṛo ke?*
A: *ghāgharo.*
Q: *thāre sāge din rāt kuṇso bhūt rahe?*
A: chhāyāṅ (*MB: 34-35*)

Q: Who came the same way you came?
A: My brothers and sisters.
Q: What strikes the ground first when you sit?

A: My glance.
Q: What do you strike when you go to your in-laws?
A: The *toraṇ*.
Q: What's in front of you and what's behind you?
A: Women.
Q: What's in your loincloth?
A: A knot.
Q: What does your father have that's long?
A: A turban.
Q: What does your mother have that's broad?
A: A skirt.
Q: What ghost follows you day and night?
A: My shadow.

Unique to the context of the 'breakfast for the groom' and riddling of a bridegroom by his female in-laws is the kind of riddle challenge in verse known as *bāṅdhaṇo-kholaṇo* (bind-and-release). Like Amar Singh, the groom is told that some object he wants (his seat, his shoes, food, a glass of water, a door he needs to get through) is "bound," i.e., that he cannot have it. In order to "release" the object, he must unravel the meaning of a convoluted narrative riddle, composing a long reply in verse that makes clever reference to one or more of the women of the family and ends with the demand to release the "bound" object. Only then can he have access to it—just as he can only have access to his bride after the women of the *zenānā* have "released" her to him.

In preparation for these *bāṅdhaṇo-kholaṇo* challenges, grooms traditionally memorized many stanzas by heart, learning thereby the patterns and formulas they would use in composing their replies. An idea of how complex *bāṅdhaṇo-kholaṇo* can be is the following exchange from *Muklāvā-Bahār*. Madanlal asks for some water, but is told by one of his sisters-in-law that the water is "bound." She starts with a riddle marker that plays on the two meanings of the word *pāṇī*: both 'water' and, by extension, 'luster, brilliance, cleverness, wits'.

chāṅbeṅ pān ugaleṅ dhāṇī
mhe bāndhāṅ mardāṅ ko pāṇī
Chew the *pān*,[15] spit out the grain.
This man's wits I bind today.

She then goes on to narrate a seemingly disjointed tale. It starts with a wealthy young man smitten by the sight of a beautiful young woman filling a water pot at the pond. Whether to protect herself from his attention or to coyly entice him, she casts the "spears" of her glances in all four directions.

gorī ghāgar śīr dharī
chālī bharaṇ tālāb
mūṅh dhove kullā kare
motiyana dīpai līlāḍ
ek motī jhaḍ paḍyo
bije liyo uṭhāy
bin per paḍjyo bijalī
is jyoṅ nāgan jāy
eḍī kī geḍī karūṅ
tan ko tarkas tīr
naiṇāṅ kā bhālā karūṅ
mārūṅ chatar amīr
chaḍtī mārūṅ rāmagaṛh
utartī lāhor
bije mārūṅ meḍate
jā pacche nāgor

Fair woman, pot on her head,
goes to fill it at the pond.
Washes her face, rinses her mouth,
on her forehead, shining pearls.
One pearl falls to the ground,
another is snatched away.
He's struck as if by lightning
or by the bite of a snake.
"My heel I'll make into a coil of rope,
my body into bow and arrows.[16]
My eyes I'll make into spears,
to strike that rich and clever man.
I'll throw a spear down to Ramgarh,
then one up to Lahore.
Then I'll throw one to Merta,
and after that to Nagore."

What the woman addressing Madanlal is describing by means of this jumble of metaphoric images is the green tie-and-dye *oḍhnī* (the veil-like half-*sārī* of Rajasthani women) she is wearing. Only intimate knowledge of the tie-and-dye process and the particular pattern being described (*pomcho*) can make sense of this.[17] The pond is the plain ground color of the garment, and the pearl-like drops of water on the woman's forehead are the white dots of the tie-and-dye pattern. Shooting the spears refers to the method whereby knots are tied in a straight line from one end of the *oḍhnī* to the other, along a single thread. The place names, Ramgarh to Lahore (west to north) and Merta to Nagore (east to south), indicate the crossing diagonal lines of white dots in the *pomcho* pattern.

The story continues. The young man follows the glance (or spear) cast in the direction of Nagore, goes there, and finds a wealthy *baṇjārin* (nomadic merchant woman) who has a spouted water vessel (*jhārī*) made of gold and offers it to him for seventy gold coins.

> *vahāṅ base lākhī biṇjārī*
> *hātha liye kaṅchan kī jhārī*
> *kah biṇjārī jhārī ko mol*
> *sattar mhor lagaiṅge bol*
> There a wealthy *baṇjārin* lives,
> with a water vessel made of gold.
> "Tell me, *baṇjārin*, how much does it cost?"
> "Seventy gold coins you'll have to pay."

Madanlal, who has guessed the answer to the riddle, introduces his reply by continuing the dialogue with the *baṇjārin*, saying that the price is too low – the implication being that it would take a much more difficult riddle to successfully "bind" his wits (and his water).

> *thaiṅ biṇjāri thoṛā kahyā*
> *merā man bahot meṅ rahyā*
> "Your price is too low, *baṇjārin*!
> I can afford much more."[18]

Then he shows he has guessed the riddle by continuing the description of the *pomcho*.

> *aglī ke eṛo ghero*
> *pāchhlī ke lāgyo bachhero*

bichlī hai va ghar kī nār
kar nikalī solā siṅgār
First the grain around the rim,
then the grazing calves.
In the middle the woman of the house,
adorned with sixteen ornaments.

The grain refers to the seed-shaped tie-and-dye designs along the border of the *oḍhnī*, the calves to larger designs in the corners. The woman of the house, with the formulaic "sixteen ornaments" of poetic tradition, is a large design in the center.

Madanlal then composes a string of verses about water, the object he wants to release and one of the most scarce resources in Rajasthan.

pāṇī hai samadar kī pāl
pāṇī kīmat motī lāl
pāṇī binā sukhtā bāg
pāṇī binā lagtī āg
pāṇī sab prāṇī kā prāṇ
pāṇī varuṇ rūp bhagvān
Water is the spirit over the sea,
water is worth rubies and pearls.
Without water gardens dry,
without water fires blaze.
Water is the life of all that lives,
water is God in the form of rain.

Finally, with one last riddle marker, or answer marker, he declares the water (and his wits) to be "released."

baiṭh dal par mainā bole
bole samay pichhāṇī
bāṅdhūṅ thāroṅ kuṭum kabīlo
chhoḍo mhāro pāṇī
bāṅdhyo thāro haryo pomcho
chhūṭyo mhāro pāṇī
Seated on a branch, the mynah bird speaks:
"Recognize your fate!
I've bound all of your people,[19]
so release my water!
I've bound your green *pomcho*,

my water must be released!"[20]

A final type of riddle is the enacted, wordless riddle. The women appear wearing costumes and enact small skits, the meaning of which the groom must guess. One well known riddle of this type is traditionally enacted at the time of the *gaunā* or *muklāvā*, when the groom comes to take his bride away to live at his father's house. The bride and three of her friends are dressed identically, with their faces veiled, each holding a metal plate with a different object in it: lac bangles, henna (*meṅhdī*), a coconut, and a bottle of perfume. The groom must guess which one is his bride. The answer is the one with the perfume, as in Rajasthani culture the other three objects are all signs of an already married woman: lac bangles and henna decorations on the hands were traditionally worn only by married women, and the coconut is a metaphor for the womb that contains a second life within it (Komal Kothari, personal communication).

Performing Rajasthani Culture

Few riddles posed to a Rajasthani bridegroom are "special knowledge" riddles requiring familiarity with a body of esoteric lore or learning. All the riddles, however, assume a general knowledge of the culture. They are constructed from its everyday material aspects, cognitive categories, social rules, artistic sense and moral values, and are potentially soluble by virtue of participation in them. The answer to the "which is the bride?" riddle requires knowledge of a particular cultural code and principles of classification. The riddles about the padlock and key, potter's wheel or *pomcho* require familiarity with the material culture, while the "twinkling seeds" and "coins on its tail" riddles rely on participation in the culture's aesthetic imagination. All the riddles involve observation of and play with the elements that constitute Rajasthani culture.

Milton Singer (1972: 67–80) has pointed to the importance of cultural performances as entry points into understanding or "charting the topography" of a culture or civilization. Observing a range of cultural performances among the Smarta Brahmans of the Madras area, he noted their centrality and recurrence in the life of the community, and concluded that these people, and perhaps all people, think of their culture as encapsulated in such performances. Cultural performances, he suggested, should be seen as the elementary constituents of a culture, as well as the most basic units through which a culture may be studied (*ibid.*, 71).

Because Singer was seeking to chart an all-India cultural consciousness shaped by the "Great Tradition" of Sanskritic Hinduism, the performances on which he chose to focus were primarily those mediated by Brahman cultural specialists identified with the "Great Tradition" – prayers, ritual readings, recitations, religious discourses, priestly rites and ceremonies, learned lectures, and classical performing arts events. A different, more democratic range of cultural performances needs to be examined when one seeks to chart the contours of the regional folk culture of Rajasthan, which is less shaped by the Brahman priesthood, and is the creation of non-professionals as well as professionals, low-status people as well as high-status people, and women as well as men.

The custom of riddling the bridegroom is one such performance. Like all cultural performances, it involves a special occasion, a setting, performers, an audience, and a specific content, "program" or "text." As with the performances studied by Singer, it reveals, encapsulates, and enacts a cultural consciousness and pattern. Thus the riddles not only *contain* metaphors, but *are themselves* metaphors for Rajasthani culture as a whole.

The typical subject matter of Rajasthani riddles, like that of riddles everywhere, is the material world and concerns of people's everyday lives. The topics range from weather, natural phenomena and regional geography to famous personages, history, legends and mythology, and proverbial and spiritual wisdom. As Rajasthani society has been historically, and is still, predominantly agricultural and pastoral, many riddles have to do with the regional fauna and flora, as well as agricultural and livestock-related products and processes. Household, field and craft implements, and activities related to these work domains, are also prominent, as are conveyances and dwellings, or parts of dwellings. Other important topics having to do with the regional way of life include clothing, social types, kinship systems and categories, along with customs, ceremonies and habitual behaviors. Many riddles, while ostensibly dealing with a concrete referent, implicitly express the society's abstract perceptual and conceptual categories, aesthetic conventions, social rules and ethical norms.

How these riddles encapsulate the culture and act as metaphors for it can be seen through examination of even the smallest representative sample. The following riddle encapsulates the geography of central Rajasthan by mentioning four of its principal towns, summarizes the *charas* well-irrigation technique characteristic of this semi-arid part of the state, and reveals the gender-based division of labor, all in the course of describing through analogy one of the daily household chores of Rajasthani village women.

> *Q*: *kuau khuḍijai Meṛtai*
> *sāraṇ Sāṅgāner*
> *pāṇatiyau Pālī basai*
> *sīṅchārau Ājmer*
> *A*: *bilovaṇau* (*K&D: I, no. 232*)

> Q: Well is dug in Merta,
> slope runs to Sanganer.
> Field-waterer stands in Pali,
> water-lifter in Ajmer.
> A: Churning (butter from curds).

The location of the four towns in relation to one another is roughly that of the well, the bottom of the slope along which the draft animals move, the work-team member who draws the leather bucket (*charas*) from the well, and the one who empties it into the irrigation channel. The leap of imagination required to guess the riddle involves seeing a similar positioning and pattern in the butter-churning task performed by women in the home: the curds are in a deep clay pot, and the action of a tall churning stick "draws" butter from the curds, as one woman squats near the pot rolling the stick between her hands while a second pours water from above.

Another riddle describes the square-shaped masonry step-well (*bāvaṛī*) characteristic of the semi-arid and arid regions of Rajasthan, and makes reference to the desert phenomenon of mirage, which can lead people and animals to their death.

> *Q*: *chār kuṇāṅ rī bāvaṛī*
> *bharī hiboḷā khāy*
> *hāthī ghoṛā dūbiyā*

piṇaghaṭa khālī jāy
A: *kāch* (*K&D: I, no. 44*)[21]

Q: Four-cornered well,
full and shimmering.
Elephants and horses drown in it,
women leave without water.
A: A mirror.

Yet another refers to Rajasthani well-irrigation with a metaphor from animal husbandry.

Q: *bhairā meṅ char-char jāvai*
A: *kue rī lāv* (*K&D: I, no. 334*)

Q: It grazes at the well.
A: The rope used to draw water from the well.

The importance of cattle in Rajasthani cultural consciousness is seen in riddles like the following.

Q: *dhoḷī gāy rāt chare*
din ūgyāṅ ghar jāe
A: *tārā* (*K&D: I, no. 146*)

Q: White cows that graze at night.
When day breaks, they go home.
A: Stars.

Many riddles about agricultural products encapsulate important aspects of the region's economy, as in one about a long-time major cash crop.

Q: *dūdh khet meṅ nīpaje*
dahī disāvar jāy
būḍhā khāvai prem sūṅ
chāṅdī mol bikāy
A: *aphīm* (*K&D: I, no. 25*)

Q: Milk grows in the fields,
curds go abroad.
Old men consume it gladly,
it sells for the price of silver.
A: Opium.

Agricultural riddles often reveal and reinforce aspects of Rajasthani social life, as in the following about one of the staple lentils of the region.

Q: *goḷa moḷa baṭiyau*
supārī rau sāraṅg
gyārah devar chhoṛa kai
chalī jeṭh ke saṅg
A: *arhar rī dāl* (*K&D: I, no. 27*)

Q: Small round pellet,
color of betelnut.
Rejects husband's eleven younger brothers,
goes off with the elder.
A: The *arhar* lentil.

The riddle puns on two meanings of *jeṭh*: 'husband's-elder-brother' and the month (Jeth) in which the *arhar* lentil is harvested. Thus, while stating with precision the harvesting time of this crop, the riddle also refers to one of the major kinship distinctions a wife must observe within the Rajasthani joint-family: that between her husband's older brothers (*jeṭh*), from whom she must remain distant, and his younger brothers (*devar*), with whom a familiar joking relationship is allowed.[22]

Another riddle whose topic is a natural phenomenon combines delicate poetic imagery with the expression of another important kinship distinction.

Q: *harī hariyālī*
motiyāṅ jālī
chāṅd kī baiṇ
sūraj kī sālī
A: *os* (*K&D: I, no. 19*)

Q: Over the greenery,
a web of pearls.
Moon's sister,
Sun's sister-in-law.
A: Dew.

Reference here is to the habitual friendship between brother and sister on the one hand, and on the other the potentially "scorching" danger to a woman from contact with her older sister's husband.

This same pattern of cultural enactment and encapsulation is found in varying degrees in all Rajasthani riddles. Two frequent topics, treated with great poetic imagination, are the beauty and expressiveness of eyes, and the small earthenware oil-lamps known as *diyā*. Until a few decades ago, these oil-lamps were the principal form of night-time lighting in most Rajasthani villages, and are still used for religious ceremonies and to light up homes for the festival of Divali. In riddles about these objects, the imagery of traditional love poetry is often used.

> *Q*: *motī jitarau māḷiyau*
> *til jitarau kiṅvāṛ*
> *māṅya paṅkherū ram rahyo*
> *rājan rai uṇiyār*
> *A*: *āṅkh* *(K&D: 1, no. 9)*

> Q: Rooms like a pearls,
> shutters like sesame seeds.
> Bird dallies inside,
> disguised as a prince.
> A: Eyes.

Two conventional poetic conceits are used in this riddle: that the pupil of the eye is like a bird, and that the woman in love holds her beloved's image captive inside her eyes. The following riddle about an oil-lamp likewsie makes use of traditional poetic conceits.

> *Q*: *nājuk nārī pīya saṅg sovai*
> *aṅg se aṅg milāy*
> *pīya ko bicchurat jāni ke*
> *saṅg satī ho jay*
> *A*: *diyau-battī* (Srivastava 1974: 284)

> Q: Tender womans sleeps by her beloved,
> body joined to body.
> Knowing her beloved will leave,
> she joins him in *satī*.
> A: Wick and lamp-oil.

Striking to an outsider, the imagery of the wick burning itself out with the oil expresses dramatically the traditional Rajput ideal of *satī* (the self-immolation of a widow on her husband's funeral pyre) – if not in its literal meaning then at least in the metaphorical sense of absolute devotion and love which it has acquired in poetry and devotional religion.

What distinguishes folk traditions from classical traditions (or from the modern popular culture impersonally transmitted by the mass media) is their intimate connection with the colloquial language, material circumstances, social relationships, and emotional experiences and mundane daily concerns of a particular community's way of life. Folk traditions also tend to be more fluid, less formal, and less self-reflective than classical traditions, transmitted by performers who are related to their audiences in an intimate, face-to-face way, and in performance contexts that are more closely woven into the texture and cyclical rhythms of daily life. Like the mother-tongue, a community's folk traditions are absorbed unselfconsciously through participation in the group's social and ritual life, and their meaning and emotional impact are heavily dependent on the traditional setting in which they are performed. By contrast, the process of "refinement" by which classical traditions are fashioned is one of universalization and abstraction, their transmission has more of the deliberateness of second-language acquisition, and the emotional and aesthetic impact of performances is more independent of the context that originally produced them.

The strength of a regional folk culture rests in the degree to which its performances are emotionally relevant to a continuing way of life. In Rajasthan, a region of relative isolation which has been less intensely subjected to outside influences over the centuries than other, more central parts of India, traditional folk performances have remained vital to this day. Modernization, the problematics of which Amar Singh was an early example, tends to undermine the importance and meaningfulness of folk customs and performances; yet, for the majority of Rajasthan's still mostly rural people, it does not represent a threat to their very survival. Unlike regions, both in India and elsewhere in the world, which are more urbanized, and in which the social and cultural dislocations of modernity have been more extreme, Rajasthan has shown a resilient capacity for adapting to change without loss of cultural identity and confidence. To the extent that Rajasthanis, including expatriate Rajasthanis, continue to adapt to change without fear of cultural loss, one can expect folk traditions, especially those as embedded in ritual contexts as is the riddling of bridegrooms, to continue playing an important part in enacting and transmitting the regional culture.

ENDNOTES

I am indebted to Padma Shri Komal Kothari, Director of Rupayan Sansthan (Rajasthan Institute of Folklore) in Jodhpur, who, while a Fulbright Scholar-in-Residence at the University of California at Berkeley in 1980, brought to my attention the importance of this riddling tradition, urged me to write about it, and made available to me source materials from Rupayan Sansthan's oral literature archive. For further assistance in understanding Rajasthani wedding customs and interpreting the riddles, I would also like to thank several San Francisco Bay Area members of the Rajasthan Association of North America: Leela Mathur, Ramesh and Arpita Mishra, Jaya Pungaliya, Motilal and Sukhchen Khemsara, and Manju Singh. Thanks are also due to Joan Erdman, Ved Prakash Vatuk, and to my husband, Raphael Shevelev, for critical comment and suggestions on earlier drafts. An earlier version of this paper was presented at the 1981 Western Association for Asian Studies meetings at the University of California-Berkeley, in a panel on "Actors and Audiences: Performing Rajasthan's Culture."

1. Extensive work on the life of Amar Singh of Kanota (1878-1942) and the history of his lineage has been done by Lloyd and Susanne Rudolph, in collaboration with Amar Singh's nephew, Thakur Mohan Singh. The summary sketch of Amar Singh's life provided here is based on Rudolph and Rudolph 1984: 81-140, 177-232, *passim*, and 1987.
2. The Amar Singh diary, 87 volumes long, is in the possession of the Kanota family, with microfilm copies at the Nehru Memorial Museum and Library in New Delhi and at the Joseph Regenstein Library of the University of Chicago. With the permission of the family, Lloyd and Susanne Rudolph and Mohan Singh are editing it, and the Rudolphs have published several articles based on it. For more information on the diary, see Rudolph and Rudolph 1984: vii, 1987, and 1988.
3. Lloyd and Susanne Rudolph have brought this section of the diary to my attention and obtained for me Thakur Mohan Singh's permission to quote from it. The text is reproduced verbatim, keeping intact Amar Singh's sometimes idiosyncratic use of the English language.
4. For more on the traditional extended family household of the Rajputana nobility, and on the meaning of Amar Singh's marriage within that context, see Rudolph and Rudolph 1984: 177-210.
5. The most complete ethnographic description of Rajasthaṇi wedding ceremonies is Gupta (1974: 78-103). Bryce (1961: 53-126), based on Ramsinha (1939), describes the sequence of ceremonies in relation to the kinds of wedding songs associated with each. For the wedding customs of particular castes in Rajasthan, see Lushington 1833 (Jats) and Vetscher 1973 (Minas). For descriptions of wedding customs in other parts of North India, see Fruzetti for Bengal (1982: 29-60 *passim*, 69-95), Archer for Bihar (1985: xiv-xviii, 3-51), and Lewis for western Uttar Pradesh (1958). Srivastava (1974: 85-123) provides a comparative account of wedding customs in Rajasthan and eastern Uttar Pradesh.
6. *Gālī* singing by women exists throughout North India. For an examination of *gālī* texts and contexts from an eastern Uttar Pradesh village, see Henry 1975: 65-66, 75, 80-81, 85-87.

7. The Rajasthani women's custom of singing riddles has been documented and studied by Komal Kothari. I have heard and used tapes and transcriptions of sung riddles he collected with his associate, Vijay Dan Detha, in the village of Borunda (Kothari and Detha 1979). The performance pattern is for three to ten riddles in verse to be strung together and sung to the same tune, with vocative phrases such as "*jī ḍholā!*" (O groom!) or "*o rāj!*" (O prince!) inserted at verse breaks, and a formulaic refrain at the end of each riddle.
8. *Juvā–juvī*, for example, has the bride and groom fishing for a ring in a shallow platter of water made murky by adding some milk to it. Another game has a woman place bits of cotton on different parts of the bride's and groom's bodies, which they must remove for each other. A mock-fighting game has the bridal pair beating each other with twigs or pieces of rope. Finally, there is the game in which the bride and groom must untie the knots in each other's *kaṅkaṇḍoro*, amulets tied to their wrists as part of the ceremonies preliminary to the wedding.
9. Riddles in neighboring areas, particularly the Hindi-speaking areas to the east of Rajasthan, have a similarity of poetics and subject-matter that is readily apparent. See Dundes and Vatuk (1974), Parmar (1973), Singh (1973), and Upadhyaya (1967a and 1967b) for riddles from Uttar Pradesh and Madhya Pradesh; for riddles from the tribal groups of Madhya Pradesh, Bihar and Orissa, see Archer (1943), and Elwina nd Archer (1943). Bhagwat (1965: 100-129), a sampling of riddles from all over India, shows subcontinental similarities. Examination of riddle collections from other parts of the world helps see by contrast what is culturally distinctive about the riddle lore of the Indian subcontinent. For riddles from Africa, see Bascom (1949), Beuchat (1965), Glazier and Glazier (1976); see Scott (1965) for Persian and Arabic riddles, Sein and Dundes (1964) for Burma, and McAllester (1964) for Native American riddles; Taylor (1951) is a vast compendium of riddles from the British Isles and all the English-speaking parts of the Western hemisphere.
10. This variation is evident in the Kothari and Detha collection of riddles from Borunda (1979).
11. It is customary for two young children, usually younger brothers or nephews, to serve as escort to the bride and escort to the groom, present at their respective sides throughout the wedding proceedings.
12. See Bascom (1949), Georges and Dundes (1963), Scott (1965 and 1969), Hamnett (1967), Haring (1971), Maranda (1971a and 1971b), Abrahams (1972 and 1980); Abrahams and Dundes (1972), Green and Pepicello (1978, 1979, 1984), and Pepicello (1980).
13. This interpretation is somewhat problematic. *Rājasthānī Sabad Kos* defines *bacchak* as the cupped palm of the hand (Lalas 1962-78: 2839). The meaning of 'belly-button' may be by analogy to the hollow formed in the palm.
14. For a critique of Taylor's definition of the "true riddle," see Georges and Dundes 1963: 111-113. For different viewpoints on the distinction between "riddling questions" and "true riddles," see Archer 1943: 145-146; Green and Pepicello 1979: 17-19; Abrahams 1972: 179-188 *passim*.
15. Betel-leaf.
16. *Geḍī* is the term used for the ring of coiled rope women place on their heads to cushion the weight of the water pots they carry. This line follows the "My

. . . I'll make into a . . . " formula, which is frequently found in Rajasthani folk poetry, and can be inserted into many different contexts.

17. Besides *pomcho*, there are three other principal *oḍhnī* patterns: *chuṇarī*, *lahariyā*, and *pīḷā*. Elements from one pattern can be brought into another, as in the case of the one in question here, which seems to combine elements of *pomcho* and *pīḷā*. *Pomcho* is characterized by parallel diagonal lines of small white tie-and-dye dots. *Pīḷā* has a yellow ground with a red border and a large red design in the center, and is worn by women who have already had a male child (Jaya Pungaliya, oral communication).
18. The literal meaning of this line is not quite clear. The translation is based in part on extrapolation from context.
19. The words rendered here as "all of your people" are *kuṭum* and *kabīlo*, meaning, respectively, 'extended family' and 'lineage'.
20. I was assisted in translating this *bāṅdhaṇo-kholaṇo* riddle by Jaya Pungaliya and her parents, Motilal and Sukhchen Khemsara. While the father, a learned and scholarly man, at first could make no sense of it, the mother, who had little formal education but had attended many weddings in her time and had participated in wedding riddling, new almost at once that a tie-and-dye *pomcho* was being described, and animatedly explained how every detail of the *pomcho* design corresponded to the riddle description.
21. This riddle is also found in *K&D* II, no. 6, and cited in Srivastava 1974: 285.
22. This riddle was also found by Ved Vatuk and Kashi Ram Kaushik in the Bulandshahr district of western Uttar Pradesh, and is discussed in Dundes and Vatuk (1974: 135-137).

REFERENCES CITED

Abbreviations

MB Arjunlal Agraval, *Muklāvā-Bahār*

K&D Komal Kothari and Vijaydan Detha, *Borundā se Paheliyāṅ*

Abrahams, Roger D.

1972 "The Literary Study of the Riddle." *Texas Studies in Literature and Language* 14(1): 177-197.

1980 "Riddles Which Tell Stories." In *Folklore Studies in Honour of Herbert Halpert*. K.S. Goldstein and N.V. Rosenberg, eds. pp. 31-53. St. John's, Newfoundland, Canada: Memorial University of Newfoundland.

Abrahams, Roger D. and Alan Dundes

1972 "Riddles." In *Folklore and Folklife: An Introduction*. Richard M. Dorson, ed. pp. 129-143.

Agraval, Arjunlal

1961 *Muklāvā-Bahār, arthāt Sasurāl Rahasya*. 7th ed. Revised by Khemraj Shrikrishnadas. Bombay: Shri Venkateshvar Press. (1st ed. 1937).

Archer, William G.

1943 "An Indian Riddle Book." *Man in India* 23(4): 267-315.

1985 *Songs for the Bride: Wedding Rites of Rural India*. Edited by Barbara Stoler Miller and Mildred Archer. New York: Columbia University Press.

Bascom, William R.
1949 "Literary Style in Yoruba Riddles." *Journal of American Folklore* 62(243): 1-16.

Beuchat, P. D.
1965 "Riddles in Bantu." In *The Study of Folklore*. Alan Dundes, ed. pp. 182-205. Englewood Cliffs, N.J.: Prentice Hall.

Bhagwat, Durga
1965 *The Riddle in Indian Life, Lore and Literature*. Bombay: Popular Prakashan.

Bryce, L. Winifred
1961 *Women's Folk-Songs of Rajputana*. Delhi: Publications Division, Ministry of Information and Broadcasting.

Dundes, Alan and Ved Prakash Vatuk
1974 "Some Characteristic Meters of Hindi Riddle Prosody." *Asian Folklore Studies* 33(1): 85-153.

Elwin, Verrier and W.G. Archer
1943 "Extracts from a Riddle Note-Book." *Man in India* 23(4): 318-341.

Fruzzetti, Lina M.
1982 *The Gift of a Virgin: Women, Marriage, and Ritual in Bengali Society*. New Brunswick, NJ: Rutgers University Press, 1982.

Georges, Robert A. and Alan Dundes
1963 "Toward a Structural Definition of the Riddle." *Journal of American Folklore* 76: 111-118.

Glazier, Jack and Phyllis Gorfain Glazier
1976 "Ambiguity and Exchange: The Double Dimension of Mbeere Riddles." *Journal of American Folklore* 89(352): 189-238.

Green, Thomas A. and W.J. Pepicello
1978 "Wit in Riddling: A Linguistic Perspective." *Genre* 2: 1-13.
1979 "The Folk Riddle: A Redefinition of Terms." *Western Folklore* 37(3): 3-20.
1984 *The Language of Riddles*. Columbus: Ohio State University Press.

Gupta, Giri Raj
1974 *Marriage, Religion and Society: Pattern of Change in an Indian Village*. Delhi: Vikas Publishing House.

Hamnett, Ian
1967 "Ambiguity, Classification and Change: The Function of Riddles." *Man* 2: 379-392.

Haring, Lee
1971 "On Knowing the Answer." *Journal of American Folklore* 84: 377-393.

Henry, Edward O.
1975 "North Indian Wedding Songs." *Journal of South Asian Literature* 11(1-2): 61-93.

Kothari, Komal and Vijaydan Detha, comps.
1979 "*Borundā se Paheliyāṅ*" (Riddles from Borunda). Part I: *Paheliyāṅ*

(Riddles). Part II: *Geya Paheliyāṅ* (Sung Riddles). Borunda, Rajasthan: Unpublished Manuscript.

Lalas, Sitaram
1962-78 *Rājasthan Sabad Kos*. 9 vols. Jodhpur: Rajasthani Shodh Sansthan.

Lewis, Oscar
1958 *Village Life in Northern India*. New York: Random House.

Lushington, C.S.
1833 "On the Marriage Rites and Usages of the Jats of Bharatpur." *Journal of the Asiatic Society of Bengal* 12(18): 273-497.

Maranda, Elli Kongas
1971a "The Logic of Riddles." In *Structural Analysis of Oral Tradition*. Pierre Maranda and Elli Kongas Maranda, eds. pp. 189-234. Philadelphia: University of Pennsylvania Press.
1971b "Theory and Practice of Riddle Analysis." *Journal of American Folklore* 84: 51-61.

McAllester, David, P.
1964 "Riddles and Other Verbal Play among the Comanches." *Journal of American Folkfore* 77(305): 251-257.

Parmar, Shyam
1973 "A Note on the Riddles of Madhya Pradesh." *Folklore* (Calcutta) 14(7): 252-256, 278-279.

Pepicello, W.J.
1980 "Linguistic Strategy in Riddling." *Western Folklore* 39: 1-16.

Ramsinha, Thakur *et al.*, eds.
1939 *Rājasthān ke Lok-Gīt*. Calcutta: Rajasthan Research Society.

Rudolph, Susanne Hoeber and Lloyd I. Rudolph
1984 *Essays on Rajputana*. New Delhi: Concept Publishing Company.
1987 "The Amar Singh Diary: A Rajasthan Voice in the Era of Paramountcy." Unpublished paper delivered at the Jaipur Conference on the Preservation of Culture and the Environment in Rajanthan.
1988 "Becoming a Diarist: The Making of an Indian Personal Document." *Indian Social and Economic History Review*, June 1988.

Schomer, Karine
1987 "The *Dohā* as a Vehicle of Sant Teachings." In *The Sants: Studies in a Devotional Tradition of India*. Karine Schomer and W.H. McLeod, eds. pp. 61-90.

Scott, Charles T.
1965 *Persian and Arabic Riddles: A Language-Centered Approach to Genre Definition*. Bloomington: Indiana University and Mouton.
1969 "On Defining the Riddle: The Problem of a Structural Unit." *Genre* 2: 129-142.

Sein, Maung Than and Alan Dundes
1964 "Twenty-Three Riddles from Central Burma." *Journal of American Folklore* 77(303): 69-75.

Singer, Milton
1972 "Search for a Great Tradition in Cultural Performances." In *When a Great Tradition Modernizes: An Anthropological Approach to Indian*

Civilization, by Milton Singer, pp. 67-80. Chicago: University of Chicago Press, 1972.

Singh, Amar

1901 "The Amar Singh Diary." "Notes about my Marriage." I-XXIV, September 17 - October 1, 1901. Typescript Manuscript.

Singh, T.R.

1973 "Hindi Riddles and Natural Objects: An Exploratory Study." *Man in India* 53(3): 305-314.

Srivastava, Sahab Lal

1974 *Folk Culture and Oral Tradition: A Comparative Study of Regions in Rajasthan and Eastern U.P.* New Delhi: Abhinav Publications.

Taylor, Archer

1943 "The Riddle." *Californai Folkfore Quarterly* 2: 129-147.

1951 *English Riddles from Oral Tradition*. Berkeley: University of California Press.

Upadhyaya, Hari S.

1967a "Botanical Riddles and Their Versions from Uttar Pradesh, India." *Southern Folklore Quarterly* 31(3): 215-235.

1967b "Material Culture in Bhojpuri Riddles of Northern India." *Tennessee Folklore Society Bulletin* 33(4): 109-120.

Vetscher, Trande

1973 "Betrothal and Marriage Among the Minas of South Rajasthan." *Man in India* 53(4): 387-414.

ART REGIONS AND MODERN RAJASTHAN

MICHAEL W. MEISTER

The present state of Rajasthan represents a recent political unity validated in part by conscious attempts to define an ancient past. Shortly after the integration of the princely states made modern India possible, administrative units were determined along linguistic and cultural lines. As Mohan Sinha Mehta – then Vice Chancellor of Rajasthan University – wrote in his introduction to *Rajasthan Through the Ages*, a volume commissioned by the Government of Rajasthan, "Soon after India became independent, all the States of Rajasthan became one administrative part of the Indian Federation. Political integration did not, however, immediately bring about psychological unity . . ." (Sharma 1966:10).

"Rajputana" had seemed perhaps more of an entity to British and Mughal administrators than to its independent and warring rulers or their subjects. "Even to this day," Mehta wrote, "while the homogeneity of Rajasthan as [a] unit of the Indian Union is clearly recognisable in social and cultural tradition, the variety and individuality of local strains can be distinguished in many ways" (*ibid.*, 9).

The myth and present reality of a unified Rajputana had been based as much on the presumed identity of Rajput clans as on territory. The sociologist G.S. Ghurye, for example, in his study of "Rajput" architecture, extended his definition of this category to include temples at Khajuraho built by "Chandella Rajputs" and to monuments in other areas of northern, eastern and central India, as well as the Deccan, tying his analysis to presumed clan patronage rather than to region (Ghurye 1968:19).[1] "We have heard and read the daring account of great warriors and patriots like Rana Sanga and Rana Pratap," wrote Mohanlal Sukhadia, the then Chief Minister of Rajasthan, in his preface to *Rajasthan Through the Ages*. "The touch of divine magic in the works of Rajasthan sculptors and painters has held us spell-bound. Behind all this, one can perceive the character and culture which has a unity of its own" (Sharma 1966:7).

Rajasthan is not populated solely by Rajputs, of course, nor are all Rajputs martial, yet the idea of the martial Rajput has contributed its part to a definition of the culture of modern Rajasthan: ". . . because of this stress upon the blood relationship between themselves and the kings and heroes of the past, one of the most basic attributes of the martial Rājpūt is the strongly held belief that he himself, at least by tradition and innate capacity, is a warrior and ruler" (Hitchcock 1959:11).

Col. James Tod can, to a large extent, be credited with creating the British image of Rajputana as a cultural and political territory early in the 19th century (Tod 1829-32). His writings also contributed to the development of a modern, unitary, Rajput self-image. Tod saw the Rajputs as a single royal "family" in a way their own tradition largely had not. He based part of his historical information on the bardic tradition of the Charans which had attempted to provide a unified past only in a fragmentary form. Rajput legends had instead concerned themselves primarily with lineage and origination, validating each ruling clan while distinguishing one from another. It is only in certain definable periods that myths that distinguished and gave identity were used to unify clans (Meister 1986a). In order to understand the gradual formation of a regional identity in Rajasthan, therefore, it would seem essential for us to determine the mechanisms at work in such myths.

Distinguishing vs. Unifying Myths

We may take as examples two of the most important heroic myths of the bardic tradition of Rajasthan, that giving the lineage of the Guhilots of Mewar – perceived in modern Rajasthan as defenders of the famed fortress at Chittor – and the more general legend of a common Rajput origin from fire on Mt. Abu. Both are used today, in part, to validate Rajputs as a group and Rajasthan as a territory. Both, however, have a history of more limited and particular uses.

Bappa Raval is credited by contemporary bards with being the founder of the Guhilots and the first Guhila ruler to occupy the Chittor fortress, seizing it from the Maurya clan (who founded the fort in the 7th century) by *ca.* 753 A.D. (a date more likely to have been associated with Pratihara occupation). No archaelogical or inscriptional remains at Chittor, however, support so early a Guhila occupation.

Bappa's legend in fact seems to have been created between the 14th and 16th centuries as an origin-myth for the Guhilot clan of Nagda and Ahar (near modern Udaipur) following their rise to a position of broad regional power in the 10th century. By the 14th century, their prestige had risen further because of their struggle with the Sultans of Delhi. By then, according to D.C. Sircar, "Bappa *began* to be represented as the ancestor of Guhila or Guhadatta. Thus the *distinction* of the Nagda-Ahar branch, having Bappa as its founder, from the other Guhila houses was made quite clear" (1966:30, emphasis mine). Sircar goes on to say:

> This also led to the development of certain legends about Bappa, which were further embellished with the enhancement of the honour of the house resulting from the struggle with the Mughals in the sixteenth century A.D. Thus, ultimately the petty *Rāval*, originally regarded as the secondary founder of the Guhila house in question, came out in folklore as one of the greatest heroes India ever produced (*ibid.*).

Each ruling family in Rajasthan created and embellished myths legitimating its origin. The legend of Bappa Raval became more important than most because of the emblematic value placed on the defense of Chittorgarh by Rajputs against generations of attackers, a heroic action that could be projected further into the past by the use of Bappa Raval's legend.

The second important Rajput legend – that of the origin of four tribes of Rajputs from a common fire pit (*agnikula*) on Mt. Abu – functions as a unifying myth in modern Rajasthan and can also be used to exemplify a process at work where differences have been synthesized and diversity used to validate a new unity.

Relatively late sources like the *Chand Rāisā* describe a common origin for the Pawar (Paramara), Parihar (Pratihara), Chauhan (Chahamana), and Solanki (Chalukya) tribes in the *agnikula* (Sircar 1965:17). Romila Thapar describes the myth in these terms:

> Rajputs rose to political importance in the ninth and tenth

> centuries A.D. when they were divided into a number of clans of which four claimed a special status. These . . . claimed a descent from a mythical figure who arose out of a vast sacrificial fire pit near Mt. Abu in Rajasthan. Consequently these four clans were described as the *Agnikula* or Fire Family. This was probably the first occasion when deliberate and conscious attempts were made to insist on their *kshatriya* status (1966: 227).

Dasharatha Sharma, as have others, however, has pointed out that "the *Agnikula* myth [was] a concoction of the sixteenth century" (1966:439).

Of the four clans, only the Paramaras have records that claim descent from fire dating back as early as the 11th century.[2] Other clans in this period had separate, and separating, origination myths. The Paramaras, according to Sircar, themselves adopted the myth of a fire-origin in the 11th century in order to *discontinue* a previous "claim of Rāṣṭrakūṭa origin owing apparently to their enmity with the later Rāṣṭrakūṭas" (1965:21). Only in the 16th century, with other political prerogatives in force, did these four major Rajput tribes see a need to be *united* by sharing such a myth.

Regional Identity

In acient Western India, both geographic regions and tribes retained individual identities. The first were fixed and largely still survive; the latter could float, moving to where each tribe carried its power. Until the rise of Pratihara hegemony in the 9th century – following the successful coalition of Western Indian tribes in the previous century to contain Muslim attacks from Sindh – Western India had little sense of itself as a unified cultural or political entity beyond the web of local alliances necessary for rule. It was primarily geographic divisions – forest, desert, mountain – that helped define cultural units, which were then woven together by clan power. Such divisions persisted under Pratihara hegemony, but were subordinated to, and partly defined by, relationships with the paramount power.

Following Pratihara decline, regional rulers in the 10th century were once more able to establish independent power bases and refresh autonomous identities. Politics in the 10th century made myth-making to locate but separate one power from another again necessary. The strength of such myth-making in Western India has been its ability to alternate between – and to integrate – unifying and differentiating roles.

The politics of later centuries, as Sultanate, Mughal and British forces threatened, made both art-making and myth-making increasingly important means of unifying the Rajput ruling classes while differentiating them as a group from non-Hindu rulers and from each other. Yet sub-regions in Rajasthan remain distinct – Maru, Uparamala, Medapata, Sakambhari, Arbuda, etc. – as have clans. The very process of integrating regions and tribes has also helped preserve and strengthen the separate identity of each.[3]

Geography vs. Clan

Western India extends from the coastal regions of Gujarat and Saurashtra and the salt marshes of Kutch to the great Thar desert in the north; the Aravalli mountains stretch from Delhi to Mt. Abu, with a spur toward the Malwa plateau beyond Chittorgarh, separating to some extent desert from forest and forest from fertile farmland. Regions held special importance according to the waxing and waning of the fortunes of specific clans. Saurashtra had great importance under the Maitrakas of Valabhi in the 6th and 7th centuries. Gurjaradesa – a region historically centered on what is now the border between northern Gujarat and southern Rajasthan, west of the Aravallis – was the original home for the Gurjara-Pratiharas as they began their rise to imperial power early in the 8th century. Several Guhila clans ruled the scrub-mountainous regions of Mewar in the 7th century, becoming the most significant regional power, however, only in the 10th century. Chahamanas were associated with Sakambhari and Sapadalaksha (Sambhar and Chatsu regions) from the 8th century, acting first as prominent feudatories of the Pratiharas in the 9th and 10th centuries and becoming independent rulers of great power from the 12th century.

While many of these clans retained their original home territory as base for expanding power, the Gurjara-Pratiharas are one example of the movability of power. Beginning first as petty chiefs in the Bhinmal-Jalor region of southern Rajasthan, by the end of the 8th century they could claim all of western Rajasthan as their *svaviṣaya* (home country, kingdom), as in the inscription dated 815 A.D. on a temple at Buchkala, east of Jodhpur (Bhandarkar 1906-07:15).

Called "Gurjara"-Pratiharas only by their neighbors, in reference to their original region, they conquered the crown city of northern India, Kanauj, early in the 9th century, from which they ruled over most of Western and Central India for more than a hundred years (Sharma 1966). The modern definition of Rajasthan sees "Rajputana" as homeland for all Rajputs. Such a modern category can find its most ancient base in the much expanded *svaviṣaya* claimed by the Pratihara dynasty early in the 9th century A.D.

The Role of Feudatories and Regional Hegemony

The Mauryas in the third century B.C. – ruling from distant Magadha – inscribed a boulder in Saurashtra to record their construction of a giant dam for irrigation. The Guptas, in the 5th century A.D., added their own inscription to record both repairs and their presence in the region. Such "marking" of a territory by a paramount ruler could establish a ritual hegemony without in fact disturbing a substantial and continuing regional autonomy. Tributary or feudatory powers were not merely at the periphery of imperial power, but made up the fabric of an Indian social order that both preceded and paralleled state organization and patronage.

Romila Thapar has characterized this fabric as "lineage" vs. "state" society and reports that, though state formation itself had begun much earlier, "the juxtaposition of the two remains . . . a continual feature of Indian history until well into the second millennium A.D." (1984:171). Her discussion of this process of state formation and its "overlapping forms" deserves substantial quotation in the context of this paper's argument:

> The lineage system did not die out with the emergence of the state. Population pressure was concentrated on areas of optimum economic activity so large tracts of less than optimum areas retained a *gaṇa-saṅga* (chiefdom) system for many centuries . . . . Even where the lineage system was absorbed into the state its identity was not entirely eliminated. Administration, except at the higher levels, remained a local concern and . . . kinship ties were still effective. Legal codes drew

> substantially on customary law and incorporated local practices. Legitimacy was frequently expressed through rituals pertaining to the lineage system . . . or through conversion of clan deities and their rituals into the religious expression of the state . . . . Thus it was not so much that the state was a segmentary system with a concentration of power at the centre shading off into ritual hegemony at the periphery as that the state system in itself was not a unitary, monolithic system . . . but . . . had a margin for flexibility in relation to peripheral areas (*ibid*, 171-172).

Of particular importance in Thapar's analysis is her definition of the shifting significance of territory in the Indian process of state formation: "The jurisdiction of the state is defined in terms of its sovereignty over a fixed territory and membership is therefore determined by residence or birthright in a territory," she says, but in ancient India "the notion of a well-defined territory was uncertain . . . . The boundaries between *janapadas* tend to be topographical features such as forests, rivers and streams and hills. Territory was seen as the clearly identifiable settlements and the more liminal areas of forests and waste land between settlements" (*ibid*., 12, 34).

Thapar further records that "the state system itself underwent a change in that the states of the late first millennium A.D. registered a more pervasive activity on the part of the state and the monarch," and goes on to say that "the culmination of this process was the recognition of territory . . . as crucial to the definition of the state and in this context regional histories began to be written" (*ibid*., 173).

It was also in the late first millennium A.D. that temple building, which had begun as part of the ritual life representing lineage society, became a major expression of state activity. It thus acts as a nexus between lineage and territory, and its survivals reflect a pattern of patronage and craft that, as Thapar says in another context, "may not record factual history but may well provide pointers to historical actuality" (*ibid*., 156)

Art Regions and Architectural Remains

Architectural remains in the territory of the modern state of Rajasthan range in date from the Maurya period (3rd century B.C.) to modern times. Temple remains date primarily from the

5th to the 15th century A.D., a period of great architectural efflorescence; palaces and urban structures also survive from the territories of Rajput states that formed alliances or found accommodation with Mughal and then British power from the 16th century onward. These states preserved and developed individual identities while yielding partial power to a "paramount" ruler. In art, also, each court tended to seek means to distinguish itself, preserving its independent identity by establishing artistic separation. From paintings to palaces, stylistic variation helped to identify each local court.

The study of these art regions can contribute to the discussion of Rajasthani regional identity in specific ways. It is important, however, that we recognize the nature of the evidence that surviving monuments provide us. A monument is a residue of patronage and available craftsmanship as well as of the social organization of its period. More than other aspects of clan identity, art remains tied to a region through its craft. The presence, distribution, and coherence of style in a region can suggest patterns of social organization available from few other sources. Because monuments are fixed, both physically and relatively well chronologically, they offer a grid, however shadowy, of practice and patronage through space and time that few other sources from ancient India provide (Meister 1982). While the attention to detail required to carry out style-analysis may seem a process suited primarily for the connoisseur, the results can have wider implications than connoisseurship alone. What, then, do monuments surviving in the territory of modern Rajasthan (see Map 1) suggest?

5th-6th Centuries A.D.

From the Gupta and early post-Gupta periods, only three monuments survive – at Darra, Charchoma, and Nagari – all in eastern Rajasthan. All seem reflections of a Malwa version of Gupta art in Central India (Meister 1981a, Williams 1981, Bhandarkar 1920), yet, as Joanna Williams has phrased it, "the process of localization was not a simple and steady one . . . but rather a constant interplay between those centrifugal and centripetal forces that created a dynamic tension in what we loosely call 'Gupta art'" (1981:52). Williams encapsulates her position on art

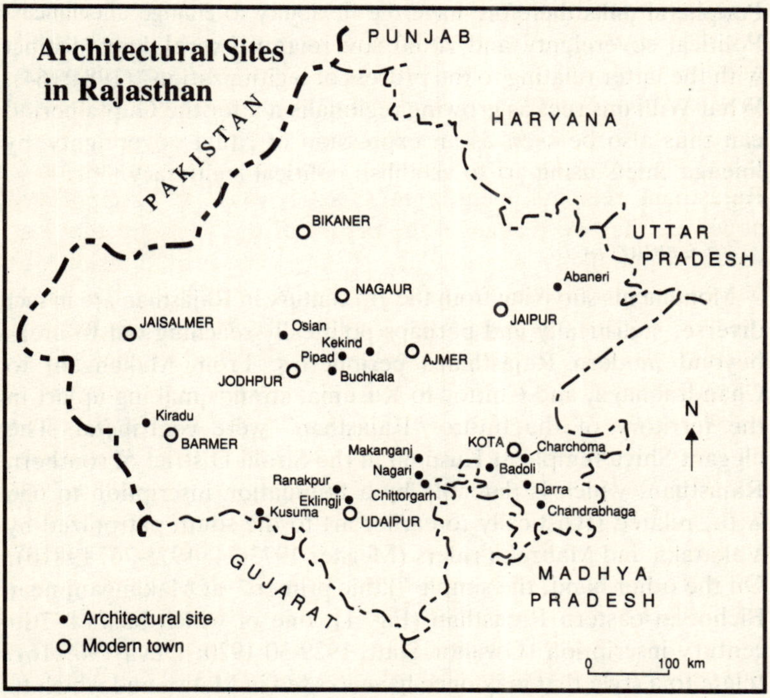

Map. 1: **Architectural Sites in Rajasthan**

and patronage in the Gupta period by the subtitle she chooses ("Empire and Province") for her important volume on the art of Gupta India (1982). Thapar, however, in her discussion of the applicability of a segmentary-state model to India, points out that the "monopoly of force at the centre was restricted at the periphery. Peripheral units therefore have the flexibility to change allegiances. Political sovereignty and ritual sovereignty [were] kept distinct with the latter relating to the process of legitimization" (1984:164). What Williams sees as growing regionalism after the Gupta period can thus also be seen as an expression of ritual sovereignty by lineage chiefs using art to establish political legitimacy.

7th Century A.D.

Monuments surviving from the 7th century in Rajasthan are in fact diverse, stylistically and perhaps politically reaching out to areas beyond modern Rajasthan's peripheries. From Makanganj to Chandrabhaga, and Chittor to Kusuma, strands making up art in the territory of the future "Rajasthan" were centripetal. The elegant Shiva temple at Kusuma in the Sirohi District of southern Rajasthan, which is dateable by a foundation inscription to 636 A.D., related stylistically to earlier art to the south patronized by Vakataka and Maitraka rulers (Meister 1973-74, 1975-76, 1981b). On the other hand, the simple "lithic primers" at Makanganj near Bichor in eastern Rajasthan (Fig. 1), one of which bears a 7th-century inscription (Gwalior State 1929-30:1920; Deva 1969:16), relate to a style that may once have existed in Malwa and which to some degree still survives in early Saurashtra shrines (Nanavati and Dhaky 1969; Deva 1969). By contrast, the "stone forest" of the Sitalesvara Mahadeva temple on the Chandrabhaga river near Jhalrapatan in eastern Rajasthan (Fig. 2), a temple that can be dated by reference to an inscription of 689 A.D. (Meister 1981b) and built by a local chief affiliated with the Mauryas of Chittorgarh, looks towards pillared wooden structures then probably extant in Central India as its model.

Little in the 7th century suggests a unifying pattern, stylistically or in terms of patronage, within the boundaries of present Rajasthan, beyond the ritual desire of chiefdoms to establish validating shrines (Meister 1986b). While the curvilinear Nagara form of temple in this period itself demonstrates the development of a

Fig. 1: **Makanganj, Dist. Chittorgarh, ruined temple, mid-7th century A.D. (Photograph courtesy Shri Krishna Deva)**

Fig. 2: Chandrabhaga (Jhalrapatan), Dist. Jhalawar, Sitalesvara Mahadeva temple, ca. 689 A.D. (Photograph by the author)

primary "modality" for such validation, and provides the principal form of architectural continuity across North India from the 7th century onward (*ibid.*), its regional rendering was largely left to the local guild.

I have spoken elsewhere of "idiom" as representing the local craft of guilds, and of "styles" as statistical averages (Meister 1983); but style, as Williams' discussion often suggests (1982), can be made consciously to represent and legitimate an "empire" (or even a chiefdom) beyond the simple fact of consistency within guild craftsmanship. Surviving style areas in the 7th century, however, suggest primarily the small-scale continuities of craft and a complex shifting of craft allegiances along peripheries that are not strictly political. Local patronage seems tied to local craftsmen and it does not seem clear that style itself, as opposed to the act of ritual construction, was seen as a matter contributing to the validation of the patron.

8th Century A.D.

Art regions early in the 8th century suggest that important local chieftains in Rajasthan were patronizing temple architecture to a degree sufficient to encourage the development of distinctive localized craft guilds with distinct styles. The earliest phases of these, however, still suggest the "shifting peripheries" of the previous century. Early 8th-century temples at Osian (Fig. 3) and Pipad, in Jodhpur District (Bhandarkar 1906-07, 1908-09), built by the Mandor Pratiharas, show clear knowledge of 7th-century Nagara formulas from Central India;[4] two shrines surviving at Menal in Chittorgarh District still suggest Malwa connections (Agarwala 1962); at Chittorgarh itself the earliest temples – the Kalika-Mata and Kumbhasyama temples – suggest that the local guild could turn toward different regions in establishing standards for those two grand ambulatory temples.[5] To what degree texts or itinerant craftsmen contributed to such differences is not easy to determine.

By the second half of the 8th century, however, under the extensive but still somewhat ill-defined regional hegemony of the Gurjara-Pratiharas over both western and eastern territories of Rajasthan, seemingly self-conscious idioms had developed that are attributed to specific regions. At Osian, the Harihara temple no. 2

Fig. 3: Osian, Dist. Jodhpur, Surya temple no. 1, ca. 700–725 A.D. (Photograph by the author)

Fig. 4: Osian, Dist. Jodhpur, Surya-Vishnu temple, late 8th century A.D.
(Photograph by the author)

Fig. 5: Chittorgarh, Dist. Chittorgarh, Kshemankari temple. 825–850 A.D.
(Photograph by the author)

Fig. 6: **Buchhkala, Dist. Jodhpur, Shiva temple, ca. 815 A.D. (Photograph by the author)**

(*ca.* 750 A.D.) already had begun to define a new idiom at the site, marked both by an elaboration of wall segments and increased sculptural ornamentation. This became by and large the "local style" for most later structures at the site, such as the Surya-Vishnu temple (Fig. 4), and in the surrounding region.

At Chittor, the centripetal elements expressed by the Kalika-Mata and Kumbhasyama temples in the first half of the century (which include variant molding, plinth, niche and pillar types) were fused into a consistent local idiom in structures built late in the 8th century and in the 9th century, as exemplified by the Kshemankari temple (Fig. 5). This Chittor idiom can be characterized particularly by the use of a sub-plinth and by offset (*bhadraka*) pilasters on the intermediate facets of the wall. Distinctive to the Chittor region, this idiom took on considerable importance stylistically as Pratihara hegemony over Central India in the 9th century allowed aspects of it to be encountered and accepted by guilds in other regions.

By the end of the 8th century, at sites such as Abaneri,[6] northeast of Jaipur (Agrawala 1955-56), idioms of considerable power already seem to have begun to represent specific feudatory powers of the Pratiharas (in Abaneri's case, the Chahamanas). Yet temples in even so extraordinarily plain an idiom as that at Buchkala, in Jodhpur District (Bhandarkar 1906-07), dated by a foundation inscription to *ca.* 815 A.D. (Fig. 6), could still ritually represent the Pratiharas' *svaviṣaya*.

9th and 10th Centuries A.D.

M.A. Dhaky (1975) has defined two major style patterns for Western India from the 8th century that seem to reflect the post-Gupta and post-Vakataka development of the Nagara mode of temple architecture in North India. These he defines as "Maha-Maru" and "Maha-Gurjara," referring to the general regions in which type sites can be found. The pattern of sites he describes in Rajasthan and Gujarat in the 8th and 9th centuries, however, shows also a grading of characteristics that reflects the idiomatic definition of localities as much as the larger imperia of styles. While Pratihara political hegemony allowed increased interchange between Western and Central India in the 9th century, local idioms continued that reflect and were perhaps increasingly meant to represent the patronage of local chiefdoms.

In the 10th century, the weakening of Pratihara hegemony led to a number of extraordinary, beautiful, and distinct regional idioms in Rajasthan such as those at Badoli near Kota (Fig. 7) (Tripathi 1975); in Mewar at sites such as Eklingji (Fig. 8) patronized by the Guhilas (Agrawala 1964, Dhaky 1972, Meister 1978); and at Kekind in Marwar (Fig. 9) (Dhaky 1973). While the growing independent authority of feudatories contributed to the building of such structures, the essential distinguishing features of these idioms seem to have been established by the early years of Pratihara rule. Their growing importance as "styles" defining regional legitimacies can best explain their separate efflorescenc in the 10th century.

11th and 14th Centuries

One of Dhaky's strongest analytic contributions (1975) has been his definition of the synthetic style he calls "Maru-Gurjara" that developed in Western India early in the 11th century. This style, often called "Solanki" in earlier literature (Brown 1959:117-127; Dhaky 1961), after the Gujarat-based power whose patronage helped to spread it widely throughout Western India, united elements of the "Maha-Maru" and "Maha-Gurjara" styles of earlier centuries in what seems to have become a self-conscious "Western Indian" style. It is possible that in this period of increasing Muslim military pressure, a common style expressing Rajput unity in the western region may have become particularly relevant.

This typical Western Indian modality (the technical morphology is known as *śkharī* and refers to the temple's typical clustered tower type) is both formally original as well as stylistically synthetic. It can be seen in the Shiva temples at Kiradu in Barmer District (Fig. 10) (Dhaky 1967). Though the style also shows regional variations of an idiomatic nature, for the first time it suggests a stylistic awareness of a broad territory as associated with the definition of a Rajput state (Thapar 1984:173). Little in this period, however, suggests "Rajasthan" as separate from "Gujarat" in Western India. Rajasthan, in fact, continues to seem largely lineage-oriented territory, while Solanki rule and style in Western India seem expressive of a more broadly defined state. Within a

Fig. 7: Badoli, Dist. Chittorgarh, Ghatesvara temple, ca. 925 A.D.
(Photograph by the author)

Fig. 8: **Eklingji, Dist. Udaipur, Takesvara temple, detail, ca. 950–975, A.D. (Photograph courtesy American Institute of Indian Studies, Centre for Art and Archaeology, Varanasi)**

Fig. 9: **Kekind, Dist. Nagaur, Nilakanthesvara temple, ca. 950–975 A.D. (Photograph by the author)**

Fig. 10: **Kiradu, Dist. Barmer, Siva temple no. 3, ca. 1050–1075 A.D. (Photograph by the author)**

broad awareness of a western region, however, lineage-based, local and idiomatic variations continued to appear. Sub-regional powers in this period seem still to have searched for independent, if also interlinking, artistic idioms by which to differentiate themselves.

15th-16th Centuries A.D.

"Rajasthan" took on the powerful regional importance it currently holds primarily from the 15th century onward, when Rana Kumbha, who ruled in Mewar, actively attempted to restore Rajput power in spite of Mughal rule over North India. His "renaissant" style (Dhaky 1966), rather than merely extending the synthetic style of the Solankis, was conspicuously self-conscious about the variety of older styles available within the territory of Rajasthan, and drew on the past in what might now seem a "post-modern" way.

While indeed to a degree creating a "renaissant" style from the region's artistic past, as in the Surya temple at Ranakpur (Fig. 11), the period also displayed an eclectic assimilation of regional forms, as in the Adbhutnath temple at Chittorgarh (Fig. 12), as a means by which recognition of existing stylistic distinctions could be used to unify a diversity of people and regions. Rana Kumbha, it has been argued by some modern writers, was concerned with creating a common "Hindu" identity as a way to unify the people within his kingdom.[7] Consciously looking to the past seems even then to have been part of a need to re-evaluate and redefine the present.

Post-16th Century

Rajput memorial monuments since the 16th century – as in the cenotaphs built for rulers of Marwar at Mandor (save for those subsumed by Mughal forms) – have stylistic roots in Rana Kumbha's period. Yet style in all its variety has retained its capacity to differentiate as well as to unite, even as new norms under new political realities came to be assimilated. In monuments, as in miniature paintings, elements of Mughal "modalities" were introduced, but a distinction between Rajput and Mughal was stylistically maintained, often by substituting Rajput elements such as *chhatrīs* (small pillared pavillions) and *jālīs* (perforated screens) for

Fig. 11: **Ranakpur, Dist. Udaipur, Surya temple, 15th Century A.D.**
(Photograph by the author)

Fig. 12: Chittorgarh, Dist. Chittorgarh, Adbhutnath temple, 15th century A.D. (Photograph by the author)

Fig. 13: **Udaipur, Dist. Udaipur, City Palace, late 16th Century A.D. and later (Photograph by the author)**

parallel Mughal forms. Within the late "Mughalizing" palaces of Rajput India,[8] for example, such variations both helped to define Rajputs as a group separate from their Mughal overlords and to differentiate Rajput from Rajput. The Udaipur City Palace (Fig. 13), for example, in its stylistic particularity, declares of its patron "I am a Sisodia Rajput from Mewar," as well as "a Rajput from Rajputana." By using Mughal (and later British) modalities, it also declares "I am a modern fellow of Rajasthan."

Conclusion

Art regions in Western India, as preserved by standing monuments, were not, in any period, contained by the boundaries of modern Rajasthan, nor do they always suggest a sense of regional unity. They do suggest the periods, however, in which centripetal forces may have begun to define a regional identity. As an art historian, I have been impressed both by the continuing cultural integrity of geographic sub-regions in Rajasthan – often, though not exclusively, tied to a single clan's patronage through many periods – and by the sense of a distinct identity the region as a whole has come to share.

In post-Independence India, a building such as the Udaipur palace can stand for an identity broader than either Sisodia or Rajput, declaring itself part of modern Rajasthan. This paper has attempted to demonstrate that the *process* of using differentiating artistic sub-styles as a basis to integrate the people of this region predates its post-Independence use.

ENDNOTES

1. "Rajput architecture is spread over a large part of Republican India. It dates from about the seventh century to about the middle of the nineteenth century. As extant specimens go it begins with sacred architecture and ends with civil palatial structures and semi-sacred mortuary monuments" (Ghurye 1968:1). It is indicative, however, that Coomaraswamy, in first defining "Rajput painting," took the position that "the term Rājput is here practically equivalent to the 'Indo-Aryan' of ethnologists, which designation covers the Rājputs, Khattris, and Jāts of Rājputāna, the Pañjāb, and the Western Himālayas, i.e. all the old Hindū elements in North-Western India, east of the Indus" (1975:11).

2. The *Navasāhasāṅkacarita* (Sircar 1965:18) is the first, but one should compare the Harsola plates of 949 A.D. (*ibid.*, 19; *Epigraphia Indica* 19:236ff.), which still claim a Rashtrakuta descent.
3. The complex web of "Rajput" styles of painting can be seen as a means of differentiating both the individual Rajput states and Rajput states from Mughal paramountcy.
4. Art historians must reconstruct these formulas from a single 7th-century temple at Mahua, slightly later shrines surviving in the Gwalior region, and by reference to extensions of the modality found in Chalukya territory. These latter have led some scholars (Handa 1984) to comment on Chalukya influence at Osian, which seems unlikely.
5. My work on Chittorgarh temples has not yet been published. A preliminary article, "Style and Idiom in the Art of Uparamala," has been given to the *Bulletin of the Museum and Picture Gallery* (Baroda) for a U.P. Shah Felicitation Volume (Meister n.d.).
6. The site of Abaneri is said to have been "the capital of the Nikumbha Rājputs before they founded Alwar" (Jain 1972:275-276).
7. "Among the Mahārāṇas of Mewār, Kumbhā perhaps was the first to have strong Hindu feelings. He called himself *Hindu-suratrāna* and bards sang of his victories as the triumphs of a great Hindu ruler " (Sharma 1966:715).
8. By "Mughalizing" I mean a process by which Rajput buildings often utilize indigenous adaptations of Mughal forms, but with conscious reference to Mughal standards and formal organization.

NOTES ON ILLUSTRATIONS

Fig. 1: **Makanganj, Dist. Chittorgarh, ruined temple, mid-7th century A.D. (Photograph courtesy Shri Krishna Deva)**

Makanganj (the village name is derived from a Mr. Mackintosh, who set up a small colony there for Mina tribals in 1844), near Bichor, north of Chittorgarh in eastern Rajasthan, contains two ruined temples, one with an inscription dateable to the 7th century. The plain walls of these temples, stunted niches, and archaic superstructural elements relate them to others that may have existed in Malwa and to Maitraka shrines that survive in Saurashtra from the 6th and 7th centuries (Nanavati and Dhaky 1969). These temples have been labeled "lithic primers" by Krishna Deva (1969:6), yet in their experimentation they are starkly different from the "stone forest" of Fig. 2.

Fig. 2: **Chandrabhaga (Jhalrapatan), Dist. Jhalawar, Sitalesvara Mahadeva temple, ca. 689 A.D. (Photograph by the author)**

Jhalrapatan, on the Chandrabhaga river in eastern Rajasthan, contains this ancient temple, dateable by reference to a foundation inscription (Meister 1981b, 1985). In contrast with the "lithic primer" of the temples at Makanganj, this structure is based on wooden pillared prototypes, no longer in existence. The basal moldings, in contrast with the vaguely post-Vataka moldings at Makanganj, are typical of post-Gupta temple architecture in North India. The dome used as superstructure is a late addition.

Fig. 3: **Osian, Dist. Jodhpur, Surya temple no. 1. ca. 700-725 A.D. (Photograph by the author)**

This Surya temple on the Sacchiyamata hill at Osian, whicn probably dates to the early years of the 8th century, reflects Central Indian Nagara norms of the 7th century in its system of base moldings, masonry walls with sunk niches at the center and applied niches on the corners, niche pediments, complex upper cornice to the wall, and Latina superstructure (reconstructed from old pieces in this century). Somewhat comparable structures can be found in the Gwalior region in Central India and in Chalukya territory in Andhra Pradesh (Alampur), where Central Indian Nagara norms were carried in the 7th century.

Fig. 4: **Osian, Dist. Jodhpur, Surya-Vishnu temple, late 8th century A.D. (Photograph by the author)**

The Surya-Vishnu temple at Osian dates to the end of the 8th century and continues the complexly oranmented and offset idiom begun at the site with the Harihara temple no. 1 from the middle of the 8th century. Temples at Osian stand on large platforms, often have subsidiary shrines, retain typical post-Gupta moldings but with added ornamentation, and, in this idiom, offset the wall in complex ways and apply niches on every offset.

Fig. 5: **Chittorgarh, Dist. Chittorgarh, Kshemankari temple, 825-850 A.D. (Photograph by the author)**

At Chittogarh, an idiom developed by late in the 8th century, typified by the use of a sub-plinth not found otherwise in post-Gupta temples, and by offset pilasters on the intermediate facets of the wall. This example, the Kshemankari temple opposite the Kalika temple, propably comes from the mid-9th century. Typical of the idiom is the lack of a second cornice above the recess acting as support of the superstructure (compare Fig. 4). This idiom remains consistent in the Chittor region into the 10th century.

Fig. 6: **Buchkala, Dist. Jodhpur, Shiva temple, ca. 815 A.D. (Photograph by the author)**

The Shiva and Vishnu temples at Buchkala in Jodhpur District are dated by an inscription. Though later than most of the temples at Osian, they show a radically simplified idiom, with only a single offset on the masonry wall. Low niche-pediments and rounded niche-pilasters, checker in the cornice recess, the lack of recesses between the spines of the superstructure, and the structure of the "web" pattern cast over the central spine of the superstructure are all idiomatic indications of 9th century style.

Fig. 7: **Badoli, Dist. Kota, Ghatesvara temple, ca. 925 A.D. (Photograph by the author).**

The Ghatesvara temple at Badoli, near Kota, dates to early in the 10th century and reflects the "Maha-Maru" idiom typical of this region. Unlike the temples at Osian, it uses square attached pilastrs on the intermediate wall-offsets and has an elaborate attached entry-porch with pent-roof superstructure. As had earlier temples in this region, this structure seems reflective of an idiom in Malwa otherwise not surviving that crossed elements of "Maha-Maru" and "Maha-Gurjara" styles even as early as the 7th century.

Fig. 8: **Eklingji, Dist. Udaipur, Takesvara temple, detail, ca. 950-975 A.D. (Photograph courtesy American Institute of Indian Studies, Centre for Art and Archaeology, Varanasi)**

The Vishnu temple at Eklingji, District Udaipur, is an elegant example of the "Maha-Gurjara" idiom patronized in this region by the Guhila rulers of Nagda and Ahar, the most famous example of which is the Ambika temple at Jagat. Base moldings show a broad recess beneath the crowning hood; intermediate facets of the wall are defined as narrow pilasters with capital elements, and elegant images are shown on the corners and in the recess, not in niches but supported by projecting platforms or lotuses sprouting from the wall.

Fig. 9: **Kekind, Dist. Nagaur, Nilakanthesvara temple, ca. 950-975 A.D. (Photograph by the author)**

The Nilakanthesvara temple at Kekind, District Nagaur, from the mid-10th century, reflects a "Maha-Maru" idiom contemporary with the "Maha-Gurjara" structure in Fig. 8. All facets of the wall as well as the recesses between have been defined as fluted pillars, each encrusted with niches. The base-moldings show no recess. The complex moldings topping the wall place a pair of cornices beneath the bulbous superstructure.

Fig. 10: **Kiradu, Dist. Barmer, Siva temple no. 3, ca. 1050-1075 A.D. (Photograph by the author)**

The Siva temple no. 3 at Kiradu, District Barmer, reflects a Rajasthani version of "Maha-Gurjara" style in the mid-11th century. Its walls resemble those of the Nilakanthesvara temple at Kekind (Fig. 9), but moldings reflect "Maha-Gurjara" norms (Fig. 8). The temple stands above a figured sub-plinth, and an awning has typically been inserted beneath the superstructure, the clustered form of which (on a non-ambulatory shrine) is a creation of Western India.

Fig. 11 **Ranakpur, Dist. Udaipur, Surya temple, 15th century A.D. (Photograph by the author)**

This Surya temple at Ranakpur, a remarkable Jain site in the mountains northeast of Udaipur, dates to the period of Rana Kumbha in the 15th century. It both extends the "Maru-Gurjara" style of the Solaṇki period and transforms it self-consciously. The "balconies" projecting in the superstructure are typical of the 15th-16th centuries. The rotating offset plans of the sanctum and entry-hall are creative extensions of earlier rotating forms.

Fig. 12: **Chittorgarh, Dist. Chittorgarh, Adbhutnath temple, 15th century A.D. (Photograph by the author)**

The Adbhutnath temple at Chittorgarh, also of Rana Kumbha's period, is typical of the eclectic assimilation of his period. Unlike the *sékharī* or clustered superstructure of the Surya temple at Ramakpur (Fig. 11), this reflects Rana Kumbha's exploration of a *bhūmija* or storied mode known from earlier centuries when it largely represented Paramara rulers (Krishna Deva 1975). Here it suggests the range of Rana Kumbha's conscious appropriation of earlier forms.

***Fig. 13:* Udaipur, Dist. Udaipur, City Palace, late 16th century A.D. and later. (Photograph by the author)**

The palace of the Guhilot rulers at Udaipur comes from several periods, but its main pile reflects a "mughalizing" formula using *chhatrīs,* screens, brackets, pillars, and other forms primarily of Rajput derivation. Though the "Rajput" nature of this palace cannot be mistaken, it is also not identical with palaces elsewhere in Mewar. It identifies both the region and the broader clan and pays respect to formulas of Mughal paramountcy.

REFERENCES CITED

Agrawala, R.C.

1955-56 "Sculptures from Abaneri, Rajasthan." *Lalit Kalā* 1-2.

1962 "Early Medieval Chapels at Menāl, Rajasthan." *Bhāratīya Vidyā* 22:43-44.

1964 "Khajuraho of Rajasthan: The Temple of Ambika at Jagat." *Arts Asiatiques* 10:43-65.

Bhandarkar, D.R.

1906-07 "Buchkala and Pipar." In *Archaeological Survey of India, Western Circle, Progress Report, 1906-06*, pp. 15, 38-39. Calcutta: Archaeological Survey of India.

1908-09 "Temples Osiā." In *Archaeological Survey of India, Annual Report, 1908-09*, pp. 100-115. Calcutta: Archaeological Survey of India.

1920 "The Archaeological Remains and Excavations at Nagari." *Memoirs of the Archaeological Survey of India* 4. Calcutta: Archaeological Survey of India.

Brown, Percy

1959 *Indian Architecture (Buddhist and Hindu Periods)*. 4th ed. Bombay: D.B. Taraporevala Sons & Co. Private Ltd.

Coomaraswamy, Ananda

1975 *Rajput Painting*. Reprint ed. New York: Hacker Books. (1st ed. 1916)

Deva, Krishna

1969 *Temples of North India*. New Delhi: National Book Trust.

1975 "Bhūmija Temples." In *Studies in Indian Temple Architecture*. Pramod Chandra, ed. pp. 90-113. New Delhi: American Institute of Indian Studies.

Dhaky, M.A.

1961 "The Chronology of the Solankī Temples of Gujarat." *Journal of the Madhya Pradesh Itihasa Parishad* 3:1-83.

1966 "Renaissance and the Late Māru-Gurjara Temple Architecture." In *Western Indian Art*, pp. 4-22. Special Number of the *Journal of the Indian Society of Oriental Art*.

1967 "Kiradu and the Māru-Gurjara Style of Architecture." *Bulletin of the American Academy of Benares* 1:35-45.

1972 "The Temple of Mahāvīra at Ahar and the Viṣṇu Temple, Eklingji." *Journal of the Asiatic Society* 14:11-17.

1973 "The Nīlakaṇṭheśvara Temple at Kekind." *Journal of the Oriental Institute* 22:397-408.

1975 "The Genesis and Development of Māru-Gurjara Temple Architecture." In *Studies in Indian Temple Architecture*, Pramod Chandra, ed. pp. 114-165. New Delhi: American Institute of Indian Studies.

Epigraphia Indica

1927-28 "Harsola Plates." *Epigraphia Indica* 19:236-244.

Ghurye, G.S.

1968 *Rajput Architecture*. Bombay: Popular Prakashan.

Gwalior State

1929-30 "Makanganj." In *Annual Report of the Archaeological Department, 1929-30,* pp. 19-20.

Handa, Devendra

1984 *Osian: History, Archaeology, Art & Architecture*. Delhi: Sundeep Prakashan.

Hitchcock, John T.

1959 "The Idea of the Martial Rājpūt." In *Traditional India: Structure and Change*. Milton Singer, ed. pp. 10-17. Philadelphia: The American Folklore Society.

Jain, Kailash Chand

1972 *Ancient Cities and Towns of Rajasthan*. Delhi: Motilal Banarsidass.

Meister, Michael W.

1973-74 "Detective Archaeology: A Preliminary Report on the Śiva Temple at Kusumā." *Archives of Asian Art* 27:76-91.

1975-76 "A Field Report on Temples at Kusumā." *Archives of Asian Art* 29:23-46.

1978 "The Sivaite Sūrya Shrine near Tūsa." *Journal of the Indian Society of Oriental Art*, Moti Chandra Commemoration Volume:60-65.

1981a "Darrā and the Early Gupta Tradition." In *Chhavi-2*. Anand Krishna, ed., pp. 192-205. Banaras: Bharat Kala Bhavan.

1981b "Forest and Cave: Temples at Candrabhaga and Kansuāñ." *Archives of Asian Art* 34:56-73.

1982 "Indian Sculptures from Rajasthan in the Fogg Museum." In *Fogg Museum Annual Report 1976-78*. pp. 73-85. Cambridge, Mass.: Harvard University.

1983 "Bīṭhū: Individuality and Idiom." *Ars Orientalis* 13:169-186.

1985 "Historigraphy of Temples on the Candrabhāgā, Reconsidered." In *Indian Epigraphy: Its Bearing on the History of Art*. Frederick M. Asher and G.S. Gai, eds. pp. 121-124. New Delhi: Oxford & IBH Publishing Co. with the American Institute of Indian Studies.

1986a "The Hero as *Yogin*: A *Vīrastambha* from Chittor." In *Dimensions of Indian Art*. Lokesh Chandra and Jyotindra Jain, eds. 2 Vols. I:283-286, II:97-100. Delhi: Agam Kala Prakashan.

1986b "On the Morphology of a Symbolic Architecture, India." *Res* 12:33-50.

n.d. "Style and Idiom in the Art of Uparamala." *Bulletin of the Museum and Picture Gallery* (Baroda). U.P. Shah Felicitation Volume. (in press).

Nanavaṭi, J.M. and M.A. Dhaky

1969 *The Maitraka and the Saindhava Temples of Gujarat*. Ascona: Artibus Asiae.

Sharma, Dashạratha

1966 *Rajasthan Through the Ages: A Comprehensive and Authentic History of Rajasthan Prepared Under the Orders of the Government of Rajasthan*. Vol. 1: *From the Earliest Times to 1316 A.D.*. Bikaner: Rajasthan State Archives.

Sircar, D.C.

1965 *The Guhilas of Kiskindhā*. Calcutta Sanskrit College Research Series 34. Calcutta: Sanskrit College.

Thapar, Romila

1966 *A History of India*. Vol. 1. Baltimore, Maryland: Penguin Books.

1984 *From Lineage to State*. Bombay: Oxford University Press.

Tod, James

1829-32 *Annals and Antiquities of Rajasthan*. 2 vols. London: Smith, Elder, and Co.

Tripathi, L. K.

1975 *The Temples at Baroli*. Varanasi: Amitabha Prakasana.

Williams, Joanna

1981 "Chār-Chomā and the Late Gupta Period in Mālwā." In *Chhavi-2*. Anand Krishna, ed. pp. 47-53. Banaras: Bharat Kala Bhavan.

1982 *The Art of Gupta India: Empire and Province*. Princeton, N.J.: Princeton University Press.

THE FRONTIER OF INDUS CIVILIZATION IN NORTHERN RAJASTHAN

HENRI-PAUL FRANCFORT

Views about the nature, origin and extent of the Indus or Harappan civilization have undergone dramatic changes since the initial excavations of Mohenjo-Daro and Harappa in the 1920s.[1] The accepted understanding up till the time of the Second World War and the partition of the subcontinent was that the Indus civilization had emerged and disappeared suddenly, without long periods of genesis and decay. Furthermore, explorations had been undertaken primarily in the Sindh plain and the valleys of Baluchistan, with the result that the eastern, southern and northern extent of the civilization was unknown. Besides Harappa, few sites were known outside the Sindh region. Finally, there was no proper knowledge about the interaction or relationships between the Indus civilization and other prehistoric or protohistoric cultures of the subcontinent – including those in the area of present-day Rajasthan.

After partition, the Archaeological Survey of India and other institutions planned systematic surveys to locate Harappan sites in the Indian Punjab (now Punjab and Haryana), Rajasthan and Gujarat. In the 30 years since that time, over 700 sites have been discovered in India, including the major site at Kalibangan, in the Ganganagar district of Rajasthan. Excavated between 1961 and 1969,[2] Kalibangan is estimated to have been inhabited from about 2900 B.C. to about 1700 B.C., beginning with a culture that has been interpreted as Early Harappan, followed by a Mature Harappan phase.[3]

Kalibangan is one of numerous sites discovered along the now dry bed of the river Ghaggar (called Hakra and Wahinda in Pakistan), which ran south-east of the Sutlej and the Indus from the Himalayas to the Rann of Kutch, becoming the Nara river in

Sindh.[4] Once a river system that may have been mightier than the Indus, and thought by some scholars to have been the Sarasvati river of the ancient Vedic texts (Allchin 1982:307-330),[5] the Ghaggar nowadays dries up west of Sirsa in Haryana. Hundreds of sites have been found along its bed, and since their discovery and exploration, our understanding of the nuclear zone of the Indus civilization has been expanded to include the Ghaggar-Hakra river system as well as the Indus system (Mughal 1981, 1982, 1984; Dikshit 1977, 1979, 1984).

The understanding of what constituted the outer limits or frontiers of Indus civilization has also had to be revised in light of new archaeological discoveries (see Map 1). Post-independence explorations in India (Joshi *et al.* 1984, see map on p. 517; Misra 1984) have uncovered sites as far east as Alamgirpur in the Saharanpur district of Uttar Pradesh, as far north as the foothills of the Pir Panjal range (Manda, 28 kilometers west of Jammu), and as far south as the Kathiawad peninsula of Gujarat (Lothal, Rangpur, Prabhas, Rojdi) and the Ahmednagar district of Maharashtra (Daimabad). Explorations in Pakistan (Mughal 1981, 1982, 1984), and beyond the western border of Pakistan, have pushed the western frontiers of the Indus civilization to beyond the Makran coast and the Iranian border (Sutkagen-dor), crossing the Gulf up to Oman, and into the mountainous area bordering on Afghanistan (Gumla, Rahman Dheri). Some sites, such as Shortughai in the Oxus basin, have been found in Afghanistan, and Harappan objects have been found at various sites throughout the Central Asian area (Francfort 1989).

In addition to all these discoveries of Indus sites, the archaeological research of the past four decades has also uncovered what are believed to be the remains of several non-urban Chalcolithic cultures (cultures characterized by the use of both stone and copper) contemporaneous with Harappan civilization that existed on the frontiers of the Indus world. Two of these, the Ahar culture of the Udaipur area, and the so-called Ganeshwar (or Ganeshwar-Jodhpura) culture of the Khetri copper-belt region in the Sikar and Jhunjhunu districts, are in the Aravalli zone of present-day Rajasthan.[6]

This paper, based on preliminary research carried out by the Indo-French Archaeological Mission during 1983-84, examines the Harappan frontier in the Rajasthan area – between the Harappan

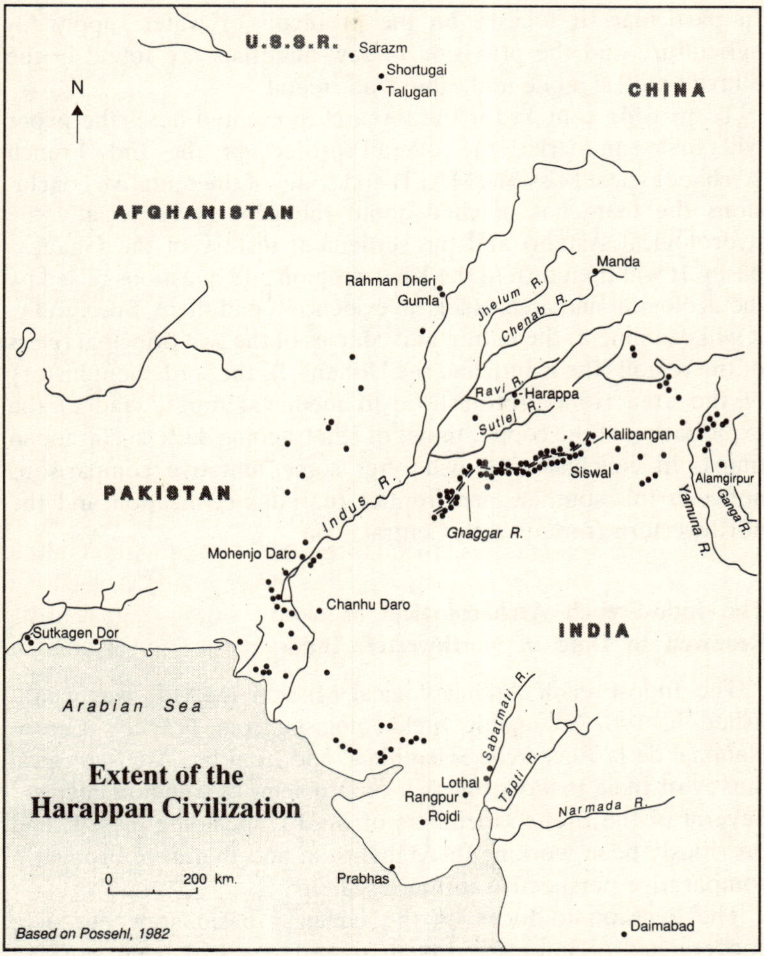

Map 1: **Extent of the Harappan Civilization**

settlements of the Ghaggar valley and the settlements of the Ganeshwar people in the mountainous Sikar-Jhunjhunu hinterland to the south (see Map 2). Its primary concern is with economic factors – one of the least understood aspects of Indus civilization. In particular, it focuses on the problems of water supply for agriculture and the provision of raw materials not found in the alluvial plains: stone and, above all, metal.

To provide context for the research presented here, the paper will first summarize the overall project of the Indo-French Archaeological Mission (MAFI) and some of the tentative conclusions the team has reached about the geology (especially the hydrological system) and the settlement history of the Ghaggar basin. It will then turn to the Khetri region and questions raised by the geological and archaeological evidence found there. Specifically, it will examine a) the nature and courses of the two principal rivers of the region (the Kantli and the Dohan), b) the settlement history of the area from protohistoric to medieval times,[7] and c) the exploitation of the copper mines of Khetri going back to Harappan times. In conclusion, it will ofter some tentative comparisons between this southeastern frontier of Indus civilization and the northwestern frontier with Central Asia.

The Indo-French Archaeological Mission: Research to Date in Northwestern India

The Indo-French Archaeological Mission (MAFI) was established in 1982 to enable archaeologists from France's Centre National de la Recherche Scientifique and from the Archaeological Survey of India to work together on problems of common interest.[8] Several of the French members of MAFI, including myself, had previously been working in Afghanistan and therefore brought a comparative perspective to the research.

The decision to focus on the Ghaggar basin grew out of a convergence of interests. Indian researchers had been working with the help of satellite photography on determining the prehistoric course of the Ghaggar and other river systems of northwestern India, with a view to establishing connections betwen these systems, both past and present, and archaeological remains in the area.[9] The French members of the team working in Afghanistan had been studying prehistoric irrigation systems in

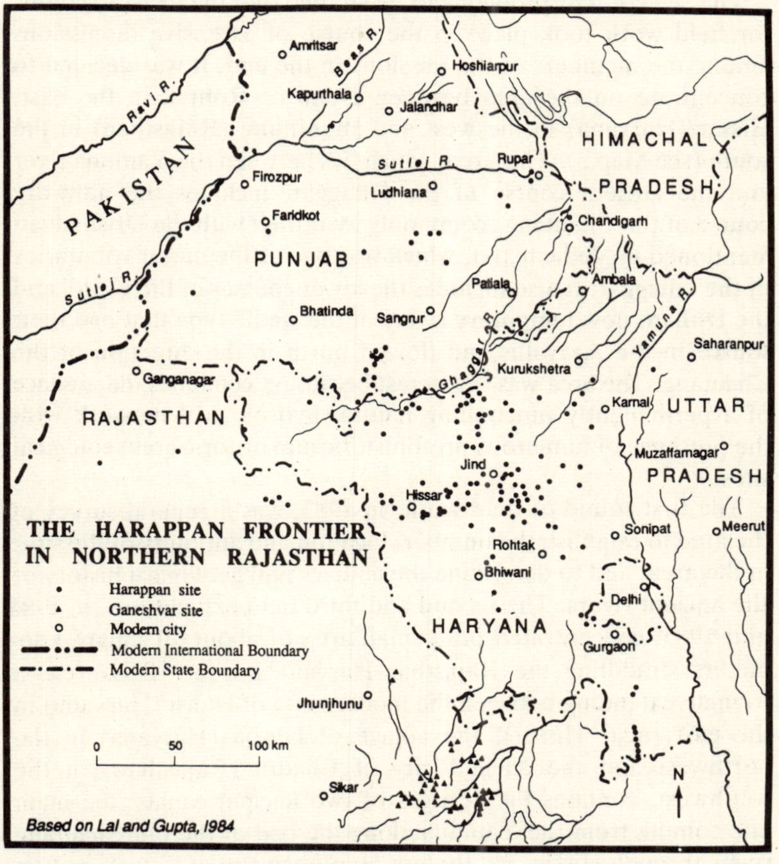

Map 2: **The Harappan Frontier in Northern Rajasthan**

conjunction with archaeological analysis of pottery at sites in the area,[10] and wanted to discover whether there had been similar irrigation systems in northwestern India.

The selection of problems to be studied and the exact locations for field work took place in the course of extensive discussions among the members of the mission. In the end, it was decided to concentrate on the area between Delhi or Rohtak in the east, Hissar (Haryana) in the west and Jhunjhunu (Rajasthan) in the south (see Map 3). This area, which lies between the Yamuna river and the ancient course of the Ghaggar, includes the now dry course of the Chautang (commonly identified with the Drishadvati mentioned in Vedic texts), which was one of the major tributaries of the Ghaggar. It also includes the lower courses of the Kantli and the Dohan, now temporary rivers of the wadi[11] type that had their source in the Aravallis and flowed north in the direction of the Chautang. The area was of interest because it combines the absence of a permanently functioning natural hydrological network with the presence of numerous protohistoric and historic archaeological sites.

The first round of field work, in 1983, was a general survey of the area to establish the number, location and antiquity of the sites in the area, and to determine the courses and geological history of the ancient rivers. The second and third field expeditions, in 1984 and 1985, concentrated on a small area of about 70 square kilometers straddling the Rajasthan-Haryana border. This area, a triangle extending between the modern city of Hansi (Haryana) in the east (near Hissar), the village of Darba (Haryana) in the northwest and the ancient city of Bhadra (Rajasthan) in the southwest, contains the vestiges of two ancient canals: the main one coming from the Yamuna along the bed of the old Chautang river, through Hissar and the pre-Harappan site of Siswal, and on to Bhadra; the second one, a branch canal, going from Siswal to Darba.[12] About 300 sites were determined in the plain around the courses of these canals and river beds. All of the sites were systematically explored, and 30 ascertained to be of the protohistoric period.

The research team that carried out the field work consisted of seven archaeologists (J.R. Batra, R.S. Bisht, Henri-Paul Francfort, K.P. Gupta, A.K. Sharma, Puran Singh, and A.K. Sinha), an ethno-archaeologist (V. Roux), a geographer whose specialty was

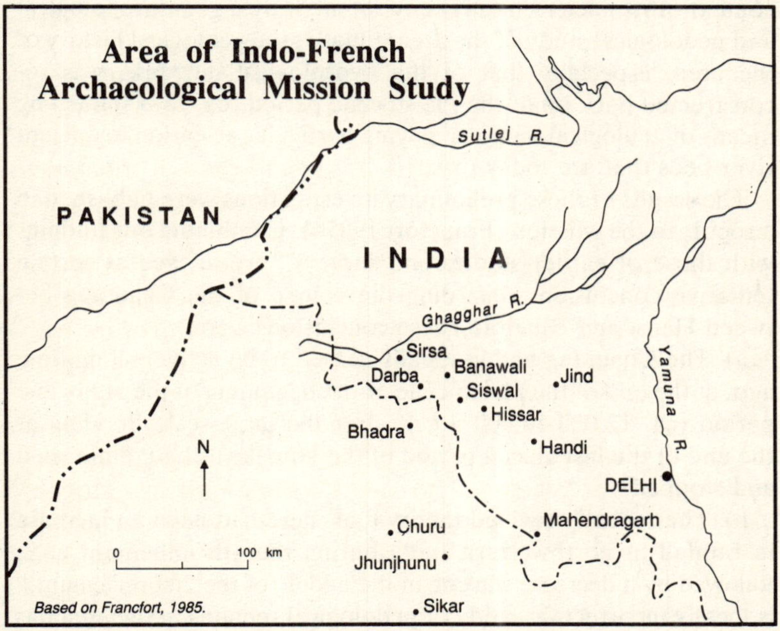

Map 3: **Area of MAFI Study**

ancient irrigation systems (Pierre Gentelle), and a geo-archaeologist (Marie-Agnes Courty) trained in geology, geo-morphology (the study of land forms) and pedology (the study of soil formations). The working method adopted by the team was to begin with an archaeological survey to mark all datable sites by means of potsherds gathered on the surface. Each site was then put into the context of its ancient natural environment by a geomorphological and pedological study of the area. Finally, the geological history of the area, especially that of the hydrological network, was reconstructed back up to the Pleistocene period (ca. 15,000 B.C.) by means of geological sections, paying particular attention to ancient river beds that are today dry.

The results of these preliminary investigations were published in a report to the Mission (Francfort 1985b). Combining our findings with those of earlier studies and surveys,[13] we arrived at certain tentative conclusions regarding the course of the Chautang between Hansi and Bhadra. These conclusions were:

a) The Chautang had gradually ceased to be active a long time ago, at the end of the Pleistocene or the beginning of the Holocene period (ca. 12,000-10,000 B.C.), after the large-scale flooding at the end of the last glacial period of the Himalayas had diminished and stopped.[14]

b) The recently revived theory that there had been an increase in rainfall in northwestern India during the 4th millenium B.C., followed by a decrease starting in the middle of the 2nd millenium,[15] is locally incorrect, as study of pedological remains in the area has revealed no important climatic changes during that period of time (Courty 1985:25-29).

c) Consequently, no evidence supports tying the settlement of the ancient basin of the Ghaggar to vast water courses traversing the region or to a period of more abundant rainfall.

d) For the moment, the only hypothesis we feel accords with the observed data is that settlement of this semi-arid zone during the protohistoric period may have been based on mastery of irrigated agriculture somewhat in the manner of Mesopotamia or Central Asia (Francfort 1985a:65).[16] Indeed, remains of ancient canals have been uncovered that belong to a very early age,[17] but we cannot propose absolute dates for them until we obtain the results of certain thermoluminescence dating analyses.

If these conclusions regarding the Chautang are correct, then the question of the water courses coming down the northern slopes of the Aravallis becomes of great importance to the protohistory of the Ghaggar basin and its relationship to the area to the south of the Aravallis. It was therefore imperative to turn to a closer examination of the Kantli and Dohan rivers. The overriding question was how far north these rivers used to run (did they ever flow into the Chautang?) and whether they were large rivers on the banks of which substantial settlement could have taken place in the Harappan period, even though the area today is arid and covered with sand dunes. It was also important to clarify the settlement history of the area around these rivers, to determine whether any of it was Harappan, whether the natural environment was different from what it is today, and whether irrigation was used. Finally, the question of the exploitation of the copper mines of Khetri during the protohistoric period needed to be further explored; in particular, there was a need to determine whether the Harappans themselves ever established themselves near the mines.

The Kantli and the Dohan: Some Geo-Archaeological Observations

The geomorphological study of the Kantli and Dohan area by MAFI members Courty and Gentelle concentrated first on the sand dunes adjacent to the Aravalli mountains, then on the valleys of the two rivers (see Map 4).[18] What it revealed was that both the dune mass and the rivers were already in place, practically the same as today, as far back as ca. 4000 B.C.

The sand dune mass as it is today can be divided into three superimposed layers of different ages. The oldest layer is rarely exposed, appearing at the surface only on the eroded slopes surrounding the peaks of the Aravalli mountains. The second layer covers the first with a mass of yellow silt and sand coming from alluvial materials, deposited possibly in the early Holocene (ca. 9800 B.C.) and shaped by the wind, and consists of dunes now fixed by vegetation and rainfall. The dunes created during this major phase in the formation of the landscape are made of a very fine, unsorted material, the nature of which will be revealed by further analysis. The third layer of the dune mass consists of active dunes that are formed from a portion of the second layer.

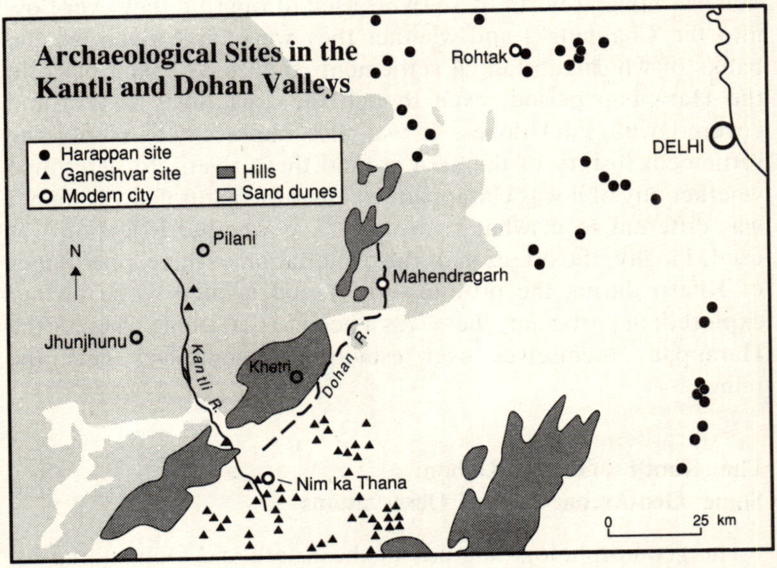

Map 4: **The Kantli and Dohan valleys: Physical features and prehistoric sites**

The traces left by the course of the Kantli show that it stopped flowing north beyond Rajgarh (about 50 kilometers south of Hissar) even before the formation of the second layer of the dune mass, or at most during its formation. The river has left clear traces of its south to north passage by cutting through the dunes southeast of Jhunjhunu, which generally run west to east. Further north, the Kantli vanishes into the dunes, leaving small depressions that will have to be dated by analyses of shells.

When Courty and Gentelle turned to geological and pedological study of the area, they came up with similar results, showing three soil formations in the dune mass. The most recent formation consists of small, active sand dunes whose pedogenesis (surface soil formation) is indicated by a brownish tint in the upper layers and some percolation of carbonates (salts). The second formation consists of recent fixed dunes, whose pedogenesis is indicated by a distinct brown coloring and a percolation of carbonates which has led to the creation of thick layers containing calcite (a rock-forming carbonate) nodules. The third formation consists of old, fixed dunes characterized by a slightly reddish pedogenesis and a loss of carbonates from the entire layer. These dunes are localized at the foot of the Aravalli range and are strongly eroded.

Examination of about 30 sections of test pits and wells in the Kantli and Dohan valleys has made it possible to state the thickness of the dune mass, and has provided information about the older pedogeneses that affected it. On the basis of borings down to approximately 30 meters, one can distinguish three layers of sandy deposits, separated by three phases of pedogenesis. These are, from top to bottom: carbonatization (replacement of minerals by carbonates), light oxidation as a result of exposure to weathering, and then again a phase of carbonatization. Below these alternating layers of fine sands and carbonates, coarser material appears, marking the last phase of major alluvial deposits by a river. In the Kantli valley, it is coarse-grained sands, which appear at a depth of 30 meters, while in the Dohan valley, it is sandy gravels, and their appearance is at a depth of 20 meters.

The Kantli ends in a group of depressions characterized by sandy lacustrian (lake-produced) clays rich in molluscs. These formations are capped by a sandy layer 1.5 meters thick apparently affected by the second phase of pedogenesis. Thus, in all likelihood, the formation of these depressions took place prior to the second phase in the stabilization of the dunes, or at the very least was contemporaneous with it.

These observations, along with those made while studying the area further north between Hansi and Bhadra clearly show that the major phases of substantial river flow in this whole region were over by the time it became settled by protohistoric populations, and that the dune mass (except for the top layer of moving dunes) was already in place. If semi-arid or arid conditions thus prevailed already at the time of the Indus civilization, it is impossible for the Kantli and Dohan to have been perennial rivers during the third and second millenia B.C. Their flow was very certainly much the same as it is today, which means that 5000 years ago, neither of these rivers had sufficient hydraulic force to continue its course all the way to the vicinity of Sirsa.

Settlement History of the Kantli and Dohan Valleys

We can now examine the history of the peopling of this region to see if it correlates with the history of the rivers. As has just been shown, neither in protohistoric times nor later did the Kantli and Dohan reach the plains region to the north; instead, they were separated from it by substantial dune masses. It is well established that the plains region was occupied, with some local variation, since the protohistoric period. A clear picture can be seen from the site distribution maps prepared by Joshi *et al.* (1984), scholars like Suraj Bhan (1973, 1975), and the MAFI team (Francfort 1985a:60-64). The question that arises, therefore, is that of the southward extension of these settlements, along the banks of the Kantli and the Dohan, towards the Aravallis.

The settlement study of this region done by MAFI was not the first. K.N. Dikshit of the Archaeological Survey of India conducted a survey between 1978 and 1980.[19] In addition, in the Sikar-Jhunjhunu area immediately to the south of Dikshit's survey, R.C. Agrawala conducted extensive surveys and excavations (Agrawala 1984; Agrawala and Kumar 1984). Dikshit's results showed an absence of Harappan sites in the Kantli valley. One of our objectives was therefore to make further observations in order to confirm or challenge this conclusion.

To obtain the most accurate data possible, we kept very close to the course of the Kantli, and explored in detail part of the zone where it loses itself in the sand, though without undertaking a systematic investigation of the surrounding dune mass. Our reasoning was that, whether one adopts the theory of settlements depending on artificial irrigation, or holds to the old hypothesis of river settlements, it is in the neighborhood of water courses or their traces that one must look for protohistoric sites.

On all the sites – most of them located with the help of local villagers, who know the territory very well – a large quantity of pottery fragments was collected. This manner of proceeding, which we had used during our survey of northeastern Afghanistan (Gardin 1984), allows one to detect traces of ancient occupation in subsequently heavily re-occupied sites, even if all that is left of the ancient occupation is a few potsherds. Marking a grid on the soil and attempting anything more than coarse surface subdivisions appeared useless for the kind of sites we were studying, which were mainly small and shapeless, as surface subdivisions for collections make sense only on relatively larger sites.

The results obtained are summarized here on Map 5, which shows the protohistoric, historic and medieval sites located in Rajasthan.[20] The sites belong to many periods and cultures. The protohistoric sites are represented by Early, Mature and Late Harappan pottery and Painted Gray Ware.[21] The historic sites are characterized by Northern Black Polished Ware,[22] Kushan or Gupta pottery, and the medieval sites include both ancient medieval and recent medieval pottery.[23]

These findings accord with our general hypotheses, and allow us to make certain generalizations about the settlement history of the area. First, since no protohistoric Harappan settlement was found in the Kantli region, Dikshit's earlier conclusion is confirmed. Second, though settlements appeared in early historic times, they were hardly significant before the Kushan and Gupta periods, which did not develop locally until the third and fourth centuries A.D. Third, the medieval settlement distribution merely strengthened the earlier ones. Finally, the seeming absence of settlements between the end of the Kantli and Dohan rivers and the plains settlements to the north may (at least for the historic and medieval period) be due as much to the fact that our survey was not systematic as to anything else.

Just as today, we concluded, the historic and medieval settlement of these valleys did not depend on irrigation using the water of the

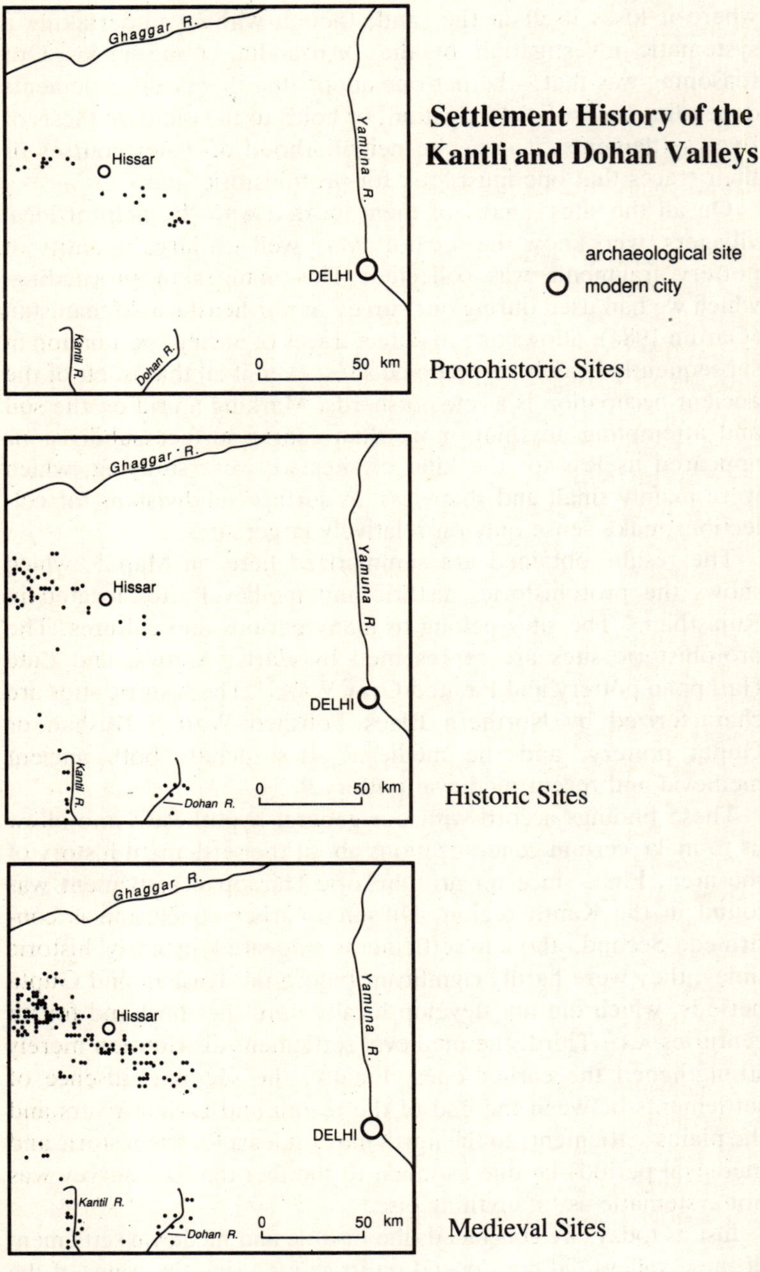

***Map 5:* Settlement history of the Kantli and Dohan valleys**

rivers. Because the Dohan and Kantli are rivers of the wadi type (remaining dry except during the rainy season they could hardly be useful for rendering productive soil which is all sand dunes. The settlements in their valleys therefore must have depended on digging wells, storing water in tanks, and dry farming the dunes. Recently, tube wells and modern watering techniques have allowed a certain improvement in land utilization, but it has been much less in both extent and yields than what has taken place in the plains north of the large dune mass.

The absence of protohistoric Harappan setllements presents a problem in light of the fact that the environment was similar to what it is today. If this absence is real, which further surveys will doubtless confirm, two questions arise: a) why did the protohistoric settlement of the Harappans not penetrate this region? and b) why did greater land utilization become possible later on?

Several plausible anthropological hypotheses could be offered in reply to the first question, but they will not be developed here, as our focus is on environmental constraints. If we look at these constraints alone, we note simply that the Kantli and Dohan valleys and the surrounding dunes were not suitable for irrigation, and thus present a sharp contrast with the large alluvial plains to the north. But couldn't the Harappans simply have established themselves around wells and tanks, the way inhabitants in later periods did (Ratnagar 1986)?

The answer to the second question may shed light on the first one. To make a sand dune productive, even on a small scale, one needs not only water but also cultivable plants that grow in sand more easily than the winter cereals that were the basic food of the Harappans. Gram, which grows well in sand, was apparently used in the Harappan period (though precise data on this is not available), but it certainly did not form the core of their diet. The same question arises for other drought-resistant plants like millet and sorghum (though it should be noted that not all of them like the sand!). There is as yet insufficient data for us to draw definite conclusions, but it is a question worth asking. Sand dunes are not the most propitious places for human settlement, even if one keeps in mind that natural obstacles have rarely stopped man, and that archaeological arguments based on absence of data are weak. Is it possible that economic motives other than agricultural development drew the protohistoric settlers of the northern plains through the dunes? Could it be the search for metals that caused the Harappans and Early Harappans to venture into this area?

The Copper Mines of Khetri

The old copper mines of Khetri, well known in the medieval period (Chakrabarti 1985-86:65-66) are still worked today. The question that arises is whether they were already being exploited in the protohistoric period, and if so, under what conditions. Some data tend to show that this was the case. Specifically, analyses of chalcopyrite (copper and pyrite) samples have been carried out and compared with both local Chalcolithic objects probably belonging to the Ganeshwar culture and with two Harappan objects from Chanhu-Daro and Mohenjo-Daro. The similarity between impurities in the ore from Khetri and that in the Harappan objects allows us to think of these mines as a possible source of raw materials for Harappan metallurgy (Agrawal 1984:166). This plausible hypothesis must be reinforced by analyses more numerous and precise than those available to us at the moment. However, one fact even now merits our attention: the mines of Khetri are situated outside the Indus civilization zone and in the zone of the Ganeshwar culture instead.

Some recent scholarship suggests a clear association of the Ganeshwar culture with production of protohistoric metal objects (Agrawala 1984). This is not the place to discuss the dating of the Ganeshwar culture, or the exact role it played in protohistoric metallurgical production. It is sufficient for our purpose to state that the mines, whatever their mode of exploitation during the Indus civilization period, were situated beyond the areas of dense settlement by the Early Harappans, Mature Harappans and Late Harappans. These settlements, according to both the maps published as a result of Archaeological Survey of India research and the site distribution maps prepared by MAFI, are situated further north and further west. Therefore, if exploitation of the copper ore at Khetri by the Harappans were to be confirmed in the future, it would mean that it was done only by way of minor settlements, seasonal or temporary expeditions, or through trade with the non-Harappan inhabitants of the Aravallis (i.e., the Ganeshwar people). A kind of frontier zone or no man's land would thus have existed between the Harappan settlements to the north and the Ganeshwar settlements in the south.

By contrast, during historical and medieval times, the areas around the lower and middle Kantli and Dohan, though consisting of large sand dune masses, were peopled by fixed settlements, and one finds more or less the same cultures both north and south of the Aravallis. The causes and modalities of this phenomenon have yet to be analyzed, but one may theorize that the introduction of drought-resistant plants able to grow in sand was not unrelated to this "colonization" of the dune mass.

The date of this penetration of the dune mass by permanent human settlements is not known exactly, but there is some likelihood it was during the first centuries of the present era. An objection could be made that the area was already occupied during the protohistoric period and that the sites were subsequently covered with sand dunes, but it does not hold, for two reasons. First, in spite of a few recent localized dune movements, the great bulk of the dune mass (the middle layer, with its brown coloring and deep layers containing calcitic nodules) has been in place and stable since before the beginning of the present era, and probably since before the protohistoric period (ca. 3000 B.C.). This is corroborated by the fact that many Ganeshwar sites (currently assumed to be protohistoric) have been found in dunes which were already stabilized at the time the sites were settled. Second, there are at the foot of the Aravallis ancient fixed dunes belonging to the oldest layer (with a slightly reddish surface and loss of carbonates from the entire layer). Moreover, the presence of microliths on the summit of these dunes shows that this surface soil formation existed before the Neolithic period, and hence the stabilization of the dunes is much older than Indus civilization.

Consequently, unless one supposes that a freak chance selectively erased all traces of Indus civilization sites from Early Harappan (ca. 2800-2500 B.C.) to Late Harappan (ca. 1800-1500 B.C.), one has to conclude that the dune mass was not at all, or hardly at all, occupied by Harappans during the protohistoric period. The implication of this would be that there existed a genuine frontier zone between the Indus civilization people of the plains and the Ganeshwar people to the south (if, as is generally accepted, the latter were indeed proto-historic).

Conclusions

The small area for which we have presented data allows us to consider certain neglected aspects of Indus civilization. The work of the MAFI research team and the evidence from earlier investigations have established that the area under consideration has not undergone any significant environmental changes since protohistoric times. The Kantli, the Dohan, the surrounding sand dune mass that hems them in close to the northern foothills of the Aravallis, the alluvial plains of Hissar, Hansi and Delhi – all these were then essentially as they are now. Geo-archaeological observation and the distribution of sites show that the possible exploitation of the copper deposits at Khetri by Harappans was either intermittent (seasonal campaigns) or mediated, possibly through the Ganeshwar people.

Considerable attention has been paid by Indus civilization archaeologists to questions of protohistoric technology, crafts and commerce. It is time to give proper importance to the agricultural component of that civilization. It is our thesis that in the area between Hissar and Hansi, Early Harappan and Harappan settlements occupied the alluvial plains in a selective and intelligent manner, by utilizing the natural northeast to southwest flow of the rivers when they revived during the monsoon, and, above all, by laying out large-scale partly artificial irrigation networks.

If this is the case, then the northern fringe of the large sand dune mass of Rajasthan formed a frontier in the true sense of the term. It is there that the Himalayan slope running from north to south encounters the slope of the Aravallis running south to north. Since water could not penetrate into the sand dune mass, the winter cereals cultivated in the plains to the north could not be grown there, as they are not adaptable to dry farming on sand in a semi-arid climate. The dune mass was in effect a no man's land between the Harappan culture in the north and the land to the south occupied by the Ganeshwar culture – a culture whose economic base was completely different. From the small area studied by our team all the way to Kalibangan in the west, and along the Thar desert in the west and northwest, the frontier between the Indus civilization and the mountainous regions of Rajasthan is marked by the sands. Even if one wants to avoid strict environmental determinism and leave room for human choice inspired by other considerations, this conclusion is not a trivial one, especially in its implications for the mode of mineral resource exploitation in Rajasthan.

It may be instructive, in closing, to compare the frontier tentatively delineated here with the other great frontier of Indus civilization, the northwestern frontier with Central Asia. There, the pattern of settlement, exploitation of the environment and exchanges with local cultures took a completely different turn. In some places in Central Asia a real Harappan colonization took place, as in Eastern Bactria (northeastern Afghanistan) during the 3rd millenium B.C. Small plains and valleys were irrigated and peopled by Harappan settlers while "highland" valleys and hills were inhabited by peoples of local cultures. These Harappan settlements of Central Asia were located on communication lines and trade roads going west towards Turkmenia and eastern Iran, such as the so-called great *lapis lazuli* road. From the Mature Harappan period, one finds a site like Shortughai in northeastern Afghanistan, which is clearly a colony of the Indus civilization (Francfort 1984, 1989; Kohl 1984). In addition to such "colonies", moreover, there are many Indus civilization finds in northern Afghanistan and Turkmenia. Therefore, I would submit, Central Asia was much more influenced by Indus civilization during the Harappan period than was the Rajasthan area which, while not being necessarily foreign to it, was yet hardly touched by it.

The reason for this lie in a long history. In Central Asia, a zone of mountains and valleys rich in minerals, one finds sites dating to the beginning of the third millenium B.C. that contain material related to that of the Early Harappan culture of Baluchistan (for example the sites of Taluqan in Afghanistan or Sarazm in the Zerafshan valley in Soviet Tadjikistan).[24]

Starting from this data, we find, surprisingly, that the penetration of the Indus civilization into Central Asia was older and deeper than its advance towards Rajasthan. The reasons for this difference are doubtless many, but it seems that one of them must have been the availability of perennial rivers and irrigable plains in Central Asia. If this was the case, then the frontier in Rajasthan must have been as much a natural frontier of sand and aridity as a cultural frontier made of agrarian practices, methods of occupying lands, social patterns, religious beliefs and artistic traditions. From the Harappan period onward, it was commerce – at first the search for copper, and later on the requirements of changing agrarian techniques and societies – that caused the frontier to be crossed.

ENDNOTES

This paper is based on the collective research of an entire team of scholars. However, I alone am responsible for the conclusions drawn and any defects that may appear in it. I am particularly grateful to Karine Schomer for the considerable editorial work she performed on my original version.

1. For a brief history of Indus civilization archaeology, see Allchin (1984) and Thapar (1984).
2. For an account of Kalibangan by the director of the excavations, see Lal (1979); another important account is Thapar (1975).
3. The problem of Indus civilization chronology is complex. The civilization begins with a phase variously named Pre-Harappan, Proto-Harappan, or Early Harappan, which can be dated from the first half of the third millenium B.C. However, in Rajasthan and Haryana, this Early Harappan phase (also known as the "Kalibangan I" phase) possibly comes later, after ca. 2500 B.C. The second phase is the Mature Harappan phase, ca. 2500-1800 B.C. according to the latest chronologies. Late Harappan is used to refer either to a sort of degenerated or provincial Mature Harappan (sometimes called Late-Mature Harappan) or to post-Harappan cultures like the "Cemetery H Culture" of Harappa itself. At present, there is no agreement on the use of the term other than the understanding that this phase begins after ca. 1800 B.C.
4. In spite of recent studies based on satellite images, it is still unclear (due to the absence of field work) whether this paleo-Ghaggar or Hakra flowed into the Rann of Kutch or joined the Indus, or both, at various epochs. See Pal *et al.* (1984) and Ghose *et al.* (1979).
5. Besides, or complementing the paleo-geographic interpretation of the Vedic Sarasvati, there is also a symbolic interpretation (Sarasvati as the goddess of knowledge and intelligence). See Indras (1968) and Witzel (1984).
6. For the Ganeshwar culture, see Agrawala (1984:160-162) and Agrawala and Kumar (1982). The first site of what came to be known as the Ganeshwar culture was discovered in 1977 by R.C. Agrawala, southeast of Nim-Ka-Thana in the Sikar district of Rajasthan, on the Kantli river about 60 kilometers from the Khetri mines. Excavations at Ganeshwar and in the vicinity yielded a large collection of distinctive pottery and copper objects. The Ganeshwar people appear to have been at a hunting and fishing stage, but to have had knowledge of copper technology. The copper implements of the Ganeshwar culture are however different in shape from Harappan copper objects. Agrawala and others maintain that the Ganeshwar culture goes back to the third millenium B.C., but the chronology is still a matter of controversy in the absence of carbon-14 dating.
7. Broad chronological divisions are being used here. Protohistory covers the

Early Harappan, Mature Harappan and Late Harappan periods, plus the Painted Gray Ware culture (2nd half of the 2nd millenium B.C.). The historical period includes all the local cultures connected with the Maurya, Sunga, Kushan and Gupta dynasties between ca. 500 B.C. and ca. 900 A.D. The medieval period refers to all local cultures between the 10th and 18th centuries. Unfortunately, unlike monuments and art objects, it is difficult to ascribe modest objects such as canals or potsherds to specific dynasties like the Tughluqs or the Mughals.

8. MAFI was originally created as the result of discussions between D.P. Agrawal, K.N. Dikshit, Henri-Paul Francfort, Jean-Claude Gardin, Pierre Gentelle, J.P. Joshi, B.B. Lal, Bertille Lyonnet, D. Mitra, and B.K. Thapar.
9. See the recent research conducted by the Physical Research Laboratory of Ahmedabad (Pal *et al.* 1984) and the Central Arid Zone Research Institute (Ghose *et al.* 1979).
10. See the field research conducted between 1974 and 1978 under the leadership of Jean-Claude Gardin (Gardin 1980, 1984).
11. Wadi: term used to refer to riverbeds that remain dry except during the rainy season, and to the rivers or streams that flow in them.
12. Ancient Persian texts mention the digging of a canal going towards Bhadra by Firuz Shah Tughluq. and the reactivation of this canal during the reign of Shah Jahan. However, the Darba branch was soon abandoned. Closer study of medieval texts will certainly bring up more evidence about irrigation systems in this period.
13. Most of this earlier work has been summarized in Joshi *et al.* (1984), which gives the most up-to-date picture of the settlement patterns in the area under consideration. No simple and regular distribution of sites along the course of the Chautang emerged from these studies and surveys.
14. The drying up of the Chautang took place gradually and must be considered in connection with the history of the monsoon in the area, because monsoon rains and floods periodically reactivated the ancient river channels over the centuries. This complex history is the subject of a detailed study presently being carried out by Marie-Agnès Courty. However, the fact remains that the Chautang was no longer a substantial river by ca. 4000 B.C. (Courty and Fédoroff 1985). It is therefore difficult to accept the theory that a sudden techtonic uplift in the 2nd millenium B.C. diverted the entire Ghaggar river network and forced the inhabitants to abandon the area (Pal *et al.* 1984).
15. The theory, originally put forth by Aurel Stein and John Marshall in the 1930s, was discredited by the 1950s, but has been recently revived by the research of Gurdip Singh (1971, 1974). Singh's evidence for a wetter climate during the Harappan period is based on analysis of pollen samples taken from three salt lakes of southern Rajasthan (Sambhar, Didwana, Lunkaransar). For a summary and discussion of Singh's hypotheses, see Misra (1984). His hypothesis of a dramatic climatic change has not received general approval from archaeologists of northwestern India, several of whom have done research that contradicts his findings (Pande 1977, Meher-Homji 1977, Dhir 1977).
16. In Mesopotamia, vast irrigation networks were in existence from the beginning of the third millenium B.C. Irrigation also began to appear in Central Asia at

that time. Technically, therefore, nothing would have prevented the Indus civilization from knowing of such networks. See Ratnagar (1986). The latest research tends to suggest irrigation based on the use of largely natural flood channels.

17. On the basis of burnt bricks discovered in 1985 in the bed of a canal near Bhadra, it would seem that at least one of these canals, apparently not the oldest, could date from the beginning of the present era.
18. This entire section is based on the work of Marie-Agnès Courty and Pierre Gentelle, only part of which has been published so far (Courty 1985, Gentelle 1985). Dr. Courty's conclusions are set forth in her unpublished doctoral dissertation (1990).
19. I would like to express my appreciation to Dr. Dikshit for giving us information from his unpublished data.
20. The map presented here is based exclusively on our field work, and covers only Rajasthan. The protohistoric sites were preliminarily dated in the course of a ceramic study in June 1984 by A.K. Sinha and myself. See Sinha's published report (1985) for a summary of the findings of this study. The comprehensive study of all the pottery collected during the three seasons (1983, 1984, 1985) has been completed.
21. Painted Gray Ware was quite rare in the area explored, however. It belongs to a material culture sometimes related to the coming of the Aryans into India. After the discoveries of J.P. Joshi at Bhagwanpura, we know that there was a period of overlap between the Late Harappan and Painted Gray Ware cultures in northwestern India. However, Painted Gray Ware culture is not represented in the Aravalli area, while it covers a vast crescent-like zone following the Yamuna, the northern Punjab plain and the Sutlej.
22. Northern Black Polished Ware is found in the Maurya levels, mostly in the Ganga-Yamuna area. It is a fine pottery, of shining black color with a red core, most similar to the Greek pottery from Attica.
23. To substantiate the division between ancient and recent medieval, we need precise excavations. Broadly speaking, the ancient medieval period refers to pre-Mughal times.
24. The main body of data for the region comes from the sites of Shortughai (Francfort 1984, 1989; Kohl 1984), Sarazm (Isakov 1981; 1985), and Taluqan (Lyonnet 1987).

REFERENCES CITED

Allchin, Bridget and Raymond

1982 *The Rise of Civilization in India and Pakistan*. Cambridge: Cambridge University Press.

Agrawal, D.P.

1984 "Metal Technology of the Harappans." In *Frontiers of the Indus Civilization*. B.B. Lal and S.P. Gupta, eds. pp. 163-167. New Delhi: Indian Archaeological Society.

Agrawal, D.P. and B.M. Pande, eds.

1977 *Ecology and Archaeology of Western India*. Ahmedabad: Concept Publishing Company.

Agrawala, R.C.

1984 "Aravalli: The Major Source of Copper for the Indus and Indus-Related Cultures." In *Frontiers of The Indus Civilization*. B.B. Lal and S.P. Gupta, eds. pp. 157-162. New Delhi: Indian Archaeological Society.

Agrawala, R.C. and Vijay Kumar

1982 "Ganeshwar-Jodhpura Culture: New Traits in Indian Archaeology." In *Harappan Civilization: A Contemporary Perspective*. Gregory L. Possehl, ed. pp. 125-134. Warminster: Aris and Phillips, Ltd.

Bhan, Suraj

1973 "The Sequence and Spread of Prehistoric Cultures in the Upper Sarasvati Basin." In *Radiocarbon and Indian Archaeology*. D.P. Agrawal and A. Ghosh, eds. pp. 252-263. Bombay: Tata Institute of Fundamental Research.

1975 *Excavation at Mithatal (1968) and Other Explorations in the Sutlej-Yamuna Divide*. Kurukshetra, U.P.: Kurukshetra University.

Chakrabarti, Dilip K.

1985-86 "The Pre-Industrial Mines of India." *Puratattva* 16:65-66.

Courty, Marie-Agnès

1985 "Le Milieu Physique et Utilisations du Sol." In *Prospections Archéologiques au Nord-Ouest de l'Inde: Rapport Préliminaire 1983-1984 (MAFI 1)*. Henri-Paul Francfort, ed. pp. 11-31. Paris: Éditions Recherche sur les Civilisations.

Courty, Marie-Agnès and Nicolas Fédoroff

1985 "Micromorphology of Recent and Buried Soils in a Semi-Arid Region of Northern India." *Geoderma* 35:287-332.

Dhir, R.P.

1977 "Palaeoclimatic Inferences from Quaternary Pedogenetic Processes in Arid Zone." In *Ecology and Archaeology of Western India*. D.P. Agrawal and B.M. Pande, eds. p. 132 Ahmedabad: Concept Publishing Company.

Dikshit, K.N.

1977 "Distribution and Relationship of Protohistoric Sites along Old River Channels of the Ghaggar System." In *Ecology and Archaeology of Western India*. D.P. Agrawal and B.N. Pande, eds. pp. 61-66. Ahmedabad: Concept Publishing Company.

1979 "Old Channels of Ghaggar in Rajasthan – Revised." *Man and Environment* 4:32-43.

1984 "Late Harappan in Northern India." In *Frontiers of the Indus Civilization*. B.B. Lal and S.P. Gupta, eds. pp. 253-269. New Delhi: Indian Archaeological Society.

Francfort, Henri-Paul

1984 "The Harappan Settlement of Shortughai." In *Frontiers of the Indus Civilization*. B.B. Lal and S.P. Gupta, eds. pp. 301-310. New Delhi: Indian Archaeological Society.

1985a "Distribution des Sites." In *Prospections Archéologiques au Nord-Ouest de l'Inde: Rapport Préliminaire 1983-1984 (MAFI 1)*. Henri-Paul Francfort, ed. pp. 55-65. Paris: Éditions Recherche sur les Civilisations.

1985b (editor) *Prospections Archéologiques au Nord-Ouest de l'Inde: Rapport Préliminaire 1983-1984 (MAFI 1)*. Paris: Éditions Recherche sur les Civilisations.

1989 (editor) *Fouilles de Shortughai: Recherches sur l'Asie Centrale Protohistorique (Mémoires de la Mission Archéologique Française en Asie Centrale, II)*. 2 vols. Paris: Diffusion de Boccard.

Gardin, Jean-Claude

1980 "L'Archéologie du Paysage Bactrien." *Compte-rendus de l'Académie des Inscriptions et Belles-Lettres*, pp. 480-501.

1984 "Canal Irrigation in Bronze Age Eastern Bactria." In *Frontiers of the Indus Civilization*. B.B. Lal and S.P. Gupta, eds. pp. 311-320. New Delhi: Indian Archaeological Society.

Gentelle, Pierre

1985 "Paysages, Environnement et Irrigation: Hypothèses Pour l'Étude des 3ème et 2ème Millénaires." In *Prospections Archéologiques au Nord-Ouest de l'Inde: Rapport Préliminaire 1983-1984 (MAFI 1)*. Henri-Paul Francfort, ed. pp. 33-41. Paris: Éditions Recherche sur les Civilisations.

Ghose, B.A., A. Kar, and Z. Husain

1979 "The Lost Courses of the Saraswati River in the Great Indian Desert: New Evidence from Landsat Imagery." *The Geographical Journal* 145(3):446-451.

Indras

1968 *The Lost Saraswati*. Wallabh Vidyanagar: Sardar Patel University.

Isakov, Abdullah

1981 "Excavations of the Bronze Age Settlement of Sarazm." In *The Bronze Age Civilization of Central Asia*. P.I. Kohl, ed. pp. 273-286. New York: Sharpe.

1985 "Sarazm et ses Rapports Avec le Sud." In *L'archéologie de la Bactriane Ancienne*. J.C. Gardin, ed. pp. 229-234. Paris: Éditions du C.N.R.S.

Joshi, Jagat Pathi, Madhu Bala, and Jassu Ram

1984 "The Indus Civilization: A Reconsideration on the Basis of Distribution Maps." In *Frontier of the Indus Civilization*. B.B. Lal and S.P. Gupta, eds. New Delhi: Indian Archaeological Society.

Kohl, Philip L., ed.

1981 *The Bronze Age Civilization of Central Asia*. New York: Sharpe.

1984 *Central Asia. Paleolithic Beginnings to the Iron Age*. Paris: Éditions Recherche sur les Civilisations.

Lal, B.B.

1979 "Kalibangan and the Indus Civilization." In *Essays in Indian Protohistory*. D.P. Agrawal and Dilip K. Chakrabarti, eds. pp. 65-67. Delhi: B.R. Publishing Corporation.

Lal, B.B. and S.P. Gupta, eds.

1984 *Frontiers of the Indus Civilization*. Sir Mortimer Wheeler Commemoration Volume. New Delhi: Indian Archaeological Society.

Lyonnet, Bertille
1981 "Établissements Chalcolithiques Dans le Nord-Est de l'Afghanistan: Leurs Rapports avec les Civilisations du Bassin de l'Indus." *Paléorient* 7(2):57-73.

Meher-Homji, V.M.
1977 "History of the Dry Deciduous Forest of Western and Central India." In *Ecology and Archaeology of Western India*. D.P. Agrawal and B.M. Pande, eds. p. 117. Ahmedabad: Concept Publishing Company.

Misra, V.N.
1984 "Climate, a Factor in the Rise and Fall of the Indus Civilization: Evidence from Rajasthan and Beyond." In *Frontiers of the Indus Civilization*. B.B. Lal and S.P. Gupta, eds. pp. 461-489. New Delhi: Indian Archaeological Society.

Mughal, Mughal Rafique
1981 "New Archaeological Evidence from Bahawalpur." In *Indus Civilization: New Perspectives*. A.H. Dani, ed. pp. 33-42. Islamabad.
1982 "Recent Archaeological Research in the Cholistan Desert." In *Harappan Civilization: A Contemporary Perspective*. Gregory L. Possehl, ed. Pp. 85-95. Warminster: Aris Phillips, Ltd.
1984 "The Post-Harappan Phase in Bahawalpur Distr., Pakistan." In *Frontiers of the Indus Civilization*. B.B. Lal and S.P. Gupta, eds. Pp. 499-503. New Delhi: Indian Archaeological Society.

Pal, Yasht, Baldev Sahai, R.K. Sood, and D.P. Agrawal
1984 "Remote Sensing of the 'Lost' Sarasvati River." In *Frontiers of the Indus Civilization*. B.B. Lal and S.P. Gupta, eds. pp. 491-497. New Delhi: Indian Archaeological Society.

Pande, B.M.
1977 "Archaeological Remains of the Ancient Saraswati." In *Ecology and Archaeology of Western India*. D.P. Agrawal and B.M. Pande, eds. Pp. 55-59. Ahmedabad: Concept Publishing Company.

Possehl, Gregory L.
1982 "The Harappan Civilization: A Contemporary Perspective." In *Harappan Civilization: A Contemporary Perspective*. Gregory L. Possehl, ed. pp. 15-28. Warminster:Aris & Phillips.

Ratnagar, Shereen
1986 "An Aspect of Harappan Agricultural Production." *Studies in History* (New Delhi) 2(2)n.s.: 137-153.

Singh, Gurdip
1971 "The Indus Valley Culture (Seen in the Context of Post-Glacial Climate and Ecological Studies in North-West India)." *Archaeology and Physical Anthropology in Oceania* 6 (2):177-189.
1974 "Late Quaternary History of Vegetation and Climate of the Rajasthan Desert, India." *Philosophical Transactions of the Royal Society of London (Biological Sciences)* 267 (889):467-501.

Sinha, A.K.
1985 "Note sur la Céramique et Autres Trouvailles Provenant d'une Zone Triangulaire Entre Siswal, Darba et Bhadra." In *Prospections Archéologiques au Nord-Ouest de l'Inde: Rapport Préliminaire 1983-1984 (MAFI*

1). Henrri-Paul Francfort, ed. pp. 43-54. Paris: Éditions Recherche sur les Civilisations.

Thapar, B.K.

1975 "Kalibangan: A Harappan Metropolis Beyond the Indus Valley." *Expedition* 17(2):19-32.

1984 "Six Decades of Indus Studies." *In Frontiers of the Indus Civilizattion*. B.B. Lal and S.P. Gupta, eds. pp. 1-25. New Delhi: Indian Archaeological Society.

Witzel, Michael

1984 "Sur le Chemin du Ciel." *Bulletin des Études Indiennes* 2:213-279.

ART AS COMMUNICATION

MUSICIANS FOR THE PEOPLE: THE MANGANIYARS OF WESTERN RAJASTHAN

KOMAL KOTHARI

The Manganiyars are hereditary professional folk musicians of the western part of Rajasthan. They are Muslims, and live mainly in Jaisalmer and Barmer, and in parts of Jalor, Bikaner and Jodhpur districts. They provide musical services to their patrons, receiving in exchange cattle, camels, goats, cash, and a share in the patrons' income from agriculture or animal husbandry. This relationship is hereditary, and entails an absolute obligation on the part of the patron families to use the services of the musicians and reward them according to traditional agreements.

The word *mānganiyār* comes from the verb *māngaṇo* ('to beg'), and means, literally, 'a person who begs'. In this context, however, it has a specific meaning and does not carry general connotations of begging. 'Manganiyar' as a name for this caste is a neutral term of reference in Rajasthani society. Of course, because the relationship between the Manganiyars and their patrons is hierarchical, the name denotes a somewhat lower social status. A more respectful name for Muslim musicians in northwestern India is Mirasi, and many Manganiyars like to be addressed and referred to as Mirasis. There is a general social feature in Rajasthan whereby each caste has three names: one which is respectful, a second which is general or neutral, and a third which is abusive or demeaning. Thus a leather worker would be respectfully addressed as Meghwal, in general as Bhambhi, and disparagingly as Dhed. Similarly, someone from a merchant caste would be known as Mahajan, Baniya or Lerh. In general communication, this threefold nomenclature for castes clearly reveals the respective social status of the persons or groups involved. Thus, for these folk musicians, Mirasi would be a respectful designation, Manganiyar a general term, and Doom or Kameen disparaging or abusive names.

Musician Castes and Patron Families

Like other occupational caste groups, musicians are economically dependent on their patrons. There are three terms used for the relationship between patrons and those who provide them with services: *birat, āyat*, and *jajmānī*. When physical and technical or craft services are provided (as in the case of carpenters, barbers, ironsmiths, etc.), the relationship is known as *birat* or *āyat*. *Birat* is generally hereditary for patrons as well as those who serve them, while *āyat* is a sort of contract. Both relationships are on a barter basis, with payment for services consisting in a share of the crop or some other economic benefit rather than cash. The word *jajmānī*, by contrast, is used for non-physical services provided by many different types of groups such as Bhats (genealogists), Raos (bards), Nats (acrobats-cum-genealogists), and musician castes such as the Manganiyars, Langas or Damanis. All groups that function as priests or conduct religious ceremonies for patrons also fall into this category. These religious and social services are of great importance for the maintenance of the social system.

Strict rules govern the relationship between the *jajmān* (patron) and the *jāchak* or *māngat* (the persons who provides the service, the 'server'). The fact that the relationship is hereditary results in certain complications. In particular, there can be many occasions when patron and server get into an argument and cease to trust each other. Often, the relationship breaks down, and many years elapse before reconciliation can be achieved. As repeated disputes and estrangement can negatively affect the social structure, the society has developed means of resolving conflict of this sort. For example, if there is a dispute between a carpenter (or ironsmith) and his patron, the craftsman can stop providing his services. Such a "strike" can seriously hamper the patron's ability to conduct his economic activities. Thus craftsmen are not powerless, but can punish their patrons if the situation demands it.

In the case of musicians, genealogists and providers of other non-physical types of services, the *jajmān* cannot be put to any physical or economic inconvenience by the 'server'. The society has therefore developed different methods by which the server can express displeasure with his patron. If a dispute arises between a musician and his patron, the musician will apply pressure by ceasing to pay respect to his patron's family. There is a tradition known as *subhrāj*, whereby a musician addresses his patron with a few poetic stanzas related to the patron's family. Every musician has to learn his fixed text, as it is through the *subhrāj* that a patron recognizes a musician attached to his family and his obligation toward him. In a dispute, a musician's first step in withholding respect is to cease reciting *subhrāj* for his patron. When this occurs, other people may try to mediate between the parties. If the conflict is not resolved, the musician buries his turban in front of his patron's house or hut. If the dispute still persists, he takes the strings off his instrument and buries them. If even this does not help, he prepares an effigy (*lolaṛ*) of the patron, ties it to a donkey's tail, and parades the donkey among the patron's relatives, insulting the effigy, beating it with shoes, and loudly abusing it. This is known as *lolaṛ bāndhaṇo* ('to tie on an effigy'). Once this happens, no musician from the caste of the plaintiff can perform at ceremonial functions of the patron's family. This results in the patron family's complete social isolation. The major consequence of this can be that the patron will be unable to marry his children within his caste. There are many reported cases where patrons have had to marry their children into lower castes and endure other social penalties as a result of '*lolaṛ bāndhaṇo*. This custom, then, followed very strictly by both musicians and patron families, makes it obligatory for patrons to accept the role of musicians in their family's affairs.

Rupture in the relationship between patrons and ceremonial, ritual or social performers may also result in the latter composing poems of censure or abuse, which remain known for many generations. Such poems or couplets are known as *bhūṇḍ* in Rajasthan. They are just the opposite of the poems of eulogy or praise usually composed for patrons. Patrons are always in fear of bequeathing such poems to their descendants. Certain *jāchak* castes have other modes of expressing displeasure with their patrons as well. The Charans (Rajasthan's bardic caste), for example, used to go to extreme lengths. In the case of a serious dispute, a Charan would take a big knife and gradually cut off first his fingers, and then other parts of his body, until he eventually died. The patron would then bear the heavy curse of having been responsible for a Charan's death. This gruesome tradition is known as *tāgā*, and there have been occasions when many Charans committed this kind of suicide together as a form of protest. Most 'server' groups, however, including musician castes, have only the weapon of their sharp wit and the power to defame a family through the composition of *bhūṇḍs*.

Musician castes and their patron families are linked by traditional arrangements that have been in place for generations and are expected to continue as a matter of unquestioned practice. If a musician has 100 families and two sons, the sons will divide the families equally between them at the time of their father's death, inheriting 50 each. If there are four or five sons, however, each son will get a smaller number of families. On the other hand, a musician family may have a line of only one son for two or three generations; in this case, the number of patron families will be very large. Another consideration in the apportioning of patron families when a musician dies is the right of his widow, widowed mother and widowed grandmother to stay with his youngest son, who therefore gets a few more families as part of his share. Finally, it should be noted that as the patron families multiply, each son heading up a new family is bound by patronage ties to the musician serving his father. Thus the number of families a musician inherits may be 50, but he may have many more to pass on to his own sons by the time he dies. Since the majority of families in rural Rajasthan are nuclear, each brother setting up his own household, the number of families "belonging" to a musician can be quite large.

In Rajasthan, every caste, whether high or low, has its traditional hereditary musicians: it is not a privilege of princely families alone. This means that most hereditary folk musicians receive patronage from ordinary people. During one field work session, I learned that a caste is only recognized as a caste when it has a genealogist and official musicians attached to it. A group without these services may exist, but it is in social limbo. This fact goes counter to the general belief that it is primarily patronage by the courts that has been responsible for preserving the society's musical traditions.

Musicians have to attend the childbirth, marriage and death ceremonies of their patron families, as well as major festivals and private functions. A musician is attached not only to individual patron families, but to entire family lines. This means that patrons are not confined to a single village, but are dispersed over a wide area. A musician is expected to keep track of the ceremonies and functions of all his patron families. During childbirth and weddings, he only has to sing. But during the death ceremonies, he has to perform other services as well. In particular, he is expected to wear saffron-colored clothes and stay at the cremation ground for 12 days, reciting laments for the departed every morning. The musician's attendance at this time is very important from the point of view of legitimizing legal succession in the family.

Jāgīrdār Patronage and Its Decline

Before 1947, each princely state of what is now Rajasthan was ruled by a king, whose court was at the apex of a pyramid of political and administrative authority. Distributed throughout the state were the king's *jāgīrdārs* (feudal lords), who represented him and ruled on his behalf, exercising both judicial and executive power. Whether his authority was over a large tract or a single village, each *jāgīrdār* had his own court, organized according to the pattern of the king's court, which in turn followed the medieval Mughal court pattern. Thus both kings and *jāgīrdārs* patronized musicians, bards, poets, dancers, painters and artisans.

The patronage relationship differed considerably, however. In the royal courts, there was no hereditary right to patronage. The kings competed among themselves in providing patronage to the best talent from all over India. Musicians and other artists would be called to the courts because of their virtuosity. During the initial period of their artistic formation, they were of no concern to the courts, coming into the picture only when they had achieved a certain level of excellence. Nor did patronage automatically extend to an artist or musician's sons. If a great musician's son turned out to be promising, he could find a place at the court, but if he was not, he was left to find his own means of support. This type of patronage had a limited purpose, and did not nurture the traditions by supporting the training and preparation of artists. If this had not been the case, the movement of musicians and artists from one state to another would not have been so prevalent.

Among the common people, the patronage ties were much stronger. If a fine musician had two sons, neither of whom could play an instrument or sing, the patron family was still obliged to maintain them, in the hope that in some future generation a good musician would be born in the family once again. In such circumstances, the men who could not perform had to enlist the services of their relatives in order to fulfil the needs of the patron family.

In the case of the *jāgīrdārs*, yet another patronage pattern prevailed. Whereas among the common people, patron families were bound to a particular family of musicians, the *jāgīrdārs* were only bound to the particular musician caste as a whole. By heredity, certain musician castes had the right to work for the *jāgīrdārs*, receiving in exchange certain rewards, ceremonial cash payments, and a small share of the crops of every farmer in the *jāgīrdār's* revenue territory. Thus the musicians from these castes had a role in the administrative arrangements of *jāgīr* villages.

All but two of the princely states of Rajputana were ruled by Rajputs, and 90% of all the *jāgīrdārs* were Rajput. The musician caste most commonly patronized by the Rajput *jāgīrdārs* and other Rajput families of high status was the Raj Damanis, a sub-group of the Dholi musicians. Because of their proximity to the *jāgīrdārs*, the Raj Damanis had higher social status than the other Dholis. Their role was to sing and play ceremonial songs, to publicly announce orders issued by the *jāgīrdārs*, and to play particular rhythmic patterns on their drums (*ḍhols*) to warn villages of floods, fire or other collective dangers.

Structurally, the Raj Damanis were part of the *jāgīrdārs'* retinues. When the *jāgīrdārī* system was abolished after India's independence, they lost their base of support. They were thus the first traditional musicians of Rajasthan to experience dislocation because of the new circumstances, and they had to seek different ways of making a living. The string instrument they played, a type of *sārangī*, ceased to be in demand, and their musical tradition came to a sudden halt. Most of the Raj Damanis found employment in urban brass bands, but many had to take jobs unrelated to music.

By contrast, professional musician groups whose base of support was broader continued to receive patronage, and thus survived the abrupt political and economic changes in the society. The Manganiyars, as well as the Dhadhis, Dholis, Langas and Nats, all belong to this second category of musicians whose support came not from kings or *jāgīrdārs*, but from the common people.

Manganiyar Oral Histories

The Manganiyars are Sunni Muslims, but sing for Hindu families. A similar group of musicians living in the same area of Rajasthan, the Langas, sing for Muslim patron families. There is a third group (who also call themselves Manganiyars) who sing for both Hindu and Muslim families. The differences between these three groups are easily discernible. The Manganiyars use a bowed string instrument called the *kāmāychā*, while the Langas play the *sindhī sārangī*. The third group play either the *pyāledār sārangī* or the *sindhī sārangī*, but their song repertoire is that of the Manganiyars. I have been told that the Manganiyars of this third group intermarry with both the first group of Manganiyars and the Langas, which establishes some kind of caste relationship between Manganiyars and Langas.

Tracing the history of a folk musician group is not easy. If we go to epigraphic sources, old literary texts or archival records, we find very little reference to these low-caste people, as most of these historical materials deal exclusively with courts and kings. It was necessary to turn to the methods of oral history. Most people can relate their family history going back three or four generations, but professional folk musicians and genealogist castes like the Manganiyars, Bhats, Raos, Dhadhis or Nats can easily recall 10 to 15 generations. Thus the best available source is the oral accounts of the musician families themselves.

Three accounts will be presented as case studies: (1) Sakar Khan Manganiyar, a *kāmāychā* player from the village of Hamira, near Jaisalmer, (2) Bhungar Khan Manganiyar, a singer from the village of Jaisindhar, in Barmer District, and (3) Misri Khan, a singer from the village of Khodal, also in Barmer District. All three are excellent musicians.

Sakar Khan Manganiyar

Sakar Khan belongs to the Babar subcaste of the Manganiyars.[1] He traces his ancestry back ten generations to a man named Babar, after whom the subcaste is named.[2] If we assume an average of 20 years for a generation, Sakar Khan's knowledge of his family goes back about 200 years.

According to Sakar Khan, his family came to Hamira at the time of his great-grandfather, Mithu Khan. Mithu Khan was invited there by Thakur Sabal Singh Bhati, a Rajput of the Raidhar Bhati subcaste. Before this, Mithu Khan had been living in the village of Dhaneli. Prior to this, the family had lived in the village of Dhaing. From there, one family member had gone to Dhaneli, another to Khuhadi, and the third to Hamira.

The village of Hamira had been established in the desert by one Hamir Singh Bhati. He was from the family of the Jaisalmer king, but was a *chhuṭ bhāī* (younger brother), i.e., not in the line of succession to the throne. (Both *jāgīrdārī* and kingship follow the rule of primogeniture, with the eldest son getting all the succession rights, and younger sons being entirely dependent on the generosity of the sole heir). Hamir Singh, the account goes, was tending a herd of cows, moving with it from pasture to pasture. While on the road from Jaisalmer to Nachna, he found a good place with water and grass, and decided to establish a new village there, which he named Hamira. With Hamir Singh came a number of people who were in his service: a Suthar (carpenter), Hazurias (illegitimate children of Rajput families), a Khavas (barber), Meghwals (leather workers), a Darji (tailor), and a Bhil (tribal watchman). Collectively, such service castes are referred to as Kasabis.

The Manganiyars from Jaisalmer did not join Hamir Singh as one of the Kasabi groups when the village was first established. It was only when the village had taken real shape and was no longer a temporary camp that the need for musicians arose. This was at the time of one of Hamir Singh's successors, Sabal Singh. Sabal Singh invited Mithu Khan, and the ceremony of *sāfā bandhāī* ('turban-tying') was duly performed. Once this ceremony has taken place, a Manganiyar becomes officially attached to a given Rajput family, and his family becomes one of the Rajput's Kasabis. The Manganiyars then have to provide services not only to the Rajput patrons but to all the Kasabi groups who were originally in the service of the patron.

Manganiyars maintain that their patrons are high-caste Rajputs. This is true, but they also have the same relationship with the Kasabi groups serving their Rajput patrons. In the case of Sakar Khan's family line, service is owed to all the families who settled Hamira with Hamir Singh Bhati. Later on, members of these families migrated to many other villages, both near and far. At present, therefore, Sakar has the right to come and perform at the ceremonies of all such families, whether they are in the direct line of Hamir Singh or in the family lines of Hamir Singh's original Kasabi families.

By tradition, the official rewards and ceremonial cash payments for musical services must go to a family's hereditary musicians, no matter how far away they live. Should the hereditary musicians not arrive for the ceremony, however, both cash payments and income-sharing rights are passed on to the Manganiyars living in the village. But whenever the official hereditary musicians arrive, they have full rights to both the official rewards and the ceremonial cash payments. A patron family that loses all contact with its hereditary musicians may adopt a new family in that capacity. If this happens, the patron's Kasabi families also come under the obligation to use the new musician family for their ceremonial needs.

When Mithu Khan came to Hamira, he was invited by two different Rajput groups, the Bhatis and the Rathors. The Rathors of Hamira also 'tied the turban' with him. As a result, Mithu Khan received patronage from both the Bhatis and the Rathors, and from the Kasabis of both. Today, Sakar Khan's patronage is spread out in the following way: Bhatis (60 families), Rathors (80 families), Suthars (10 families), Meghwals (16 families), Kumars (4 families), and Bhils (12 families).

Sakar Khan is not the only Manganiyar musician to serve these patron families. He and his younger brother, Pempa Khan, have not yet divided these patron families among them. Also having claim to these families are two cousins. Sakar Khan's great-grandfather had five sons: Nabho, Sumar, Haji, Dungar, and Bahadar. Sumar and Bahadar had died young, thus leaving three family lines to continue. In Nabho's line, the performing musicians at present are Sakar Khan and Pempa Khan; in Haji's line is Kadar Khan, and in Dungar's line Haider Khan. All four are actively engaged in music, and also in the story-telling tradition. Only Sakar plays the *kāmāychā*; Pempa plays two wind instruments, the *muraḷī* and the *shehnāī* (or *surnāī*); Kadar and Haider sing. All the other cousins are engaged in building and construction work, but this non-musical occupation does not deter them from claiming their hereditary income from the family's patrons.

Bhungar Khan Manganiyar

Bhungar Khan belongs to the Gunsar subcaste of the Manganiyars. He traces his family lineage back eight generations.[3] Jaisindhar, the village in which he now lives, is on the Pakistan border. His ancestral village, about 12 miles away, is presently in the Umarkot District of Pakistan. Jaisindhar was originally established by Dalleji, a Rajput of the Sodha subcaste. Dalleji had two sons, Raichand and Bhagchand. While Raichand remained in Jaisindhar, his younger brother established another village, Naidusar.

It was a very disturbed time in the history of the area, with many well organized bands of robbers. During the time of Dalleji, robbers once attacked Jaisindhar, and both of Dalleji's sons fought in defense of the village. Bhungar Khan's ancestor Gulle Khan, who was associated with Dalleji through patronage, also fought, and was killed. Because Gulle Khan had given his life for his patron's family, his descendants became entitled to a certain amount of money in addition to the other contractual rewards and payments. This money is still paid to Bhungar Khan's family, in a ceremony known as the "dagger" ceremony.

There are about 261 families in Jaisindhar. The caste distribution is as follows: 60 Sodha Rajputs, 60 Ravana Rajputs (illegitimate children of Rajput families), 40 Banias (merchants), 60 Garudas (providers of Brahmanical services to the lower castes), 12 Suthars (carpenters), 6 Dhati Brahmans, 6 Meghwals (leather workers), 2 Darbus (Muslim Nais, i.e. barbers), 5 Darjis (tailors), and 10 Manganiyars. The Manganiyars provide musical services to both the Rajputs and the Kasabi groups. Even though all but one of the Manganiyar families have by now gone into other occupations, they all still receive the customary rewards they are entitled to by tradition. Thus at the time of weddings, childbirth or death ceremonies in their patrons' families, they always receive a turban and a set of clothes.

Bhungar Khan has inherited the patronage of only 20 families of Sodha Rajputs and their Kasabis. However, as he is the only practicing musician in Jaisindhar in his family line, he sings for almost all the patron families, and receives a share of the customary rewards. "Patronage is property," he explains, "like a field under cultivation. The owner of a field has the right to rent it out, or to share it with a cultivator on certain terms. The share here is always 50-50, and the same is the practice with us. I can't take the place of musicians who can't perform without their specific permission and without sharing the rewards with them." In the past, Bhungar's family also served the *jāgīrdār* by calculating the amount of harvest that came in, in exchange for which they would get three quintals of grass and a quintal of millet (*bājrā*) from the farmers. This practice has come to an end, however.

Misri Khan Manganiyar

Misri Khan belongs to the Gehla subcaste of the Manganiyars, and traces his lineage back ten generations.[4] He lives in the village of Khodal in Barmer District. His father, Sadi Khan, came there from the village of Kodiyasar in Jaisalmer District, where all his other relatives still live.

According to Misri Khan, Sadi Khan's move to Khodal is part of a complex history. The Gehla Manganiyars have traditionally been the exclusive musicians for the Paliwal Brahmans of Jaisalmer District. The Paliwals were agriculturalists of the desert region. They had developed a technique of erecting stone *bunds* (embankements) that followed the contour and watershed patterns of the region. Rain water would be collected and stored in this way, and allowed to seep for a month or two. They would then prepare the field and, without irrigation, would grow a winter crop of wheat. The Paliwals were a major source of revenue for the Jaisalmer state. About 135 years ago, the Paliwals and the princely bureaucracy came into conflict, and the Paliwals decided to leave Jaisalmer en masse. The legend is that the whole community drank water mixed with salt in the evening, and by the next morning were beyond the boundaries of the state.

This sudden departure of the Paliwals left the Gehla Manganiyars of Jaisalmer without any means of support. According to Misri Khan, the Paliwals ordered their musicians to join them, but the Gehlas hesitated. The Paliwals therefore cursed them with barrenness. All this happened at the time of Misri Khan's grandfather, Dhuloji. Dhulo, who was then living in Kodiyasar, had three brothers: Buddho, Haji and Chautho. All but Dhulo were childless, and Dhulo had only one son, Sadi Khan. Worried that the curse of the Paliwals would bring the family line to an end, they decided to move out of Jaisalmer state. There were four families of Paliwals in the village of Khodal at the time, who had left Jaisalmer prior to the mass exit, because of marriage connections. Dhulo's family decided to join them, and shifted to this new village. Thus, according to Misri Khan, his family of Gehla Manganiyars has continued in the exclusive service of Paliwals.

Misri Khan's case differs in several ways from that of the two

Manganiyar musicians already discussed. He states that his family turned to music only seven generations ago, starting with his ancestor Karamchand. Prior to Karamchand, the family had been a Paliwal Brahman family. Karamchand learned to play the *dhol*, however. One day, at a Paliwal gathering, he was asked to play. Because he put the *ḍhol* on his shoulders, they declared him to be their Manganiyar. This is not the whole story, however. Misri Khan also relates that Karamchand used to eat non-vegetarian food with the Jangh Muslims of the village. Paliwal Brahmans were strict vegetarians, avoiding even onions, garlic and other root vegetables; it is thus likely that Karamchand was outcasted. Misri Khan also says that Karamchand married into a Manganiyar family. Misri Khan's overall claim, that on his paternal side he is descended from Paliwal Brahmans, is not made by any other Gehla Manganiyars.

These three oral histories tell us a lot about the relationship between *jajmān* and *jāchak*, how it originates and continues along hereditary lines, and what the mutual obligations of patrons and musicians are. It is clear that professional musician castes practice music as a means of livelihood, and transmit their tradition from father to son just as other crafts and service castes do. Like these other castes too, they become formally attached to patron families and groups, and prosper or deline with them.

Musical Services: Childbirth Ceremonies

The Manganiyars are expected to be present at all the life passage ceremonies of their patrons. When a child is born in a patron family, the musician comes with his instrument and sings songs having to do with the birth of the child, wishes the child a long life, and congratulates the family upon this addition of a new member.

One kind of song sung on this occasion refers to all the child's relatives, and to their joy at the family having produced a child who is as great as Krishna or Ram. There is a saying about these compositions that suggests that the larger the extended family is, the longer the song will be: *gīt baṛā yā got*? ('Which is bigger, the song or the family?'). This kind of song can go on endlessly, repeating each stanza for every relative.

A second type of song is about the auspicious arrival of people involved in the childbirth ceremonies or the people who provide for the child's essential needs. Thus the musician is described as arriving with pious songs, the carpenter with a cradle, the Brahman with a blessing, the goldsmith with ornaments, the perfume seller with perfume, and so on.

The Manganiyar musician is also expected to be present at all the ceremonies the mother of a newborn child has to perform.

Musical Services: Wedding Ceremonies

After childbirth, the next important ceremonial occasion in an individual's life is marriage. Wedding ceremonies involve two families, and musicians have to provide services for both. By tradition, the bridegroom's party goes to the bride's place, which is usually in a different village. From start to finish, a wedding takes from two weeks to a month. The patron families' musicians are expected to be there the entire time, singing songs for all the different ceremonies that make up the marriage ritual.

The marriage ritual formally begins with an invocation to the god Ganesh and the installation of his image. Among the many subsequent ceremonies requiring songs are the massage of the bride and groom with *pīṭhī* (a paste made of ground pulse) and *haldī* (turmeric), *bindoḷī* (meal invitations by relatives and family friends), the arrival of guests, the departure of the wedding procession from the groom's village, the journey to the bride's village, the arrival at the bride's home, the wedding ceremony itself, the farewell to the bride, the journey back, and the homecoming ceremonies. Besides these major events, there are also ceremonial occasions in between when a song or two must be sung. The *māyaro*, for example, when the bride or groom's maternal uncle gives gifts to his sister (i.e., to the mother of the bride or groom), is an occasion at which many songs are sung. Similarly, when the bride's and bridegroom's families meet, a lot of joking songs about relatives are sung.

For all of these ceremonial occasions, the musicians sing, but there is no specified group of listeners. The musicians sit somewhere near the ceremonial area and go on singing without any concern for audience. By contrast, there are occasions in the evenings when a group assembles around the Manganiyar musicians, and a serious music session gets underway. Such a session is known as *kacheṛī*. This is the prime opportunity for musicians to perform at their best. During a *kacheṛī* session, the audience responds to the songs by handing the musicians cash donations while they sing. Musicians earn a substantial amount during a *kacheṛī* session, above and beyond their customary payment in cash.

As a performance institution, a *kacheṛī* provides the opportunity for a musician to show his artistic skill, the beauty of compositions, the quality of his improvisation, and the large repertoire of songs and compositions he knows. As the listeners are themselves steeped in the tradition of the songs, and connoisseurs of the music, they are very discriminating and critical. They demand of the musicians very high standards in both repertoire and performance. All their lives, Manganiyars practice and work hard to be successful in these sessions.

We thus see that there are two kinds of occasions during weddings when Manganiyars are expected to sing. In one, the musicians sing ceremonially, without audience. In the second, the musicians play for a keenly discriminating audience. In the first kind of occasion, the ceremonial function is paramount, whereas in the second, it is the subject matter of the songs and the musical composition. Some songs are exclusive to one or the other, but there are also many songs common to both.

While the Manganiyar men are busy with the singing of ceremonial songs, the women are also engaged in singing, as a group and in a separate place. Because both men and women are singing for a wedding, the subject matter of their songs is similar. Some of the main categories of ceremonial wedding songs are the following:

bano/banaḍo	song in praise of the bridegroom
banī/banaḍī	song in praise of the bride
kāmaṇ	song to ward off the evil that could befall the couple
goṛhī	song sung when the bridegroom is riding his mare
toraṇ	song sung when the bridegroom, arriving at the bride's house, touches the *toraṇ*, a triangular ritual object that hangs over the entrance
gālī	song of teasing, joking and abuse sung about relatives of the bride or bridegroom

pīṭhī	song sung during the massage of the bride and groom with *pīṭhī* paste
haldī	song sung during the massage of the bride and groom with turmeric
mehendī	song sung during the application of henna (*mehendī*) to the hands of the bride and groom
pherā	song sung during the seven rounds around the sacred fire taken by the groom and bride
bidāī	song sung when the bride leaves her parents' home
māyaro	song sung when the bride or groom's maternal uncle gives gifts to his sister
badhāvo	auspicious welcome song
khamā/khamāj	couplet or song sung during the wedding procession
chaṅvaṛī	songs about the temporary canopy (*chaṅvaṛī*) under which the wedding ceremony takes place
āḍiyāṅ	riddle song sung to the groom, which he must solve

All of these are generic names for a particular aspect of the wedding ritual, or for an important actor in it. In each category, there are many songs. For example, there are hundreds of *bano* and *banī* songs. There are also numerous songs in the *kāmaṇ* category. The *gālī* songs, exchanged between male and female groups, are also numerous.

After the wedding ceremony is completed, and sometimes even before, an all night ceremonial session known as *rātījagā* is held. The songs are principally about ancestors or deified heroes. At a *rātījagā*, the songs are mainly sung by the women of the patron family, or by the Manganiyar women. Sometimes the Manganiyar men also participate, singing devotional songs or songs about the lore of folk deities.[5]

Musical Sessions *(Kacheṛī)*

The songs performed by the Manganiyars during *kacheṛī* sessions are very different from the ceremonial wedding songs. To begin with, they are referred to not by their function or thematic content, but by the name of the *rāga* (musical mode) in which they are sung.[6] The musician states the name of a *rāga* and then sings the composition in that *rāga*. The composition is divided into two musical sections. First, there is a stylized but metrically free rendering of one or more *dohās* (couplets). Through musical improvisation, the singer strives to express as many shades of emotion and poetic meaning as possible. Then comes the song or composition, set to a metrical pattern (*laya*). The song always consists of several stanzas, repeatedly ornamented by a refrain line.

The subject matter sung about in a *kacheṛī* session is extremely varied. There are love songs, songs of separation, festival songs, ceremonial songs, heroic songs, songs describing female beauty, songs about the beauty of nature. There are songs about the deeds of great men and women, noble examples of service, sacrifice for a social cause, mercy shown to the poor and needy, and other meritorious acts. There are songs stating philosophical truths through enigmatic metaphors, songs on devotional and religious topics, and songs about folk gods and goddesses. The repertoire also includes songs taken from traditional romantic tales.[7]

A particular musical game is also played during *kacheṛī* sessions. It has its origin in the contest situation between the bride's party and the groom's. Several non-musical ceremonial contests take place in the course of a wedding. For example, when the groom's party arrives at the boundary of the bride's village, a messenger (*baṛbadhāū*) is sent to the host family. The men from the bride's family come out on horseback to welcome the guests. After the welcome, a contest follows in which the bridegroom races someone in the bride's party. This horse race, most common among high-caste groups, is considered a very auspicious contest. Another contest involves weight lifting. The bride's relatives sit facing the groom's party, and a heavy stone with a carved handle is placed between them. The contestants from both sides have to lift the stone above their heads with a single swing of the hand, without bending. It is a show of strength, and it is expected that the groom's party should win the game. Many other games of this sort are popular with different caste groups.

The musical game played during the *kacheṛī* session is initiated by the bride's party. An elder in the family calls the family's

Fig. 1: Manganiyar musician group performing at Umaid Bhavan in Jodhpur, October 21, 1990. Left to right: Nyaz (*ḍholok*), Barkat Khan (vocal), Sakar Khan (*kāmāychā*), Sadiq (vocal and *khartāl*), Multan (vocal), Chanan (vocal and *kāmāychā*) (Photograph by Larry Goodfriend)

Fig. 2: **Manganiyar musician group performing at Umaid Bhavan (side view). (Photograph by Rephael Shevelev / A Thousand Words © 1990)**

Fig. 3: Four Manganiyar musicians. Left to right: Nyaz (*ḍholok*), Barkat Khan (vocal), Sakar Khan (*kāmāychā*), Sadiq (vocal and *khartāl*) (Photograph by Larry Goodfriend)

Fig. 4: Portrait of Sakar Khan Manganiyar
(Photograph by Raphael Shevelev / A Thousand Words ©1990)

Manganiyar instrumentalist and tell him in secret the location of some object that has been hidden, either in the house or outside. For example, the object could be a black bottle filled with white liquor lying on top of a storage cabinet. The object is not visible from the place where the game is being played. The musician seats himself before the groom's party and starts playing a melody. Two or three experts in the groom's party concentrate on the music being played. By means of a musical code, the instrumentalist indicates to them that they should move in a certain direction, for instance east, to find the object. He might then change melody, indicating that they should go no further. Then he might start up another melody, indicating another direction, for instance north. In this manner, the musician keeps on playing, and the experts follow him as directed. Once they have arrived at the right place, the musician begins to sing songs hinting at the identity of the object, and the experts have to guess what it is. This game is known as the 'pebble' (*kāṅkarī*) game.

The secret of the *kāṇkarī* game is expert knowledge of the *rāgas*. There are ten *rāgas* which signify the ten directions, and one is selected to indicate stopping. Both the musician and the listeners must have a perfect knowledge of the directional significance of the *rāgas* in order to participate in the game. Musically, the *rāgas* of the Manganiyars have very subtle and minute distinctions, and people who are very adept at recognizing these *rāgas* greatly enjoy the game of *kāṇkarī*.

The performance context of the *kacheṛī* thus encourages high standards of excellence in traditional music. It is here that Manganiyar musicians have to shine and show their skill, and where they receive the approbation of an audience. The ceremonial occasions do not provide the musicians with any challenge. In the institution of the *kacheṛī*, expertise is appreciated and economically rewarded. Skilful musicians are given the opportunity and the motivation to create complex metric patterns, add new songs to their repertoire, and produce new compositions. In the repertoires of Manganiyar families, there are many compositions associated with individuals who created them for performance in the *kacheṛī*. Similar opportunities for virtuosity and creativity also exist for the Langa, Dholi and Dadhi musician castes.

Instruments of the Manganiyars

All Manganiyar musicians must have two essential sets of instruments. The first consists of *ḍhol* and *thālī*. The *ḍhol* is a large, two-headed cylindrical drum. The *thālī*, which always accompanies the *ḍhol*, is a small circular instrument made of bell metal. *Ḍhol* and *thālī* are considered auspicious, and are required for all ceremonial occasions. Thus Manganiyars will lead a family procession playing *ḍhol* and *thālī*, and all ceremonies must begin with the beat of these two instruments. The second set of auspicious instruments consists of the *surnāī* (a form of oboe), accompanied rhythmically by *ḍhol*, *ḍholak* or *nagārā*. The *ḍholak* is a barrel-shaped wooden drum, both heads of which are covered with parchment; it is smaller than the *ḍhol*, and both sides are played with the hands. The *nagārā* consists of two kettle drums, one large and one small, and is played with two long, thin sticks.

The *ḍhol* is a simple rhythm instrument and does not require much practice. The player suspends the *ḍhol* from his neck and usually plays in a standing position. The right side, considered female (*mādā*), is played with the fingers and palms of the hand, and produces a high pitch. The left side, considered male (*nar*), provides the base tone and is played with a small stick that is thick and curved. Usually, an assistant joins in on the male side of the drum with two thin bambo sticks. Some Manganiyar *ḍhol* players use sticks for both sides, one small and thick, the other with a sharp point. They play at a very fast tempo, and when the parchment vibrates loudly, a sudden stroke with the pointed stick causes a sharp, cracking sound. This is a feat that only a few drummers can execute.

Several different rhythmic patterns are played on the *ḍhol*. *Gāgarā* and *maṭakī* (or *maṭaku*) are played for particular women's dances, *chakkar* for men's sword dances. The rhythm for wedding processions is known as *bandoḷī*. *Tājiyā* or *tābūt* is played during the processions of the Muslim Muhurram festival, and *kaṭak* when getting ready for combat. Two very powerful rhythms are *satī* and *vāru*. *Satī* is played when a widow performs the rite of *satī*, and *vāru* to announce a calamity and call people to gather together. In rural areas, *vāru* has tremendous sanctity and is played only at times of crisis. No one is allowed to play it just for pleasure, and if someone does, there is heavy punishment. These different rhythmic patterns are all understood by village people, and they respond to them readily.

While Manganiyars play *ḍhol*, *thālī* and *surnāī* for ceremonial occasions, their true musical virtuosity lies in the *kāmāychā* and the *pyāledār sārangī* . The *kāmāychā* is a bowed string instrument played to accompany vocal singing. Two types of *kāmāychā* players are found among the Manganiyars. One only accompanies himself as he sings, while the other accompanies another singer or plays the instrument solo. The difference between the two is noticeable. The singer-instrumentalist does not play the vocal melodies, but plays instead a repetitive *chālā* (pattern of notes), with rhythmic bowing stresses on certain beats. When the second type of *kāmāychā* player accompanies a vocalist, he follows every nuance of the melody. When he plays solo, he uses techniques that are purely instrumental, improvising on the melody in many different ways. The *pyāledār sārangī* is a variant of the *sindhī sārangī* played by the Langas. The two instruments differ in the arrangement and tuning of their strings, as well as in the method of fingering.

Other string instruments played by the Manganiyars are the *sirimaṇḍal* (a trapezoid box polychord), the *jagtārā* (a drone instrument with a single or double open string), and the *chautāro* (a drone instrument with five strings). Nowadays, there are only two old men left who play the *sirimaṇḍal*. The reason for this is that for an entire generation, the children of men who learned the *sirimaṇḍal* died, a coincidence that frightened people away from this instrument.

The *jagtārā* provides not only the drone but also the basic rhythmic pattern, as its playing technique involves a strong right-to-left stroke. It is usually played by those Manganiyar musicians who are adept at religious, devotional and Sufi songs. The *chautāro* is also known as *bīn* or *tandūro*. *Chautāro* actually means 'four strings', but the instrument has five strings. The name probably comes from the tuning pattern, in which two strings are tuned in unison and are therefore counted as one. This instrument is connected with religious and devotional songs, and with certain epics and ballads. The compositions sung with it have to do with Ramdeo, the popular regional deity worshipped by low-caste groups from Rajasthan, Madhya Pradesh, Gujarat, Haryana and Punjab. The *chautāro* is always played to accompany group singing, and supplemented rhythmically with *ḍholak*, *manjīrā* and *khartāl*.

Among the wind instruments played by the Manganiyars is the *surnāī*, a double-reed instrument. It is considered auspicious, and is always accompanied by *ḍholak*. Another wind instrument is the *muralī*, a double-reed gourd-pipe. Though elsewhere, *muralī* is the name used for the transverse flute, in the desert region it has come to refer specifically to the gourd-pipe. It has been adopted by the Manganiyars and Langas from the Jogis, a nomad group. The Jogis call the instrument *pungī* or *bīn*. There are three types of *muralī*, each with a different pitch. The lowest-pitched *muralī* is called *āgor*; its tonic is suitable for the singing voices of older women. The medium-pitched *muralī*, pitched at a level suitable for the voices of young girls, is known as *mansurī*. The third type, known as *ṭaṅkī*, is pitched very high and cannot be used to accompany any vocal music. The Manganiyars and Langas mostly use the *ṭaṅkī*, though the *āgor* may be used to accompany *āḍā gīt* (see below).

The final wind instrument used by the Manganiyars is the *ghaṛā*, a clay pot whose belly is supported by both hands and kept high over the head so that the musician can blow into it forcefully. It produces a deep sound and rhythmic beat. It is used for devotional music, and is usually accompanied by the *chautāro*. The *ghaṛā* is played by ordinary people as well as by Manganiyar professionals, but in seated position rather than standing.

Songs of the Manganiyars: The Women's Ceremonial Tradition

The songs sung by the Manganiyars are of two kinds: those from the women's ceremonial tradition, and those sung exclusively by the male professionals. The question arises: did Manganiyar women ever sing professionally? Manganiyars today deny this, but in my opinion, the exclusion of women from professional singing is a recent, post-independence phenomenon related to the question of caste prestige. It was only a few years ago that this consideration led the Manganiyar community to pass a resolution entirely stopping the practice of women being sent to sing for patron families.

Previously, when women did sing professionally for patrons, their role was limited to ceremonial singing. There is no suggestion that they ever participated in *kacheṛī* sessions. They mostly sang for the women in the patron families, in separate *zenānā* (women's) assemblies. I have attended a few weddings in the interior parts of the desert where men and women sing these ceremonial songs together even today. In the past, it may have been the common practice. This would explain why Manganiyar women have quite a different repertoire of wedding songs than do women from the general population. The ceremonial songs they sing are more complex, and singing them requires special cultivation and practice.

The repertoire of Manganiyar women singers is limited to ceremonial songs. Musically, they consist of a single melodic line, repeated again and again. When they sing these songs, the women do not announce any particular *rāga* name. By contrast, when Manganiyar men sing these same songs, they identify a *rāga* name and embellish the composition with additional improvised melodic material. There is also a difference between the rhythmic patterns used by men and those used by women. Finally, there is a difference in accompaniment. When Manganiyar women sing, they either sing in a group without accompaniment, or solo, accompanying themselves on a large *ḍhol*; there is no additional instrumentation. Men, on the other hand, perform with a *ḍholak* accompanist and another accompanist playing the *kāmāychā*, the *pyāledār sārangī* or, more recently, the harmonium.

An example of a women's ceremonial wedding song will be presented here, and analyzed in terms of literary form and content.

he nimbūḍo levo annadātā thai
narangī ro tel lyo
hā jī mhārā madchhakiyā re mārū, jiyo bāg maiṅ
hame nimbuḍo lyo

jodhane helo ai annadātā thai
lahariyā lyāy do
hā jī re nandalbāī rā bīrā, jiyo bāg maiṅ
chhoṭā nimbūḍā uṛā lyo

ai sonigār helo badīlā ḍholā
gahaṇiyo to lāy
lumbąjhaḍ ladī rā ḍhola, jiyo bāg maiṅ
hame nimbūḍā lāy do

ai pātanpūr helo annadātā thai
paṭulā thai lyāy do
hame dhīmā bolī rā bālam, jiyo bāg maiṅ
limbūḍā chhoṭā lyāy do

kalālī ghar helo annadātā thai
dāruro thai lyāy do
miragā naiṇī rā bālam, jiyo bāg maiṅ
hame limbūḍā lāy do

Take the lemon, my lord,
Make juice from the sweet limes;
My passionate dear, from the garden,
Take the lemon.

Go to Jodhpur, my lord,
Bring a wavy scarf;
Sister-in-law's brother, from the garden,
Pick small lemons.

Go to the goldsmith, strong-willed groom,
Bring ornaments;
Lover of the ornament-laden one, from the garden,
Bring lemons.

Go to Patanpur, my lord,
Bring heavy bangles;
Lover of the soft-spoken one, from the garden,
Bring small lemons.

Go to the tavern, my lord,
Bring wine;
Lover of the doe-eyed one, from the garden
Bring lemons.

This song can be sung at any time during the wedding ceremonies. Its language is the standard Rajasthani of folk songs, understandable all over Rajasthan in spite of dialect differences. The song consists of five stanzas, edited here to reduce the extensive improvisational repetition of words, lines and meaningless syllables that is characteristic of Manganiyar singing. Each stanza has a formulaic verse-and-refrain structure, with only two words or phrases changing in each verse, and slight variations in the refrain. All the rest remains the same. The melody is also stanzaic, with meaningless syllables thrown in to adjust the words to the metric line.

Thematically, the song consists of a list of objects to be brought by the groom for the bride, a common theme in women's folk songs. All of these – the scarf (*lahariyā*), ornaments (*gahaṇiyā*), bangles (*pāṭulā*), wine (*dāru*) – are ceremonially significant in the wedding. The song can be lengthened by including many other objects (perfume, shoes, combs, etc.) and their makers or sellers, and by listing the ornaments individually. The song thus has a definite beginning but no definite end, though usually only four or five stanzas are sung.

The first stanza differs from the others. In it, the groom is told not to bring presents, but to take the bride – symbolically referred to as a lemon freshly picked from the orchard, youthful, full of juice, and with a tinge of sharpness to her taste. Her breasts are compared to sweet limes – small, firm, to be pressed for juice. This sexually suggestive theme provides the refrain for the rest of the song.

In this song, as in many wedding songs, the groom is referred to by many different terms: *annadātā* (lord, lit. 'giver of bread'), *madcchakiyā* (passionate, lit. 'intoxicated'), *mārū* (a term of address meaning 'dear'), *nandalbāī rā bīrā* (sister-in-law's brother), *badīlā ḍholā* (strong-willed groom), *lumbājhaḍ ladī rā ḍholā* (lover of the ornament-laden one), *dhīmā bolī rā bālam* (lover of the soft-spoken one), and *miragā naiṇī rā bālam* (lover of the doe-eyed one).

Songs of the Manganiyars: The Men's Professional Tradition

Manganiyar men usually divide their professional repertoire into *chhoṭā gīt* (small song) and *moṭā gīt* (big song). This division is based on the complexity of the melody and the use of metric patterns. In terms of text, *chhoṭā gīts* have short stanzas and a strongly rendered refrain, while *moṭā gīts* have longer stanzas and tend not to have refrains. Some *moṭā gīt* stanzas take the form of couplets or quatrains in particular poetic meters. All songs composed in formal poetic meters belong to the *moṭā gīt* category, but *moṭā gīt* also includes other kinds of poetic compositions. Manganiyar musicians say the women's repertoire also includes both *chhoṭā gīt* or *moṭā gīt*. However, most of women's *moṭā gīts* are not composed in formal poetic meters, but are considered *moṭā gīts* because, musically, they go beyond the middle octave.

This relates to the second Manganiyar classification of songs, based on musical scales. This classification distinguishes between *āḍā* (horizontal or oblique) and *khaḍā* (vertical or standing). *Āḍā* songs are usually sung in the middle octave alone, may move a little into the lower octave, but never go into the higher octave. All *āḍā* songs are *moṭā gīts*. *Khaḍā* songs, by contrast, go way up into the higher octave. The terms *āḍā* and *khaḍā* are used principally by the wind and string instrumentalists who accompany the vocalists. *Chhoṭā* and *moṭā* are terms used to refer to the vocal rendering of a song.

The third musical classification used by the Manganiyars is that of *rāga* (musical mode). Every *rāga* can have both *chhoṭā* and *moṭā* compositions. As the concept of *rāga* among traditional musicians such as the Manganiyars, Langas and Dholis differs considerably from the classical concept, it will be treated below in a separate section.

The Manganiyars begin their singing with a number of couplets, followed by the song or main composition. The couplet is known as *dohā*, an independent verse form of the *mātrik* (moraic) variety. *Mātrik* meters are quantitative, based on total moraic count of short and long syllables (*mātrās*) rather than feet, while *vārṇik* meters are based on fixed arrangements of poetic feet. The *dohā*, of which there are many varieties, has 24 *mātrās* in each line, with a caesura after the 13th and different rhyming possibilities. *Dohā* is the most popular meter in Rajasthani folk poetry. An example of *dohā* follows:

ko luvā kita jausiyo, pāvasa dhara padiyāha
hīya nābodha nāra re, bālama bichhaṛiyaha

Hot wind, where will you go
  when the rain comes for shelter
In the heart of the grieving woman
  whose lover has gone?

A *moṭa gīt* always starts with metrically free singing of several *dohās*. Depending on the audience's interest, the singer's memory, and his repertoire, this can continue for a long time: there is no limit to the number of *dohās* that can be performed before the *gīt* itself. The text of the *dohās* is always poetic and emotional, and agrees in mood with the *gīt* that will follow. Frequently, as will be seen below, it has as its subject matter the *rāga* in which the composition is being performed. Every word or phrase is beautifully rendered to convey the image and emotion. Musically, this non-metrical singing of *dohās* must keep within the formal bounds of the *rāga* being sung. No two *dohās* are sung in the same way, and the singer is free to improvise and develop the musical material as he pleases to embellish the meaning and message of the poetic composition.

The songs sung by the Manganiyars have specific names. Announcing the name before the singing begins helps communication between the lead singer, other singers and accompanists, and the audience. There are six different categories of song names, which may overlap.

1) *Generic names for certain types of songs*. Some of these, relating to weddings, have already been mentioned. Others include *halāriyo* (childbirth song), *jacchā* (song addressed to the new mother), *gūṛho* (enigmatic religious song expressing an esoteric spiritual message), *phāg* (song sung during the Holi festival), *bhajan* (devotional song), *barsālo* (rainy season song), and *gaṇgaur* (song sung during the festival of the goddess Gangaur).

2) *Names which are the titles of particular songs*. These titles are often the names of gods and goddesses, heroes and heroines, poets or composers, other well-known characters, or regional castes. Names of aṇimals, plants, natural objects, man-made objects of different sorts, festivals, rituals, and relationship terms are also found as song titles.[8]

3) *Names referring to particular song topics*. For example, *kariyō* (camel song), *ghoro* (horse song), *kurjan* (song about the curlew – a messenger bird), or *kalālī* (song about a woman who sells wine). For each of these, there are subcategories with different names. There are thus songs about different kinds of camels: *kāchhī kariyo* (camel from the Kutch region), *loṭan kariyo* (camel who lies down), *rāte rānghai ro kariyo* (dark colored camel), *Haimal kariyo* (Haimal, the camel in the Dhola-Maru story).

Likewise, songs about horses include *banko ghoṛo* (spirited horse), *bhāṅvarjī ro ghoṛo* (husband/lover's horse), *Gangājal ghoṛo* (the horse Gangajal), etc. *Kalāḷī* songs break down into subcategories such as *Nāgaur rī kalāḷī* (wine seller from Nagaur), *rāṇā rī kalāḷī* (king's wine seller) or *Jhumā De kalāḷī* (the wine seller Jhuma De). With *kurjan* songs, the subcategories have to do with the content, sender, recepient or destination of the message. For example *bhāībahiṇ* (message between brother and sister), *Jaisalmer* (message to Jaisalmer), or *bhāṅvar milā do* (message asking husband/lover to come back).

4) *Names that refer to types of religious songs*. For example, *bhajan* (devotional song), *harjas* (song of praise), *helī* (invocation), *virahaṇī* (song of the soul yearning for God like a woman for her departed lover), *parbhātī* (morning song), *vāṇī* (words of the saints), and *fakīrī* (song of renunciation).

5) *Names consisting of the first line of the song*.

6) *Names derived from the titles and characters of folk narratives*. *Mārū*, for example, would be a song having to do with the popular Dhola-Maru love story.

Some of the songs bearing these kinds of names are also referred to by the name of the *rāga* in which they are habitually sung. Others, however, may have only a thematic title, as they are not sung in a particular *rāga*. Most children's songs and songs relating to life-cycle topics fall into this latter pattern.

In classical music, rendering a composition in a certain *rāga* involves two distinct melodic sections. *Sthāī* (the refrain section) moves in the lower middle octaves, *antarā* (the verse or stanza section) in the middle and upper octave. Very few songs in the Manganiyar tradition follow this pattern. Most of their compositions are limited to a range of one and a half octaves at the most, and there is no sectioning into *sthāī* and *antarā*. *Bandish* (melodic form) as known in the classical tradition is absent from their music.

Many songs consist of a single melodic line repeated over and over to accommodate a developing poetic theme. But within this limited compositional framework, there are many places where improvisation or additional melodic material can be added by a good musician. The musician can also elaborate metric matterns in a virtuoso style.

The *Rāga* Concept in Manganiyar Music

The Manganiyar's repertoire of *rāgas* differs from that of North Indian classical music. Some *rāga* names – Kalyan, Jog, Paraf, Sindhi Bhairavi, Bilawal, Todi, Salang (Sarang) – resemble those of certain classical *rāgas*. However, with the exception of Sindhi Bhairavi, these *rāgas* do not have the same characteristics as the classical *rāgas*.

Some *rāgas* of regional origin (Sorath, Des, Maru, Pahadi) are shared by both traditions. They are, however, *rāgas* which play a minor role in classical music, where they are used only for the *chhoṭā khayāl* genre or the semi-classical genres of *ṭhumrī, ghazal, dādrā* and *bhajan*. There are a few true classical *rāgas* in the Manganiyar repertoire, such as Asa and Dhani, but they are rarely performed. Finally, there are *rāga* names (Suhab, Sameri, Birvas, Mangh, Khamayachi) which are not found in the classical tradition at all. Some of these *rāgas* exist in the classical tradition, but are known there by other names. Khamaychi, for instance, also known as Khamaji, is the Khamaj of classical music. It is sung by the Manganiyars when they lead a wedding procession or welcome guests.[9] Several *rāgas* of the Manganiyars (Rano, Sasvi, Sindhi Bhairavi, Mangh, Kohiyari) are of Sindhi origin.

Entirely absent from the Manganiyar repertoire is *rāga* Mand, a popular *rāga* of folk origin that has become incorporated into the classical North Indian repertoire. This is especially surprising in view of the fact that the Jaisalmer region may have been this *rāga's* place or origin. Mand is known in Rajasthan, but is associated with the Hindu Dholi singers rather than with the Manganiyars.

In classical Indian music, *rāgas* are defined by at least ten elements, the most important of which are the sequence of ascending and descending notes (*āroha-āvaroha*), notes defined as consonant or dissonant (*samvādī-vivādī*), characteristic repetitions of certain notes (*pakaṛ*), and characteristic end phrases (*nyās*). In rendering their *rāgas*, the Manganiyars observe these rules, but they do not have a theoretical understanding of notes and intervals. Though they use the seven-note scale of classical music, at the conceptual level they recognize only two notes: *dādar* (the tonic, corresponding to classical *sā*), and *āgor* (the fourth, or sometimes the fifth, corresponding to classical *ma* or *pa*). All other notes are explained by numbers. Their situation is similar to that of beginning students of classical music, who may have mastered some compositions, but do not understand the theory of the music.

The *dohās* sung by the Manganiyars as prelude to compositions are the key to understanding their general concept of *rāga* and the particular *rāgas* of their repertoire. Many of these *dohās* have the *rāgas* themselves as subject matter. Unlike the *lakṣaṇ gīts* ('trait songs') of the classical tradition, which provide verbal information about the *rāga*'s definition while demonstrating it musically, the Manganiyars' *dohās* only demonstrate. The text makes reference to the *rāga*, but deals with a wide range of poetic subject matter. Thus a *dohā* may be in praise of a *rāga*, about the time of day in which a *rāga* is sung, or about musicians and their patrons.

nadiyā meṅ Gangā baṛī, tīratha baṛo Kedāra
rūṅkha meṅ chandana baṛo, rāga Gūṇḍa Malhāra

Greatest of rivers is the Ganga,
of pilgrimage sites Kedarnath;
Greatest of trees is the sandalwood tree,
the greatest *rāga* Gund Malhar.

eka Bilāvala phājarakī, dūjī Bilāvala bepāra
tījī Bilāvala sāmakī, chauthī Bilāvala adharāta

One Bilaval is for the morning,
the second Bilaval for noon;
The third Bilaval is for evening time,
the fourth Bilaval for midnight.

Soraṭhiyo dūho bhalo,kapaṛo bhalo sufeda
ṭhakariyo dātā bhalo, ghuṛalo bhalo kumeta

Sorath as a couplet is good,
as is white cloth,
a patron who is generous
and a horse the color of lac.

As in the classical tradition, certain *rāgas* (Salang, Malhari) are especially associated with the rainy season, and rendered by *dohās* on this theme. Certain other *rāgas* are habitually rendered by *dohās* expressing wisdom, devotion or moral values. Among these are *rāgas* Asa, Todi, Kafi, Bhairavi and Sindhi Bhairavi. Bhairavi and Sindhi Bhairavi, two *rāgas* sung in the early morning hours, are deeply devotional in mood. *Dohās* in these ragas are especially associated with the symbolic theme of swans being drawn to the holy lake Mansarovar.

The most important kind of *dohā* about *rāgas* is that in which the *rāga* is personified as the heroine of a traditional epic or tale. Thus all *dohās* rendered for *rāga* Maru come from the Dhola-Maru love narrative.

> *Ḍholājī begā āvajo, Sāvana pelī tīju*
> *darapa mare dhana Māravī, dekha khivantī bīja*

> Come quickly, Dhola,
>   it's the third day of Savan;
> Your beloved Maru will die of fear,
>   seeing the lightning flash.

For *rāga* Sorath, the *rāga* most sung by the Manganiyars, there are two different narratives with a heroine by that name: the love story of Sorath and Rao Kangar, and the story of Sorath in the Beenjha narrative. *Dohās* from both are sung.[10]

> *Soraṭha mhe thane oḷakhiyā, jājhe jhūlāra meṅ*
> *jāne chamakī bijalī, gurale bādala meṅ*

> Sorath, I recognized you
>   in the midst of the large crowd;
> You were like a flash of lightning
>   in the middle of the thick clouds.

Some of the Manganiyars' special *rāgas* (Suhab, Sameri) are personified as heroines too, though there are no known narratives attached to these figures. *Dohās* for the *rāga* Rano come from the romantic tale of Mumal and Rano, popular in the neighboring Sindh region of Pakistan, and are in Sindhi rather than Rajasthani. *Dohās* for *rāga* Sasvi (also called Lodau) also come from a Sindhi narrative, the love story of Sasi and Punnu.

Finally, there are *rāgas* for which no particular *dohās* or *dohā* subject matter are used. Jog, Birhas, Tilang, Paraj, Kamod, Puriya, Kalingada, Pahadi, Kedara, Bhup, Des, Shyam Kalyan and Durga Kalyan are examples of these.

There is a connection between certain *rāgas* of the Manganiyars and certain kinds of songs. This connection is especially obvious in the case of *rāgas* (e.g., Suhab, Sameri, Sorath, Maru, Rano, Sasvi, Asa) whose very names indicate a particular subject matter. What this suggests is a process whereby simple, non-*rāga* melodies gradually find a place in the Manganiyars' *rāga* repertoire. Songs originally from the women's tradition or from the world of children become adopted by the male professionals, who then render them as *rāga*-based compositions.[11] The way this is done is to begin with a *dohā* in a *rāga* close to the melody of the song, then to perform the song in that *rāga*. Different musicians will take the same song and develop it in terms of different *rāgas*.

Competent musicians can render *dohās* in any *rāga*. This is not done much with *dohās* that specifically mention a *rāga* name, but many *dohās* can move from one *rāga* to another. The same is true of many types of song, especially devotional songs like *harjas*. As many Manganiyars serve patrons in both Rajasthan and Sindh, they are adept at performing such songs in the *rāgas* of both regions.

Finally, there is the question of the relationship between the Manganiyars' folk *rāgas* and the *rāgas* of the classical tradition. The core of the Manganiyars' music was developed in the context of village and *jāgīrdār* life-cycle ceremonies, and is basically 'Marvari', with an admixture of 'Sindhi'. The royal courts, where classical 'Hindustani' music was cultivated, had little or nothing to do with patronage of the Manganiyars. However, there were two ways in which the Manganiyars had some musical contact with the courts. First, some families accompanied court musicians as percussionists. At the Jodhpur court, this was usually the role of the Raj Damanis, but at the Jaisalmer court, there was at least one Manganiyar family in regular service. Secondly, Manganiyars often accompanied the prostitute singing women who travelled around with armies. Through these contacts, they were exposed to *rāgas* of the classical tradition, some of which (e.g., Durga, Bhup, Durga Kalyan, Shyam Kalyan, and different forms of Todi) became part of their repertoire.

Rhythmic Patterns in Manganiyar Music

There are two main rhythmic patterns in Manganiyar music: *kalvāṛā* (a rhythm of 8 beats or *mātrās*) and *tīntār* (a rhythm of 7 beats or *mātrās*). In classical music, the corresponding patterns would be *kaharvā* (8 beats) and *chāchar, rūpak* or *addhā dīpchandī* (all 7 beats). Some Manganiyars use *jhaptāl* (a 10-beat pattern) or *dīpchandī* (a 14-beat pattern), though only with certain compositions. *Dādrā*, the 6-beat rhythmic pattern of classical music, is well known to the Manganiyar musicians, but they have very few compositions in it.

Manganiyars use rhythmic patterns as the basis for extremely elaborate improvisation. Excellent percussion accompaniment (on the *ḍholak*) is always very important for a successful performance. A good percussionlist is expected to follow all the rhythmic nuances of the lead vocalist or instrumentalist, while at the same time maintaining the fixed rhythmic pattern.

Though many of the terms just used here are the same as those in the classical tradition, there is a major difference. The rhythmic patterns of classical music, called *tāl*, are consistently cyclical, with the point at which the melodic composition and rhythmic accompaniment come together (*sam*) occurring with absolute, repetitive regularity. In addition, different sections of the *tāl* are defined as *khālī* (empty) or *bharī* (full), depending on whether the leading beats are light or heavy; these marked beats serve to further establish the rhythmic cycle. Thus *tīntāl*, the most common classical *tāl*, consists of 16 beats divided into sections of 4 each. The first, second and fourth sections are designated as *bharī*, the third as *khālī*; when the *khālī* sound is heard, *sam* is always 9 beats away.

In the rhythmic patterns of the Manganiyars, there is also a point at which instrumentalist/vocalist and percussionist meet on a common stress. This point is referred to as *muddā* or *gur*. However, the point of convergence is not based on the principle of a regularly returning *sam*. If classical *tāls* are cyclical, the movement of Manganiyar rhythmic patterns can best be described as spiral.

The rhythmic patterns of Manganiyar music are not defined by the percussion accompaniment alone, but by an interplay between these rhythms and those created by the verbal text. It is the words and phrases of the refrain or first line (referred to as *mukhaṛā*) that dictate the rhythmic accompaniment by creating a certain pattern of stresses. Though not all songs sung by the Manganiyars have this *mukhaṛā* feature, all their *moṭā gīt* compositions do. The *mukhaṛā* and the spiral pattern of rhythmic stresses created by it are a distinguishing feature of Manganiyar music. By contrast, the community folk songs of the general population (especially women's folk songs) have a single, steady beat and a rhythmic movement that is straightforward and linear.

Manganiyars as Genealogists

It should be mentioned in conclusion that Manganiyars are not only musicians, but also keep the genealogies of their patron families. No Manganiyar is worthy of the name if he cannot remember and recount the history of 20 to 25 generations for each of his patron families. Patron families also have other genealogists, known as Bhats, who keep a written or oral record of each new-born child in the family. The Bhat comes around every two or three years, records all the new births, and leaves after receiving a suitable reward. But the Bhat is not in regular contact with his patrons for their life-cycle ceremonies. This role is played by the Manganiyars instead.

Nearly all marriages arranged by patrons need to have the sanction of the family's Manganiyar, who is taken to be an authority on marriage relations. Because of the complex rules of kinship and marriage, ascertaining what degrees of relation allow or prohibit marriage is extremely difficult. All the details involved in preventing "incest" within the caste or subcaste are the responsibility of the Manganiyar. This responsibility places him at a level higher than that of mere entertainer or ceremonial singer.

Life-passage ceremonies are not only rituals, but also help maintain the social structure. Birth, marriage and death are crucial events for every family. With birth, an heir comes into being; through a socially acceptable marriage union, the progeny obtains certain rights; at death, the heir succeeds his parents and takes over their property. No society can do without specific rules to govern family and inheritance. Modern societies have complex written laws, but these are a recent phenomenon.

In Rajasthan, the societal rules are medieval, and hardly touched by modern laws. The contradictions between modern laws and customary practice are many. For example, contemporary law provides girls with rights of succession and inheritance, but they are hardly operative in actual life. As long as Rajasthani rural society is able to maintain its traditional organization, the role of professional caste singers like the Manganiyars will persist. And as long as this role continues, their musical tradition has every chance of surviving, in some form or other. But the day Rajasthani society abandons its social traditions, the musical tradition will also wither. The Manganiyars live in and serve the desert region of Rajasthan, where modernity is coming only at a very slow pace. Manganiyar music therefore seems to have more chance than other musical traditions to continue existing in the future.

ENDNOTES

This paper presents the results of many years of field work on the Manganiyars. For their careful reading and suggestions on the final draft, I am grateful to Reis Flora, Joan Erdman and Karine Schomer.

1. Manganiyars follow the Hindu practice of avoiding marriage within one's subcaste, that of one's mother, or that of either grandmother. This rule is contrary to Islamic personal law, which allows cousin and cross-cousin marriage.
2. Sakar Khan lists his paternal ancestors as follows: Chuhad (Sakar Khan's father), Nabho, Mithu, Bhano, Ridmal, Salemo, Appo, Tajo, Mirkha, Babar.
3. Khangar Khan (Bhungar Khan's father), Khano, Naggo, Alladan, Aso, Gullo (Gulle Khan), Nirbhavo, and Hafat.
4. Sadi Khan (his father), Dhuloji (Dhulo), Piroji, Motiji, Alladin, Bhupalji, Karamchand, Suroji, Hiroji.
5. Similar all-night singing sessions are also held during childbirth ceremonies and when a child's hair is cut for the first time. A night-long musical wake also follows the completion of death ceremonies. The same kinds of songs are sung on all three occasions.
6. The difference between the classical *rāga* system and the concept of *rāga* in folk traditions will be discussed below.
7. These tales are told in prose interspersed with musical episodes, some of which become independent songs.
8. Examples of song titles: *gorbandh, dhumālṛī, madkar, araṇī, hichakī, kachhavāī, rāydhaṇ, kāchhabiyo, Savāī Singh ro soḷo, Dharam Singh rī bhāvan, luṇāgar, ḍoro, chiramī, miṇiyāro, nāgjī, riṛmal, bālochaṇ, Lākho-Phūlāṇī, jheḍar, paṇihārī, helo, sokaṛlī, Javāhar Singh rī bhāvan*.
9. The word *khamā* derives from Sanskrit *kṣamā* (mercy). In the expression *khamā ghaṇī* ('have great mercy [on me]'), it is used in Rajasthan as a respectful form of address for older persons or persons of higher status. The text of a song in *rāga* Khamayachi elaborates on this salutation.
10. Sorath is also the name of a region (Saurashtra in Gujarat) and of a poetic meter similar to the *dohā*.
11. The song "*Nimbūṛo*" presented above is an example of this.

CONTINUITY OF TRADITION IN THE MUSIC OF NATHDVARA: A PARTICIPANT-OBSERVER'S VIEW

ANNE-MARIE GASTON

Compared with contemporary artistic traditions in the west, the arts of India are heavily influenced by religion. Until recently, the situation was reminiscent of Europe prior to the Renaissance. Even today, the content of India's classical arts is taken largely from Hindu religious texts, and many current performance genres evolved from religious rituals. They are now performed frequently in most of the large metropolitan centers, or sent abroad as ambassadors of Indian culture (Gaston 1983a:297), yet their adaptation to the concert stage has taken place only in the 20th century.

While the setting for classical performance arts has thus shifted away from temples and other religious venues to the theatrical stage, film and television screens, some remnants, or even large portions of the religious heritage have been carried over into these secular contexts. In some cases, new religious rituals have even been introduced. Thus in most Odissi and Bharata Natyam dance recitals today, public worship (*pūjā*) is performed to an icon placed on the stage. Worship of the icon has recently been incorporated into the choreography of the opening dance as well. While some dancers questioned this innovation, most felt it was important. They rationalized that audiences had come to expect it (Gaston: 1990a). This is but one example of the growing trend whereby religious content is being manipulated by artists and the demands of audiences rather than following traditional patterns (Ahmad 1984:7-8).

In the current situation, it is increasingly difficult to distinguish the traditional religious heritage from recent accretions. This difficulty is aggravated by the increasing scarcity of arts still performed in their traditional contexts by hereditary specialists (Gaston 1983a, 1990b, Marglin 1985:28-29, Neuman 1980). It is therefore of particular interest to examine an artistic tradition which exists in a temple context still largely unmodified by outside influences. The music played in centers of worship of the Vallabhacharya or *puṣṭimārg sampradāy* (sect)[1] is such a tradition - one that continues to be a major component of their religious observances.

For the Vallabhacharya *sampradāy*, founded in 1494 A.D. by Vallabhacharya, the Shri Nathji shrine in Nathdvara, Rajasthan is one of the most important (Barz 1976:27). All the centers of worship of the Vallabhacharya *sampradāy* are called *havelī*, because they are modeled after the *havelī* or large manor house typical of the royal houses of Rajasthan. Although *havelī* is more precise, the term temple is often used interchangeably to describe a building that houses an image venerated by the sect. The music played in the sect's temples is called *havelī sangīt*.

The presence of music in the Shri Nathji *havelī* in Nathdvara is mentioned in eight earlier scholarly works (Tod 1978, Skelton 1973, Barz 1976, Jindel 1976, Maduro 1976, Talwar and Krishna 1979, Verdia 1982 and Ambalal 1987), but none deals in detail with the music and its role in temple ritual. Tod, writing in the 19th century, supplied the earliest account of Nathdvara in English, but as he did not gain entry to the temples, he does not mention music or its role in worship. Jindel gives the most accurate comments on the role of music in worship, although her remarks are cursory. Verdia mentions the musicians but does not describe the context in which the music was presented. Barz provides an excellent account of the historical background of the Vallabhacharya *sampradāy* and of the main composers of its musical tradition, known as the *aṣṭacchāp*. However, he is not concerned with the current practices of the Vallabhacharya *sampradāy*, or the context of music today. The miniature paintings illustrated in Ambalal are invaluable as historical documents for showing where the music was played and the type of instruments; however, he does not include comparisons with the present-day situation. Skelton, Maduro, and Talwar and Krishna concern themselves entirely with the tradition of painting and *pichhvāī* making, and therefore refer to the music only incidentally.[2]

The focus of this study is on what the music and musicians of Nathdvara can tell us about the functioning of temple music traditions in India and how these contexts can influence performance. In it, I have sought to document the role of music in the Vallabhacharya *sampradāy havelīs* of Nathdvara, in particular the Shri Nathji shrine, and what the current state and prospects of the tradition are. I have also examined who the musicians are, how they are recruited, what their financial status is, and what level of commitment their musical profession requires.

Most of the information presented here was obtained by interviews and observations in the course of eight visits to Nathdvara between 1981 and 1987. I was first introduced to the music of Nathdvara in 1970, when I began to study the *pakhāvaj* (a two-headed barrel drum) with Guru Purushottam Das, the hereditary *pakhāvajī* (*pakhāvaj* player) in the Shri Nathji temple at Nathdvara, a post that had been held by his family for four generations. Between 1957 and 1981, when he retired and returned to Nathdvara, he taught in Delhi at two music and dance institutions, Bharatiya Kala Kendra and Kathak Kendra, and obtained national and international recognition as one of India's leading *pakhāvaj* players.[3]

My research began as a project to collect and record the music of Guru Das (Gaston 1983b).[4] It soon became evident that to fully appreciate this tradition, I would have to study it in its context, during the religious rituals in the Shri Nathji temple.

The Vallabhacharya *sampradāy* is generally exclusive and closed to outsiders.[5] Through the influence of Guru Das, I was initiated by the present spiritual head of the Shri Nathji temple, His Holiness the Tilkayat,[6] Maharaj Shri Govind Lal, and granted permission to visit the Shri Nathji *havelī* and take *darśan* with the devotees.

The Tilkayat personally conducted the initiation ceremony,[7] which was held in his palace, Moti Mahal, part of the *havelī* complex that also contains Shri Nathji's image.[8] It was very simple. First, I was required to give a small donation. Then, while kneeling in front of the Tilkayat, I was asked to repeat after him the words "*Śri Kṛṣṇa śaraṇam mama*" (Shri Krishna is my refuge). Finally, the Tilkayat presented me with some betel and a *tulsī* necklace (*kaṇṭhī*), which I was to wear at all times.

After this first initiation, I was only allowed to enter the Shri Nathji temple once, at the time of the *Rāj Bhog darśan* (see below). The next year I was initiated again by one of the Tilkayat's sons and given free access to the *havelī*. On both occasions, the ceremony was performed in the evening around 8:30 P.M., one of the two times of day at which the Tilkayat is available to meet devotees (10:30-11:30 A.M. and 8:00-9:00 P.M.). Other devotees were present and several made small donations to the Tilkayat in cash, kind or in the form of their own poems describing Krishna. The atmosphere was always relaxed.

By virtue of having been initiated by the Tilkayat, I was also granted access to the other two *havelīs* under his direct control: Navanitapriyaji (which is in the same compound as Shri Nathji) and Madanmohanji. I was also allowed access to five Vallabhacharya *sampradāy havelīs* at Nathdvara administered by other families: Banamaliji, Jamunaji, Govindraiji, Kalyanraiji, and Gopallaji (see Fig. 1).

The only *havelī* I could not enter was Vitthalnathji, the second largest in Nathdvara, which is controlled by another spiritual head, Maharaj Kalyanrai, and his two brothers, Shri Gokulutsav and Shri Devkinand.[9] To visit this temple, I was required to get special permission directly from Maharaj Kalyanrai. It was refused in 1983, but granted with no difficulty in 1985. I attribute this change of heart to the fact that Kalyanrai had witnessed one of my dance performances for the Tilkayat a few months earlier and was convinced of my sincerity by its devotional content.[10] I have therefore been able to enter all of the temples and observe the role music plays in each one.

Background: The Vallabhacharya *Sampradāy*

The Vallabhacharya *sampradāy* that built the Shri Nathji *havelī* is a Vaishnava sect that worships Shri Nathji, the form of Krishna as a child lifting Mount Govardhan (Vaudeville 1980:6). Braj (the Vrindaban-Mathura area) was the center of the cult for nearly 200 years, but in 1670 the image was transported to Nathdvara, where it was installed in 1672. The town of Nathdvara was created by the arrival of Shri Nathji. It developed near the village of Sirnar, about 20 miles from Udaipur (Tod 1978:I,415-422; Richardson 1979:73).

The families of many of the musicians who still perform in the temples accompanied the image from Braj. Even today there is a continuous exchange of musicians between Braj and Nathdvara, both important centers of Krishna worship. The cultural links with Braj are close, and one can find remnants of Braj culture in Nath-

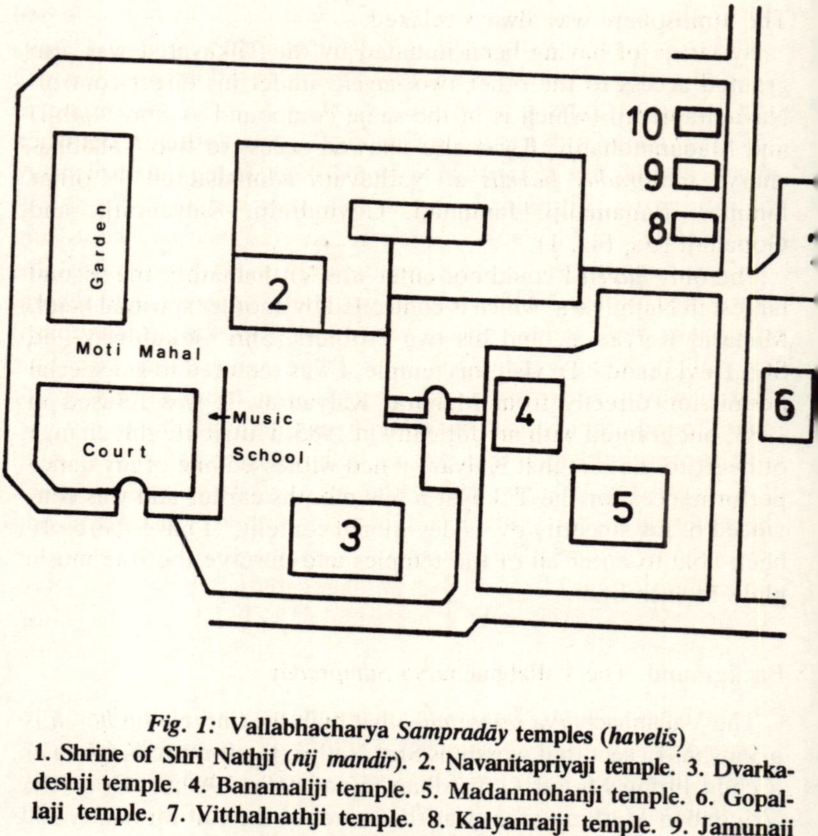

Fig. 1: **Vallabhacharya *Sampradāy* temples (*havelis*)**
1. Shrine of Shri Nathji (*nij mandir*). 2. Navanitapriyaji temple. 3. Dvarkadeshji temple. 4. Banamaliji temple. 5. Madanmohanji temple. 6. Gopallaji temple. 7. Vitthalnathji temple. 8. Kalyanraiji temple. 9. Jamunaji temple. 10. Govindraiji temple.

dvara, some of which have died out in Braj. The connection is particularly evident in the music, the songs sung in the temple being largely in the Braj dialect (Braj Bhasha), the literary language of the 16th century.

Various reasons are given for the departure of the image from Braj. The most popular is that in 1670, fearing the iconoclastic zeal of the emperor Aurangzeb, Vallabhacharya's son and heir, Vitthalnath, and hundreds of his followers were forced to flee with the image of Shri Nathji (Tod 1978:I, 415-422).[11] According to Tod, the image took refuge in Chaupasni, near Jodhpur, but when the local ruler felt he could no longer risk incurring the displeasure of Aurangzeb, Vitthalnath and his followers were forced to leave. Fortunately, the Maharaja of Mewar answered their call for asylum and sent troops to conduct them safely to the borders of his territories. Not all of the original party left, however, and several musicians were among those who decided to stay in Chaupasni (Jindel 1976:45, Verdia 1982:50). Their connection with Shri Nathji was never severed and several generations later some of them found employment in the temples of Nathdvara.[12]

The present head of the sect, the Tilkayat, Shri Maharaj Govind Lal, traces his ancestry to the founder, Vallabhacharya, through his eldest grandson, Giridhar. Giridhar's father, Vitthalnath, had seven sons, and the descendants of each control separate Vallabhacharya *sampradāy* establishments located all over India (Barz 1976:52-55). The Tilkayat is pre-eminent over all of them. Thus, even though the Shri Nathji *havelī* is administered by a temple board, the Tilkayat still determines much of what goes on.[13]

The essential ingredients of worship in the Shri Nathji *havelī* are common to many Krishna temples: *bhakti* or personal surrender to God (Chatterjee 1981:115-131), and *sevā* or service (Barz 1976:46-52; Hardy 1983:12-31; Parekh 1943:237-240). Shri Nathji's devotees share his daily routine by coming to see him at specific times. These occasions are known as *darśan* (literally 'seeing'). There is no English equivalent for the word *darśan*, because it implies not only that the worshipper observes the deity (or great person), but that the god transmits some part of his holiness to the beholder (Eck 1985:6-7).

All the activities in the Vallabhacharya *sampradāy* temples at Nathdvara revolve around preparing the deity for *darśan* and honoring him with objects of aesthetic pleasure. All the work in the temple is regarded as *sevā* to Shri Nathji, and music, performed by a professional group of musicians from a small number of hereditary families, is one of the principal components of religious worship in the temple,[14] taking place up to 17 times a day: before and during the eight periods when Shri Nathji may be seen by his devotees, and as the last ritual at night when Shri Nathji is put to sleep (see Table 1).

Havelī Sangīt

All the music performed during worship in the temples of Nathdvara is referred to as *puṣṭimārg bhakti sangīt*, or *havelī sangīt*. The temple musicians state that *havelī sangīt* is closely related to the classical *dhrupad-dhamār* form of music. Srivastava, in her book on *dhrupad*, agrees with this. She states that in the late 15th century, around the time the Vallabhacharya *sampradāy* was founded, and contemporaneous with the *bhakti* revival, *havelī sangīt* evolved from the *dhrupad* form in response to the need for religious music in the *havelīs*. Hence the name, *havelī sangīt* (*havelī* songs) (Srivastava 1980:131).

Havelī sangīt as performed today in Nathdvara is a religiously inspired genre and places a greater emphasis on enthusiasm and devotion than on musical intricacy. The formal setting provided by royal courts, with their lavish patronage and discerning audiences, gave *dhrupad-dhamār* the impetus to develop greater complexity Audiences devoted their full attention to the appreciation of this music (Wade 1979:159-179). This is quite unlike the situation at the Shri Nathji temple, where music is only one of several forms of devotional offerings made simultaneously. *Dhrupad-dhamār* is more acceptable for the concert stage, where aesthetic considerations are more important. Furthermore, lack of reliance on devotional context allows *dhrupad-dhamār* songs to be appreciated by a wider audience. While the richness of the *dhrupad-dhamār* tradition has attracted exponents from outside hereditary families, singing *havelī sangīt* has not (Owens 1983:161, 163-165).

From all accounts, the audiences of the courts not only expected excellence, but also demanded new forms (Ahmad 1984:97; Owens 1983:159; Prajnananda 1973:80-84; Srivastava 1980:22). However, unlike *darbārī dhrupad*, the branch of *dhrupad* that was patronized by the courts, *havelī sangīt* continued to be more conservative in content and technique. Many of the older styles of vocal and percussion music have been preserved in temples or in other religious contexts long after they have disappeared from the repertoire of court musicians (Seetha 1981:21-22). *Havelī sangīt* is a striking example of this phenomenon.

Although *havelī sangīt* and *dhrupad-dhamār* share many of the same characteristics, *havelī sangīt* as performed in the temples of Nathdvara is simpler and more straightforward. The temple musicians stressed the emphasis *havelī* places on the text. This is in contrast to *dhrupad-dhamār*, where the text is subordinated to the music (Srivastava 1980:46).

According to the Nathdvara musicians, the chief structural difference between the two styles lies in the use of *ālāp* (development of the melodic line where the rhythm is apparently free) (Saxena 1981:130-134, 145-152; Widdess 1981:167-168). *Havelī sangīt* when sung in the Nathdvara temples only occasionally uses *ālāp*. On those occasions when I have heard *havelī sangīt* sung in concert situations, the *ālāp* occurs in the middle of the song. In *dhrupad-dhamār*, *ālāp* is featured at the beginning of most pieces and can be as long or longer than the rhythmic rendering of the text (Srivastava 1980:47, 58).

The purpose of *havelī sangīt* is to stir the imagination and devotion of the worshipper, and thus it can not be judged by the same criteria as *dhrupad-dhamār* or other strictly performance music. The songs are delivered in a robust, up-tempo style suited to the frenetic atmosphere of public *darśans*. However, we should not dismiss the skill of musicians trained in the environment of the Nathdvara temples, as evidenced, for example, in the person of Guru Das.

Music has been part of worship almost from the beginning of the Vallabhacharya *sampradāy*. Their traditions recount that Vallabhacharya initiated four poet-singers to sing the praises of Shri Krishna: Kumbhandas in 1500, Surdas in 1511, Krishnadas in 1512 and Paramanandadas in 1521. Though Vallabhacharya encouraged singing in the first Shri Nathji temple on Mount Govardhan, which was completed in 1520, it was not until the Tilkayatship of his son Vitthalnath (1531-1586) that music was formally integrated as part of worship (Barz 1976:50). Vitthalnath initiated four more poet-singers: Nandadas, Govindasvami, Chhitasvami and Chaturbhuj. These four musicians, along with the four initiated by Vallabhacharya, became known as the *aṣṭachhāp* ('the eight seals'), and their compositions form the core of the devotional music in the Shri Nathji *havelī*. Each is considered the pre-eminent, though definitely not the exclusive composer for one of the *darśans* (see Table 1; also Dallapiccola 1982:188-195, Jindel 1976: 158).[15] Many of the songs presently sung in the Shri Nathji *havelī* are by other composers, but those of the *aṣṭachhāp* are still regarded as exceptional in their literary and devotional merit.

The *aṣṭachhāp* poets composed out of religious fervor, to recount and share the ecstasy they experienced. Their songs describe the events surrounding Krishna's life and are taken from the *Bhāgavata Purāṇa* (Mulji 1865:48-77; Readington 1983; Sheth 1984:43-87). While the *Bhāgavata Purāṇa* is written in Sanskrit, however, the songs of the *aṣṭachhāp* are in Braj Bhasha, as it was believed to be more appropriate to praise Krishna in his own language (Barz 1976:97). The resurgence of the Vaishnava *bhakti* movement at the time ensured that their songs would become widely disseminated (Barz 1976:103-256; Srivastava 1980:22; Bryant 1978:4-5). The importance of the *aṣṭachhāp* poets, and an indication that their poetry still holds real significance for devotees, is reflected in the fact that even today, most of the townsfolk in Nathdvara can readily recall their names.

It is a fundamental belief of the Vallabhacharya *sampradāy* that all beings have the potential for a unique experience with Krishna (Marfatia 1967; Barz 1976:87-90; Chatterjee 1981:116-122). First, however, they must be receptive and believe that the stories of the *Bhāgavata Purāṇa* are the result of divine inspiration. The poetry in the songs awakens this potential by helping devotees visualize actually participating in the life of Krishna. Language and music create the scene and the listeners are once again transported to the sacred land of Braj (Barz 1976:98-100; Bryant 1978:3). On the rare occasions when the temple singers perform outside the temple, they speak the text of the song before it is sung, so that the audience can savor both the poetry and its meter when integrated into the music.[16]

Five instruments accompany *havelī sangīt* in the Shri Nathji temple: *bīn, pakhāvaj, sārangī, tānpūrā* and harmonium.[17] The *tānpūrā* is used only by the solo singer, generally in the early morning to wake up Shri Nathji or in the evening to lull him to sleep. Ambalal provides an illustration of a painting dated 1883 of the *tānpūrā* being played along with other instruments during *darśan* (1987:134, 158), and Jindel also mentions that it is played along with the other instruments (1967:75). However, I observed that when other instruments were played, the harmonium replaced it. The *bīn* is played unaccompanied[18] two or three times a day: when Shri Nathji wakes up in the morning, after his afternoon nap, and when he retires at night. *Bīn* and *pakhāvaj* are played without vocal accompaniment while Shri Nathji eats his mid-day meal, but are more frequently used to accompany *havelī sangīt* during the pre-*darśan* and post-*darśan* periods (see Table 1, below). Since Nathdvara is especially known for *havelī sangīt, bīn* and *pakhāvaj* (Das 1911; Das 1983), it is likely that *sārangī* and harmonium, both versatile instruments for accompaniment, were introduced into the music of Nathdvara at a later date, and may have entered the temple via performances for the Tilkayat.

During the month of Phalgun (February-March), in which the festival of Holi is celebrated (Ambalal 1987:27), a genre of song heavy with erotic content, the *rasiyā*, is sung by specialists known as *rasiyās*, who are originally from Braj (Growse 1979:95-96, 183). *Rasiyās* are sung during *darśan* as well as at other, unfixed times in the *darśan* hall (*ḍol tibārī*), and throughout the temple complex. They are accompanied by the *daph*, a spherical drum about one meter in circumference (Jindel 1976:159). For the whole month of Phalgun, the *daph* is played during *darśan* in the shrines of Shri Nathji and Navanitapriyaji, supplementing the other instruments. In the Shri Nathji *havelī*, only hereditary *rasiyās* play the *daph*, while in Navanitapriyaji, two sons of that temple's *kīrtankār mukhiyā* (head musician) often perform this function.[19]

Darśan in the Vallabhacharya *Sampradāy Havelīs* of Nathdvara

All the Vallabhacharya *sampradāy havelīs* in Nathdvara are normally open seven or eight times a day for *darśan* (see Table 1). The most widely attended are those in the Shri Nathji *havelī*. Devotees go to see and be seen by Shri Nathji's luminous, white, crescent-shaped eyes with downward looking pupils. His gaze emphasizes that he watches over his devotees as they take shelter beneath Mount Govardhan (Barz 1976:20-22; Vaudeville 1980:6), which he holds in his left hand. Shri Nathji is said to be 11 years and 60 days old. As he is a child, the ceremonies prior to

***Table 1* : Timing of *Darśans* at the Shri Nathji Temple**

No.	*Darśan*	Approximate time	Duration	Activity	Music	Main Poet
1	*Mangal*	4:00-5:00 A.M. (winter) 5:00-6:00 A.M. (summer)	30-40 minutes	the waking of Shri Nathji in the early morning	pre-*Mangal* : *bīn* unaccompanied, conch blown, 2 songs sung by *bīnkār* and/or *kīrtankār* *mukhīya* unaccompanied *Mangal* : 1-2 songs sung by *kīrtankār* *mukhīya* and *bīnkār* unaccompanied	Paramanandadas
2.	*Śṛṅgār*	7:00-7:30 A.M.	10 minutes	dressing Shri Nathji	pre-*Śṛṅgār:* all musicians except *bīnkār* in *kīrtankār galī*, 2-3 songs sung at the same time as *bīnkār* plays in *darśan* hall *Śṛṅgār*: 1 song sung by all musicians	Nandadas
3.	*Gvāl*	8:00-9:00 A.M.	10 minutes	Shri Nathji leads the cows to graze	pre-*Gvāl*: 1 accompanied song, then only *bīn* and *pakhāvaj* *Gvāl* : 1-3 songs	Govindasvami
4.	*Rāj Bhog*	10:00-11:00 A.M.	1 hour	Shri Nathji eats his mid-day meal	pre-*Rāj Bhog* : *bīn* and *pakhāvaj* 11 songs *Rāj Bhoj* : 1 song	Kumbhandas

5.	*Utthāpan*	3:15-4:45 P.M.	10 minutes	awakening Shri Nathji from his mid-day nap	pre-*Utthāpan* : *bīn* unaccompanied conch blown, 1 song sung by *bīnkar* or *kīrtankār mukhiyā* unaccompanied *Utthāpan* : 1 song sung by *bīnkar* and *kīrtankār mukhiyā* unaccompanied, Sometimes *bīnkār* plays	Surdas
6.	*Bhog*	4:00-4:15 P.M.	10 minutes	Shri Nathji's afternoon meal	pre-*Bhog* : *bīn* unaccompanied, 1 song *Bhog* : *bīn*, *sārangī* and *pakhāvaj*, and/or all musicians sing 1 song	Chaturbhuj
7.	*Āratī* or *Sandhyā*	5:00-5:30 P.M.	30-45 minutes	Shri Nathji leads the cows home	pre-*Āratī* : 1 song sung by all musicians *Āratī* : 1 song sung by all musicians	Chittasvami
8.	*Śayan*	6:00-7:00 P.M.	10 minutes	putting Shri Nathji to sleep	pre-*Śayan* : 3 songs *Śayan* : 1 song sung by *kīrtankār mukhiyā* or *bīnkar* accompanied by *tānpūrā*, *bīn* unaccompanied played under *dhruv bārī*	Krishnadas

darśan are modified to suit his age, but being also a god, other more adult rituals are also observed. As a *svarūp* (a literal embodiment of the Lord), Shri Nathji is regarded as the divine entity, not merely a likeness (Eck 1985:34). Worship centers around presenting him with good food, decorating him in opulent clothes and singing songs in his honor.

While most of the townsfolk of Nathdvara report attending at least one *darśan* daily, pilgrims try to attend all of them. It is a full-time task just to attend those at the Shri Nathji temple, let alone those at the less important shrines. The first *darśan* of the day, somewhat surprisingly, occurs earlier in winter than in summer. This is explained on grounds that, when the days are shorter, the child Krishna goes to bed earlier and therefore, like his mortal counterparts, gets up earlier. Other *darśans* are fairly evenly spaced, except for a period of a few hours in the early afternoon when Shri Nathji takes an afternoon nap.

Each *darśan* represents one of Shri Nathji's daily activities (see Table 1). At *Mangal* his devotees greet him just after he has awakened; in winter he appears wrapped in a blanket (*razāī*), while in summer he is covered only by a thin cloth (Jindel 1976:64). In the next *darśan, Śṛṇgār*, he appears in the fine clothes he will wear all day; the dress worn is appropriate to the season and there is great attention to detail (Talwar and Krishna 1979:9-10, 133; Ambalal 1987: 102, 110, 111, 112, 113, 114.). Each *darśan* period includes some visual symbol, in the form of particular toys and implements, by which worshippers can identify Shri Nathji's activities. For example at *Gvāl*, he is shown with a stick and cows as he leads the cattle off to graze. At *Rāj Bhog*, the fourth and most elaborate *darśan*, he receives the main meal of the day; this food becomes sanctified (*prasād*) and some portion of it is given to the temple employees later as payment for their service to the deity (*neg*) (Khare 1976:25). At *Śṛṅgār* and *Rāj Bhog*, Shri Nathji is honored as a prince, while *Gvāl* recalls his peasant origins in Braj.

The duration of each *darśan* varies according to how long the preparations take. *Rāj Bhog* is generally considered the most important of the eight *darśans*. On festival days such as Divali, unusually elaborate preparations are made for it. The huge numbers of devotees wishing to take *darśan* necessitate that it remain open considerably longer, often two or more hours. On such occasions, *Gvāl* (the *darśan* between *Śṛṅgār* and *Rāj Bhog*) will not be open. Instead, the priests perform it alone; even then, with the public absent, music is played. The temple is always closed for a few hours at mid-day. An extended *Rāj Bhog darśan* affects the later *darśans*, and usually results in *Bhog* and *Āratī* being combined. *Śayan darśan* is closed for six months of the year during the hot season when Shri Nathji sleeps out of doors.

During the festival of Annakut, which commemorates the occasion on which Krishna as Giriraj raised Mount Govardhan (Growse 1979:60, 81, 89, 300; Sheth 1984:30-33; Vaudeville 1980:1-6, Entwistle 1987:283),[20] huge quantities of food are prepared and mounds of rice fill the *darśan* hall (Tod 1978:I,436; Toomey 1984:147-171; Ambalal 1987:106-107, 141, 153, 160; Gaston 1990c). Late at night, at about 11:00 P.M., after Shri Nathji has eaten, devotees are allowed into the temple to see the food. This lasts well into the early morning, which results in *Mangal* the next day beginning later than usual. Because of uncertainty concerning the timing of *darśans*, particularly on festival days, pilgrims have to be alert and ready to rush to the temple. To ensure that they are aware of the *darśans*, announcements are broadcast over loudspeakers, while kettledrums (*naubat* and *naqqārā*) and *śahnāī* (a clarinet-like reed instrument) play from the *naubat khānā* (see below. More affluent pilgrims hire a guide whose duty is to come to their lodgings and keep them informed. Waiting for and attending all *darśans* can be both time-consuming and very tiring.

The *svarūp* of Shri Nathji is decorated by the head priests (*mukhiyās*), the only ones who have been granted permission by the Tilkayat to touch the image. Before they report for duty, they must bathe within the temple and exchange their clothes for clean ones, which they leave within the temple.[21] Devotees perform *sevā* in the various departments of the temple that specialize in producing the goods (garlands, *pān*, etc.) required for each *darśan* (Jindel 1976:113-120). The *sevāvālās*, who touch the articles that will later be offered to Shri Nathji, must follow the same bathing procedures as the priests. The running of the temple thus depends on the *sevā* that is performed by townsfolk as well as by pilgrims. Divali is a particularly important time for devotees, as the Tilkayat is usually in Nathdvara for this festival. Many families also come each year to spend the Dassehra (Eck 1983:174, Entwistle 1987:488) vacation working in the temple.

While the image in the Shri Nathji temple is being prepared, the devotees wait in the outer courtyard (*kamal chauk*) or the inner courtyard (*ratan chauk*) (See Fig. 2). The privilege of waiting in *ratan chauk* is given to those who have made a sizable donation to the temple (approximately Rs. 300 or more) or else is obtained through the good will of employees who help them past the guards whose duty it is to restrict entry to members of the Vallabhacharya *sampradāy* and maintain order in the temple. Guards include both soldiers belonging to the Tilkayat's personal army and *jhapaṭiyās* — men from town, either employed by the temple, or performing this function for a limited period as part of their *sevā*. Only *jhapaṭiyās* are stationed in front of the shrine, and it is their duty to keep pilgrims moving so that more may come in for *darśan*.[22] Soldiers, who are permanently employed, paid for their work, and not from Nathdvara, are always on duty at all three entrances to the temple. At night several of them sleep in small corridors on either side of the entry points. During the day they station themselves in strategic positions such as in front of the doors that guard the main *chauks*. They wear a military uniform and carry guns of ca. 1900 vintage, with fixed bayonets.[23]

The shrine is accessible through both *ratan chauk* and *kīrtankār galī* (the musicians' lane) (see Fig.2). If one is especially privileged, it is possible to wait in *kīrtankār galī*, a hallway about four yards wide that stretches the full length of the *darśan* room, through which devotees exit after viewing the image.[24] In *kīrtankār galī*, the musicians sing during the pre-*darśan* period, wait before going in for *darśan*, and store their instruments. The instruments are either hung on the wall or locked in special cupboards which also contain their turbans, song books and some of the *prasād* they receive from the temple. Hanging on the wall are four *bīns*, two to four *pakhāvajs*, and eight pairs of *jhāñjh* (cymbals). Interspersed between them are paintings of the child Krishna.

While the devotees wait for *darśan* to open, the musicians play and sing enthusiastically in *kīrtankār galī*. During this pre-*darśan* period, they sit informally and engage in what appears to be a spontaneous 'jam session'. The public is not allowed in, but visiting musicians, either from other Vallabhacharya *sampradāy* temples or professional musicians visiting Nathdvara, are admitted. For these pre-*darśan* periods I was allowed to sit with the musicians, but when the *bīn* player (*bīnkār*) played alone in the *darśan* room, he was the only musician admitted. At those times I had to make observations by peeping through the bars that divide *kīrtankār galī* from the *darśan* room. At the start of each *darśan*, the musicians have only a few seconds to pick up their instruments, and move rapidly via the door on the right side of Shri Nathji to their positions in front of the *svarūp*. As they did this, I would enter the *darśan* room from *kīrtankār galī*, through the doors that are normally the exit after *darśan*, and was therefore able to get in the front row. I was often assisted by the *jhapaṭiyās* and soldiers, who pulled me in and made sure I had a good view. The usual entrance is via *ratan chauk* (see Fig. 2).

The music begins just as the devotees rush into the hall. Visiting musicians who wish to sing while *darśan* is taking place enter with the regular musicians. Only male musicians can participate in the *darśan* singing. Permission for this honor is requested from the Tilkayat, and the men who receive it must wear the required dress of *angarkhī* (a long-sleeved jacket that fits tightly around the chest and falls loosely to waist level), *dhotī* and turban (Ambalal 1987:99, 152).

The musicians stand beside the image but do not touch it, or anything that will be offered to it. Therefore, unlike the priests and *sevāvālās*, they are not required to take a bath inside the temple. Instead, they bathe at home before reporting for duty, and need only do it once a day. The same rule – a general practice for all Hindu shrines – governs the devotees who want to enter the temple.

The musicians usually stand on both sides of the image, with the *kīrtankār mukhiyā* closest. The *sārangī* player sometimes sits and at other times rests against the wall, with one knee raised supporting the instrument. The *pakhāvaj* player either sits or stands with the drum slung from a cord around his neck.[25] The arrangement of the musicians is very flexible and there is much variation in the combinations used. Thus on special occasions, when several *pakhāvajīs* are present, two or three drums may be played simultaneously. The *bīn* is not always played, and the *bīnkār* sometimes sings instead. The *sārangī* player may also sing or play the harmonium.

If the *darśan* period is particularly long, as in the case of the Chhappan Bhog celebrations, the festival at which Shri Nathji is offered 56 varieties of foodstuffs (Talwar and Krishna 1979:140; Vaudeville 1980:1-2, Entwistle 1987:84, 162, 260), not all the

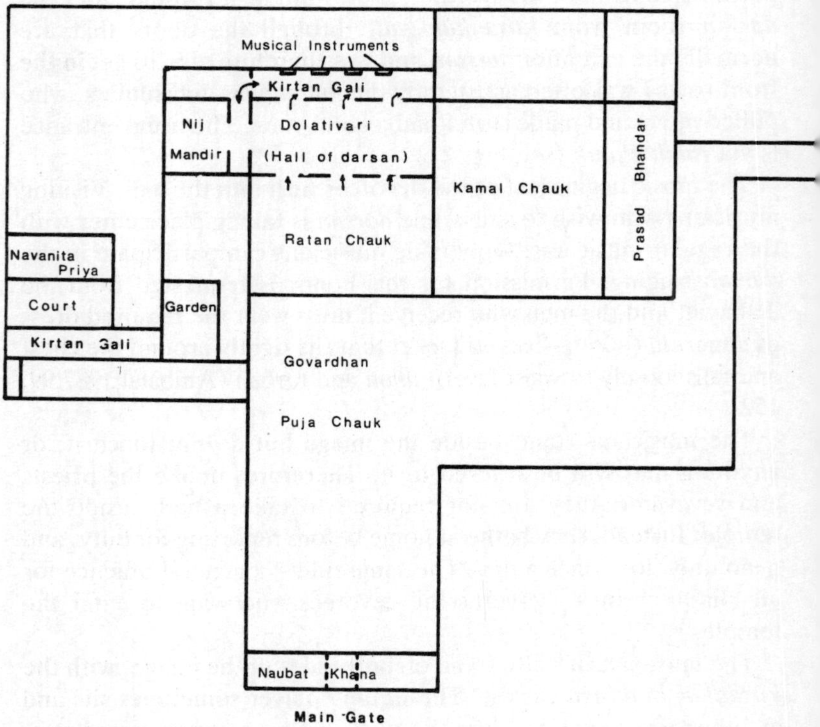

Fig. 2: **Detailed plan of the Shri Nathji temple (*havelī*)**

musicians stay for the entire musical presentation, which may last an hour and a half. Generally, most musicians are present for the first half of the *darśan*. Guru Das, as a senior musician, often left early, particularly during the month of Phalgun when, at the end of *Rāj Bhog*, the head priest and, if present, the Tilkayat and his family, throw colored powder (*gulāl*) at the devotees.[26]

The musicians usually finish playing well before *darśan* is over. They either wait in *kīrtankār galī* for the next pre-*darśan* period, standing pressed against the wall and cradling their instruments to avoid the devotees on their way out, or they hang their instruments on the wall and walk around the temple. When the doors in front of the image are shut, signifying the completion of *darśan*, all except musicians must vacate *kīrtankār galī*. The function of removing stragglers is carried out by the *jhapaṭiyās*, and the entrance door to *kīrtankār galī* is guarded either by one of them or by a soldier.[27] Within five minutes of *darśan* being closed, the musicians reassemble and begin to play for the next pre-*darśan*.

Playing or dancing in front of the image by visiting artists always precedes *Śṛṅgār darśan*, and requires prior permission from the Tilkayat. The usual procedure is to play or dance in his palace beforehand and then personally request from him the honor of performing in the *darśan* hall. At that time, a curtain hides Shri Nathji while he is being dressed for *Śṛṅgār darśan*. Only those people with special permission from the Tilkayat may watch and listen to the visiting artist; the maximum number I have seen present is 20. Most of the *kīrtankārs* come; occasionally one of them provides accompaniment on *sārangī*, harmonium, or even *tablā*, despite the fact that *tablā* is never played during *darśan*.[28]

At the beginning of *darśan*, the three purple wooden doors leading to the *darśan* room are unlocked and opened. This is the signal for the devotees to enter. The door closest to the image is reserved for women, and their space is divided from that of the men by a horizontal bar. The floor is made of wooden steps raised about six inches and about one yard wide. To some extent, this helps viewing, but the uneven surface can make balance uncertain. Within seconds the room is full and there is a seething mass of people pressing against each other. Small children are lifted up onto shoulders, and the old and infirm are carried or supported.

Prior to entering the *darśan* area, I noticed that several women had removed their silver anklets. I removed my head cloth, for fear it might be tightened around my neck as the crowds pulled, push and grabbed onto anything for leverage in their efforts to see Shri Nathji better. While the rush is intense, it is also somewhat orchestrated and helps augment the religious fervor. In the center of the crowd, which sways back and forth and sideways, one can easily become swept up in the collective emotion. It is the job of the *jhapaṭiyās* to maintain order, preventing devotees from being trampled and to keep the crowd moving. This is achieved by snapping long strips of cloth: a slight snap at the shoulder is the signal that your time is up and that you should move on to make way for others.[29]

While music is played for each *darśan*, it is practically impossible to hear it because of the noise of the devotees, shouting in ecstasy or pushing and jostling to get a closer look at the image. Many devotees are unaware that music is being played. This became apparent to me when a member of the Vallabhacharya *sampradāy*, a science research scholar in the Oxford college to which I am affiliated, expressed surprise at my topic of research. "How can you study music in the Nathdvara temple?" he asked. "I have taken *darśan*, and did not hear or notice any musicians."

During *darśan* the music may last anywhere from five minutes to one and a half hours, as is the case during Chhappan Bhog. However, *darśan* may continue long after the music has stopped. When the cloth on which Shri Nathji stands is folded, it is a signal for the music to end and for the musicians to walk off. *Darśan* may continue for another half hour, however, and if there are many devotees the priests may have to make several attempts to close the *darśan*, prevented each time by cries from the crowd.

The Musicians: Hereditary Position and Current Situation

Music is played regularly in three main areas of the Shri Nathji temple (see Fig. 2): in the *naubat khānā* or *naqqārā khānā* (the open platform above the main gate of the temple), within the inner temple in *kīrtankār galī*, and in *maṇī koṭa*, the area in front of the niche where Shri Nathji is installed (*nij mandir*). On festival days such as Holi and Divali, music is played throughout the temple complex, in *ratan chauk*, on the terrace in front of the adjoining Navanitapriyaji shrine, and in the garden behind Moti Mahal, the Tilkayat's palace which is also part of the *havelī* complex.[30]

Havelīs mimic many Mughal architectural features. One of these is the *naubat* or *naqqārā khānā* (Nath 1985:243),[31] where ceremonial music is played on kettledrums (*naqqārā* and *naubat*) and *śahnāīs* (Erdman 1978:357-359; Wade 1979:111-113; Singh 1981:9). All of these instruments were an integral part of the court tradition and were once used to rally troops to war, or draw attention to major events such as a royal birth. Even today, music from the *naubat khānā* in Jaipur's City Palace announces that it is noon (Erdman 1985:39). In Nathdvara, I often retreated to the *naubat khānā* while I waited for the gates of the shrine to open or to hear the military band of the Tilkayat's bodyguard, who assemble there during major festivals such as Janmashthami, the birth of Krishna (Jindel 1976:68-69). Perched high above the *havelī* complex, the *naubat khānā* affords an excellent view of both *sūraj pōl* (the third entrance gate) and *Govardhan chauk*, the first courtyard. Music is played there daily prior to *Rāj Bhog darśan*, to call the pilgrims to worship. On festival days it is played more frequently.

The various drums (*naubat, naqqārā, ḍhol*) and reed instruments (*śahnāīs*) are stored in the *naubat/naqqārā khānā*. Five *śahnāī* players and three drummers are employed by the temple. The musicians who play in the *naubat khānā* are all hereditary, and play the same instruments as their fathers, from whom they also received instruction. They form a separate groups from those who perform in the inner temple. The two groups do not intermarry, nor does one group learn the music of the other. One exception was Amrit Lal, the present *sārangī* player in the Shri Nathji temple, who studied this instrument with Daya Ram, the father of Bansi Lal, who now plays *śahnaī* in the *naubat khānā*.[32] On the several occasions on which I visited the *naubat khānā*, I noticed that some of the general servants of the temple were filling in by playing a simple beat on the *ḍhoḷ*.

All of the musicians who work in the *naubat khānā* live in the village of Sirnar, which existed before Nathdvara was founded. It seems likely, therefore, that the custom of *naubat khānā* was adopted by the temple after the installation of the image at Nathdvara. By contrast, many musicians who play inside the temple during *darśan* trace their ancestry to Braj, where the Shri Nathji temple had been before the migration to Rajasthan.

The musicians who play during *darśan* belong to seven families closely interlinked by marriage. Aside from musicians, these families include watch and clock repairers, tailors, building contractors, stenographers and farmers. The younger generation includes college graduates, medical doctors and businessmen. Clearly, the group exhibits the tendency to increasing education and diversification of employment which is common to contemporary Indian society as a whole.

The majority of the musicians are known by the generic name *kīrtankār*, and belong to the Kumavat caste. There are two groups of Kumavats: those of strictly Rajasthani origin and those who trace their ancestry to Braj, the Brajvasis. Not all Brajvasi musicians are Kumavats, however, for among them is also a family of Sanadhya Brahmins. While the Sanadhyas stay separate, the two branches of Kumavats intermarry.[33] The Brajvasis trace their families to various villages in Braj such as Gantholi (Entwistle 1987:144) and Karahala/Karhela (Growse 1979:74, 79; Entwistle 1987:87, 216, 268, 271, 383, 487). The majority arrived in Nathdvara at its foundation. Some, such as the family of Mathura Das, the former *kīrtankār mukhiyā* of the Shri Nathji temple, arrived at a later date, from Chaupasni. His two sons are presently employed in the Shri Nathji temple: Ram Das has succeeded his father as *kīrtankār mukhiyā*, and Amrit Lal, Ram Das's younger brother, is employed as the *sārangī* player.

Kīrtankār mukhiyās are highly regarded. They are appointed by the spiritual head in charge of each temple and traditionally chosen from among the *havelī* singers. The musicians report that selection is based on seniority, but in practice other factors such as their father's position, their talent and the Tilkayat's own preference decide who will hold this post. *Kīrtankār mukhiyās* decide which songs are to be sung in the temple and coordinate the music. They usually hold the song book and always lead the singing. For their seniority and added responsibility they receive more remuneration.

The number of musicians employed in each temple varies. In 1988 there were five *havelī* singers attached to the Shri Nathji temple, four to Navanitapriyaji, and one to Vitthalnathji. All of the singers played *jhāñjh*, two cymbals about eight inches in diameter which are held in either hand, played only during certain festivals and at certain prescribed times of the year (Ambalal 1987:107, 115). There was one *pakhāvaj* player in each temple, and only the Shri Nathji temple employed separate *bīn*, harmonium and *sārangī* players. The *bīnkār* of the Shri Nathji temple was required to play *bīn* only at specific times, and at other times sang *havelī*. The *kīrtankār mukhiyā* in the Vitthalnathji temple had to compensate for the lack of a permanent *bīnkār* there by combining the duties of singing *havelī* with playing *bīn*. Three or four other musicians also reported having received instruction on *bīn*.[34]

Many of the musicians have worked in several of the Nathdvara temples, including Vitthalnathji, even though it is administered separately. Examination of the succession in particular positions suggests that heredity is very important. Several recent replacements have involved sons following their fathers. The career of Guru Das, who was the honorary *pakhāvajī* of the Shri Nathji temple, is a case in point (Das 1911; Das 1983; Gaston 1989). His great-grandfather (Vallabhdas), his grandfather (Shankar), and his father (Ghanshyam) had all been *pakhāvajīs* in the Shri Nathji temple (see Figs. 3 and 4). Guru Das was only nine when his father died, and consequently the post fell to someone else. However, through the good will of the Tilkayat, he eventually regained his family's prerogative, occupying the post from 1932 to 1957, when he left to teach in Delhi.[35]

All the musicians reported that music was declining in importance at Nathdvara. The fact that it continues at all is a measure of the ritual role it plays in *darśan* (Parekh 1943:256-258). In some temples, it has practically disappeared. In 1985 two temples, Madanmohanji and Banamaliji, employed only one musician, whereas 25 years ago both had employed two, one to sing and one to play *pakhāvaj*. Two of the smaller temples, Kalyanraiji and Govindraiji, had informal arrangements whereby they employed musicians who worked at Shri Nathji and Navanitapriyaji, where all *darśans* must have musical accompaniment.[36] These musicians had to adjust their hours of work, rushing to the smaller temples between engagements at the larger ones. Consequently, music was usually presented only once a day at the smaller temples, most frequently at *Rāj Bhog*. Since these musicians played solo, they had to provide their own accompaniment by playing *jhāṅjh*, and on occasion, *pakhāvaj* as well. Singing or playing the *bīn* without rhythmic accompaniment is unknown in the musical tradition of Nathdvara, except when Shri Nathji is being awakened or put to sleep.

In the less endowed temples, posts today are occupied by older musicians. 25 years ago, when there were more positions available, the musicians in these smaller temples were younger and less experienced. This situation allowed them to do their daily practice and gain experience. At that time, the Kalyanraiji temple employed two musicians, Shyam Lal (*pakhāvaj*) and Radhakrishṇa (*havelī sangīt*). Both received their training on the spot and were then able to move to more lucrative and prestigious temples. Thus Radhakrishna left the Kalyanraiji temple 40 years ago to become *kīrtankār mukhiyā* of the Vitthalnathji temple, a post he held until his death in 1987. Since then his son, Bhanwar Lal, has assumed his duties, which include playing *bīn*. No other *havelī* singer has been appointed to the Vitthalnathji temple, even on a temporary basis.

The training of earlier generations of musicians usually included a period of employment in the smaller, less endowed temples, or in the Shri Nathji temple while seated in *kīrtankār galī* during the pre-*darśan* periods, or during the less important *darśans* such as *Gvāl*. Today, however, the children of the musicians attend school or college and are not available at a young age to devote the same time to playing in the temples. As a result, the youngest musicians in active service in the temples of Nathdvara are in their early 40s. With the cutting back of posts, there is less opportunity for younger artists to stay in the field while waiting for a good position to become vacant. Instead, most of the young men are working in shops where crafts are sold, some made by their own families and others by fellow *kīrtankārs*. It appears that more money is available for material goods than for nurturing and encouraging younger musicians to take up the profession.

Hours of Work and Remuneration for the Musicians

Music must be played for all *darśans* (See Table 1), and also while the priests are preparing the deity for *darśan* and while the deity is eating. The normal order of events is 8 *darśans* per day, coupled with 8 pre-*darśan* periods, and one post-*darśan* period at the end of the day, making a total of 17 times when music is required. Normally 7 of the 8 *darśans* are open to the public;[37] none of the pre-*darśan* periods are.

Except for festival days, *darśan* periods are short, the longest being *Rāj Bhog*, which usually takes 45 minutes to an hour. On festival days, however, such as Chhappan Bhog, *Rāj Bhog darśan*

Fig. 3: **The Musicians of Nathdvara, ca. 1911.**

Back row, L to R: (1) Jamnadas, holding *jhāñjh*, (2) Unidentified *sāraṅgī* player, (3) Raghunathji. Front row, L to R: (1) Arm of Govindram playing harmonium, (2) Ramnarayan, standing with arms crossed, (3) Manuji, playing *bīn*, (4) Gangadas, playing *tānpurā*, (5) Ghanshyam Das, playing *pakhāvaj*, (6) Jaikrishan, holding child, (7) Unidentified child. Gangadas was *kīrtankār mukhiyā* of Shri Nathji; Govindram succeeded him; Manuji, *bīnkār* of the temple, was originally from Chaupasni; Ramnarayan was *pakhāvajī* of Navanitapriyaji; Jamnadas, later *pakhāvajī* of Shri Nathji, adopted Vallabhadas, *bīnkār* of Shri Nathji, in 1987; Raghunathji's grandson is Bhanwar Lal, *kīrtankār mukhiyā* of Navanitapriyaji in 1987; Jaikrishan, *kīrtankār mukhiyā* of Navanitapriyaji, had a daughter who married Shyam Lal, *pakhāvajī* of the temple in 1987; Ghanshyam Das was the father of Guru Purushottam Das, honorary *pakhāvajī* of Shri Nathji in 1987. (Photograph courtesy Guru Purushottam Das)

Fig. 4: **Guru Purushottam Das and his father Ghanshyam Das, *pakhāvajī* of Shri Nathji, ca. 1911–14 (Photograph courtesy Guru Puroshottam Das)**

can take up to two hours. On such days, the musicians are required to play for a longer period. Even when *darśans* are not taking place, however, all musicians are required to be on duty in the temple from 7:00 A.M. to 11:30 A.M., beginning with pre-*Śṛṅgār* in *kīrtankār galī*. Their duty in the afternoon begins around 4:00 P.M. and lasts until about 5:30 P.M. All of these times are approximate and generally much longer during festival days. The *kīrtankār mukhiyā* and the *bīnkār* in the Shri Nathji temple have longer hours. In the morning their duty begins with pre-*Mangal*; depending on the season, this is any time between 4:00 A.M. and 5:00 A.M. Their afternoon sessions begin around 3:30 P.M., with pre-*Utthāpan*.

Vallabh Das, the *bīnkār* of the Shri Nathji temple, recounted his duties for September 14, 1984. At about 3:00 A.M. a temple servant arrived at his home to wake him, and at 4:00 A.M. he woke Shri Nathji by playing *bīn* in *ḍol tibārī*, standing alone on the right side of the closed doors to the *nij mandir*. During *Mangal*, the first public *darśan* of the day, he and Ram Das, the *kīrtankār mukhiyā*, presented two songs in *maṇi koṭa*, the usual place for musicians to be during public *darśans*. By 7:00 A.M. all the musicians had gathered in *kīrtankār galī*. There, before the second *darśan, Śṛṅgār*, three songs composed by Surdas, Kumbhandas and Paramanandadas (all *aṣṭachhāp* poets) were sung. At the same time, Vallabh Das played the *bīn* in the *darśan* hall. During *Śṛṅgār darśan* only one song, by the poet Vitthal, was sung. After *Śṛṅgār darśan*, when the doors were closed, Ratan Lal, the brother of the harmonium player Mul Chand, sang a song in *kīrtankār galī* for the pre-*Gvāl* session. It was not his duty that day, but he did so because he had free time and it was his responsibility that day to sing for *Gvāl*, the next *darśan*. During *Gvāl*, he sang only one song, though he said he could have sung two or three.[38]

After *Gvāl, bīn* and *pakhāvaj* were played in *kīrtankār galī* for about 20 to 25 minutes. This is the period (pre-*Rāj Bhog*) during which Shri Nathji eats his main meal of the day. *Rāj Bhog* (11:30 A.M. to 12:00 noon), the fourth *darśan* of the day, is the most elaborate. On that day, when all the musicians had assembled in front of Shri Nathji, they sang only one song. After *Rāj Bhog*, the musicians received a portion of the *prasād* as partial payment for their *sevā*. The temple was then closed and the musicians went home to have their mid-day meal and rest.

By 3:30 P.M. the *bīnkār* and *kīrtankār mukhiyā* were in the temple again for *Utthāpan darśan*, to wake Shri Nathji with the music of *bīn* and *havelī sangīt. Pakhāvaj* is never played at this time. By 4:30 P.M. all the musicians had assembled again for *Bhog darśan*. On that day, they sang one song in the presence of Shri Nathji and one in *kīrtankār galī*. For *Śayan*, only *bīn* was played.

Musicians officially employed by the temples receive remuneration in kind. Their 'salary' (*neg*) is a portion of the *prasād*. Some of this food is consumed by the musicians' families, and the rest is handed over to local shops that sell it to pilgrims and townsfolk. Once a month the musicians collect a percentage of the selling price, which fluctuates considerably as more *prasād* is prepared on festival days. The amount the musicians eventually receive varies from Rs. 180 to Rs. 800 a month.

The Shri Nathji temple is considered pre-eminent, and its musicians receive the most remuneration. The next most prestigious are Navanitapriyaji and Vitthalnathji, followed by Madanmohanji and Banamaliji. Upward and downward mobility are both possible. In 1984, a singer, Pyare Lal, was re-assigned from the Navanitapriyaji temple to Madanmohanji. He refused to report for duty, as he interpreted it as a demotion both in status and in remuneration. He now earns his living selling religious articles in a shop near the entrance of the Vitthalnathji temple.

Visiting musicians play for the deity without remuneration. It is different when they perform for the Tilkayat, as many expect their professional fee and usually reject the idea that this might also be regarded as *sevā*. As honorary *pakhāvajī* of the Shri Nathji temple, Guru Das did not receive remuneration for playing *pakhāvaj* in the temple. However, as part of his *sevā* to Shri Nathji, he played at least twice a day at *Rāj Bhog* and *Bhog*. Several other musicians also play in the temple from time to time without remuneration, as their *sevā* to Shri Nathji. If they are substituting for a regularly employed musician, however, they receive the *neg* normally given to the absent musician.

There is no provision for sick leave. If a musician is sick, or required to be away for personal business, it is his responsibility to get someone to stand in for him. Mul Chand, the harmonium player in the Shri Nathji temple, was frequently ill, and whenever this happened his brother Ratan Lal would come from Bhilvara, a city about 20 miles away, as a substitute. Although Ratan Lal normally earns his living repairing watches, he has received training in *havelī sangīt, pakhāvaj* and harmonium; his proficiency in all of these is of a professional standard. On another occasion while I was there, Sohan Lal, the *pakhāvaj* player from the Navanitapriyaji temple, handed over his duties to Kanhaiyalal, one of the *havelī* singers of the temple. Kanhaiyalal sang and played *pakhāvaj* simultaneously, something most *havelī* singers can do, as they always have some rudimentary training in *pakhāvaj*, which gives them flexibility.[39]

Other than employment in the temples, *havelī* singers have limited options for earning a living through music. Three hereditary *kīrtankārs*[40] teach music in government high schools, but most of the other musicians have to supplement their meager income by making and selling articles of decoration that serve to enhance the workship of Shri Nathji.

All these handicrafts, just like the music and painting of Nathdvara, revolve around Shri Nathji. They include peacock feather fans (*morchhal*), fly whisks (*chamar*), small cushioned seats, decorative crowns (*mukuṭ*) and jewelry. All these objects are miniature replicas of items used in worship, which pilgrims purchase for use in the Nathdvara temples, in shrines at home and in Vallabhacharya *sampradāy* centers of worship throughout India and abroad. The export market for these items has been growing, particularly to the Gulf states and the United Kingdom (Skelton 1973:23-25, Talwar and Krishna 1979; Ambalal 1987:168).

The best known among the arts of Nathdvara is that of making *pichhvāīs*, decorated pieces of cloth which are used as backdrops behind the various Vallabhacharya *sampradāy* images. The designs on them vary from abstract motifs to specific incidents in the life of the youthful Krishna (Dhamiya 1965; Skelton 1973:35; Talwar and Krishna 1979:15-72). They can be either painted or embroidered. According to Talwar and Krishna, Shri Nathji and the other seven centers (*gaddī*) of the Vallabhacharya *sampradāy* use mostly printed, brocaded, or embroidered *pichhvāīs* (Talwar and Krishna 1979:12-13; Barz 1976:55). The painted ones are used only for the less important holidays of the sect's smaller temples. The making of painted *pichhvāīs* is reserved for a group of professional Brahman painters (Maduro 1976:50-54), while embroidered *pichhvāīs* are made by two brothers from a Kumavat *kīrtankār* family: Panna Lal, *havelī* singer in the Shri Nathji temple, and Jamna Das, *bīnkār* in the Shri Nathji temple. They also make patchwork *pichhvāīs* and *bangalās* (small replicas of houses), as well as other articles used for worship.[41] Other musicians act as guides for pilgrims, or repair watches.

All the tasks involved in producing and selling crafts are shared among family members. Women too take part in this work, particularly the production of crafts, though they are limited to tasks performed at home.[42] Without this cooperation, the pursuit of several simultaneous occupations would not be possible. From selling *prasād* to making souvenirs, the musicians are completely dependent on the pilgrims. Their entire economy is thus either supported directly by the temple, or indirectly by the pilgrims.

A school of music, the Shri Nathji Shikshan Kendra, is attached to the Shri Nathji temple. Except for Guru Das, who was the principal, and the secretary, his grandson Prakash, all the staff are also employed in the temple. Consequently the hours of instruction are 2:00-4:00 P.M., and 7:00-9:00 P.M. so as not to conflict with temple duty. One of the teachers, Bhanvar Lal, is *kīrtankār mukhiyā* in the Vitthalnathji temple; as his hours of work in the temple are longer, he is occasionally late for his teaching duties. Bhanvar Lal replaced his late father, Radhakrishna, both as *kīrtankār mukhiyā* and *havelī* teacher in the school. The other *havelī* instructor is Kanhaiya Lal, who is employed in the Navanitapriyaji temple.

Several teachers are employed by the temple for a skill different from what they teach in the school. Shyam Lal plays *pakhāvaj* in the Shri Nathji temple but is employed to teach *tablā* in the school, while Mul Chand plays harmonium in the Shri Nathji temple but teaches *pakhāvaj* in the school. Guru Das also taught *pakhāvaj*, and two of his students, his own grandson Prakash and Balmukund, Shyam Lal's son, had Government of India scholarships to study *pakhāvaj* with him.

While musicians are rewarded in kind for their service in the temple, those who teach in the music school are given a fixed salary which varies from Rs. 150 per month for all the teachers to Rs. 800 for the principal. About 30 students are registered in the school, half of whom come from *kīrtankār* families.

All the musicians reported that their standard of living had fallen because of inflation, as a result of which many of them were not teaching their own children. Thus, while a few of the *kīrtankār* children are studying in the schools, most of the parents are encouraging their children to qualify in new professions. None of the older generation see the life of a musician as secure. A frequent complaint heard from Nathdvara musicians is that in the past, their work was given more generous patronage and was held in higher esteem (Jindel 1976:162; Ahmad 1984:7-8; Owens 1983:166; Erdman 1978:343-344; Verdia 1982:94; Gaston 1990b, 1990c).

Conclusions

Music as *sevā* is still an important tradition in the temples of Nathdvara. All the musicians presently employed in the temples entered the Vallabhacharya *sampradāy* and the musical profession by virtue of their birth. Even today, it is unlikely that anyone from outside the *kīrtankār* families could obtain a position there as a temple musician.

This situation makes an interesting comparison with the state of dance and dance music in southern India, which was once governed by the same rules as those still in effect in Nathdvara. Prior to the banning of dance in the temples, all the dancing was performed by hereditary dancers (*devadāsīs*) and the dance was part of temple ritual; the teachers and musicians associated with the dance were also hereditary. Now that the dance has left the precincts of the temple, all caste and religious restrictions have disappeared. This has had a profound effect on the art, its practitioners and its audiences. What is available today is a tradition that is being re-created and is rapidly changing (Gaston 1983a:301-304; Gaston 1990a).

In Nathdvara, by contrast, restrictions of caste and sect continue, giving the music continuity of purpose, and allowing it to resist the changes and modernization occuring elsewhere. The musical and family links among members of this tightly-knit social group are the kind of social structure that was typical of Indian musical traditions in the past, but is becoming increasingly obscured in the modern context by the mobility of artists and the breakdown of caste restrictions (Gaston 1990b) that once determined who could join the profession.

Studying a traditional system that is still operative is of considerable historical interest, because many of the artistic traditions of present-day India cannot claim to be more than re-creations. The venues of performance have changed, and the audiences have been cultivated rather than absorbed as a way of life. Much of the art available to the outside world and to urban India is being packaged and "cleaned up" to make it more accessible. In this process, the balance has shifted from religious to social and aesthetic values.

The music presented at *darśan* in the temples of Nathdvara is entirely in the hands of the musicians. The songs performed, their duration and the type of accompaniment used are extremely flexible. In addition, music is liable to "break out" at other times and in other parts of the temple if the musicians feel disposed to perform. This spur-of-the-moment attitude toward the music derives from the great familiarity of the musicians with the entire establishment of the temple. Almost from birth, they become accustomed to the rituals of the temple, so that they never need to think about what should be happening. They are so much a part of the temple's functions that, within certain limits, whatever they consider appropriate is *de facto* correct. This freedom from strictly defined procedures may well be characteristic of hereditary traditions in which the general format of the art is absorbed at a very young age.

The music in the Nathdvara *havelīs* will continue as long as it is a recognized ingredient of *darśan* and is considered an important part of *sevā*. However, the number of musicians supported by the *havelīs* is declining, and only three continue to support several musicians. Whether music will continue to be regarded as an occupation with sufficient status and remuneration to attract talented recruits is questionable. Already, many of the musicians' children have chosen to enter other professions. The fact that some of the young people are studying *pakhāvaj* is probably a measure of the influence Guru Das had on them rather than an indication of a general revival of interest. For *bīn* and vocal, there do not appear to be any seriously committed students in the 20s age group.

The decline in the importance of music in the temples, which almost all the musicians perceive, might eventually lead to a dilution of the Nathdvara tradition and a falling off of standards. On the other hand, the musical success of Guru Das has given great encouragement to those who aspire to become top musicians themselves. His presence at the music school has lent the profession of music at Nathdvara a greater prestige than before. As a result, visiting musicians have been more likely to perform there, knowing they shared a platform with an acknowledged master. This also tends to create greater enthusiasm for the art within the community.

Yet the music of Nathdvara, which depends entirely on the patronage of the temple, is not likely to be exported elsewhere. Its flavor is bound up with the Vallabhacharya *sampradāy* faith, rituals and setting. I am reminded of two Ras Lila recitals, one in London in 1984, the other in Vrindaban in 1983, both by the same troupe of traditional actors. The London recital at the Commonwealth Institute did not make any impact: the actors looked disaffected, the costumes garish, and the audience was either unable to interact or felt it improper, even though their spiritual head, Purushottam Gosvami, was present. In Vrindaban, by contrast, when viewed by devotees in Purushottam Gosvami's home and with him in attendance, the same performance had purpose and meaning, making its aesthetic shortcomings acceptable.

The music of Nathdvara, lacking the ingredients for a lasting concert stage presentation, is entirely dependent on the temples for venue and patronage. Should this support be withdrawn, it would lose its whole purpose and financial basis. In the final analysis, it is the attitude of the temple hierarchy, particularly the Tilkayat, towards the standard of musicianship within the temple retinue, which is likely to determine the fate of Nathdvara's *havelī sangīt* tradition.

ENDNOTES

Without the assistance of Padma Shri Guru Purushottam Das (1907-1991) and Maharaj Shri Govind Lal, the Tilkayat of the Shri Nathji temple, this research would not have been possible. I would also like to thank all of the musicians of Nathdvara and their families for their cooperation. For assistance with interpretation and other help, I would like to thank Prakash Chandra and Sushil Paliwal. John Erdman and Karine Schomer gave me extensive advice in the preparation of the manuscript. Bryan Wilson, Rupert Snell, Richard Widdess, Joep Bor, Mukund Lath, Stephen Inglis and Andrew Topsfield offered comments. Tony Gaston helped me in many ways, including recording the music, drawing the maps and sustaining my enthusiasm. I am grateful to all of them. Part of this research was carried out with the support of the Canadian Social Sciences and Humanities Research Council and the International Society for Traditional Art Research (ISTAR).

1. For lack of a better English equivalent, I use the word sect as equivalent to *sampradāy*, although this is not strictly speaking correct, as a sect is a breakaway group whereas the Vallabhacharya *sampradāy* has not broken away from mainstream Hinduism. It does however share certain features with a sect in that it is an exclusive group and members have to be initiated. See Barz 1976:40.
2. Barz makes only one reference to music in the Vallabhacharya *sampradāy havelīs* of Bombay. He refers to hearing music played by Mukund Goswami on the *sitār* but not in the *havelī*. I have never heard or seen *sitār* being played as part of the rituals during the *darśan* in the Shri Nathji *havelī* or any of the *havelīs* in Nathdvara. Ambalal, however, illustrates the *sitār* being played during *darśan* (1987:134, 158). I have heard it played during the pre-*Śṛṅgār* period. Maduro too appears not to have been allowed into the Shri Nathji shrine, and has had to resort to second-hand accounts of the music. From his description (1976:34), one gets the impression that the *bīn* was played in the *naubat khānā*. This is not the case, nor, as he suggests, is the *tablā* played during *darśan* in the temple. The *tablā*, like the *sitār*, can however, be played prior to *Śṛṅgār darśan*, as I have heard visiting musicians on several occasions accompany singers and Kathak dancers on the *tablā* while they performed in the *ḍol tibārī* (*darśan* hall).
3. Among other honors, Guru Das received the Sangeet Natak Award in 1979 and the Padma Shri in 1983.
4. See Gaston 1983b:II,565; also Gaston 1984, an unpublished manuscript available at the American Institute for Indian Studies, New Delhi. In Gaston 1984, the music of the *pakhāvaj* is integrated with that of the *havelī* song recorded by the Sangit Natak Akademi (recording number 1535). The artists are Guru Purushottam Das, giving *pakhāvaj* accompaniment to *havelī sangīt*, sung by the late Manna Lal, who held the post of *kīrtankār mukhiyā* (head musician) in the Shri Nathji *havelī*. (In 1987, Manna Lal's son, Shyam Lal was the *pakhāvajī* in the Shri Nathji *havelī*). The song and the musical notation are given in Srivastava 1980:70-89.
5. Growse writes about the difficulty encountered in trying to meet His Highness: "In the official world, however, he is barely known even by his name . . . he declines all social intercourse with Europeans, even of the highest rank: so much so, that when the Lieutenant-Governor of these Provinces visited the station in 1873, and being unware of this peculiarity, expressed in writing a desire to see him, the invitation was not accepted. The compliment was prompted by the Gosain's annual gift of a prize of Rs. 300 for the student who passes first in the general Entrance Examination for Calcutta University . . ." (1979:290).
6. The title "Maharaj" was used from the time of Vallabhacharya's son, Vitthalnath (d. A.D. 1586) (Motivala 1935; Barz 1976:41). The title Tilkayat came later, and was first given to Vitthal Rai, the fifth lineal descendant of Vitthalnath in 1663 (Jindel 1976:41).
7. Mulji (1865:120-121) describes the initiation ceremony; see also Growse 1979:286-287.
8. "A Vallabhacharya Temple consists of three successive compartments. The central one is larger and more open than the other two to accommodate the

worshippers. One is the residence of the Maharaj, the other is dedicated to the worship of the image of Krishna." (Mulji 1865:99).

9. The family of Maharaj Kalyanrai, which controls the Vitthalnathji temple at Nathdvara, traces its descent to Govindrai, the second son of Vitthalnath. Neither the Tilkayat Govind Lal, nor Kalyanrai and his brothers, live permanently in Nathdvara. The former lives in Bombay, the latter in Indore. Both visit Nathdvara only for special occasions and at those times reside in the respective palaces which are part of the *havelī* complex.
10. Dance and music continue to be important ingredients in the celebratory events associated with the Tilkayat's family. My own recitals for him were on two occasions: during his second son's ten-day wedding celebrations in Mathura in 1972, and in 1985, when he invited me to perform in his palace (Moti Mahal) adjoining the Shri Nathji *havelī* on the occasion of his eldest son's birthday and his grandson's *mundan* (tonsure) ceremony. These events illustrate the continuing tradition of using dance and music both in the worship of Shri Nathji and to entertain his intermediary, the Tilkayat.
11. Richardson (1979:1-10) offers a different interpretation.
12. Personal communication from the musicians of Nathdvara.
13. Personal communication from Mr. Tripathi, secretary to the Tilkayat in 1983.
14. An incident illustrating the importance attached to music by the temple hierarchy occurred in 1983 when a member of the musician community died. Because of this death, nearly half of the community was barred from entering the temple for ten days, the prescribed period of ritual impurity. In order to maintain the necessary musical accompaniment, musicians were hurriedly imported from outside Nathdvara, mainly from the Vallabhacharya *sampradāy havelīs* in Bombay.
15. Previous accounts of the *darśan* music have stated that for each *darśan* the music of a particular *aṣṭachhāp* composer predominates. However, my own experience does not bear this out. On many occasions the music of the prescribed composer was omitted from the *darśan* altogether (Gaston 1990c).
16. Personal communication from Mukund Lath. He also informed me that his vocal teacher, Pandit Jasraj, has made a cassette of *havelī* songs. This is in keeping with the growing trend of introducing religious music into the concert repertoire. See also Gaston 1990a concerning this same trend in classical Indian dance.
17. *Bīn* and *pakhāvaj* are used in the *dhrupad-dhamār* tradition. According to Wade (1979:113), *bīn* was originally used mainly for accompaniment, not as a solo instrument. The *pakhāvaj* is still the percussion instrument for the *dhrupad-dhamār* style (*ibid.*, 104; Neuman 1980:118), and is much older than the more common *tablā* which is currently used in the temples of Vrindaban (Wade 1979:137). Since the mid-18th century there has been a steady decline in the use of the *pakhāvaj*. This eclipse is linked to the increasing popularity of the *khyāl* and *ṭhumrī* genres and the *sitār*, which the *tablā* is better suited to accompany (*ibid.*, 82-85).
18. Solo *bīn* recitals as performed in public today derive from the court tradition, which is quite different from what is normally played during worship in the Nathdvara *havelīs*. It is only on rare occasions that one hears *bīn* recitals of high quality in the *havelīs*. Once, in 1987, I did hear a superb performance

during pre-*Gval darśan*, by Ratan Lal, a member of one of the *kīrtankār* families employed in the temple who earns his living as a watchmaker in nearby Bhilvara and was just filling in on that day.

19. For further description of Holi celebrations at Nathdvara, see Jindel 1976:159 and Mulji 1865:4-5. For a description of Holi in Braj, see Growse 1979:91-102.
20. The festival of Annakut (lit. 'mountain of food') is the day after Divali. This day is sacred to Krishna and he is worshipped as Giriraj ('king of the mountain'). The festival commemorates the day Krishna raised Mount Govardhan to protect the cowherds from the rain storms sent by the angry Vedic deity Indra. Annakut is important all over North India, but particularly in Nathdvara, as Shri Nathji represents Krishna holding up Mount Govardhan. In Nathdvara, not only is Krishna worshipped with a mountain of food, but the local indigenous people, the Bhils, take an active role in the celebrations by "looting" the food from the shrine (Tod 1978:I, 436; Ambalal 1987:141, 160). For a general description of Annakut see Eck 1983:271; Growse 1979:27, 68, 169, 279, 300-301; Talwar and Krishna 1979:12, 15, 37-40, 43, 75). Ambalal 1987:160 includes an early 20th-century painting of the event that approximates exactly the event today.
21. The bathing takes place in a special area about four foot square. Hot water from a pot is poured out ("like a shower") while the priests are still fully clothed. They do not use soap. They wear wooden sandals and must not step on the ground. If they do they must bathe again. They then change their clothes, leaving the wet ones hanging on bamboo poles. Each person is allotted two bamboo poles to hang clothes on. All the servants that deal with the cooking of the food bathe there as well. The procedure must be repeated if they leave the temple. (Personal communication from the second *mukhiyā* of the Shri Nathji *havelī*). This was the one area of the temple I was not permitted to visit.
22. The *jhapaṭiyās* as described by Mujli, were much more brutal than I experienced: "To accelerate the devotion of those who have got in, and to induce them to make room for other devotees, who are anxiously waiting outside, one of the guardians of the temple mounts on a rail, with a thick cord in his hand to whip them along. Many of the devotees receive a very severe beating; and it has even happened that an eye has been lost, or other severe and permanent injuries inflicted" (1865:103).
23. In 1988 the soldiers no longer carried vintage muskets, but single shot rifles.
24. See Fig. 2 and note the discrepancy in Skelton's plan (1973:220).
25. Guru Das sat when he played *pakhāvaj*, but his nephew Shyam Lal, who is younger, sometimes stands, with the drum slung from a cord around his neck. See Talwar and Krishna (1979:20) for an illustration of *pakhāvaj* carried in this manner. Ambalal provides illustrations of *pakhāvajīs* sitting and standing while playing for Shri Nathji (1987:99, 106, 107).
26. To my knowledge, the custom of throwing *gulāl* for a whole month is peculiar to the Shri Nathji *havelī*. The powder is believed to have a cooling effect and to cause respiratory troubles. Certainly most of the musicians had colds during this time of the year. However, no one mentioned that Shri Nathji too might suffer side effects. The throwing of *gulāl* by the Maharajas at the end of the *darśan* was objected to by many. We get some insight into this reaction from

Mulji: "It is not considered among our people equivalent to adultery to throw gulāl on the breast of a woman" (1876:4). Ambalal illustrates a mid-18th century painting that is an exact replica of the *darśan* today during Holi when *gulāl* is thrown.

27. The guards on duty have discretionary power to grant access to *kīrtankār galī*. Needless to say, their cooperation was essential to my work.
28. Although Muslims are not encouraged to enter the temple (Jindel 1976:17, 137-138), I heard a violin recital there in March 1985 by Shri Satya Dev Pawar (of All India Radio-Delhi), accompanied on *tablā* by Ustad Faiyaz Khan (also of All India Radio-Delhi). At that time, only musicians and music connoisseurs were present. We sat on the steps of the *darśan* hall, facing the sanctuary of Shri Nathji (*nij mandir*). The music recital lasted about 20 minutes, with the musicians from the Shri Nathji temple making requests and signifying their approval by the customary "*Vah! Vah!*". While the music was being played, the image of Shri Nathji was being decorated, concealed from our view by a bamboo and cloth curtain. At intervals, the priests would peek out at us. Just before the curtain was opened to reveal Shri Nathji, the steel bar separating us from the sanctuary was raised to allow the temple musicians to move forward quickly and take up their appointed places. They began playing immediately, just as the devotees came rushing in. The visiting musicians picked up their instruments at once and we all took *darśan*. If we had remained seated, there would have been a risk of being trampled by the crowd.
29. See also the description of *darśan* by Jindel (1976:95-96).
30. The garden was built over during the period that this paper was being written. Ambalal gives a mid-18th century illustration of Lord Vitthalnathji in his garden. The arrangement was similar for Shri Nathji's garden (Ambalal 1987:98). I witnessed the Holi celebrations in this garden in 1985.
31. The *naubat khānā* is a Mughal architectural feature present in the royal palaces and *havelīs* of Rajasthan. Its specific purpose is to serve as a platform on which musicians sit and play. Playing music in the *naubat khānā* is a Mughal court tradition that was adopted by the Rajput royal houses. In the Shri Nathji *havelī* in Nathdvara, it is a rectangular room above the main gate to the shrine, open on two sides with a fire in the center that is used to tune the drums by warming their heads. For more on the *naubat khānā* see Parekh 1943:274 and Wade 1979:110-111.
32. Daya Ram, who also played *śahnāī*, worked in the *naubat khānā* in the Shri Nathji temple and, as a *sārangī* player, accompanied dancing girls (*tawāīfs*) in the court of the Maharana of Udaipur.
33. One example is the daughter of Guru Das, Radha, whose ancestry through her father's line is Rajasthani, his ancestors having originally come from Jaipur (Das 1911:1-5). Radha married Damodar, a Brajvasi. While their son, Prakash, has become a *pakhāvaj* player, most of the other Brajvasis, including Damodar, have concentrated their musical training on *havelī sangīt*. Prakash has recently married a Kumavat from Jaipur whose family has no connection with music.
34. The playing of *bīn* is a ritual necessity in the morning while waking the deity and at night while putting him to sleep. This makes the hours of work longest for *bīn* players.

35. Guru Das reported that the recommendation of Mohinuddin and Aminuddin Dagar helped him receive his appointment at the Bharatiya Kala Kendra in Delhi. See also Owens 1983. See Gaston 1989 for more details concerning Guru Das' musical lineage and family history.
36. The Kalyanraiji temple was using the services of Tola Ram, *havelī* singer in the Shri Nathji temple, and the Govindraiji temple had employed Bhanwar Lal, *havelī* singer in the Navanitapriyaji temple.
37. *Śayan* is the exception, open to the public at some times and closed at others.
38. *Gvāl* is important in the early stages of a musician's career. Many younger musicians reported having their first musical performance experience at that time, either singing or accompanying. Guru Das reported that from age 18 to 25, before he became the official *pakhāvajī* of the Shri Nathji temple, he accompanied singers at this *darśan* to get exposure and practice in accompaniment.
39. Except for two *pakhāvaj* players, Guru Das and his great-nephew, Sohan Lal, all the musicians are trained in *havelī sangīt*. Guru Das's family appears to restrict its musical training to *pakhāvaj*.
40. Mishri Lal, who is the middle brother of Damodar (*kīrtankār mukhiyā* of the Navanitapriyaji *havelī*); Kanhaiya Lal, a *havelī* singer, also of the Navanitapriyaji temple; and Shyam Lal, son of Ram Das (*kīrtankār mukhiyā* of the Shri Nathji *havelī*).
41. Surprisingly, although the art of *pichhvāī* is the main theme in the work of Skelton (1973), Talwar and Krishna (1979) and, to some extent, Maduro (1976), none of them refer to the role of the musician community in the industry. This is in spite of the fact that much of this work is of exceptionally high quality. One explanation may be that the identity of the Nathdvara musician community is as musicians (*kīrtankār*), and they think of themselves as such even when engaged in other types of work.
42. There is an instance of the art of *pichhvāī* being introduced into a family via a new wife (personal communication from Chotibai). Many daughters and wives do this type of work, as it is easily done at home.

REFERENCES CITED

Ahmad, Najma Parveen
1984 *Hindustani Music: A Study of Its Development in the Seventeenth and Eighteenth Centuries*. Delhi: Manohar Publications.

Ambalal, Amit
1987 *Krishna as Shrinathji: Rajasthani Paintings from Nathdvara*. Ahmedabad: Mapin Publications.

Barz, Richard
1976 *The Bhakti Sect of Vallabhacarya*. Faridabad, U.P.: Thompson Press.

Bryant, Kenneth E.
1978 *Poems to the Child God: Structures and Strategies in the Poetry of Surdas*. Berkeley: University of California Press.

Chatterjee, Chinmayi
1981 *Studies in the Evolution of the Bhakti Cult with Special Reference to Vallabha School*. Part 2. Calcutta: Jadavpur University.

Dallapiccola, Anna
1982 *Krishna the Divine Lover: Myth and Legend Through Indian Art*. New Delhi: B.I. Publications.

Das, Ghanshyam
1911 *Mṛdanga Sāgar*. Bombay.

Das, Purushottam
1983 *Mṛdang Vādan*. New Delhi: Sangit Natak Akademi.

Dhamiya, Jasleen
1965 "The Pechwais of Nathadvara." In *The Times of India Annual*, pp. 73-80. Bombay.

Eck, Diana
1983 *Banaras: City of Light*. London: Routledge and Kegan Paul.
1985 *Darśan: Seeing the Divine Image in India*. Chambersburg: Anima.

Erdman, Joan L.
1978 "The Maharaja's Musicians: The Organization of Cultural Performance at Jaipur in the Nineteenth Century." In *American Studies in the Anthropology of India*. Sylvia Vatak, ed. pp. 342-367. New Delhi: Manohar Publications.
1985 *Patrons and Performers in Rajasthan: The Subtle Tradition*. Delhi: Chanakya Publications.

Gaston, Anne-Marie
1983a "The Effect of Changing Social Structures in Indian Classical Dance." In *Contribution to the Sociology of the Arts: Reports from the 10th World Congress of Sociology, Mexico City, 1982*. ISA Research Committee 37. pp. 297-308. Sophia, Bulgaria: Research Institute for Culture.
1983b "North Indian Drumming: The Pakhavaj Tradition of Guru Purushottam Das." 2 vols. Report to the Social Sciences and Humanities Research Council, Ottawa, Canada. Typescript.
1984 "Research on the Music of Purushottam Das." Unpublished manuscript prepared for the International Society for Traditional Arts Research. New Delhi: American Institute of Indian Studies. Typescript.
1989 "The Family History of Guru Purushottam Das, Hereditary Pakhavaji of the Śri Nathji Temple, Nathdvara, Rajasthan." In *Dhrupad Annual*. Banaras: Banaras Hindu University.
1990a "Dance and the Hindu Woman: Religion and Ritual in Bharata Natyam." In *Roles and Rituals for Hindu Women*. Julia Leslie, ed. London: Pinter Publishers.
1990b "Bharata Natyam: A Classical East Indian Dance Style in Transition." *South Asian Studies* (Cambridge).
1990c *Drumming for the Child God Krishna: Guru Purushottam Das and the Nathdvara Pakhavaj Tradition*. New Delhi: Oxford University Press. (in press)

Growse, F.S.
1979 *Mathura: A District Memoir*. 3rd ed. Reprint ed. New Delhi: Asian Education Services. (1st ed. 1874)

Hardy, Friedhelm
1983 *Viraha Bhakti: The Early History of Kṛṣṇa Bhakti in South India*. New Delhi: Oxford University Press.

Jindel, Rajendra
1976 *Culture of a Sacred Town: A Sociological Study of Nathadvara*. Bombay: Popular Prakashan.

Khare, R.S.
1976 *Culture and Reality: Essays on the Hindu System of Managing Foods*. Simla: Indian Institute of Advanced Studies.

Maduro, Renaldo
1976 *Artistic Creativity in a Brahmin Painter Community*. Berkeley: Center for South and Southeast Asia Studies, University of California.

Marfatia, Mrudula I.
1967 *The Philosophy of Vallabhacharya*. Delhi: Munshiram Manoharlal.

Marglin, Frédérique Apffel
1985 *Wives of the God King: The Rituals of the Devadasis of Puri*. New Delhi: Oxford University Press.

Motivala, B.N.
1935 *Karsondas Mulji*. Bombay: Karsondas Mulji Centenary Celebration Committee.

Mulji, Karsondas
1865 *History of the Sect of Maharajas or Vallabhacharyas in Western India*. London: Trubner.

Nath, R.
1985 *A History of Mughal Architecture*. Vol. 2. New Delhi: Abhinav Publications.

Neuman, Daniel M.
1980 *The Life of Music in North India: The Organization of an Artistic Tradition*. New Delhi: Manohar Publications.

Owens, Naomi
1983 "The Dagar Gharana, With Special Reference to Ustad Nasir Aminuddin Dagar." In *Performing Arts in India: Essays on Music, Dance, and Drama*. Bonnie Wade, ed. p. 158-170. Berkeley: Center for South and Southeast Asia Studies, University of California.

Parekh, Bhai Manilal C.
1943 *Sri Vallabhacharya: Life, Teachings and Movement (Ạ Religion of Grace)*. Rajkot: Harmony House, Shri Bhagavata Dharma Mission.

Prajnananda, Swami
1973 *Historical Development of Indian Music*. Calcutta: Firma K.L. Mukhopadhyay.

Readington, James D.
1983 *Vallabhacharya on the Love Games of Kṛṣṇa*. Delhi: Motilal Banarsidass.

Richardson, Edwin-Allen
1979 "Mughal and Rajput Patronage of the Bhakti Sect of the Maharajas: The Vallabha Sampradaya, 1640-1760." Ph.D. Dissertation, Department of Oriental Sudies, University of Arizona.

Saxena, S.K.
1981 *Aesthetical Essays*. Delhi: Chanakya Publications.

Seetha, S.
1981 *Tanjore as a Seat of Music*. Madras: University of Madras.

Sheth, Noel
1984 *The Divinity of Krishna*. Delhi: Munshiram Manoharlal Publications.

Singh, Chandramani
1981 "Performing Arts from Amber and Jaipur (A Study Based on Paturkhana and Naqqarkhana." In *Cultural Contours of India: Dr. Satya Prakash Felicitation Volume*. V.S. Srivastava, ed. pp. 1-10. New Delhi: Abhinav Publications.

Skelton, Robert
1973 *Rajasthani Temple Hangings of the Krishna Cult*. New York: American Federation of Arts.

Srivastava, Indurama
1980 *Dhrupada: A Study of Its Origin, Historical Development, Structure and Present State*. Delhi: Motilal Banarsidass.

Talwar, Kay and Kalyan Krishna
1979 *Indian Pigment Paintings on Cloth*. Ahmedabad: Calico Museum of Textiles.

Tod, James
1978 *Annals and Antiquities of Rajasthan*. 2 Vols. Reprint ed. New Delhi: M.N. Publishers. (1st ed. 1829-32)

Toomey, Paul Michael
1984 "From the Mouth of Krishna: Sacred Food and Pilgrimage at Mount Govardhan." Ph.D. Dissertation, Department of Anthropology, University of Virginia.

Vaudeville, Charlotte
1980 "The Govardhan Myth in Northern India." *Indo-Iranian Journal* 22:1-45.

Verdia, H.S.
1982 *Religion and Social Structure in a Sacred Town: Nathdwara*. Delhi: Researchco.

Wade, Bonnie
1979 *Music in India: The Classical Traditions*. New Jersey: Prentice Hall.

Widdess, Richard
1981 "Aspects of Form in North Indian Alap and Dhrupad." In *Music and Tradition: Essays on Asia and Other Music*. Richard Widdess and R.F. Wolpert, eds. Pp. 148-183. Cambridge: Cambridge University Press.

A JOKER IN THE DECK: THE MANY FACES OF A RAJASTHANI *BAHURŪPIYĀ*

JOHN EMIGH WITH ULRIKE EMIGH

Hajari Bhand of Chittorgarh is renowned throughout the Mewar region of southern Rajasthan as a *bahurūpiyā* – a wandering mimic and comic. For two months in 1982-83, he graciously gave up semi-retirement so that we could document his work and took to the road again – visiting some of the 460 towns and villages that have comprised his circuit and performing 25 different roles, including some routines with his son, Janakilal Bhand. In the months that followed, we visited his home to share raw footage from the film we were making and to interview him concerning his life as a *bahurūpiyā* and – prior to Independence – as a jester, praise singer, and wit in the Mewar courts.

Using Hajari Bhand's life and work as an example, this essay is an inquiry into the art and function of the now vanishing *bahurūpiyās* and Bhands of Rajasthan. In *The Fool and His Scepter: A Study in Clowns and Jesters and Their Audience*, William Willeford notes that "fools have generally lacked the kind of fully established personal and social identities that can be made the subjects of biography and history" (1969: xix). In some ways, Hajari Bhand's life has followed a scenario of trials and choices that we might think of as typical of the unchronicled jesters who worked at court and on the road in medieval Europe, and thus an account of his life and art may also provide an imperfect window to an irrecoverable Western past.

The term *bahurūpiyā* derives from the Sanskrit *bahu* (many) and *rūpa* (form). Hajari Bhand claims to have portrayed several hundred characters over the past 45 years – creating and recreating a vast assortment of Rajputs and holy men, professional men and tribals, gods and goddesses, tradesmen and rogues, beggars and fools. As one who assumes many forms and playfully takes on different identities, he is aided by the fact that, in Rajasthan, a great deal about a person's occupation, social standing, expected behavior and speech patterns can still be predicted by the clothing worn. Great emphasis is placed on a *bahurūpiyā*'s skill at costuming and makeup. A *bahurūpiyā*'s disguise is known as a *veś* (from the Sanskrit *veṣa* for clothing or dress) and the art of presenting himself in make-up and costume is referred to as 'doing a *veś*'. The usually comic actions that accompany the wearing of a *veś* are known as *sāṅg* or *svāṅg*. Derived from the Sanskrit *svāṅga*, 'having graceful action' (Dash 1979:14), this term now signifies a comic routine. One may refer almost interchangeably to a *bahurūpiyā*'s *veś* or his *sāṅg*, with a slight shift of emphasis from his appearance to his actions.

Using the streets, courtyards and market places of Mewar as venues for his *veśas* and *sāṅgs*, Hajari Bhand imitates, exaggerates, and sometimes violates stereotypical expectations for comic and dramatic effect. He drops old roles, adds new ones, and frequently changes his patter as the times, his changing interests, and those of his audience require. His art is fashioned from a detailed knowledge of the dress and behavior patterns appropriate to the castes, character types, and figures from mythology that have traditionally comprised the Rajasthani world, and his playful portrayals reflect and help to shape the Rajasthani public's sense of its own identity in its most human terms.

Bhands and *Bahurūpiyās*

The history of the Bhands in India is sketchily known at best. The Sanskrit *bhāṇa* denotes a jester or a comic monodrama in which the actor plays many parts (Raghavan 1981:40), while *bhāṅḍa* is a Sanskrit word used for jester (Russell and Lal 1975:I, 349). Historical connections with the pot-bellied, irreverent Brahman *vidūṣakas* of Sanskrit drama, as well as with the witty parasites mentioned in Vatsyayana's *Kāmasūtra*, may well be valid (Welsford 1968:63-64); but ancestors of the present-day Bhands are said to have entered India from Persia with the Muslim courts, and are especially associated with Timur-leng (Tamburlaine), who invaded India in 1398 (Russell and Lal 1975:I, 349). As a result of these historical movements, there is still a substantial concentration of

Bhands in Kashmir, where a form of farcical drama, Bhand Pather, is performed on Islamic saints' days and other festive occasions; many of the Bhands presently in North India seem to have come down from Kashmir at a later date (*ibid.*; Motilal Kemmu 1980, personal communication). Like the Kashmiri Bhands, most Bhands in North India are Muslim. Thus, in 1896, Crooke cited figures for Uttar Pradesh, Punjab, and Haryana showing over 14,000 Muslim Bhands living in these areas, but only 14 Hindu Bhands (1974:I, 259). In Rajasthan, however, because of strong resistance to the spread of Islam, a separate Hindu caste arose, including Hajari Bhand's ancestors, who served the courts of Mewar as jesters.

The existence of Bhands in the region seems to be of considerable antiquity. G.N. Sharma quotes the *Samyaktva* of Taruna Prabha Suri, written in 1354, as already mentioning "bhands and troupes of professionals of both sexes performing buffoonery and farce, accompanied by music, dance, and dialogue" (1968:149). The *A'in-i Akbari* of Abu'l Fazl'Allami makes note of Bhands playing percussion instruments, and "singing and mimicking men and animals" in 16th century India (Jarrett 1978: III, 272). In a 1983 conversation, Prof. Sharma expressed his belief that Bhands played a vital role in developing the dramatic aspect of the Bhavai theatre in Gujarat, as well as much of the popular theatre of Rajasthan.

Up until recently, Bhands have corresponded closely both in their function and in their activities to the professional buffoons and "artificial fools" of medieval Europe. The *Ethnographic Atlas of Rajasthan* states that, "known for their ready wit and humor, their art of story telling, jokery and buffoonery, the Bhands provide entertainment and fun to the people at festivals and feasts with the aid of their exciting fables and satires" (Mathur 1969: 60-61). A traditional Hindi proverb has it that a Bhand is "as essential at an entertainment as a tiger in a forest" (Crooke 1974: I, 258). Within the Rajput courts, Bhands entertained in the evening hours in military encampments or on hunting expeditions, singing out praises for a good shot or jibing at a missed one. Similarly, they accompanied rajas into battle – sometimes dressed as a Rajput ancestor – praising brave deeds or making jokes at the expense of both sides. Tulsinath Dabhai of the palace at Udaipur puts the case simply: "Their main function was to make the raja laugh" (1983, personal communication).

Rawat Kesari Singh, a patron of Hajari Bhand since the days

before Independence, stresses that "financially [Bhands] were completely dependent on Rajputs. They were given food, grains, and clothes, and at the marriages and deaths of their family members all the expenses were paid by the rajas and *jāgīrdārs*." To earn this support, the Bhand provided his royal patron with amusement, flattering praise, and at times witty and stinging criticism. "It was," says Singh, "a very necessary part of court life" (1983, personal communication).

Like medieval jesters, the Bhands were privileged men; but such privileges have limits and, like their European counterparts, they were in constant danger of losing their livelihood by failing to amuse or overstepping the boundaries of royal humor. K.S. Ada of the Bharatiya Lok Kala Mandal in Udaipur tells a story that illustrates the skills required for survival (1982, personal communication). A Bhand in Jaipur had fallen out of favor with his raja and been told never to show his face to the ruler again. After he departed in shame, a great procession was scheduled out of Jaipur. The Bhand coated his buttocks with wheat powder, stationed himself on a hill at the front of the crowd, and bent over, exposing his rear as his monarch paraded by. When asked to explain this extraordinary behavior, the Bhand said that he felt an overwhelming desire to present himself and pay proper homage to his king, but alas, since he was forbidden to show his face, what else could he do? He was immediately restored to favor.

The practice of performing as a *bahurūpiyā* is now associated with Bhands; but formerly members of various castes, including Brahmans, practiced this art, in villages as well as at the courts. The *A'in-i Akbari* lists the "Bahurupi" as separate from the Bhands and notes that in their daytime mimicry, "youths disguise themselves as old men so successfully that they impose on the most acute observers" (Jarrett 1978: III, 272). The term denotes a professional activity rather than a caste and not all Bhands have been gifted at this particular set of skills: "It is an art, and a gift. Not all can do it," says Hajari Bhand (1983, personal communication).[1]

Central to the art of the *bahurūpiyā* is the ability to create convincing impersonations of identifiable types. Impersonations of deities at Hindu temple festivals may have led to performances involving the comic mimicry of social types among such castes as the Rawals by the end of the 14th century (Bhanawat 1979: 26-27).

Bhands may have adopted these skills to increase their repertory as jesters. These origins are argued for by the fact that in Orissa, where the Muslim courts had far less influence, the term *bahurūpiyā* is applied exclusively to those impersonating Hindu deities (Dash 1979: 15 and 1983, personal communication); and both Hindu and Muslim Bhands who act as *bahurūpiyās* in Rajasthan now sometimes represent Hindu deities. The combination of mimicry with court jests is a natural one, with or without evolution from divine impersonation. The 14th-century Italian buffoon, Gonello, for instance, is said to have "carried various disguises about with him" and to have depended upon his gifts for mimicry and impersonation for the success of many of his jests (Welsford 1968:14). Whatever their religion, their caste, or the origins of their art, *bahurūpiyās* from Gujarat to Bengal have traditionally prided themselves on the accuracy of their impersonations of men and women from all walks of life and on their ability to deceive even those who know them well. In the Punjab Census Report of 1881, Denzil Charles Ibbetson describes how these abilities might be put to use: "One of their favorite devices is to ask for money, and when it is refused to ask that it may be given if the Bahurupiya succeeds in deceiving the person who refused it. Several days later, the Bahurupiya will again visit the house in the disguise of a peddler, a milkman, or what not, sell his goods without being detected, throw off his disguise and claim the stipulated reward" (cited in Russell and Lal 1975:I, 349).

Enid Welsford summarizes the conditions that made the professions of court jester and wandering buffoon possible in medieval and Renaissance Europe as follows: "It was the existence of the small cultivated court, the sharp distinction but close connection between all classes of society and the comparative rareness of books which made buffoonery so lucrative and popular a profession. The jest books of the 16th century depict variegated but compact little societies, where king, burgher, priest and peasant are perpetually jostling one another, and the buffoon slips in and out licking up something from them all" (1968:22). This description applies as well to the princely states of Rajasthan before 1947. With Independence, the social and political system that had sustained the Bhands as court jesters was significantly altered, and the capacity of the courts to offer patronage drastically weakened. For a time, Bhands skilled in the art of the *bahurūpiyā* could earn their living through public performances, but the popularity of films and now of television have undercut the support available from the general populace.

Bahurūpiyās are becoming scarce, but they have not yet vanished. Babulal Bhand of Gauri in the Swayambhadpur District of Rajasthan travels with two younger members of his family throughout the Hindi-speaking region of North India, following "his own sweet will" and earning 5,000 to 10,000 rupees a year. Babulal claims that 2,000 to 4,000 people – most of them Bhands or Naqqals – still earn a substantial part of their income as *bahurūpiyās* (1982, personal communication).[2] Of the over 4,000 Bhands in Rajasthan listed in the 1961 census, R.S. Ashiya of the Bharatiya Lok Kala Mandal estimates that 50 or 60 families still make a substantial part of their income through their traditional skills (1983:14). Bhands have taken up agriculture, government services, and many other walks of life in order to survive. As members of a Scheduled Caste, younger Bhands receive educational aid, and Kesari Singh notes a tendency among the educated youth to despise the traditional work of their caste: "They regard it as a shameful profession and feel they should give it up" (personal communication, 1982). This attitude is reinforced by those who regard Bhands and *bahurūpiyās* as beggars.

In response to the tendency among townspeople to regard the Bhands as mendicants, Hajari Bhand speaks with dignity, pride and unconcealed anger: "I am the Bhand of rajas and maharanas. We have been Bhands for a long time. All my forefathers were Bhands. . . . I have an allotted area of 460 villages, and I am respected in all these 460 villages. Everyone greets me with respect and I greet them with respect also. I am not a beggar. I am a Bhand. I live in Chittor. . . . Now, after the death of the Maharana,[3] I have created my own patrons, and I am recognized and respected by all of these people."

A Bhand's Life

Hajari Bhand was born in March, 1922. He does not know the exact date. His father, Kaluji, was 46 years old when Hajari was born, and Hajari's elder brother, Mohan, was 17 years his senior. His father performed four or five roles, which he taught Hajari, and his brother taught him more; but he has been largely self-taught, and unlike other *bahurūpiyās* he has never studied under a guru. Both Kaluji and Mohanji were better known as experts at *bhāṅḍāī*: praising the patron by reciting verses in his honor, or else, if the occasion called for it, criticizing, exposing, or ridiculing him in verse. Kaluji was also head (*paṭel*) of the Bhand community in the Chittorgarh area and his responsibilities included keeping discipline within the community and organizing ritual functions. As Hajari recalls, "Wherever he went, whatever he did, every sort of work, two or four hundred people would gather. He would hold council and they heeded his word. He would treat everyone with respect."

Hajari's grandfather was Moraji Bhand, who originally lived with his brother Jhoraji in Bhandakakhera – on lands ceded to the Bhands after one of their number had posed as a holy man and tricked Maharana Sajan Singh of Udaipur himself into becoming a disciple (Bhanawat 1974: 15). Family legend has it that Jhoraji became a particular favorite of Maharana Svarup Singh when he appeared dressed as a golden lion at a *śikār* (hunting expedition) held by the ruler. Seeing the "lion", Svarup Singh shot at Jhora Bhand, who was wearing iron plates on his chest for protection. As Hajari Bhand tells the story, "The Maharana fired and the lion stood up on two legs. As soon as he was hit, he fell to the ground. After five minutes he stood up again. Then he declared 'I am Jhora Bhand!' The Raja cried out, 'He is killed! How did he get here as a lion?'" Jhora Bhand was smeared with animal blood. He had a glass bullet in his hand and showed it to the hunt master. Finally, he removed his disguise and revealed himself, saying, "I fooled you, and now I am your Bhand." He was given over 200 *bīghās* of land (about 120 acres) near Mandal, in Bhilwara District.

This event took place in the mid-19th century, beginning a long association of Hajari Bhand's family with the highest courts of Mewar. During the rule of Maharana Fateh Singh, Moraji brought his family to Chittorgarh, while Jhoraji's family moved to nearby Bassi, where the local *zamīndārs* gave them more fertile land. Every year during the Navaratri festivities preceding Dasahara, members of Kaluji Bhand's family, along with other Bhands, would appear at the *darbār* of the Maharana of Mewar at Udaipur – a custom Hajari continued until recently. During the rest of the year, ten families of Bhands would alternate attendance at the Maharana's court, but the Bhands of Chittorgarh were regarded as particular favorites of the Maharana (*ibid.*, 15-16). Silver coins were placed on lances and given to the Bhands as payment for a good joke or comic routine. During the Navaratri visits, Hajari would receive up to 1,000 rupees in addition to costumes, food, emergency funds to meet specific needs and, occasionally, more land. At other times, the Maharana would visit their area and the Chittorgarh Bhands would come to entertain. They also worked under the patronage of the local Rajputs of the Bassi and Chittorgarh areas, gave occasional public performances, and were engaged by temples to play gods in religious processions.

In 1936, at the age of 14, Hajari was married to the daughter of a Bhand from Indore. He started living with her when he was 15, in the house where he still lives. At about this time, Hajari began to perform as a *bahurūpiyā*—first in supporting roles and then for a year under the patronage of the Thakur of Bhatyankakhera. Each day he would go to the Thakur's house to eat, and while there he also started to learn the art of bone-setting from the Thakur—a skill he still practices in addition to his work as a *bahurūpiyā*.

When he was 17, Hajari Bhand came to the court of Maharana Bhupal Singh at Udaipur. While at the court, a famous *bahurūpiyā* from Jaipur, Ramchandra, arrived. Ramchandra was not a Bhand, but a Brahman who went from court to court practicing the art of the *bahurūpiyā*. His paraphernalia and costumes filled an entire railway baggage car. At Udaipur, Hajari saw him win great favor and two hands full of silver rupees by pretending to be a crocodile in the palace lake, frightening and delighting the Maharana. This is how Hajari tells the story: "The *bahurūpiyā* Ramchandra dressed up as a crocodile and plunged into the lake. Someone cried, 'Oh, where has this beast come from? Bring a gun, someone!' By the time they brought the gun the crocodile had dived back into the lake, letting only its snout stick out. As soon as the people handed the gun to the Maharana, the crocodile said, 'I am the *bahurūpiyā* Ramchandra from Jaipur!'" The officer in charge of entertainment praised Ramchandra's bravery, derided the Bhands of Chittorgarh as having little talent or imagination, and challenged them to appear in a novel disguise or return to Chittorgarh in shame.

Owing to his already evident skills in mimicry, young Hajari was chosen to represent his family. "The next day, I disguised myself as a demon (*rākṣasa*) first of all. I went among the crowd and many men and women were really frightened. Next, I dressed as a pregnant Pinjari (a woman who cards unspun cotton). I went before the Raja and said, 'Oh, what has happened to me? You, Bhupal Singhji, you have deprived me of my honor!'" As Bhupal Singh tried to conceal his laughter with a handkerchief, Hajari pointed to the Maharana, who had been crippled by polio as a youth, and addressed the crowd: "That one, sitting there, even though he can't walk a step, he still got me pregnant!" Bhupal Singh seems to have been delighted at this flattering abuse. "So Bhupal Singhji gave me 125 rupees and said, 'You did a *sāṅg* which made us convulse with laughter. Now don't do this any longer.' The Maharana was choked with laughter and he told them, 'Give them 125 rupees and give them good food and treat them well.'"

Young Hajari was not through, however. He disguised himself next as a Gaduliya, an itinerant maker and vendor of iron wares whose caste claims descent from Rajput blacksmiths and swordsmiths of ancient Chittor – a claim Rajputs deny and resent. His account of his work in this disguise further illustrates how a Bhand exercised his privilege and flirted with disfavor in order to gain greater favor. After many obscene puns about furnishing the assembled lords with iron tools, Hajari shouted out, "I am a Gaduliya: I am one of your ancestors." As Hajari Bhand continues the story, "I said I was a Rajput and shouted all the time. Some two, three people tried to stop my mouth, but the Maharana was very pleased. They said, 'Don't shout! We'll give you whatever you demand.' The next day the Maharana gave me a reward of 250 rupees. He said the Bhands of Chittorgarh may freely come to the court." Hajari had successfully gauged his patron's sense of humor and his daring had won him favor. Before the stay was over, he had also performed as a washerwoman, an Afghani aphrodisiac salesman, a shepherd and a dancing girl. Ramchandra, defeated in competition by the young Bhand, offered Hajari's father 300 rupees a month if he would turn the boy over to him. Kaluji Bhand refused this offer and Bhupal Singh gave Hajari 600 more rupees in appreciation of his skill and heaped gifts of clothing upon him. "Then he told me to come to the palace dressed in those things. I went dressed in them and he said, 'Now you look like a Rajput.' Then I said, '*Khamā dhaṇī* – excuse me, Your Highness,' and went back home." Hajari remained a great favorite with Bhupal Singh, and over the years until his death in 1955, Bhupal Singh rewarded and encouraged Hajari's talents by giving him money, a ceremonial sword, and costumes valued at over 20,000 rupees.

Hajari still visits some of his former patrons, such as the Thakur of Orli, Kalyan Singh, and Rawat Kesari Singh, now the elected mayor of Bassi. They express great affection for him and invite him to perform at family weddings and other gatherings. As recently as 1971, Hajari dressed his large family as a group of Bhil tribals and entertained the present Maharana Pramukh of Udaipur, Bhagwat Singh. The grateful descendant of the Maharanas rewarded Hajari with 400 rupees. Still, Bhagwat Singh does not share the passion of his ancestors for the Bhands' jokes, disguises, and comic turns, and in any case, he does not command his ancestors' treasury (G.L. Sharma 1983, personal communication).

With the dwindling of royal patronage after Independence, Hajari Bhand has had to rely more on village audiences, and especially the merchant castes for support. Despite their spectacular success at Bhupal Singh's court, the Bhands of Chittorgarh had anticipated this problem, and by the time Hajari Bhand was 20 years old, he, his brother Mohan, and a neighbor, Champalal Bhand, had begun to go out into the villages to perform publicly. Eventually, their travels included villages in the Udaipur, Kapesan, Bhilwara, and Chittorgarh areas, and ranged as far as Banswara, 120 kilometres away, creating a circuit of 460 villages. These villages were shared out among six families of Bhands working out of Chittorgarh, while another 250 villages were allotted to a group of Bhands from Devli. Sometimes, villages would be alternated from year to year between cooperating families, and family members would be assigned to play their *veśas* at specific villages. In the event that a *bahurūpiyā* performed his *veśas* in a place assigned to another, he would have to pay a share of his earnings to the person whose territory he had infringed upon. This practice seems to be less in force now, as fewer Bhands are working in the villages. In any case, Hajari did not need to seek permission to enter the villages we visited, since his high status within the community exempted him from these restrictions.

As Hajari grew older, sometimes one or two children from his growing family would accompany him for *veśas* involving more than one character. Other times, he would perform with his brother Mohan. Most of the time, however, he traveled alone, leaving bundles of costumes at relatives' houses scattered throughout the district. When arriving at a new place, he found accommodation at a caste member's home a *dharamśālā* (public guest house), or sometimes with the local nobility. In a small village, Hajari Bhand usually performed two *veśas* a day, one in the morning and one in the afternoon. In large towns, a single *veś* might take all day. His stay in a village would ordinarily last one or two weeks. As he performed from shop to shop and door to door, he accepted payment offered by onlookers, and also kept a ledger recording the names of shop-owners and householders he entertained. At the end of his stay, he usually appeared in the disguise of a money-lender or Bania, and collected from those he had entertained, marking the amounts of payment in his record book. Those entertained are expected to give something, be it money, rice, wheat, corn or other payment in kind according to the season. He estimates that the income from touring half the year amounted to 3,000 to 4,000 rupees.

During his travels, Hajari kept expanding his repertory, picking up ideas from other wandering mimics and inventing new roles based on people he observed in the courts, towns, and villages. "Where I could, I learned, and where I couldn't learn, I taught." Often, he built up characters by observing real-life models over extended periods of time. He tells of attaching himself to a Muslim Fakir for two weeks in order to study his ways. The lengths he might go to in order to master a new role, as well as his adventurous spirit, are shown in his acquisition of the costume of a Bheru Jogi, a mendicant Hindu holy man. After approaching a Bheru Jogi about obtaining the costume, he was told that he must wear it for one hour a day for 12 years without accepting money before he could earn the right to use it in his work. "12 years long, I wore the costume every morning for one hour. While I was acting the role, people would give me flowers and money, but I didn't accept anything from them. If a flower was given, I gave it to the dogs, and if money was given, I distributed it to children." After this long apprenticeship, Hajari Bhand not only acquired the right to use the costume as a *bahurūpiyā*, but also "the spiritual powers (*siddhi*) of a Bheru Jogi." Hajari once put on the costume to face down a local practitioner of black magic who had threatened a relative of his, drawing a protective circle around the intended victim. He believes that the powers accruing from his disciplined apprenticeship with this costume have helped him gain respect and relative prosperity. "In its name, I am earning my living and working as a *bahurūpiyā*."

Hajari Bhand's life has not been spent entirely on the road or at royal courts. He is a leader of the Bhand community in Chittorgarh, has married twice, and has fathered 13 children—the youngest being four years old at the time of our visit in 1982-83. Hajari's first wife died when he was 24. He was remarried to a daughter of Ambalalji Bhand of Jaipur, a Bhand noted for his poetic skills. Of his two children by his first wife and 11 by his second, 9 sons and one daughter are still alive. To support this large family and supplement his earnings as a *bahurūpiyā*, Hajari Bhand supervises cultivation of the family lands (now ten *bīghās*). He also earns additional income from assisting with make-up at school plays and "fancy-dress" competitions. Most importantly—and quite apart from his work as a *bahurūpiyā*—he also practices as a bone-setter, and his house is frequently visited by people who have broken, sprained, or dislocated a limb. After being introduced to this skill by the Thakur of Bhatyankakhera, he developed it while achieving distinction as an amateur wrestler. He does not accept cash payments for his services, but grateful patients and their parents have given him goats, cows, and building materials through the years. He also performs frequently in the streets of Chittorgarh. Here, Hajari Bhand does not need to keep a record book. Well known by the local merchants, he collects his fees twice a year, at the holidays of Divali and Holi.

Festival occasions are important workdays for *bahurūpiyās*. Bhands may be hired by temples to represent gods and goddesses, or they may appear on their own accord. As a younger man, Hajari used to appear on Divali as the goddess Lakshmi, though he now considers himself too old to successfully perform this *veś*, and during our stay he substituted portrayals of Hanuman and Shiva. On the Muslim holiday of Id, Hajari dresses as a Muslim Fakir, gently satirizes these holy beggars, and collects at least 500 rupees from the amused celebrants. Both Muslim and Hindu Bhands often perform this *veś* on Id, and there seems to be no sacrilege or resentment felt by the Muslim community regarding Hajari's comic portrayal, nor on the part of the Hindu community when Muslim Bhands portray Hindu deities.

In addition to performing from shop to shop in towns and villages, Bhands appear as invited or uninvited guests at the weddings of the wealthy merchant castes—these castes having taken over (to an extent) the patronage of the Bhands. While Babulal Bhand most frequently appears at such an occasion as a Bania, making jokes about the merchant caste's historical involvement with the practice of usury and on the new couple's coming economic plights, Hajari usually goes dressed as a policeman. He starts from his home already disguised as an officer, often commandeering bus rides along the way. "Sometimes a policeman shakes hands with me. Sometimes even a police inspector shakes hands. 'Where have you come from?' he says. 'Where have you been transferred from?' 'I've been transferred from Durgapur.'" In this manner, he makes his way to the wedding festivities, sometimes revealing the joke and sometimes not. "Then I address the people of the wedding party. I frighten and threaten people. 'Hey mister! What do you think you're doing?' 'Oh no, Sir. I'm not doing anything.' 'Remove this bus from here! Ho, where is the license for this vehicle?' 'We don't have all of the necessary papers.'" At times, Hajari Bhand will encounter a real policeman at the wedding. "I tell him, 'The number on your belt is upside down.' He corrects the belt and salutes me." At large receptions, he may invoke a public law designed to reduce wasteful expenditures on wedding feasts and order the reception disbanded. "I call the bridegroom's father and ask him: 'How many persons have you assembled here?' '150 persons, Sir.' 'Why did you assemble 150 persons? The government's law does not allow that. The law allows only 51 persons to assemble for a wedding feast. Why have you done this?' 'Oh Sir, we'll never do it again.'" As protests mount, angry words are exchanged, and bribes offered, he reveals his disguise and collects liberal fees from the relieved relatives.

Hajari recognizes that fewer and fewer Bhands are now able to sustain themselves by the traditional skills of their caste, and he has exerted no pressure on his children to take up his work. Although many of these children are still quite young, so far only one of Hajari's nine surviving sons, Janakilal (the second son by his first wife) has taken up the work of the *bahurūpiyā*, and his activities are limited to festival days. In Bhilwara, where he works in a flour mill to make ends meet, Janakilal Bhand usually performs for 20 days during the Divali season, six days during Holi, and occasionally travels to the weddings of well-to-do merchants and bankers of the Maheshwari and Oswali Bania castes.

Although he sometimes regrets the drying up of royal patronage, Hajari enjoys working the village crowds. He is regarded with great affection, and mentioning his name evokes smiles, anecdotes, and words of appreciation for his skills as a comic artist and his standing in the larger community. Hajari says that when he was a young man he was offered a contract for performing in the then fledgling film industry of Bombay. Taking his father's advice, he turned down the offer. He has no regrets.

The Art of *Bhāṅḍāī*

The ability to give both flattering priase and stinging abuse was central to a Bhand's skills. Both the praise and the abuse are referred to by the generic term, *bhāṅḍāī*. *Bhāṅḍāīs* praising a patron might be given as a salutation or as an expression of gratitude. The formula for these *bhāṅḍāīs* involves naming valued ancestors, praising the patron's worth, and proffering blessings on the patron and his family. These encomiums are often lavish in hyperbolic praise. This is a *bhāṅḍāī* Hajari Bhand composed and recited in our presence to one of his traditional patrons, Kalyan Singh, Thakur of Orli:

> Oh Sir, you are the Protector of the Earth, like Chhatrapati Shivaji! The whole earth becomes free and their bonds are broken the moment they look at you! You are like Mahadev in appearance and all baseness flees at a single glance from you! You are more liberal in charity and braver in warfare than any other! You can transform a worthless shell into a jewel worth hundreds of thousands of rupees, such is your worth-enhancing power! This village of Orli where you Rathors rule is like heaven on earth. May God keep you happy forever!
>
> The whole world knows that you are like an incarnation of God. Your name is known everywhere in the universe. . . . May your illustrious Rathor family shine like the sun! Hajari Bhand will go on singing your virtues forever.
>
> Your household estates are like those of a Lord of the Earth. Your heart is large and generous. Oh Kalyan Singh, you are peerless on this earth. Many people come to you with prayers for help in distress and thousands stand in attendance for you. You are Lord of the Earth, Ocean of Mercy, and Giver of Food to us all![4]

While these paeans of flattering praise could be extreme, the abuse of a Bhand who had been offended was to be feared. A

Hindi proverb singles out "the rage of a widow, a Bhand, and a bull" as being awesome to behold (Crooke 1896 1: 258). Sometimes, this anger could take the form of withering curses aimed at an offending patron. Hajari gave this example:

> Oh patron, may you have a long life. But may you be blind in both of your eyes. May you travel forth to foreign lands and be set upon there by thieves and robbers. May all your 32 teeth get broken, just as you near your door. May you be sent to jail and rot there for life after life. May the ominous swallow-wort and acacia trees grow outside of your home. Oh my lord, may I never again seek even a grain of corn or a bundle of grass from you!

In these appeals to magic powers for vengeance on an ungrateful patron, the Bhands stand as living examples of a satiric tradition that stretches beyond the wandering bards of Ireland (who were credited with rhyming rats and, sometimes, kings to death), all the way to Archilochus, whose poetic invective was said to have driven King Lycambes to his death (Elliott 1960: 3-48). It is interesting to note that, while most of the Bhands' professional activities are clearly secular, Hajari Bhand – in learning the skills of bone setting and in earning the right to the Bheru Jogi's spiritual powers – has independently taken upon himself some of the functions and qualities of the shaman or wizard. Paradoxically, still another link with the traditional procedures of sacred magic may be seen in the use of blatant obscenity in the imagery of this *bhāṅḍāī* that Hajari once used to upbraid a Thakur for his lack of generosity:

> Thakur Sahib, *rājpūtī* (the courage and benevolence of the Rajputs) is no more. It has gone far beyond the seas. All virtuous Rajputs have been cooked to death in a whore's fart. Poor *rājpūtī* moves about, crying, "Where should I go now? Everywhere I wander, I see nothing but prostitutes' legs spread wide!"

The use of graphically obscene imagery is made all the more shocking and effective by its juxtaposition with *rājpūtī* – a chivalric code of values that traditionally operates as an unwritten standard of ethics for the Rajput castes. In further upbraiding and insulting the ungenerous Thakur, Hajari Bhand continues to make use of this normative frame of values:

> You are a Rajput. I came to your door to ask for your patronage, but you didn't even offer me water. You are the resident Thakur. A fortunate man worth two, three or four *lākhs* [hundreds of thousands of rupees], and still you don't invite me for a little food. What sort of Thakur are you? You and your kind are not Thakurs, but the thieves and swindlers of the world. And if the Thakurani had given birth to a real Thakur, he would have looked quite different from you!

More frequently, abuse in a critical *bhāṅḍāī* was clothed in wit. Kesari Singh says that court ministers would sometimes try to withhold payment to a Bhand that had been promised by a raja, but they did this at the risk of being made a laughing stock in front of the court (personal communication, 1983). The following *bhāndāī* in Hajari Bhand's repertory is an example of the kind of abuse such a minister would risk:

> Your father is a great slave. Your son is nothing but a slave. And your uncle is a slave to paupers. Your brother is a slave to beggars. Your maternal uncle is a slave to men with monkey shows. Your elder brother wears the sky for his clothes. Your brother-in-law is a slave to fools. Your son-in-law is a slave to Jogis. This is the kind of family you come from, and you have only increased their baseness. And now I have lost my own honor as a Bhand by requesting money from the likes of you!

In the rough and tumble of court life, the Bhand's skills at abusive rhetoric could be turned to sport. Sometimes a Bhand would be threatened with the loss of all he had earned if he could not make the raja laugh, and Hajari Bhand remembers his brother finally winning such a dare by cleverly and outrageously abusing the raja himself. Motilal Kemmu, who has worked for many years with the Bhands of Kashmir, tells of a mean-spirited raja who was blind in one eye from battle and threatened a Bhand with death if he could not make him laugh. After going through his entire comic repertory, the desperate Bhand went up to the king and whispered in his ear: "Why don't you laugh, you blind bastard?" The king roared in appreciation of this mention of a taboo subject and handsomely rewarded the fortunate Bhand (1981, personal communication).

As use of the ethical framework of *rājpūtī* in addressing the ungenerous Thakur suggests, the *bhāndāī* could extend beyond sport or leverage for payment in its significance. Kesari Singh notes that the acerbic remarks of the Bhand were often warranted, and that a wise raja would listen carefully for words of warning and wisdom in the privileged man's jibes. "Some very courageous Bhands used to point out to the rajas where they were mistaken and what their wrong actions were. Clever or wise rajas would never get angry at them, but would reward their service. Some unwise rajas at times would get angry and turn them out of their kingdom. Such things also happened" (personal communication, 1983). It is starting for those familiar with Renaissance drama to discover such close cousins to Calderon's *graciosos* and Shakespeare's wise fools still alive in this century.

Hajari Bhand now recites *bhāṅḍāīs* for generous patrons among the merchant castes in the same manner as he did for his royal providers, sometimes even retaining titles appropriate for Rajputs. Thus, the generous payment of cash and a turban by a merchant at Divali was greeted as follows:

> Oh Bhandari Raja, you are merciful to the poor and a most lucky King of Kings. Oh Great and Fortunate Raja, you have brought renown to your family and land. You are like a supreme ruler of the world and your heart is as kind as that of King Hamir. Oh Bhandari Raja, you are incomparable on this earth and there are no limits to your charity. So many persons stand before you, putting forth their requests, begging for alms and help. Thousands of people stand ready to execute your orders. May the goddess Lakshmi and the god Satyanarayan keep you happy and prosperous. Oh World-Renowned One, may you bathe in milk and prosper in children, as a fortunate King of Kings.[5]

Sometimes the concerns of the merchants form an odd mix with the formulaic compliments and good wishes traditionally extended to royal patrons.

> You also are a fortunate King of Kings. May you also swim in milk and prosper in progeny. May the goddess Lakshmi keep your coffers and stores perennially filled to the full. May you make a net saving of 35 *lākhs* rupees in the coming year! Oh Master of the World, Bestower of Food and Sustainer of the Poor, I, your Bhand, have come to the door of your palace!

If the merchant class has inherited the flattering praise offered to generous royalty, however, they have also become vulnerable to the sarcasm and humiliation that can be caused by a Bhand who feels himself slighted. By "raising the *bhāṅḍāī*" against a wealthy merchant who has refused payment, embarrassment can be heaped upon him and his entire family. Hajari told a story which exemplifies this power of the Bhands to enforce their means of livelihood: "In our Chittor, ——— (an influential merchant) once stopped our being invited to weddings. Four or five of us made a decision. We all gathered and formed a procession. We made Onkarji Bhand ride a donkey, while my brother disguised himself as a witch. We went to the market-place. All the members of the merchant community gathered there, and they asked us: 'What are you doing?' 'I am ———'s mother, I am a witch!' We were using a shoe as a fan, and Onkarji Bhand was wearing a shoe instead of a bridegroom's crown. Like that, we passed through the market." In these costumes, they arrived in front of the wealthy merchant's house and began to hurl curses against him, adding the following ill wishes to the recycled curses already cited:

> Lord of the Earth, may you never get food or wife, and may your cattle starve for want of fodder! You are killing us, the poor and needy people. May you never enjoy well-being in life! And now this one of us has become a witch in order to take your wife from you so that you may never enjoy life again. As I have said this, so may it be!

The merchant stayed at home for five days, ashamed at being publicly abused. The women begged him to pay off the Bhands, and finally his caste relations gave the Bhands their fees and assured them that they would always be welcome at Maheshwari weddings.

At times, *bhāṅḍāīs* can be pointedly satiric, exposing the

skeletons in family closets. One Bania who refused to allow payment to Hajari Bhand and his family at a wedding was reputed to have slept with his son's wife and fathered a child. Adapting the *veś* that had won him such favor with Maharana Bhupal Singh, Hajari dressed as a pregnant peasant woman and came up to the man in public, accusing him of being the father of the child "she" was carrying, and making not so veiled references to the money-lender's extra-commercial exploits. Although this practice is now rare and the Bhands' power has declined with the weakening of the feudal order, Komal Kothari, director of the Rupayan Sansthan Institute, says that in extreme instances Bhands can still make it difficult to marry daughters of families known to have incurred their wrath and scorn, for fear of the scurrilous abuse that might be offered by the uninvited guests at such weddings (1981, personal communication).

On the Road: The Artistry of a *Bahurūpiyā*

In discussing the criteria for a good *ves*. Hajari Bhand stresses care in costuming and make-up, accuracy in the choice of details, and the clear presentation of a character type recognizable to the audience. To meet these goals, first his looking glass and then his wife and family are consulted before presenting a role publicly. His costumes and properties – his huge coconut-shell begging bowl, for example – are frequently purchased from people he has studied, and his mastery of dialects and accents is particularly impressive – ranging from the rough vernacular of a Pathan street vendor to the polished speech of a Hindi-speaking doctor. Mohan Singh Shaktawat and Tulsinath Dabhai of the Udaipur Palace testify that his characterizations were so accurate that he would often go unrecognized at the palace until he revealed his true identity (personal communication, 1983). He enjoys testing the truthfulness of his portrayals by circulating among those he imitates without being detected, and once he infiltrated a group of Gaduliyas sent to Chittor fort for an audience with Prime Minister Jawaharlal Nehru. He was selected as one of the spokesmen before revealing himself as a *bahurūpiyā*.

Even in his public *veśas*, where it would be difficult and eventually self-defeating to disguise his identity for long, Hajari often goes out of his way to play to members of the caste or social group he is mimicking. Thus, his iron vendor will call out to female smiths of the Gaduliya caste with the peculiar falling inflections typical of Gaduliya intonation, and his garrulous Banjara will seek out members of other castes involved with cattle droving:

> Good morning, brother, where are you from? Kanore? How far's Kanore from here? Are these young bullocks yours or not? Brother, we'll meet again if we manage to stay alive. What's the certainty of this life? Any minute, your breath might stop coming out. What's the going rate for salt around here?

More complex is his portrayal of a wealthy Marwari money-lender and wholesaler, commonly referred to as a Bania, while collecting for his services as a Bhand from the Maheshwari merchants.

> Hello shopkeeper, which village do you come from? What? You're a Babil? I'm a Porwal. I live in Jaipur. All your accounts with me have to be cleared. Your grandfather took goods on credit and hasn't paid me yet. What's the matter with you? Laughing won't work. You'll have to pay me anyway. Tell me, where should I throw these account books? In a well or in a trough? You tell me where. Remember when you asked me for credit? Oh no, you ask the price of chillies later. First settle your accounts!

Hajari goes from store to store – wool-vested, a red account book under his arm, the sign of Vishnu on his forehead, and a fine patterned turban wrapped immaculately around his head – threatening to charge 4% monthly interest on imaginary accounts, complaining about the dwindling of honor among the merchants of Chittorgarh as shown by their lack of zeal in paying their Divali "debts," and citing sometimes exaggerated information on the wealth and earnings of specific merchants being dunned for payment:

> You are very rich, too, running those cinema houses. Your son-in-law owns a cinema at Kapasan. Your father has been honored by Maharana Bhupal Singh himself and you are very well off yourself. No wealthy man can ever compare with you!

The accuracy of his impersonation of the Maheshwari money-lender makes this public dunning potentially tense, but usually good humor prevails. Sometimes in his banter, Hajari Bhand will make sport of a familiar merchant, inventing comical failings:

> What should I do? Make up for past losses with future profits? We have always been kind, even though we have *lākhs* of rupees. And Sethiji, you too are very well off in every respect, except in education. The only thing causing us losses and trouble now is your illiteracy!

Shop by shop, he incites laughter, pockets small amounts of money for his past services, and stops his patter only to salute generous patrons of long standing with *bhāṅḍāīs* of flattering praise, or perhaps to share a cup of tea.

The specificity of Rajasthani dress and speech patterns, together with the public nature of much of Rajasthani life, helps Hajari to create easily recognizable character types. Working in the hurly-burly of Rajasthani streets and marketplaces, he must first attract attention – "make a scene." Itinerant vendors hawking their wares are particularly suitable for large crowds, since they also must attract and hold the attention of the milling public. Hajari builds comically on the extroverted behavior natural to these vendors. In these publicly performed *sāṅgs*, laughter is even more important than accuracy. "60 per cent comedy, 40 per cent accuracy" was a formula Hajari once offered us – with a huge grin that belied its mathematical precision. The garrulous old Banjara mixes the street cries of the salt seller with his humorous homilies, and the Gaduliya alternates between hawking non-existent bits of ironware and making sexual puns about iron tools or offering to fix up a shop-keeper's worn-out bottom with a good copper nail.

The first *veś* that Hajari performs in a new town or village is usually that of a Pathan selling asafoetida, or *hīṅg* – a bitter powder used in cooking and in medicine that is believed to kill germs, cure toothaches, and restore sexual vigor. Wearing white leggings (*salvār*) and a bright orange turban wrapped in the Pathan manner, Hajari accosts people in a broad Afghani accent and uses the stereotype of the Pathan as a rough, proud and bawdy individual in order to aggressively move out into the public, assess their mood and humor, and announce his presence as a performer:

> The strength of horses, the quickness of peacocks, the power of a bull can all be yours! I've got *hīṅg!* Pathani *hīṅg*, Pishori *hīṅg*, Peshawari *hīṅg*! Four rupees a *ṭolā!* Excellent *hīṅg*! Try it once and you'll never forget it! A taste of this *hīṅg* and a man becomes young and virile again! You'll ring those chimes at night like a glorious bell! Yes, my man, this *hīṅg* comes straight from Peshawar! Take some and you'll be ready to go the whole night long! Take it at night and you can ring those chimes in the day! Would you take it from a Pathan? Strong like a horse, quick like a peacock, powerful like a bull! This'll make you so hot that you won't even want to leave your bed! Genuine *hīṅg*! Just one *ṭolā* and you'll keep it up all night! Stiff and steady all through the night like a Pathan! Four rupees a *ṭolā*! Look, yours is longer already![6]

The *hīṅg* vendor's salacious patter, repeated with variations and with more and more asides to audience members, creates a highly charged field of energy and short circuits all sense of propriety. It thereby opens up future possibilities for a playful "putting on" of the conglomerate of attitudes and attributes that constitute Rajasthani culture and creates an aura of expectation and appreciation for the *sāṅgs* that are to follow.

Like vendors, religious mendicants must also call attention to themselves in public. Imitating these holy beggars gives the *bahurūpiyā* the opportunity to play with the ways in which sacred and secular values interface each other in Rajasthani life. Although Hajari Bhand takes the powers of his Bheru Jogi's *veś* seriously, the figure cut is that of a jovial mendicant moving through seas of grinning and shouting children like some well-fed and wondrously beneficent pied piper, shouting out praises to Shiva like a divine fool: "Bom, bom, bom! Bhole Nath! Jai Shankara! Hail to Lord Shiva!" His Muslim Fakir is similarly jovial, but his good nature and touch of divine joyfulness and grace is accompanied by an appreciation for cash contributions, thus creating good-humored satire. Hajari moves about accosting the crowd wearing a black *dhotī* and *kurtā*, a black Muslim hat, a huge black mustache, beads around his neck and earrings in his ears, and carrying an animal skin to sleep on, a set of tongs (*chimṭā*) to use as a noisemaker and for defense, and his all-purpose coconut-shell begging bowl:

> Good health to you and your children, too! I'll take alms only if you wish to give alms. Money jangles and returns to the giver! I need my fare to get to Ajmer! He who gives alms buys good health for his family! Oh, Ali, Oh, Haider! Partridges and pigeons, beware the cannon! He who renounces money is granted salvation! Oh, Ali! Oh, Haider! Bless all of you and your children, too! Send me a *paisā* [coin] and a handkerchief edged with gold! I'll take alms only if you want to give alms! Partridges and cows, never ride a wild horse! Give unasked in the name of God! I need my fare to get to Ajmer! He who remembers God prospers and he who forgets God finds ruin! Oh, Ali, send me alms! And make these foreigners here my disciples. I won't go without alms!

Less ambivalent in its satiric play with religiosity is Hajari Bhand's depiction of a wealthy Khakiji Sadhu. Amidst invocations to Rama and Narasimha, this prosperous holy man announces that he has come with 350 other Sadhus from Ayodhya on their way to Rameshwaram.[7] "Get ready," he warns "there are hungry and thirsty Sadhus in your village here. Devotees of God must be well looked after by the people." And so, he adds, must their 350 cows. "And we've got a few elephants with us, too!"

This strain of social satire, directed against the hypocrisy, greed, and overbearing pride of the wealthy and powerful, is also found playing beneath the mimicking of the Bania, the police officer, a doctor who suggests removal of vital organs and sexual abstinence, and a sanctimonious Congress Party politician. Though satire rarely dominates, it surfaces often, as, for example, when the Gaduliya mentions that people call his caste vagrants and beggars because they sleep in wagons, whereas "the real beggars are the bureaucrats who live in their new houses built with the money of the poor."

Hajari Bhand not only portrays and sometimes satirizes holy men, he represents the deities themselves. Thus, within a tradition that may relate back to the origins of mimetic performance in India, he represents Hanuman, Kali, Shiva—and, when he was younger, Lakshmi in non-comic *veśas* frequently given on religious holidays. For Hanuman, he uses a papier-mache Ramlila mask, along with a great deal of red dye, a "tail" improvised from materials about the house, and a picture of Rama and Sita cut from a calendar at his home and glued to his chest. He leaps and shouts "Shri Ram!" as he moves through the Divali market, animating the vision of Hanuman generated by calendars, comic books, and popular religious films.[8] His Shiva glides through the market in a jovial, ecstatic state, blessing goods and people, accepting alms, and dancing joyfully outside of the Shiva *liṅgam* and shrine in downtown Chittorgarh. This affinity of the fool with the divine manifests itself around the world. The privilege of the fool to rail and satirize is surely related to these touches of divine grace.

The ecstatic quality associated with divinities has its darker, demonic side, as well. Several middle-aged men told us of childhood nightmares occasioned by seeing a *bahurūpiyā* as the fierce goddess Kali or as a *rākṣasa* (demon). Divine inspiration also finds its disturbing and sometimes cruelly comic counterpoint within the *bahurūpiyā*'s repertory in the portrayal of secular madness. The madman, or *pāgal*, who calls attention to himself through his own eccentric looks and behavior, is a familiar figure in India. Hajari portrays a variety of such characters, adding touches of poignancy and comic zest to his professional fool's enactment of the natural fool's behavior. Thus, one such fool sits in the middle of the street with blood pouring from his head, pounding rocks together, breaking into manic laughter, and repeatedly shouting out doggerel verse:

> Come children, come! Come on out to play!
> I've found a white pebble, made of Pushkar clay!

Another portrayal of madness occurs in a two person *sāṅg* based on the Persian story of Leila and Majnun. Majnun, a poor young man, falls in love with Leila, a princess. Though love may care little for such distinctions, societies do, and the lovers are not allowed to marry. Majnun goes mad and spends his life crying out for his lost love, haunted by her memory, searching for her everywhere. In the performance, the spectre of Leila is played by a young performer, often a son or apprentice of the *bahurūpiyā*, and Majnun carries the dialogue. With Janakilal playing Leila, Hajari cried out for her up and down the street, reached for her in the crowd, tore his clothes into shreds, beat his breast with rocks so hard he couldn't perform for two days after, and "mistakenly" embraced bicycles commandeered from shops and children pulled from the audience – combining melodramatic passion with a Quixote-like single-mindedness:

> I cry Leila, Leila in the wilderness! Leila haunts my mind, day and night! Where should I look for my Leila? Leila Oh, Leila! I am ruined for Leila, gone mad for her, drunk with the thought of her! Leila!

Real private affairs often spill out into public space in Rajasthan, and since Hajari Bhand's home is next to the old police station in Chittorgarh he has witnessed many such events. He takes advantage of this in a number of *veśas*—particularly those involving women. The role of the pregnant Pinjari played before Bhupal Singh and used to expose a philandering merchant is also adapted as a street routine—humorously blaming dignified merchants as the father, calling out for public assistance in collecting support payments, and threatening to give birth in the street. Kesari Singh expresses particular admiration for both the veracity and comic skill of Hajari's portrayal of a Kanjari woman seeking money from the crowd, claiming police brutality, and flirting outrageously with those who will stop to listen. From a caste traditionally notorious as prostitutes, thieves, and repeat criminal offenders (O.P. Joshi 1982, personal communication), Hajari's Kanjari is a non-stop talker—pleading, cajoling, protesting innocence, and playing upon the audience's sympathy with a glint of humor in her eyes. The laughter generated comes from delight in the play with sexual identity, exploitation of the stereotypical behavior associated with a traditional outlaw caste, satirical allusions to police brutality, and by-play with individual audience members:

> We're innocent, Sir, but the officer has broken every bone in my husband's body. We don't steal, Sir, we're just camping in the neighborhood. We get by begging scraps of food. We keep little puppies and calves, Sir, we don't steal. And then the officer comes wearing his shorts and takes away my husband. The sergeant has broken every bone in my husband's body, Sir. My daughter, my mother-in-law, her daughter, they're all weeping bitterly, one tear after the other, Sir. Come to our camp and we'll feed you some eggs. Sir, if you put up bail for my husband, I'll let you sleep with my daughter.

The technique of bringing private affairs into the public arena is combined with the extroverted bawdiness of the Gaduliya and his wife in a *sāṅg* performed by Hajari and his son, Janakilal, in which private squabbles overwhelm the vendors' professional concerns:

Gaduliya: Bring your scrap iron to me! Buy that ladle you need! Give me your broken scrap iron!
Wife: Oh mother, would you buy a ladle?
Gaduliya: Why do you always shout and create a disturbance?
Wife: Strange! If I sell my wares or do nothing at all, you still say I shout!
Gaduliya: Oh, let me burn your mouth! Look at that, Sethji, just because the country is ruled by a lady, this woman is shouting![9] I've told her clearly that, being a woman, she shouldn't shout, but she shouts anyway, can't keep her face straight or her mouth shut!
Wife: Lovely language you're using in front of everyone in the middle of the market!
Gaduliya: How dare you interrupt when I'm speaking?
Wife: You don't want me to sell any goods?
Gaduliya: Sell goods? Goods are sold by men, not women!
Wife: Oh, if a woman shouldn't shout to sell goods, maybe she should stuff a pestle in her mouth!
Gaduliya: What's that about a pestle? Still shouting? I'll brand you yet! Have you seen my tool?
Wife: Watch out for your tool, it's blunt!
Gaduliya: You want me to sharpen my tool? Have you felt it lately? If you go to another man, I'll get another wife! Shopkeeper, the rains have failed, we're out of fodder, the children need food. How can I feed them when all she thinks of is clothing and jewelry?
Wife: Are you going to buy me a skirt or not?
Gaduliya: See how she shouts!

Perhaps most startling and complex of all the *sāṅg*s bringing private matters into public spaces is that of the Nakhti – a woman whose nose tip has been cut off by her husband in a jealous rage – a practice of punishing unfaithful wives once fairly common and still occasionally heard of in villages according to R.C. Pancholi, a Chittorgarh jurist (1982, personal communication). With the cut nose created by tying a piece of cardboard soaked in red dye over his real nose, and a liberal use of stage blood, Hajari enters the streets shouting for help:

> Oh sir, my nose has been lopped off! When I was nursing my child, he came and said that I slept with other men! Damn my husband! What'll become of my children now? Where should I go? How could I be an adulteress when I'm the mother of three children?!

The audience's astonishment and shock is gradually turned to uneasy comedy as Hajari names one after the other of the onlookers as among the "few" exceptions that she had shared her favors with, praising the discretion of some, disparaging the sexual services of others, and finally stating that the husband's claim that she had slept with every man in the village was preposterous, given the smallness of their home. In the process, both the husband's vicious action, the wife's hypocrisy and prodigality, and the audience's own gullibility and discomfiture become targets for satiric attention and laughter.

These examples show certain artistic principles at work in the construction of the *bahurūpiyā*'s *sāṅgs*. Since he is a street performer and must play to a constantly changing audience, the repetition of key phrases abound in the playing—far more so, in fact, than in the limited examples given. Thus, street cries, bits of doggerel, and repeated lamentations are used to specify the character and situation for new onlookers as well as to sustain dialogue and character for those who follow the performance from street to street and shop to shop. These key strips of dialogue provide a base for the *sāṅg* and are then departed from as Hajari improvises within the circumstances offered by the audience's reactions. Many of these improvised bits of repartee with the audience have already been tested in other performances, while a few may be evoked by the particularities of the moment.

Entire performances are built up by recycling old material within new contexts. Thus, the *veś* of the pregnant Pinjari, originally created for Bhupal Singh's amusement, can be used to humiliate an antagonistic merchant or to provide public entertainment. Elements worked out for one-man *veśas* can be built upon in expanded *sāṅgs* involving two or more *bahurūpiyā*s. Janakilal, for example, teamed with his father to perform as a protesting Kanjara being led to the police station by Hajari's stern Police Officer:

> *Kanjara*: I fall at your feet, Sir! We walk the straight and

narrow path, Sir! We don't steal! We are your Kanjaras, completely innocent!

Policeman: Shut up, motherfucker! Keep moving! If you talk too much, I'll whack you with this stick!

Kanjara: Oh, Sir! Please don't drag us into the station! What have we stolen? We only steal little things. Have we stolen gold so you're taking us to the police station?

Policeman: Move it! Walk!

Kanjara: Oh, Sir! We don't steal. Ask him! We won't steal anymore, Sir! We're innocent. Except for a few little necessary thefts. Oh, Sir, we didn't steal the goats.

Policeman: How many goats did you steal? Who did you sell them to?

Kanjara: We sold them to Mama, the butcher. But he just died yesterday. What can we do?

Policeman: How many goats? Tell the truth!

Kanjara: Oh, Sir, I only took three goats. And still people say we steal gold! Oh, Sir, we don't even eat mutton! We are your Kanjaras, getting by begging cold stale food!

Policeman: It'd better not happen again! Sit here on the ground, motherfucker! And shut up!

Kanjara: Oh, Sir, I repent, I put my hands in my mouth. What do we steal, Sir? By your throat I swear, Sir!

Policeman: You dare swear by my throat?

Kanjara: I'll never swear by your throat again, Sir. We're your Kanjaras, camping in your area, living on food we beg, Sir. By your throat, I swear, Sir. We only steal very small things or gold. Except for gold and small things, we never steal at all!

Though "situation" becomes far more important than "plot," and characters have little chance to "develop" as the street audience comes and goes, it is important to note that – at least in Hajari and Janakilal Bhand's treatments – there is a dramatic progression involved in these *sāṅgs*. The initial dialogue establishes the situation and character – usually ones familiar to the audience. Often, there is an initial "taking in" of the audience. Thus, the Doctor and Police Officer convince many at first by their seeming authenticity, and we have seen the *sāṅg* of the Nakhti send people calling for help. Gradually, the joke is revealed by greater and greater audacity in the portrayal of character and manipulation of dialogue – as in the Pathan's harangue or in the fight between the Gaduliya and his wife – or through comic by-play with the audience. Thus, the Doctor moves from suggesting pills to telling the "patient" that he should only have sex once a year. The performative play involved in the *sāṅg* of the Nakhti is revealed by her more and more outrageous allusions to supposed secret affairs with audience members. Janakilal's Kanjara goes from protesting complete innocence to pleading with the arresting officer that "except for gold and small things, we never steal at all."

The overall sense of spontaneous and enlivening play may be more important to a *bahurūpiyā*'s performance than any of the specific techniques and effects that have been pointed out. To celebrate the end of our work together, and to mark the end of a period of mourning following the death of his elder brother Mohan, Hajari Bhand dressed up his sons and recreated the *veś* of the tribal Bhils – a people known for their bravery, loyalty, and zestful appetite for life. With Hajari impersonating a Bhil matriarch, carrying his two-year-old son, and spinning in feverish circles with a broad grin on his face, the infectious joy was picked up by the citizens of Chittorgarh as Hajari and his family sang this song:

The king is coming,
Beat the drums and *thālī*!
The Bhils are dancing,
The Bhands are dancing, too!

To an unusual degree, Hajari Bhand strives for originality while devising his *sāṅgs* – even when his *veśas* are shared by other *bahurūpiyās*. He takes pride in the fact that he has developed his own repertory and in his efforts to keep his material fresh. During our travels, we had the opportunity to observe the creation of a new character. While Hajari was performing the *veś* of the Nakhti, a real life *pāgal* began to interact with Hajari, saying he would beat up the woman's husband and inviting her to move in with him. Hajari afterwards reflected that the *pāgal's* intervention had been welcome at first, since it gave him something new to respond to in his improvised play. As the *pāgal* began to follow us around, however, demanding money, throwing stones, and taking attention away from the performance, Hajari found his presence annoying. Later that night, we asked him if he could make up a character based on the *pāgal*. Hajari immediately showed us how he would do this, beginning by rearranging his clothes and then assuming a stance that was a slight exaggeration of the *pāgal*'s. He then started to repeat a few key actions and phrases of the *pāgal* that had rankled him: imitating the demands for money and swinging his arms in a wide arc as if throwing a stone. As we laughed, he began to elaborate, keeping the words and actions first chosen as touchstones in his widening portrayal. A character that was both an accurate reflection and a comic comment on the *pāgal* began to take on life, as though he was being recreated in the distorting glass of a fun-house mirror.

If the mirror that the *bahurūpiyā* holds up to nature is a distorting one, often sustaining stereotypes and poking fun at man's pretensions to dignity, the *bahurūpiyā*'s playful census of Rajasthani types also provides a dynamic method of airing tensions within the culture. Beyond this, in its cumulative effect, the artistry of the *bahurūpiyā* challenges the fixed nature of the very categories that it uses for its field of play. Plato, who distrusted mimetic skills, refers in *The Republic* to wandering "pantomimic gentlemen, who are so clever that they can imitate anything" and suggests sending story-tellers with such skills promptly away as disruptive influences, "sweet and holy and wonderful beings" though they may be (Jowett 1944:155). Plato feared that the mimic would further distort life—already imperfectly comprehended—for the sake of a good laugh or a dramatic effect, and that the net result of his fooling with identities would be chaos. The anarchic juggling of identities by the *bahurūpiyā* as a "pantomimic gentleman" is particularly striking against a social background traditionally dominated by principles of *karma* and *dharma*—principles which dictate the obligations and duties, as well as social rank, dress, and occupations of caste members. Plato is at least potentially correct in pointing out the anarchic impetus latent in the mimic's art; but then, perhaps, an heretical touch of anarchy has more to do with a comprehensive and humane picture of the world than he would readily admit. The *bahurūpiyā*'s adroitness at shifting identities while maintaining his comic (and moral) perspective may strike us as particularly commendable in a world that often calls for dizzying shifts of roles that make the unitary sense of self harder and harder to sustain.

Feudal societies in general have tried to answer the call of anarchy by sponsoring pockets of disorder within the system itself. The fool chained to the throne of the king served as a reminder of common frailty, but the chain must also have functioned as a means of keeping this human symbol for disorder fixed within the compass of the court. The natural fools and dwarves that so fascinated the European medieval and Renaissance courts as lessons in humility and images of a disorder that cried out for containment seem to have been less popular (though not entirely missing, to judge by the *vidūṣka's* distorted shape) in the courts of India. In Hindu caste society, the *bahurūpiyā*'s ability to take on many identities is similarly appealing and threatening. It can be no accident that, of all the Bhands, the Hindu Bhands of Rajasthan seem to have taken particular delight in tapping this tradition to add to their repertory as jesters. If the rigidities of dress and behavior in caste society facilitate the *bahurūpiyā*'s work, these same rigidities give added meaning to his ability to function.

The *bahurūpiyā*'s heretical play with the principles of *karma* and *dharma* points to a deeper stratum of Hindu philosophy that insists that each human being contains in microcosmic form the powers and potentialities of the macrocosmos. As a joker in the deck, a "wild card" in an otherwise carefully labeled pack, the *bahurūpiyā* serves as a reminder that, even in the most rigid societies, identities are not fixed. The wheel of *karma* takes many turns and a prince in one cycle may find himself a pauper in another as the *līlā* or play of life continues. Small wonder, then, that the rich and powerful would strive to contain and control this disruptive presence through patronage, and that the Bhand's sycophantic flattery is sought after, while his curses are feared. The Bhand as *bahurūpiyā* serves not only as an entertaining reflection and distortion of a Rajasthani "human comedy," but as a reminder and immediate demonstration of the mutability of the human soul and the liveliness of the human spirit.

This is, of course, neither a new nor a peculiarly Indian (or Asian) enterprise. At the end of the middle ages in Europe, Erasmus followed a similar line of thought while meditating on the fool and writing his *Praise of Folly*:

> Now what else is the whole life of mortals but a sort of comedy, in which the various actors, disguised by various costumes and masks, walk on and play each one his part, until the manager waves them off the stage? Moreover, this manager frequently

bids the same actor go back in a different costume, so that he who has but lately played the king in scarlet now acts the flunky in patched clothes (Hudson 1941:37).

We do not know, of course, how much of this analysis would ring true to Hajari Bhand, who in his day-to-day behavior is as polite and modest as he is outrageous in his professional roles. It is appropriate to end this study with his own joking protest about our work with him:

> I wander about. I meet everybody. I get along with everyone. By making people happy, I earn some money. I eat and I drink. I have no problems. Then you people come along and hire me to do all this work and ask me all these questions about this and that. Now, I've got problems!

ENDNOTES

This paper originally appeared, with minor differences, in the Spring 1986 issue of *The Drama Review*, 30(1), as "A Joker in the Deck: Hajari Bhand of Rajasthan." Research was funded by the Smithsonian Institution in 1981 (for investigations jointly undertaken with Amy R. Catlin and William O. Beeman), and by the Indo-US Subcommission in 1982-83. This funding was administered by the American Institute of Indian Studies, whose help is gratefully acknowledged. In addition to the individuals cited in the text, and many others who must go unrecognized, we are indebted to the people of Bassi, Bhilwara, Chittorgarh, Gangapur, Renwal, Pushkar, Kacheriawas, Jaipur and Udaipur, where we filmed and conducted research: the *bahurūpiyās'* work and our own would be impossible without their good will and sense of humor.

A 40-minute video tape, *Hajari Bhand of Rajasthan: Jester without Court* (NTSC color standard) is available for rental or purchase through Documentary Educational Resources, 101 Morse Street, Watertown, MA 02172, USA (Tel. 617/926-(0491). VHS copies of this video tape are also available for viewing in India at the Archive and Research Center for Etnomusicology, American Institute of Indian Studies, B-29, Defence Colony, New Delhi 110 024, and at the Rupayan Sansthan Institute in Jodhpur, Rajasthan.

1. Quotations from Hajari Bhand come from taped interviews and conversations held from November 1982 to March of 1983. Translation assistance was provided at various times by Komal Kothari, who first introduced Hajari Bhand to us, Rawat Kesari Singh, O.P. Joshi, Ranchor Singh Ashiya, Dinesh Chandra

Bhanawat, Shadashiv Shrotriya, Amrit Singh and Kanilal M. Bhandari, whose good faith and assistance were invaluable. Further translation advice was provided by Robert Hueckstedt. Karine Schomer and Joan Erdman offered helpful suggestions for writing and editing. The sections of Hajari Bhand's *sāṅgs* quoted in this paper have been reworked from Dinesh Chandra Bhanawat's literal translations made from our field recordings.

2. Naqqals are frequently equated with Bhands (Russell and Lal 1975:I, 349). In usage, though, the term seems to be a more generic term for itinerant actors; it derives from an Urdu term for imitation, or copy, and is more frequently used in Uttar Pradesh.
3. The patron referred to is Bhupal Singh, who was Maharana of Udaipur from 1931 to 1950 and died in 1955.
4. Some of the references made by Hajari Bhand in this *bhāṅḍāī* may require explication. "Thakur" roughly corresponds to "lord" and is traditionally used both as a respectful term of address for Rajput noblemen and as a designation for prominent local landowners and overlords. Chhatrapati Shivaji is one of the many appellations for Shiva – that aspect of the godhead associated with destruction and renewal. Mahadev is yet another name for Shiva, stressing his preeminence among the gods. The Rathors constitute one of the dominant Rajput clans. Rathors have ruled in various localities in Rajasthan since at least the 10th century A.D., but are particularly associated with Jodhpur; since the time of Akbar, they have been celebrated especially for their prowess in battle.
5. Divali, or the Festival of Lights, is a festive holiday held in autumn. It is traditionally a time when both ancestral spirits and the goddess of wealth (Lakshmi) are honored; hence, it is a particularly appropriate time for Bhands to collect for their services and to offer up *bhāṅḍāīs* that praise a family's lineage and wealth. Other terms in this *bhāṅḍāī* may need explication. The Bhandaris are a subdivision of the Oswali Bania caste of merchants and bankers. King Hamir (Maharana Hamir Singh) ruled in Udaipur from 1300 to 1363 and was known for both his vigorous defense of Mewar and his generous patronage of the arts. Lakshmi is understandably important in the worship of the Bania merchants – particularly at the time of Divali. Satyanarayan refers to Vishnu, Lakshmi's consort and one of the principal manifestations of the Hindu godhead; he is especially associated with the preservation of a divinely determined order on earth and in the heavens. Though some Banias are Jains, most consider themselves Vaishnavites.
6. Id-ul-Fitr is a festive Islamic holiday that marks the breaking of the Ramazan fast. The term Fakir comes from the Arabic *fakr*, poverty; Id would be a particularly propitious day for these mendicants to seek alms. Ajmer is a pilgrimage site for Muslims, since it houses the Chishti Dargah, shrine to the 13th-century Sufi saint, Mu'in al-Din Sanjari, whose memory is honored by many Hindus as well. Ali (b. Ali Talib) was the Prophet Mohammad's son-in-law and heir, the fourth Caliph of Islam (656-660 A.D.); he is revered by Shi'ites, who hold that the legitimate succession of the Caliphate was through Ali and his martyred son, Husain. Ali is also widely held to be a founder of the Fakir orders. Haider is another name for him.

7. Khakiji Sadhus are itinerant Vaishnavite holy men who travel in groups; they can be quite prosperous. Narasimha is the man-lion *avatār* (incarnation) of Vishnu, who saved the tripartite world order by destroying the ambitious demon Hiranyakashipu. Rameshwaram is a celebrated place of pilgrimage in Tamil Nadu, where Rama is said to have set up one of the 12 great *lingams* to honor Shiva.
8. Ramlila performances are held in September-October to celebrate Rama's victory over the demon Ravana, as chronicled in the *Rāmāyaṇa* and its more recent retellings, especially Tulsidas's *Rāmcharitmānas*. While the largest of these ceremonies takes place over 30-31 days in Ramnagar, outside of Varanasi, smaller celebrations are held throughout northern India. Rama (an *avatār* of Vishnu) is aided in his struggle by an army of monkeys under the leadership of the loyal Hanuman; this legendary monkey-general has assumed an important place in the Hindu pantheon. Masks for Hanuman may be made of wood, hammered copper, or, like the one used by Hajari Bhand, of papier mâché.
9. In 1982, when this *sāṅg* was recorded, Indira Gandhi was Prime Minister of India. Seth(ji) is an honorific used in addressing merchants.

REFERENCES CITED

Ashiya, Ranchor Singh
1983 "*Mulākāt Hajārī Bhāṅḍ se.*" *Rangayan* 16(10): 13-19.

Bhanawat, Mahendra
1974 "*Nakal ko Bhāṅḍ kī.*" *Ranguyog* (Journal of the Rajasthan Sangeet Natak Akademi).
1979 "Overview of the Folk Theatre of Rajasthan." *Sangeet Natak* (Journal of Sangeet Natak Akademi) 53-54: 26-32.

Crooke, William
1974 *Tribes and Castes of Northwestern India*. 4 vols. Delhi: Cosmo Publications (1st ed. 1986).

Dash, Dhiren
1979 "Jatra: People's Theatre of Orissa." *Sangeet Natak* (Journal of the Sangeet Natak Akademi) 52: 11-26.

Elliot, R.C.
1960 *The Power of Satire: Magic, Ritual, Art*. Princeton, N.J.: Princeton University Press.

Hudson, Hoyt Hopewell, transl.
1941 *The Praise of Folly by Desiderius Erasmus*. Princeton, N.J.: Princeton University Press.

Jarrett, Col. H.S., transl.
1978 *The A'in-i Akbari of Abu'l Fazl 'Allami*. 4 vols. Sir Jadunath Sarkar, ed. Reprint of 2nd revised ed. New Delhi: Oriental Books Reprint Corporation. (First ed. 1894)

Jowett, B., transl.
1944 *Plato: The Republic*. 3rd ed. New York: Heritage Press. (First published 1892)

Mathur, V.B.
1969 *Ethnographic Atlas of Rajasthan with Reference to Scheduled Castes and Scheduled Tribes*. Jaipur: Rajasthan Census Operations.

Raghavan, V.
1981 "Sanskrit Drama into Performance." In *Sanskrit Drama into Performance*. Rachel Van M. Baumer and James R. Brandon, eds. pp. 9-44. Honolulu: University of Hawaii.

Russell, R.V. and Rai Bahadur Hira Lal
1975 *Tribes and Castes of the Central Provinces of India*. 4 vols. Delhi: Rajdhani Book Centre.(1st ed. 1915)

Sharma, G.N.
1968 *Social Life in Medieval Rajasthan: 1500-1800 A.D.* Agra: Laxmi Narain Agarwal.

Welsford, Enid
1968 *The Fool: His Social and Literary History*. London: Faber and Faber. (1st ed. 1935)

Willeford, William
1969 *The Fool and His Scepter: A Study in Clowns and Jesters and Their Audience*. Evanston, Ill.: Northwestern University Press.

TIMELESS SYMBOLS: ROYAL PORTRAITS FROM RAJASTHAN 17TH-19TH CENTURIES

VISHAKHA N. DESAI

One of the most important cultural consequences of the interaction between the Mughal and Rajput courts was the development of Rajput portraiture in Rajasthan,[1] beginning in the first half of the 17th century. Previously, the production of images under Rajput patronage had consisted primarily of illustrations of religious and literary manuscripts such as the *Bhāgavata Purāṇa, Rāmāyaṇa*, and the *Rāgamālā*. Now, the Rajput rulers also began to commission paintings of themselves, alone or in a courtly setting – watching a performance, hunting, sitting in a *darbār*, or smoking a *huqqā*.

In a culture that had traditionally emphasized connections with the past and the eternal qualities of life rather than empirical observation of everyday reality, pictorial representation of an individual's reign was something entirely new. In order to understand this development in Rajasthani painting, we need not only to examine its antecedents and distinctiveness, but also to understand it in the broader context of Rajput culture. Conversely, a careful analysis of these portraits can provide us with a better understanding of Rajput cultural concepts and values.

Though pictorial representation of individual Rajput rulers was a new phenomenon, the literary and bardic accounts give us a fairly clear picture of how ideal kings were defined and understood. In this literature, whose viewpoint is reflected in James Tod's *Annals and Antiquities of Rajasthan*, the chief characteristics which define a model ruler are his genealogy, his courage in defending the honor of his land and lineage, and his munificence. It is important that a ruler be brave (*vīra*), magnanimous (*udāra*), and generous (*dānī*). His kindness to his subjects and his role as protector of his people (*lokapāla*) are also emphasized. These bardic descriptions are characteristically exaggerated in their praise and adulation of a virtuous king, the emphasis being not so much on the specific actions of the ruler as on general attributes of kingship and on a Rajput ruler's traditional role as a virtuous inheritor of his ancestors' rule and land.[2]

This stress on the timeless virtues of kingship and the notion of a king's role as hereditary protector of his subjects stand in sharp contrast to the notion of an ideal ruler as described in the Mughal chronicles. Study of the *Akbarnāma* and the *Tuzūk-i Jahāngīrī* reveals a strong emphasis on the absolute authority of the king. "King of kings", "Glory over the head of mortals", or "Paramount over famous sovereigns and mighty" are the characteristic descriptive phrases.[3] Additionally, the fact that such historical chronicles, integral to Mughal notions of history and of a ruler's legitimacy, are completely absent in the Rajput world also suggests a very different view of time and history. By and large, the Rajput view, rooted in certain fundamental concepts of Hindu thought, does not emphasize specificity of events, or even the personalities shaping the events. It is this lack of interest in the observation and recording of actual events and activities, and in the specific description of physical attributes of historical personages, combined with the absence of the concept of a ruler's absolute authority, which account for the lack of physiognomically-specific royal portraiture in pre-Mughal India.[4]

With the advent of imperial Mughal culture under the emperor Akbar and his successors, the Rajput rulers of Rajasthan came in close contact with another way of looking at the world. This new view was infused with Akbar's preoccupation with the establishment of his authority in the form of incessant documentation of his actions, and his genuine interest in the observation of the actual world of nature, events, and individuals – a view which had given rise to and shaped the whole development of Mughal portraiture.

In examining the Rajput tradition of royal portraits that grew out of contact with the Mughals, there are two central questions. First, what aspects of Mughal portraiture were adopted by the Rajput court painters, what themes and elements were borrowed only selectively, and what was left out altogether? Secondly, what is the significance of the selection and adoption process in the context of traditional Rajput cultural values?

The 17th Century

It is not surprising that the earliest Rajput portraits are greatly indebted to Mughal prototypes. The degree and nature of the Mughal influence varies from court to court, depending on the Rajput ruler's relationship with the Mughals, his willingness to adopt new ideas and fashion and his artists' awareness of and ability to create new kinds of pictures. Thus, some of the early portraits are directly based on Mughal works and may have been done by Mughal artists who had migrated from Delhi. Others are in the Mughal idiom but reflect Rajput sensibilities. A third group borrows only the concept of rendering likenesses from the Mughal tradition but develops a much more thoroughly Rajput vision, with only a slight trace of Mughal style.

The earliest known group of Rajput portraits come from areas that had developed strong political connections with the Mughal empire at a fairly early stage. Thus, Bikaner, Bundi and Marwar are among the most important centers of early portrait painting in the Mughalized idiom.[5] Raja Rai Singh of Bikaner (r. 1571-1611) had succeeded in breaking away from the state of Marwar and in establishing an independent kingdom only with the help of Akbar, who successfully invaded Marwar in 1569 and guaranteed Rai Singh free possession of Bikaner (Tod 1971:II, 958). The alliance was further strengthened by the marriages of Rai Singh and Akbar to princesses of Jaisalmer who were sisters (*ibid.*, II,1133). Maldeo of Marwar (r. 1532-1568) had been defeated by Akbar in 1568-69, but a close connection between Marwar and the Mughal emperor was established by Maldeo's successor Udai Singh, who sought Mughal support to weaken the claims of his bother to the Marwar throne (*ibid.*, II,959-961). For Rao Surjan Singh of Bundi (r. 1533-ca. 1575), an alliance with Akbar after the fall of his fort at Ranthambhor in 1569 meant freedom from vassalage to the Rana of Mewar (*ibid.*, III, 1480-1482).

Significantly, each of these Rajput rulers opted to accept Mughal sovereignity with the hope that he would gain power over or independence from his Rajput foes. In other words, the actions of these rulers were determined by their attitudes toward their own world, the Rajput world, with little regard for the resultant subjugation to the Mughal throne. They responded to Akbar's political and military overtures in order to support their own new claims or settle old scores within the context of a quintessentially Rajput world. Similarly, it can be argued that the Rajput adoption of Mughal portrait conventions was not simply a formal or pictorial development but the result of a conscious selection process whereby new conceptual and visual ideas were incorporated into a preexisting Rajput framework.

Early portraits from these three kingdoms consist primarily of single figures, bust and "balcony" (*zarokhā*) portraits, equestrian images, and occasionally of entertainment scenes.[6] The earliest of these images were most likely painted by the artists at the Mughal court while others were painted by artists who may have migrated from the imperial centers to the regional Rajput courts. For example, a line drawing of Raja Karan Singh of Bikaner (r. 1631-1669/71), dating from the mid-17th century, is attributed to a leading Muslim artist trained in the Mughal idiom (see Fig. 1).[7] In its sensitive treatment of the face, particularly the eyes, modeling around the chin, delicate hair line, and the three-dimensional folds of the garment, this lifelike sketch is very close to contemporary Mughal works.[8] Lack of stylization and the freshness of the picture suggests that it was done from life. Such an execution would not have been possible for an artist who was not used to transforming observations from the physical world into a convincing visual image on the two-dimensional surface of paper. It is unlikely that in the first half of the 17th century, this transformation could have been achieved by a court artist not trained in the Mughal tradition.[9]

When artists from non-Mughal milieus attempted to create a Mughalized image, the effect was somewhat different. There was a departure from visual specificity, and a greater abstraction of natural forms, reflecting Rajput preferences and aesthetics. A posthumous portrait of Raja Gaj Singh of Marwar (r. 1619-1638), though highly Mughal at first sight, upon closer examination reveals certain characteristically Rajput or native Indian predilections (see Fig. 2). Gaj Singh's prominent nose, folds under the eyes, and double chin reflect the artist's indebtedness to the Mughal notion of physiognomic specificity. In fact, the close similarity between this image and several other Mughal portraits of the same ruler suggests that it may have been based on a Mughal work. But when comparing it with Mughal examples, one is struck by the stylized lines of the inner ear and wavy whiskers, and the idealized, lotus-petal shape of the eyes. A Rajput preference for

Fig. 1: Raja Karan Singh of Bikaner. Bikaner mid-17th century, 26.2 x 17.2 cm. Ink on paper. (Private Collection)

Fig. 2: Raja Gaj Singh of Marwar. Jodhpur region, mid-17th century. 26.8 x 18.3 cm. Ink and gold washes on paper. (Courtesy National Museum New Delhi, 63. 1789)

transforming specific features into generalized forms begins to be apparent.

A large group of single-figure portraits dating from the first half of the 17th century comes from Bundi.[10] Although these images use such Mughal conventions as green backgrounds, floral foreground, and a few lines of colorful sky at the top of the picture, their implicit Rajput qualities are clear. Most of them portray long deceased kings, and are not directly based on Mughal prototypes.[11] There is very little visual distinction between each of these portraits. The only way we are able to identify them individually is through their different attributes and inscriptions.

Clearly, the purpose of these pictures was not to provide a specific visual rendering of an individual. Rather, the intention of the patron, and consequently of the artist, was to create a series of genealogical portraits which would work as a cohesive group. This is further corroborated by the stylistic unity of the pictures, suggesting that most of the images were created as a group for one ruler. Although stylistically related to the Mughal prototypes, conceptually and thematically such portraits are only indirectly related to the Mughal world. The artists who produced these works had thus begun to adapt the Mughal concept of portraiture to Rajput intentions and purposes, and to use Rajput conventions such as the iconographic treatment of the rulers' features. It is likely that such changes in subject, style and use of portraiture were directly related to the preferences and predilections of the patrons and the corresponding abilities of their artists.

Strong Mughal influence can also be discerned in entertainment and *zenānā* (women's quarters) scenes from Bikaner, Bundi, and Marwar.[12] In almost all of these scenes, the compositional formulae of flower gardens in the foreground, pavilion-like spaces in the middle ground, and landscaped backgrounds recall Mughal paintings of the first half of the century. The female types, particularly in the Bikaner and Marwar paintings, are direct descendants of Mughal painting. And yet, none of these "contextual" portraits, showing a ruler in the company of women and enjoying music, is based directly on Mughal prototypes.[13] All of the Rajput images are more lush in vegetation and busier in surface details than their Mughal counterparts. That there are far more entertainment scenes from the Rajput courts of Rajasthan than from the imperial Mughal world suggests that themes were not simply borrowed from the Mughals but developed further and given a distinct flavor. This phenomenon has important implications for visual developments in the portraiture of the succeeding century.

While Bundi, Bikaner and Marwar adopted the concept of portraiture from the Mughals at an early stage,[14] the court of Mewar was one of the last major centers to accept this empirically oriented art form. One of the last Rajput states to surrender to the Mughals and accept their sovereignty,[15] Mewar was culturally conservative as well, extolled by later eras for having preserved traditional Rajput values rather than adopting Mughal ways.

The earliest known Mewari portraits, based largely on contemporary Bundi images, date from the reign of Rana Raj Singh (r. 1652-1680; Topsfield 1980:10). Significantly, these images form a very small part of the Mewar painters' repertoire, and the Mughalized style of these pictures does not seem to have had a significant impact on the more prolific production of religious and literary manuscript illustrations. For manuscripts, artists continued to use the traditional, hieratic style with only minor modifications.[16] Both the illustrated manuscripts and the secular court pictures were commissioned by royal patrons, and it is very likely that they were painted by the same group of court artists. From the study of Mewari painting at the end of the century it is clear that Mewar artists, unlike their contemporaries at Bundi and Bikaner, did not infuse all of their pictures with Mughalized idioms. Rather, they selectively borrowed motifs and styles when appropriate for a particular theme or subject. Just as in the political history of the 17th century, Mewar's stance was one of conservatism and resistance to the new order, in the realm of painting as well, it can be argued, Mewar exhibited the characteristic Rajput pattern of selective adaptation to the outside world without any fundamental departure from the traditional world view.

This pattern of selective borrowing, present to varying degrees in the different traditions of Rajasthani painting, is most evident in the conspicuous absence of historical or event-specific portraits. By contrast, a large number of the portraits of Mughal emperors come from historical manuscripts such as the *Jahāngīrnāmā* and the *Pādshāhnāmā*. Even the *darbār* scenes showing these emperors are usually illustrations of specific events described in the chronicles (Desai 1985a:12-14). The answer to this lack of historical portraits in 17th-century Rajasthani painting lies in the Rajput character itself. As suggested earlier, Rajputs were accustomed to a traditional Indian view of temporal reality as only a small part of a universe with infinite time cycles. What appealed to them were the notions of timelessness and of an enduring link between the present and the past. Their notion of history was bardic, with no inclination to separate facts from legends, or historic present from mythic past. For them, there was no great virtue in emphasizing historical description over visionary or idealized expression. Even under the strong influence of 17th-century Mughal empiricism, these quintessentially Rajput rulers resisted the Mughal notions of kingship that emphasized the temporal power and the historical position of rulers. The 17th-century Rajput rulers selected and patronized those aspects of Mughal portrait painting which could be adapted to their own concept of royalty, while avoiding others which were alien to their world view.

The 18th Century

In the 18th century, portraits and works on other secular themes greatly increased at the Rajput courts, gradually eclipsing religious and literary manuscript illustrations. By the second quarter of the century, depictions of rulers in a variety of settings, ranging from Holi celebrations to hunting scenes, became predominant themes. Stylistic innovation and artistic excellence are clearly evident in works on these courtly subjects, whereas the manuscript illustrations of the period appear increasingly formulaic and repetitive. However, this new emphasis on secular or courtly subjects does not mean that the royal portrait tradition in Rajasthan was coming under a stronger influence of the Mughal tradition. On the contrary, most innovations in 18th-century Rajasthani court portraiture had little to do with the Mughal tradition. Instead, it was at this time that royal portraiture in Rajasthan truly came of age.

A late bloomer in the portrait tradition, Mewar became the leading center of contextual portraiture in the first half of the 18th century. This change is first evident in the paintings from the reign of Rana Amar Singh II (b. 1672, r. 1698-1710). Even before coming to the throne, Amar Singh seems to have been an active patron, commissioning portraits of himself in the Mughalized *grisaille* style.[17] However, from around 1705 onward, paintings from his reign display a new vision of courtly themes. *Maharana*

Amar Singh Celebrating Holi with his Couriers (see Fig. 3) exemplifies this new tradition of contextual portraits. In a luxuriant garden filled with cypresses and richly foliated trees, the haloed Maharana, larger in scale than everyone else, presides over the formal Holi celebrations. Such large panoramic depictions of rulers had no precedent in Mughal painting. Even though the image may represent a specific Holi *darbār*, there is little suggestion in the composition of a specific moment in time. One feels as if this is a prototypical representation of a Holi *darbār*. Rather than depicting a particular historical moment, it is imbued with a sense of timelessness. And yet the individualization of figures and their careful placement suggests that the artist has attempted to record the scene carefully. His observation is further corroborated by the detailed inscription on the reverse which identifies the scene as the celebration of Phag (Holi) in the royal pavilion of the Sabrat Vilas garden. Also given are the names of every figure in the picture, including those of the musicians. Although the detailed inscription imparts a sense of specificity to the scene, thus recalling the Mughal aesthetic preference for empirical observation, its content as well as the painting's spatial organization are radically different from Mughal examples.

When we compare the Amar Singh *darbār* with that of the Mughal emperor Jahangir (see Fig. 4), both appear formal and hierarchical. The central placement of the haloed rulers and the devices that set them apart from other figures, have similarities. However, conceptually and spatially these images are products of two very different worlds. In the Mughal *darbār* the hierarchy is established in a linear placement of the figures. Closest to the emperor are members of his immediate family and his most trusted advisors.[18] As we move away and downward from the locus of power we meet such petty functionaries as the accountant of the elephant stables. In characteristic Mughal fashion, the only seated person in the composition is the emperor himself: all authority emanates from him and everyone else is subservient to him.

The Amar Singh *darbār* displays a radically different spatial organization and a correspondingly different hierarchical system. The closest members of the Maharana's family – the heir-apparent Sangram Singh, and Maharaja Umed Singh, the closest and seniormost relative of the Maharana – are placed not near the ruler, but at the cardinal points of the square. Seated closest to the ruler

Fig. 3: Maharana Amar Singh Playing Holi with Courtiers. Udaipur, ca. 1708–1710. 47 x 40.5 cm. Opaque watercolor on paper. (Courtesy National Gallery of Victoria, Melbourne, Felton Bequest)

Fig. 4: Darbar of Jahangir. Attributed to Manohar. Mughal, North India, ca. 1620. 34.5 x 19.5 cm. Opaque watercolor on paper. (Courtesy Museum of Fine Arts, Boston, Francis Bartlett Donation of 1912 and Picture Fund)

are the priest and the seniormost grandees of the vassal states (*thikānās*) of Mewar. Although the Maharana is distinguished from others by a halo and such royal emblems as the shield, fly whisk, and *huqqā*, he is seated among equals. In sharp contrast to the Mughal *darbār*, where all but the emperor are standing, the Maharana's courtiers are all shown seated as well. The standing figures in the Mewar painting, primarily attendants, servants and musicians, are clearly from inferior social groups. Instead of the purely linear hierarchy and absolute power accorded the Mughal emperor in the *darbār* of Jahangir, *Rana Amar Singh Celebrating Holi* suggests a more spatially arranged system of power in which the Rajput ruler acknowledges the support and power of his feudatories, who are fellow clansmen. He sees himself as a "first among equals."

Portraits of this kind, set in distinctively Rajput contexts, began with the reign of Amar Singh and continued to be produced in increasing numbers throughout the century. In Mewar, the focus was on large panoramic pictures of Maharanas celebrating festivals, watching dance and music performances, or hunting with full regalia (Desai 1985a:66-70, Topsfield 1980:81-135). Stylistically, these pictures display a somewhat confusing combination of superficial Mughal conventions and predominantly Rajput features. For example, following the Mughal tradition, there is some attempt at rendering perspective in the architectural backgrounds of these pictures. However, more often than not, the diagonal lines suggesting depth diverge rather than converging on one point, and create an effect of aerial or isometric perspective. Such bird's-eye views of palace interiors and courtyards allow the artists to include a large amount of anecdotal imagery. Details – an attendant dozing off, another one fanning a fire, a courtier offering a flower – give an air of observed reality to such pictures. However, it would be impossible to observe such microscopic forms within large panoramic scenes in the real world. The artist in this tradition paints what he knows, not what he sees, or rather, he translates what he sees into what he knows, and then proceeds to create a conceptual rather than a perceptual view of the world. This is in keeping with the Rajput predilection for universal rather than temporal visual symbols.

Such an approach allows the artist not to feel bound by a "rational" view of things or by naturalistic conventions for creating compositions. Ultimately, it makes him better suited to visualize the conceptual framework of his Rajput patrons. Indeed, multiple viewpoints and sequential actions within a single composition are a reflection of the non-empirical tendencies of the Rajput and traditional Hindu world view. For all their visual details, these court portraits are more like archetypal visualizations of a given scene. As B.N. Goswamy has observed, "one senses that in rendering a moment the painter is not losing sight of the moments that have gone by and those that are yet to come" (in Desai 1985a:xxi). Much as in the illustrations of literary and religious manuscripts, the emphasis in these pictures is on clarity and comprehension of the narrative.

The lack of specificity in relation to historical or linear time in these picures of court life is also seen in the treatment of individual figures. Facial expressions and specific physical appearances from only a minor part of the distinguishing characteristics of an individual. In most cases, we identify the rulers through attributes such as the halo, ornaments, clothing, and weapons. Often, eyes are idealized, and it is through the outlines of a figure's forehead, nose or chin that we begin to differentiate between individuals. That almost all of these figures are rendered in profile, devoid of specific human emotions and without any sense of temporal connection with the viewer, also lends a sense of timelessness to them.[19] It is fair to say that such figures are treated as idealized iconographic symbols of royalty in the same way as images of deities. Even though the royal figures are historical and have the potential to be carefully observed, the artists at the Rajput courts again and again turn to ageless conventions to add a touch of generality to their specific rendering of a given patron. Indeed, the Rajput patrons seem to have preferred such an idealized and selective rendering of their lives, often in direct contradiction with the harsh political realities of their times.

These characteristics of 18th-century Mewar painting occur in the portraits produced in other princely states of Rajasthan as well. At most of the courts, there is a dearth of single-figure portraits and a preponderance of contextual portraits in which the kingship of the ruler is suggested through his actions in society. Predominant themes include *darbārs*, hunts, entertainment, festivals, and *zenānā* scenes. In Bundi and Kota, hunts seem to occupy a primary position throughout the century (see Figs. 5 and 6).[20] In

Fig. 5 : Raja Umed Singh Hunting Tigers. Hans Raj Joshi. Kota, 1787. 43.2 x 70.5 cm. Opaque watercolor on paper. (Collection of Catherine and Ralph Benkaim)

Fig. 6 : Raja Umed Singh Hunting Tigers (detail)

Bikaner, the most Mughalized of the Rajput painting centers, one finds a greater number of small-scale equestrian and hunting portraits in which the ruler is surrounded by a few attendants (Goetz 1950:110-112). In Jodhpur, large *darbārs* in richly textured interiors are popular subjects (Welch and Beach 1965:75). This proliferation of contextual portraits at the Rajasthani courts thus reflects a thorough assimilation of portraiture into the traditional Rajput view of royalty.

Our understanding of Rajput ideas of kingship and their portrayal in the 18th century can be further refined through comparison of royal portraits from Rajasthan with contemporary Mughal works. Like their Rajasthani counterparts, 18th century Mughal paintings are stylistically different from the Mughal paintings of the preceding century. Illustrated historical manuscripts, central to the development of imperial Mughal portraits, are now absent. Whether at the imperial center in Delhi or at a provincial court such as Oudh, a majority of portrait painting now consists of single portraits, lovers, and entertainment scenes. Codification of royal attributes, as seen in the Rajasthani paintings, is also found in the Mughal works. Even with these apparent similarities, 18th-century Mughal and Rajput works are conceptually and visually quite different. A Mughal sense of linear hierarchy and singular authority is seen even in portraits of such ineffectual rulers as Muhammad Shah. Either on a throne or carried in a palanquin, Muhammad Shah is always the only seated person in the composition. His courtiers stand in attendance, as if ready to take advice from their emperor, in direct contradiction with the political reality of the period (Desai 1985a:20). The emperor's authority is a given: he does not derive any special power from his surroundings. By contrast, in Rajasthani works, the emphasis is invariably on the contextual statement of royal power. The king establishes his authority and his virtues as a model ruler through his heroic and generous actions and through his social context, which includes a complex system of hierarchy among his nobles.

Stylistically as well, there are distinctions between these two types of royal portraits. It is true that neither of them possesses the naturalism so prevalent in 17th-century Mughal painting. Frozen figures with vacant stares, truncated bodies, and full-bodied *jāmās* (gowns) with diaphanous texture are shared by both traditions. It is in spatial organization and color scheme that the two styles of painting diverge most consistently. Mughal paintings of the period by and large use a cooler color palette with a greater number of secondary colors. Muted color combinations work better with the suggestion of depth in these compositions. Their spatial organization is also in keeping with a view of the world more grounded in empirical reality. Even if the 18th-century Mughal artist does not convey the kind of depth or perspective found in the imperial painting of the previous century, his works still echo the earlier prototypes associated with the ateliers of the emperors Jahangir and Shah Jahan. One does not find the multiple perspectives or simultaneous narratives commonly seen in contemporary Rajput works.

In the color scheme of the Rajasthani paintings of the period, there is much greater variety and vibrancy. Bright yellow and polished white backgrounds, forcing the surface of the picture to become two-dimensional, are frequently seen (Desai 1985a:42). The bright colors of textiles (red, yellow, and orange), the lush greens of the landscape, and the red borders of these pictures further enhance their two-dimensionality. Even when the artist renders figures in a very sensitive and realistic manner, he feels perfectly comfortable in "floating" them on a picture plane with no suggestion of ground or sense of space beneath or around them. The multiple spatial viewpoints of these compositions also emphasize the abstract and conceptual nature of the aesthetic. As suggested earlier, such stylistic distinctions between Rajput and Mughal works, rather than being arbitrary, further illuminate the differing philosophical frameworks of the two traditions.

This analysis of the Rajput understanding of kingship and its expression in the portraiture of the Rajasthani courts can be further refined through a comparison of 18th-century Rajasthani portraits with similar works from the Punjab Hills, which differed in their receptivity to Mighal conventions.[21] As in the Rajasthani traditions, 17th-century Pahari portraits were largely inspired by Mughal prototypes.[22] The most significant difference is seen in the paintings of the 18th-century. As previously explained, the Rajasthani images of the period consisted primarily of "contextual" portraits, depicting crowded *darbārs* and hunting scenes in large compositions. There was a gradual decline in religious and literary manuscript illustration, stylistic innovations being confined primarily to royal portraits. Pahari portraits in the 18th century have a very different flavor, which may be a reflection of the modified Rajput character of the royal culture of the Punjab Hills. Depictions of Pahari rulers and their courtiers typically consist of small groups – two rajas conversing with each other, smoking *huqqās*, listening to music, watching a dance performance, or worshipping a deity (W. Archer 1973:II, 63-64, 108, 112). There are very few images of kings hunting or in large *darbār* scenes (*ibid.*, II,146, 200-203). None of these royal portraits displays the multiple perspectives or bird's-eye views so prevalent in Rajasthan. The royalty of the figure in Pahari portraits, as in Rajasthani paintings, is established through such attributes as the flywhisk (made out of peacock feathers, yak tails or cloth), and a special plumed hat. Significantly no Pahari royal figure is shown with a halo. This absence of the halo, one of the most significant iconographic conventions of Rajasthani court pictures, combined with a more naturalistic treatment of the figures, makes the Pahari rulers seem more of this world than their Rajasthani brethren. In Pahari royal portraits there is less emphasis on the heroic, brave, or passionate demeanor of the ruler. This stands in direct contrast with contemporary Rajasthani works in which large, dense, compositions show royalty in its grandest moments.

Stylistically, these purely secular Pahari images are close to their religious and literary counterparts. In other words, the visual changes and innovations found in portraiture are also carried out in Pahari manuscript illustrations of the 18th century. This stylistic cohesion and a move toward a more naturalistic rendering of a scene suggests that both the artists and the patrons in this region were more likely to embrace the Mughal preference for depicting temporal reality and ultimately may have been more receptive to new ideas.[23]

Rajasthani painters began in the 17th century by emulating Mughal conventions of descriptive likenesses, then adapted them to suit their own visual and conceptual framework, and ultimately created their own versions of portraiture, quite independent of the Mughal prototypes. The Pahari painters also followed the Mughal examples initially, while simultaneously developing their own brand of iconographic portraiture. However, at the Pahari courts, the trend in the 18th century was almost the opposite of what happened in Rajasthan. By mid-century there was a fresh impetus from the Mughal court, due either to the migrations of artists, or to the arrival of 17th- and 18th-century Mughal works at the Pahari courts.[24] In this sense, Pahari painting, rather than moving away from the Mughal tradition, actually came closer to it in the second half of the 18th century.

What accounts for these two distinct developments in Rajasthan and the Punjab Hills? Since both geographic areas received the influx of the Mughal aesthetic in the form of pictures and through the migration or artists trained in the Mughal mode, geographic proximity or the movement of artists cannot solely account for the greater "Mughalization" of the Pahari portraits. In fact, the greater political connections of the Rajasthani rulers with the Mughal emperors should suggest an opposite development. The answer may be found in the differing ideas of kingship in these two areas.

It seems that in Rajasthan, especially at principal courts such as Mewar, Marwar, and Kota, the archetypal concept of a Rajput ruler was so strong that it overpowered the initial impact of the Mughal conventions of naturalism and descriptive specificity. Depiction of the physiognomic likeness of an individual was modified, turning a portrait into an "ideal" rendering of a king. In the Punjab Hills, there was less depth to the rulers' dynastic histories, and therefore, perhaps, less preoccupation with proving legitimacy and antiquity. The absence of elaborate accounts of hunts, festival celebrations and narrative descriptions of the legendary past, in both the textual and visual traditions of the Punjab Hills, may be indicative of a relative lack of interest in aggrandizing the status of the ruler.[25] It may be this modification of the Rajput ideal which gave the Punjab Hills rulers greater flexibility and a greater willingness to embrace new ideas.

By contrast, the Rajasthani concern for representation of the "ideal" king seems to have become further emphasized during the 18th century in the face of the rulers' growing political and military troubles and gradually declining powers. Their kingdoms came under increasing attacks by the Marathas and Afghans, and they faced ever stronger threats to their authority from their vassal states. To compensate for their diminishing power, a large number of rulers seems to have become even more preoccupied with grand pictorial statements of their glory and opulence. Toward the end of the century, the royal portraits of Rajasthan were becoming more and more ossified, the thematic and stylistic innovations of the early part of the century becoming more rare. It was almost as if the traditional Rajput culture of Rajasthan, which had been responsible for the development of a unique genre of royal portraiture, was unable to sustain it.

The 19th Century

Traditional portraits in the style of the preceding century continued to be produced at most of the courts of Rajasthan during the 19th century. Generally, however, they lack vitality and display a strong tendency towards stereotyped equestrian images of rulers who are disproportionately larger than the truncated attendant figures (Topsfield 1980:149-166).[26] Colors are thinner, faces mask-like, and compositions stilled. Even if the ruler is shown with a halo and heavily bejeweled, his power rings hollow, reflecting his political and social decline. Now, symbols of royalty – the halo, swords and shields, royal cushions, richly ornamented horses – become important in themselves. Instead of the contextual portraits of the preceding century, in which the rulers' actions, along with their insignia, conveyed significant elements of their political and cultural power, royal symbols in 19th-century protraits seem isolated and without a sense of authority or authenticity.

Such developments in painting may indirectly reflect political realities. Beginning in the early 19th century, the British had begun to negotiate complex political treaties with the Rajput rulers. Some were designed to create a careful balance of power between the feuding *ṭhākurs* (vassals) and the ruler, others limited a ruler's ability to declare war on neighboring kingdoms without the intervention of the British.[27] In almost all cases, the net effect of these treaties was to rob the ruler of his key function as heroic protector of his subjects, ready to die a passionate death in a battle. Stripped of his primary source of power, and financially ill-equipped to stage elaborate functions, festivals and rituals, an average 19th-century Rajput ruler, amidst a rapidly declining court culture, could hardly have been expected to commission anything but the dry, dull portraits that are characteristic of the latter half of the century.

While the British divested the Rajput rulers of their political power, they were also partially responsible for bringing to the portrait tradition of Rajasthan the new phenomenon of photography to create likeness. Indeed, the most significant development in 19th-century portraiture is found not in traditional works but in images that incorporate photographic techniques and western conventions, creating a new vision of royalty that reflected the political changes of the time.

In the second half of the 19th century, traditional painters were gradually moving into the orbit of photography (Gutman 1982:108-109). Most of the major courts had begun to maintain studios with artist-photographers who would not only photograph royalty, but also "embellish" the images appropriately. These new groups of artists, calling themselves "royal" or "court" photographers, were well aware of the potential of the camera for capturing "reality" as defined by the British photographers in India; many were trained by the British. But their function at the court was to create a "perfect" or "ideal" image of the ruler, not to capture a moment in time, one of the primary functions of the medium in the west. Not unlike their predecessors these artist-photographers once again incorporated a new concept and a new technology into the traditional Indian vision. Their primary function continued to be the creation of idealized images of their patrons, devoid of physical imperfections and psychological vulnerabilities, and without any reference to a temporal sense of reality.

If photography allowed the artists to capture a more precise physiognomic likeness of a person, the use of vibrant opaque colors on top of photographic images deemphasized perceptual reality and brought the pictures back into the realm of traditional portraiture. It is significant that one of the major characteristics of modern photography – capturing a moment – which we take for granted today, was specifically avoided by the court photographers. Such a graphic rendition of time would have been at odds with the traditional Rajput and Indian predilection for the visualization of eternal, or non-specific time. Similarly, the manipulation of light to create shadows and a sense of depth around the figures, central to traditional western photography, was irrelevant to the Indian photographer. In fact, he manipulated light so it would flood an entire area, creating a picture that was simultaneously devoid of depth while generating a sense of limitless space (Gutman

1982:118, 124). The resultant abstraction of these painted photographic portraits and paintings based on photographs fits perfectly into the Indian tradition of timeless portraiture.

Though conceptually similar to earlier images, visually and culturally these new portraits suggest some changes in the notion of Rajput kingship. No longer do we witness the self-absorption of the king and his courtiers in elaborate hunts, *darbārs*, or festivals. In most of the painted photographs we see the ruler in his royal garb, usually without his retinue of courtiers and attendants, looking directly at the camera and ultimately at the viewer *Maharaja Jaswant Singh of Marwar* (see Fig. 7) can serve as a characteristic example of the new developments in 19th-century Rajput portraiture. Seated on a Victorian chair and wearing British medallions and necklaces, this ruler is surrounded by western objects. An English table with a flower vase, books, or even small cameo photographs are his new accoutrements. In keeping with the new photograhic sense of reality, we no longer see the characteristic halo around his face.

The only traditional attribute consistently visible in these new pictures is the sword, often painted in elaborate pure-gold pigments. The solitary presence of this royal symbol of Rajput chivalry poignantly evokes the pathetic nature of Rajput power at the time. Just as the sword had become an outmoded weapon and a royal symbol without any protective power, the rulers themselves had become largely ceremonial heads of state under British overlordship. Robbed of their most fundamental role as protectors, the Rajput rulers had become a political anachronism. Their extravagant life style and its visual display was not only tolerated by the British, but was encouraged. "Pampered and petted favorites," as they were often referred to by the British, these rulers continued to live in a world of hollow power, while the new rulers of the subcontinent acquired ever greater political control.

The changed role of the Rajput rulers is also evident from the proliferation of photographic portraits for the rising merchant class in British India. No longer was the tradition of portraiture reserved for royalty. By the 1880s, as photography spread into new arenas of Indian life, it began to reflect everyday, non-aristocratic reality. Just as India was moving away from its courtly, feudal past and into the modern era, the painted photograph was moving beyond the prescriptive descriptions of beauty and royalty that had

Fig. 7: Maharaja Jaswant Singh of Marwar. Attributed to Narsingh. Jodhpur, ca. 1880. 33.5 x 25.5 cm. Opaque watercolor on paper. (Courtesy the Brooklyn Museum)

been adhered to for centuries. Indeed photography, while briefly providing a new direction for royal portraiture, ultimately contributed to its decline.

Conclusion

Through this survey of royal portraiture in Rajasthan, from its inception to its decline, it is possible to understand not only the essential visual characteristics of this important genre of Indian painting, but also offer suggestions regarding the Rajput character as reflected in the visual development and conceptual framework of the pictures.

The idea of portraying likeness in an empirical sense, "the way a man is seen", is not indigenous to Rajput culture, or for that matter to the traditional Indian world view. Developed under the patronage of the Mughal emperors Akbar and Jahangir, this concept of empirically determined and psychologically sensitive portraiture was selectively adopted by the Rajasthani courts in the Mughal orbit. After an initial stage of emulation, the tradition was gradually assimilated to become a thoroughly Rajput phenomenon. Rather than challenging or changing fundamental Rajput assumptions, portraiture was ultimately used to illustrate the traditional Rajput notions of idealized kingship.

The notions of verisimilitude, and of the specific physical and psychological state of the sitter, were avoided in favor of the universally recognized iconographic attributes and features of the ideal king. The identity of the ruler and his power were thus established in broadly defined historical and societal terms rather than through illustrations of specific times and events in his reign. Even when the artists at the Rajput courts set out to document a specific event, or capture the likeness of a living ruler, they incorporated the age-old prescriptive conventions of painting into their vision. Observation of a specific scene or a specific ruler was not abandoned, but was adjusted to include the patron's and the painter's knowledge of an ideal ruler in an ideal setting. In other words, only those elements of empirical reality were used which did not challenge the archetypal, ahistorical nature of courtly depictions, and could enhance the realms of metaphoric meaning. The meticulous manner in which artists rendered details also emphasized conceptual rather than perceptual interest in the subjects and objects of paintings, imparting a sense of timelessness, and ultimately revealing very little of the psychological state or personal predicaments of the individuals being portrayed.

Cultural analysis and study of the historical development of royal portraits in Rajasthan reveals the traditional and conservative nature of both Rajput painting and Rajput society. When new painting themes and, through them, new ideas were introduced or accepted, they were channeled through a selective adoption process. Even when necessary changes were made, either consciously or unconsciously, fundamental cultural principles were not altered. Without a dynamic social and political structure which could face new realities, confront challenges, or relish innovative aesthetics, Rajput culture, with its traditional adherence to age-old conventions, was more likely to alter the form and nature of such "exotic" themes as empirically-oriented portraiture and incorporate them into long-held beliefs rather than be altered by them.

ENDNOTES

Written in 1987, this study is closely based on the exhibition and catalogue, *Life at Court: Art for India's Rulers, 16th-19th Centuries* (Museum of Fine Arts, Boston, 1985) which I organized on the occasion of the Festival of India in the United States. I am greatly indebted to Dr. B.N. Goswamy for initial discussions on the nature of Rajput portraiture and for his essay in the exhibition catalogue. I would also like to thank institutions and individuals for their permission to use photographs of paintings in their collections.

1. The term "Rajput" painting refers simultaneously to works created at the Rajput courts of Rajasthan, Central India, and the Punjab Hills, and to the style of these pictures, which is usually defined in contradistinction to imperial Mughal painting. For further discussion of the stylistic features of Rajput painting, see Coomaraswamy 1916:5-12. In the present essay, the term "Rajput" painting is used when the pictures are discussed stylistically and culturally. In the discussion of the works in their geographic context, "Rajasthani" painting or "painting at the Rajput courts of Rajasthan" is used to further differentiate between the two main geographic areas of Rajput painting, Rajasthan and the Punjab Hills.
2. For a detailed discussion of traditional Indian portraiture with its emphasis on the cognitive attributes of the ruler, see Goswamy 1986:193-202.
3. For selected examples of such phrases, see Beveridge 1912:I,85, 223; and Rogers and Beveridge 1968:I,33-34, 225.

4. Depictions of royal and religious figures are found in the temples of the Chola kings in South India from the 10th century on, but they are generally shown with little physiognomic specificity; their individual identification is dependent primarily on the inscription accompanying the image and its contextual placement. For further information on South Indian royal portraiture, see Kaimal 1987.
5. Amber, being one of the earliest Rajput courts to accept the Mughal power, is also likely to have been an important early center of portrait painting. However, 17th-century Amber painting, most of which is in the royal collection in Jaipur, has not been accessible to scholars.
6. Though stylistically datable to the first half of the 17th century, none of these early portraits is actually dated. For examples see Desai 1985a:28-31.
7. From the available names of the court artists from Bikaner in the 17th century, it seems that many were Muslims. In the inscription on the earliest dated Bikaneri work, it is mentioned that the leading artist, Ali Raza, had come from Delhi. It is likely that other Muslim artists also migrated in mid-century. For further information on Bikaner artists, see Khandalavala *et al.* 1960:48-51 and Krishna 1985:23-27.
8. For examples of similar Mughal drawings, see Archer and Falk 1981:78-80.
9. For slightly more stylized and later versions of the same portrait, see Desai 1985b:xvi, 38, and Khandalavala *et al.* 1960:50.
10. Most of the pictures in this largely unpublished collection are to be found the collection of the late Shri Gopi Krishna and Vinod Krishna Kanoria in Patna. For a discussion of early Bundi portraits, see Bautze 1986:168-175.
11. One major exception to this pattern is found in the portraits of Rao Ratan (r. 1607-1631) on the walls of Badal Mahal at the Bundi palace and in their painting style. The wall paintings and a few of the known portraits of this Bundi ruler may be contemporary with his reign. For further discussion, see Bautze 1986.
12. For examples, see Welch 1973:60, Beach 1974:72, and Topsfield 1980:36.
13. An instructive example of the conscious selection process by which Mughal compositions are adapted to Rajput use is *Girls Celebrating Holi* in the Cleveland Museum of Art (71.83). Closely based on an imperial Mughal composition showing the emperor Jahangir playing Holi (Chester Beatty Library, Dublin), the Bikaner painting not only omits Jahangir from the composition, but successfully compensates for this change by adding trees and a water fountain in the background. See Leach 1986:122-123.
14. As mentioned before, a similar case could also be made for Amber, but it awaits further research.
15. Even the Mughals acknowledged the Mewar rulers to be their most important Rajput foes. For Jahangir's reaction to the final defeat of Mewar by Khurram, the future emperor Shah Jahan, see Bèveridge 1968:I,285-286.
16. For an understanding of the use of divergent but contemporaneous styles for two different kinds of subject matter, see Chandra 1955:8 and Topsfield 1980:54-58.
17. *Grisaille* refers to a style of painting which, using only shades of gray and black, tries to create an effect of three-dimensionality. Mughal artists first used it in the late 16th century while emulating similar effects in European prints which had recently reached the Mughal court.

18. The only exception is Prince Parwiz, the saluting figure in the center. For a detailed discussion of the identification of the scene, see Desai 1985a:13-14.
19. For further discussion of profile images in art, see Schapiro 1972:22-26.
20. For other examples, see Desai 1985b:56-58, and Beach 1974:50-52.
21. In this context, the most "typical" Rajasthani traditions are defined as those 18th-century schools which are least related to the Mughal traditions – for example, Mewar, Bundi, Kota, and Jodhpur. They are distinguished from such court centers as Bikaner and Kishangarh, which follow the Mughal examples more closely. Painting from the Punjab Hills during the same time reveals a much more cohesive and consistent relationship to the Mughal tradition.
22. For further discussion of Pahari portraits in the 17th century, see Desai 1985a:34, 99.
23. In the absence of written records regarding the production processes of Indian painting, it is difficult to be precise about the respective roles of artist, patron, and subject matter in determining specific style or composition. Preliminary studies of the images themselves suggest that while all three played a part, patrons may have exerted a great deal of control over what was painted and the manner in which it was executed.
24. For a detailed discussion of contrasting views regarding mid-18th century developments at the Punjab Hills courts, see Goswamy 1968:17-62.
25. For more information on the history of the Punjab Hills rulers, see Hutchinson and Vogel 1933.
26. Painting under the patronage of Raja Ram Singh II of Kota (r. 1827-1865) is a major exception. For a detailed discussion of painting under his reign, see Desai 1985a:116-120.
27. For an example of a British treaty with a Rajasthani court, see Tod 1971:III,1833-1834.

REFERENCES CITED

Archer, Mildred and Toby Falk

1981 *Indian Miniatures in the India Office Library*. London: Sotheby Parke Bernet.

Archer, William G.

1959 *Indian Painting in Bundi and Kotah*. London: Victoria and Albert Museum.

1973 *Indian Painting from the Punjab Hills*. 2 vols. London and New York: Sotheby Parke Bernet.

Bautze, Joachim

1986 "Mughal and Deccani influence on Early 17th-century Murals of Bundi." In *Facets of Indian Art*. Robert Skelton *et al.* eds. pp. 168-176. London: Victoria and Albert Museum.

Beach, Milo Cleveland

1974 *Rajput Painting from Bundi and Kota*. Ascona, Switzerland: Artibus Asiae.

Beveridge, Henry, transl.
1912 *The Akbarnāma of Abu-l-Fazl*. 3 vols. Calcutta: Asiatic Society of Bengal. (1st ed. 1897-99)

Chandra, Moti
1955 *Mewar Painting*. New Delhi: Lalit Kala Akademi.

Coomaraswamy, Ananda K.
1916 *Rajput Painting*. London: Oxford University Press.

Desai, Vishakha N.
1985a *Life At Court: Art for India's Rulers, 16th-19th Centuries*. Boston: Museum of Fine Arts.
1985b "Portraits, Hunts, Harems, and Darbars: Courtly Paintings of Rajasthan." *Orientations* 16 (11):35-46.

Goetz, Hermann
1950 *The Art and Architecture of Bikaner State*. Oxford: Cassirer.

Goswamy, B.N.
1968 "Pahari Painting: The Family as the Basis of Style." *Marg* 21:17-62.
1985 "Of Devotees and Elephant Fights: Some Notes on Subject Matter in Rajput and Mughal Painting." In *Life At Court: Art for India's Rulers, 16th-19th Centuries*. Vishakha N. Desai, ed. pp. xix-xxiii. Boston: Museum of Fine Arts.
1986 "Essence and Appearance: Some Notes on Indian Portraiture." In *Facets of Indian Art*. Robert Skelton *et al.*, eds. pp. 193-202. London: Victoria and Albert Museum.

Gutman, Judith Mara
1982 *Through Indian Eyes*. New York: International Center of Photography.

Hutchinson, John and P. Vogel
1933 *History of the Punjab Hill States*. Lahore.

Kaimal, Padma
1987 "Royal Portraits in South India." Ph. D. dissertation, Department of Art History, University of California, Berkeley.

Khandalavala, Karl, Moti Chandra, and Pramod Chandra
1960 *Miniature Painting from the Sri Moti Chand Khajanchi Collection*. New Delhi: Lalit Kala Akademi.

Krishna, Naval
1985 "Bikaneri Miniature Painting Workshops of Ruknuddin, Ibrahim and Nathu." *Lalit Kala* 21:23-27.

Leach, Linda York
1986 *Indian Miniature Paintings and Drawings*. The Catalogue of Oriental Art, Part One. Cleveland: The Cleveland Museum of Art.

Rogers, Alexander, transl. and Henry Beveridge, ed.
1968 *The Tuzūk-i Jahāngīrī; or, Memoirs of Jahangir*. 2 vols. 2nd ed. New Delhi: Munshiram Manoharlal. (1st ed. 1909-14)

Schapiro, Meyer
1972 *Words and Pictures*. The Hague: Mouton.

Skelton, Robert, *et al.*, eds.
1982 *The Indian Heritage: Court Life and Arts under Mughal Rule*. London: Victoria and Albert Museum.

1986 *Facets of Indian Art*. A symposium held at the Victoria and Albert Museum. London: Victoria and Albert Museum.

Tod, James

1971 *Annals and Antiquities of Rajasthan*. 3 vols. 3rd ed. New Delhi: Motilal Banarsidass. (1st ed., 1829-32).

Topsfield, Andrew

1980 *Paintings from Rajasthan in the National Gallery of Victoria*. Melbourne: National Gallery of Victoria.

Welch, Stuart Cary

1973 *A Flower from Every Meadow*. New York: The Asia Society.

Welch, Stuart Cary and Milo Cleveland Beach

1965 *Gods, Thrones, and Peacocks*. New York: Asia Society.

SIGNS OF THE DIVINE: *SATĪ* MEMORIALS AND *SATĪ* WORSHIP IN RAJASTHAN

WILLIAM A. NOBLE AND AD RAM SANKHYAN

According to the well-known classical Hindu myth, Sati, the wife of Shiva, committed suicide because her father had insulted her husband. Though there are different versions of the myth, the principal one holds that she did so by throwing herself into the sacrificial fire.[1] Her name, Sati, is the feminine form of the Sanskrit adjective *sat* ('true'), and the word *satī* came to be applied specifically to the widow who immolated herself on her husband's funeral pyre. The rite of *satī* (referred to as 'suttee' in the 19th-century British literature on the subject)[2] is of uncertain origin, and appears to have developed in India during the post-Vedic period.[3] Though there are instances of *satī* in the classical epics (Walker 1968:II,461), *satī* was not condoned by the Code of Manu, which may not have been written until the 1st or 2nd centuries A.D. Instead, it recommended a simple and austere life for the widow (Manu 1886:195-198). *Satī* as a voluntary act appears to have slowly spread throughout India from the 3rd century A.D. onward, and became more prevalent and popular after the 8th century A.D. (Chattopadhyay 1975). Thereafter, sacred works increasingly advocated the rite as a religious duty for women and a way by which the wife might even ensure salvation for both her dead husband and herself (Altekar 1962:115-142; Rao 1933:219-240; Thakur 1963:126-184).

The practice of *satī* naturally attracted the attention of foreign observers. The earliest account of a *satī* cremation, which took place in Media (northwestern Persia), is that provided by the classical historian Diodorus of Sicily.[4] Brief mention of *satī* occurs in the writings of Muslim and early European travelers to India, starting with Marco Polo and Ibn Batuta (Polo 1903:II,341; Ibn Batuta 1976:21-23; Barbosa 1918:I [XLIV in Series 2], 213-217;

Valle 1892:II (LXXXV in Series I), 266-277; Tavernier 1889:I, 209-216, 219, and II, 219-222; Manucci 1957:II, 89-90, and III, 57, 62-63; Thévenot 1687: third part, 85; Bernier 1916:307-314; Modave 1971:171-174; Dubois 1906:361-367). There are also accounts and reports by the British (Beveridge 1872:II,184-187; Smith 1883:78-79; Hamilton 1930:I,157, and II,5; Buckland 1902:I, 160-161; Caunter 1834:94-98; Sleeman 1973:18-31; White 1838:86-87; Campbell 1864:219-224; Edwardes and Merivale 1872:II,36-37). Prior to the British takeover of India, the dictates of their faith caused the Mughal rulers to generally discourage *satī* whenever possible.[5] The custom, viewed with abhorrence by the British, became a political issue during the early 19th century. In 1829-30, in response to pressures from Christian missionaries and Hindu reformers, the British administration, under the reformist leadership of Governor-General William C. Bentinck, prohibited the practice of *satī* within the territories administered by the Raj.[6]

An extensive literature thus exists concerning the practice of *satī*. In addition to descriptions of the rite itself, there are numerous records of British reactions to it and their efforts to stamp it out.[7] There have also been extensive investigations into the origin of *satī*, the reasons underlying it, and its social implications (Thompson 1928; Gandhi 1977; Misra 1973; Modi 1924; Mukhopadhyay 1956-157; Stein 1978; Stietencron 1967). Two aspects of *satī*, however, have received comparatively little attention:I) the commemoration or memorialization of *satīs* and 2) their worship.

Satīs in India have been commemorated in various ways, from preserving the imprint of the doomed widows' hands on gateways to carving their images on memorial pillars, and to placing such pillars within elaborate cenotaphs (*chhatrīs*) built to honor deceased rulers and their *satīs*. Such memorials, whether dedicated entirely to *satīs* themselves or primarily commemorating their deceased consorts, are visible reminders in the modern Indian landscape of an ancient custom which has continued to the present, despite its outlawing over 150 years ago. They are more than mute records of specific historic events, however. Their form, and the symbols and motifs with which they are adorned, can tell us something about the nature of the Hindu society of the past, its philosophical and religious beliefs, and its attitudes concerning the relationship between men and women. Yet, even though some specific memorials have received attention from scholars, a systematic examination of *satī* memorials has yet to be undertaken.

The deification and worship of *satīs* have received even less scholarly attention than *satī* memorials. While scattered accounts are found in the early ethnographic literature (e.g. Crooke 1968:I, 186-189; Yule and Burnell 1903:878-883), the subject had been largely ignored by recent scholars interested in Hindu religion and society. Research by us, however, has shown that the deification and worship of *satīs* are significant processes in Hinduism at both the local and regional levels. In the Nilgiri Hills of Tamil Nadu, for instance, *satī*-related dolmens are objects of veneration among the Badagas, some dolmens even being integrated into temples. The worship of local *satī* deities along with that of the Badagas' ancestral goddess Masthi Hethai, herself a great *satī* (*mahā* + *satī*), whose annual festival at Bergani attracts people from all over the Nilgiris, is linked to integrative processes in Shaivite Badaga society throughout the region (Noble 1976, 1988). In general, however, consideration of *satī* worship, the processes whereby *satīs* become deified, and the broader implications of these processes is lacking in the scholarly literature to date.

Satī has occurred in most parts of India, and the practice has been associated with all levels of Hindu society. Traditionally, however, the rite has been identified more with the upper castes, especially the ruling aristocracy, and with certain regions more than others. Rajasthan, for example, became a major stronghold of the custom.[8] The rite of *satī* was the norm for the ruling families of Rajasthan, and there are many accounts of Rajput queens and concubines following their lords to the funeral pyre.[9] In addition to individual *satīs*, there are also accounts of mass *jauhars*, such as the three at Chittorgarh in 1303, 1535, and 1568, and the one at Jaisalmer in 1299 (Tod 1920:I,215, 249-250, 261-262; II,200-201; Kipling 1891: 106-112). These were occasions when thousands of women are said to have perished by fire before or during the time their men rode out to meet their death in battle.[10] *Satī* continued in Rajasthan for close to 30 years after its prohibition in British India, until it was finally outlawed in a majority of the states of Rajputana in 1846.[11] Even as late as the 1980s, however, an occasional *satī* has take place in Rajasthan. Information about some recent *satīs* is given toward the end of this paper.

This study is offered as a contribution to the interpretation of *satī* memorialization in India and the process involving the deification and worship of *satīs*. It focuses on Rajasthan and is based on a preliminary field survey conducted there and in other parts of India during 1977-78.[12] Its core is an illustrated areal survey of *satī* memorials in Rajasthan, with a view to identifying subregional similarities and differences within Rajasthan and – though only to a limited degree and by way of comparison – between Rajasthan and neighboring regions. A general consideration of the forms, symbolism, and motifs found in these memorials is also undertaken. Because the *satī* memorials of the Rajput nobility are conspicuous and usually more accessible, they have received the most attention, though some aspects of *satī* among non-Rajput castes are briefly addressed. Since general features are largely shared by Rajput memorials and those of non-Rajputs, detailed examination of these latter memorials could help determine subregional differences more accurately, but this remains a task for further research. Because of the significant number of deified *satīs* and *satī* temples we encountered (especially in the Shekhawati region), and the fact that in the rest of Rajasthan and elsewhere in India as well, *satīs* of all castes are deified and worshipped, our study closes with a consideration of *satī* worship today.

Satī Memorials in Rajasthan: Forms, Symbolism, and Motifs

The simplest form of *satī* memorials found in Rajasthan consists of carved outlines of the hand prints left on walls by *satīs* before their deaths – an expression of the common folk belief that supernatural power is contained in the palm of a woman about to become a *satī*. Pillars, sometimes square, but more generally rectangular, are the principal form of free-standing memorials, and may be found standing alone, in rows, or on platforms reached by steps. In the form of the *liṅga*, there are also round pillars, which we found only in cenotaphs. The most elaborate memorials, typically located near bodies of water, consist of pillars inside cenotaphs (*chhatrīs*) surmounted by one of several styles of roofs. With the exception of a more specialized system with Nandi, centered *liṅga*, and square memorial (aligned from east to west), the memorial pillars in these cenotaphs are typically located at their exact centers.[13] The earlier memorials and cenotaphs for the nobility were mostly made of red sandstone, but white marble dominates in later examples. Most cenotaphs reflect later Islamic architectural influences such as the dome (Goetz 1950:65), but some earlier ones have multifaceted peaked roofs with sides resembling steps. Curved eaves and curved cornices, structural forms probably derived from Bengali folk architecture,[14] also surmount some of the cenotaphs in Rajasthan. More rarely, cenotaph roofs assume the form of *śikharaṣ*.[15]

The principal human figures carved on memorials are the deceased male and the woman or women (both wives and concubines) who became *satīs* with him. Attendants, musicians, and dancers may be portrayed as well. The male figure is often represented as a Rajput warrior, with turban and mustache. Some males are standing, and may then be in the *namaskār* (two palms together) pose. It was also a common practice to depict the Rajput male on a horse. Standing or mounted males might hold a sword and, less frequently, a shield as well. If the memorial is a royal one, an umbrella is often placed over him, and it may be held by a servant. An alternate depiction of one or two servants standing nearby with a whisk and umbrella (both being emblems of royalty) also occurs.

The female figures are most often in the *namaskār* pose, which expresses devotion to the attainment of a spiritual after-life and devotion to one's husband. Free-standing statues of *satīs* with their right hand raised in blessing also exist, but only in temples. A distinctive type of representation found in both Rajasthan and Gujarat (and as a rare occurrence in Maharashtra) shows the *satī* wife holding her deceased husband in her arms. This may be a symbolic representation of the immortal wife, now a goddess, bearing her husband to the supernatural realm. But it could simply be a depiction of the devoted wife, sacrificing her life out of a desire to be with her husband, and then bearing him to the supernatural realm.

The iconographic conventions of *satī* memorialization in Rajasthan are characterized by symbolism and motifs that are widespread in Hindu culture, and which have thrived elsewhere as well (e.g., in ancient Mesopotamia). Thus the umbrella, which is both carved on pillars and structurally repeated in the cenotaph roofs protecting memorials, has a long history as a symbol of royalty and the sacred.[16] While the utilitarian advantage of shade provided by these roofs is obvious, their added symbolic dimension is no less important.

Another symbol found in the *satī* memorials of Rajasthan is the *liṅga*, the phallic emblem associated with Shiva. Some *liṅgas* have four faces carved into their sides, facing the four quadrants, and thus symbolize the all-seeing Siva who is at the center of all things. Other *liṅgas*, which are modified miniature *śikharas*, surmount square memorials whose sides face the four quadrants. The principal significance of this iconographic feature is related to the fact that, as a symbol, the *liṅga* functions as an *axis mundi* (an axis through which the world is thought to be centered) where the earthly and secular realm is linked to the supernatural, divine realm (Spink 1973:103-108; Munro 1982:115-118).[17] However, the *liṅga* has other complex symbolic associations as well. Conjoined with its female counterpart, the *yoni*, it commemorates men and their *satīs* through the union of the male and female principles, and is linked to the Hindu system of opposites. It is also a symbol of creation and, as a representation of Shiva, is assoicated with universal creation and destruction.

Most memorial pillars in Rajasthan, as elsewhere in India, have carved on their upper section representations of the sun and the moon. The sun may be shown with distinctive rays, and occasionally has a human face, while the moon may be represented either full or crescent-shaped and recumbent. The two may also be represented together, the sun's orb either large or as small as a dot in the hollow of the recumbent moon. Symbolically, the moon in its recumbent form represents the essence of femaleness, the womb, while the sun, the prime giver of light and warmth, is the fertilizer and nurturer and, when symbolizing the *biṅdu* of the Hindus, is the ultimate and eternal supernatural center of creation and destruction.[18] As sun and moon symbolism is frequently associated with sacred pillars, mountains, and trees,[19] its presence on *satī* memorials further reinforces the concept of these memorials functioning as *axes mundi*.

Among the secondary symbolic motifs used in *satī* memorialization are footprints, a pan-Indian way of representing the departed's last connection with the earth. Lotuses, as traditional emblems of enlightenment, and swastikas, representing the extension of cosmic evolution from a fixed center to the four quadrants, also occur.

Vegetation, in the form of trees and plants, is also present, signifying association with the tree of life, the most common and universal representation of the *axis mundi*. Another symbol, more frequent as a ritual object in *satī* temples than carved on memorials, is the *triśul* (trident). It too functions as an *axis mundi*, and represents the conduit through which the earthly is transformed into the supernatural and through which *śakti* (female energy) flows. All these, and other motifs such as coconuts, eyes, headcloths, and sari lengths, are pan-Indian, but are combined in ways that reflect regional patterns characteristic of *satī* memorialization in Rajasthan.

Satī Memorials in Rajasthan: An Areal Survey

In the course of our field research, we were able to visit most of the major *satī* sites associated with the former princely states of Bikaner, Jaisalmer, Jodhpur, Udaipur, Begun, Bundi, Kota, and Alwar in Rajasthan (see Map 1). While we searched in the Jaipur area, and visited royal cenotaphs there, we did not find any memorials on which *satīs* were represented. A time restraint prohibited us from visiting the Ajmer area. Jaipur and Ajmer are thus not included in the areal survey presented here.

Bikaner and Jaisalmer

Many cenotaphs and memorials commemorating the Rajput nobility of Rajasthan typically have a picturesque location near a body of water, and at a distance of several kilometers from the state's capital city. This pattern is obvious at sites such as the Devikund near Bikaner (Pl.I-A) and the Badabagh near Jaisalmer. The roofs of the Bikaner cenotaphs clearly reflect later Islamic influences, as they have one, two, or five domes (Pl. I-B). Though some of the cenotaphs at Jaisalmer have domes, many have roofs of the earlier kind, ranging in shape from pyramidal (4-sided) to sexa-decagonal (16-sided) (Pl. I-C). While the cenotaphs at Jaisalmer are made of red sandstone, thus blending into the red glow of the landscape at sunrise and sunset, many of the cenotaphs at Bikaner are made of white marble and stand out in stark contrast to the surrounding landscape.

At the Devikund near Bikaner, what appears to be an original memorial to Maharaja Kalyan Singh (d. 1571) (Pl. I-D) stands on

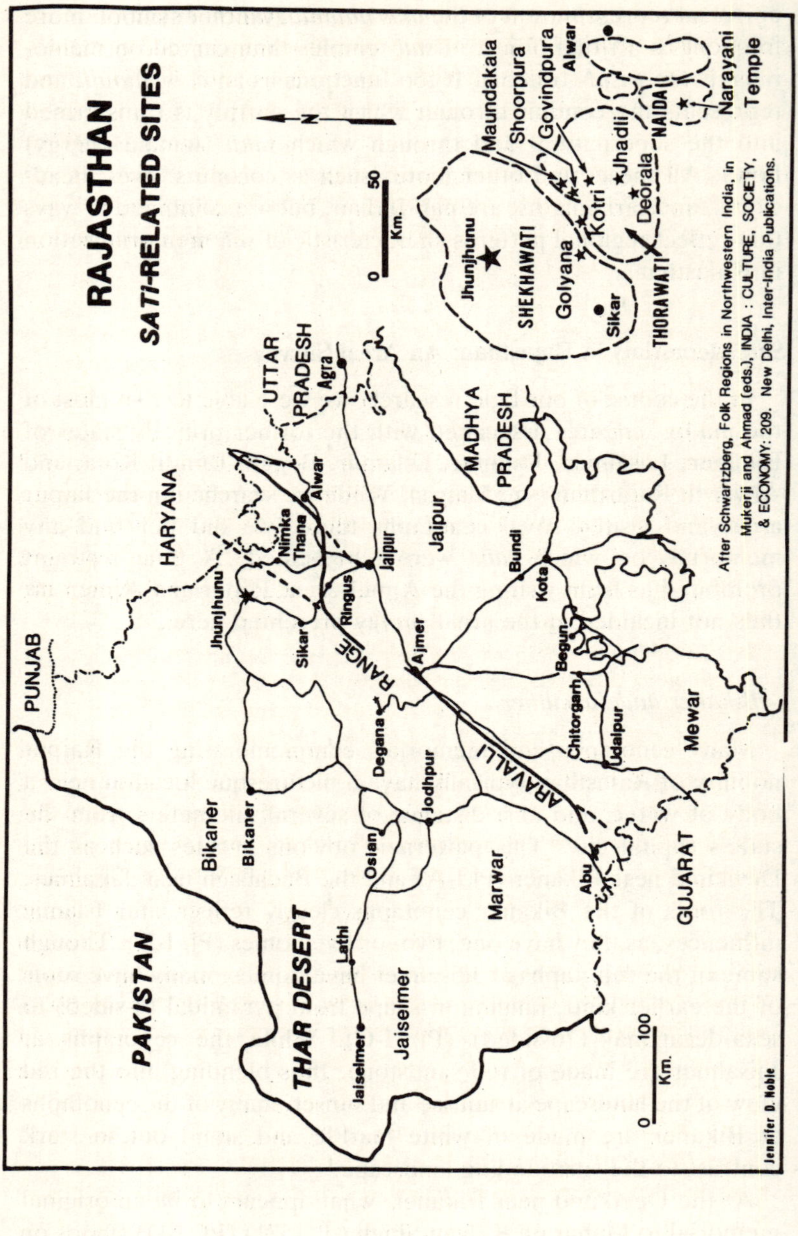
RAJASTHAN
SATI-RELATED SITES
PUNJAB
HARYANA
UTTAR PRADESH
MADHYA PRADESH
PAKISTAN
GUJARAT
THAR DESERT
ARAVALLI RANGE
Bikaner
Jaiselmer
Marwar
Mewar
Jaipur
Jhunjhunu
Sikar
Ringus
Nimka Thana
Alwar
Agra
Ajmer
Degana
Jodhpur
Osian
Lathi
Abu
Udaipur
Chitorgarh
Begun
Kota
Bundi
0 100 Km.
0 50 Km.
N
SHEKHAWATI
THORAWATI
NAIDA
Golyana
Kotri
Deorala
Jhadli
Maundakala
Shoorpura
Govindpura
Narayani Temple
After Schwartzberg, Folk Regions in Northwestern India, in Mukerji and Ahmad (eds.), INDIA : CULTURE, SOCIETY, & ECONOMY: 209. New Delhi, Inter-India Publications.
Jennifer D. Noble

its own close to the water of the pond. It thus may reflect an earlier time when memorial slabs commemorating rulers and *satīs* stood in the open. This red sandstone memorial depicts the mounted ruler with his sword (sacred to Rajput warriors) and a royal umbrella. In an adjacent small panel, four *satī* wives are shown in the *namaskār* pose. A fifth figure in a different and more sensual pose may represent a favorite concubine who became a *satī*. In two panels below, there are atypical depictions of five female musicians and five female dancers, probably representing females who danced and provided music as part of the funeral rites.[20]

Later marble memorials at Bikaner follow a similar format. It can be seen in the memorial commemorating Maharaja Moti Singh (d.1825) and his wife, Deep Kunwar, the last Maharani *satī* in Bikaner (Pl. I-E).[21] The upper panel is surmounted by a sun and a good example of a recumbent crescent moon, the ruler with his sword rides from left to right on a horse, and the Maharani in the *namaskār* pose stands in front of the horse. The sun contains a human face.[22] At the center of the upper panel there is a depiction of Shiva as ascetic – a departure from the usual iconography, yet one which would appear to reinforce the concept of memorials as *axes mundi*. A panel below contains an inscription in Sanskrit – as is typical of most pillars commemorating royalty in Rajasthan.

Another memorial pillar at Bikaner commemorates Maharaja Zorowar Singh (d.1746) and at least *21 satīs*, the most who perished with a single ruler in Bikaner (Pl.I-F). It is organized on the same pattern as that for Moti Singh. Three *satī* queens are depicted in the upper panel, along with a female servant who is shown with a lion's mane whisk and an umbrella with a curved handle that enables it to be held above a rider on horseback. It is probable that her presence on the panel indicates that she became a *satī* also. On two additional panels below, 18 more women are depicted. They represent the concubines and servants who became *satīs* with the ruler. Except for the bearer of the whisk and umbrella, all the female figures are in the *namaskār* pose.

The memorial pillars at Jaisalmer are simpler, and a warrior with a sword and shield riding on a horse is emphasized enough to make this a characteristic motif there. While some of the pillars have both the warrior and his related *satī* or *satīs* carved on them, it is more common for the *satīs* to be depicted on side extensions of the basic memorials (Pl.I-G) or on separate pillars (Pl.I-H). While the sun and moon found elsewhere are conspicuously absent, female figures are shown in the characteristic *namaskār* pose.

As mentioned above, a basic form of memorial consists of the carved outlines of hand prints left by royal *satīs*. Typical examples of this are the hand prints on the side of the massive gateway to the fort palace of Jodhpur (Pl.I-I) and those found in Jaisalmer, on either side of the fortified palace's *satī* gateway, located at the bottom of a long flight of steps (Pl.I-J). In Bikaner, too, there are hand prints carved at the well known Hathi (Elephant) Gate, and several groups of them can also be seen at the second massive gateway to the palace. Among the latter is one that was carved around a hand print left by Maharani Deep Kunwar.

Jodhpur

At the old capital site of Mandor just north of Jodhpur, *śikharas* rise above cenotaphs commemorating past rulers and their *satīs*. These cenotaphs stand next to a lake and are surrounded by gardens. One of the most impressive of these cenotaphs commemorates Maharaja Ajit Singh (d. 1724), with whom there were six queens and 58 concubines who perished (Tod 1920:II,71-72).[23] Another group of cenotaphs near Mandor is close to the Panch Kund. They have domes and curved eaves, and are surrounded by desert growth (Pl.II-A).

An intriguing aspect of the Mandor site, and of other sites in and around Jodhpur, is the apparent absence of pillars in the memorialization. Thus while there are shrines in each of the cenotaphs by the Panch Kund, there are no memorial pillars in any of them. A question for further research is whether memorial pillars were never common in this area, or whether they were destroyed by some invading force and never replaced, or whether some liberal modern ruler opposed to *satī* had them systematically removed.

Udaipur and Chittorgarh

The royal cenotaphs at Udaipur are generally domed and made of white marble (Pl.II-B). Most are within a royal enclosure where the dated evidence of more recent construction or the major renovation completed in 1928 is most clear. Some of the later work appears never to have been completed, as in the case of the cenotaph commemorating Maharana Amar Singh II (d. 1710), which is without a dome. Among other cenotaphs outside the royal enclosure, there appears to be an original one of red sandstone commemorating Maharana Amar Singh I (d. 1620), the son of the famous Rana Pratap.

The *liṅga* plays a fundamental symbolic role in the memorialization of *satīs* in southeastern Rajasthan, east of the Aravallis. In the fully developed system of memorialization at Udaipur, the *liṅga*, placed on an east-west alignment, is clearly emphasized. A stone Nandi (Shiva's bull) lies in alignment due east of the *liṅga*, which stands on the axis at the exact center of each cenotaph. The Nandi faces toward the *liṅga*. In the same alignment and due west, there is a square memorial stone with four panels (Pl.II-C), each with different portrayals of the ruler and his *satī* or *satīs*. Each *liṅga* has four carved faces oriented toward the four quadrants, and the sets of four faces exhibit considerable stylistic variation.

On the memorial pillar for Maharana Amar Singh I (d. 1620), which is probably the original one, we see a pattern that gets repeated later in this part of Rajasthan: the eastern panel is used to represent the ruler with his sword and his *satīs* (six of them in this case, all in the *namaskār* pose), the southern panel for the ruler lying on a bed with standing females waiting on him, and the northern panel for a *liṅga* upon which the ruler and his *satīs* focus their worship. The six lissome females carved onto the western panel (Pl.II-D) are a variation from the standardized motif for the western panel which was established with the death of the next ruler. From the sacred ash smeared onto the foreheads of the figures, we can assume that local worshippers consider them to be representations of *satīs*. They reaffirm, through repetition, that six women became *satīs* when the ruler was cremated.

With the memorial pillar for Maharana Karan Singh (d. 1628), the pattern was set for having the ruler on a horse in the western panel, and for a tree or part of a plant to be included in the northern panel. Contrary to the pattern elsewhere in Rajasthan, where the mounted warriors are shown moving from left to right (as the viewer looks at the pillar), the rider on this pillar, as in Udaipur generally, is shown moving from right to left. In this particular memorial, the sun and moon symbols are present, but they are usually not depicted in Udaipur memorials.

At the same site, the memorial pillar for Maharana Jagat Singh II (d. 1751) has fully developed panels which commemorate the largest number of *satīs* to have perished with one deceased ruler at Udaipur. The eastern panel shows the ruler with sword, mustache, and jewel-badecked turban (Pl.II-E). Four queens are depicted to his right (the traditional position for wives) and the 16 females carved in smaller size to his left probably represent concubines and servants who became *satīs*. The southern panel shows the ruler on a bed, with his four queens waiting on him. In the western panel, the ruler is shown on a horse, with two male attendants who follow him, bearing a wisk and fan with long handle. On the northern panel, he is depicted in a worshipping pose, with a tree spreading from the right in the background, his four queens in attendance, and a female pouring water over a *liṅga*.

Inside the fort of Chittorgarh, there are a few domed cenotaphs close to the Tower of Victory. Most memorial pillars at Chittorgarh are undated, but one of four within or close to the cenotaphs is dated 1565 A.D. It seems possible, therefore, that at least this memorial commemorates one of the Sisodias, the sept of the Guhila clan which ruled from Chittorgarh before Udai Singh founded Udaipur in 1568 (Sehgal 1977:44). The system of memorialization here may have provided a model for Udaipur. The same order of Nandi, *liṅga* and square memorial pillar on an eat-west alignment is in evidence within the cenotaphs. In the most clearly executed example, the simple stone *liṅga* is on the axis extending through the peak of the dome and is set in a low, rounded stone *yoni* base. The memorial pillar, due west on the alignment, has four panels which face the four quadrants. The carved *satī* queen in the eastern panel stands to the ruler's right, and two servants or concubines stand to the ruler's left. All are depicted in the *namaskār* pose. In the southern panel, there is a depiction of the ruler on his horse (moving from left to right). In the western panel, the ruler lies on a bed, and two standing female attendants hold a whisk and a fan. In the northern panel, the ruler pours water over a *liṅga*. The same general sequence of four motifs is repeated on the dated pillar at Chittorgarh. The same is true of the third one, within a cenotaph, if turned by 90 degrees, and of the fourth, standing outside, if the southern and northern panels are reversed.

Begun, Bundi and Kota

The royal cenotaphs at Begun, Bundi and Kota are generally surmounted by domes (Pls.II-F, II-G, and II-H). While the elephants and horses carved into the bases of the cenotaphs at Bundi and the free-standing elephants at Kota make these cenotaphs distinctive, there are also a few elephants and horses on the sides of the cenotaphs at Begun. The Begun site differs from the others in that the dominant motif on its rectangular memorial pillars is that of rulers standing next to their *satī* wives and concubines, all in the *namaskār* pose (Pl.III-A). This iconography is more typical of memorials other than those of the nobility. Like most non-royal memorials, moreover, the Begun pillars have the sun and moon above the figures. The suns usually have faces while the moons are plain, but Begun also has some instances of faces carved above the moons.

The *liṅga* as *axis mundi* is most conspicuous at Kota. Centered beneath the main dome in each cenotaph, a *liṅga* rises above a massive *yoni* base with which it is conjoined (Pl.III-B). As is the pattern throughout India, water spouts extending outward from each *yoni* base face toward the north. Representations of the *satīs* being memorialized are carved in one or two rings around the *liṅga*.

In the cenotaph for Maharao Ram Singh I (d. 1707), who died in battle near Jajau after siding with Prince Azam in the war of succession after Aurangzeb died (Gupta 1982:31), the women form a single ring around the *liṅga* (Pl.III-C). While several figures are in the *namaskār* pose, others are either holding or carrying objects. The cenotaph for Maharao Mukund Singh (d. 1658), who was slain with three brothers in the battle at Fatehabad near Ujjain (Gupta 1982:30), has a *liṅga* with two rings of women. The upper ring has representations of wives in the *namaskār* pose and a wife bearing a *liṅga* (III-D), while dancers, musicians, and other females in the *namaskār* or other poses stand in the ring below.

At Bundi there are cenotaphs which have centered *liṅgas* rising from *yoni* bases. Because there is no way of visually knowing from such memorials the number of *satīs* who may have perished with particular rulers, we bypassed them and recorded other, more complex ones in which *satī* representations were clearly associated with deceased rulers. Each of these latter memorials is still basically a *liṅga*, elaborated by a small surmounting *śikhara* (i.e., a stylized *liṅga*) above and the addition of four planes below which face the four quadrants. An example of this pattern, the memorial pillar commemorating Maharaja Shribharat Singh (d. 1658) and four *satīs*, stands in a simple cenotaph covered by an oblong dome (Pl. III-E). The order of motifs in the four planes of this memorial is found in other memorial pillars as well. In this example, each plane has a single panel. A Rajput warrior holding a sword and riding a horse (moving from left to right) and four *satīs* in the *namaskār* pose are carved into the eastern panel (Pl. III-F). The southern panel has a sun with a face and radiating rays, and a moon carved into the basal portion, in both its full phase and its crescent, recumbent phase (Pl. III-G). The western panel has a male worshipping a *liṅga* and four *satīs* in the *namaskār* pose (Pl. III-H). The northern panel has the ruler lying on a bed, two *satīs* in the *namaskār* pose, another *satī* fanning the male, and a fourth *satī* waving a whisk above him (Pl. III-I).

Another cenotaph and memorial at Bundi commemorate Rao Raja Shrishatru Shalya (or Chhatrasal Hada, in non-Sanskritic popular terminology), who, like Maharaj Shribharat Singh, died in 1658. The two warriors were father and son, and were among the 12 Hada Rajputs who, dressed in saffron-colored clothing as was the custom, charged to their deaths in battles against Aurangzeb at Dharmat and Samugarh (Dhoundiyal 1964:41-42). On the eastern plane of the memorial to Rao Raja Shrishatru Shalya, the carving in the top panel depicts a mounted warrior (with his horse moving from left to right) and 6 *satīs*, while there are representations of 12 *satīs* in the middle panel, and 13 *satīs* in the bottom panel. The southern plane has the standardized depiction of the sun and moon. The western plane has a male with a *liṅga* and 7 *satīs* in the top panel, 12 *satīs* in the middle panel, and 12 *satīs* in the bottom panel. The northern plane has a male reclining on a bed and 10 *satīs* in the upper panel, 10 *satīs* in the middle panel, and 11 *satīs* in the bottom panel. Thus, because 31 *satīs* are depicted on all three planes that have the male and *satī* combination, we know that 31 women perished with the ruler. Of these, six were probably queens, and the rest would have been either concubines or servants.

The same basic sequence is found in the memorial for Maharaj

Kumar Shrikrigham (d. 1678), which commemorates this ruler and his 15 *satīs*. Although it appears that the eastern plane has 17 *satīs*, only the two females before the horse in the top panel and the female directly behind are likely to represent *satīs*. The two female figures farther behind the horse probably represent servants (one with a fan and the other with a whisk) who did not become *satīs*, and this supposition tends to be confirmed by the fact that worshippers placed sacred ash on the foreheads of all the female figures except the last two. A count of three added to the count of 12 for *satīs* represented in the panels below brings the total to 15, a count confirmed by the 15 *satīs* on the western plane and the 15 on the northern plane. As in the rest of the carved memorials at Bundi, the sun and moon again appear as standardized depictions on the southern plane.[24]

Alwar

The last example of a royal *satī* memorial we will present here is the one found in the largest cenotaph in Rajasthan, next to the City Palace in Alwar (Pl. IV-A). The square cenotaph has a lower portion of red sandstone and a superstructure of white marble. There are both Bengali and Mughal influences in its design. It is basically a *navaratna* ('nine jewels') structure, and is part of a design sequence which is most clearly exemplified in the Hindu temples of Bengal.[25] In conformity with the principles of *navaratna* construction, the superstructure of the cenotaph has a large dome in the center and four smaller ones in the corners (adding up to five 'jewels'), while the lower portion has four corner domes, for a total of nine 'jewels'. Bengali arched roofs run between the four smaller domes in the superstructure, while four kiosks with Bengali arched roofs and curved eaves pointed toward the corners are centered on each side of the lower portion. The main entrances to the superstucture have Mughal arches.

The cenotaph commemorates Maharaja Bakhtawar Singh (d. 1815) and his *satī* wife, Maharani Musi. Their horizontally inset memorial slab, on the floor directly below the top of the main dome of the superstructure (Pl. IV-B), is a square of marble with a raised rim. A gun, shield, sword, and thrusting dagger, primary emblems of the Rajput warrior, are carved in its corners. In the exact center of the square, there is a raised dot in the middle of a sculptured lotus. A pair of footprints are carved to each side of the dot, and are aligned next to each other within the lotus. The lotus symbol and a dot representing the *bindu* set in the absolute center of the cenotaph cause this complex to have one of the finest Indian examples of centering upon a centered axis, which is symbolically an *axis mundi*. While the footprints represent the departed couple's last connection with the earth, the lotus combined with the dot indicate that the couple became enlightened through absorption into the *bindu*.

Non-Royal *Satī* Memorials

Memorials commemorating the *satīs* of men other than rulers are, as might be expected, less elaborate than those in the royal cenotaphs. Women from a broad caste spectrum have traditionally become *satīs* in Rajasthan, but most of their deaths are unrecorded and many of their memorials are undated. Most ordinary memorials are stone pillars which stand by themselves, but some are on raised stone platforms. Cenotaphs protecting a few typically have four supporting columns, and a few small shrines are enclosed with walls; roofs over these are either flat, pyramidal, or domed in the Islamic manner. Stone available locally is the usual construction material for such memorials, whereas royal cenotaphs, especially in the later stages, tended to be made of marble.

There are *satī* memorials in many different kinds of localities. At the historical cult site of Osian (see Map 1), for example, there are memorial pillars standing singly and in rows near a temple (Pl. IV-C), while others are scattered or stand inside cenotaphs and shrines in the city (Pl.IV-D, IV-E), and yet others are scattered in the desert sands of the adjacent countryside.[26] Near the Lathi Fort that overlooks the site, two memorial pillars are inside a cenotaph with the older kind of pyramidal roof (Pl.IV-F). At Begun, there are many memorial pillars on platforms (especially where the terrain is rougher) or within domed cenotaphs. Near Jaisalmer, on a hill next to the road running between the Badabagh and the city, a series of memorial pillars commemorating only Brahmans are protected by cenotaphs with mostly pyramidal but also domed roofs. In Udaipur, a free-standing memorial pillar commemorating a male and his *satī* belonging to the Dhobi (washerperson) caste stands on the grounds of the present-day Tourist Bungalow.

Highly stylized motifs are carved into most memorials of this kind. The most common representation has a male and *satī* combination, with both in the *namaskār* pose, and a symbolic sun and crescent moon above (Pl. IV-G). A recumbent moon is sometimes incorporated into the lower segment of the sun. However, the memorials to Brahmans at Jaisalmer (paralleling those in the royal cenotaphs at the Badabagh) exhibit a conspicuous absence of the symbolic sun and moon. Some memorials elsewhere (at Osian, Udaipur, and Chittorgarh) also lack these symbols. In a few examples, the male figure and the *satī* are represented with their hands on their hips rather than in the *namaskār* pose. In a few others (at Begun and Bundi), the male is shown as a warrior with sword and shield or with sword only, but the *satī* is still in the *namaskār* pose. Though it is rare for the male and his *satī* to be represented on separate stones, a few examples of this can be seen in the Brahman cenotaphs at Jaisalmer. A few depictions of a male with two or more *satīs* indicate that a deceased male was sometimes cremated with more than one *satī*. The depiction of a rider mounted on a horse, with his *satī* or *satīs* in the *namaskār* pose, is reserved for Rajputs and is thus less frequently seen. In southeastern Rajasthan, one finds a few non-royal memorials depicting a male and his *satī* with a *liṅga* (Pl. IV-H). Both the man and the woman may be shown pouring water over the *liṅga*, or one or both may be depicted in the *namaskār* pose. Carved outlines of paired feet to commemorate the deceased man and woman also occur. The motif of the *satī* holding her deceased husband in her arms is found in a few scattered examples (Pl. IV-I; see also Sahni 1937:13-14).

Satī Memorials in Regions Adjacent to Rajasthan

While this paper is primarily concerned with Rajasthan, field research on *satī* memorials elsewhere allows us to make a few comparisons between Rajasthan and the regions immediatetly surrounding it. In this section we will present some general observations and speculations about patterns in the Punjab-Haryana region, the central Gangetic plain (mainly in Bihar and Uttar Pradesh), Central India (mainly in Madhya Pradesh), and Gujarat.

The Punjab-Haryana Region

Satī-related memorials in the Punjab-Haryana region to the north of Rajasthan are generally quite different from those in Rajasthan. Since they are located in the central portion of the alluvial Indo-Gangetic plain, they are of necessity made of bricks rather than stone. They are either solid or hollow, and the hollow memorials typically have enclosing walls. Even the more elaborate cenotaphs commemorating rulers have these enclosing walls.

Most memorials in this region have a pyramidal or convex pyramidal roof, but Islamic influence has resulted in domes surmounting some. Standing rectangular stone pillars are not standard, but carved stones are sometimes placed in or close to the hollow memorials. This is the case, for instance, in the area near the northern Siwalik Hills. Such stones are usually laid flat or are leaned against a wall. Their carving tends to be crude. While a male rider on a horse is most frequently depicted, there is considerable variation in their iconography.

The practice, more common to the east in the central Gangetic plain, of using two *liṅga*-like knobs to commemorate a husband and his *satī* wife (a larger knob for the man and a smaller knob for the woman) is occasionally found in the hollow memorials of the Punjab as well. Another practice more typical of the Gangetic plain, that of erecting small mounds to commemorate males and their *satī*s, is also sometimes found in the Punjab-Haryana region.

Whether or not any of the memorial types typical of this region are to be found in the extreme northerly portions of Rajasthan remains an unanswered question, and demonstrates the need for a more detailed and systematic field survey in Rajasthan.

The Central Gangetic Plain

In the central Gangetic plain, from the Yamuna River to the Bihar-Bengal border, people traditionally used earthen mounds to commemorate males and their *satī* wives. Those who were wealthier constructed brick platforms instead. We surmise that as economic conditions improved, and bricks became less costly and more easily available, earthen mounds were gradually replaced by platforms made of bricks. Earthen mounds are now relatively rare and brick platforms are more common.

Fanny Parlby, an English woman who boated up the Ganga over

150 years ago, has left us a valuable description of *satī*-related memorials and pottery objects in the region. The objects she described, called *kalaśas*, were inverted pots to which projections were attached before firing. Most *kalaśas*, according to Parlby's description, had a small female figure (representing the *satī*) and a small male figure (representing the husband) attached to them (Parlby 1850:I,65, 93, 95-96; II,417-423). The making of such pottery objects was long ago abandoned, and we have no evidence that they were ever made in Rajasthan. The only surviving *kalaśa* which we managed to locate, after a widespread search in the Ghazipur District of Uttar Pradesh, was going to be installed as the most sacred object at the center of a *satī* temple then under construction.

The whole central Gangetic "heartland" region of India has always been strongly identified with Shiva, with its most ancient city of Varanasi specifically dedicated to the god (Eck 1978; Havell 1905:71-87, 90-105). The *liṅga* has thus naturally played a dominant role in the *satī* memorialization of that region. Among the memorials observed by Parlby, and still visible today, are hollow *liṅga*-like structures measuring up to over two meters in height. They are typically domed and with small arched entrances that permit offerings for the departed to be made. *Satī*s in the region are also commemorated with solid *liṅga*-like memorials made of bricks. In addition, a male and his *satī* are commonly memorialized through the use of two rounded stones, "like a cannon ball split in two" (Parlby 1850:II, 420), rising in tandem from brick platforms or placed within the hollow *liṅga*-like memorials.

While the memorials of Rajasthan differ considerably from those of the central Gangetic plain to the northeast, it is probably from this "heartland" region that such a conspicuous use of the *liṅga* in Rajasthan's memorial imagery was derived. The *liṅga*-related memorials in southeastern Rajasthan thus seem to be the result of cultural influences from the Gangetic plain "heartland." Conversely, the memorial pillars with carved male and female figures in the *namaskār* pose which occasionally occur in the Gangetic plain may be the result of cultural influences emanating from Rajasthan.

Central India

Eastward from Kota, in a transitional area from Rajasthan into Central India, one increasingly encounters memorials which have in their uppermost part a carving of a raised right arm, with a sun to one side and a crescent moon to the other (Pl. IV-H). This type of memorial dominates over much of Madhya Pradesh, and dated pillars show that the sun, vertical arm and moon started to be the hallmark motif in the region over 700 years ago.[27] Below this motif are depictions of the deceased male and his *satī* in a variety of poses. Both the male and the *satī* may have their arms raised, and the holding of hands or crossing of arms is frequently portrayed. A depiction of the two jointly holding a vessel and pouring water over a *liṅga* below is also common. The *satī* may also be depicted as bearing a lime, a mirror, a pot or a coconut.[28] While most of these memorials are free-standing, the few which are protected are usually in cenotaphs that are open-sided or with enclosing walls. The cenotaphs are either square or octagonal, and are most often domed.

In the iconography of the region, a few memorial pillars indicate development toward a narrative type of memorialization. On such pillars, there may be a reclining male in the bottom panel (perhaps with a female at his feet), the couple may be pouring water over a *liṅga* in the panel above and, in the highest panel, the typical raised arm separating the sun from the crescent moon will be present. A few scattered and comparatively rare memorial stones can be said to be of the fully developed narrative type. In these, the upward progression from how the warrior met his death to his ultimate presence in the supernatural realm with his *satī* wife or wives is depicted in super-imposed panels. This narrative type of memorial stone is best developed in Maharashtra and Karnataka. Though none of the narrative memorials in Madhya Pradesh is a counterpart of the memorial pillars which stand near Belur and Halebid in Karnataka, with six or even seven superimposed panels, they can still be impressive.[29]

Gujarat

Particularly in the western part of Gujarat, but in other areas as well, there are many *satī* memorials with the raised arm motif. At the great cult and pilgrimage center of Halvad, where people of different castes and lineages still come to cremate their dead, the large number of memorials with raised arms create a monotonous impression.[30] Added motifs, however, give variety to the iconography. A memorial pillar may have a plain arm, or an arm loaded down with wrist and upper-arm bangles. A figure representing the *satī's* husband may be carved onto either the same stone or a separate stone. If on the same stone, the husband may be shown as a mounted warrior on a horse to one side of the arm, or as a male with arms down to both sides and positioned above the horizontal portion of the *satī* arm. A symbolic sun and crescent moon are commonly present in the uppermost part of the memorials, while in some, there is also a stylized Pleiades inserted between the two. Representations of *triśūls* (tridents) are also carved on a few of the memorials. A stylized representation of a sari length used by women to enfold and swing their infants is also included in some memorials. A stylized representation of a *sārī* length used by having been pregnant at the time of their husband's death, generally committed *satī* after the birth of the infants.

Though fewer in number, and in some instances unique, there are other memorials in Gujarat which reveal considerable diversity and varying local traditions. Memorial stones may have depictions of single females in a variety of poses: sitting in the lotus position with a rosary, standing with their arms down, standing with a pot in one hand and a rosary in the other, or standing with both arms raised. If the female figure is accompanied by a representation of a deceased male, both may have their arms raised or down to the side, or they may be holding each other's hand. At Degam, close to Porbandar, depictions of males and *satīs* with both arms either raised or down to the side are common. In the royal cenotaphs at Bhuj, one finds the pattern of a mounted warrior on a taller pillar and of single standing *satīs* on separate stones to each side, each holding a pot in one hand and a rosary in the other. In the southwestern coastal region of Kathiawar, extending westward to the Rann of Kutch, the focus is sometimes on representations of the *satī*'s hand (in which supernatural power is believed to be centered). A memorial of this type may have one hand, two hands next to each other, or two hands and a female figure with arms down to each side. In one of the royal cenotaphs at Jamnagar, there is a tall, now defaced pillar[31] flanked on each side by individual *satī* memorials, each with two sculptured hands. The motif of the *satī* carrying her deceased husband also appears in Gujarat, as does that of a *satī*, alone or with her husband, riding a bullock cart.

While we have some evidence that this last theme was used in Rajasthan at some point (Goetz 1978: Pls. XIII, XIV), we need more positive evidence of this. But the raised arm motif that dominates in Gujarat is clearly found in the transition region of southern Rajasthan. An example is even found on one of the square memorial pillars that stand next to the Bhimlat Kund in Chittorgarh.[32]

Satī Worship

After the British made *satī* illegal within the territories they controlled, the practice began to fade away. As time went on, even the ruling elite of the princely states came to reject it. Thus, when Maharana Sarup Singh of Udaipur died in 1861, no queen would volunteer to join him on the funeral pyre. The lone slave who agreed to perish with him became the last legally permissible *satī* linked to royalty in Rajasthan, and may well have been the last legal *satī* in India. W.F. Eden, Agent of the Governor-General, described the event as follows (Thompson 1927:284-285):

> . . . the funeral procession, composed of all loyal subjects of the State, one and all, high and low, even the successor to the throne, proceeded the whole distance on foot; one alone of this vast multitude was allowed to ride, and she had but a short time to live. Mounted on a gorgeously caparisoned horse, herself richly attired as for a festive occasion, literally covered with jewels and costly ornaments; her hair loose and in disorder [as was the custom]; her whole countenance wild with the excitement of the scene and the intoxicating effects of the drugs she had swallowed, she issued forth with the body . . . .

At the cremation site, while final preparations were being made behind canvas walls, the woman ascended the pyre and placed the deceased ruler's head on her lap. After the pyre was further built up around her and the wood was steeped in oil, the canvas walls were removed. The pyre was ignited, and many in the assembled crowd cried out as they watched the ensuing cremation and devotional suicide.

Though the practice of *satī* is nowadays rare in Rajasthan, the worship of *satīs* has persisted, and is both common and widespread. The northeastern Shekhawati region (see Map 1), with its cult center at Jhunjhunu, has an unusually large number of deified *satīs* who are regularly worshipped. Rani Sati of Jhunjhunu is the most widely known *satī* goddess in India, for her worship has been extended by diffusion to temples in Bhagalpur, Bombay, Calcutta, Delhi, Imphal, Kanpur, Patna, Manipur and Varanasi in India, and even as far away as Hong Kong. The 14-year old Rani Sati, named after a faithful attendant called Rana, is said to have been deified and then worshipped continuously from the time she became a *satī* in 1295 A.D. The large temple complex that honors her (Pl. V-A) has an impressive facade. Pilgrims are accomodated in 400 rooms that surround a central courtyard. As Rani Sati was an ancestor of one of the important merchant subcastes of Shekhawati, the Jhunjhunwalas, other *satīs* believed to be in the later ancestral line of this subcaste are also venerated in 12 subsidiary shrines aligned next to the main temple (Pl. V-B). Worship in the temple is conducted by a chief priest and eight other priests. While daily periods of visitation by pilgrims run from 4:00 A.M. to 1:00 P.M. and from 3:00 P.M. to 11:00 P.M., there is formal viewing (*darśan*) and worship of Rani Sati five times a day. During a normal day, an average of 150 to 200 people visit the temple, but the number of pilgrims in daily attendance during the great annual festival in the month of Bhadrapad (August-September) averages over ten times more.

There are at least 25 more *satī* temples in the Jhunjhunu area. Though they are not as impressive in size as the Rani Sati temple, and typically have only two formal worship periods each day, some have a substantial architectural infrastructure. The modernized *śikhara* rising above the innermost sanctuary of the Khemi Sati temple (Pl. V-C), for example, compares well with that of the Rani Sati temple. As in other *satī* temples, several symbolic objects are used to represent the goddess: a *triśūl*, eyes, a *bindu* dot, four swastikas, a head shawl and a breast cloth (Pls. V-D, V-E). The Khemi Sati temple has 84 rooms for pilgrims around the central courtyard. Within the seven to ten days of the annual fair which occurs in August-September (Bhadrapad), a total of between 2000 and 3000 persons occupy the rooms in turn.

In addition to the older temples to *satīs* of the past, there are also temples to recent *satīs*. While the *satī* cults of the Jhunjhunu area of Shekhawati have primarily urban links, new cults which seem grounded in rural revivalism have emerged in recent years in the nearby Thorawati region (see Map 1). In Thorawati and an adjacent part of Shekhawati, six women became *satīs* within a period of eight years: 1) Savitri of Kotri (April 1, 1973), 2) Neh Kunwar of Govindpura (September 15, 1973), 3) Savitri of Golyana (October 3, 1973), 4) Sataj Kunwar of Shoorpura (February 25, 1974), 5) Son Kunwar of Maundakala (October 11, 1975) and 6) Om Kunwar of Jhadli (August 30, 1980). No other region in India has had such a high incidence of women becoming *satīs* in recent times.

During our field work in 1977, we visited the sites related to the Golyana and Kotri *satīs*. Only four years after their deaths, both *satīs* had already been deified, and temples were in advanced stages of construction (Pls. V-F, V-G). In the main shrine of the Golyana temple, there were a *triśūl* and other symbolic objects covered by a shawl, and paintings depicting the *satī* with her relatives were spread out on both sides of the objects (Pl. V-H). In a side room, there was a statue of Golyana Sati sitting in a posture of blessing, with a swastika on the palm of her opened hand and a representation of her deceased husband lying on her lap (Pl. VI-A). At Kotri, the display of the *triśūl* and related symbolic objects was also present (Pl. VI-B). The main difference between this shrine and the one at Golyana was the stylized representation of the *satī* by means of skirt and shawl wrappings. Photographs recording the *satī*'s final activities on earth were hung on both sides of the central image.

A diverse assortment of deified *satīs* are worshiped in the rest of Rajasthan, and there is always the potential for the worship of a new *satī*. Already mentioned above is Sati Deep Kunwar at the Devikund near Bikaner. Besides the year-round worship at the memorial pillar commemorating the *satī* and her ruler husband, there is also an annual festival held in her honor during the month of Bhadrapad. At the memorial pillar on the grounds of the Tourist Bungalow in Udaipur, likewise already mentioned, Dhobis have placed a stone with two carved feet before the representation of that *satī*, and regularly come to worship her. Southwest of Alwar, just beyond the Sariska Game Sanctuary and within the traditional region called Naida (see Map 1), there is a temple dedicated to Sati Narayani (Pl. VI-C). Because this *satī* was a member of the barber caste, she has become a special goddess of that caste in northeastern Rajasthan. For example, she is worshipped daily by the barbers of Jaipur right after they have arrived at their work places. Near Ringus, located in the Shekhawati region (see Map 1), there is a temple to Sati Poochi, in which the focus of worship is a worn memorial pillar with a warrior and female carved in the *namaskār* pose (Pls. VI-D, VI-E). It is said that Poochi had her nose and ears cut off by the thieves who killed her husband. Hand prints on the wall testify to the belief that this *satī* goddess will bless and make fertile the recently married women who come to worship her.

Temples also honor recent *satīs* in Jodhpur and Osian. The Jodhpur *satī* is Sagan Kunwar Bai. The wife of a brigadier named Thakur Jaba Singh who died in 1954, she was able to commit *satī* before the police arrived to prevent it. She is now considered to be the *satīmātā* ('*satī* mother') of Jodhpur. Inside her temple (Pl. VI-F), a photograph of her face (Pl. VI-G) has become the focus of worship. The *satī* worshiped near Osian is named Desu. After her husband died and was cremated on October 26, 1977, she died of a broken heart. So more wood was piled at the cremation site, and her remains were cremated. Because of the nature of her death, the villagers living near Osian decided that she was a *satī*. After a woman had brought her child and prayed at the cremation site five days later, she claimed that the child, who had been speechless, had miraculously started to talk after they returned home. As a result of this, the villagers built a memorial shrine to her (Pl. VI-H). When we visited the site, people were praying as they circumambulated the *satī*'s remains, and mothers were lifting up their infants and imploring the *satī* to bless them.

One of the most recent *satīs* to have become an object of worship is Sohan Kunwar of Nimbari Kotharia near Degana (see Map 1). She became a *satī* on February 29, 1980. According to newspaper accounts (Purohit 1980:21, 23; Chhabra 1980:20-21), she first took a purification bath, then dressed in the clothes of a bride, and informed her family members that she intended to become a *satī*. In one account, she is said to have also imprinted hand prints with vermillion powder on the outer walls of her house so that all who saw them would know of her intent (*Sāptāhik Hindustān* 1980:13). Then she walked with the rest of the villagers behind the people carrying her husband's body in the funeral procession, holding her hands in the *namaskār* pose, and absorbed in prayer. After reaching the pyre, she climbed and sat on it, then placed her husband's head on her lap after his body had been passed up to her. Some villagers swear that divine fire from her hand then ignited the pyre (a common folk belief related to *satīs* elsewhere as well). In reality and according to custom, her sons lit the pyre. Hundreds of people watched as she was consumed by the flames. At least seven days passed before policemen reached the village. Some impression of the thousands who came to worship her can be gained from an estimate of 100,000 coconuts sold within the first 15 days. By the end of that period, a committee had already been set up to plan for the construction of a temple.

The most recent *satī*, in Thorawati, sharply contrasts with the former in the public protests and legal responses which followed (Ali 1987; Badhwar 1987). On September 4, 1987, Roop Kunwar became a *satī* in Deorala (see Map 1). Dressed in her wedding outfit and holding a coconut, she first walked around the village and then circumambulated the funeral pyre for about 15 minutes. In the customary fashion, she perished while holding her husband in her arms on the inflamed pyre. A crowd of at least hundreds (4,000 according to another estimate) observed. While some policemen probably wished to prevent the incident, legal action became difficult because of the Rajput youths who vowed that any interference would be over their dead bodies. No other woman of Deorala had become a *satī* in 69 years . The father-in-law claimed that he and other family members could not change the *satī* from her fixed resolve to accompany her deceased husband. The father, Pal Singh Rathore, learned of his dauthter's death after the fact. He thinks his daughter is a goddess, and wishes to donate money for her temple.

By September 16, when the *chunaṛī* ceremony was held, pilgrims had been visiting the cremation site up to a probable rate of 10,000 per day. The money deposited by the worshippers in collection boxes, which sometimes had to be emptied close to every hour, in all likelihood exceeded US $100,000. A woman's social action group, objecting to the well-advertised ceremony, petitioned the Rajasthan High Court. Despite the High Court's ruling in favor of the women, police trying to stop all public transportation at a distance of over ten kilometers from the village were totally frustrated in their efforts. In addition, if necessary, a "defénse force" of about 1000 volunteers had pledged to lay down their lives to prevent any interference (Raghavan 1987:102). The overwhelming horde came on in the 200 buses provided by Roop Kunwar's father (who was in the transportation business), tractors, bullock and camel carts, and by foot. At the cremation site, a village dominated by Sakhtawat Rajputs, four swordsmen surrounded by a ring of other swordsmen, all with weapons drawn, kept a vigil. The crowd in attendence may have exceeded 200,000. Agitation by human-rights groups all over India, the possibility of the Janata Party taking legal action against some of its leaders who attended the *chunaṛī* ceremony, and Communist agitation demanding the dismissal of the Rajasthan government, led Prime Minister Rajiv Gandhi to send Union Minister of State P. Chidambaram to Rajasthan to investigate the matter. Roop Kunwar's 15 year-old brother-in-law, who had lit the pyre, his younger brother (age 10), her father-in-law, the officiating priest, and the barber who had shaved the heads of the family members before the ceremony – all were arrested. After much agitation against the building of a temple and even demands that the Rajasthan government confiscate the money given for a temple, P.Chidambaram was assuring women's groups that the construction of a temple would not be permitted. As a direct response to the events surrounding the Deorala *satī* incident and the widespread protest against *satī* which arose all over India as a result, the Government of India passed the Commission of Sati (Prevention) Act of 1987, which provides the death penalty or life imprisonment for the abetment of *satī*, and the minimum imprisonment of one year for the glorification of *satī*.

When one of us visited the cremation site at 8 A.M. on October 11, 1987, about 50 people (mostly women) were circumambulating it at a distance. Shouting "*Satī Mātā kī jai!*" (Hail Mother Sati!), five young men wearing yellow turbans were circumambulating in a tighter circle around the raised platform, on which a priest sat next to an image of Sati Roop Kunwar with a *triśūl* behind it. The priest murmured *mantras* and performed rituals on behalf of the worshippers. Two piles of smashed coconuts stood close to the shrine, and two nearby tents offered shade to pilgrims. Five children sold pictures of the *satī*, and many visitors watched the proceedings. An array of red flags commemorating the *satī* flapped from bamboo poles, and signs over drawn red cloth read "*Om Roop Kunwar Mahāsatī Sthal*" (Sacred Site of the Great *Satī* Roop Kunwar). A bus came with pilgrims from Jaipur, and local private buses running back and forth brought more pilgrims. Police, under a Deputy Superintendent of Police, were staying in the local primary school. Six police trucks were seen, and there were police patrolling in jeeps.

Conclusions

Some tentative conclusions can be drawn from the findings reported in this paper. First, the most characteristic visual aspects of *satī* memorialization in Rajasthan are: 1) hand prints, 2) pillars, 3) cenotaphs, 4) horse-riding warriors, 5) males and their *satīs* in the *namaskār* pose, 6) *liṅgas* or miniature *śikharas*, and 7) representations of the sun and moon.

Second, there are some clear subregional differences within Rajasthan in the patterns of memorialization. Cenotaphs (primarily connected with memorials honoring rulers and their *satīs*) and the *namaskār* pose (especially for female figures, but often for male figures as well) are found throughout Rajasthan. The representation of warriors on horseback, however, occurs in its clearest and simplest form to the west of the Aravallis, especially in northwestern Bikaner and western Jaisalmer. Memorials based on the *liṅga* symbol or with the miniature *śikharas*, on the other hand, occur mostly in southeastern Rajasthan, east of the Aravallis.

Third, the patterns of memorialization to the north of Rajasthan (Punjab-Haryana), the northeast (the Gangetic plain), the east (Central India), and the south (Gujarat) differ from those found in Rajasthan, but there also appear to have been mutual influences in the transitional border areas.

Finally, Rajasthan as a region is to this day strongly associated with the worship of *satīs*. The concentration of *satī* temples in the folk regions of Naida, Shekhawati and Thorawati in northeastern Rajasthan is unmatched in the rest of India. The number of temples recently constructed for deified *satīs*, particularly in or close to the Thorawati region, is similarly unmatched, as is the degree to which the Rani Sati of Jhunjhunu, in Shekhawati, is widely worshipped in India.

This study has focused upon Rajasthan, and has emphasized the distinctive patterns of *satī* memorialization and worship within this cultural region. However, it has also brought out commonalities shared across regional boundaries, as well as general patterns that are pan-Indian. It has suggested that the symbolism of *satī* memorials is related to broader concepts in Hinduism and, in some cases, to similar symbolism elsewhere, especially in ancient Mesopotamia and the Mediterranean world. It has also made it clear that the deification and worship of *satīs* is not an isolated curiosity, but part of a functioning system of popular religion that needs to be better understood. More questions have been raised than answered, suggesting that there is a need for further research into this whole subject, both in Rajasthan and in other parts of India as well.

ENDNOTES

1. One version of the legend relates that when Daksha, Sati's father, arrived late at a feast thrown by Brahma for the gods and rishis, Shiva did not rise with all the other gods to greet him. In revenge, Daksha arranged a great sacrifice to which he invited all the gods except Shiva. Sati, mortified at this treatment of her husband, went to visit her father and, in the presence of many deities, created the sacrificial fire known as *jvālā-mukhī*, into which she threw herself and was consumed (Walker 1968:I,260; II,357). A version in the *Bhāgavata Purāṇa* (IV.4, 1-34) has Sati perishing through self-immolation by yoga (1970-80:II,438-444).
2. The word *satī* originally referred to the woman who committed suicide by self-immolation and not to the act itself. Edward Thompson, however, used *satī* for the woman and the anglicized "suttee" for the act (1928:15-16), a usage followed by most later English-language writing on the subject. In this paper, for simplicity, the term *satī* is used for both the act and the female involved.
3. According to the *Atharvaveda* (XVIII.3, 1-4), the widow should pay her final respects to her deceased husband, but was then to be taken home before the pyre was ignited (1982:695-696). For a translation and discussion of the appropriate stanzas in the earlier *Ṛgveda* (X.18, 1-20), see Wilson (1858) and Lanman (1927:86-87, 382-385). Lanman refers to a time in which the dead were buried and when wives of the deceased, through levirate marriage, afterwards became the wives of brothers still living.
4. Diodorus records that in 316 B.C., one of the wives of Ceteus, an Indian general killed in battle during the struggle for power that followed Alexander's death, perished in the flames of her husband's pyre (1957-67:X,317-325).
5. In a case recorded in poetry around 1606 A.D. by Muhammad Riza Nau'i, at the request of Akbar's son Daniyal and shortly after the death of Akbar, a lady who pleaded before the emperor to become a *satī* was finally granted permission. Prince Daniyal also pleaded with the lady at the cremation site, but without success (Nau'i 1912).

6. Baptist missionaries William Carey, John Marshman and William Ward observed the *satī* rites, and their Serampore Mission became the base of devoted opposition to *satī* (Marshman 1859). The examples of *satī* in William Ward's book (1818:II, liii-iv, 298-312) were particularly influential, and were used repeatedly to fuel the fires of opposition by people in India and Britain. Mrtyunjay Vidyalankar, who demonstrated that *satī* was not condoned by the most sacred *śāstras*, became the first Bengali to publicly denounce the practice by publishing a pamphlet attacking it (Kopf 1969:205-206). Ram Mohan Roy, who suffered great emotional anguish when his brother's wife became a *satī*, became famous for his opposition to the custom (Collet 1962:33-34, 252-266, 461-467). Lord William Bentinck, after seeking advice from many sources and concluding that little resistance was likely, especially from Indian soldiers, outlawed *satī* in the Bengal Presidency on Sunday, December 6, 1829. In the following year, *satī* was outlawed in the Bombay and Madras Presidencies (Potts 1967:144-157; Seed 1955).
7. The British reaction to *satī* was stimulated by a highly influential book by Peggs (1828), who included in it a personal description of a *satī* witnessed in India. The single most informative document, covering different aspects of *satī*, was one published in Great Britain under governmental orders (Great Britain, House of Commons 1821-30). For the Bengal Presidency alone, it documents over 8000 *satī* cases. It also sets forth the moral and legal issues *satī* posed for members of the highest court in India, the Nizamat Adalat, and for the local legal representatives (primarily magistrates) who were often struggling to change the laws.
8. The strength of the institution of *satī* in Rajasthan is clearly related to the Rajput presence in the area. The practice fits well with medieval Rajput conceptions of chivalry and honor, and has been particularly embraced by the Rajput community. It may, however, represent the evolution of a much more ancient tradition. While the debate over whether the ancestors of the Rajputs were Huns, Kushans, Shakas, Scythians, or a combination of such tribal people is endless (e.g., Asopa 1976; Bingley 1978; Singh 1975), there is a consensus that at least some of their ancestors were horse-riding nomads who came from Central Asia. There is substantial evidence that some form of widow-sacrifice or widow-suicide was widespread among these horse-riding nomads of Central Asia. A description by Herodotus (5th century B.C.) of a Scythian chief's funeral in which a woman was strangled to death (1952:136) has been validated by findings at archaeological sites from that period in the southern Soviet Union (Rostovtzeff 1922:45-49; Rice 1957:92-123). Far to the east, at Pazyrik in Siberia, excavations of frozen nomad tombs have revealed the existence of the same custom (Rudenko 1970:293-294). In India, however, cremation was the dominant funerary practice. Nomadic horsemen penetrating the region would thus have intermingled with people who burned rather than buried their dead. Consequently, the burial of strangled females would have eventually been replaced by their immolation on the deceased male's funeral pyre. While the Rajput use of stone pillars (*devalīs*) to commemorate males and their *satī* wives cannot be positively linked to ancient nomadic custom, this form of a memorial, and the sculptures often found on it, may well represent symbolic links with the pre-Indian past.

9. Tod (1920:II, 1029-1032) wrote a description of a royal funeral in Rajasthan: "On Asar, the 13th., the dark half of the moon [of 1724 A.D.], seventeen hundred warriors [with uncovered heads and feet] . . . , for the last time marched before their lord [Ajit Singh, ruler of Marwar]. They placed his body in a boat [i.e., a bier shaped like a boat], and carried him to the pyre, made of sandalwood and perfumes, with heaps of cotton, oil, and camphor." Then six queens married to Ajit Singh and 58 concubines perished with him in the ensuing holocaust. While it did not occur in Rajasthan, the funeral of the Sikh ruler Ranjit Singh in the nearby Punjab is interesting for its similarities (see Steinbach 1846:17-19).
10. In a dry environment with a dearth of firewood, could such mass suicides have been carried out by fire alone? Kipling, in his brief coverage of the *jauhars* at Chittorgarh, has suggested that women perished by stabbing, poison, asphyxiation, and in explosions as well as by fire (1891:106-112).
11. For accounts of the the outlawing of *satī* in Rajputana, see Thompson 1927 and Wilson 1851.
12. We are thankful for the fellowship from the American Institute of Indian Studies that supported our field work. The field work was inspired by initial work in the Nilgiris of Tamil Nadu (Noble 1976, 1988) and the resultant desire, for comparative purposes, to see *satī*-related memorials and temples elsewhere in India. After a search through the literature and the development of a site file, key sites were chosen for visitation. While in the field, our main goal was to visit as many sites as possible within a period of a little more than six months. We primarily depended upon buses for our travel and were so mobile that often, when starting in the morning, we did not know where the next night would be spent. Many more sites with *satī* memorials and *satī* temples were found than those in the original proposal. When the time available was ended, we had visited sites from the Himalayas to northeastern Kerala, and from Jaisalmer and Jammu into Bengal. Photography was our main tool for gathering data, and over 1500 photographs were obtained. We tried to photograph as broad a representation as possible, and would typically stop taking photographs when a combination of features was being repeated. However, as one may discern from the result of our efforts in Rajasthan, when there was a need for the repeated photography of certain themes, we continued to photograph and gather related data. We also obtained the opinions of country folk, and were most interested in their interpretations of symbols and belief in *satī* goddesses. We interviewed the priests of *satī* temples, some of whom had also officiated when women became *satīs*. We also managed to interview the family members of women who had become *satīs*. While our field survey represents a hasty random sampling over a vast region, we feel that we are now able to discern some patterns of *satī* memorialization and worship in India.
13. Centered *liṅgas* and centered pillars thus symbolically form *axes mundi* (each at the center of the earth) along which the worldly is vertically transformed into the supernatural. In the words of Mircea Eliade, "no world can come to birth in the chaos of the homogeneity and relativity of profane space. The discovery or projection of a fixed point – the center – is equivalent to the creation of the world" (1959:22). "A universe comes to birth from its center; it spreads out from a central point that is, as it were, its navel" (*ibid.*, 44).

14. During the period of Mughal rule, the use of these features spread from Bengal into northern India, into the Punjab, and even into the Kangra valley. That a portion of the palace built in Agra for Akbar was called the Bengali Mahal is indicative of this Bengali influence. Man Singh, Akbar's famous Rajput general who was involved in the conquest of Bengal, brought a Kali image back and had a Bengali-style temple built to house it in the fort at Amber. The Rajput Kacchwahas of Amber and Jaipur have since worshipped the image as their *iṣṭa-devī*. Later, when Aurangzeb's fanatacism caused craftsmen to leave Delhi, many went to work for Rajput rulers. Thus curved cornices and curved eaves appeared even more frequently in the architecture of Rajputana from the early 1700s onward (Datta 1975:17, 44).
15. A *śikhara* is typically a convex-curved and stylized *liṅga*-like tower surmounting the *garbhagṛha* (the *sanctum sanctorum*, lit. 'the womb house') of the standard North Indian temple.
16. Umbrellas demonstrate the symbolic significance of centering. They have been used from the time of the ancient Egyptians to focus the attention of observers upon secular or sacred sources of power, or upon objects representing such powers. However, while the Assyrians, Persians, and Greeks adopted this symbolic system, the Romans did not, and thus the system generally died out in the West. In the East, on the other hand, it became increasingly important, and especially so in the sacred context. While the Greek-influenced Ghandaran sculptures in northwestern South Asia have depictions of ceremonial umbrellas, it may have been the earlier Persians who introduced the system into South Asia. In India, umbrellas or symbolic representations of umbrellas became an integral part of Buddhist *stupas*, while symbolic representations of umbrellas (called *stupīs*) eventually surmounted the *vimānas* (towers, with parallel horizontal levels, rising above *garbhagṛhas*) in South Indian temples (Longhurst 1979: frontispiece, 1-28). The umbrella was the main symbol of kingship in India, and has therefore been used in ceremonial contexts to indicate the presence of rulers. As a parallel, the roofs of royal cenotaphs in Rajasthan – with the exception of the uncommon *śikhara* roofs – symbolically represent umbrellas which shade and protect the centered royal and sacred memorials within.
17. The majority of cosmologies in the world prior to the "Age of Reason" held that, at the center of the universe, there exists an "axis of the world" which is a conduit between the underworld, the earth, and the sky. The *axis mundi* has been most commonly associated with a pillar, mountain or world tree (Eliade 1964:259-271). It may thus be argued that every memorial pillar and cenotaph in Rajasthan represents a cosmological construct. The *liṅga*, as an erect human penis, can also be seen as a form of *axis mundi* pillar, especially as it is often depicted as having four planes facing the quadrants – a special expression of the cosmological view that space radiates outward from the center.
18. The concept of female moon bestowing fertility and male sun nurturing growth was widespread in ancient times. Probably originating in ancient Mesopotamia, it spread throughout the countries bordering on the Mediterranean (Harding 1955:21-22, 29, 132-133, 229). In India, it appeared later and has continued to the present. The parallelism between the use of this paired symbolism in the ancient Mediterranean world and in India is striking. For example, compare the illustration of the sun and moon on a Carthagenian pillar (Burland 1972:36)

with illustrations of these symbols on pillars in Gujarat (Fischer and Shah 1973:photos 31-42, 52-54).

19. In ancient seals of Mesopotamia, the sun (either round or rayed) and the recumbent moon are shown at the end of the 4th millennium B.C. In the Akkadian era they not only appear together upon occasion, but for the first time are depicted with the sun lying within the recumbent crescent. Between approximately 2280 and 2180 B.C., the orb is shown as filling the whole hollow of the recumbent crescent. This combination occurs frequently during the First Babylon Dynasty (about 2100 to 1750 B.C.) and afterwards. The sun and moon were sometimes between two representations of deities (Butterworth 1970:107-108 and Pl.XV). From Mesopotamia into the Mediterranean basin, primarily in small depictions either on seals or jewelry, the sun and moon theme frequently accompanied representations of a pillar, mountain or tree. In Egypt, a boat carrying a recumbent moon filled with an orb also appeared in sacred settings (Harding 1955:39-45, 87-90, 222, 229; Evans 1901). A cut gem found by Layard at Nineveh, the capital of ancient Assyria, is of great interest, for it has the clear depiction of a *liṅga-yoni* altar. While the *liṅga* has a radiant sun above, a *yoni* pillar is with a lenticular *yoni* emblem and a recumbent moon above (Hannay 1971:70).
20. It is conceivable that these ten other females also became *satīs* with the Maharaja, but it is not likely. According to an account by the British Resident in Udaipur, a golden hookah, sword and water vessel were left after the Maharana was cremated near the cenotaphs. They were intended for the use of the departed ruler's spirit, until its departure 12 days after the cremation. Dancing women danced before the ashes, and musicians (gender not mentioned) played among the cenotaphs during this period of time (Kipling 1895:69-70). It thus seems likely that this same practice was followed elsewhere.
21. As the last Maharani *satī* in Bikaner, Deep Kunwar is the one most frequently worshipped, as if she stands in some way for all of the *satīs* of the royal line. This is apparent from the dots of sandal paste spread over the pillar by people who come to worship daily.
22. The representation of a human face in the sun may be a device to help legitimize the ruler by associating him with the sacred *biṅdu*.
23. An even larger number of *satīs*, 84 (probably the record for Rajasthan), perished with Raja Budh Singh of Bundi (d. 1701). See Tod (1920:II, 837-838) for this record.
24. That local worshippers appreciate the deeper symbolic significance of the sun and moon is revealed by their application of sacred ash to the faces in the suns and as spots above the crescent moons in the memorial pillars commemorating Maharaj Shribhavat Singh and Maharaj Kumar Shrikrigham.
25. The *navaratna* design sequence used in Bengal is a device which focuses attention on the center by progressively building out from it. As a pattern for temple construction, it is better developed in Bengal than in any other part of India. Starting with one major roof at the center, directly above the square space with a sacred source of power (i.e., usually a deity's image), other roofs are added to the corners in sets of four. Thus, Bengali temples with one, five, nine (*nava*), 13, 17, 21, 25, or even 29 jewels (*ratna*), i.e., roofs, result from the

sequence. David McCutchion (1972) has described this development sequence and classified temples in Bengal according to it. Michell (1983) later used McCutchion's data and photographs to produce a better illustrated volume, which also contains data added by Michell and others.

26. Osian is a counterpart, albeit not as impressive, of Halvad in Gujarat. In addition to being a pilgrimage center of long standing, it is a place to which members of different castes and lineages have traditionally come to be cremated. Through the centuries, women also came there to become *satīs*. Although Osian has declined, a series of 16 Hindu and Jain temples there are associated with a flourishing period from the 8th to the 12th century (Brown 1956:140-142).
27. At the Dhubela Museum, near Chhattarpur in Madhya Pradesh, there is a memorial pillar from Nawa Talav which commemorates the *satī* Hira and her husband Sama, a carpenter. The raised arm-sun-moon motif is clearly portrayed in the upper part, and the date 1286 is given. The same motif depicted on a memorial pillar at Kolaras, near Gwalior in Madhya Pradesh, is dated 1670. The similarity between the two memorials also includes the depiction of husband and wife jointly holding a vessel from which water is poured over a *liṅga*.
28. While lime, mirror and pot motifs are more typical of *satī* memorialization in Dravidian South India, the coconut motif, though infrequent, is pan-Indian.
29. For example, a memorial at Kolaras in Madhya Pradesh has four superimposed panels on a tall and narrow memorial pillar capped by a small stone umbrella. This memorial has been standing since 1427.
30. This unique and spectacular site thoroughly merits the term 'memorialopolis', and should some day be studied in thorough archaeological detail.
31. What is presumed to have been a representation of the ruler mounted on a horse now appears to have been entirely scratched out.
32. The Bhimlat Kund appears to have been a traditional place for *satī* memorialization at Chittorgarh, as pillars were erected on all sides of this pond. The square memorial pillar which we studied there has a left raised arm, which represents a departure from the right arm norm. In general, we found square memorials to be rare now in Rajasthan, but they may have dominated in earlier times (the 9th and 10th centuries). Only a comprehensive survey will reveal the reality, and we hope that someone will in the future organize such a survey for the entire state of Rajasthan. If all the memorial pillars at Chittorgarh were to be photographically recorded, some valuable insights into the past would be forthcoming for at least this limited area.

Plate I

A

E

F

B

G

C

H

D

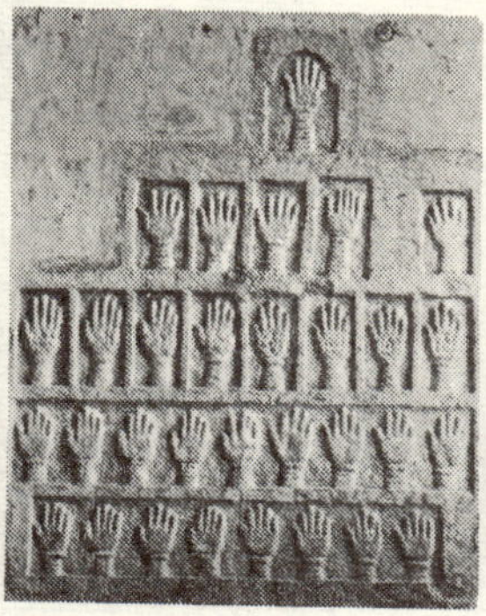

I

J

Plate

A

E

B

F

C

G

D

H

Plate III

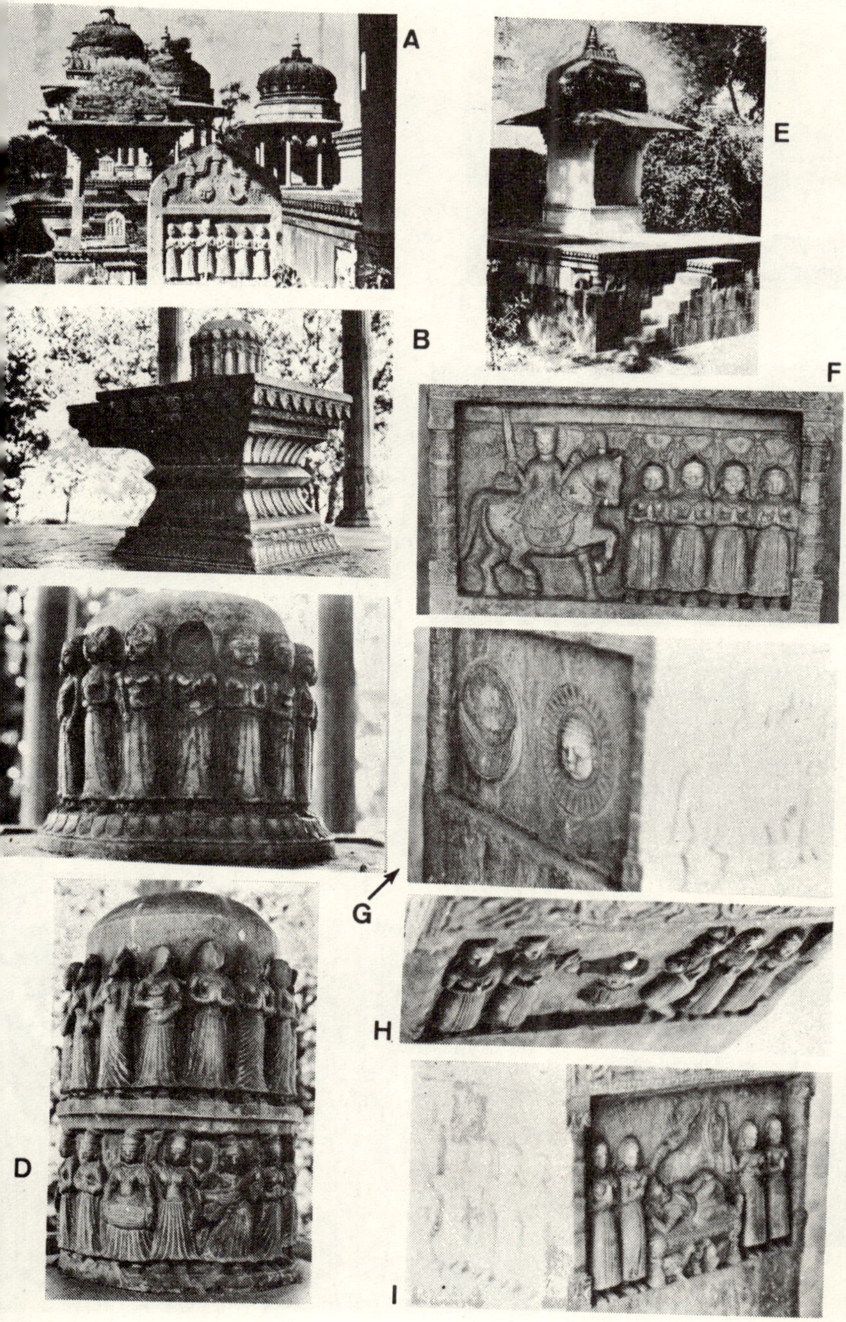

Plate

A

B

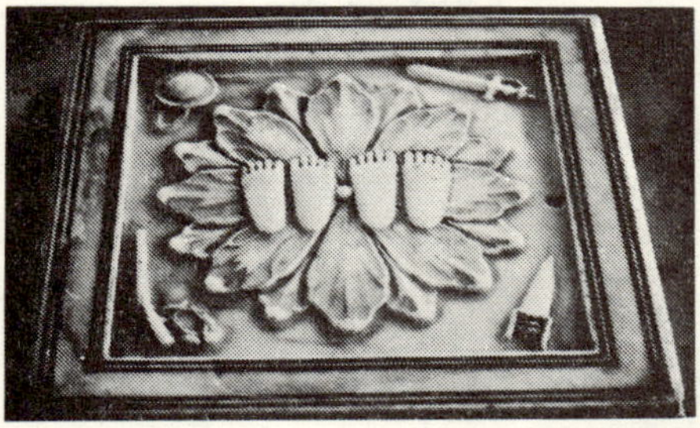

C

D

E

F

G

H

I

Plate V

E

F

C

G

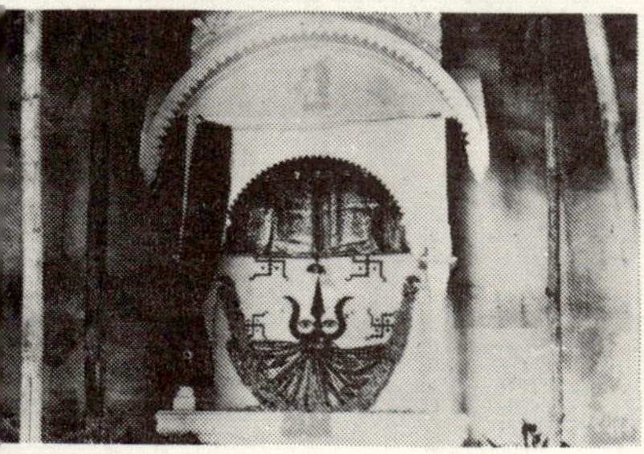

H

Plate

A

B

C

D

E

F

G

H

NOTES ON ILLUSTRATIONS

Plate I

(A) The Devikund and royal cenotaphs at Bikaner. *(B)* A cenotaph near the Devikund *(C)* Cenotaphs at the Badabagh, Jaisalmer. *(D)* Memorial pillars for at least 4 *satīs* and Maharaja Kalyan Singh, Bikaner. *(E)* Stone commemorating Deep Kunwar and Maharaja Moti Singh, Bikaner. *(F)* Memorial pillar for 22 or more *satīs* and Maharaja Zorowar Singh, Bikaner. *(G)* Marble memorial pillar for three *satīs* and a ruler, Jaisalmer. *(H)* Aligned memorial pillars for 11 *satīs* and two rulers, Jaisalmer. *(I)* Carved *satī* hand prints at the palace gateway, Jodhpur. *(J)* Gate with carved *satī* hand prints at the palace within the fort, Jaisalmer.

Plate II

(A) Royal cenotaphs near Mandor, the former capital of Jodhpur State. *(B)* The Maharana Sangram Singh II (d. 1734 A.D.) cenotaph, Udaipur. *(C)* Memorial pillar, *liṅga* and Nandi in the Maharana Jagat Singh II cenotaph, Udaipur. *(D)* Panel commemorating 6 *satīs* in the Maharana Amar Singh I cenotaph, Udaipur. *(E)* Panel commemorating 20 *satīs* and Maharana Jagat Singh II, Udaipur. *(F)* Royal cenotaphs at Begun. *(G)* Cenotaph commemorating 31 *satīs* and Rao Raja Shrishatru Shalya, Bundi. *(H)* Royal cenotaphs at Kota.

Plate III

(A) Memorial pillars within cenotaphs, Begun. *(B)* Centered *yoni* and *liṅga* within the Maharao Ram Singh I cenotaph, Kota. *(C)* Carved representations of *satīs* surrounding the *liṅga*. (D) *Satī* representations on the *liṅga*, Maharao Mukund Singh cenotaph, Kota. *(E)* Cenotaph commemorating 4 *satīs* and Maharaja Shribharat Singh, Bundi. *(F)* Eastern panel of the memorial pillar within: 4 *satīs* and a mounted warrior. *(G)* Southern panel: symbolic sun (with human face) and recumbent moon. *(H)* Western panel: 4 *satīs* and the ruler worshipping a centered *liṅga* (I) Northern panel: ruler lying on a bed and 4 standing *satīs*.

Plate IV

(A) The Musi Maharani and Maharaja Bakhtawar Singh cenotpah, Alwar. (B) The memorial stone within. *(C)* Three aligned memorial pillars at the Bhawani Mandir (Durga temple), Osian. *(D)* A *satī* shrine in the midst of Osian. *(E)* Within the shrine, a memorial pillar commemorating 6 *satīs* and a male on a horse. (F) Cenotaph with two pillars honoring *satīs* and mounted warrior couples, Lathi Fort. *(G)* Stone platform with a memorial pillar, next to the Royal Way, Begun. *(H)* Memorial pillar: couple next to be a *liṅga*, upraised arm with sun and moon, Kota. *(I)* Memorial pillar with *satī* holding husband, Bhawani Maṇdir (Durga temple), Osian.

Plate V

(A) The facade of the Rani Sati complex at Jhunjhunu. *(B)* The Rani Sati Temple and accompanying shrines. *(C)* The Khemi Sati Temple at Jhunjhunu. *(D)* The goddess Khemi Sati image. *(E)* The goddess Mauli Sati image at Jhunjhunu. *(F)* The Golyana Sati (d. 1973 A.D.) Temple. *(G)* The Kotri Sati (d. 1973 A.D.) Temple, under construction. *(H)* Image of the deified Golyana Sati, the officiating priest, and a painting to one side.

Plate VI

***(A)* Image of the Golyana Sati, in the blessing pose. *(B)* The goddess Savitri Sati image. *(C)* The Narayani Matha Temple, beyond the Sariska Game Sanctuary. *(D)* Poochi Sati Temple, Ringus. *(E)* Within, a former priest, memorial pillar, and hand prints of women. *(F)* The Sagan Kunwar Bai (d. 1954 A.D. Sati Temple at Jodhpur. *(G)* The decorated photograph of Sagan Kunwar Bai. (H) *Satī* Shrine under construction at a site near Osian.**

REFERENCES CITED

Ali, Salamat

1987 "A Young Widow Burns in Her Bridal Clothes." *Far Eastern Economic Review*. October 8, pp. 54-55.

Altekar, A.S.

1962 *The Position of Women in Hindu Civilization: From Prehistoric Times to the Present Day*. 3rd ed. Delhi: Motilal Banarsidass.

Asopa, Jai Narayan

1976 *Origin of the Rajputs*. Delhi: Bharatiya Publishing House.

Atharvaveda

1982 *The Atharvaveda*. Translated by Devi Chand. Delhi: Munshiram Manoharlal.

Badhwar, Inderjit

1987 "A Pagan Sacrifice." *India Today*. October 15, pp. 58-60.

Barbosa, Duarte

1918 *The Book of Duarte Barbosa*. Translated by Mansel L. Dames. London: Hakluyt Society.

Bernier, François

1916 *Travels in the Moghul Empire, A.D. 1656-1668*. Translated by Archibald Constable, revised by Vincent Smith. 2nd ed. London: Oxford University Press.

Beveridge, Henry

1872 *A Comprehensive History of India*. 3 vols. London: Blackie & Son.

Bhāgavata Purāṇa

1970-80 *The Bhāgavata Purāṇa*. 5 vols. Translated by Ganesh Vasudeo Tagare. Vols. 7-11 of J.L. Shastri, ed., Ancient Indian Tradition & Mythology Series. Delhi: Motilal Banarsidass.

Bingley, A.H.
1978 *Caste, Tribe and Culture of Rajputs*. Delhi: Ess Ess Publications.

Brown, Percy
1956 *Indian Architecture: Buddhist and Hindu Periods*. 3rd ed., revised and enlarged. Bombay: D.B. Taraporevala Sons & Co.

Buckland, Charles E.
1902 *Bengal Under the Lieutenant-Governors*. 2 vols. 2nd ed. Calcutta: Kedarnath Bose.

Burland, Cottie A.
1972 *Beyond Science: A Journey into the Supernatural*. New York: Grossett & Dunlap.

Butterworth, E.A.S.
1970 *The Tree at the Navel of the Earth*. Berlin: Walter de Gruyter & Co.

Campbell, Walter
1864 *My Indian Journal*. Edinburgh: Edmonston & Douglas.

Caunter, Hobart
1834 *The Oriental Annual, or Scenes in India*. London: Edward Bull.

Chattopadhyay, Aparna
1975 "Position of Widows in Early Medieval India in the Light of the Kathasaritsagara." *Journal of the Oriental Institute* (Baroda) 24:393-402.

Chhabra, Rajender
1980 "Rajasthan: Where Women Become *Satīs* Even Today!" *Dharmayug*. April 20-26, pp. 20-21.

Collett, Sophia D.
1962 *The Life and Letters of Raja Rammohan Roy*. Edited by Dilip K. Biswas and Prabhat C. Ganguli. Calcutta: Sadharan Brahmo Samaj.

Crooke, William
1968 *The Popular Religion and Folk-lore of Northern India*. 2 vols. Reprint of 2nd ed. Delhi: Munshiram Manoharlal.

Datta, Bimal Kumar
1975 *Bengal Temples*. New Delhi: Munshiram Manoharlal.

Dhoundiyal, B.N.
1964 *Rajasthan District Gazetteers: Bundi*. Jaipur: Government Central Press.

Diodorus
1957-67 *Diodorus of Sicily*. Edited by C.H. Oldfather *et al*. 12 vols. London: William Heinemann Ltd.; Cambridge, Mass.: Harvard University Press.

Dubois, Abbe Jean A.
1906 *Hindu Manners, Customs, and Ceremonies*. 3rd ed. Oxford: Clarendon Press.

Eck, Diana L.
1978 "Kasi: City and Symbol." *Purana* 20 (2):169-192.

Edwardes, Herbert and Herman Merivale
1872 *Life of Sir Henry Lawrence*. London: Smith, Elder & Co.

Eliade, Mircea
1959 *The Sacred and the Profane: The Nature of Religion*. New York: Harcourt Brace Jovanovich.
1964 *Shamanism*. New York: Bollingen Foundation.

Evans, Arthur J.
1901 *The Mycenaean Tree and Pillar Cult*. London: Macmillan & Co.

Fischer, Eberhard and Haku Shah
1973 *Vetra ne Khambha: Memorials for the Dead*. Ahmedabad: Gujarat Vidyapith.

Gandhi, Raj S.
1977 "Sati as Altruistic Suicide: Beyond Durkheim's Interpretation." *Contributions to Asian Studies* 10:141-157.

Goetz, Hermann
1950 *The Art and Architecture of Bikaner State*. Oxford: Bruno Cassirer.
1978 *Rajput Art and Architecture*. Wiesbaden: Franz Steiner Verlag.

Great Britain, House of Commons
1821-30 *Papers Relating to East India Affairs: Copies of All Communications Received from India . . . Relating to the Subject of the Immolation of Hindoo Widows [or Relatitve to the Burning of Females on the Funeral Piles of Their Husbands]*. Ordered by the House of Commons, to be printed. 3 vols. File W2263 in India Office Library, London.

Gupta, Savitri
1982 *Rajasthan District Gazetteers: Kota*. Jaipur: Directorate of District Gazetteers.

Hamilton, Alexander
1930 *A New Account of the East Indies [1688-1723]*. Edited by Sir William Foster. 2 vols. London: The Argonaut Press.

Hannay, James B.
1971 *Symbolism in Relation to Religion*. Port Washington, N.Y.: Kennikat Press.

Harding, M. Esther
1955 *Woman's Mysteries*. New York: Pantheon.

Havell, E.B.
1905 *Benares: The Sacred City*. 2nd ed. London: W. Thacker & Co.

Herodotus
1952 *The History of Herodotus*. Vol. 6 in Great Books of the Western World. Edited by Robert M. Hutchins, pp. i-xii, 1-342. Chicago: Encyclopaedia Britannica, Inc.

Ibn Batuta
1976 *The Rehla of Ibn Battuta*. Translated by Mahdi Husain. Baroda: Oriental Institute.

Kipling, Rudyard
1891 *Letters of Marque*. Vol. 9 in the Sahib Edition of Rudyard Kipling's Writings. New York: P.F. Collier & Son.
1895 *Out of India*. New York: G.W. Dillingham.

Kopf, David
1969 *British Orientalism and the Bengal Renaissance*. Berkeley: University of California Press.

Lanman, Charles R.
1927 *A Sanskrit Reader*. Cambridge: Harvard University Press.

Longhurst, A.H.
1979 *The Story of the Stupa*. New Delhi: Asian Educational Services.

McCutchion, David
1972 *Late Medieval Temples of Bengal*. Calcutta: Asiatic Society.

Manu
1886 The Laws of Manu. Translated by George Buhler. Vol. 25 of *The Sacred Books of the East*. Edited by Max Muller. Oxford: Clarendon Press.

Manucci, Niccolao
1957 *Storio do Mogor; or Mogul India, 1653-1708*. Translated by William Irvine, 4 vols. Reprint ed. Calcutta: Editions Indian. (1st ed. 1907-08).

Marshman, John C.
1859 *The Life and Times of Carey, Marshman and Ward, Embracing the History of the Serampore Mission*. 2 vols. London: Longman, Brown, Green, Longmans & Roberts.

Michell, George, ed.
1983 *Brick Temples of Bengal, From the Archives of David McCutchion*. Princeton, N.J.: Princeton University Press.

Misra, Bani Prasana
1973 "A Note on the Origin of Satī." In *Journal of Indian History, Golden Jubilee Volume*. Edited by T.A. Ravindran. pp. 283-389. Trivandrum: University of Kerala, Department of History.

Modave, Comte de
1971 *Voyage de Inde du Comte de Modave, 1773-1776*. Edited by Jean Deloche. Paris: École Française d'Extrême-Orient.

Modi, Jivanji Jamshedji
1924 "The Antiquity of the Custom of *Satī*." *Journal of the Anthropological Society of Bombay* 13:412-424.

Mukhopadhyay, Amitabha
1956-57 "*Satī* as a Social Institution in Bengal." *Bengal: Past and Present* 75:118-126; 76:99-115.

Munro, Eleanor
1982 "Shiva: The Armed Vision." *Art in America* 70:111-121.

Nau'i, Muhammad R.
1912 *Burning and Melting: Being the Suz-u-Gudaz of Muhammad Riza Nau'i of Khambushan*. Edited by Ananda K. Coomaraswamy and Dawud. London: Old Bourne Press.

Noble, William A.
1976 "Nilgiri Dolmens." *Anthropos* 71:90-128.
1988 "Nilgiri Prehistoric Remains." In *The Nilgiris: The Ethnography of an Indian Mountain Region*. Paul Hockings, ed. Delhi: Oxford University Press.

Parlby, Fanny
1850 *Wanderings of a Pilgrim*. 2 vols. London: P. Richardson.

Peggs, James
1828 *The Suttee's Cry to Britain; Showing From Essays Published in India That the Custom of Burning Widows is Not an Integral Part of Hinduism and May Be Abolished With Ease and Safety*. London: Seely & Son.

Polo, Marco
1903 *The Book of Ser Marco Polo, The Venetian*. Translated by Sir Henry Yule. 2 vols. London: J. Murray.

Potts, E. Daniel
1967 *Baptist Missionaries in India, 1793-1837: The History of Serampore and Its Mission*. Cambridge: Cambridge University Press.

Purohit, Anmol
1980 "Back to the Dark Ages!" *Blitz*. March 29, pp. 21, 23.

Raghavan, C.V.V.
1987 "*Shocking Sati*." *Frontline*. October 3-16, pp. 100-105.

Rao, Sakuntala
1933 "Suttee." *Annals of the Bhandarkar Oriental Institute* 14:219-240.

Rice, Tamara T.
1957 *The Scythians*. London: Thames and Hudson.

Rostovtzeff, Mikhali I.
1922 *Iranians and Greeks in South Russia*. Oxford: Clarendon Press.

Rudenko, Sergei I.
1970 *Frozen Tombs of Siberia: The Pazyryk Burials of Iron Age Horsemen*. Berkeley: University of California Press.

Sahni, Daya Ram
1937 *Archaeological Remains and Excavations at Bairat*. Jaipur State: Department of Archaeology and Historical Research.

Sāptāhik Hindustān
1980 "Another *Sati*: Sohan Kunwar." *Sāptāhik Hindustān*. April 6-12, p. 13.

Seed, Geoffrey
1955 "The Abolition of Suttee in Bengal." *History (n.s.)* 40 (140):286-299.

Sehgal, K.K.
1977 *Rajasthan District Gazetteers: Chittaurgarh*. Jaipur: Directorate of District Gazetteers.

Singh, R.B.
1975 *Origin of the Rajputs*. Buxipur: Sahitya Sansar Prakashan.

Sleeman, William H.
1973 *Rambles and Recollections of An Indian Official*. Reprint ed. Karachi: Oxford University Press. (1st ed. 1844)

Smith, George
1883 *The Life of William Carey*. London: J.M. Dent & Co.; New York: E.P. Dutton & Co.

Spink, Walter M.
1973 *The Axis of Eros*. New York: Schocken Books.

Stein, Dorothy K.
1978 "Women to Burn: Suttee as a Normative Institution." *Signs* 4 (2):253-268.

Steinbach, Lt. Col.
1846 *The Punjaub*. London: Smith, Elder & Co.

Stietencron, Heinrich von
1967 "Suicide as a Religious Institution." *Bharatiya Vidya* 27:7-24.

Tavernier, Jean Baptiste
1889 *Travels in India*. Translated by V. Ball. 2 vols. London: Macmillan & Co.

Thakur, Upendra
1963 *The History of Suicide in India*. Delhi: Munshi Ram Manohar Lal.

Thévenot, Jean de
1687 *The Travels of Monsieur de Thévenot. The Third Part. Containing the Relation of Indostan, the New Moguls, and of Other People and Countries of the Indies*. Translated by A. Lovell. London: H. Clark, for booksellers H. Faithorne, J. Adamson, C. Skegnes and T. Newborough, St. Paul's Churchyard.

Thompson, Edward
1927 "The Suppression of Suttee in Native States." *Edinburgh Review* 245:274-286.
1928 *Suttee: A Historical and Philosophical Enquiry Into the Hindu Rite of Widow-Burning*. London: George Allen & Unwin Ltd.

Tod, Col. James
1920 *Annals and Antiquities of Rajasthan*. 3 vols. Oxford: Oxford University Press. (1st ed. 1829-32)

Valle, Pietro della
1892 *The Travels of Pietro della Valle in India*. Translated by G. Havers, edited by Edward Grey. 2 vols. London: Hakluyt Society.

Walker, George B.
1968 *The Hindu World: An Encyclopaedic Survey of Hinduism*. 2 vols. New York: Praeger.

Ward, William
1815-18 *A View of the History, Literature and Mythology of the Hindus*. 2 vols. Serampore: Mission Press.

White, George F.
1838 *Views in India, Chiefly Among the Himalayan Mountains*. Edited by Emma Roberts. 2nd ed. London: Fischer, Son & Co.

Wilson, Horace H.
1851 "The History of British India, from 1805 to 1835." *Quarterly Review* 89:257-276.
1858 "On the Supposed Vaidik Authority for the Burning of Hindu Widows, and On the Funeral Ceremonies of the Hindus." *Journal of the Royal Asiatic Society of Great Britain and Ireland* 16:201-214.

Yule, Henry and A.C. Burnell
1903 *Hobson-Johnson*. New ed. Edited by William Crooke. London: John Murray.

APPENDIX

CONTENTS OF VOLUME II

LOCALES AND SOCIAL STRUCTURES

POWER AND HEGEMONY

NOTES ON CONTRIBUTORS

JAMES WARNER BJÖRKMAN, Ph.D.). (Yale University), formerly Director of the American Studies Research Centre in Hyderabad, is now Professor of Public Policy and Administration at the Institute of Social Studies, The Hague, Netherlands. He has published extensively on Indian politics and comparative health policy. (Vol. II)

B.D. CHATTOPADHYAYA, M.A. (Calcutta University), Ph.D. (Cambridge University), is Professor of Ancient Indian History at the Centre for Historical Studies at Jawaharlal Nehru University. He is the author of *Coins and Currency Systems in South India* (1977, awarded the Prix Duchalais by the Institut de France in 1978), *A Survey of Historical Geography of Ancient India* (1984) and *Aspects of Rural Settlements and Rural Society in Early Medieval India* (1990), and the editor of D.D. Kosambi's *Indian Numismatics* (1981), *Essays on Early Indian Economic History* (1987), and (with B.M. Pande) *Archaeology and History: Essays in Memory of A. Ghosh* (1987). His current research focuses on the state and society in early medieval India. (Vol. II)

HET RAM CHATURVEDI (1932-1988), Ph.D. (Poona University), was Senior Fellow at the Centre for the Study of Developing Societies, Delhi, at the time of his demise. After graduating from Delhi University in 1952, he earned a Master of Social Work degree in 1955 at Baroda University and then an M.A. in Sociology in 1963 at Poona University. In 1966 he joined CSDS and in 1973 received his Ph.D. for a doctoral thesis published as *Bureaucracy and Local Community: Dynamics of Development*. A prolific writer of field reports and articles, he has also authored and/or edited three other books on citizen participation, rural development and Panchayati Raj. Known to his friends as 'Panditji', Chaturvedi was also a classical scholar of *Rāmāyana* and *Mahābhārata*. (Vol. II)

VISHAKHA N. DESAI, Ph.D. (University of Michigan), is Director of the Asia Society Galleries in New York and Associate Professor of Asian Art at the University of Massachusetts, Boston. She has worked extensively on the political and literary context of Rajasthani painting and on the nature of Rajput-Mughal interactions as seen in the visual arts. She was principal organizer and author of the catalogue for the exhibition *Life at Court: Art for India's Rulers, 16th-19th Centuries* (1985). Her recent research projects include an exhibition of Asian portraits from the collection of the Museum of Fine Arts, Boston (1989-90), and an international exhibition of sculptures from the temples of North India which will take place in 1993. (Vol. I)

JOHN EMIGH, M.F.A., Ph.D. (Tulane University), is a director, playwright and performer, and Chair of the Theatre, Speech and Dance Department of Brown University. He has written on the masked theatre of New Guinea, Bali and Eastern India, as well as on contemporary Western theatre. Among his publications are *Masking and Playing: Studies in Mask Performance* (in press). He is currently involved in documenting the Bhand Pather theatre of Kashmir and the Prahlada Nataka of Orissa. He has served as Chairperson of the Asian Theatre Program, of the American Theatre Association and of the Association for Asian Performance. (Vol. I)

ULRIKE EMIGH, M.A. (Brown University), was born in Stuttgart, Germany. She studied Classics and English at Heidelberg University and came to Brown University in 1982 on a Fulbright Fellowship. She has directed medieval and contemporary Western dramas and acted the role of Padmini in Girish Karnad's *Hayavadana*. In 1982-83 she worked with John Emigh on the research and documentation of theatrical traditions on Orissa and Rajasthan. (Vol. I)

JOAN L. ERDMAN, Ph.D. (University of Chicago), is Research Associate in the Committee on Southern Asian Studies at the University of Chicago and Professor of Anthropology in the Department of Liberal Education, Columbia College Chicago. Her research has focused on the social organization of Indian performing arts, arts patronage, and cultural policy in India. She is the author of *Patrons and Performers in Rajasthan: The Subtle Tradition* (1985), and the editor of and a contributor to *Arts*

Patronage in India: Methods, Motives and Markets (1991). She is currently working on a co-authored autobiography of actress Zohra Segal, and a book on the life and artistic achievement of dance choreographer Uday Shankar. (Vol. I)

HENRI-PAUL FRANCFORT, Docteur-ès-Lettres in Archaeology, is Directeur de Recherches at France's Centre National de la Recherche Scientifique, and Director of the Research Team on Irrigation and Settlement in Central Asia. His publications based on research in Afghanistan include *Les Fortifications en Asie Centrade de l'Age du Bornze à l'Èpoque Kouchane* (1979), *Fouilles d'Ai Khanoum III* (1984), *Les Palettes du Gandhara* (1979), and *Fouilles de Shortughai* (1989). In 1982, he founded the Indo-French Archaeological Mission, which worked for six years on the archaeology of the Ghaggar basin. He edited the Mission's first report, *Prospections Achéologiques au Nord-Ouest de l'Inde* (1985), and is currently preparing the final publication. (Vol. I)

ANNE-MARIE GASTON, D.Phil. (Oxford University), is a professional performer of the Bharata Natyam, Odissi and Kuchipudi styles of classical Indian dance. Under the stage name Anjali, she regularly performs in Canada, India, the United States and Europe. She is the author of *Śiva in Dance, Myth and Iconography* (1982). Her doctoral research centered on the sociology of Indian performing arts, and is being considered for two publications by Oxford University Press: *The Makers of Modern Bharata Natyam* and *Drumming for the Child God Krishna: Guru Purushottam Das and the Nathdvara Pakhavaj Tradition*. (Vol. I)

ANN GRODZINS GOLD, Ph.D. (University of Chicago), has done anthropological field work on Hindu pilgrimage, women's songs and stories, and Nath oral epics in Rajasthan's Ajmer District. Her first book, *Fruitful Journeys: The Ways of Rajasthani Pilgrims* (1988) received the Hans Rosenhaupt Memorial Book Award from the Woodrow Wilson Fellowship Foundation. A second book, *A Carnival of Parting* (forthcoming), is an annotated translation and interpretation of two related oral epics performed by a Rajasthani bard. She is currently completing a coauthored volume on women's lore and lives in rural North India and beginning a comparative research project on farmers and the environment in New York and Rajasthan. (Vol. I)

DANIEL GOLD, Ph.D. (University of Chicago), is Director of the South Asian Program and Associate Professor of South Asian Religions in the Department of Asian Studies at Cornell University. He has written *The Lord as Guru: Hindi Sants in North Indian Tradition* (1987) and *Comprehending the Guru: Toward a Grammar of Religious Perception* (1988). His current research interests include the relationships between religious imagination and literary form in India and the development of Nath tradition in Rajasthan. (Vol. II)

EDWARD S. HAYNES, M. Phil. (Jawaharlal Nehru University), Ph.D. (Duke University), is Associate Professor of History at Winthrop College, Rock Hill, South Carolina. He has served in teaching and research positions at Kansas State University, Skidmore College, the University of Northern Iowa, and Duke University. He is the author of a number of articles on the modern history of India, especially on Rajasthan and the Indian princely states. He is completing a manuscript entitled "Jagirdars and Government: Rajput Kingship and Kinship Polity in Alwar State Under British Paramountacy. 1775-1947." (Vol. II)

CAROL HENDERSON, Ph.D. (Columbia University), has taught Anthropology at Columbia University and Emory University. She had done field research in the Jodhpur district of Rajasthan. Her doctoral dissertation was entitled "Life in the Land of Death: Famines and Droughts in Arid Western Rajasthan." Forthcoming publications focus on desertification and human response to natural disasters. Her current research is on wool production in Rajasthan. (Vol. II)

PAULINE KOLENDA, Ph.D. (Cornell University), is Professor of Anthropology at the University of Houston. She has done ethnographic field work in Indian villages in Uttar Pradesh, Rajasthan and Tamil Nadu, and has written *Caste in Contemporary India* (1985). Many of her papers appear in *Regional Caste, Cult and Hierarchy* (1981) and *Regional Differences in Family Structure in India* (1987). (Vol. II)

KOMAL KOTHARI, M.A. (Calcutta University), was co-founder and is Director of Rupayan Sansthan (Rajasthan Institute of Folklore), established in 1960 in the village of Borunda to collect, preserve and disseminate the oral traditions of Rajasthan. He has investigated and documented numerous Rajasthani folk traditions, given expert guidance to film makers, ethnomusicologists and other scholars, and has become known in international folklore study circles as a key source for the understanding of Indian folklore. Among his interests are folk professional musician communities, the relation between ecology and folk customs, and changes in patronage patterns since Indian independence. He has travelled abroad extensively to present Rajasthani folk artists and to deliver papers at scholarly conferences. He has received from the Government of India the honor of Padma Shri. He is the author of *Monograph on Langas* (1972) and a variety of articles on the folk arts, religion and literature of Rajasthan. For many years, he co-edited with Vijay Dan Detha the journal *Lok Sanskriti* (Folk Culture). (Vol. I)

DERYCK O. LODRICK, Ph.D. (University of California, Davis), was born in Ajmer, Rajasthan, and spent his early childhood in India. He was educated in England (Reading and St. Andrews) before completing graduate studies in Geography in the United States. His publications include *Sacred Cows, Sacred Places: Origins and Survivals of Animal Homes in India* (1981) and articles in geographical and anthropological journals focusing on the relations between religious values, behavior and the environment in South Asia. Ongoing research includes studies of animals and culture in South Asia, the cultural ecology of cattle-keeping in Rajasthan, and fairs and festivals of India. He is currently visiting Lecturer in the Department of Geography at the University of California, Davis, and a Research Associate of the Center for South Asia Studies at the University of California, Berkeley. (Vol. I)

MICHAEL W. MEISTER, Ph.D. (Harvard), is Professor of the History of Art and South Asia Regional Studies and Chair of the Graduate Group in Art History at the University of Pennsylvania. His research and publications have largely been on the symbolic morphology of the Indian temple. He has done field research in western and central India as well as in the Deccan and the south. He is general editor of the *Encyclopaedia of Indian Temple Architecture* (1983, 1986, 1988) and Curator of the South Asia Art

Archive at the University of Pennsylvania. Other edited volumes include *Discourses on Śiva* (1984) and *Making Things in South Asia: The Role of Artist and Craftsman* (1988). (Vol. I)

WILLIAM A. NOBLE, Ph.D. (Louisiana State University), was born in Nagarcoil, South India, and received his early education in Ootacamund. He is Associate Professor of Geography at the University of Missouri. His research has been in the prehistory and traditional peoples of the Nilgiri Hills of Tamil Nadu, the symbolic dimensions of sacred and folk architecture in India, and the memorialization and worship of *satīs*. His publications have appeared in geographical and anthropological journals, and in several edited volumes. He is currently working on a monograph on the momentous economic and technological changes which the Todas of the Nilgiri Hills have undergone since their first contact with the British in the early 1800s. (Vol. I)

R. THOMAS ROSIN, Ph.D. (University of California, Berkeley), is Professor of Anthropology at Sonoma State University in northern California. He has been researching the adaptive capabilities of the rural peoples of Rajasthan for the past 25 years. His major work is *Land Reform and Agrarian Change: Study of a Marwar Village from Raj to Swaraj* (1987). Other writings have appeared in anthropological journals and collections on India such as *American Studies in the Anthropology of India* (1979) and *Dimensions of Social Life* (1983). With photographer Gail Wread, he has presented several exhibits, which they plan to develop into an illustrated volume on the peoples of rural Rajasthan. (Vol. II)

LLOYD I. RUDOLPH, Ph.D. (Harvard), is Professor of Political Science and the Social Sciences at the University of Chicago. With his wife, Susanne Hoeber Rudolph, he is the author of *The Modernity of Tradition* (1967), *Education and Politics in India* (1972), *The Regional Imperative* (1980), *Gandhi* (1983), and *In Pursuit of Lakshmi: The Political Economy of the Indian State* (1987). He has edited and contributed to a book on cultural policy in India, and has contributed many articles on a wide range of subjects to scholarly journals and books in the United States, Britain and India. The Rudolphs have spent seven of their nine research years in India in Rajasthan, and they are the authors of

Essays on Rajputana: Reflections on History, Culture and Administration (1984).

AD RAM SANKHYAN, M.A. (School of Urban Planning, Punjab University), is completing a Ph.D. in the Department of Geography of Guru Nanak Dev University. He is currently Assistant Town Planner in the Town and Planning Organization for Himachal Pradesh, General Secretary of the Himachal Town Planners Association, and an Associate of India's Institute of Town Planners. He has been involved in the preparation of numerous development master plans for urban centers in Himachal Pradesh, and has contributed to the Uttar Pradesh Town and Country Planning Department's volume *Growth Centers in Jhansi-Lalitpur-Jalaun Region*. **(Vol. I)**

KARINE SCHOMER, Ph.D. (University of Chicago), formerly on the faculty of the Department of South and Southeast Asian Studies of the University of California at Berkeley, is now Dean of the School of Arts and Sciences at Golden Gate University, San Francisco. She has done field research on the *Ālhā* epic of North India, Rajasthani language and literature, and the modern Hindi literary community. She is the author of *Mahadevi Varma and the Chhayavad Age of Modern Hindi Poetry* (1983), and senior editor of *The Sants: Studies in a Devotional Tradition of India* (1987), and has contributed articles on the medieval, modern and folk literatures of the Hindi area and Rajasthan to scholarly journals and books. She was the founder and first president of the Rajasthan Studies Group of the Association for Asian Studies. Her current research interests include the preservation of Rajasthani culture among expatriates. **(Vol. I)**

FRANCES R. TAFT, M.A. (University of California, Berkeley), M.A. (Georgetown University), has research interests in the Rajput states during the Mughal and British periods. Her publications include an article on royal marriages in Rajasthan and forthcoming articles on rajas and *ṭhākurs* in Bikaner, the Shekhawati *ṭhikānās* of Jaipur, and the history of Mayo College, Ajmer. She is currently a Project Officer at the India Department of the World Bank. **(Vol. II)**

NORMAN P. ZIEGLER. Ph.D. (University of Chicago), has taught South Asian History at the University of Denver. He currently resides in Denver, where he works in a hospital while attending Nursing School. His doctoral research focused on the social and cultural history of the Rathor Rajputs of Marvar. His publications include articles in journals and in collected volumes such as *Kingship and Authority in South Asia* (1978). In collaboration with Richard Saran, he is the author of *Merto, Rajasthan, and Its Rulers, the Mertiyo Rathors* (forthcoming), a book of translations from 17th-century Marvari historical material, linguistic and historical annotations and biographical notes. (Vol. II)

INDEX

(Combined index for Vols. I and II)

THE IDEA OF RAJASTHAN

EXPLORATIONS IN REGIONAL IDENTITY

Vol. II
INSTITUTIONS

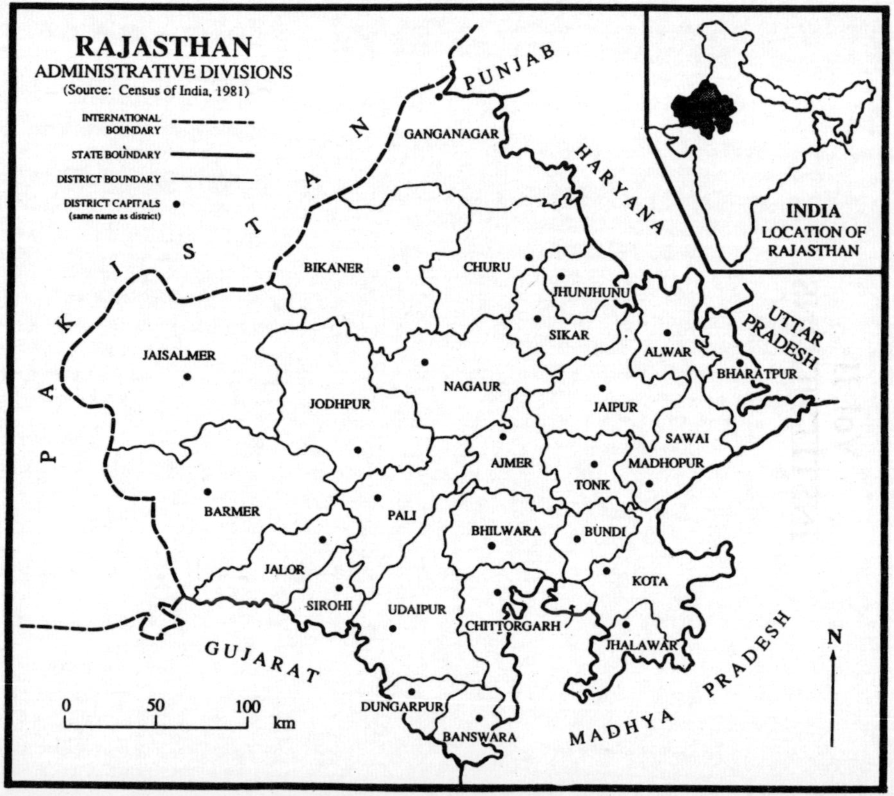
RAJASTHAN
ADMINISTRATIVE DIVISIONS
(Source: Census of India, 1981)
INTERNATIONAL BOUNDARY
STATE BOUNDARY
DISTRICT BOUNDARY
DISTRICT CAPITALS (same name as district)
INDIA
LOCATION OF RAJASTHAN
PAKISTAN
PUNJAB
HARYANA
UTTAR PRADESH
MADHYA PRADESH
GUJARAT
GANGANAGAR
BIKANER
CHURU
JHUNJHUNU
SIKAR
ALWAR
BHARATPUR
JAISALMER
NAGAUR
JAIPUR
JODHPUR
AJMER
SAWAI MADHOPUR
TONK
BARMER
PALI
BHILWARA
BUNDI
KOTA
JALOR
SIROHI
UDAIPUR
CHITTORGARH
JHALAWAR
DUNGARPUR
BANSWARA
N
0
50
100
km

THE IDEA OF RAJASTHAN

Explorations in Regional Identity

Volume II: CONSTRUCTIONS

Edited by

KARINE SCHOMER
JOAN L. ERDMAN
DERYCK O. LODRICK
LLOYD I. RUDOLPH

MANOHAR
American Institute of Indian Studies
2001

First published 1994
Paperback edition 2001

ISBN 81-7304-304-3

Published by
Ajay Kumar Jain for
Manohar Publishers & Distributors
4753/23 Ansari Road, Daryaganj
New Delhi 110 002

Printed at
Rajkamal Electric Press
B 35/9 G T Karnal Road Indl Area
Delhi 110 033

To the People of Rajasthan

CONTENTS

INTRODUCTION

Despite the rapidly spreading cosmopolitanism of the late twentieth century, regional identities are assuming increased significance in many parts of the world, and the study of regions is becoming more, not less, important. In India, with its exceptional cultural diversity and range of physical environments, regional traditions and the implications of strong regional identities are central issues and contemporary concerns. Over the past thirty years, scholarship on India has shown a marked shift away from the all-India perspectives of classical Indology, with their emphasis on Sanskrit texts and Brahmanical culture. Historical studies have moved away from the external perspectives of the British Raj and the Mughal Empire. At the same time, anthropological study has turned from a focus on isolated "little communities" such as villages, castes and tribes to the examination of supra-local patterns and networks. Conceptualizations of Indic civilization as a whole increasingly stress the significance of regional and areal components, as evidenced by Maureen L.P. Patterson's unique bibliographic synthesis, *South Asian Civilizations* (1981), which is organized as a complex architectonic scheme of geo-cultural areas, cultural-linguistic regions, and sub-regional areal units.

Both Indian and non-Indian scholars have turned their attention to regions of the subcontinent. The focus of their research, however, has been largely on specific topics in the humanities and social sciences rather than on questions of regional distinctiveness and regional identity. On the other hand, scholarship addressing questions of regions and regionalism, which has been mostly in the social sciences, has been primarily concerned with definitions, typologies, models, problems of region versus center in the modern nation-state, and broad theoretical formulations about regional patterns in Indic civilization.

Among the early landmark works on the issue of regions are Selig Harrison's *India: The Most Dangerous Decades* (1962), which saw India's regional diversity as a threat to national unity, and Robert S.

Crane's *Regions and Regionalism in South Asian Studies* (1967). An edited volume, the latter work grew out of a symposium held at Duke University to examine methodological questions in the study of regions and the role of regions in South Asian political, social and economic affairs. More recent works include the history symposium *Region and Realm in Traditional India* (1977) edited by Richard G. Fox, geographer David E. Sopher's *An Exploration of India* (1982), a comparative work on South and Southeast Asia by scholars in Holland entitled *Focus on the Region in Asia* (1982), Akhtar Majeed's *Regionalism: Developmental Tensions in India* (1984), and *Region and Nation in India* (1985), edited by Paul Wallace.

We acknowledge these works for the concerns they have raised, their clear definitions of concepts, and their subcontinental, comparative and disciplinary perspectives on the subject of Indian regions. Our aim, however, is not so much to enter and further the theoretical debate about regions as parts of a whole, but to consider in depth a particular regional identity. This collection thus bears closer kinship to works such as *The Cult of Jagannath and the Regional Tradition of Orissa* (1978) or the older work on Maharashtra by G.A. Deleury, *The Cult of Vithoba* (1960), both interdisciplinary studies of the role of cults and pilgrimage centers in the formation of particular regional cultures of India.

Every human collectivity has a sense of place, a subjective connection to its natural and man-made environment, with its physical features, institutional and social patterns, historical traditions and cultural landscapes. While regions are grounded in objective realities, they are also subjective constructs, for both outsiders and insiders. To explore a regional identity is thus to explore an idea. At the heart of our approach is such an exploration, the attempt to discover and understand more deeply what is distinctive about the region of northwestern India known as Rajasthan.

Accordingly, while the writers here consider theoretical issues in their own disciplines, each paper also addresses the subject of Rajasthan's regional identity. Thus the work as a whole provides a composite, interdisciplinary, multi-faceted picture of Rajasthan. Not intended to be all-inclusive, its aim is to stimulate further thinking about this particular region's identity. Our theoretical contribution is to suggest that the study of regions is incomplete if it does not go beyond the analysis of generic variables determined by *a priori* definitions. To understand a regional identity in all its uniqueness requires informed and sensitive insight into the complex and subtle characteristics of the particular geographical area, its inhabitants, and the cultures they have created. Environmental influences and limitations, remembered histories, language, literary styles, cultural traditions, common institutions, mutually recognized social structures, shared symbols – all need to be carefully considered, in their interrelations, with plural perspectives, and in comparison with other regions.

The Idea of Rajasthan originated on a beautiful afternoon in November 1981, when a group of seventeen scholars attending the West Coast regional meetings of the Association for Asian Studies convened in Karine Schomer's home at 1 My Way, high above Berkeley, California. Through large picture windows, we could see the dry hills on the far side of Wildcat Canyon, a landscape uncannily reminiscent of the hills of Rajasthan. Our purpose was to discuss current directions in research on Rajathan, to test interest in developing a network of scholars working on the region, and to enlist participation in a project to explore the nature of Rajasthan's regional identity. We represented a number of disciplines – anthropology, art history, ethnomusicology, folklore, geography, history, language studies, literature, and political science. Though we all shared an interest in Rajasthan, many of us were strangers to one another. None imagined then that this gathering would result in a decade of scholarly collaboration and the present two-volume work.

At that time, there were individual scholars working on Rajasthan in several American universities, especially the University of Chicago, but a number of special initiatives were taking place at the University of California at Berkeley. Komal Kothari, Director of the Rajasthan Institute of Folklore (Rupayan Sansthan) had spent a semester on the campus as a Fulbright Scholar-in-Residence. In collaboration with Leela Mathur of the Rajasthan Association of North America, Karine Schomer had initiated Rajasthani language instruction in the Department of South and Southeast Asian Studies. Faculty members and graduate students in other disciplines were turning their attention towards Rajasthan as well. Karine Schomer had just been awarded a three-year grant from the U.S. Department of Education to produce a language primer for the major Rajasthani dialects and an edited volume of essays on Rajasthan. Just before our meeting several of us had presented a panel entitled "Performing Rajasthan's Culture," which embodied in embryonic form the project we were gathering to discuss.

It was the recognition of Rajasthan as a distinctive cultural region of India that had inspired our meeting. Deeply involved with our own research, we had been working in relative isolation, generally unconnected to the work of scholars outside our particular disciplines. We therefore lacked a sense of our scholarship's relevance to an overall understanding of Rajasthan. As we discussed the project, a consensus emerged that a descriptive survey or commissioned essays on particular topics was not our goal. Instead, we would seek to provide a focus and a broader context for current research by asking scholars to consider what their work could contribute to the exploration of Rajasthan's distinctive regional identity. Contributions would be sought from a wide spectrum of disciplines, ranging from sciences concerned with the natural environment to the humanities and social sciences. Each scholar would be asked to work from individual research towards statements about Rajasthan as a region and comparative issues raised by the study of Rajasthan. We envisioned a work that would explore facets of Rajasthan's distinctive regional identity, place specialized research within a broader context of inquiry, and provide a model for the interdisciplinary study of regions.

The story of *The Idea of Rajasthan* is inseparable from that of the scholarly community of which it is a product and which it helped create. At our 1981 gathering, we had agreed on the need for networking. We decided to revive a scholarly association started by Lloyd and Susanne Rudolph at the University of Chicago in the late 1960s, which had been dormant for many years. At the 1982 Association for Asian Studies (AAS) meetings in Chicago, the Rajasthan Studies Group-AAS was formally constituted, and an executive committee elected. Plans were laid for gathering and disseminating information, encouraging scholarly contacts, promoting research, and formulating panels and seminars.

In 1983, Joan Erdman and Ann Gold conducted a survey and prepared a report entitled "Current Directions in Rajasthan Studies." In the same year, a panel entitled "Rajasthani Regionalism: Natural and Cultural Signs of Distinctiveness" was presented at the Association for Asian Studies meetings in San Francisco. Papers from this session, like those of the earlier Berkeley panel, eventually found their way into *The Idea of*

Rajasthan. Other panel presentations followed, and a bibliography of recent work on Rajasthan by scholars in North America and Europe was prepared and distributed.

The Rajasthan Studies Group-AAS gradually expanded to include an international membership. Following networking efforts by the Rudolphs and Karine Schomer in India in 1983-84, the group entered into a collaborative relationship with a new Jaipur-based Rajasthan Studies Group-India, led by Prof. Satish Chandra and Dr. Rajendra Joshi. This led to our participation in two international seminars focusing on conservation of the environment and culture in Rajasthan, the first held in Jaipur in 1987, the second in Udaipur in 1991. Through these seminars and panels, collaborative work on *The Idea of Rajasthan,* and the organizational efforts of both Rajasthan Studies groups, a vital international community of scholars interested in Rajasthan has developed.

To ensure that *The Idea of Rajasthan* would benefit from breadth of vision and the advantage of multiple disciplinary critiques for each contribution, the Rajasthan Studies Group-AAS appointed a panel of four editors to oversee the project. Each editor offered particular expertise: Karine Schomer (language, literature, folklore and cultural history) as editor-in-chief, Joan Erdman (anthropology, cultural performance and cultural policy), Deryck Lodrick (geography and cultural ecology), and Lloyd Rudolph (political science and intellectual history).

In the spring of 1983, the call for contributions went out to an international list of scholars, followed over the next few years by additional solicitations as more scholars working on Rajasthan came to our attention through the expanding Rajasthan Studies Group network. Every paper received was critiqued by each editor, was discussed by the editorial panel as a whole, and became the subject of extensive scholarly dialogue with the author. As papers and comments travelled back and forth between editors and contributors, *The Idea of Rajasthan* grew from one to two volumes, at the same time developing more precisely its focus and structure.

Thus *The Idea of Rajasthan* is the product of extensive and intense scholarly exchanges over a decade. We have had ongoing dialogues about Rajasthan as a geographical entity and way of life, shaped by its physical, historical and cultural environments, their interactions, and how they have been constructed and institutionalized. With two editors in Chicago, two in the San Francisco area, and contributors dispersed over several continents, our dialogues have been conducted through letters, long-distance telephone calls and face-to-face sessions at conferences and other meetings. We often disagreed, but we remained convinced that there was wisdom in our original idea, and that, out of the diversity of our scholarship, we were forging an integrated perspective on Rajasthan and breaking new ground in the study of regions and regional identity.

Our papers, grouped into two volumes and four thematic sections, offer interrelated perspectives on various aspects of Rajasthan's regional identity. The volume subtitled *Constructions* looks at how Rajasthanis and outsiders have created and defined Rajasthan, and examines the processes through which a Rajasthani regional identity has evolved and is performed. The volume subtitled *Institutions* analyzes enduring structures, adaptations, arrangements, and ways of life and thought that have characterized and shaped the lives of Rajasthanis in their region. The numbering of the volumes does not indicate a logical sequence but a complementarity.

"Identity as Process" opens the *Constructions* volume with a group of papers which consider how a sense of regional identity is created and reinforced. In the opening paper by Deryck Lodrick, definitions of Rajasthan as a bounded geographical area by outside observers and administrative authorities are contrasted with subjective awareness of regional and sub-regional identities. Taking the perspective from within Rajasthan, Joan Erdman shows how a modern multi-media production, "*Dhartī Dhorāṅ Rī*" (Land of Shifting Sands), seeks to develop a regional identity for all Rajasthanis through a program incorporating the stories and symbols of sub-regions and distinctive communities into a pluralistic whole.

The reinforcement of regional identity through shared religious performance is the subject of Ann Gold's study, which shows that Rajasthanis make clear distinctions between the quality of pilgrimage to regional shrines and pilgrimage to pan-Indian sacred places. The role of cultural performances in encapsulating and enacting a regional way of life is examined in Karine Schomer's paper on the Rajput wedding custom of riddling the bridegroom and the content of Rajasthani riddle repertoires.

The evidence historical monuments provide about the formation of a Rajasthani regional identity is considered by Michael Meister. Focusing on the evolution of architectural styles under the patronage of Rajput rulers, he sees an ongoing alternation between sub-regional differentiation and regional unification which has led to a gradual integration of styles. Finally, on the basis of archaeological site analysis, Henri-Paul Francfort shows that ancient Harappan civilization did not penetrate the natural frontiers separating the arid and mountainous area of present-day Rajasthan from the surrounding alluvial plains, thus suggesting that Rajasthan's regional distinctiveness has roots in prehistory.

How the arts represent and reflect regional cultural identity is addressed in the section on "Art as Communication." Rajasthan's musical traditions are deeply embedded in the society through hereditary patronage arrangements. Komal Kothari reports on the Manganiyars of western Rajasthan, folk professionals who perform at life-cycle ceremonies of their village patrons and carry forward a sophisticated musical tradition that differs significantly from the classical "Hindustani" music patronized by the more cosmopolitan royal courts. The musical tradition associated with temples in the regional cult center of Nathdvara is the subject of Anne-Marie Gaston's paper. Showing that the music derives its meaning and continued appeal from the ritual context, she argues that without this context, it could not survive.

Artistic representations reveal the Rajasthani predilection for archetypes and timeless ideals. The art and role of the now vanishing street performers known as *bahurūpiyās,* whose satirical portrayals of familiar castes, occupations and character types hold up a mirror to the society, is the focus of John Emigh's contribution. In the court tradition of royal portraiture, Vishakha Desai finds a persistent preference for timeless, iconographic representation of idealized kingship rather than depiction of the observed physiognomy of individual rulers. The final paper of the *Constructions* volume, by William Noble and Ad Ram Sankhyan, seeks to interpret the religious meaning, symbolism and sub-regional stylistic variation of the *satī* memorials that are such a poignant part of the visual landscape of Rajasthan.

The *Institutions* volume opens with a section on "Locales and Social Structures," which examines grass-roots economic, social and political adaptations to Rajasthan's limited-resource environment and the legacy of its traditional feudal polity. The adaptive strategies employed by villagers in western Rajasthan to survive the severe droughts endemic to the region, and the dynamics of a Rajasthani village under drought conditions, are the subject of Carol Henderson's paper. Thomas Rosin looks at long-term adaptive trends among rural peoples in the Aravalli hills of central Rajasthan, analyzing both local agrarian management strategies and the historical significance of migration. Demographic and ethnographic data are correlated with ecology by Pauline Kolenda to explain the high proportion of joint-family households found in Rajasthan, particularly in the state's semi-arid zone. In the last paper of this section, James Björkman and the late Het Ram Chaturvedi trace the history of Rajasthan's experiment with local self-government after India's independence. Their thesis is that it succeeded initially because the old princely order had been discredited, but was gradually undermined by competing interests of state-level politicians and administrative agencies.

"Power and Hegemony" examines dimensions of the Rajputs' historic dominance in the area which is now Rajasthan. The political, economic and social processes whereby Rajputs rose to prominence in the early medieval period, and the stages by which their distinctive clan structure evolved are examined by B.D. Chattopadhyaya. Using local primary sources, Norman Ziegler traces the emergence of Rajput state systems in the 15th and early 16th centuries, and demonstrates a close connection between increased availability and use of horses, campaigns of conquest, and the evolution of centralized rule. Mughal-Rajput marriage alliances, still a controversial subject, are considered by Frances Taft, who analyzes their origins, their recently documented extensiveness, and their political role as seen from both Mughal and Rajput perspectives.

The influence of Rajput ideals and institutions on religion and the arts is the subject of the last two papers of the *Institutions* volume. The history and institutional structures of a regional sect, the Dadu-*panth,* are shown by Daniel Gold to have been significantly shaped by Rajput values and the environment of Jaipur court patronage. Finally, Edward Haynes considers the traditional expectation that Rajput rulers should be patrons of the arts, and examines the use of arts patronage by the rulers of Alwar state to enhance their status and legitimacy.

Our papers thus include topics ranging from prehistory to the present, and examine issues as varied as ecological adaptation, cultural continuity and political legitimacy. Individually and in mutually reinforcing ways, they touch upon many interweaving themes of Rajasthani life. Ultimately, however, they are concerned with a common underlying purpose: exploring the multiple dimensions of Rajsthan's enduring regional identity. While establishing certain fundamental characteristics of the region as both objective realities and subjective constructs, they raise as many questions as they answer – not only for Rajasthan, but for the comparative study of regions and regional identity as well.

ACKNOWLEDGEMENTS

As a long project comes to fruition, there is a sense of accomplishment, but also a sense of loss. During its ten-year gestation period, *The Idea of Rajasthan* sustained strong scholarly interaction over time and across continents, in which all involved gained susbtantial breadth and depth in their understanding of Rajasthan and of regions in general. Because the interaction was so strong, and editorial involvement with each contribution so thoroughgoing, shared perspectives have permeated the final product and given it a unity uncommon in collections of scholarly papers. Without this mode of engaged collegiality, the outcome would have been very different.

The position of editor-in-chief suggests a sense of grand orchestration, but conceals the reality of large quantities of midnight oil and strong tea, tightrope diplomacy, and the burden of ultimate responsibility for the most minute of details. The list of people who have made this project possible is long. My first thanks go to my indefatigable co-editors, who persisted with me in this time-consuming labor of love. Without Lloyd Rudolph's breadth of knowledge and keen critical insights, Joan Erdman's sharp mind for conceptual constructs, Deryck Lodrick's meticulous scholarly precision, and the painstaking care each of them expended on every contribution submitted, the editorial task would have been overwhelming. They join me in thanking the contributors, whose patience with the constantly evolving editorial vision and willingness to accept our demanding requirements represents collegial forbearance at its best. We are also grateful for the continued interest and support of the Rajasthan Studies Group-AAS membership as a whole, whose repeated question, "When will the book come out?" urged us to presevere.

We acknowlege with appreciation the financial support of the U.S. Department of Education's International Research and Studies Program, whose initial grant made possible the launching of the project. Our thanks go to the University of California's

Center for South and Southeast Asia Studies, which administered the grant. We are grateful to the American Institute of Indian Studies for inclusion of this work in their publications series. Our publishers, patient in working with our complex production needs and unexpected delays, deserve our thanks as well. Permission to use illustrations was generously granted by the National Museum (New Delhi), the National Gallery of Victoria (Melbourne), the American Institute of Indian Studies Centre for Art and Archeaology (Varanasi), the Boston Museum of Fine Arts, the Brooklyn Museum, and the private collections of Catherine and Ralph Benkaim, Guru Purushottam Das, and Shri Krishna Deva. With a few exceptions, the supporting maps were conceptualized and developed by Deryck Lodrick, and produced by Shelby Hall, Molly Block and Mary Cunha. Clerical and logistical support was ably provided by Maria Firmacion.

Among the many scholars whose encouragement, interest and advice sustained our collective effort are Professors N. Gerald Barrier, Frank F. Conlon, John S. Hawley, Maureen L.P. Patterson, Joseph E. Schwartzberg, and Joanna G. Williams in the United States, and our Indian colleagues Professor Satish Chandra, Dr. Rajendra Joshi, and Padmashri Komal Kothari. The list of all the other people each editor and contributor would like to acknowledge individually is far too long to include here. My own most heartfelt thanks go to my husband, photographer-writer Raphael Shevelev, who not only gave me steady personal and intellectual support in the final years of the project, but became passionately involved in the exploration of Rajasthan's distinctive visual identity.

KARINE SCHOMER

El Cerrito, California
December 10, 1992

NOTE ON TRANSLITERATION

The scheme of transliteration followed in this work is the standard system internationally used for Indic and Perso-Arabic languages, with a few modifications designed to make the text less forbidding to non-specialists and to reflect Hindi and Rajasthani pronunciation. To bring the transliteration closer to pronunciation, the palatal consonant *c* and its aspirate *ch* are rendered, respectively, as *ch* and *chh*. A nasal before a consonant (*anusvara*) is rendered by *n* for all classes of consonants except the retroflexes (*ṭ*, *ṭh*, *ḍ*, *ḍh*) and the labials (*p*, *ph*, *b*, *bh*); before these, it is represented by *ṇ* and *m*, respectively. Nazalization of vowels is rendered by *ṅ*. In transliterating Hindi and Rajasthani words, latitude has been exercised in omitting the inherent *a* in both word-final and medial syllables. A few words (e.g. *purdah, zenana*) appear in their commonly accepted transliteration. Finally, when italicized words embedded in the English text are pluralized, the English plural *s* is also italicized. All proper names appearing as part of the English text are given in their generally accepted anglicized form, as are Indian words that have come into general English usage (e.g., raja, guru). Only italicized words in Indian languages are formally transliterated.

LOCALES AND SOCIAL STRUCTURES

FAMINES AND DROUGHTS IN WESTERN RAJASTHAN: DESERT CULTIVATORS AND PERIODIC RESOURCE STRESS

CAROL HENDERSON

If famine was "the grand natural disease" of western Rajasthan in the eyes of the 19th-century visitor (Tod 1914:II, 264), for today's scientist the single largest threat to human existence in the area is desertification (Mann 1980; CAZRI 1977).[1] For the agriculturalists in the region, the problem is frequent and unpredictable droughts which destroy crops, fodder and water supplies. Drought, famine and desertification are all related aspects of the interaction between human populations and the environment. Now, as in the past, low rainfall, blazing heat, sandstorms, inadequate underground water supplies, sandy soils and a capricious monsoon limit agriculture and constrain its expansion. One year, rainfall may be good or excessive; the next, even the most drought-resistant crops may wither due to lack of moisture. Survival in the region depends, to a considerable extent, on the ability of the inhabitants to adjust their behavior and agricultural strategies according to the availability of resources.

Although subjected to criticism (Orlove 1980; Vayda and McCay 1975), dominant models of human-environment relations stress the stability of outputs in systemically related regimes. As I have discussed elsewhere (Henderson 1987:257-258), this model permits only short resource variation cycles. The emphasis is clearly on balancing energetic inputs and outputs and achieving equilibrium. In regions where unpredictable or recurrent resource crises occur, variability is compressed by applying the assumption of some minimum level of production, achievable in all but the very worst agricultural seasons and hypothetically sustainable as a kind of lowest common denominator. Hence, the system of production is seen as geared to obtaining agricultural outputs at or near this level, through positive and negative feedback mechanisms that maintain a condition of homeostasis. In unstable environments, the risks of production failures may be lowered by exploiting a variety of habitats, by utilizing different areas through seasonal migration, or by spreading the costs of failures within the population through institutionalized sharing. Less productive but hardier varieties of crops may be preferred to those for which higher yields are possible, but at the risk of more frequent crop failures. Resource crisis is relegated to the status of an aberration that disrupts existing social and economic relations. Adjustments made by the affected population are viewed as responses to temporary malfunctions: the goal of surviving such an event is the resumption of normal affairs.

In variable environments such as the Thar desert, the theoretical attempt to reduce variation may lead to such a broadening of the level of analysis that the final statement is as statistically improbable as the engineer's "average man." There is danger of losing sight of factors that may have important consequences for the residents of the area. Additionally, the statement of the problem as one in which variation does not occur ignores the fact that human activities themselves help create and sustain variability (Burton, Kates and White 1978:11; Rindos 1980). The level of risk from a specific hazard is, in part, a function of the pattern of resource exploitation, even when the stated goal is risk reduction. Even if a stable system is identified, it does not mean that the behavior of individual components does not incorporate a high degree of risk, which may be transferred from one sector to another. In this, losses may be concentrated in part of the population (Greenough 1980; Maclachlan 1983), allowing an increased level of production for others. Alternately, the production system may be geared to high variability, capable of retrenchment during poor years and rapid expansion when the weather permits. One possibility connected with this systematic adaptation is that losses borne during a poor year may be outweighed by benefits accruing from a suspension of particular activities, such as increased soil fertility which may occur as a consequence of the enforced fallowing of land (Kirkby 1974).

From this perspective, it is not logically necessary to assume that stability is system wide, attached to a constant level of risk evenly spread throughout the population, or inherent in the production strategies of individual operating units. Instead of viewing the population as a homogeneous unit, as is the case with systems models, it is necessary to examine population differentiation to understand how adjustment to risk takes place, its consequences, and its effect on resources. At this level of analysis, the focus is on ways in which people respond to environmental crises of various kinds, and how natural and social resources are mobilized to meet a crisis. One benefit of such an approach is that it permits consideration of a range of activities, not just production in "normal" years, which actually may occur infrequently. More important, it may be possible to examine factors that promote or inhibit cultural change, and in this way avoid treating systems stability or change as mutually exclusive events (Orlove 1980:245).

The socio-cultural study of arid western Rajasthan[2] is important because the high frequency and severity of droughts presents an opportunity to examine interaction between external constraints and behavior. Climatological studies find abnormal rainfall (droughts and floods that threaten agriculture) common; it seems as if "normal" rainfall exists more as a normative construct than in reality. Monsoon failures occur during 40% of years, and "normal" rainfall during the monsoon occurs only during 26% of the weeks when it is expected (CAZRI 1977:7; Ramdas 1968:248). Since droughts leading to agricultural failures have occurred throughout the historical period of settlement, it is evident that the adaptive strategies of residents are adjustable to circumstances. How this adjustability affects shifts in, or the reconstitution of, prior socio-economic relationships is explainable with respect to internal differentiation, the connections of the community and its components with the surrounding area, and the ability of residents to take advantage of economic opportunities, both environmental and institutional.

This paper focuses on the adaptive strategies adopted by residents of arid western Rajasthan in response to drought. General adaptations to drought, such as migration, cultivation of drought-resistant crops, and dependence on livestock are documented in other studies, most prominently those carried out by the Central Arid Zone Research Institute in Jodhpur (P.L. Jaiswal 1977; Mann 1980; CAZRI 1977; Spooner and Mann 1980; see also Dhir 1982; Jodha 1975; Chouhan 1979). District and state level information on the effects of droughts is available in Famine Commission Reports and government records (Indian Famine

Commission 1880, 1898; *Rajputana Gazetteer* 1879). For the most part, these sources do not explore intra-community relations (particularly economic stratification) and drought, nor do they address adjustments made by individual households on the basis of existing local resources. Despite these limitations, however, such studies provide valuable background information. As will be seen, the utilization of resources that are external to a specific household or village – grass eaten by livestock during migration, payment derived from famine relief programs, and reliance on social ties to surrounding regions – suggests that the locus of investigation is not a single household, village or locality, but rather the collocation of relationships linking residents of a deficit area to others. This may be most immediately and practically demonstrated with respect to a village and its relationship with others, to illustrate the connected nature of ties, habitat variation, and the relationship between wealthy and poor households.

Environment, Drought and Famine in Western Rajasthan

The problem of drought is acute in the regions bordering the Thar desert. Historically, drought is the main cause of famine in the area. Here, where annual rainfall averages from 250 mm to 350 mm, crop cultivation is carried out for subsistence production of food and fodder, along with livestock rearing. The average rainfall in Jodhpur district,[3] which falls in this climatic zone, is 325 mm per year. The average annual total number of days on which rain falls averages less than 18 for the district (*Rajasthan District Gazetteer* 1979:13). This rainfall average represents a point on a transitional cline between the desert and more humid areas. As aridity increases, dependence on cultivation declines and the economy shifts to pastoralism. Production of crops is possible here, but is limited by the lack of water.

The only water course of even a semi-permanent nature is the Luni river, which passes through the southern portions of the area. Water tables are low, ranging from 60 to more than 100 meters. Ground water tends to be saline, brackish, and unfit for drinking or irrigation. Irrigation is almost nonexistent, as is the introduction of modern crops and technology. The spatial variability of rainfall occurs almost at a sub-village level. Under these conditions, agricultural settlements are small, and frequently deserted after water supplies dry up or deteriorate to an unacceptable level. One characteristic of the monsoon in this region is the association of aridity with increased monsoon unreliability: as mentioned previously, droughts occur in two out of five years (CAZRI 1977:7). Within the desert, it may be as high as one out of three years. Since rainfall totals are themselves low, any downward variation in rainfall severely curtails production. Even in years when precipitation is at or near normal levels, the timing of rainfall will impair production if it does not occur in accordance with crop requirements.

The region is characterized by dunes and stretches of sandy plains interspersed with small rocky hills. The soils are classified as light-textured, grey-brown desert soils, which are alkaline and saline. None of these soils is particularly fertile. In some areas, hardpan deposits inhibit the subsurface percolation of water and cause the formation of saline crusts. The soils found in a locality generally consist of a variety of types, ranging from sandy dunes to light alluvium near water sources. All these soils are highly susceptible to erosion; many are deposited through wind action. During the dry months from March to July, sandstorms, accompanied by hot violent winds, may deposit an inch or more of soil. Sandstorms can also destroy newly-germinated crops. Each year, re-sowing is often necessary because of heavy dust and sand deposits that cover the plants.

The vegetation consists of drought-adapted, xerophytic scrub and thorns, with large patches of bare soil. From a height, the plains are seen to be covered with widely spaced *khejṛī* (*Prosopis cineraria)* and acacia species. Large thorny shrubs line field rows and are scattered over dune areas. Consisting of little more than branches, stumps and thorns during the dry season, these plants are capable of a remarkable change because of their sensitivity to minuscule amounts of water (Mertia and Bhandari 1980:155). In an area of drought, a fall of rain is followed within 24 hours by changes in vegetation color and the appearance of new shoots. Perennials bud, transforming the dull, grey-green *khejṛī* to a bright shade, followed by a rapid growth of branches and foliage. During the rainy season, the landscape undergoes a transformation as the most important period of plant growth unfolds, and the barren landscape becomes deceptively and all too briefly lush, as the rapidly growing plants sprout, carry out their life cycles, and die (Bhandari 1978:10).

The ability to survive drought, and the coupling of plant growth to a temporarily restricted period of moisture availability (some 10 or 11 weeks) are the major adaptations of the vegetation. Cultivation is made possible by selecting plant species that are adapted to this water regime. The ability to exploit the brief period of moisture availability for agriculture creates the main erosive hazard resulting from human activities. Soil is disturbed by plowing. The use of crops and their residues as fodder may lead to livestock populations that are greater than what could be maintained on uncultivated areas alone, and are capable of denuding the surrounding territory. In combination with drought, such adaptations may lead to an intensification of desertification pressures: resource regeneration is hampered by overutilization of plant species for food and fodder. Surface soil dries out and is unprotected by vegetation. Livestock congregates near water sources and destroys surrounding plant growth. In the event of showers, the land may be plowed, adding to the potential for later wind erosion.

While desertification presents a long-range worry to planners concerned with the effects of drought, the subsistence producers of the area view its immediate impact as almost synonymous with a state of famine. Today, famine relief administration, modern transportation, and a well developed network for communicating information about potential shortages have eliminated mass starvation. Up to the middle of this century, however, famines caused high human, as well as livestock, mortality. The worst famines are remembered by name, such as the *chapaniya kāḷ* of 1899-1900 (Chouhan 1979:100) or the "Panchkal" of 1812-17 (*Rajputana Gazetteer* 1879:109).[4] The first British emissary to the region, Col. James Tod, arrived during a dry spell about this time, and the not yet recovered landscape influenced his perception of the region as one of drought, dust and poverty. Tod's expedition to the area in 1814 reported disruption of the livestock industry and depopulation (Tod 1914:II, 243, 247). Indeed, Tod was constantly reminded that the names for the region – "Marwar," "Maroost'hali," "Maru-desh" – mean "the land of death" (1914:I, 15, 536, 552; II, 234).

Marwar experienced famine in 1833-34, 1837-38, 1848-49, 1850, 1853-54, 1868-69, 1871-72, 1877-78, 1891-92, 1896-97, 1899-1900, 1915-16, 1924-25, and 1936-37 (*Rajasthan District Gazetteer* 1979:130ff; Adams 1899). After Independence, droughts occurred in 1949-50, 1950-51, 1951-52, 1953-54, 1957-58, 1960-61, 1963-64, 1964-65, 1966-67, 1968-69, 1969-70, and 1971-72. A drought that affected most of Rajasthan occurred in 1974-75, and from 1977 to 1982, there was almost continuous failure of the monsoon (see Table 1). The worst famines have usually occurred after two or more years of drought, and often at the same time as monsoon failures have affected the entire subcontinent. In comparison with drought, extended periods of good rainfall have been rare.

Table 1: **Famines in Rajasthan, 1967-1982**

Year	Number of Affected Districts
1967-68	12
1968-69	26
1969-70	23
1970-71	8
1971-72	12
1972-73	26
1973-74	—
1974-75	25
1975-76	—
1976-77	—
1977-78	18
1978-79	24
1979-80	26
1980-81	26
1981-82	26

(Source: Dandia 1981:5)

Examples of adjustments to drought are seen in the 1868-69 famine, as well as throughout the decade 1891-1901. The 1868-69 famine which affected most of northern India, was experienced in the desert states as well. Previous agricultural seasons had experienced irregular rainfall, causing crop deficits in 1864, 1865 and 1866. No rain fell in Marwar during the monsoon of 1868, and in other areas there was not enough rain to sow crops. As soon as the drought was certain, the people began to migrate. So much livestock died or was driven out of the area in search of fodder that it was impossible to import grain on overland routes (*Rajputana Gazetteer* 1879:109-110). Nearly all of the cattle were removed from the region, and it is estimated that three-fourths died (Adams

1899:147). Two-thirds of the population of Marwar, about one million people, are estimated to have migrated (Indian Famine Commission 1880:14). In 1869, villagers returned to the area to wait for the monsoon. It arrived late, and the ripening crops were destroyed by locusts. Cholera and fever decimated the population. The famine did not end until the harvest of 1870.

In 1890-92, the monsoon failed in Ajmer-Merwara. The building of a railroad across this region made it possible for the first time to import grain by rail, reducing starvation mortality, though cattle losses were high (Indian Famine Commission 1898:36). Marwar was also affected. About 200,000 people and 661,000 cattle are estimated to have migrated. The worst famines to affect the subcontinent occurred in 1896-97 and 1899-1901. In the first famine, 59,000,000 people in central and northern India were affected during 1896-97, and 28,000,000 people were in affected regions during 1899-1901. Rajputana was one of the areas that experienced almost continuing drought during this period. The census for the Rajputana states estimates that there was an 18% decline in population from 1891 to 1901, attributable to the effect of crop failure, drought and famine (Saxena 1975:86).

Marwar experienced a food and fodder famine during 1896 (Adams 1899:151). Barely had recovery begun, when drought appeared again in 1899. Less than one inch of rainfall was recorded for Jodhpur city in that year. There was a partial drought again in 1901, and rainfall was less than half the area average in 1902, 1904 and 1905. In 1907-08 another crop failure occurred. The last famine before Independence occurred in 1937-38, when there was a severe famine in Marwar (Saxena 1975:87). Drought conditions prevailed during the 1950s. During the decade from 1977 to 1982, the longest period of almost uninterrupted drought in the 20th century took place. Drought conditions caused crop failures, livestock mortality and the drying up of local water supplies. However, famine deaths and starvation did not occur, because famine relief was widely available in the form of loans, food, water, fodder aid, work relief, and tax remissions in the affected villages.

It is obvious that drought is no stranger to western Rajasthan. Famine reports document disruptions of land revenues, and dislocations caused by widespread migrations. Historically, migration – primarily to Gujarat in the south, Malwa and the Chambal valley to the east, and west across the desert to Sindh – represented one solution to famine conditions. Since the partition of Pakistan and India, however, the route to Sindh has been closed. Other traditional responses include the funding of water conservation measures such as the construction of earthen dams (*bunds*), tanks and reservoirs. Social and economic adjustments also provide ways of coping with drought conditions. The degree of success of these solutions is based to a considerable extent on the ability of any group to control local resources. Family organization, political factionalism, differential wealth, and the ability to exploit economic opportunities are important factors that affect all these responses to drought. These aspects of village dynamics under famine conditions will be examined in the following pages.

Environmental Resources in a Desert Village

Along the desert margins, villages are small and sites are limited by the availability of water. Networks of dusty roads and trails link villages and scattered homesteads, which are surrounded by cultivated fields and sandy or dune areas overgrown by scrub. Renupur is the name given to one such village lying in the belt where rainfall is slightly more than eight inches per year. Rainfall is the only source of water for drinking and agriculture. There is no well, and none of the land is irrigated. The economic pattern of the village is based on the production of a single annual crop of millet, and livestock is raised for subsistence purposes and for sale. Little modernization of agriculture is seen; the village has no electricity, and the costs of improvements are beyond the means of most residents.

The village is 35 miles southwest of Jodhpur city, and situated four miles off the highway linking Jodhpur with Jaisalmer. It is connected to nearby villages by dirt paths and roads. During the rains, these roads become impassable due to mud or flooding, and during the hot season, sand deposits make travel by motor vehicle or cart difficult. The surrounding villages are within a walking distance of four to six miles. The nearest local center of marketing and administration is located on the highway and has a population of about 2,000. The villages surrounding Renupur have populations ranging from 600 to 1,000 residents. In 1982, the population of the village was approximately 823. This represents an increase from a population of approximately 450 in 1961.

The village contains two small shops that buy and sell grains, dry goods and small items. Their main business is money-lending. Rates vary from 24% to 36% per year, and may spiral upward, depending on repayments. Wealthier villagers also lend money, at the same rates. There are 75 villagers who live and work in other areas, returning only for holidays or to work during the harvest season. Most are employed outside agriculture, as menials in shops or factories. Two wealthy households own small shops in Jodhpur city, and family members are in permanent residence there.

The village lands total approximately 4,000 acres. Most residents live in the main settlement, but 16 households are scattered among the rolling sand hills and flat terrain with sparse vegetation typical of the area. The main settlement is located on a mound that marks the south end of a gradient extending from four small rocky hills located three miles to the north and west. The water runoff from these hills provides drinking water for the village pond, and feeds fields on the north and west sides of the village. These lands, called *relo*, are the best agricultural land in the village. Toward the west, the land becomes sandier and is called *magro*, up to the hill, where it is known as *udeso magro*, *magro* lands on the hillside. The eastern and southern lands consist of rolling, sandy dunes, called *dhoro*.

The productive potential of these lands reflects both the soil type and moisture availability. Crops grown on *relo* are the least vulnerable to annual rainfall fluctuations, because this soil is the most likely to receive moisture if some rain occurs. This is due to the land's position in local runoff patterns, for after a heavy storm it may be under a foot or more of water. This overflowing and flooding is a consequence of the desert-like conditions. Rocky and gravelly soils, covered by a low amount of surface vegetation – a characteristic of the pre-monsoon environment – contribute to potentially high rates of surface runoff following a storm. This is a problem if sheet erosion and channelling occur, but the runoff may benefit downslope fields. Areas that are a considerable distance from cultivation sites, and themselves non-cultivable, may contribute moisture through surface runoff and the subsurface percolation of water. In years of deficient rainfall, this type of water collection at various sites may facilitate agriculture, even when nearby lands are too dry for plowing and sowing. Residents take advantage of this runoff by constructing *bunds* to increase the collection of water at such favored spots.

Pearl millet (*Pennisetum typhoideum*) is the staple food and most important crop grown in the region. Locally named *bājrā* or *bājrī*, over 96% of sown land in the arid zone is under this crop (Sen and Abraham 1966:113). Millet is extremely resistant to drought, heat and salt. It is grown where annual rainfall varies between 125 mm and 900 mm (Rachie and Majumdar 1980:126), and is almost never irrigated. Large year-to-year variations in yields are normal. In Rajasthan, the annual average yield per hectare varied from a low of 1.0 quintal in 1974 to 3.6 quintals in 1976 (Government of Rajasthan 1981:41). In the arid zone, the average output is around 1.8 quintals per hectare (Mann and Singh 1975:353). So far, the adoption of high-yielding varieties by cultivators is less than 3% of the sown land in unirrigated areas (CAZRI 1978:157). Local knowledge recognizes the superiority of these high-yielding varieties, but cultivators are reluctant to grow them except when favorable monsoon conditions permit it. In dry years, indigenous varieties are preferred.

The second most important crop in the arid zone is sorghum (*Sorghum vulgare*), locally called *jawār*. Although it is usually grown where annual rainfall averages are between 500 mm and 770 mm (Sen and Abraham 1966:107), in the desert sorghum is grown in the depressions where water settles. Since the maturation period for this crop is shorter than for millet, sorghum is sown for fodder if the rains are so delayed that good yields of millet cannot be expected. This was the case in 1982, with much of the fodder actually being sold to dairymen from Jodhpur city.

Mung beans (*Phaseolus mungo*), *moṭh* (*Phaseolus aconitifolius*), and sesame (*Sesamum indicum*) are intercropped with millet. *Guār* beans (*Cyamopsis psoralioides*) are sown on rockier and drier soils. Sesame is grown to provide oilseeds. *Guār* can be added as a feed concentrate for livestock. *Matīro* (*Citrullus lanatus*), a melon, may be encouraged and its seeds sold as a cash crop, or stored for use as a food supplement. The crops are ordinarily planted in July and harvested in September and October.

In a normal year, millet is planted on the *relo*. *Moṭh*, *mung* beans and millet are planted on the *magro*. Millet and *moṭh* are planted on the *dhoro*. Customarily, millet is intercropped with *moṭh, mung* beans and sesame. In a year of good rainfall, hybrid millet and *mung* beans are sown on the *relo*, and if it is an exceptional year, a second crop can also be grown after the fall harvest. Sesame, *mung* beans and *moṭh* are sown on both the *magro* and the *dhoro*, along with millet. In a terrible year, sorghum is planted on the *relo*, while the remaining crop land is sown in *guār* beans. In addition to adjusting planting to climatic conditions, the crops are customarily rotated and lands are periodically fallowed. Millet and sorghum are considered "strong" crops that weaken the soil, so they are followed by planting *guār*. The length of the fallow period on the *relo* is shorter than on the *dhoro*, which, according to the villagers, requires four times as much rest as other soils.

Average yields are highly variable, depending on the type of soil. In a good year, the *relo* is capable of yields of millet that are more than twice the yields from the *dhoro*. Production on the *dhoro* is the most unstable, since these lands not only are the worst quality and receive the least water, but also appear to be the most vulnerable to sandstorms. During 1982, the greatest resowing of crops due to sandstorms was that of crops planted on *dhoro* lands. In 1982, crop production varied from nonexistent on the *dhoro* lands to excellent on portions of the *relo*. During the previous year, only two households in the village produced crops, and in both cases, the land was outside the village limits. The closest field, about two miles distant, was in a favored position at the foot of a hill, and enclosed by a *bund*. It was the only nearby land to produce a crop.

Livestock is as important as crops in the local economy. Livestock capital is flexible according to circumstances, and cultivation provides fodder when grazing resources are depleted. During droughts, animals can be moved to areas where fodder and water are available. Livestock is raised for both subsistence and commercial purposes. Cattle, buffaloes and goats are kept for milk. Camels and bullocks are used as draft animals, and sheep are raised for wool. Milk, *ghee*, hair or wool, and both young and adult animals can be sold. The milk produced by cattle and goats is a critical source of protein in the diet. Goats are important milk producers for households that are unable to support a cow. During periods of drought, goats are better able to survive than cattle. Recent increases in the proportion of goats within the livestock population, from one-fifth to roughly one-third of the total population, are attributed to the drought conditions that prevailed during most of the past decade (Ghosh and Khan 1980). Although the water buffalo is not considered a desert animal, its population is increasing as dairy marketing cooperatives spread and it becomes possible to produce milk for urban markets.

Social Differentiation in a Desert Village

The 105 households residing in Renupur are divided among 19 caste groups: Gujar-Gaur Brahmans, Purohit Brahmans, Paliwal Brahmans, Jains, Bisnois, Suthars, Rajputs, Sads, Jats, Sonars, Kumhars, Nais, Pitals, Lohars, Meghwals, Beldars, Sindhis, Nayaks, and Dadhis (see Table 2). Two of these, the Bisnois and

Table 2: **List of Castes, Number of Households, and Membership, Listed in Order of Population (data from village Renupur, 1982)**

Jāti (Caste)	Number of Households	Total Members
Purohit Brahman	27	193
Jat	16	136
Gujar-Gaur Brahman	13	106
Bisnoi	6	59
Paliwal Brahman	9	49
Sindhi	5	42
Suthar	1	37
Beldar	4	27
Meghwal	4	26
Nai	3	23
Kumhar	3	21
Rajput	4	20
Lohar	3	19
Pital	1	17
Sad	2	16
Bhil (Nayak)	1	8
Dadhi	1	8
Baniya (Oswal Jain)	2	2
Sonar	1	1
Total Membership	105	811

the Jains, are high-ranking non-Hindu groups, and two, the Dadhis and the Sindhis, are Muslim groups. Purohits, Suthars and Gujar-Gaur Brahmans trace their groups' residence in the village to its founding, while others came at different times and for different reasons. The two most important recent in-migrations occurred following the famine of 1899-1901, and after India's Independence. The principal reasons given for settling in Renupur are economic opportunities, a quarrel or famine which drove a household's ancestors from their previous village, or the presence of relatives – a factor which helps encourage settlement within particular villages.

Before the land reforms of the 1950s, the village landlords were Purohit Brahmans, who had been granted the village as a revenue-free *sāṇsaṇ* holding. Somra Purohits, members of the *gotra* (exogamous patrisib)[5] that received the grant, were from a village that is about 20 miles distant. Sewar Purohits emigrated from 20 miles to the north because of a quarrel. The Suthars' ancestors had fled to Renupur after murdering a Rajput. Kumhars and Dadhis had moved to Renupur from adjacent villages. The remaining castes trace their settlement to the past 100 years, either shortly after the 1901 famine, or after Independence. Jats came to join relatives 80 years ago because of a quarrel in their previous village, which is adjacent to Renupur. Beldars migrated in at the same time, because of famine. Sads also established their lineage in the village at that time, when their ancestors fled from bandits. Meghwals arrived while grazing animals, and were invited to remain and herd the village cattle.

After Independence, there was an influx of refugees from Pakistan. Overall, Rajasthan experienced an 18% increase in population. The land reforms of the 1950s included programs to grant lands to members of Scheduled Castes and Tribes. In the village, several households benefitted from this. A family of formerly nomadic Gadulia Lohars settled, and became the village blacksmiths. They came from a village where many of the Purohits have relatives. A Bhil family was given a small amount of land. The Beldars obtained grants of land. Sindhi Muslims came to live with their relatives following Partition. At this time, too, Bisnois bought land and settled on the perimeters of the village.

The process of settlement is an ongoing feature of social and economic life. Lineages have died out or left and others have replaced them. Households with the strongest economic position are the least likely to move. These households may meet their needs for adult males by recruiting a man – a member of the same *jāti* (subcaste) but from a different *gotra*, according to the rules governing such matches – through an uxorilocal marriage to one of their daughters. The poorest households are generally drawn *en masse* by anticipated economic benefits. Since the land of the latter is the worst in the village, they are the most easily tempted to move on. Even when economic benefits are a drawing point, the household may cement the move by marriage, which helps to guarantee the claim to land.

Affinal and maternal connections are especially important in this society where village exogamy and the male inheritance of land are the rule, because such ties are the main basis for creating and maintaining links between different villages. Kin in other villages are expected to help in disaster, give information about outside economic and social opportunities, and lend support during migrations. When villagers state that they are going to visit relatives in other villages, almost invariably it means they are visiting maternal or affinally related kin. Most of these ties are concentrated within a 15-mile radius of the village, or are focused within one or two different villages. For example, the Purohits' marriages are contracted almost exclusively between Renupur and a cluster of three villages in the northeast.

Women married into a household, or into the households of brothers, tend to be from the same village and may be sisters (Kolenda 1978). Daughters often marry into the same villages as those from which their sisters-in-law come. Over time, these relationships are retained as a woman moves to the village where an aunt is resident, or even the village of her mother's parents. Most women maintain close ties to their natal kin. Women often spend a month or more at their parents' village, or are visited frequently by their brothers and sisters, especially during the years when their first children are born.

The effect of these practices is that connections between specific pairs or clusters of villages are concentrated spatially and maintained through time. Overall, most affinal ties are inside the northeast to southwest zone of arable land that lies between two belts of sand dunes in western Jodhpur district. Relations of affinity show up as distinctive clusters uniting the village with specific areas. In a sample of 179 marriages in which the village of a wife or daughter's husband is stated, 35 linked Renupur to adjacent villages, 30 represented villages with a 5- to 10-mile radius, and another 30 marriages joined households that were between 10 and 15 miles from Renupur. Only two marriages linked the village with Jodhpur city. It may be that urbanization is too recent to permit many such alliances, or it may reflect the preference of households for spouses knowledgeable about local farming conditions.

This concentration of ties, and their continual renewal, adds to the stability of relationships linking particular villages. These ties assume great importance in times of hardship. At such times, livestock may be transferred to relatives until the crisis is over. Members of a household may move in with their relatives. Kin are expected to permit their relatives to plant part of their land for food, if it is cultivable.

The most important factor affecting the survival of villagers during periods of drought, however, is their control over resources. Land ownership is inequitably distributed among the households in the village. The nine households with the largest landholdings own 28% of the cropped land (see Table 3). The bottom third of households in terms of size of landholding hold only 9% of the land, and most of this is of low quality. Although the average acres *per capita* is 5.09 overall, for the poorest 30 households, *per capita* availability of land is only 1.84 acres. The number of acres *per capita* rises steadily from this level to 11.9 acres *per capita* in the highest category. Household size is also positively associated with landholding, varying from 5.6 members in the lowest category, to over 10 for households owning more than 80 acres of land.

The Purohits are the wealthiest caste group in the village. Before land reform, they controlled about three-fourths of the land. Today, they control 1,440 acres, or about 41% of the total cropped land. The Purohits are also numerically dominant, with 27 households and 193 members. The *per capita* landholdings of the Purohits average approximately 7.6 acres, compared to 4.17 acres *per capita* for members of other caste groups. The Purohits, together with the Gujar-Gaur Brahmans and Suthars, comprise an economic and political faction that controls about half the cropped land.

The second most important land-owning caste in the village is the Jats, who control 560 acres of land. There are 16 Jat households,

Table 3: **Population and Landholdings per Household and per Capita, by Land Ownership Category, Renupur Village, 1982**

Category (Acres)	Total Acres	Population	Acres per Capita	House-holds	Acres per Household	Average Household Size
0–20	313	170	1.84	30	10.4	5.60
21–40	771	195	3.95	23	33.5	8.47
41–60	626	120	5.22	12	52.2	10.00
61–80	802	106	7.56	11	72.9	9.60
81–100	492	55	8.94	5	98.4	11.00
100 +	500	42	11.90	4	125.0	10.50
Total	3,506	688	5.09	85	41.4	8.09

making them the second largest local caste group. Jats and their followers (the rest of the village) form another economic and political faction, and the split between the two factions affects all village affairs. For example, a proposal to sink a well was blocked because each faction wanted the well to be located on its side of the village. Even selection of the village schoolmaster is subject to this conflict, and dealings with outsiders are likely to become merely another arena for this internal schism. At the same time, the existence of two strong factions helps ensure that all members of the village are included in government programs, as the factional leaders compete for the support of the village's households.

Land ownership also influences livestock ownership. In this area, where droughts are a frequent if not seasonal hazard, the amount of land controlled by a household determines in large part its access to fodder and ability to maintain livestock. Each species of domestic animal is characterized by differences in drought resistance, use, value, and cost of upkeep – factors which affect the utility of animals to households of different levels of wealth. Important considerations include the practicability and desirability of owning an animal relative to the cost of its upkeep, the value of its production, and the need for its labor or other products. In addition to animal products such as milk, wool, hair, *ghee* and traction power, the animals themselves may be sold. In fact, the marketability of certain types of animals is often exploited by cultivators during droughts.

The villagers of Renupur own goats, sheep, buffaloes, camels, bullocks and cows. By the end of June 1982, the livestock owned by villagers consisted of 259 cows. 40 calves under the age of three, 50 buffaloes, 9 buffalo young, 14 camels, and 9 bullocks. Villagers also owned 145 goats and 300 sheep. The poorest households owned primarily goats. Goats cost less than cows, are cheaper to maintain, are more salt tolerant, and are hardier than cows during droughts. In 1982, 60% of the goats were owned by households with 40 or fewer acres of land. 35% of the goats were owned by households with fewer than 20 acres of land. Households owning goats averaged 23.8 acres per household, compared to an overall average acreage of 41.4 acres per household.

In contrast with goats, only 9.8% of cows were owned by households with fewer than 20 acres of land, and 35% of cows were owned by households controlling between 20 and 40 acres. Buffalo ownership was concentrated in households with 40 or more acres of land, as was the ownership of camels. Comparing cow and buffalo ownership, households that owned only cows averaged 35.2 acres, while households that owned a buffalo averaged 63.2 acres. Households that owned both cows and buffaloes were in the most favorable position, having an average of 70.8 acres per household.

Adaptive Strategies in the 1979–82 Drought

From 1979 until the crop season of 1982, Renupur experienced almost continuous drought. The biggest problem was lack of water. The village pond shrank to a puddle containing about ten cubic meters of muddy water. Two-thirds of the village households were forced to buy water at an average cost of Rs. 528 per household, which is more than a month's wage for a laborer. As part of a famine relief project, the villagers had constructed a water tank that was connected by pipe to a village 25 kilometers away. It was impossible to actually pump the water, because there was no electricity, and the tank had never been filled.

Next to the shortage of water, the greatest hardship was caused by lack of fodder. By the third year of the drought, stored fodder was almost exhausted. Available fodder and food grains sold for the same price. Three-fourths of the households bought fodder at an average cost of Rs. 3,200 per household. Half the debt incurred in Renupur during 1981-82 can be accounted for by the need for fodder, but despite this, one third of the cows died of starvation.

Animals were sold or abandoned, and most of the cattle were herded to other areas in search of water and feed.

Only the wealthy households could afford to maintain non-productive animals – growing heifers and young bullocks, non-milk producing or non-pregnant cows. Since bullocks would be of no use from the fall of 1981 until the next monsoon, they were sold to reduce losses. 200 sheep, 51 bullocks, 11 male calves, 13 cows, 3 female calves, 2 buffaloes and 2 male buffalo calves were sold. The prices received for animals, particularly bullocks, were below normal market rates because of the flood of sales at the time.

Another strategy to reduce cattle losses was migration. 300 cattle were sent to areas where it was hoped fodder would be found. Two trends were evident. The first was migration to distant areas. In the past, villagers would go to Sindh, but this is no longer possible. Two parties of men and livestock set out in October 1981, after it became certain that the monsoon had failed. One group went to southern Barmer district, and the second travelled toward Sanchore. In all, 31 households sent cattle on the migration. Along migration routes, fodder was scarce or nonexistent, and many animals died. One or two men from a household herded their cows. Widows without adult sons sent cows with their husbands' relatives. In some cases, related households or neighbors sent their cattle in the charge of several men.

This kind of migration is common when local resources are exhausted. In some areas, migration is annual, except when there is a good rainfall, and the migrants follow regular routes and maintain contacts with villagers at their destinations. A large proportion of the village population thus may be absent from late fall until the next monsoon. As the migrants travel, they sell animals, milk and *ghee*, herding the animals into a field to obtain grass or water in return for the manure left behind.

The second trend was the movement of livestock between relatives in nearby villages. Undramatic and ignored in accounts of famine, this type of migration provides a temporary mechanism for the transfer of resources within the local kin group. 18 households participated in these transfers. As long as the animal remained with relatives, any milk that was produced could be used by them. Three households sent their cows to Jodhpur city, where one household kept a dairy business. One cow was sent back from the city to a wealthy village household, because the household owned fodder and the cow was expected to calve soon. In addition, one household sent a team of bullocks to Jodhpur city to be hired out.

Those households that could not migrate, or ran out of fodder and could not afford it, or lacked credit to buy it, were forced to watch their animals starve or to abandon them. This was done by taking the animals so far from Renupur that they could not find their way home. By June of 1982, only productive animals, such as pregnant or lactating cows, were being maintained, while the others were given smaller rations. Out of the 350 cows owned by the villagers, 100 died. 20 of these deaths were attributed to illness, old age or injuries, and the rest were due directly to weakness and starvation. 45 calves – 20 females and 25 males – died. About one third of the sheep, 180 head, died from lack of fodder and water. 7 of the 10 buffalo deaths were attributed to the famine. Two bullock deaths were reported, both from famine. There was practically no famine mortality among the goats, however, and no camels were lost because of the famine.

The effect of the drought on agricultural production was that there was almost none for three years. During 1981, only two households in the village obtained any crops, and both did so by cultivating outside land. Almost nine-tenths of the cropped land was plowed in 1981, but it produced nothing. In 1982, the crop failure was partial, and affected production in two ways. First, because the monsoon was late, the *magro* lands were sown in sorghum rather than millet. Second, while near normal crops were grown on the *relo*, those planted on the *dhoro* represented an almost total loss.

The agricultural strategies purused in 1982 – as I have discussed in detail elsewhere (Henderson 1987:270-271) – closely followed on, and were adjusted to, rainfall conditions during the monsoon. A small amount of rain fell near the end of June. This was sufficient to partially refill the pond and cause farmers to initiate plowing and the sowing of millet. A dust storm deposited about an inch of dust on June 22. Plowing operations continued that week. By the first week of July, some millet had sprouted in an uneven fashion. Millet requires additional moisture at this point in its growth cycle, but the crop had to wait almost until the end of the month. In the meantime, on July 13, a dust storm buried most of the crops on the *dhoro* and resowing was necessary. In fact, on the *dhoro*, nearly all the fields were sown twice, and in about 10% of cases, three times. By using bullocks or a camel, a cultivator can plow around undamaged plants – an activity that is not feasible with a tractor. Up to this time, rainfall had been very poor. On July 14, it rained for half an hour, with drizzles the next morning. A rainstorm passed by on the horizon three days later, but no rain fell on the village lands.

On July 24, several weeks late, the monsoon arrived. It rained throughout the afternoon and most of the night and morning of the next day, flooding the *relo* and *magro*. The village pond overflowed. Cultivators plowed and sowed sorghum on the *magro* lands west of the village. This crop was expected to be used as fodder. Eventually, about one-fourth of it was sold to village shopkeepers or dairymen from Jodhpur city. In all, the lateness of the monsoon led cultivators to plant almost half the village's lands in sorghum and *guār*, rather than the staple food, millet. One household with only *dhoro* land migrated to a relative's village and abandoned their crop. Men from a nearby village sharecropped 12 acres of *magro* land belonging to a brother-in-law in Renupur, because of drought in their own village. The harvest, so eagerly awaited, was poor. Three-fourths of the expected crop failed.

Not surprisingly, villagers depended heavily on credit and famine relief. Relief consisted of a small monthly grain ration, and work for a small wage. During the famine, about 150 people from Renupur and nearby villages worked in the stone mines near Jodhpur city, and about 400 on famine relief construction in the village. During 1980-81, Renupur's pond was deepened, so that it would store increased amounts of runoff following a rain. The soil that was dug out of the bottom of the pond was used in the construction of a *bund* that protected 80 acres of *relo*. Additionally, two underground tanks to store water were dug. The earnings from work on these projects, as reported by individuals, averaged about Rs. 600 per household. In Renupur, 46 households reported income from this source. 80% of these households were in the poorest group, owning 40 or fewer acres, while only 11 households with more than 40 acres participated. On the project, women, men and children all worked.

During this time, 56 households earned income from the activities of its members who worked outside Renupur. The overall average for such work was Rs. 5,232 per household – almost ten times the average earnings for famine relief work. Median earnings, probably a more representative figure, given the wide range of responses, was Rs. 2,400 per household. Outside work was widely regarded by the villagers as more lucrative. The ability to engage in it, however, was sharply limited to households with at least two adult males – one to stay in the village, and one to migrate in search of work. In addition to earning by work migration, 15 of Renupur's households earned income from sales through the dairy cooperative, though most stated that this did not cover their production costs.

The average reported debt of wealthier households was larger than that reported by poorer ones. As previously noted, half the reported debt could be accounted for because of the need for fodder, and the amount of debt that was attributed to social obligations, such as weddings, was small. Another social obligation – *jajmānī* (the customary annual grain payments to the village's service-providers based on traditional caste work), frequently suggested as a source of survival for poor client villagers (Epstein 1971) – was simply suspended for the duration of the drought. Only one houshold in Renupur, that of the Brahman priest, received such payments. The biggest problem, villagers continually stated, was the lack of rain for agriculture and drinking, pointing to a string of recent "worst years" when they had suffered from droughts.

Conclusion

Villagers in the Thar desert survive droughts and extreme environmental variation by adjusting their activities to seasonal conditions. Cultivators mimic natural flora events, by utilizing crops that are drought-adapted and capable of growth within the restricted limits of moisture availability. The high risk of drought encourages production strategies that permit flexible resource use. Cropping strategies take into consideration type of land, crop characteristics, and the amount and timing of rainfall. Passive water-harvesting technologies, such as *bunds*, maximize the availability of water to favored sites. The differences between crop strategies in 1981 and 1982 provide some evidence as to the extent to which cultivators adjust their crop schemes depending on circumstances. In 1981, almost all the crop land in Renupur was planted. Most of the land – 80% – was sown with a subsistence crop of millet. In 1982, because the monsoon was late, only about 70% of the village's crop land was sown, and about half of this was planted with fodder crops.

Reliance on livestock is probably as great as reliance on crops. Animals may be moved to regions where fodder is available. Since certain animals, such as bullocks, are closely tied in to market relations, strategies of livestock management depend on the owner's ability to sell animals that would constitute a drain on resources during dry periods, and to purchase new ones as needed to fulfil traction requirements. At times when it is not possible to produce food grains, fodder may be planted to support a household's livestock and permit continued production of milk or other animal products. The need for fodder is demonstrated by the large amounts spent on it, debt incurred for this purpose, and high livestock mortality. The livestock held by a household is adjusted to available resources by sale, gift, abandonment, and the death of non-favored animals.

Social connections provide access to resources not directly controlled by households. Within the village, sharecropping arrangements are frequently made between households with land that is surplus, relative to their subsistence needs, and those that lack enough to support their membership. The basis for such arrangements may be kinship, friendship, or patron-client relationships. Kinship provides channels through which animals and workers are transferred between villages. Indeed, relatives whose own land is uncultivable because of drought may be permitted to share some land in Renupur during this season. Village-based money lenders provide credit for seed, grain and other household needs.

The result is that strategies are adjustable to prevailing local conditions and reflect not simply shifts in rainfall, but also kinship and economic institutions. Within this context, the behavior of a household largely depends on the resources it controls. Impoverished, powerless households may simply have to move out. These households tend to own poor land, which intensifies the shortage of food and fodder, and encourages the ownership of goats in place of cows. Their land is the least likely to receive water in the event of a drought and is the most susceptible to erosion. The small size of the poorest households means that their ability to take advantage of outside work opportunities – or even to migrate with the cattle – is limited. It is not possible to easily divide the household into migrant and non-migrant constituents, so that a part stays to look after local property while others are absent. The earnings of these households tend to be restricted to famine relief. They are the most tied to the local resource base and are the most vulnerable to the fluctuations of the monsoon.

Wealthy households are able to survive the drought with less impairment of productive resources than poor households. The ability to maintain currently non-productive, but potential replacement stock, gives these households an advantage in reconstituting their herds, and also allows them to serve as the source of purchased replacement cows for poorer villagers. The land owned by wealthier villagers is of better quality, less susceptible to erosion and more likely to receive runoff topsoil, because of its topographic situation. Wealthy households also have higher outside income than poorer households. Their larger membership is easily divided for the purposes of labor or cattle migration, so that they are in a better position to take advantage of more lucrative external opportunities. Wealthy households engaged in moneylending to poorer households. Finally, the well-to-do, politically important families were able to ensure that their poorer relatives received famine relief.

Unequal onwership of resources exacerbates trends underlying economic differentiation of rich and poor because of famine. While both rich and poor housholds benefit from the return of good weather, the wealthy are more likely to have conserved resources on which to base their recovery of assets. Thus the rich can recover faster. Furthermore, the poor are dependent on wealthier households for replacement cows, seed and loans. Land improvements sponsored by development schemes have benefited households whose land is the most easily improved – the best land, which is owned for the most part by the wealthy. Tractorization is another instance where modernization has unequal benefits. Only a few households own tractors. Their poorer neighbors, lacking bullocks, must hire the tractor's services for plowing.

Similarly, efforts to reduce the level of resource use on vulnerable lands affects the rich and the poor differently. In Renupur, a goat control program would affect the poorest 30% of households, who are unable to afford to keep a cow, and depend on goats for milk and meat. Cow control, on the other hand, affects the wealthier households in the village. Attempts to shift the worst-quality soil from crop production to grazing affects the poorest households, for their small plots are concentrated in this land.

Equilibrium is constantly thwarted by climatic conditions, population migration, and factors that promote economic stratification. Conservative measures such as sharing between relatives in different villages, cattle migration, and support of clients by village patrons redistribute resources between areas of adequacy (if not surplus) and deficit. A high adjustability of strategies is demonstrated in the combination of livestock husbandry, wage-earning activities, and grain, fodder or cash crop production. The ability to migrate and norms supporting cooperation between units dispersed in many villages add flexibility in the use of outside resources. Economic stratification within the community creates different pressures and possibilities. To say that residents somehow survive a famine does not mean that they are terribly successful, or that one can see this as a balanced system. Poverty, lack of resources, and limited options are pervasive constraints faced by all members of the community.

This paper thus suggests that models of human-environment relations that posit a balanced equation are of limited utility for understanding events and processes within highly variable environments. In such regions, the key to survival appears to lie in the ability of households and communities to adjust to constantly shifting circumstances. Drought is a highly unpredictable event, random in its occurrence, not based on stable cycles. The attempt to delineate a geographic area within which an ecosystemic balance occurs may fail if community adaptation actually involves the exploitation of outside markets and external resources, and further, is highly responsive to shifts in these factors. The situation implies, moreover, that the question of desertification, which most studies approach in terms of the size of populations (human and animal) relative to the environment, or simple ratios of "crop land" to "grazing land," do not provide an adequate basis for understanding the actual pressures in the region. Without incorporating economic differentiation as a variable, salient differences in access to, and control over resources, are ignored.

This paper represents an attempt to characterize responses to the problem of drought more finely than is possible under the broad rubric of adaptation, and to permit the use of measures that examine differentiation within the community being studied. Western Rajasthan, like unstable and variable environments elsewhere in the world, is a region where demographic, political and economic shifts are transforming rural-urban relations and the connections between communities in the countryside. The focus on responses and adjustments to a variety of conditions may help to provide clues, not just to the effects of variable resources on behavior, but also to the nature and variety of community life itself.

ENDNOTES

1. Research for this paper was supported by a Junior Fellowship of the American Institute of Indian Studies in 1981–1982.
2. Present-day Barmer, Bikaner, Churu, Ganganagar, Jaisalmer, Jalore, Jhunjhunu, Jodhpur, Nagaur, Pali and Sikar districts of Rajasthan State (Mann and Singh 1975).
3. Jodhpur district comprises the central portions of the former princely state known variously as Jodhpur State or Marwar State. "Marwar" is the common name for the region. Previous to Independence, the state also included today's Barmer, Nagaur, Jalore, Pali and Sikar districts.
4. Residents of the area regard drought and famine as linked, but distinguish between several types of famines. The general term, *kāḷ*, is modified so that one sees also *ankāḷ* (shortage of grain), *jalkāḷ* (shortage of drinking water), *trinkāḷ* (shortage of fodder), and *trikāḷ* (shortage of all three). This last is the worst and generally appears if rain has failed for more than one year in a row.
5. A patrisib is comprised of individuals who claim agnatic (patrilineal) descent from a common ancestor, but may not be able to demonstrate all ties to the ancestor. This differs from a patrilineage, where these connections are demonstrable.

REFERENCES CITED

Adams, Archibald
1899 *The Western Rajputana States: A Medico-topographical and General Account of Marwar, Sirohi, Jaisalmer*. London: Junior Army & Navy Stores, Limited.

Bhandari, M.M.
1978 *Flora of the Indian Desert*. Jodhpur: Scientific Publishers.

Burton, Ian, Robert W. Kates and Gilbert F. White
1978 *The Environment as Hazard*. New York: Oxford University Press.

CAZRI (Central Arid Zone Research Institute)
1977 *India: Case Study on Desertification, Luni Development Block*. United Nations Conference on Desertification, 19 August-9 September, 1977. Jodhpur: Central Arid Zone Research Institute.
1978 *Annual Report*. Jodhpur: Central Arid Zone Research Institute–Indian Council of Agricultural Research.

Chouhan, Tej Singh
1979 "A Geographical Study of the Impact of Drought Hazard and Relief Measures in the Mallani Region: Rajasthan." Ph.D. dissertation, Department of Geography, University of Jodhpur.

Dandia, Milap Chand
1981 "Why is Rajasthan Backward?" *Yojana* 25 (22): 4ff.

Dhir, R.P.
1982 "The Human Factor in Ecological History." In *Desertification and Its Control: Dryland Ecology and Social Perspective*. Brian Spooner and H.S. Mann, eds. pp. 311-331. New York: Academic Press.

Epstein, T. Scarlett
1971 "Customary Systems of Rewards in Rural South India." In *Economic Development and Social Change*. G. Dalton, ed. pp. 99-120. Garden City, New York: The Natural History Press.

Government of Rajasthan
1981 *Statistical Abstract, 1979*. Jaipur: Shri H.N. Printing Press, for Government of Rajasthan Directorate of Economics and Statistics.

Ghosh, P.K. and M.S. Khan
1980 "The Goat in the Desert Environment." *Research Bulletin* 12. Jodhpur: Central Arid Zone Research Institute.

Greenough, Paul R.
1980 "Indian Famines and Peasant Victims: The Case of Bengal in 1943-44." *Modern Asian Studies* 14 (2):205-235.

Henderson, Carol
1987 "Famines, Droughts and the "Norm" in Arid Western Rajasthan: Problems of Modeling Environmental Variability." In *Research in Economic Anthropology*, vol. 9. Barry L. Isaac, ed., pp. 251-280. Greenwich, Conn.: JAI Press, Inc.

Indian Famine Commission
1880 *Report of the Indian Famine Commission, 1878. Part I: Famine Relief*. London: George Edward Eyre and William Spottiswoode.
1898 *Report of the Indian Famine Commission, 1898*. Simla: Government Central Printing Office.

Jaiswal, P.L., ed.
1977 *Desertification and Its Control*. New Delhi: Indian Council of Agricultural Research.

Jodha, N.S.
1975 "Famine and Famine Policies." *Economic and Political Weekly* (Bombay) 10:1609-1623.

Kirkby, Anne V.
1974 "Individual and Community Responses to Rainfall Variability in Oaxaca, Mexico." In *Natural Hazards: Local, National, Global*. Gilbert F. White, ed. pp. 119-128. New York: Oxford University Press.

Kolenda, Pauline
1978 "Sibling-Set Marriage, Collateral-Set Marriage, and Deflected Alliance Among Annana Jats of Jaipur District, Rajasthan." In *American Studies in the Anthropology of India*. Sylvia Vatuk, ed. pp. 242-277. Delhi: Manohar.

Maclachlan, Morgan D.
1983 *Why They Did Not Starve*. Philadelphia: Institute for the Study of Human Issues.

Mann, H.S., ed.
1980 *Arid Zone Research and Development*. Proceedings of the Symposium on Arid Zone Research and Development, by Arid Zone Research Association of India at the Central Arid Zone Research Institute, Jodhpur, 14-18 February, 1978. Jodhpur: Scientific Publications.

Mann, H.S. and R.P. Singh
1975 "Crop Production in the Arid Zone with Special Reference to Western Rajasthan." *Annals of Arid Zone* 14 (4):347-357.

Mertia, R.S. and M.M. Bhandari
1980 "Vegetational Adaptation in the Extremely Arid Regions of the Indian Desert." In *Arid Zone Research and Development*. H.S. Mann, ed. pp. 155-164. Jodhpur: Scientific Publications

Orlove, Benjamin S.
1980 *Pearl Millet*. University Park, Pennsylvania: The Pennsylvania State Uni-

Rachie, Kenneth O. and J.V. Majumdar
1980 Pearl Millet. University Park, Pennsylvania: The Pennsylvania State University Press.

Rajasthan District Gazetteer
1979 *Rajasthan District Gazetteer. Jodhpur*. Jaipur: Government of Rajasthan, Directorate of District Gazetteers.

Rajputana Gazetteer
1879 *The Rajputana Gazetteer.Vol. II*. Calcutta: Office of the Superintendent of Government Printing.

Ramdas, L.A.
1968 "Monsoon and Rainfall Pattern in the Indian Sub-Continent." In *Mountains and Rivers of India*. B.C. Law, ed. Calcutta: National Committee for Geography.

Rindos, David
1980 "Symbiosis, Instability, and the Origins and Spread of Agriculture: A New Model." *Current Anthropology* 21 (6):751-772.

Saxena, M.
1975 *Impact of the British Sovereignty on the Economic Conditions of Rajasthan*. Jaipur: Research Publications in the Social Sciences.

Sen, Amal Kumar and C.T. Abraham
1966 "Crop Belts and Cropping Patterns of Rajasthan." *Annals of Arid Zone* 5 (1):105-116.

Spooner, Brian and H.S. Mann, eds.
1980 *Desertification and Its Control: Dryland Ecology in Social Perspective.* New York: Academic Press.

Tod, James
1914 *The Annals and Antiquities of Rajast'han.* 2 Vols. London: George Routledge & Sons Ltd. (1st ed. 1829-32).

Vayda, Andrew P. and Bonnie J. McCay
1975 "New Directions in Ecology and Ecological Anthropology." *Annual Review of Anthropology* 4:293-307.

LOCALITY AND FRONTIER: SECURING LIVELIHOOD IN THE ARAVALLI ZONE OF CENTRAL RAJASTHAN

R. THOMAS ROSIN

The northern zone of the Aravalli hills includes a vast stretch of savanna merging into steppe desert that is one of the most densely populated arid and semi-arid regions of the world (Malhotra 1977:302). This population density rests on the development of land and water as resources to support human habitation. A series of long established, locally initiated adaptations that have modified the environment over the centuries to improve these resources have made possible year round settlement and even irrigation in areas once less utilized. Such improvements in turn have made possible the extension and intensification of animal husbandry and crop cultivation.

The intensified use of this fragile, rain-dependent environment, however, has made its population increasingly vulnerable to crises. Drought or flood, excessive winds removing topsoil, a cloud-occluded winter season – not to mention civil calamities precipitated by military conflict – are eventualities the peasantry must anticipate. Events that threaten their livelihood for a season, a year, or even longer, compel many people in this area (and indeed, Rajasthanis in general) to extend their attention beyond their immediate locale. As well as using customary, organizational and institutional supports in times of crisis, they share information about adaptive opportunities available across political and ecological boundaries. Such areas, whether in neighboring regions or distant lands, thus become a "frontier," where the opportunity for further development, involving both variations in and alternatives to existing means of livelihood, is seen to be present.

This paper examines the manner in which the peoples of the central hills of Rajasthan have adapted over time to environmental change initiated by increasingly intensive use of resources. Focus is on the sequence and range of human modifications of the physical environment brought about by the extension and intensification of animal husbandry and crop cultivation. Adopting an approach that stresses a time perspective of generations rather than the short term, change and crises over stable and recurrent features of the environment, and family and community rather than territory, the study identifies long-term adaptive trends in the Aravalli region of Rajasthan. It is based on direct observation of the adaptive strategies utilized by rural families in villages in Nagaur District over a 20-year period after Independence (Rosin 1978, 1987a), as well as a field survey of variations in settlement patterns and adaptation along the length of the Aravallis. These data, which introduce findings about cognitive skills previously unreported in the literature, are combined with historic sources recording local conditions from the pre-Independence period to infer stages of adaptation antecedent to the contemporary system's level of complexity.

A clear distinction must be made between adaptive strategy and adaptive trend. "Adaptive strategy" refers to the activities of families or corporate groups who manage the resources of land and water, social relations, capital, equipment, knowledge and expertise to secure their livelihood in the face of both natural and socio-political change. As so defined, strategy refers to the actors, their perceptions, calculations, choices and planning for future contingencies to realize their long-term objectives. "Adaptive trend," on the other hand, refers to the long-term aggregate results of people executing their strategies for adaptation, with emphasis on results involving changes in relationships between humans and the environment. Some trends may represent a feedback loop between a changing environment and human actions that are correspondingly altered or intensified, thereby causing further changes in the environment. A trend may thus prove accumulative and/or reinforcing.[1]

In examining long-term trends in the management of land and water resources in the Aravallis, this study touches on an issue that has received scant attention from scholars researching Rajasthan: the significance of the wetter southern reaches of the Aravallis to adaptive strategies in the harsh conditions of the more arid north. The arid and semi-arid zones of Rajasthan sit astride the Aravallis, which increase not only in altitude and massiveness, but also in rainfall, as they reach southward toward the wetter, forested fastnesses of central India and the tableland of Malwa. Furthermore, the forests of southern Rajasthan remain even today a densely populated tribal belt, parts of which were not fully integrated under state control until the late 19th century. This close proximity of a forested tribal domain to the south warrants examination as a frontier region for the people inhabiting the intensively utilized semi-arid environment to the north. Did the progressive opening up of the tribal areas provide alternatives in livelihood for the peoples of the neighboring dry zone? While historical sources are scant in recording the emerging relations between settlers and tribal peoples, the contemporary nature of the process can be studied today in the outposts of immigrants settled in tribal areas and in the development of modern systems of water management initiated and constructed by the state.

This opening up of the forested southern Aravalli region to exploitation by peoples from surrounding areas was but one of the adaptive strategies open to the inhabitants of the northern zone. They also implemented traditional adaptive capabilities – as seen in the complexity of their social relations, managerial competence and awareness of opportunities in more distant regions – that are of significance to more than just coping with environmental change. As will be seen in this paper, these very same capabilities are of relevance to understanding the ability of the region's inhabitants to adapt to the emergent economic and political conditions of the modern Rajasthan state.

Natural Precipitation and Rain-Fed Crop Cultivation

The Aravalli hills bisect Rajasthan, separating the savanna and desert to the northwest from the more humid regions of the east and southeast. Rising as scattered ridges and outcroppings of low elevation in the north, the Aravallis become massive hills in the south, reaching elevations as high as 1722 meters at Mt. Abu. Rainfall during the monsoon increases rapidly along a northwest-southeast gradient perpendicular to the range. The seasonal rainfall in the north and west creates temporary streams, springs and briny pans, while the rains in the south sustain perennial rivers, lakes and springs. Without development of water resources, the limitations in the natural hydrology in the north would restrict human adaptation to temporary settlements, cultivation of a single rain-fed crop, and a transhumant pastoralism[2] wherein herds must be shifted seasonally out of the dry zone into the better watered surrounding areas.

The population density and permanence of settlement in the north rests on a series of long established, locally initiated developments that have modified the environment to improve water resources, directly benefiting rain-fed crop cultivation and animal husbandry. Dams built across the beds of temporary streams or across land depressions serve to impound run-off water for surface storage, recharge ground water through soakage, or provide moist and silted catchment areas (*khāḍiṇ*) that may be ploughed and seeded as the surface waters recede (Malhotra and Mann 1982:308). Embankments and levees, often built and extended by successive generations of workers, expand water catchment areas. In addition, many dams or bunds were intended not for storing water but for distributing surface run-off to flood a neighboring region (*Rajputana Gazetteer* 1879:I, 152-153).

Excavation of wells and deepening of depressions to create artificial lakes or tanks helped to provision humans and domesticates with water during the drier months. Wells dug for public drinking and bathing were often enhanced by elaborate masonry steps leading down to the shifting water level (Jain 1972:467-468, 110-111, 138-140, 173, 260). Such wells, called *bāvaṛī* in eastern Marwar, often achieved wondrous forms: arches hanging over the descending staircase to reinforce the side walls, descent by means of a series of right-angled turns in the staircase, double or quadruple staircases leading to a single passage at the lowest level (Jain-Neubauer 1981:xiii, Plates 1 & 2). Such designs celebrated the contribution of the princely, warrior or priestly elite, who funded these well-monuments in order to extend the seasonal or permanent settlement of farmers, craftsmen or shepherds on their lands.[3]

The extensive cultivation of a rain-fed crop, in turn, directly supports pastoralism in the region. Crops of millet, sorghum, pulses and melons, seeded over as much land as possible, add fodder to supplement the jungle grasses, leafy bushes and trees on which the animals graze. Even in rain-scarce years, crops that do not mature to grain are valuable for the chaff and straw they provide for livestock feed. Improvements in water, feed and human food reserves permit half-year settled residence in a home village or hamlet in the savanna, a pattern which today characterizes a vast number of pastoral families (whether Jat, Gujar or Rebari). The extensiveness of crop cultivation by a people often classified as pastoral is evident today in the high percentage of land brought under single crop cultivation in the regions identified with pastoralism.[4] For the pastoralist, food, feed and water reserves often prove inadequate for full, year-round settlement. A high population of cattle in relation to available browsing and grazing area (the local commons, tree-studded fields or uncultivated jungle) and available fodder from croppage may necessitate shifting herds from rain-scarce regions to surrounding, better-watered areas. (Sheep, goats and camels, however, are generally able to sustain themselves longer on the local resources.) Depending on their location, pastoralists may move their herds during the dry season toward the Gangetic plain and the Doab, across the ridge of the Aravallis toward the Malwa tablelands, or toward the Sindh or Gujarat, where they may graze near the salt barrens and in the forests, on the range between villages, or on farmlands rented in order to harvest leaves and pods from pruned trees.

The combination of single crop cultivation and transhumance increases the density of the human and domesticate population during the monsoon and winter season. As the dry season begins, however, herds in the desert and savanna zone start exceeding local needs. Since it borders on this zone, the western Aravalli belt is the site of scores of fairs throughout the year that bring together buyers and farmers from the wetter lands east with sellers of livestock from the west (Rosin 1987a:465-466, Lodrick 1984). Peasants and shepherds (particularly from the regions of Marwar, Shekhawati and Ajmer-Mairwara) gather at fairs attracting buyers from as far away as the Gangetic plain and the Doab. Likewise, peasants from Jhalawar and Chittorgarh participate in the fairs of Malwa. The various fairs in each sector are held throughout the year, enabling peasants and shepherds to adjust the size of their herds in relation to the rains which determine the adequacy of grasses and chaff for feed. Both transhumance and cattle fairs are important mechanisms for adjusting herd size to the seasonal availability of water and feed, to natural disasters such as floods, and to long-term climatic anomalies such as drought.

Intensification of Cultivation Through Irrigation

Further increase in population density and permanence of settlement in the Aravallis rests on the expansion of cultivation to a second season of cropping. A second crop supported by rainfall without irrigation is possible in certain parts of the hills where soils remain moist during the winter season because of an impervious stratum close to the surface, the moisture rententiveness of the soil, decreased evaporation rates or abundance of rainfall.[5] But in general, such an intensification of cultivation depends on the development of irrigation works.

One may contrast two kinds of irrigation systems in Rajasthan: 1) surface storage of water impounded behind dams with delivery of water through canals, and 2) ground water reserves recharged by soakage from artificial lakes, reservoirs and rivers, with water delivered to the surface by percolation wells.[6] The traditional system dominant throughout the Aravallis used artificial lakes, tanks, and reservoirs to recharge ground water to improve reserves to be tapped by wells. In the north, the porosity of the beds of lakes and streams, along with high evaporation rates, make most surface reserves temporary and hence less available for canal delivery. While dams and reservoirs along with perennial streams become more common as one moves southward through the Aravallis, their contribution in supplying water directly to the fields by canals has tended to be overestimated by recent western observers keen to visualize a hydraulic system similar to the grand dam and canal construction that the British favored in the 19th and 20th centuries.[7]

a) *Surface storage systems.* Late 19th-century accounts by British agents in gazetteers present information useful to assessing the nature of the previous surface storage systems in the south. Among such great artificial lakes in the south as Jai Samand, Raj Samand, Udai Sagar (all close to Udaipur, the capital of Mewar) and Dugari (in the neighboring state of Bundi), Dugari stands out with the largest acreage of land irrigated (1500 *bīghās*) (*Rajputana Gazetteer* 1879:I, 216). Of the Jai Samand or Debur lake, it is written that "The water has hitherto been little used for irrigation, but sluices are now being introduced to supply canals along the hillsides and irrigate the plains below" (*Rajputana Gazetteer* 1880:III, 13). The vast potential for canal delivery had not begun to be realized until British conceptions influenced traditional practices.[8]

Irrigation did occur, but neither on the scale nor in the manner often conceived by British observers.[9] In some cases, what was considered irrigation in the late 19th-century gazetteers was a matter of soil saturation in the bed of the reservoir or tank site itself.[10] After reviewing the various artificial lakes of the states of Mewar, Bundi and Kota, the *Rajputana Gazetteer* concludes:

> All these artificial lakes have been built with the object of storing water, without looking to its subsequent distribution. The area which they can irrigate for cultivation is therefore very insignificant, and lies mainly within the lake's bed, which yields excellent crops as the water subsides, if it subsides in time" (1879:I, 37).

Thus earlier British accounts of the indigenous system do not appear to have recognized the broader function of the artificial tanks and reservoirs as facilitating soakage and recharge of ground water. However, they did recognize their importance in providing drinking and bathing water to large, concentrated settlements of humans and domesticates, and in irrigating some lands and gardens.

b) *Well irrigation*. Throughout the Aravallis, wells have traditionally been central in providing irrigation for a second season of cropping, with artificial lakes, tanks and reservoirs being used to recharge ground water and thus improve the reserves to be tapped by wells. However, considerable variations exist between north and south in seasonal rainfall, soil absorption and evaporation rates, and the depth and abundance of ground water. Water storage, retrieval and delivery for an irrigated crop vary accordingly, along with the technology and organization of social relations for production.

In the northern Aravallis, lesser rainfall and the greater depth of impervious layers of rock or clay necessitates deeper wells which are less quickly recharged. The technology for water-lifting varies from the most labor-intensive potted leather bag (*poṭalya charas*) to the nozzled vessel (*soṇḍiya charas*) and the Persian wheel (*araṭh*). All of these utilize bullock or camel power. Deeper wells use draft animals drawing a bag or vessel to provide a slower and discontinuous flow of water, while the more abundant shallow wells use animals on a turnstile, cranking a chain of buckets to give a continuous flow.

The necessity of animals for draft, and the year-round maintenance of cattle made possible by the abundance of fodder available from two crops a year, makes the activities of crop cultivation, irrigation and animal husbandry highly interdependent. This interrelationship is expressed by the term "churrus, chursa, or skin of land" (Tod 1957:II, 518) used in Mewar to refer to a parcel of leased land including both dry land for the monsoon crop and irrigated land for a winter crop. The word *charas* is the same as that used for the skin or hide taken from one's dead cattle and fashioned into a water bag. Thus the land parcel allocated is the amount of acreage that may be watered by draft teams drawing the *charas* from the well at a rate and volume that permits repeated irrigations during the *rabī* (spring) season.

Deeper wells of the type dug in the north require a prodigious organization of labor for initial excavation, deepening and continued operation. In Marwar and Shekhawati this is made possible by a tradition of joint family life and strong ties of affinity among the cultivators. In addition, enduring ties of partnership around each well also join sets of families that may share neither kinship nor affinity, nor even caste.

Initial construction of wells may be ordered and executed by the land-title holder, using hired laborers like the Baori, who specialize in quarry and well excavation. In other cases, construction is directly undertaken by the cultivator (*Rajputana Gazetteer* 1879:I, 79; 1880:III, 38), to whom a title holder might extend interest-free loans (*Rajputana Gazetteer* 1879:III, 257). To deepen wells already dug and to improve wells once abandoned, tenant families acting as partners with some assurance of continuity in tenure undertake the task, making use of the considerable human and bullock labor they have available through the family members and affines of each partner. To drain a well adequately, so that men can work below to deepen it, often requires twice the work force needed for crop irrigation.[11]

The utilization of the *poṭalya charas* for irrigation, as is common in the Marwar and Shekhawati regions of the northern Aravallis, involves a four-man work team. Each worker comes from a different family, which also supplies a pair of bullocks (or camels) and the labor of its other able-bodied members, and even their affines, for peak periods of weeding and harvesting or for the activities of well and land improvement. Such families are usually patrilineally extended, brothers with their wives and children often remaining together in household farming operations even after the death of their parents. Sons are ranked but share equal rights of inheritance. Sibling-set and collateral-set marriages are preferred (Rosin 1968:255, 268; Kolenda 1978), for in this manner the in-marrying women, as well as the patrilocally resident men, are bound by ties of kinship to enhance the solidarity of the joint family.

The affinal ties binding each joint family to other families are extensive. Each person is bound through their spouse to each member of the spouse's family through specifically defined relations of affinity. Furthermore, each is bound through a generic tie of affinity (expressed in eastern Marwar through the *byāījī* term of address for males and the *byāṇjī* term for females) to members of other families through the marriages of their brothers and sisters, their own sons and daughters and their nieces and nephews (Rosin 1987a:256-257). Those related as *byāījī* or *byāṇjī* (in-laws) are joined in a relationship of generalized equality, mutual support and emotional solidarity.

Among the priestly, moneylending and Rajput elite of Rajasthan, the lower status of the bride's family vis-à-vis that of the groom is ritually affirmed and expressed in common discourse. Among the cultivating communities, however, the affinal relationships created by the linking of two families are strikingly egalitarian, informal and emotionally supportive.

Joint families, their internal weave made firm by kinship binding the women together as well as the men, with their radiating warp of affinity binding each family to other families, provide a remarkable organizational resource among the peasantry. When such families are further joined by ties of partnership, they are able to meet the demands of two-crop farming and animal husbandry for the livestock markets, supply the work force to convert rain-fed fields (*bāranī*) into fenced and soil-enhanced fields (*chāhī*) irrigated by excavated wells, and provide social security in times of natural or civil calamity.

Cooperation and solidarity among the families working as partners at each well are based on an assumption of equity. Each partner shares equally the costs, risks and gains of production.

Through a system of rotation, they share the different tasks at the well, as well as the ensuing responsibilities and authority. Furthermore, they also share in efforts at long-term improvements of well and soil quality.

Equity does not rest simply on good faith among the co-workers, but involves skills in measurement, counting, recording and calculation. The rotation of work shifts is based on an elaborate digital system of "counting the stones" (*kankaṛī giṇaṇo*) for the potted leather bag,[12] or on an analogic system of measuring turns around the turnstyle by unwinding a spindle of string tied to the vertical axle of the Persian wheel. The accumulating pile of stones or the unwinding spindle is thus a public record of work accomplished. In sharing the harvest, the record is kept by chanted counting of each measure allocated from the grain heap to each partner, with all members present to witness the division. Where partners work as a foursome, the men become adept at calculations based on quadrupling shares for time, materials and funds contributed by each to cover cost, and quartering shares for the division of profits (Rosin 1984). Even bullock teams are characterized by their relative work capacity, measured in terms of their proven ability to draw a certain number of waterbag loads from the well. Disputes, if they occur, are reduced to arguments over measured quantities and are thus liable to rational resolution.

The amount of acreage partners choose to seed each year depends on the anticipated supply of ground water. For labor intensive irrigated crops, farmers want to seed only as much acreage as can be brought to harvest. Cultivators are able to calculate the actual volume of water lifted and delivered for an entire crop during prior seasons. Furthermore, they do reflect on how water delivery over the years relates to changes in rainfall and ground water levels. They seed their acreage accordingly, maximizing crop yield and diminishing the likelihood of over-expending seed and labor on acreage that cannot be brought to fruition because of limited water reserves that year.

Irrigated farming, particularly as practiced by peasants in the northern part of the Aravallis, encourages increased use of counting and recording devices and improved calculation skills. The initial impetus for this local tradition may have been the desire to make the assessment of fair shares among partners increasingly objective and free from dispute. When this information is routinely calculated, it is put to use to increase efficiency, minimizing efforts and expenditure in relationship to harvest yield. The effect is to increase the managerial capability of a peasantry already unusual in its ability to mobilize a well-coordinated work force for both annual production and the long-term improvement of water and land resources.

Factors of Resource Management Favoring Long-Term Tenancy

The Aravalli zone, particularly in its drier, more intensively exploited northern section, has required long-term investment not only in irrigation facilities, but in land improvement. The irrigated land of Marwar, for example, is known as *chāhī* ('dear land'), as great effort has been required to maintain its productivity. Likewise, in Mewar, irrigated land that is temporarily abandoned is called *banjar* ('sterile soil'), affirming local conceptions that relate human effort to the fertility of soil (Tod 1957:II, 498-499). The peasants of eastern Marwar, for example, perceive their sandy loam soils as low in humus and nutrients, and improve their fields through cumulative manuring and transportation of silt from ponds and tanks. Dust storms can whisk away the friable topsoil, so high earthern ridges are constructed along plot boundaries as both wind shield and soil trap. Because irrigation requires gravity flow from distant well to field, cultivators maintain earthern ridges in order to support irrigation channels as well, occasionally constructing elevated masonry bridges or siphons to extend water flow across arroyos. Irrigated crop cultivation, with its dependency on manure and draft animals, requires animal husbandry as well, and farmers must maintain extensive thorn fencing to protect maturing crops from grazing animals.[13] Because of deep-rooted devil grasses (*dobṛī*) that have adapted well to an environment degraded and disturbed by centuries of cultivation, only deep plowing and weed removal can limit the competition of cultigen and weed for water, nutrient and sunlight. To manure, weed, maintain earthern ridges and fencing, and to perform all the activities directly connected with irrigation, there is need for a work force committed to long-term improvement of resources.

Historically, both landlords and peasants have favored long-term occupancy, for such security encourages irrigation and land improvement, which in turn maintains productivity. Accordingly, the bulk of the peasantry are long-term tenants. Even rural artisans tend to cultivate a rain-fed crop as tenants, as do transhumant pastoralists during their half-year residency in a home village or hamlet. The percentage of artisans or laborers providing only agricultural services or temporary labor to tenants or to the landed rural elite is small in the dry, irrigated regions, but increases in the wetter, less irrigation-dependent southeast.

The institution of long-term tenancy has given stature to the primary producer by recognizing and depending on his managerial and supervisory abilities. To this day the status of shepherds and farmers is honored through commensal rules that permit their inter-dining with local Rajput landlords.[14] This respect for the tribal, the pastoralist and the cultivator is also evident in the historical lore of conquest and early rituals of dominion. Tod, for example, records conquerors inter-dining with the people they subjected: "the conquest of this tract (in the mid-sixteenth century) was made from the Koteah Bhils of the Oojla, the 'unmixed,' or aboriginal race. From these the Rajpoot will eat, and all classes will 'drink water' at their hands" (1957:II, 409). Tod also documents the fact that those who had been subjugated were granted recognition of their rights in the land. He cites not only the aboriginal Bhils and Minas, but the pastoral Jats as well, of whom he states that they applied as *tilak* "the unguent of royalty to the forehead of the successor" of the invested Rajput chieftain (1957:II, 141; Saxena 1964).[15]

One could argue that the contests and battles that fill the chronicles of Rajput history were fought not for control over land and resources, but for the right to reap the harvest, cull the livestock and tap the labor of those who resided in the conquered land. The natural resources of the savanna, desert and forest zone required the hardiness, initiative and developmental efforts of primary producers if a land so harsh was to produce value worthy of conquest.

In pre-Independence Rajputana, such a dependency on their productive capability gave tenants some leverage in adjusting their relationships with their landlords. In post-Independence Rajasthan their prior continuity and rights in tenure provided the basis for gaining primary title to the lands they worked, a gain made possible by their successful mobilization to participate in the modern electoral and judicial process – points to which we will turn in the concluding sections.

Migration and Occupational Alternatives for Long-Term Survival

We have argued that long-term investments in improving land and water resources has augmented utilization of a water-scarce environment. Improvements in water resources has made seasonal settlement possible and temporary settlements permanent. Such improvements have also contributed to extending and intensifying pastoralism through increasing rain-fed crop cultivation in the more arid savanna. Where ground water has proved adequate, they have made possible further intensification of cultivation through irrigation of a second (often cash) crop. Given the marginality of the environment and the vicissitudes of climate in the Aravalli zone, however, such extension and intensification of production has had its limits.

Such intensified exploitation has resulted in progressive degrading of the environment (Jodha 1982:345) through defoliation, salinization (CAZRI 1977:43), erosion and soil loss. Local people faced recurrent drought (Bharara 1982), flood, famine (Timberg 1978:101) and epidemics (Tod 1957:II, 552; CAZRI 1977:14), as well as, in previous centuries, depradations by foreign troops or marauders or the planned consequences of military action by their own elites – as in the strategic destruction of the countryside in Mewar by Rana Pratap (G.N. Sharma 1968:342-344) to deprive the enemy forces of food, fodder and water. As long as the borders of states and *ṭhikānās* (estates) were insecure, and lords and nobles made battlefields of the countryside, the peasantry was bound to suffer not only from the ravages of war, but from the heroic ethos that supported diversion of the wealth of the land to support the self-proclaimed noble adventures of the warrior class. As a consequence, one can document recurrent losses in population (Tod 1957:II, 508; R.C. Sharma 1972:53, 87),[16] followed by periods of recovery with the reopening of opportunity (R.C. Sharma 1972:183; Tod 1957:I, 398-399).

The vicissitudes of climate, pestilence and military adventure experienced in the Aravalli zone, and the subsequent crises of famine, plague and plunder have been a perennial challenge to long-term survival. Among the range of practices used to alleviate distress or provide recovery from crises, several are cumulative in their effect and serve to improve productive options and capabilities for long-term survival.

Families who accumulate assets in stored grain, jewelry, and livestock during good years gain security for years of dearth. Likewise, when the state or *ṭhikānā* accumulates and stores grain surplus, it is able to provide famine relief. Thus when assets have been accumulated by landlords or the state, actual crises can become occasions to launch public works. Grain payments are made to peasants to excavate reservoirs or improve dams and levees, thereby enhancing *khāḍiṇ* lands and ground water reserves for percolation wells downslope. Funds given as loans permit peasants to further deepen wells made temporarily dry by drought. Such continuous improvements in developing water resources, or recharging and retrieving ground water reserves, lessen the impact of subsequent droughts. Roads or rail construction, in turn, improves transportation and marketing, so that subsequent crises can be better met by bringing in relief or seeking it in more distant, unaffected regions, while at the same time helping diversify the local economy with employment opportunities outside agriculture.

Central among strategies for long-term survival in the face of recurrent crises is the development of occupational practices and alternatives that integrate the local area with more distant regions. Pastoralism stores mobile wealth on hoof, which can be shifted to other areas with adequate grazing and browsing resources. Livestock fairs attracting distant buyers assure liquidity through frequent opportunities to sell stock in excess of available feed. Craft specialization producing marketable commodities augments or replaces earnings from dryland farming. The migration to long established jobs in mining, quarrying (Rosin 1987b), salt extraction and construction are as important, perhaps, as the state and *ṭhikānā* sponsored public work programs for famine relief.

Placing a family member in secure employment outside the region assures a flow of income that helps weather the austerity of local conditions. In general, the migration pattern does not weaken local traditions but strengthens them instead. While much of the laboring, service and commercial population may move out for employment, their family members – the elderly, younger brothers, women and children – lodge secure in joint family households in the home village or town.[17]

Emigration is probably a long established pattern. In earlier centuries, a vast expanse of partially forested terrain in the Aravalli zone, abandoned by state or *ṭhikānā*, or occupied by such aboriginal groups as Bhils and Minas, or such long established settlers as the Sahariyas, Gerasias or Mers, offered opportunities for people of all strata in the surrounding caste society. An aspect of the history of Rajputana that has received little attention is the progressive or recurrent penetration of tribal sovereignties by chiefs, feudal lords and rajas, the exploitation of their resources, and the incorporation of their peoples into the expanding caste society,[18] often preceded or accompanied by internal differentiation and stratification among the tribal people (Sinha 1962).

On the basis of historic and ethnographic accounts of the southern region, supplemented by the extensive literature on the incorporation of tribal peoples elsewhere in South Asia,[19] it is possible to reconstruct in rough outline the process in Rajasthan, and to suggest the kinds of opportunities the southern, wetter regions of the Aravallis may have made available to the peoples living in the drier north. Rajas, princes, feudal lords and desperadoes sought sovereignty over tribal territory through conquest, treaty or intrigue. They, in turn, could confer their sovereignty on lesser lords or priests, as land grants for services rendered.[20] Warriors, priests and commerical castes established outposts, from which they could assert an exploitative and inegalitarian ideology supportive of the expansion of caste society into the tribal area. Through trade and moneylending, they could penetrate economically the tribal sea surrounding them, in some cases gaining land through mortgages foreclosed for indebtedness (G.B. Sharma 1976:177-178; Mathur 1976:64-65). Priests could perform their religious, ritual, and astrological functions, while the concern for purity in the growing multi-caste towns required the services of untouchable outcastes to remove defilement. As documented by Brij Raj Chauhan in recording the origins of Ranawaton-ki-sadri village from a hamlet granted to a dispossessed warrior in 1811 by the Rana of Udaipur, warriors and priests with land grants encouraged colonialization by peasant, shepherd, craft and service castes (1967:8-19). The accretion of peasant villages to tribal hamlets and homesteads provided a citizenry from which taxes, rent and labor could be extracted, while providing new opportunity for shepherds and cultivators fleeing oppression, insecure tenure or more austere conditions in neighboring regions.

Thus the southern Aravallis had available territory, resources, and a population for exploitation, offering to the peoples of the drier north opportunities to colonize a more attractive ecological region. That such colonization and exploitation did occur may be documented from the historic record of southward migrations from just one of the drier regions of the north, Marwar. Warriors from various clans of Rajputs, for example, took territory in such southern reaches as Banswara, Dungarpur, and Kusalgarh; Chauhan Rajputs from Sambhar conquered the Jawas and Para tracts of Mewar (*Rajputana Gazetteer* 1880:III, 62); Rathor Rajputs numbered 8 of the 16 noble houses holding lands in Banswara (1879:I, 106); Mertiya Rathors from Nagaur gained land grants in Banswara to protect the Talwara pass (*ibid.*, 108); a Rathor Rajput, descendant of the founder of the Jodhpur state, is said to have conquered Lalgarh from the Bhils in Kusalgarh further to the south (*ibid.*, 127).

The migration of primary producers from Marwar to the south is more difficult to document. Historic accounts show that, as part of marriage negotiations, the rana of Mewar demanded from the raja of Jodhpur ten thousand Jat cultivators, who migrated upon being assured of hereditary proprietary rights (Tod 1957:I, 394). Adrian Mayer also documents "a tradition of immigration" for a village in Malwa to the south, referring in one case to the "emigration of the whole subcaste from Mewar" (1970: 4, 13, 14). G.D. Sharma reports that in the 13th century, cultivators were invited to settle around the caravan town of Pali, on the southwestern edge of the Aravallis, to make the area secure from Mer tribesmen and to extend cultivation (1977:2). Chauhan records that in the later stages in the settlement of the Mewar village he studied, artisans and service caste members came from distant Marwar and Mairwara (1967:8-19).[21] Early in the 1800s, Tod as British Political Agent had arranged to restore the crown lands and estates of Mewar by attracting back cultivators to tracts plundered by Maratha incursions and local exploitation (Banerjee 1951:310). Generally, whenever lawfulness and security were restored, as in Sirohi, which had been raided by Rajputs from Marwar in the late 19th century,[22] cultivators were likely to be attracted to abandoned lands, with wells dug but deserted (*Rajputana Gazetteer* 1880:III, 90).

Throughout the 18th century, the increased movement of Marwari traders southward to Malwa as shopkeepers and moneylenders, "financing the production of crops demanded by the British, at first opium, and then especially cotton" (Timberg

1978:44), suggests that they may have stimulated similar movement by cultivators. Those immigrating could join local peasants cultivating not only rain-fed and irrigated crops of staples, but sugar cane in the late 18th century and increasingly, as the British expanded their exports to markets in China, opium and cotton. The pervasiveness of opium crop cultivation in Rajasthan in the 19th century is conveyed by a single sentence in Tod: "Poppy oil is more used for the cherag'h (lamp) than any other in Mewar" (1957:II, 509). So large was the volume of poppy harvested for the intoxicating resin of its flower that the remaining stalks provided ample oil for lamps to light peasant homes! While Mewar state officially alloted one out of every 25 *bīghās* of land to opium production, two *bīghās* out of 25 were in fact seeded with poppy (*ibid.*, 507-511).

Movement southward by peasants was facilitated not only by the presence of Marwari traders and the opportunity to restore abandoned lands, but also by the nature of the economic activities and settlement pattern of tribals such as the Bhils. The Bhils favor *valar* (slash and burn) cultivation, cutting and burning forest scrub and trees to clear fields for planting. On land thus fertilized by ash, they produce crops of rice, sesame seed and corn for several years before abandoning the land and clearing new fields for cultivation (*Rajputana Gazetteer* 1879:I, 109). Both Bhils and Minas in the southern Aravallis favor neolocal residence in homesteads separated from parental hamlets, with quick access to the resources of jungle, pasturage and field. Their population dispersion, their slash and burn cultivation, and their non-continuous usage of resources made easier the infiltration of peasants. As military dominance and settlement by non-tribals became established on bordering lands, their own population increase, now on a circumscribed and diminished domain, encouraged more intensified forest clearance, increased irrigation that used a counter-weighted dipstick (*denkolī*) and continued re-use of cultivated land that limited forest regrowth. Supplying forest products to neighboring multi-caste outposts would further accelerate the opening up of the forested hills and valleys of the southern and eastern Aravallis for pasturage by transhumant shepherds and farming by immigrating colonist.[23]

Such a conversion of the forest belt and incorporation of its inhabitants into a caste and state dominated society is a process that has fluctuated in accord with the fortunes of states, *ṭhikānās* and tribal chiefs. Lands once settled and made secure might again be devastated by weather, exploitation or political misfortune. Far from being a process that had run its course by the turn of the last century, moreover, it is one that continues today under new conditions.

Since India's Independence and the formation of the state of Rajasthan, the empowerment of tribals through democratic institutions and modern administration has placed limits on the usefulness of the remaining tribal belt interior of Rajasthan as niches for exploitation by those from surrounding regions. Elections are a new arena for the reemergence of tribal political consciousness and mobilization. Furthermore, legal changes in post-Independence Rajasthan – the reservation of seats for scheduled tribes in administration and governance, legal restrictions on land purchases and on foreclosure of mortgages for tribal indebtedness, the emancipation of bonded labor – limit continuing exploitation of tribal people and resources.

Nevertheless, the layering of dominion over the rights of tribals to their ancestral lands is occurring in a new manner as the modern generation of irrigation facilities, the great new dams constructed by the state, are thrown across the rivers and stream beds of south-central Rajasthan. The great Mahi Dam on the confluence of the Erau and Mahi rivers in northwestern Banswara, for example, is nearly complete. This has become a modern outpost, a planned community constructed for engineers, planners and contractors. Grid-line streets and middle class homes, with cement-floored patios and wrought iron gates, occupy the very lands of several removed Bhil villages. Over 97 other registered Bhil villages have been inundated and their inhabitants resettled in the remaining inhabited forest zone just to the north, where increased numbers will quickly accelerate the final reduction of the forest, as has already occurred over the scarred red hills to the southeast on the road to Ratlam. At the construction site, Bhils join laborers from other provinces to work on a dam that is impounding water over the dissolved mud walls of their previous homes.[24]

While such massive state-planned and implemented irrigation systems are intended to intensify agrarian production, in part through encouraging outsiders as colonists, few involved in their design realize or acknowledge that people such as those displaced by the impounded water of the Mahi dam are often the cultivators who have traditionally irrigated the lands of the area,[25] achieving higher levels of productivity than many of their caste neighbors to the north.[26] As in the past, an unstated objective of such state projects is the political and administrative penetration of the tribal area, which will be consolidated by the influx of peasants, commercial and financial agents, and officials.[27]

The search for options and occupational alternatives in the drier north has not, however, been restricted to the southern forested zone of the Aravallis, or even to the states of Rajputana. In the period at the turn of the 18th century marked by British contact and treaties with the various princely states, the pathmakers were men of the commercial classes in the towns on caravan routes between princely states or in their capitals. By the late 18th century they became involved in opium trade from Malwa and the grain trade from the Doab, expanding by the early 20th century into the port cities of Bombay and Calcutta (Timberg 1978). Others pursued trade and moneylending in more distant tribal regions in Madhya Pradesh, Assam, and into the foothills of the Terai of Nepal. The expansion of global markets under the British Raj opened up new occupations. Those who realized success in banking, international commerce, stock speculation and manufacturing in turn provided opportunities to fellow Rajasthanis as clerks, accountants, sweepers and household servants and guards of the establishment. At their sides moved cultivators, pastoralists and petty Rajput lords pursuing direct employment in armies serving British interests. Today the frontier extends into the Middle-East, where those skilled in crafts, engineering or management join an international work force constructing the new harbors, high-rises, industrial facilities and suburbs surrounding the Persian Gulf.

Strikingly, Rajasthan remains even for those most successful a homeland and community of reference. In the towns and villages they have left, they build schools, hostels, temples, *dharmaśālās*, *gośālās*, dispensaries and even universities – each to bear witness to a community of others they still regard as significant.[28] The frontier that was once within Rajputana is now found in other states and even other nations. Those who go take with them a tradition evolved for long-term survival in their own marginal home environment: family level initiative and managerial capability, a keenness to track options both inside their homeland and outside it, and a strategic sense of planning for one's family's future. These traits or attitudes of mind are common to both primary producers and their neighbors specializing in commerce, finance or priestly activities.

The Contemporary Political Significance of Peasant Adaptive Strategy

The adaptive strategies by which peasants in the Aravalli zone have historically survived the vicissitudes of an arid and semi-arid environment are directly relevant to post-Independence economic and political development in Rajasthan. Out of the earlier Rajputana period of princely states has emerged a people capable of taking advantage of opportunity at the regional, provincial, state, and global levels of the modern world.

The peasants of Rajputana have faced not only the challenges of a marginal and constantly changing environment, but that of imposed systems of feudal, and later state, domination. The same social relations, mobility, planning and values that have made possible strategic adaptation to land and climate have also provided peasants and tribals with the leverage to adjust or reorder their relationship to the dominant power (Rosin 1982). To gain access to resources, maintain his security of tenure, and limit the onerous extraction of both his labor and its fruits, the peasant has had the advantage of his landlord's dependence on his productive capacity and initiative. Threats to work other estates or migrate to other states, documented particularly for Mewar state (Ray 1978:219), where an earlier history of actual emigration depopulated the land (Tod 1957:II, 508), made more effective peasant protests that recurred throughout the 19th and early 20th centuries. The value of the opium crop produced may further explain the effectiveness of the Jat and Dhakr refusal to plough their lands in 1880, 1905 (Ray 1978:218-221) and 1916 (*ibid.*, 226-231), but also suggests how reluctant in practice peasants were to relinquish the irrigated fields enhanced for cash production by manuring and soil transport. In Bijolia in 1922, for example, the Dhakr abandoned *only* their unirrigated land during their long but successful protest against enhanced rents (*ibid.*, 231).

The primary producers have been able to turn their organizational and managerial capabilities to political advantage through massive mobilization to protest increased rents or cesses, resist extraction of free labor or services, or withdraw from productive activity. During the regime of the princely states, peasants as well as tribals mobilized on many occasions, the tragic consequences of which are well recorded in history because of the repressions that ensued (Saxena 1971, Rudolph 1981:161-164, Choudhry 1968, Government of Rajasthan 1975:74-81, 1977:50-53). Names such as Neemuchana, Shekhawati, Bijolia, Rikhabdeo and Govindpura in Begun *ṭhikānā* are recalled in the lore of local resistance to the oppression of landlords, officials and princes.

The foundations for such resistance can be found in the repertoire of social relations utilized in production and trade. While varying in their distribution along the Aravalli zone, these provide, in different local combinations, a powerful potential for political organization. Throughout the region, among the middle peasants of the Jat, Sirvi, Bishnoi and Dhakr, patrilineally extended families are reinforced by sibling-set and collateral-set marriage. The extension, elaboration and equality of affinal relations further strengthens such communities, while localized marriage networks serve to integrate them across estate and even state boundaries (Ray 1978:218). In the north, the technology and social organization for well irrigation necessitates partnerships that often cut across solidarities afforded by kinship, affinity and caste. In the south the more simplified form of single family organization for production is complemented by class homogeneity of peasant settlements and ethnic homogeneity of the tribal region. These hamlets and villages have been less effectively penetrated administratively and politically by the landholding elite and local officials (*ibid.*, 216), who normally reside in feudal towns, along with artisans, shopkeepers and the scheduled castes serving their interests. Such residential separation of the elite from the affairs of the village partially explains the vitality of intervillage caste councils to adjudicate matters of marriage, divorce and inheritance (Chauhan 1967:119-147). In the north, by contrast, the presence in the villages of the landholding elite has often involved their intervening in the affairs of the cultivating castes (Rosin 1987a:374-378).

Throughout the region, livestock fairs are held, often in association with pilgrimages as at Pushkar in Ajmer and Martri Kundiya in Mewar (Ray 1978:220), attracting peasants and buyers from hundreds of miles. The fairgrounds are laid out like a map of the region, each village having its own site, and site distances and directions from one another approximating on a reduced scale their actual locations in the countryside. The fairs complement tighter networks of kinship, marriage and village solidarity by bringing together unrelated caste members and rural folk of different castes who normally reside at great distances from one another. Through these fairs the regional peasantry recognizes its commonalities, for it is their life style and values as a class of primary producers that dominate the affair. In addition, despite dialectal differences, they share a similar language, in contrast to many of the buyers who come as foreigners from the Doab, the Gangetic plain or Malwa.

Livestock fairs and pilgrimage centers, transhumant pastoralism, commerce (Russell 1975:II, 164-165) and the out-migration of men seeking employment -- all have provided opportunities for the dissemination of information. In the early 20th century, these institutions, along with the influx of social reformers, helped link up the countryside with the ferment of Arya Samaj social reform (Sisson 1972:76) and the nationalism and *satyāgraha* strategy developing in British India (Saxena 1971:116-161). Ajmer-Mairwara, as a province first dominated by Muslims from Delhi and later by the British (Jain 1972:301-308), was centrally located as an island of influence and political refuge within Rajputana (Saxena 1971:147-149, 218-227). Also of importance was the outflow of men from Shekhawati seeking commerce, employment and military service in a larger world.

In the northern states, peasant movements crystallized into permanent associations as peasants in the period of post-Independence parliamentary democracy and land reform increasingly adapted their relations for production and trade to further the ends of political participation (Sisson 1969; 1972:73-96; Rosin 1978; 1981; Singh 1964). In the northern Aravallis, for example, kinship, affinity and partnership for production, along with recurrent participation in livestock markets, facilitated local-level organization for electoral politics. This repeatedly placed representatives of farming interests into elected office in such key northern constituencies as in Nagaur, Jhunjhunu and Sikar Districts (Sisson 1972:136-138, 142, 160-172). This large block of representatives within the Congress Party succeeded in adding to such laws as the Rajasthan Protection of Tenants Ordinance, promulgated by the new Government of Rajasthan in 1949, one in a series of ordinances and acts culminating in the Rajasthan Tenancy Act of 1955 (Dutt 1979). The new laws empowered the state to resume all lands and confer the primary title of *khatedār* to cultivators on the basis of long term tenancy, while recognizing rights of previous landlords to the lands they had personally cultivated (*khudkāsht*). By basing land entitlement on long-term tenancy, the laws benefited the bulk of cultivators throughout the Aravalli zone, for, as argued above, their ability to both enhance resources and manage agrarian production had encouraged practices that provided continuity in tenure.

The success of the Rajasthan land reform program in removing intermediary landlords and transferring land titles to peasants (Singh 1964; Rosin 1978:477; Rudolph and Rudolph 1984:50-56) rests not only on effective legislative action to fill loopholes in the law, and effective administrative implementation in the subsequent resumption of tenures, but also on the peasant community's use of the revenue courts to challenge *khudkāsht* titles granted to their landlords. In the decade following the initiation of land reform, intermediate tenancy continued to decrease as previous landlords were reluctant to hire tenants to work their *khudkāsht* lands for fear of litigation, with many of their lands falling into disuse and eventually sold on the market. Peasants, by contrast, further intensified cultivation through irrigation by means of well construction and soil improvements. The significance of all this for contemporary Rajasthan has thus been a peasantry that recognizes the relevance of direct political and judicial participation in the modern institutions of Rajasthan state to their own local-level agrarian interests.

Conclusion

The rural peoples of the northwestern Aravallis demonstrate remarkable complexity in their social relations supporting production, in their management of land and water resources, and in their computation for and planning of agrarian enterprise. The long-term outcome of such local activities has been the intensification and extention of agriculture in a region already vulnerable to the vicissitudes of weather and politics. The threat of recurring crises wrought by nature or man has encouraged the people of this region to think not only about their immediate locale, but to perceive neighboring areas as a frontier offering opportunity and alternatives for livelihood in time of stress.

This paper has introduced as a problem the possible significance of the wetter southern reaches of the Aravallis for the peoples residing in the more arid north. Sections of the wetter forested areas – occupied by a more homogeneous and less stratified population of either Bhil or Mina tribals, or such ethnically homogeneous settlers as Gerasias or Mairs – have for long periods of time resisted princely or, in the last century, British control. Such enclaves, or areas previously depopulated, offered opportunities for the people residing in surrounding areas. Historic and ethnographic sources, for example, provide evidence of movements of population into the area from Marwar, the arid region on the northwestern edge of the Aravallis. Various groups of Rathor Rajputs moved south to gain control of lands and villages. Pastoralists entered the area in search of new grazing, and some full-time cultivators settled new lands. Artisans, shopkeepers, moneylenders and priests relocated into commercial and administrative outposts, often established in tribal areas, throughout the southern zone.

Accordingly, a study of long-term adaptation in the northern sector of the Aravallis has extended our review of adaptation across the whole sweep of the Aravallis. Such a survey crossed the now unmarked boundaries of the former princely states and *ṭhikānās* of the pre-Independence British province of Rajputana. Such princely states as Marwar, Kishangarh, Kota, Tonk, Mewar and Jhalawar, as well as the British-administered Ajmer-Mairwara, differ historically not only in the composition of their ruling elites, but often in the dialect, customs and manners of their people. One of the ways to explore Rajasthan as a region, I have assumed, is to review sub-regional similarities, differences and interconnections in adaptation. Such a review, conducted here for the Aravalli zone of central Rajasthan, has provided information on land tenure patterns, and on rural social relations, management and strategic skills. This has then set the stage for understanding the contemporary level of rural participation in the judicial, electoral and administrative institutions of the modern Rajasthan state – a participation that has increasingly integrated the countryside into the modern state system.

In reviewing similarities and differences in adaptation across central Rajasthan, we have argued common principles of soil soakage and acquifer recharge utilized in the development of water resources for more intensified farming. We have described differences in technology and social relations for irrigation, with the greatest complexity shown to be in the northwest and decreasing from north to south. Throughout the Aravalli zone, we have seen the role of the peasantry in developing land and water resources and in managing production is recognized in local traditions that favor the cultivator's long-term tenancy rights. The managerial competence of the primary producers, their propensity for strategic thinking, and the security of tenure granted them by the land-holding elites are thus characteristic of the entire region. However, adaptive strategies in this zone extend beyond intensification of production to the exploitation of resources outside the immediate area. By examining how peoples securing their livelihood in the north may be engaged outside their locale in areas they experience as culturally and politically different, we have suggested the nature of the integration that has linked people across some of the former political units and differing environmental zones.

The evidence provided here is suggestive of the role peoples from the more arid north played in opening up the southern regions of the Aravallis to more intensive exploitation. The testing of such assertions much await the detailed reconstruction of the settlement history of central Rajasthan. Such a study would involve analysis of the areal distribution of castes, tribes and their respective clans; oral histories of their origins and movements; archival records of land grants, settlements and revenue collection; and chronicles of military actions, intrigues and conquests. Reconstructing the history of some of the southern towns might reveal their early stages as outposts within tribal domains. Raising the question of the strategic significance of the southern forested regions for peoples of neighboring states and estates would probably reveal that the interrelationship is not a simple, progressive opening up of the so-called tribal belt, but a fluctuating expansion and contraction of state and colonial intrusions into the area, with periods of population loss, weakened administration and reforestation.

This paper has also suggested that those who have been traditionally attentive to environmental and economic opportunity have proved to be equally alert to the political opportunity unfolding with the dissolution of the Rajputana states and the creation of the state of Rajasthan. Their very capabilities in managing and planning agrarian enterprises to secure their livelihood in an arid environment gave them the predisposition and organizational capability to make effective use of the modern instruments of democratic government. Specifically, one may cite such areas as Nagaur District, where elaborate relations of production and a vital inter-regional livestock market, along with computative skills and strategic thinking among the cultivating population, coincides with a high level of peasant mobilization and successful participation in the modern electoral process. This tendency of cultivators to manage their own enterprise as tenants with some measure of security of tenure provided the basis for legislating a land reform program that conferred on the bulk of cultivators primary title to the lands they work. That land reform benefited so many of the tenant class demonstrated the value of modern institutions of state to the interests of the rural community, thereby encouraging their continued active participation. Thus, I suggest, the peasants of central Rajasthan have adapted to the vicissitudes of Independence and the establishment of a democratic polity by learning to perceive their own interests in the new emerging frontier of the modern state.

ENDNOTES

1. As John W. Bennet states in his explication of a similar use of terms, "Adaptive strategies are generally at the conscious level in the behavior of the people involved; adaptive processes [or trends] are formulated by observers and analysts . . . " (1969:14).
2. My use of the term "transhumant" for the seasonal migrations of livestock and the people who tend them includes not only the usual application restricted to shifts between mountains and surrounding lowlands, but also shifts between an arid/semi-arid zone and better watered regions with more plentiful grazing land. During the dry season in western Rajasthan, the latter kind of migration routinely occurs.

3. Local lore, writtern records and stone memorials celebrating such public works provide records for analysis of early states in settlement history. For a well documented study in the neighboring state of Gujarat see Jutta Jain-Neubauer, *The Stepwells of Gujarat in Art-Historical perspective* (1981).
4. Today in Churu, Barmer and Jodhpur, western districts where pastoralism is central to livelihood, the percentage of total acreage cultivated is very high: 74.2% in Churu, 55% in Barmer, 52.8% in Jodhpur (Government of Rajasthan 1979: Table 3.3; R.C. Sharma 1972:34, 60).
5. For example, a semi-pervious layer of clays close to the surface near Merta city in Nagaur District enhances the retention of moisture in the soils above to permit surrounding villages a *rabī* crop of wheat and barley. Black soils in Kota District are also noted for their moisture retentiveness which makes possible two seasons of harvest (*Rajputana Gazetteer* 1879:I, 98).
6. The principle of soakage and ground water recharge tapped by percolation wells is stated in 19th-century British accounts in regard to the effect of natural rivers and streams, but is not extended to the man-made lakes and reservoirs:

   > It is in relation to the wells that the rivers may truly be said to fertilize the country. On each side of the streams the water percolates for a considerable distance, and large supplies are retained in the soil, comparatively near the surface: it is here that the wells are numerous and least expensive. They are called "seja," or spring wells, from the belief that the spring is reached; but the constant supply seems solely due to the more rapid percolation. "Akara" is the other kind, avowedly percolation wells; they are sunk much deeper and are therefore much more expensive, and the supply of water is more precarious, than in "seja" wells (*Rajputana Gazetteer* 1880:III, 14-15).

   Such a pattern of well concentration alongside both perennial and temporary streams is visible today in Landsat satellite remote-sensing imagery of the irrigated winter wheat crop over Rajasthan during the months of December and January, when the luxuriousness of the crop stands out in sharp contrast to the surrounding barrenness of the unirrigated lands. The crop land clusters along smaller streams coalescing into the larger river beds, surrounds lakes and tanks, and concentrates in the long valleys between the ridges of the Aravallis where subterranean water flow is channeled by the impervious strata of the ridges reaching under the alluvium.
7. One of the earliest dam and canal delivery systems for irrigation in Rajputana constructed in consultation with British engineers was completed under the maharaja of Kota in 1877 to water 12,000 acres along the Parvati river, predating by decades the grander and better known Ganganagar canal project initiated by the maharaja of Bikaner and completed in 1927.
8. The great artificial lakes served a variety of purposes. They were often constructed, as was Raj Samand in 1681, to provide relief work for subjects destitute because of famine (*Rajputana Gazetteer* 1880:III, 13). While providing water to support great towns and capitals, they created magnificent settings for temples, royal pavillions and gardens. Canals such as those constructed at Phul Sagar in Bundi were often to bring "the source of water-supply to the adjoining pleasure-garden, said to have been constructed by, or for, a concubine of Rao Raja Bhoj Singh in Sambat 1659" (1879:I, 218). In other cases, as in Nainwa,

the very embankments impounding the water may have been constructed with "the view of strengthening the fortifications of the town" (1879:I, 217).

9. For Mewar, the *Rajputana Gazetteer* stated, " . . . almost every village may be said to have a tank, some very large: the water is used considerably for irrigating the fields below the dam, but, being conveyed only in channels dug in the soil, the waste is very great" (1880:III, 14).
10. Thus the gazetteer for Mewar stated the following: "The extensive plains of the Meywar plateau are fertile when irrigated. Almost every village has its artificial lake or tank. Behind the retaining embankments, or in the beds of these tanks, and wherever there are wells, large crops of wheat are grown, and here and there cotton, opium, and sugarcane" (*Rajputana Gazetteer* 1879:I, 98). In this quote, "irrigation" is applied to direct soakage received in the bed of the tank or the lands behind the embankment, not to those lying below it.
11. The extensive occurrence of partnerships in eastern Marwar may prove to have been more a direct response to the labor required from men and bullocks to deepen wells already dug, than to the labor required annually for irrigation. Since Independence, the replacement of human and animal power by the use of pumping sets made possible by rural electrification has resulted in the breaking up of partnerships at the wells. An emerging problem among farmers today is obtaining the manpower necessary to deepen their wells in order to tap a lowering water table. In the past, partners provided such improvements during the dry season, which saved the cost of hiring others as laborers.
12. In Nagaur District, I have observed the use of a set of 80 stones to compute a cycle of 320 deliveries of water by leather bag from a well. Two of the four partners at a well take turns at driving their respective teams of bullocks down the ramp away from the wellhead in order to draw the line lifting a leather bag of water from the well. One partner keeps count of both of their deliveries, by moving one pebble in a pile of 80 to a second pile on each circuit he makes in driving his bullock down the ramp. When the first pile has been emptied of pebbles, each marking a double delivery of water, he replaces them in turn on the original pile, which when filled records a total of 320 deliveries. This completion of 320 deliveries marks the end of a shift, at which point all the partners rotate their work positions and shift their teams of bullocks between work and rest. Three rotations, totalling 960 deliveries, constitute a normal day of irrigation, with two additonal rotations occurring during the night during the peak of the growing season. Using a water-bag that holds four maunds (or 352 pounds) of water, this totals 281.67 tons (i.e., 67,555 gallons) of water per 24-hour day, drawn from depths of 60 to 100 feet!
13. Thorn branches are available for fencing as a result of the extensive pruning of such indigenous trees as the *khejaṛī* (*Prosopis spicigera*) for pod and leaf as livestock feed – a practice that is a part of the "agro-forest system" involving interdependencies between trees, field crops and animal husbandry analyzed by Michie (1984:30-34) for the rain-fed *kharīf* lands. The complexity of the pattern and recognition of its benefits by those who practice it further highlights the sophistication of the cultivating tenants.
14. This practice is not distinctive to Rajputana, but extends southward into Malwa and central India for those communities Adrian Mayer calls the "allied castes" (1960:33-60). Such practices are also recorded in South India by Brenda Beck,

in the case of a peasant community similarly capable in the management and extension of production (1979:56).

15. In the succession rites of a Rajput chieftain to territories previously conquered, the Bhil, Mina and Jat inhabitants were ritually recognized. At a crucial point in the proceedings, their representatives stepped forward to apply a *tilak* to the chieftain's forehead. Thus to be invested as Rajput chieftain required symbolic recognition by the original inhabitants, an act that assumed their important position and rights as inhabitants under him.
16. Short-term shifts in population in Marwar are evident in Dhir's fascinating study, "The Human Factor in Ecological History" (1982:311-331). While he documents a population increase in Marwar state from the year 1660 to the year 1891 (as recorded by the then chief revenue officer, Muhanot Nainsi), a closer look at his data in graph form (pp. 322-323) suggests a loss of approximately 400,000 people between 1820 and 1881 (in a state with a previous high of 2 million persons). Another decrease in population between 1891 and 1921, as corroborated by Malhotra (1977), resolves into two periods of delcine: 1891 to 1901, which coincides with the severe drought and famine of 1899 (Bharara 1982:353-355; Timberg 1978:101), and 1911-1921, a period of population decline for Rajasthan and India as a whole (Dhir 1982:324).
17. Rajasthan and Kerala are the only two states in India in which the out-migration of women exceeds that of men. This reflects not only the fact that women relocate after marriage in accord with rules of village exogamy and virilocal residence, but that women, "largely illiterate and unskilled," migrate in response to "the demand in Delhi and other northwestern Indian cities for cheap Rajasthani female labor" (Libbee 1980:82). This movement of women form the laborer castes does not weaken the family, but rather supports the nuclear family traditions favored by such castes by keeping husband, wife and children together during their urban employment.
18. While accounts of early contact are recorded for Rajasthan (Tod 1957:I, 137-138, 181-183; II, 141, 280-283), the actual process of penetration, exploitation and incorporation of such tribal zones into caste society is poorly recorded. For example, in describing the settlement of the Pali region, abutting the edge of the Aravallis in the southwest of Marwar, G.D. Sharma states, ". . . in order to extend cultivation and to populate the area, the Jats, Rajputs, etc., were invited from the neighboring territories to settle in the villages of Pali. This could be the immediate cause of the hostility of the Mers" (1977:2). Such accounts of the developing relations between colonists and previously settled peoples only introduce the process, with all further reference shifting to the higher levels of political contest and control among overlords, nobles, chiefs and rajas.
19. For the process in other regions of South Asia, see the works of F.G. Bailey, C. von Furer-Haimendorf, M. Orans, S. Sinha, G.D. Berreman, V. Elwin, S. Fuchs.
20. Utilizing many sources on neighboring Uttar Pradesh, Thomas Metcalf provides a valuable analysis of Rajput settlers gaining control over land tracts from the lower Doab across Oudh to Banaras (1979:3-16). See particularly the role of intrigue and "guile" (*ibid.*, 3-5).

21. The founding stage, however, involved only a localized movement of settlers from neighboring villages and towns.
22. "Owing to the disorganization and lawlessness which so long prevailed in Sirohi, the cultivating classes [probably Kilis, Kunbis and Ganchis] must, judging by the number of deserted wells, have left in considerable numbers. Those who remained here, apparently through a feeling of insecurity, cultivated but little more land than was sufficient to supply their own wants; so fully nine-tenths of the land is still uncultivated and covered with dense jungle, a secure refuge for outlaws and plunderers" (*Rajputana Gazetteer* 1880:III, 90). For Mewar raids on Sirohi, see pp. 90, 100.
23. One can observe various stages in the establishment of multi-caste towns seeking to incorporate a tribal hinterland by studying the town of Sohagpura among the Minas on the border of the former state of Pratapgarh, or Bhoongra and Khamera among the Bhils in the northeastern forests of Banswara District. As revealed in the 1971 census, Bhoongra, which is located off a dirt track, is comprised of 87% non-scheduled castes, surrounded by countryside comprised of nearly 100% tribal peoples. In the heart of Bhil country, in a district comprised of 73% tribal peoples, the city of Banswara has a population of only 6.4% tribal peoples (86.1% non-scheduled castes), while surrounding villages have 100% tribal peoples.
24. The small Bhil village of Jhumpriya in Chittorgarh Tehsil is the site of a tragedy demanding investigation. Once intensively cultivated lands in the valley reappeared from under water in 1982, after only two years of drought in the area. During wet years, the Bhil village borders a man-made lake from which they can derive no livelihood, while their multi-caste neighbors in the village of Begariya across the eastern ridge receive irrigation waters through an elevated aqueduct from the base of the 50-foot high dam completed by the Rajasthan government. The tribal villages upstream from the Ujar river dam under construction at Mora might be a similar example of this process.
25. In 1882,.prior to their subjugation by the maharana, for example, the Bhils in Udaipur state were irrigating a second annual crop. Dr. Stratton, the official British Resident in Mewar, records their losses in resisting the state forces: "They sacrificed their spring crops, which withered on ceasing to be watered. They lost also the produce of the mango and 'mahwa' trees this season . . . Beyond this they have left a location which, for a Pal [hamlet], is singularly well favoured, from its extent and excellence both for cultivation, grazing, and jungle produce" (Saxena 1971:175).
26. Today, the areas in Rajasthan with the greatest percentage of tribals (districts Banswara 72.9%, Dungarpur 63.6%, Udaipur 33.7%) have the largest percentage of sown area that is double-cropped or multi-cropped, with the highest productivity (6.47 maunds of wheat per *bīghā* in Banswara, 6.23 in Dungarpur, 5.77 in Udaipur) and the highest percentage of cultivated area irrigated (Banswara 12.07%, Dungarpur 13.3%, Udaipur 42.3%) (*Census of India* 1971: Tables 3.1, 3.3, 4.2).
27. Fürer-Haimendorf states the problem for the whole of India: "Yet the drive for modernization and industrialization pursued by all Indian governments committed to the improvement of the country's standard of living does not augur well for the future of the tribal populations affected by projects promising

to raise industrial output. This applies in particular to hydroelectric and irrigation projects located in hilly country inhabited by tribals whose land is to be submerged by the construction of reservoirs" (1982:321).

28. The most recent wealth, mostly remittances from the Middle-East, is invested in improved homes and irrigation facilities, and stereo cassette decks to tape local devotional music. Next in the offing are videocassette recorders.

REFERENCES CITED

Banerjee, Anil Chandra
1951 *The Rajput States and the East India Company*. Calcutta: A.K. Mukherjee.
Beck, Brenda E.F.
1979 "Centers and Boundaries of a Regional Caste System." In *Perspectives on a Regional Culture*. Brenda E.F. Beck, ed. pp. 54-92. New Delhi: Vikas.
Bennett, John W.
1969 *Northern Plainsmen: Adaptive Strategy and Agrarian Life*. Chicago: Aldine.
Bharara, L.P.
1982 "Notes on the Experience of Drought: Perception, Recollection and Prediction." In *Desertification and Development: Dryland Ecology in Social Perspective*. Brian Spooner and H.S. Mann, eds., pp. 351-361. New York: Academic Press.
Census of India
1971 *Census of India. Series 18 (Rajasthan). Part V. Special Tables and Notes on Scheduled Castes and Scheduled Tribes*. Jaipur: Census Operations.
CAZRI (Central Arid Zone Research Institute)
1977 *Case Study on Desertification: Luni Development Block*. United Nations Conference on Desertification. UNESCO.
Chauhan, Brij Raj
1967 *A Rajasthan Village*. New Delhi: Associated Publishing House.
Choudhry, P.S.
1968 *Rajasthan Between the Two World Wars (1919-1939)*. Agra: Sri Ram Megra and Company.
Dhir, R.P.
1982 "The Human Factor in Ecological History." In *Desertification and Development: Dryland Ecology in Social Perspective*. Brian Spooner and H.S. Mann, eds. pp. 311-331. New York: Academic Press.
Dutt, S.K.
1979 *Tenancy Law in Rajasthan*. Jaipur: Western Law Publishers.
Furer-Haimendorf, Christoph von
1982 *Tribes of India: The Struggle for Survival*. Berkeley: University of California Press.
Government of Rajasthan
1975 *District Gazetteers: Bhilwara*. Jaipur: Government Central Press.
1977 *Rajasthan District Gazetteers: Chittaurgarh*. Jaipur: Government Central Press.

1979 *Statistical Abstracts*. Jaipur: Directorate of Economics and Statistics.

Jain, Kailash Chand

1972 *Ancient Cities and Towns of Rajasthan*. Delhi: Motilal Banarsidass.

Jain-Neubauer, Jutta

1981 *The Stepwells of Gujarat in Art-Historical Perspective*. New Delhi: Abhinav Publications.

Jodha, N.S.

1982 "The Role of Administration in Desertification: Land Tenure as a Factor in the Historical Ecology of Western Rajasthan." In *Desertification and Development: Dryland Ecology in Social Perspective*. Brian Spooner and H.S. Mann, eds. pp. 333-350.

Kolenda, Pauline

1978 "Sibling-Set Marriage, Collateral-Set Marriage and Deflected Alliance among Annana Jats of Jaipur District, Rajasthan." In *American Studies in the Anthropology of India*. Sylvia Vatuk, ed. pp. 242-277. New Delhi: Manohar Press.

Libbee, Michael J.

1980 "Territorial Endogamy and the Spatial Structure of Marriage in Rural India." In *An Exploration of India*. David E. Sopher, ed. pp 65-104. Ithica: Cornell University Press.

Lodrick, Deryck O.

1984 "A Cattle Fair in Rajasthan: The Kharwa Mela." *Current Anthropology* 25:218-225.

Malhotra, S.P.

1977 "Socio-Demographic Factors and Nomadism in the Arid Rajasthan." In *Desertification and Its Control*. P.L. Jaiswal, ed. New Delhi: Indian Council of Agricultural Research.

Malhotra, S.P. and H.S. Mann

1982 "Desertification and the Organization of Society." In *Desertification and Development: Dryland Ecology in Social Perspective*. Brian Spooner and H.S. Mann, eds. pp. 305-310. New York: Academic Press.

Mathur, H.M.

1976 *Development Administration in Tribal Areas*. Jaipur: The HCM State. Institute of Public Administration.

Mayer, Adrian C.

1970 *Caste and Kinship in Central India: A Village and Its Region*. Berkeley: University of California Press.

Metcalf, Thomas R.

1979 *Land, Landlords, and the British Raj: Northern India in the Nineteenth Century*. Berkeley: University of California Press.

Rajputana Gazetteer

1879 *The Rajputana Gazetteer. Vols. I & II*. Calcutta: Office of the Superintendent of Government Printing.

1880 *The Rajputana Gazetteer Vol. III*. Simla: Government Central Branch Press.

Ray, Rajat K.

1978 "Mewar: The Breakdown of the Princely Order." In *People, Princes and Paramount Power: Society and Politics in the Indian Princely States*. Robin Jeffrey, ed. pp. 205-239. Delhi: Oxford University Press.

Rosin, R. Thomas
1968 "Changing Land Tenure and Village Polity in Rajasthan, India: An Interractional Perspective." Ph.D. Dissertation, Anthropology Department, University of California at Berkeley.
1978 "Peasant Adaptation as Process in Land Reform: A Case Study." In *American Studies in the Anthropology of India*. Sylvia Vatuk, ed. pp. 460-495. New Delhi: Manohar Publications.
1981 "Land Reform in Rajasthan." *Current Anthropology* 22:75-76.
1982 "The Social Foundation for Mobilized Peasant and Tribal in Rajputana." *Political Science Review* (Rajasthan University) 21:73-82.
1984 "Gold Medallions: The Arithmetic Calculations of an Illiterate." *Anthropology and Education Quarterly* 15:38-50.
1987a *Land Reform and Agrarian Change: Study of a Marwar Village from Raj to Swaraj*. Jaipur: Rawat Publications.
1987b "Quarry and Field: Sources of Continuity and Change in a Rajasthan Village." In *Dimensions of Social Life: Essays in Honor of David Mandelbaum*. Paul Hockings, ed. Berlin: Mouton de Gruyter.

Rudolph, Susan Hoeber
1981 "The Search for 'The Indigenous' in the Study of Indian Princely States." *Reviews in Anthropology*: 157-165.

Rudolph, Susanne Hoeber and Lloyd I. Rudolph
1984 "The Political Modernization of an Indian Feudal Order." In *Essays on Rajputana*, by Susanne Hoeber Rudolph and Lloyd I. Rudolph, pp. 38-78. New Delhi: Concept Publishing Company.

Russell, Robert Vane
1975 *The Tribes and Castes of the Central Provinces of India*. 4 vols. Delhi: Cosmo. (1st ed. 1916)

Saxena, K.S.
1971 *The Political Movements and Awakening in Rajasthan (1857 to 1947)*. New Delhi: S. Chand and Company.

Saxena, Ranvir Prakash
1964 *Tribal Economy in Central India*. Calcutta: Firma K.L. Mukhopadhyay.

Sharma, G.B.
1976 "Abolition of Bonded Labour in Rajasthan." In *Agrarian Reform and Rural Development*. Hari Mohan Mathur, ed. pp. 173-189. Jaipur: The HCM State Institute of Public Administration.

Sharma, G.D.
1977 *Rajput Polity: A Study of Politics and Administration of the State of Marwar, 1638-1749*. New Delhi: Manohar Press.

Sharma, G.N.
1968 *Social Life in Medieval Rajasthan (1500-1800 A.D.)*. Agra: Lakshmi Narain Agarwal.

Sharma, R.C.
1972 *Settlement Geography of the Indian Desert*. New Delhi: Kumar Brothers.

Singh, Dool
1964 *Land Reforms in Rajasthan*. New Delhi: Government of India, Planning Commission, Reserved Programmes Committee.

Sinha, Surajit

1962 "State Formation and Rajput Tribal Myth in Central India." *Man in India* 42:35-80.

Sisson, Richard

1969 "Peasant Movements and Political Mobilization: The Jats of Rajasthan." *Asian Survey* 9:946-963.

1972 *The Congress Party in Rajasthan: Political Integration and Institution Building in an Indian State*. Berkeley: University of California Press.

Timberg, Thomas A.

1978 *The Marwaris: From Traders to Industrialists*. New Delhi: Vikas Publishing House.

Tod, James

1957 *Annals and Antiquities of Rajast'han*. 2 vols. London: Routledge and Kegan Paul Ltd. (1st ed. 1829-32)

THE JOINT-FAMILY HOUSEHOLD IN RURAL RAJASTHAN: ECOLOGICAL, CULTURAL AND DEMOGRAPHIC CONDITIONS FOR ITS OCCURRENCE

PAULINE KOLENDA

One of the most characteristic social institutions of Rajasthan is the rural joint-family household. Often considered to be one of the most characteristic social institutions in India as a whole, the joint-family takes it place beside caste and the arranged marriage as close to universal in India. The 1961 Census of India was one of the first to collect data on household composition, enabling comparative analysis of family household structure between different states, regions, and districts. Comparison of the 1961 household composition tables for 326 districts and territories was reported in an earlier paper (Kolenda and Haddon 1987). Mapping of various measures of the occurence of joint-family households revealed that in proportion to the population, there were more rural joint-family households in Rajasthan than in any other state (Kolenda and Haddon 1987:227-238; see Maps 1 and 2 below.)

What accounts for this high occurrence of joint-family households in Rajasthan? This is the probelm I try to solve in this paper. I draw on three kinds of data – cultural, derived from ethnographies of various villages in Rajasthan, most done by Census ethnographers, others done by other anthropologists and by myself; demographic, namely statistics derived from a variety of tabulations in the 1961 Census; and ecological, derived from Census District Gazetteers, geographical works, and especially important, from mapping done by A.K. Sen of the Central Arid Zone Research Institute in Jodhpur, Rajasthan.

The Concept of Joint-Family Household as Used in the Census of India

There are two aspects to the definition of the joint-family household, that of composition – who belongs to a joint-family? – and that of location and boundaries – how does one locate a joint-family and distinguish it from other families and other social units? There has been much more agreement about the functional location and boundaries of the family than about its composition. The problem of definition of family structure is one I addressed in the past (Kolenda 1968:344-349; also Kolenda 1987:8-16); the conclusions of that effort are briefly stated here and are used in the present analysis.

The functional definition of the joint-family established by the Census of India more than a hundred years ago is relatives who eat from the same kitchen (*chūlhā* in Hindi), or the 'hearth-group'. This definition has been used by many social scientists, as well as the Census, and its use has made for consistency, enabling comparability between studies. This is not the ideal definition of joint-family for all research purposes, as a *chūlha*-group is almost always linked socially and economically to others, and it is a wider *set* of *chūlhā*-groups that functions in many contexts as the joint-family. The households in the C-I Tables of the Census of India, central to this study, are *chūlhā*-groups, however, and the ethnographers who studied hundreds of villages in the 1960s for the Census also used that functional definition. The problem of this paper is thus, more precisely: why, according to the Census of India-1961, were there more joint-family hearth-groups in Rajasthan in proportion to the population than in other Indian states?

As for composition of the joint-family household, while Indians are often inconsistent in their use of the term 'joint-family', they are usually referring to a household consisting of two or more related couples. English-speaking Indians generally use the one term 'joint-family', but there are various terms for it in Indian languages. The villagers in the village I studied in Jaipur district used the expression *pūṇā parivār* (literally 'the complete family').

Usually a joint-family is composed of parents and one married son, his wife and their children (the patrilineal joint-family), but there can also be more than one married son (the patrilineal-collateral joint-family). While most Indians trace their descent and structure their families along the father-son line, the culturally prescribed structure among some communities in the northeast and southwest is along the mother-child line (the matrilineal joint-family). In Rajasthan, the norm is the patrilineal joint-family. Consistent with my previous work (1967, 1968, 1987:1-154; Kolenda and Haddon 1987), I will follow the Census definition: a joint-family is a household composed of two or more related couples. While anthropologists might consider the Indian joint-family to fall under the more general rubric of 'extended family', I prefer here to be consistent with Indian usage.

Household Tables in the Census of India-1961

The 1961 census examined a 20% sample of all households (hearth-groups) within every district and territory of India, tabulating their composition under the rubrics of head, spouse of head, other married relatives (sons, other males, other females), unmarried relatives (never married, widowed or divorced, separated) and unrelated persons. The data are presented in the C-I Tables of the Census, entitled "Composition of Sample Households by Relationship to Head of Family Classified by Size of Land Cultivated."[1] These tables divide each district or territory's population into rural and urban. In this paper, I am concerned only with the statistics for rural populations. Since over 80% of the Indian population lived in rural areas in 1961, we are concerned with the households of the vast majority of Indians at that time.

The reader may ask why I report a study done with data from the 1961 Census rather than the 1981 Census. One answer is that conditions in Rajasthan a generation ago were probably closer to those which fostered joint-family households in past centuries than are the changed conditions of the 1980s. For example, land reform, which began in Rajasthan in 1952, significantly affected household structures, at least as these were reported to Census-takers in 1961, and it is likely that it continued to stimulate changes for a decade or more. While it would add greatly to this study to compare the 1961 figures with those of 1981, this study involved reference to scores of different volumes of the Census of India 1961, and sufficient comparable volumes from the 1981 Census have only recently become available in United States libraries. It might be possible at present to replicate this study with 1971

Census data if the enterprise proved worthwhile. The 1961 analysis should, in any case, serve as a 'baseline' against which to compare changes in household distribution in 1971 and 1981 and in subsequent censuses.

The 1961 data showed marked regional differences in family structure. These were revealed by mapping two indices derived from the C-I Tables. By dividing the total rural population in the 20% sample of all households in a district into the number of Married Sons residing with the heads of those households, the resulting percentage was used as an index of the prevalence of the patrilineal joint-family, as one can expect that where a larger percentage of the persons in the sample households are Married Sons of the household head, there are more patrilineal joint-families. In the same way, the total number in the 20% sample of households was divided into the total for Other Married Relatives (excluding the spouse), as one can also expect that where a larger proportion of the persons in the sample households are Other Married Relatives, there is a larger proportion of lineal, collateral, lineal-collateral and other types of joint-families. (Note, of course, that one kind of Other Married Relative is the Married Son.)

The method used for mapping these two variables and others based on Census data was to rank all districts and territories on the variable and then divide them into quintiles. The 326 districts and territories of this study[2] are divided into 4 quintiles of 65 districts each, and one quintile (Quintile 3) with 66 districts. The districts with the highest values on a variable are in Quintile 1, those with the lowest in Quintile 5. Thus, Maps 1 and 2 show the districts in Quintile 1 and Quintile 5 for the two measures of joint-family, the *proportions of Married Sons* and the *proportions of Other Married Relatives* in the household sample populations. Mapping of these two indices of joint-family should be a reasonably sound guide to those regions where joint-families occur with high frequency and those where they are more rare.

Looking first at Map 1, we see that districts in Quintile 1 on proportions of Married Sons, indicating high proportions of patrilineal joint-families, form a belt of 62 districts across northern India – 15 in Rajasthan, contiguous with 14 in Madhya Pradesh, 25 in Uttar Pradesh, and 8 in Bihar. Districts in Quintile 5 cluster in two blocks, one in the northeast, composed of all the districts of Assam, some territories beyond Assam, and some of the districts

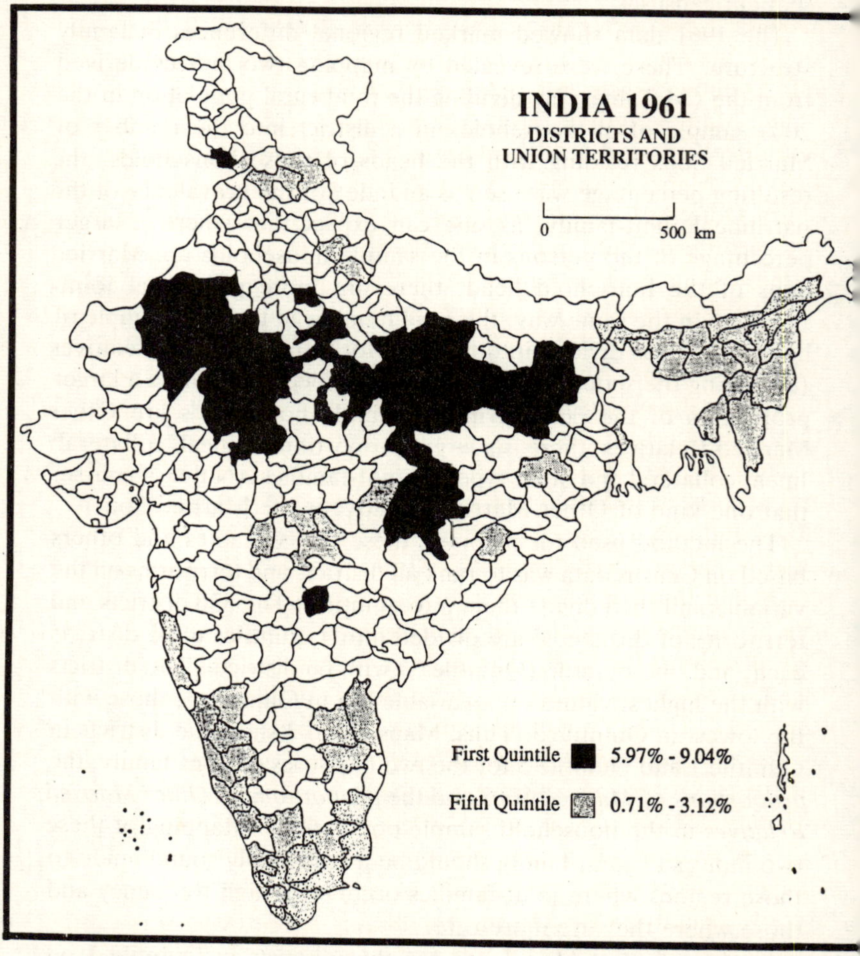

Map 1: **Proportions of Joint-Families in India as Measured by Proportions of Married Sons in 20% Sample of Households (Census of India 1961)**

of West Bengal, the other in the southwest, composed of Kerala and parts of Madras, Andhra Pradesh and Mysore. Map 2, showing quintiles based on Other Married Relatives, indicating high proportions of all types of joint-families, shows a similar pattern of a Quintile 1 belt across the waist of India and two Quintile 5 clusters, one in the northeast and one in the south, with a few Quintile 1 and Quintile 5 districts scattered elsewhere.[3]

On Map 3 and on subsequent maps, each district outside Quintile 1 has within its outline the quintile number to which it belongs. Map 3 shows the 15 districts out of Rajasthan's 26 which fall in Quintile 1 on Married Sons, an index of the occurrence of the patrilineal joint-family there. This is the highest proportion of Quintile 1 districts for a single state (58%), as compared to 25 out of 54 districts (46%) for Uttar Pradesh, 14 out of 43 (33%) for Madhya Pradesh, 8 out of 17 (47%) for Bihar, one district each for Jammu Kashmir, Andhra Pradesh and Himachal Pradesh, and no districts in the other eight states and nine territories. In addition to the 15 districts of Rajasthan in Quintile 1, there are five in Quintile 2. Thus 20 out of Rajasthan's 26 districts (76%) are above average in frequency of joint-family households in the all-India perspective, since Quintiles 1 and 2 constitute together the upper 40% of all districts and territories. Three of the remaining districts in Rajasthan are in the third or 'average' quintile, and three in the fourth, a below average quintile; none are in Quintile 5, the lowest.

Map 4 shows the 11 districts in Rajasthan which fall in Quintile 1 on Other Married Relatives, and eight other districts that are in Quintile 2. Thus 19 out of Rajasthan's 26 districts (73%) are above average in joint-family households as indexed by Other Married Relatives. Of the remaining districts, one is in Quintile 3, five are in Quintile 4, and one is in the lowest, Quintile 5.

Thus, according to the figures of the 1961 Census, there were at that time more rural joint-family households (hearth-groups) in Rajasthan in proportion to the population than in any other state of India. What accounts for this high proportion? The remainder of this paper is devoted to exploring this question through analysis of demographic, cultural and ecological factors.

Ethnographic Fieldwork in Rajasthan

My own ethnographic fieldwork in Rajasthan was guided by preliminary, incomplete versions of Maps 1 and 2 that I prepared

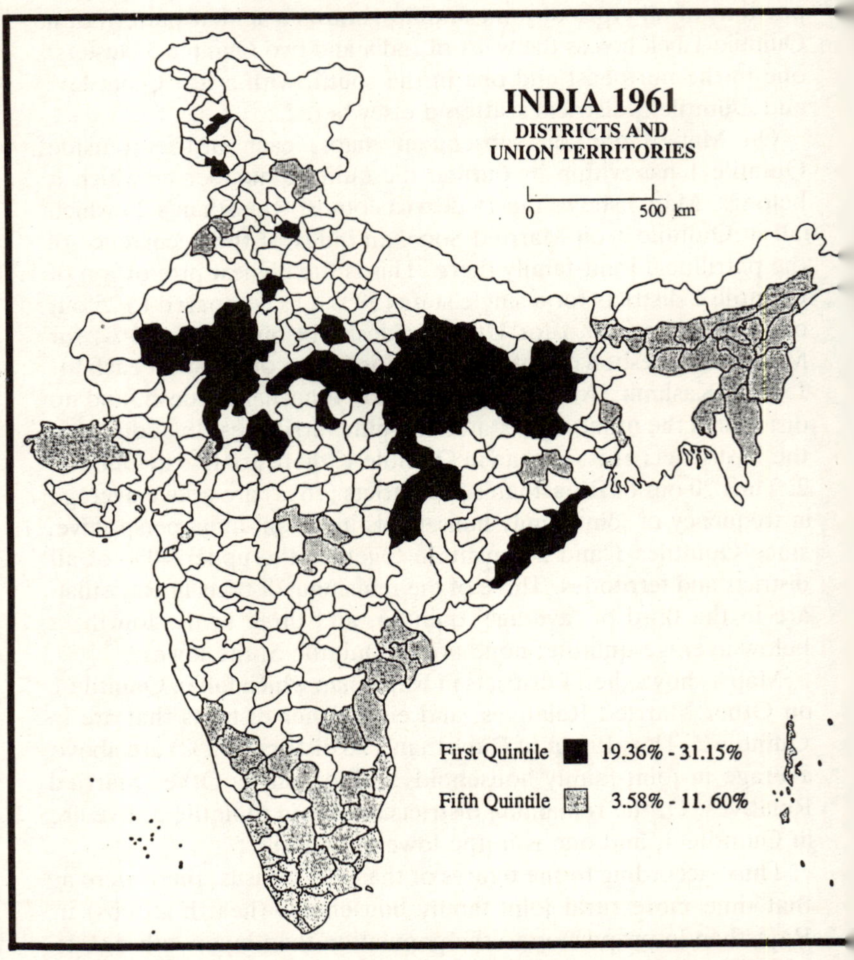

Map 2: **Proportions of Joint-Families in India as Measured by Proportions of "Other Married Relatives" in 20% Sample of Households (Census of India 1961)**

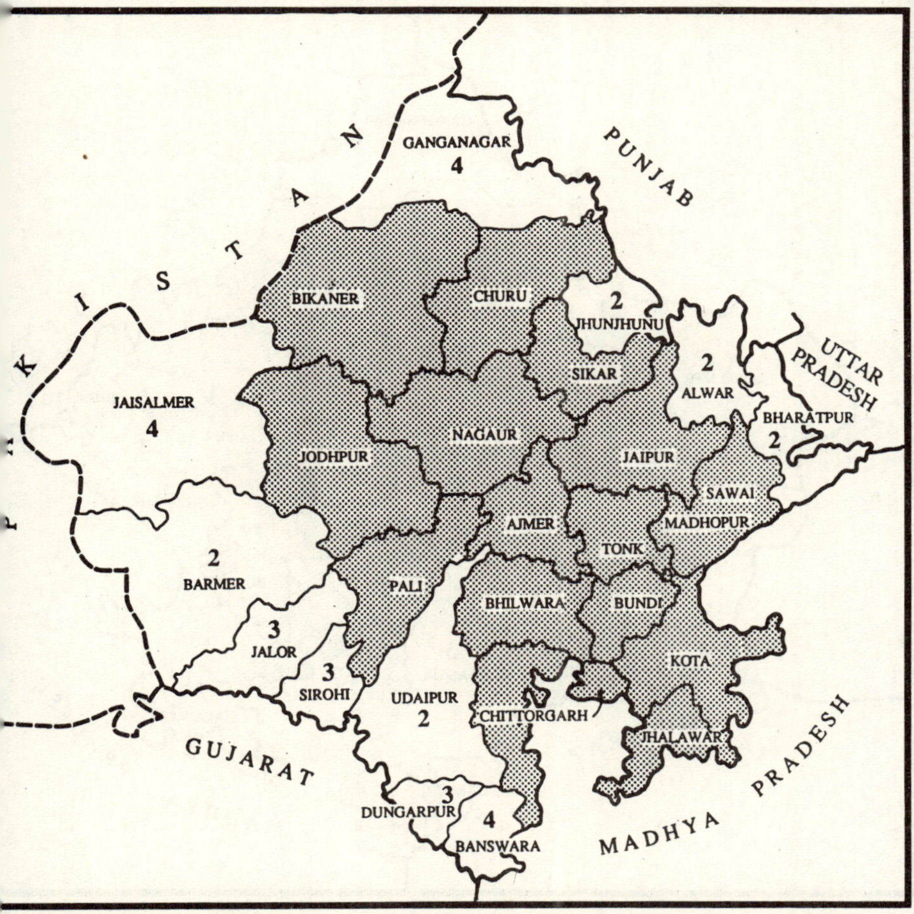

Map 3: **Districts in Rajasthan with Highest Proportions of Joint-Families as Measured by First Quintile Rankings on Proportions of Married Sons in 20% Sample of Households (Census of India 1961). Quintiles to which other districts belong are noted by numbers within the district boundaries.**

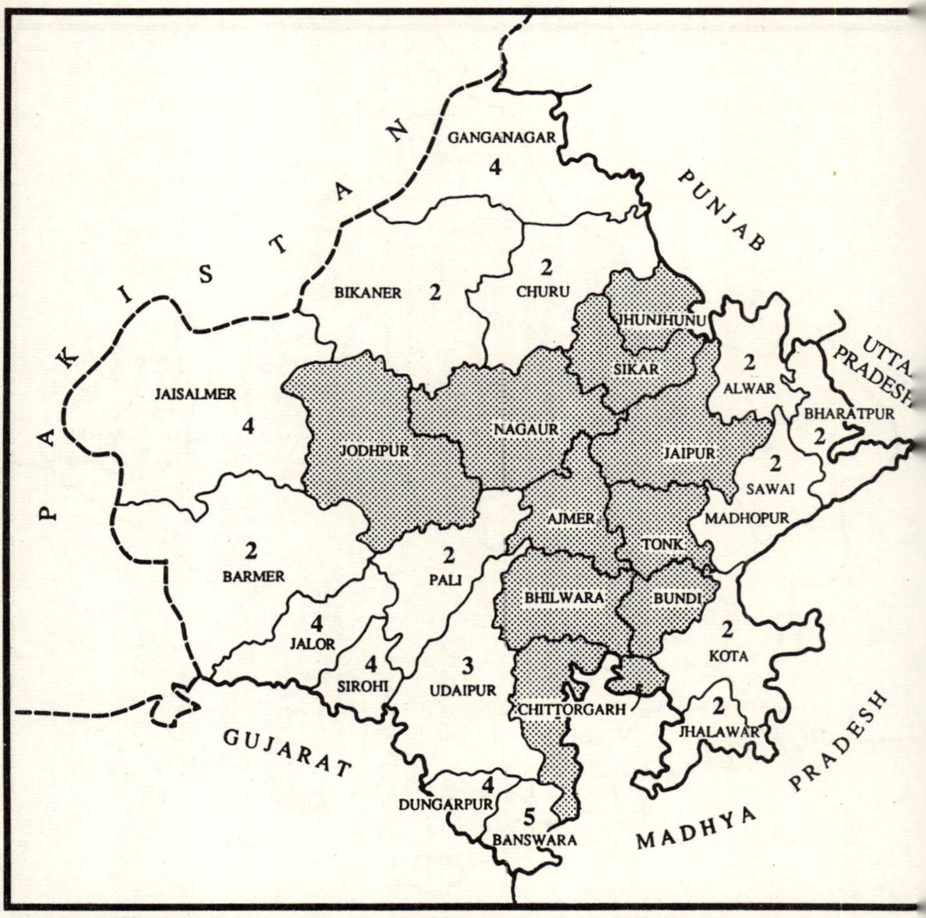

Map 4: **Districts in Rajasthan with Highest Proportions of Joint-Families as Measured by First Quintile Rankings on Proportions of "Other Married Relatives" in 20% Sample of Households (Census of India 1961). Quintiles to which other districts belong are noted by numbers within the district boundaries.**

in the summer of 1966, using the 1961 Census volumes then available. On the basis of these maps, I chose six districts in various parts of India in which to do fieldwork, one of them Jaipur district in Rajasthan. By observation of families in their villages, I hoped to discover the essential conditions for joint-family structure. In this paper, I draw on my field notes and published and unpublished articles (Kolenda 1969, 1978a, 1978b, 1987:178-213) concerning the linked villages of Maharajapur-Kishanpur, 13 miles west of the city of Jaipur, where my research assistant, Indira Sapru, and I worked for five months in 1966-67. Mrs. Sapru has gone back to Maharajapur-Kishanpur several times to gather further data, and we have worked there together for brief periods in 1969, 1974, 1978 and 1985.

In Maharajapur-Kishanpur, with a population of 367 in 1966, consisting almost entirely of the two well-known Rajasthani ethnic groups, Jats (63% of the population) and Minas (25%), I expected to find high proportions of joint-families. There were indeed high proportions – 31% of the Jat families and 49.5% of the Jat population lived in joint-families, as did 21.5% of the Mina families and 46.5% of the Mina population. (See Tables 1 and 2 for the full distributions).

***Table 1*: Proportions of Joint-Families among the Jats of Maharajapur-Kishanpur (from Kolenda 1987b: 243; 1987: 179)**

Type of Family	Families		Persons	
	no.	%	no.	%
Joint	12	31	131	49.5
Supplemented nuclear	9	25	66	24
Nuclear	12	31	51	20
Polygynous	1	3.25	6	3
Supplemented sub-nuclear	1	3.25	3	1.5
Sub-nuclear	1	3.25	3	1.5
Single person	1	3.25	1	.5
	37	100	261	100

An unexpected factor emerged, one not previously highlighted in Indian or other ethnography: the existence of very high proportions of sibling-set and collateral-set marriages. This was the custom of a set of two or three brothers marrying a set of two or

Table 2: **Proportions of Joint-Families among the Minas of Maharajapur-Kishanpur (from Kolenda 1969: 29)**

Type of Family	Families		Persons	
	no.	%	no.	%
Joint	3	21.5	39	46.5
Supplemented nuclear	3	21.5	22	26
Nuclear	5	35.5	19	22.5
Single-person	2	14	2	2.5
Other	1	7.5	2	2.5
	14	100	84	100

three sisters or 'cousin-sisters' (father's brother's daughter to each other), or other sets of women who were close relatives.[4] The male set might be 'cousin-brothers' (father's brother's son to each other) or other sets of men who were close relatives. Almost two thirds (63%) of Maharajapur-Kishanpur Jat daughters were married in sibling- or collateral-sets (Kolenda 1978b:253; 1987:190), as were 60% of Mina wives (Kolenda, 1969:53). This very strong marital pattern double-bonded the joint families of Maharajapur-Kishanpur, so that not only were the adult males of a family brothers, but the adult females were sisters or cousin-sisters as well as sisters-in-law (brothers' wives). A newly in-married woman would not be entirely among strangers, because her older sister might be in the same household; her aunt (father's sister) might live in a household nearby, as might other women from her village. She could thus, presumably, make an easier adjustment to her life as a married woman and be less likely to develop hostile relations with her sisters-in-law. Such double-bonding might ensure greater harmony between women and, hence, a joint-family would be less likely to fragment into its component nuclear units.

The villagers themselves did not emphasize joint-family double-bonding through sibling-set or collateral-set marriages; rather, they emphasized the economy in affinal ties thus established. The expenses of the wedding and of subsequent gift-giving and hospitality are indeed curtailed if two married daughters share the same set of affinal kin, or two daughters-in-law share the same set of natal kin. Furthermore, the difficulty of seeking bridegrooms for daughters is less if two or three marry into the same family. Despite the villagers' ability to cite some sisters married into the same family who quarreled, my comparison of Jat joint-families in Maharajapur-Kishanpur indicated that families in which sisters or cousin-sisters were sister-in-law endured longer (Kolenda 1978a, 1978b:265, 1987:201; see also Rosin 1987:26).

Other anthropologists have noticed sibling-set marriage. Brij Raj Chauhan, in his book on a village in Chittorgarh district, mentions that it is "permissible in southern Rajasthan, to find two brothers marrying two sisters" (1976:212). Drs. Anandlaxsmi and Carol Henderson have mentioned to me the prevalence of the custom in the villages they have studied, respectively in Jaipur and Jodhpur districts (personal communication). Bhargava and Gupta, writing about Rangmahal village in Ganganagar district, refer to the Scheduled Caste Meghwals and Nayaks (together composing 54% of families) "among whom younger sisters of a grown up girl are sometimes married along with her. This is done with a view to economise" (1965c:20). Similarly, writing about Mudh village (in Bikaner district), a multicaste Hindu village in which 31% of the population was Scheduled Tribe Meghwals, the same authors say that "a person having more than one daughter may arrange their marriages simultaneously in order to effect economy. In such cases girls even of tender age might be married along with his elder daughters" (1965a:22). In the Nagaur village he studied, Thomas Rosin mentions that "The high frequency of sibling- and cousin-set marriages strengthens joint-family solidarity" (1978:490; 1968:255, 268).

Rosin (1987), in the only other analysis of sibling-set and collateral-set marriages in Rajasthan, found that 24% of all married couples in the Nagaur District village of Undhyala were married in sibling- or collateral-sets in 1964-65. This proportion of such marriages, 24%, is much lower than the three-fifths or more of such marriages I found among the Jats and Minas of Maharajapur-Kishanpur. This comparison raises the question of why there were higher proportions of sibling- and collateral-set marriages in one village rather than in the other. As in Maharajapur-Kishanpur, the Jats were the largest caste group in Undhyala (22% of the total population). Though sibling- or collateral-set marriages occurred in Undhyala among all of the larger castes (*ibid.*, 11), there were relatively high proportions (40%) of such marriages among the

Jats (*ibid.*, 3, 19). Joint-families composed of such sets also tended to endure (*ibid.*, 26), and motivation for such marriages was "cost cutting" in performing weddings (*ibid.*, 25). Rosin is especially concerned with the relationship between sibling- and collateral-set marriages and the endurance of joint-families. When his analysis is ready for publication it will undoubtedly shed much light on this relationship.

In Jaipur district (Agarwal and Gupta 1965:16) and other parts of Rajasthan (Singh and Pendharker 1976:15 for Jodhpur District; Rosin 1987:4 for Nagaur District), it is customary to hold all weddings on only a few specific days during the year. In Maharajapur-Kishanpur, the two wedding days were Akha Tij (the third day of the bright half of the month of Baisakh) and Pipal Purnima (the full-moon day in Jeth). In 1967, Akha Tij fell on May 12, when there were five weddings of Maharajapur-Kishanpur children and, according to newspapers, thousands in and around Jaipur city, and Pipal Purnima fell on May 22, when there were four weddings of Maharajapur-Kishanpur children.

As a result of this custom, a wedding guest invited to more than one wedding has to stay at each wedding only briefly or else must choose among his invitations. The many weddings occurring on the same day in a region therefore helped save on wedding costs by limiting the number of guests. The reason villagers gave for having weddings only on these two days – that they were auspicious and hence one did not have to consult a Brahman *paṇḍit* to find an auspicious day – appears to be another economy measure. In addition, there are many double or triple weddings. In Maharajapur-Kishanpur, there have been as many as seven weddings taking place together. Sisters and/or cousin-sisters are often married at the same time.

One cannot reconstruct precise composition of families from C-I Tables of the Census, and it is therefore not possible to find sibling-sets or collateral-sets in joint-families there. However, as we will see later, the factor with which the Census measures of joint-family (Married Sons and Other Married Relatives) correlates most strongly is young adolescent marriage. As Bhargava and Gupta suggest, and as I have found in Maharajapur-Kishanpur, the practices of sibling-set and collateral-set marriage and of multiple weddings on the same day tend to encourage the marriage of much younger girls along with their older sisters or 'cousin-sisters'. The matching bridegrooms are often similarly apart in age. Thus, these customs contribute to the high proportions of married young adolescents in Rajasthan. Young adolescent marriage, in turn, contributes to the high proprortion of joint-families in Rajasthan, as the high correlations between the indices of joint family structure and the proportions of males or females aged 10-14 who are reported as married show.

Young adolescent marriage or even child marriage is prescribed by some influential Hindu law books. Some speak of brides as young as six (Kane 1958:614), eight and twelve (Buhler 1886:355). A frequent prescription is that a daughter should be married before or immediately after her first menstruation (Kane 1941:438-447). As Kane points out, with respect to the recommended young ages (6-12) for brides, "There was no question of consummation which took place only after puberty" (*ibid.*, 446), and some law books prescribe celibacy for the married couple for some time after marriage (*ibid.*, 441), which is consistent with the continuing physical immaturity of one or both members of the couple for some time after the wedding.

Traditionally, Rajasthani Hindu custom has tended to be consistent with the law books. In the mid-1960s it was customary in Maharajapur-Kishanpur and in surrounding villages for marriage to be celebrated by two major sets of ceremonies usually a year or more apart, the *shādī* and the *muklāvā*. The first established an alliance between the two families, and often took place before a girl reached puberty. The second usually took place one or more years later, usually after the bride had reached puberty, and preceded the couple's commencement of sexual relations.

Among the Jats of Maharajapur-Kishanpur, the custom was for the *shādī* to take place before the age of 12 for both sons and daughters, and for the *muklāvā* to take place one to seven years later; exactly how soon after the *muklāvā* a bride began to live with her husband and his family depended upon her age and physical maturity. For example, one Jat wife who had come to live with her husband four years before told us that she had been married at the same time as her older sister, 15 years before, and the *muklāvā* for both had been one year later. While the older sister came to live with her husband's family immediately, our informant, married at age "five or seven," did not come until 11 years after the *muklāvā*. We may guess that the older sister was 11 or 12 at the time of the *shādī* and 13 at the time of the *muklāvā*, and that her younger sister probably did not come to reside with her marital family until age 16. Another girl of about 12 had still not gone to her mother-in-law even though she had had her *muklāvā* four or five years before, again as the junior bride in a double sibling-set marriage with her sister. True to their proclivity for economizing, many Jats dispense with the *muklāvā* ceremonies entirely and allow one or more men from the groom's family to come and escort the bride to her mother-in-law when she is mature, or if the bride is already mature at the time of the *shādī*, the *muklāvā* takes place immediately after the *shādī*, before the bride departs with the new husband and his party for his village.

Lushington wrote about the weddings of the royal Jats of Bharatpur:

> On the expiration of her three days residence at the home of her lord and master, the bride returns to her relations for a period of one, three or five years, and she is then brought home by the bridegroom to assume the duties of the married state. This second bringing home of the wife is termed *gona* or *gaman*, and is usually the consummation of the marriage; but the *gaman* may be altogether dispensed with by the performance of *phir-pattah*, or changing the stools of the bride and bridegroom when the *Hom* is celebrated. (1833:294-295)

The customs Lushington described for royal Jats are consistent with those followed by Maharajapur-Kishanpur Jats 133 years later.

Thus both Hindu domestic law and long tradition support the Maharajapur-Kishanpur Jats in their child-marriages. Since there is no real lower limit in age for marriage, and a considerable feeling that there must be something wrong with an unmarried person who is over the age of 16 (for girls) and 20 (for boys), the custom of sibling-set or collateral-set marriages for children several years apart in age make good sense, especially in the context of Jat penury and adherence to Brahman advice. I should add that some families are so poor that sons among them may not marry until they are mature, when a man can earn enough to pay a brideprice himself.[5] We attended one Jat wedding in Maharajapur-Kishanpur at which the bride appeared to be 12 and the groom 25 or 30.

There are some men who get only a leviratic bride when a brother dies; some men never marry.

Among the Minas, on the other hand, there appeared to be two patterns. Among the wealthier Minas, the grooms tended to be 17 to 20, and the brides 15 to 16; among poor Minas, grooms tended to be 25 to 30 and brides 10 to 14. Among both Jats and Minas, the marriages of men in their twenties to young girls were likley to be brideprice marriages in which a very poor man gave his daughter to a bachelor, also from a poor family, who had managed to raise enough money (about 2000 to 4000 rupees in the mid-1960s) to pay the brideprice. Especially important in evaluating a bridegroom's status was whether his family owned land and how much land, and whether the men of the family had outside jobs from which they earned money.

The first factor discovered to be related to joint-family households, then, was sibling-set and collateral-set marriages, and the second was child or young adolescent marriage. Both are facilitated by the Rajasthani custom of holding multiple weddings on the one or two days a year deemed by astrological almanacs to be auspicious for them to take place. A third factor was one often mentioned by anthropologists: the joint-family as work-team. This was a factor I was aware of from writings about Japanese families (Johnson 1964:846; Nakane 1967). In Maharajapur-Kishanpur, the joint-family functioned as a well-team consisting of two adult men, who were almost always related, either as father and son, or as brothers, plus one of their wives and some of their older children. I described the system as follows

> . . . an incline is built in front of a well down which a pair of bullocks is driven, their downward movement pulling a leathern pouch (*charas*) full of water from the well. One man drives the bullocks, a second man empties the pouch of water into a sink from which it drains along dried-mud channel-bunds built above the fields. A third person, often a woman or older child, releases the water from the channel at the desired point to enter the fields . . . . Almost three-quarters of the Jat well-teams (74 percent) – seventeen out of twenty-three – are composed of patrilineally-related men. Two-thirds (65 percent) – fifteen out of twenty-three – are composed either of brothers or of father-son combinations. Thirteen, 56 percent, are composed of

> brothers or of father-sons who share the same house and eat from the kitchen. There is thus a majority tendency for Jat men who compose well-teams to be members of the same commensal extended families.
>
> Jat women not only work in the house caring for children and cooking for the family, but they work in the fields irrigating the patches of garden. They also harvest and winnow grains such as *bājrā*, and vegetables such as *moṭh*. They cut and carry thorn bushes used for barriers. They gather foliage for fuel. They cut, carry, and chop fodder for animals. They water and feed the animals, as well. Jats and Minas have herds of sheep and goats. They and villagers of other castes have some cows and buffaloes. It is the children who are in charge of herding.
>
> Joint families make possible a division of labor among the members. One wife can care for small children, while another works in the field or collects and chops fodder. It makes possible a division of labor among men, as well, either on the well – one driving the bullocks, the other emptying out the water pouch – or by some men doing agricultural work in M-K and others working outside. Older children similarly can be assigned different tasks – some in the fields, or herding, or caring for the babies, some attending school. (Kolenda 1978a:248-249; 1987:183-185)

This Jat and Mina pattern illustrates the hypothesis of Pasternak, Ember and Ember (1976), that joint-families often occur in pre-industrial societies where and when an adult has incompatible tasks to perform. The incompatibility is solved by having more than one man or more than one woman to do the tasks which would be incompatible for one man alone or for one woman alone to do.

Also related to the joint-family as a work-team was the paucity of agricultural labor employed by the landholding Jats and Minas. Only at peak labor times, as when the sowing of the winter crop was taking place at the same time as the harvesting of the summer crop, did they employ untouchable Balais to help them in the fields. Map 5 shows the distribution of Scheduled Castes by district in rural Rajasthan in 1961. These communities, who often serve as agrestic servants, were not heavily concentrated in the high joint-family districts; of the 11 Quintile 1 districts shown on Map 4, only one, Tonk, had more than 20% of its population among the

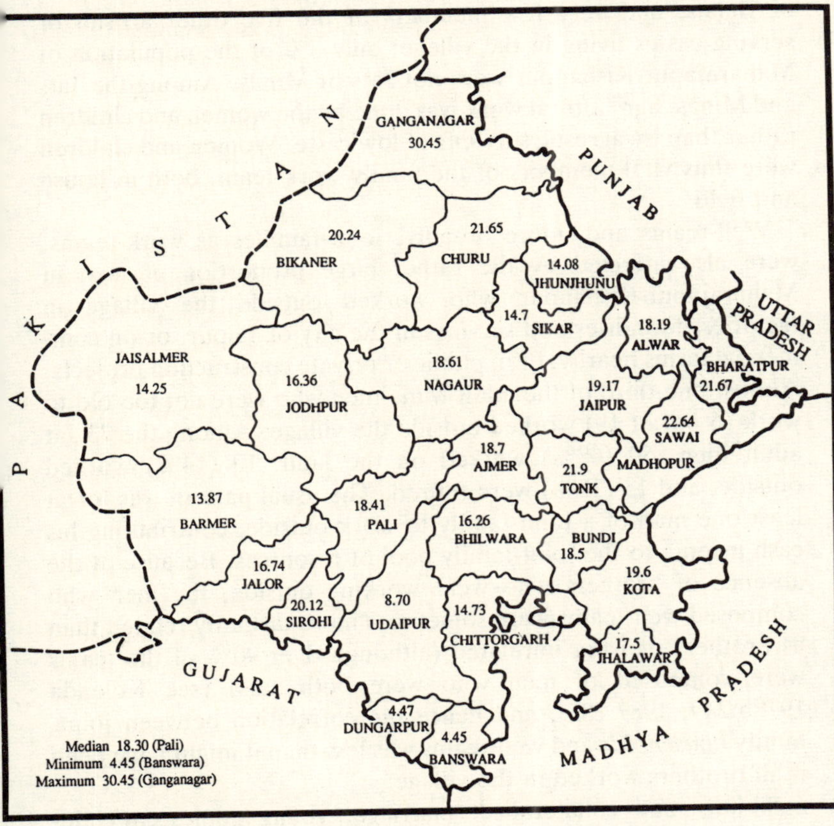

Map 5: **Proportion of Scheduled Caste People in Each District of Rajasthan (Census of India 1961)**

Scheduled Castes. The correlation coefficient between Married Sons and Scheduled Castes was +.22, that between Other Married Relatives and Scheduled Castes was +.28, both low relationships. The most economical way to farm, the Jats and Minas of Maharajapur-Kishanpur knew, was to have all work in the fields done by family members. Thus, there were only two extended families of Balais, and very few members of the five other artisan or serving castes living in the village; only 3% of the population of Maharajapur-Kishanpur were not Jats or Minas. Among the Jats and Minas, agricultural work was done by the women and children rather than by agrestic servants of low caste. Women and children were thus vital members of the family work-team, both in house and field.

Well-teams and, more broadly, joint-families as work-teams, were also affected by the rather large proportion of men in Maharajapur-Kishanpur who worked outside the village in factories, foundries and services in the city of Jaipur, or on commercial farms nearby, or in public or private construction projects. Almost one-third of the adult Mina men who were not too old to work (6 out of 19) worked outside the village. Among the 73 Jat adult men, 50 (68%) worked on the land, 10 (14%) worked outside, and 13 (18%) were retired. The usual pattern was for at least one man of a joint-family to work outside, contributing his cash income to the joint-family pool of resources. Because of the absence of brothers who were working outside, the men who composed well-teams were sometimes more distantly related than as brothers or were unrelated (although over 90% of the teams were composed of men who were both Jats) (see Kolenda 1978b:249, 1987:185), and hence the correlation between joint-family *households* and well-teams was less than it might have been if all brothers worked in the village.

Sibling- and collateral-set marriage, young adolescent/child-marriage and work-team requirements thus all supported the organization of joint-families in Maharajapur-Kishanpur. A fourth factor was the role of the former *jāgīrdār* (hereditary estate-holder) and *ināmdār* (rent-free landholder), and the *mahant* (head priest) of the Krishna temple in Kishanpur, in influencing household structure before the implementation of the Rajasthan Land Reforms and Resumption of Jagirs Act of 1952. Maharajapur had been *khālsā* village (a village belonging to the Maharaja of Jaipur), while Kishanpur had been partly an *ināmdārī* and partly a *jāgīrdārī* village. Most of its lands had belonged to the Krishna (locally, 'Kishan') temple. The former *mahant* told us that his predecessors had tried to encourage cultivation by tenants by building houses and wells for them, or else they would give tenants wood or lend them money toward the cost of building houses. But he also stated that "during *jāgīrdārī* days the cultivator's life was very unstable, because *jāgīdārs* threw cultivators off the land whenever they pleased. Therefore no cultivator could build a *pakkā* (fired-brick) house" (Field interview by Indira Sapru, April 1, 1968). Since building new houses was by permission of the *jāgīrdār*, *ināmdār*, or Maharaja's official, tenants may not have built houses as soon as they felt they were needed for expanding families. There is thus the possibility that more families lived in a house or shared a *chūlhā* in the past than might have chosen to do so.

That the requirement of the village landlord's permission to partition joint households may have considerable impact upon the pattern of family structure among tenants or agrestic servants is indicated by the study of Peter Czap (1983) of serf households in Mishino, Russia, between 1814 and 1858. Among the serfs, 75% of households were joint (Hajnal 1983:91), and as many as 65% were composed of three or more generatioins (Czap 1983:133).[6] It was part of the authority of the *seigneur* to inhibit household fission (*ibid.*, 122, 136), possibly from a belief in the benefits of the large family system either for their members or for the estate managment. The role of the *jāgīrdār*, *ināmdār*, or royal official in Rajasthan may have included a similar inhibition.

Evidence for the unwilling persistence of some joint-families in Maharajapur-Kishanpur is indicated by the fact that some of eldest brothers of Jat and Mina families left their joint-family households in Maharajapur to build separate houses in Kishanpur or elsewhere as soon as land reform permitted it (Kolenda 1987:181). (Eldest sons are likely to have the largest numbers of children first in the joint-family's development, and hence may feel crowded earliest.) By the Land Reform Act, Kishanpur land went to the Minas who had previously tilled it, while Maharajapur land went to the former Jat tenants of the Maharaja. After almost all the Minas had left Maharajapur to live in Kishanpur, some of the eldest sons of Jat joint-families moved into the vacant houses, establishing separate *chūlhās* there. Since so much building of new houses and moving out had taken place in the eight years since land reform (1958-1966), the proportions of joint-families and the number of people in them may well have been higher in Maharajapur-Kishanpur prior to that time. The fact that none of the former tenants of the former *jāgīrdār* and *ināmdār* of Kishanpur lived in Kishanpur until after Land Reform raises the question: did the *jāgīrdār* and *ināmdār* forbid their tenants to live near the fields they tilled? This was possible since the Kishanpur tenants were Minas who had supported themselves as "protectors" of the Jats of Maharajapur and thus lived in Maharajapur, until in 1928 an epidemic in Kishanpur motivated the *mahant* and the *jāgīrdār* to take them on as tenants. The *mahant* could thus insist that the Minas continue to reside in Maharajapur rather than moving to Kishanpur.

The fieldwork conducted in Maharajapur-Kishanpur thus suggests four major factors contributing to the occurrence of joint-families: 1) sibling-set and collateral-set marriage, 2) young adolescent/child-marriage, 3) well-teams composed of members of the same joint-family, and 4) the need, in the past, for permission from *ināmdārs*, *jāgīrdārs* or other officials in order to build houses. Sibling-set and collateral-set marriages serve to strengthen the joint-family by bringing together as daughters-in-law women who are sisters or cousin-sisters; hence quarrels between co-daughters-in-law are less likely to be serious enough to lead to demands on their part for dissolution of their common joint-family. The need to economize in wedding expenses, along with Hindu teachings on the desirability of marrying daughters before puberty, encourages these sibling- and collateral-set marriages, as do multiple weddings and a very young age of marriage for brides and grooms – a crucial factor which will be taken up again below. The well-team/work-team formed by the joint family serves as a functional cause for the persistence of the joint-family. Finally, the former requirement that tenants get permission from their landlords to build new living quarters is an oppressive cause of joint-family households: people shared house and *chūlhā* because of a shortage of living space. Since land became allotted to former tenants in the 1950s, the landlord's permission is no longer necessary, but the cost of building a new house or even adding on to an existing house may still be prohibitive enough that some joint-families continue to live together despite their preference for division into separate households.

Family Structure in the 1961 Census Village Surveys of Rajasthan

As part of the 1961 Census, representative villages were surveyed for every state and territory of India. For Rajasthan, 36 village surveys were done, of which 24 were obtained for this study.[7] These are listed at the beginning of the References Cited at the end of this paper. Map 6 shows the location of the 24 villages. In the surveys, four types of families were tabulated: simple, intermediate, joint, and other. Two of the Census ethnographers, Gupta and Pendharker, define these as follows:

> A simple family consists of husband, his wife and unmarried children; an intermediate one consists of a married couple and an unmarried brother, sister or one of the parents; whereas the joint family consists of a married couple with married sons/daughters, or with married brothers/sisters. The types of families not covered by any of the above have been classified as 'others' (1969:27).

Given these definitions, it is reasonable to equate the Census categories of simple, intermediate and joint with those of nuclear, supplemented nuclear and joint as I have defined them in my earlier work (Kolenda 1967:346-347; 1987:11-13). Table 3 shows the proportions for the four types of families in the 24 village surveys, as well as quintile rank on proportion of married females aged 10-14 and married males aged 10-14.

In my 1968 comparative study of the Indian joint-family, based on a comparison of 26 studies from 14 different states of India, I developed a principle of what constitutes high, medium and low proportions of joint-family households in India. A proportion of 30% or more is high, 20% to 29% is medium, and 19% or less is low (Kolenda 1968:375; 1987:57). By this principle, 9 (38%) of the Rajasthan villages considered here were high (with Mudh, Bikaner District, a largely Scheduled Caste village consisting mostly of Meghwals, the highest at 51%), 8 were medium, and 7 were low. Thus 17 villages out of 24 (70%) showed medium and high proportions of joint-families, confirming the district statistics for Rajasthan presented earlier and showing that the state has a higher than average proportion of joint-family households.

Two of the 'low' villages, Ramnagar Kanjar Colony (Bundi

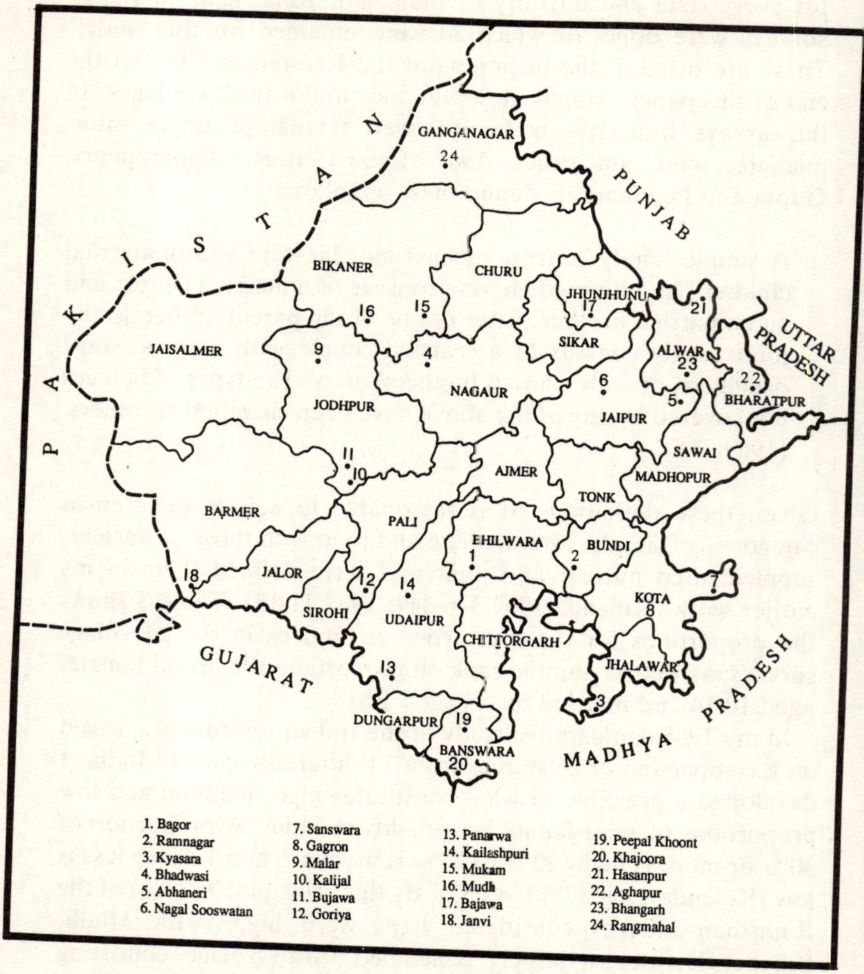

Map 6: **Locations of 24 Villages in Rajasthan Surveyed by the Census of India 1961**

in Rajasthan and Quintile Rank on Proportions of Married Adolescents

Village	Tehsil	District	Family Types: Simple	Inter.	Joint	Other	Quintile Rank: F	M	Ref.
1 Bagor	Mandal	Bhilwara	43 (81%)	3 (6%)	7 (13%)		1	1	p. 26
2 Ramnagar Kanjar Colony	Bundi	Bundi	168 (93%)	12 (7%)			1	1	p. 30
3 Kyasara	Dag	Jhalawar	31 (33%)	20 (21%)	37 (39%)	6 (6%)	1	1	p. 39
4 Bhadwasi	Nagaur	Nagaur	35 (61%)	1 (2%)	21 (37%)		1	1	p. 27
5 Abhaneri	Baswa	Jaipur	66 (41%)	50 (31%)	41 (27%)	1 (1%)	1	2	p. 30
6 Nangal Soos-watan	Amber	Jaipur	52 (41%)	31 (25%)	41 (33%)	2 (1%)	1	2	p. 31
7 Sanwara	Shahbad	Kota	24 (55%)	5 (11%)	15 (34%)		1	2	p. 31
8 Gagron	Kanwas	Kota	23 (40%)	7 (12%)	19 (33%)	8 (14%)	1	2	p. 26
9 Malar	Palodi	Jodhpur	77 (55%)	25 (18%)	39 (28%)		2	1	p. 35
10 Kalijal	Jodhpur	Jodhpur	55 (48%)	23 (20%)	36 (31%)	1 (1%)	2	1	p. 28
11 Bujawa	Jodhpur	Jodhpur	16 (44%)	9 (25%)	11 (31%)		2	1	p. 36
12 Goriya	Bali	Pali	94 (69%)	8 (6%)	35 (25%)		2	1	p. 33
13 Panarwa	Phalasia	Udaipur	18 (58%)	1 (3%)	9 (29%)	3 (10%)	2	1	p. 32
14 Kailashpuri	Girwa	Udaipur	119 (66%)	21 (12%)	27 (15%)	13 (7%)	2	1	p. 25
15 Mukam	Nokha	Bikaner	41 (63%)	14 (22%)	10 (15%)		2	2	p. 32
16 Mudh	Kolayat	Bikaner	38 (49%)		39*(51%)		2	2	p. 41
17 Bujawa	Udaipurwati	Jhunjhunu	16 (59%)	1 (4%)	8 (30%)	2 (7%)	2	3	p. 81
18 Janvi	Sanchore	Jalor	72 (53%)	23 (17%)	39 (29%)	1 (1%)	3	2	p. 58
19 Peepal Khoont	Ghatol	Banswara	129 (77%)	17 (10%)	17 (10%)	5 (3%)	3	2	p. 49
20 Khajoora	Kushalgarh	Banswara	18 (51%)	5 (14%)	8 (23%)	4 (12%)	3	2	p. 31
21 Hasanpur	Tijara	Alwar	68 (80%)	9(11%)	8 (9%)		3	2	p. 25
22 Aghapur	Bharatupur	Bharatpur	64 (54%)	27 (23%)	25 (21%)	3 (2%)	3	2	p. 33
23 Bhangarh	Rajgarh	Alwar	33 (55%)	10 (16%)	16 (26%)	3 (3%)	3	2	p. 34
24 Rangmahal	Suratgarh	Ganganagar	63 (76%)	10 (12%)	9 (11%)	1 (1%)	4	3	p. 83

(* including 32 lateral, 4 collateral, and 3 others; of the 3, 2 have sons-in-law residing with fathers-in-law and 1 is an outcasted couple)

District) and Bagor (Bhilwara District), were composed almost entirely of Kanjars, an erstwhile nomadic criminal tribe which the government had tried to sedentarize. The ethnographers of Ramnagar Kanjar Colony, Sharma and Gupta, explained the absence of joint-families as customary as follows:

> The reason is that it is customary among the Kanjars for a boy who is about to be married to receive a separate piece of land, a residential house and other necessary articles for his maintenance from his parents. After the marriage the newly married couple lives in a new house, and not with the parents (1967a:30; see also p.12).

According to Sharma and Gupta, the age of marriage among the Scheduled Caste sedentarized Kanjars of Ramnagar Kanjar Colony was 20-29 for males and 15-24 for females. While they did not specify the connection between the couple setting up their own house immediately upon marriage and the older age of marriage among these Kanjars as compared to other Rajasthani communities, it would appear to be much easier for a couple to run a household if they are older.

Concerning the Kanjars and Sansis (another former nomadic criminal tribe) who composed Bagor village, Bhargava and Pendharker wrote:

> The preference for the simple type of family is a natural consequence of the settlement of the communities on land. Separate families were allotted separate holdings and it was advantageous for the settlers to claim to belong to separate rather than joint family type (1968:26).

According to this explanation, the low proportion of joint-family households in Bagor was not due to either custom or older age of marriage, but to the recent redistribution of land under the Land Reform Act, as a result of which the Kanjars and Sansis found it advantageous to maximize the number of families among them in order to qualify for the most land possible. In fact it is clear that at the time of the survey young adolescent marriage for girls prevailed in Bagor. According to Bhargava and Pendharker, there were no unmarried females over the age of 14 among the

Kanjars (*ibid.*, 24), and the usual age of marriage was 15-16 for boys and 12-13 for girls (*ibid.*, 12).

The influence of land redistribution on family composition, encouraging the maximization of nuclear families, may well have taken place as well in the joint-family village of Kailashpuri (Udaipur District), where Bhil cultivators had recently been allotted former Eklingji Temple lands.

The village with the lowest proportion of joint-family households (9%) was Hasanpur (Alwar District), where almost two-thirds of the population (63%) were Muslim Meos. The explanation offered by Sharma and Pendharker was that "The large number of families of the simple type is due to the fact that land holdings are small and they cannot bear the burden of joint families" (1969:25). This explanation is questionable, because as will be seen below in Table 11 showing types of families among *landless* Chamars, those represented in the Rajasthan villages surveyed had high proportions of joint-families. Since some proportion of Hasanpur's population had departed for Pakistan at the time of the Partition of the sub-continent into India and Pakistan in 1947 (*ibid.*, 23), it is more likely that joint-families had been fragmented by out-migration of one or more of their nuclear family components. Out-migration may also have been important in the low joint-family village of Mukam (Bikaner District), a pilgrimage center of Jambheswarji (the founder of the Bishnoi sect), composed only of Bishnois and their Meghwal servants. Mukam had little agricultural land, so that some Bishnoi cultivators tilled land in nearby villages, and many other Bishnois migrated out.

In the cases of both Hasanpur and Mukam, it is likely that entire nuclear families migrated out, not just male members. It is a common pattern in many rural areas of India for men to work outside the village for months or years at a time, leaving their wives and children on the land or in the house owned there, sometimes in the care of the remaining men of their joint-families, the man returning to live with his family upon his retirement from his outside work. (For an example of such a pattern, see Dandekar 1986 for a village in Maharashtra.) While such out-migration may have occurred in Hasanpur and Mukam, it also seems likely that entire nuclear families or components of joint families migrated out permanently.

Rangmahal (Ganganagar District) and Peepal Khoont (Banswara

District), two other villages low in joint-families, were in districts ranked in either the fourth or fifth quintile on Married Sons and Other Married Relatives. Their low 12% and 10% of joint-family households were consistent with their districts' low quintile ratings on measures of joint-family living (to be discussed below).

We thus see that, side-by-side with the factors *encouraging* joint-family living (sibling- and collateral-set marriage, young adolescent/child-marriage, well-teams/work-teams, and need for official permission to build new homes), there are two factors (land reform and permanent out-migration) that tend to *fragment* joint-families and reduce their proportion in a village. Of the villages low in joint-family households, two were in districts of Rajasthan with below-average quintiles on joint-family measures, but three seemed to have a low proportion of joint-families because of government land redistribution, and two seem to have been disrupted by departure, permanent out-migation. In only one was there clear evidence that the custom was for marriage to be at an older age, with the couple occupying its own new house immediately after marriage.

Caste or Tribal Preference for Joint-Family Living

A popular hypothesis concerning joint-family living is the ethnic one – that joint families are preferred by certain communities (in Rajasthan, by Rajputs and Jats) and rejected by others (in Rajasthan, by Bhils and other tribals). The ethnographic material in the 1961 Census village surveys provides an opportunity to test this hypothesis. Though a few of the 24 villages were populated by a single ethnic community (nos. 2 and 17) or by two (no. 15), most were multicaste communities (see Table 4).

The villages surveyed included 65 different caste and tribal communities. The fragmentation of the caste system is such that only seven out of these 65 had members in as many as six different villages. Jats, Chamars and Kumhars appeared in 6, Nais in 8, Bhils in 9, Rajputs in 10, and Brahmans in 12. The possibility of comparison of members of the same caste or tribal community living in different places is thus limited. Such comparison is further limited by the absence, in some of the surveys, of reports or tables showing the breakdown of household types by caste and tribal community. Comparison for Nais and Kumhars are precluded by the very small number of families of each in any one village. It has been claimed that Rajputs prefer to live in joint-families. The data from the village surveys can be examined to test this, as Rajputs were to be found in 10 of the villages, ranging from one family (in Mudh, Bikaner District) up to 23 (in Janvi, Jalor District). Unfortunately, the breakdown of family types of caste is not provided for three of the villages (nos. 10, 14, 16). But for the other seven villages, the proportion of Rajput families which were joint ranged from 0% to 100% (see Table 5).

Applying the principle that if the proportion of joint-families is 30% or more in an Indian village, it probably means that about half the people live in joint-families, we see that in five out of the seven villages, most Rajputs lived in joint-families, but that in two villages (Gagron in Kota District and Janvi in Jalor District) they did not.[8] The figures for Janvi, showing that none of the 23 Rajput families there was joint, are puzzling, as the proportion for total number of families in the village (135) was 29% joint. Janvi included 18 different ethnic communities. The largest caste, the Bishnois, had 50% joint families (18 out of 36 families), as did the Brahmans, Kalbis and Suthars. Why, then, were there not joint-families at all among the Rajputs, the second largest ethnic group of Janvi?

The answer once again seems to be the effect of land reform. The *bhūmīchārā jāgīrdārī* (jointly held estate) land owned by the Rajputs in the past had recently been redistributed. 60% of the land had gone to Bishnois (the former tenants of the Rajputs) and members of other castes, and 40% had been subdivided among the former Rajput joint-owners. It may well have been beneficial for the Rajputs to maximize the numbers of their families when it came to this redistribution of land. In addition, a number of the Rajput young men of Janvi had become sufficiently educated to become office workers in the town of Sanchore, and some Rajput men had gone into business. Thus, it seems plausible that the breaking up and partial loss of the *jāgīrdārī* previously shared by the Rajputs of Janvi removed the support that had existed for joint-family living among them (Singh and Gupta 1966b:48–49, 58, 60). Unfortunately, we do not have the distribution of household types among them before land reform, so we can only postulate that there were more joint-families earlier.

A further characteristic of the Rajputs of Janvi that militated

***Table 4:* Caste Composition of 24 Villages Surveyed by the Census of India-1961 in Rajasthan**

Village	Tehsil	District	Castes and Number of Families
1 Bagor	Mandal	Bhilwara	Sansi (32), Kanjar (21)
2 Ramnagar Kanjar Colony	Bundi	Bundi	Kanjar (180)
3 Kyasara	Dag	Jhalawar	Rajput (46), Nath (18), Chamar (12), Brahman (4), Suthar (3), Nai (2), Balai (2), Darzi (2), Dholi (2), Teli (1), Bania (1), Kumhar (1)
4 Bhadwasi	Nagaur	Nagaur	Mali (23), Rajput (10), Jat (10), Nayak (7), Bhambi (4) Muslim (3)
5 Abhaneri	Baswa	Jaipur	Brahman (69), Gujar (35), Kumhar (16), Mali (11), Chamar (8), Mahajan (4), Nai (4), Rajput (3), Koli (3), Jain (2), Khati (2), Mina (2), Bhangi (2)
6 Nangal Sooswatan	Amber	Jaipur	Mina (87), Balai (13), Brahmabhat (7), Mali (6), Khati (5) Brahman (4), Dholi (Rana) (2), Mahajan (1), Jogi (1)
7 Sanwara	Shahbad	Kota	Sahairya (32), Ahir (10), Brahman (1), Muslim (1)
8 Gagron	Kanwas	Kota	Muslim Rajput (25), Mali (7), Chamar (7), Bhil (6), Rajput (5), Moghia (3), Brahman (2), Bhangi (2)
9 Malar	Palodi	Jodhpur	Pushkaran Brahman (121), Darzi (5), Sewak Brahman (3), Nai (3), Bhil (3), Bhambi (3), Bawari (2), Suthar (1)
10 Kalijal	Jodhpur	Jodhpur	Jat (51), Rajput (33), Rebari (10), Bhil (8), Bhambi (7), Suthar (3), Sadh (1), Daroga (1), Bhangi (1)
11 Bujawa	Jodhpur	Jodhpur	Rajput (21), Raika (4), Bhambi (4), Sadh (3), Suthar (2), Darzi (1), Nai (1)
12 Goriya	Bali	Pali	Girasia (104), Bhil (28), Lohar (2), Kumhar (1), Hargada (1), Muslim (1)

13 Panarwa	Phalasia	Udaipur	Bhil (13), Rajput (7), Daroga (6), Girasia (5)
14 Kailashpuri	Girwa	Udaipur	Bhil (96), Brahman (55), Mali (18), Rajput (3), Darzi (2), Nai (2), Muslim (1), Jogi (1), Manihar (1), Jat (1)
15 Mukam	Nokha	Bikaner	Bishnoi (58), Meghwal (7)
16 Mudh	Kolayat	Bikaner	Meghwal (21), Darzi (15), Kumhar (11), Nayak (10), Sadh (6), Lohar (4), Nai (2), Khati (2), Dholi (1), Muslim (1), Paliwal (1), Sunar (1), Rajput (1), Pushkarna Brahman (1)
17 Bujawa	Udaipurwati	Jhunjhunu	Chowkidari Mina (27)
18 Janvi	Sanchore	Jalor	Rajput (23), Kalbi (16), Daroga (12), Bhambi (9), Rebari (7), Bhil (5), Brahman (4), Mahajan (3), Garuda (3), Ghanchi (3), Koli (3), Swami (3), Suthar (2), Mirasi (2), Jat (2), Bishnoi (2), Sadh (1), Honi (1)
19 Peepal Khoont	Ghatol	Banswara	Bhil (131) (92% of population), remainder are Bhoi, Jogi, Chamar
20 Khajoora	Kushalgarh	Banswara	Bhil (34), Gasa (1)
21 Hasanpur	Tijara	Alwar	Meo (53), Chamar (23), Sindhi (4), Bhangi (3) Faqir (1), Mahajan (1)
22 Aghapur	Bharatpur	Bharatpur	Gujar (43), Kachhi (19), Jat (15), Banjara (15), Brahman (10), Sikh (6), Kumhar (3), Nai (3), Lodha (2), Gadariya (1), Kadera (1), Bhangi (1)
23 Bhangarh	Rajgarh	Alwar	Koli (24), Kanphata Jogi (10), Brahman (10), Banjara (6), Chamar (5), Mina (4), Khati (1), Nai (1)
24 Rangmahal	Suratgarh	Ganganagar	Nayak (27), Jat (18), Meghwal (18), Baori (10), Jogi (5), Kumhar (4), Brahman (1)

Table 5: **Rajput Family Types in Seven Villages Surveyed by the Census of India-1961 in Rajasthan**

Village	District	Total no. Families	Simple	Inter.	Joint	Other
3 Kyasara	Jhalawar	46	10 (22%)	15 (33%)	18 (39%)	3 (6%)
4 Bhadwasi	Nagaur	10	5 (50%)	1 (10%)	4 (40%)	
5 Abhaneri	Jaipur	3			3 (100%)	
8 Gagron	Kota	5	2 (40%)	2 (40%)	1 (20%)	
11 Bujawa	Jodhpur	21	6 (29%)	7 (33%)	8 (38%)	
13 Panarwa	Udaipur	7	3 (43%)		3 (43%)	1 (14%)
18 Janvi	Talor	23	20 (87%)	3 (13%)		

against joint-families was the late age of marriage reported for them – 18-20 for boys and 14-18 for girls. These were much higher ages than those for the Bishnoi and Kalbi children, who were reported to marry boys as young as five and girls as young as three (*ibid.*, 32). This factor of child-marriage will be taken up in greater detail below.

The other village lacking a high proportion of joint-family households among Rajputs (Gagron, Kota District) had a medium proportion of 20% – one out of five families. The number of persons in each category of family was not given in the Gagron survey report, so it is not possible to say what proportion of the 29 Rajput individuals in the village belonged to the one joint family. This, of course, is also a small population with a small number of families.

Before land reform, 30% to 100% of the land in five of the seven villages (nos. 3, 4, 8, 11, 18) had been controlled by the Rajputs. The Rajputs in the other two villages (nos. 5 and 13) were few in number, living in villages controlled by other dominant castes. There is here again the suggestion that large landholdings encourage a joint-family structure.

A feature of Rajput life that is important in terms of family structure is that, along with Brahmans, Mahajans (Hindu merchants and bureaucrats) and Bishnois, they forbid the remarriage of widows. This tends to create a category of dependent women to be cared for by some family. Rajputs also tend to have especially distorted sex ratios (see Table 6 for sex ratios in the 24 villages surveyed),[9] which leads to some adult men remaining bachelors throughout life, another category of dependents to be cared for by some family, as it does not seem to be a common Rajasthani custom to permit a single person to live alone, or more precisely to eat from her or his own kitchen. Prohibition on widow remarriage and the greater number of males may result in a sizeable number of permanently unmarried people of both sexes to be included in 'intermediate' (supplemented nuclear) or 'joint' families. The addition of a single adult to a family does not make it a joint-family, since, by definition, a joint-family consists of two or more related married couples. Thus the addition of a permanently unmarried adult to a joint-family can only 'supplement' it and increase its size, but does convert a nuclear family into an 'intermediate' family.

Table 6: **Sex Ratios for 24 Villages Surveyed by the Census of India-1961 in Rajasthan**

Village	Tehsil	District	Total Population	Females no.	Females %	Males no.	Males %	Quintile Rank F	Quintile Rank M
1 Bagor	Mandal	Bhilwara	229	105	42%	124	58%	1	1
2 Ramnagar Kanjar Colony	Bundi	Bundi	655	275	42%	380	58%	1	1
3 Kyasara	Dag	Jhalawar	514	250	49%	264	51%	1	1
4 Bhadwasi	Nagaur	Nagaur	363	162	45%	201	55%	1	1
5 Abhaneri	Baswa	Jaipur	1005	459	46%	546	54%	1	2
6 Nangal Sooswatan	Amber	Jaipur	708	339	48%	369	52%	1	2
7 Sanwara	Shahbad	Kota	222	116	52%	106	48%	1	2
8 Gagron	Kanwas	Kota	282	121	43%	161	57%	1	2
9 Malar	Palodi	Jodhpur	648	296	46%	352	54%	2	1
10 Kalijal	Jodhpur	Jodhpur	689	317	46%	372	54%	2	1
11 Bujawa	Jodhpur	Jodhpur	229	101	44%	128	56%	2	1
12 Goriya	Bali	Pali	782	376	48%	406	52%	2	1
13 Panarwa	Phalasia	Udaipur	146	67	46%	79	54%	2	1
14 Kailashpuri	Girwa	Udaipur	664	316	48%	348	52%	2	1
15 Mukam	Nokha	Bikaner	298	131	44%	167	56%	2	2
16 Mudh	Kolayat	Bikaner	419	206	49%	213	51%	2	2
17 Bujawa	Udaipurwati	Jhunjhunu	149	79	53%	70	47%	2	3
	+Chowkidari Minas		190	88	46%	102	54%		
18 Janvi	Sanchore	Jalor	685	342	50%	343	50%	3	2
19 Peepal Khoont	Ghatol	Banswara	830	400	48%	430	52%	3	2
20 Khajoora	Kushalgarh	Banswara	206	103	50%	103	50%	3	2
21 Hasanpur	Tijara	Alwar	356	164	46%	192	54%	3	2
22 Aghapur	Bharatpur	Bharatpur	599	254	42%	345	58%	3	2
23 Bhangarh	Rajgarh	Alwar	341	156	46%	185	54%	3	2
24 Rangmahal	Suratgarh	Ganganagar	355	161	45%	194	55%	4	3

When the 24 village surveys are compared on the proportions of their populations which fall into the categories of unmarried males over the age of 25, widowers, and widows (see Table 7), we find high proportions (10% to 20%) in seven villages. Three of these were dominated by Rajputs – two by Hindu Rajputs (nos. 3 and 11) and one by Muslim Rajputs (no. 8). Two were dominated by Hindu religious specialists – one by Brahmans (no. 9) and one by Bishnois (no. 15). The other village with high proportion of unmarried adults (Aghapur, Bharatpur District) was predominantly Gujar and Jat. According to its ethnographers, Agarwal and Gupta,

> The presence of 19 unmarried males in the age-group 25-29 and the age group 30-34 is perhaps due to the fact that the economic position of the households is not strong enough to pay the high bride price demanded by the parents of the girl (1969:32).

Aghapur's high proportion of single adults seems to have been composed largely of unmarried adult males (34 out of 73), rather than by the widows so characteristic of villages with large Rajput or other high caste populations.

The village with the lowest proportion of its population in these permanently unmarried categories was Goriya, in Pali District, in which three-quarters of the population were members of the Scheduled Tribe of Girasias. The sex ratio was also less unequal (52% male, 48% female) than in half the other villages. Among the Girasias, the common form of marriage is elopement, after which the bridegroom pays some brideprice; exchange is also allowed, requiring neither brideprice nor dowry; both widows and widowers are allowed to remarry, and extramarital relationships are not "much looked down upon" (Gulati and Gupta 1966:16, 32). These Girasia tribal norms seemed to result in few adults remaining unmated, hence a lower proportion of permanently unmarried adults and fewer intermediate families. Conversely, the high proportions of permanently unmarried adults among Rajputs and other high castes help account for the high proportions of 'intermediate' families among them.

What about the other major castes and tribes in the villages surveyed – the Jats, Brahmans, Bhils and Chamars? Tables 8, 9, 10 and 11 show the distribution of family types in the villages in which each community was to be found. A perusal of these tables indicates that there was no consistent pattern for Jats, Brahmans or Bhils. There were both high and low proportions of joint-families among each of these ethnic groups. Clearly, therefore, Jats and Brahmans do not have consistently high proportions of joint-families, nor do Bhils have consistently low proportions. Thus the popular idea that Jats and high castes have high proportions of joint-families, and that tribals do not, is not sustained by these village surveys.

Any suggestion that joint-family living is most characteristic of high castes is belied not only by the Bhil figures in Table 10, but also by the figures in Table 11 for the low-caste untouchable Chamars. Consistently, Chamars had high proportions of joint-families, as high as 88% (Abhaneri, Jaipur District) and 80% (Bhangarh, Alwar District). The number of Chamar families in each village was small, however, between 5 and 12 families. Moreover, it should be noted that both Abhaneri and Bhangarh are well-watered villages on the Sanwar river, and that the Chamars there were agricultural laborers living in one-room houses (Agarwal and Pendharker 1965:3, 9, 20; Gulati and Pendharker 1965c:11, 21). Possibly, then, the Chamars' high proportion of joint-families was not entirely the result of choice, but also of lack of resources to build more housing. Thomas Rosin has pointed out to me that possibly the Chamar joint-household may also be a work team when it is pursuing the Chamars' traditional leather craft. He writes:

> The jointness of leather workers' families also has struck me, but their structure seems consistent with their elaborate activities in hauling, flailing, tanning, and crafting leather (personal communication).

The importance of the joint-family as a work-team was mentioned for Maharajapur-Kishanpur above and will be discussed in more detail for Rajasthan as a whole below.

Comparison of a caste's family structure in different Rajasthani villages thus suggests variation within the caste. In the village surveys examined here, only the Scheduled Caste Chamars showed consistently high proportions of joint-family living, followed by the high-caste Rajputs. While the high proportions for Rajputs may have been the result of large landholdings in the past, in 24 Villages Surveyed by the Census of India-1961 in Rajasthan

Village	District	Unmarried Males	Widowers	Widows	Population Size	Total Unmarried	% Unmarried
1 Bagor	Bhilwara	2	5	4	229	11	5%
2 Ramnagar Kanjar Colony	Bundi	many	7	20	655	27	?
3 Kyasara	Jhalawar	3	12	41	514	56	11%
4 Bhadwasi	Nagaur	4	4	3	363	11	3%
5 Abhaneri	Jaipur	26	34	31	1005	91	9%
6 Nangal Sooswatan	Jaipur	3	9	36	708	48	7%
7 Sanwara	Kota	1	2	5	222	8	4%
8 Gagron	Kota	3	15	11	282	29	10%
9 Malar	Jodhpur	15	17	41	648	73	11%
10 Kalijal	Jodhpur	5	14	35	689	53	8%
11 Bujawa	Jodhpur	6	5	17	229	28	12%
12 Goriya	Pali	1	7	8	782	16	2%
13 Panarwa	Udaipur	0	1	3	146	4	3%
14 Kailashpuri	Udaipur	3	8	33	664	44	7%
15 Mukam	Bikaner	8	13	12	298	33	11%
16 Mudh	Bikaner	1	11	20	298	33	11%
17 Bujawa	Jhunjhunu	3	2	7	149	12	8%
18 Janvi	Jalor	1	11	23	695	35	5%
19 Peepal Khoont	Banswara	3	14	35	830	52	6%
20 Khajoora	Banswara	4	3	7	206	14	7%
21 Hasanpur	Alwar	1	5	9	356	15	4%
22 Aghapur	Bharatpur	34	20	19	599	73	12%
23 Bhangarh	Alwar	3	13	12	341	28	8%
24 Rangmahal	Ganganagar	6	8	9	355	23	6%

Table 8: **Jat Family Types in 4 Villages Surveyed by the Census of India–1961 in Rajasthan**

Village	District	Familes	Simple		Inter.		Joint		Other	
			no.	%	no.	%	no.	%	no.	%
4 Bhadwasi	Nagaur	10	7	70%			3	30%		
18 Janvi	Jalor	2	2	100%						
22 Aghapur	Bharatpur	15	8	53%	1	7%	5	33%	1	7%
24 Rangmahal	Ganganagar	18	12	67%	5	28%			1	5%

Table 9: **Brahman Family Types in 11 Villages Surveyed by the Census of India-1961 in Rajasthan**

Village	District	Familes	Simple		Inter.		Joint		Other	
			no.	%	no.	%	no.	%	no.	%
3 Kyasara	Jhalawar	4	3	75%			1	25%		
5 Abhaṇeri	Jaipur	69	40	58%	25	36%	5	7%		
6 Nangal Sooswatan	Jaipur	4			1	25%	3	75%		
7 Sanwara	Kota	1			1	100%				
8 Gagron	Kota	2			1	50%	1	50%		
9 Malar	Jodhpur	124	69	56%	23	33%	32	26%		
14 Kailashpuri	Udaipur	55	35	64%	6	10%	7	13%	7	13%
18 Janvi	Jalor	4			2	50%	2	50%		
22 Aghapur	Bharatpur	10	2	20%	4	40%	4	40%		
23 Bhangarh	Alwar	10	4	40%	1	10%	3	30%	2	20%
24 Rangmahal	Ganganagar	1	1	100%						

Table 10: **Bhil Family Types in 8 Villages Surveyed by the Census of India-1961 in Rajasthan**

Village	District	Familes	Simple		Inter.		Joint		Other	
			no.	%	no.	%	no.	%	no.	%
8 Gagron	Kota	46	10	22%	15	33%	18	39%	3	6%
9 Malar	Jodhpur	3	2	67%			1	33%		
12 Goriya	Pali	28	20	71%			8	29%		
13 Panarwa	Udaipur	13	8	62%			4	31%	1	7%
14 Kailashpuri	Udaipur	96	65	68%	10	10%	15	16%	6	6%
18 Janvi	Jalor	23	20	87%	3	13%				
19 Peepal Khoont	Banswara	155	120	77%	15	10%	15	10%	5	3%
20 Khajoora	Banswara	34	18	53%	5	15%	7	20%	4	12%

Table 11: **Chamar Family Types in 5 Villages Surveyed by the Census of India-1961 in Rajasthan**

Village	District	Familes	Simple		Inter.		Joint		Other	
			no.	%	no.	%	no.	%	no.	%
3 Kyasara	Jhalawar	12	5	42%	1	8%	4	33%	2	17%
5 Abhaneri	Jaipur	8					7	88%	1	12%
8 Gagron	Kota	7			1	14%	4	57%	2	29%
19 Peepal Khoont	Banswara	7	3	43%			3	43%	1	14%
23 Bhangarh	Alwar	5	1	20%			4	80%		

those for Chamars may have been due to crowded housing. The common beliefs about the relationships between ethnicity and family structure in Rajasthan are sustained by these Census village survey data only with respect to Rajputs, not with respect to Jats or Bhils.

Early Adolescent Marriage and the 'Protective Joint-Family'

In the late 1960s and early 1970s, Lorraine Haddon, a graduate student at the University of Houston, calculated measures of over 60 variables in the 1961 Census. These measures fell into three groups: variables related to family, variables taken to be indices of modernization, and other social-cultural variables such as religion, occupation, and caste or tribe membership. Only a few of these variables were found to have strong (positive or negative) correlations of +/−.60 or better with the indices of joint-family living discussed above (Married Sons and Other Married Relatives).[10] On an all-India basis, negative relationships were found between proportions of joint-families and various educational variables and measures of modernization (Kolenda and Haddon 1987:276, 279-286). These negative relationships were not found in Rajasthan, however, probably because the districts of Rajasthan in which there were low proportions of joint-families (the Gujarat border districts, Jaisalmer, and Ganganagar) were not highly modernized and did not have, except possibly in some towns and in some of the more modernized parts of Ganganagar, especially good educational facilities. The largest number of schools with the most school-goers are in the districts east of the Aravallis, the very districts which are high in joint-families.

The variables with which the indices of joint-family were found to be most strongly related were the proportions of females and males aged 10-14 reported as married. The correlation coefficients between the proportion of Married Sons and the two measures of adolescent marriage were +.912 for females and +.856 for males; the same relationships for proportion of Other Married Relatives were +.848 and +.761. These two variables of adolescent marriage were also highly interrelated, with a correlation coefficient of +.90.

Maps 7 and 8 show the districts in Rajasthan in Quintile 1 on proportions of married females and males aged 10-14. The nine

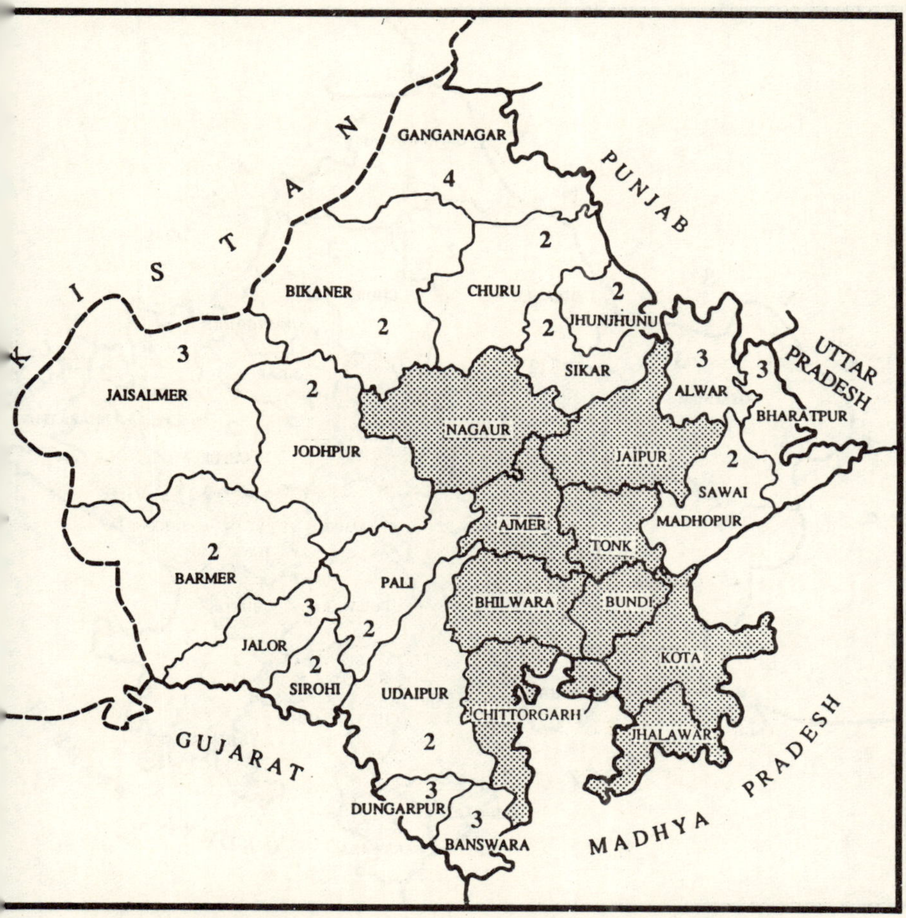

Map 7: **Districts in Rajasthan in First Quintile on Proportions of Females Aged 10–14 Reported as Married (Census of India 1961)**

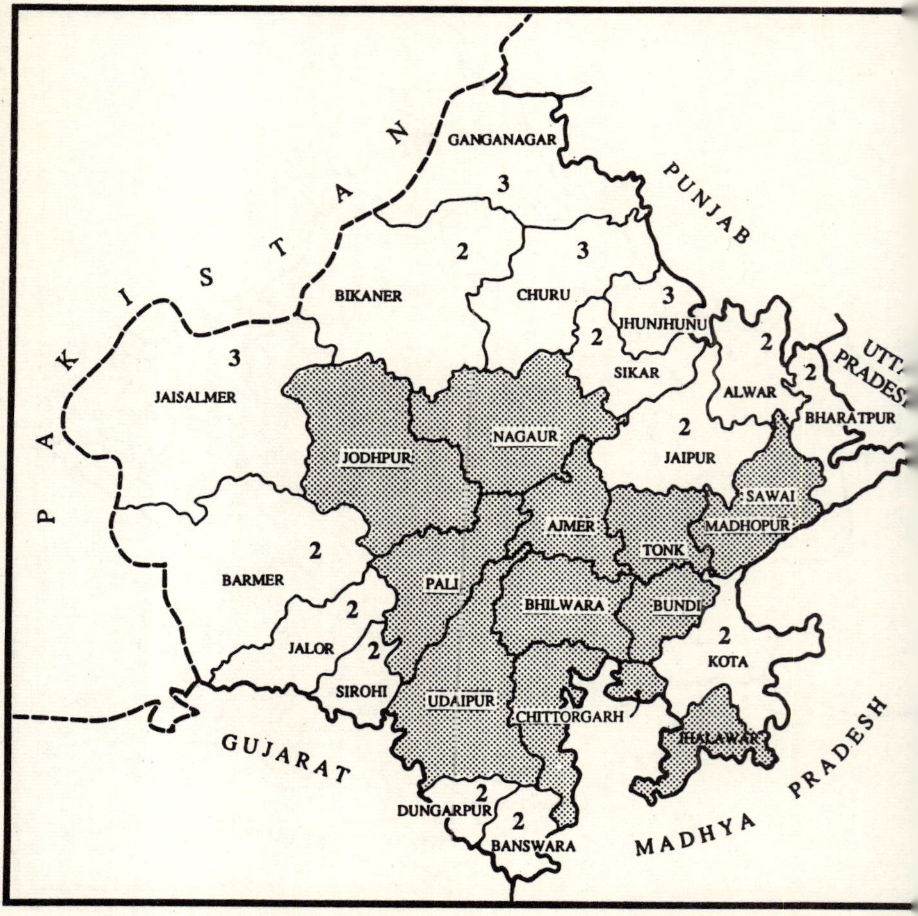

Map 8: **Districts in Rajasthan in First Quintile on Proportions of Males Aged 10–14 Reported as Married (Census of India 1961)**

Map 9: **Seven Districts in Rajasthan in First Quintile on Four Measures: Proportions of Married Sons, "Other Married Relatives," Females 10–14 Married, and Males 10–14 Married (Census of India 1961)**

districts shown on Map 7 ranged between 63.92% (Bhilwara District) and 42.26% (Jaipur District) for females aged 10-14 reported as married; 10 other districts were in the second quintile. Thus in 19 districts of Rajasthan, the proportion of females aged 10-14 reported as married was well above all-India averages. In addition, six districts were in the third quintile and one in the fourth; none was in the fifth quintile.

Map 8 shows 11 Rajasthan districts that fell into the first quintile on proportion of married males aged 10-14, ranging from 32.48% (Bhilwara District) to 13.69% (Udaipur District). Moreover, with 12 districts falling into the second quintile, 23 of the districts of Rajasthan were well above average in proportion of married males 10-14. The other three districts fell in Quintile 3.

A comparison of Maps 3 and 4 with Maps 7 and 8 indicates that young adolescent marriage is more characteristic of Rajasthan than are joint-families. That is, more districts fall above the all-India average on the two measures of adolescent marriage than on the two measures of joint-family. Map 9 shows seven districts which rank in the first quintile on all four of these measures. Spatially contiguous except for Jhalawar, separated by a small section of Kota from Chittorgarh, they form a central core in which there is a high proportion of joint-family households, explained to a considerable extent by the high proportions of married young adolescents.

While the proportions of married 10-14 year olds were recorded in the 1961 Census, it was not noted whether those counted were living with their spouses or not. The meaning of the 1961 Census figures is thus questionable. Were these young adolescents married only in the sense of having had their *shādīs*, or had their *muklāvās* taken place already and were they living together in the husband's household? It is noteworthy that none of the Census ethnographers ever addresses this issue or the question of what is meant by a Census report of "married" 10-14 years old.

Here it is useful to turn to ethnographic evidence. That marriages took place at early ages in Rajasthan is supported by Rama Mehta's memoir about the Oswals (Vaishya bureaucrats) (Mehta 1982:141) attached to the Maharana of Udaipur's court. She writes:

> . . . it must be remembered that the age of marriage in the Oswal community was between nine and twelve years prior to

> 1947, and the age at which a woman came to her husband's home was usually about thirteen to fourteen . . . . Among the Oswals, child marriage was widespread.
>
> . . . purdah becomes a means for minimalizing family disputes, allowing the child bride to function under the supervision of elders without the possibility of contradicting their commands. This was necessary, since a child bride had not been tutored to assume responsibility before she entered marriage. For the young bride, the early years of her marriage constituted a period of training and education. (*ibid.*, 146–148)

According to Rama Mehta, the young Oswal brides were ignorant of housekeeping and were trained by their mothers-in-law, as they were too young to have been properly trained before marriage. In Maharajapur-Kishanpur, too, new brides complained that they did not know how to do the tasks assigned them by their mothers-in-law. They were often so young that they had to be trained to do household chores by their mothers-in-law or older sisters-in-law. If a girl was the junior daughter-in-law in a joint household in which her own sister was the senior daughter-in-law, the latter might even do the work *for* her.

Young age for marriage was noted in 13 of the 1961 Census village surveys (nos, 1, 3, 4, 6, 7, 8, 9, 12, 15, 16, 18, 19, 22). In Kyasara village, Jhalawar District, for example, in which almost half the population was Rajput, another 20% Nath and 10% Chamar, with nine other small caste communities (Singh and Gupta 1965a:2), three-quarters of the females aged 10-14 and one-third of the males aged 10-14 were recorded as married. According to the ethnographers, "There is no unmarried female above the age of 14 in the village" (Singh and Gupta 1965a:37). In only three villages were there any reports of marriage for girls normally occuring after age 14. Two reports refer to Rajputs (4, 18), and one to Kanjars (2).

That marriage ceremonies may take place at extremely young ages is suggested by the report from Kalijal village in Jodhpur District:

> Among the Jats of this village it is customary to hold the marriages of the girls of the family without consideration of their age at the time of performance of death-feast of some

> elderly person. The main consideration behind this custom is economy. Even girls in arms who belong to the family are married on the occasion. It is not unusual to see a small girl seated on a brass plate to be married to a boy who may be a little bigger than her. The children are lifted by the parents who go round the fire to complete the *pheras* [circumambulations of the sacred fire by the bride and groom]. (Singh and Pendharker 1967:14)

In his book on the village of Awan in Kota District, Giri Raj Gupta explains the custom of early age of marriage as follows:

> It is a common practice for girls to marry before reaching puberty. There are several arguments advanced in favour of early marriage. The people believe early marriages tend to protect the chastity of women, ease the transfer of a girl from her father's domain to that of her husband, and make it easier for a girl to adjust to her husband and in-laws. Pre-puberty marriages are also considered to be more sacred and pure than a marriage which takes place later in a girl's life, since the girl has not been contaminated by the pollution associated with menstruation. It is also feared that a girl's approaching sexuality will lead her to relinquish her sacred status as a virgin. It is well known that the Sanskritic scriptures of the Vedic times state that a girl should be married as a virgin and before menarche.
>
> The economic consideration is also very important. A girl married before puberty becomes an economic partner in her conjugal family much earlier. This, in turn, reintegrates the economy of her natal as well as conjugal family.
>
> Traditionally, each incipient family begins with the support of an old family. The young people are responsible for bringing new people into the family, both by marriage and by birth, to replace the old members. Since marriages are expensive events, the family's economy must be preserved by spacing marriages several years apart. The earlier the marriage is organised, the better it is for the family. Parents like to see their responsibilities fulfiled before they retire. Most marriages cost somewhat more than a year's income of the family. In some cases, as among the Rajputs, a marriage may take two to three years of the family's income. Early marriages of the children help the family to space the marriages evenly.

> Another advantage of early marriages is that a person benefits immediately from any advantages he has achieved through the marital alliance.
>
> However, on an average, the boys are usually married between the age of 12 and 16 years, while the girls are married between the age of 9 and 14 years. Analysing the caste rank and its relationship with age at marriage, it appears that there is little association between the two. One of the major inferences could be that it is not the rank of the caste, but its involvement in agricultural activities which could explain the distribution of age at *sagai* [betrothal] and marriage. For purposes of broader generalisation three perceivable trends can be delineated: 1) upper castes marry relatively late, 2) agriculturalists and artisans marry relatively early, and 3) most of the boys and girls among all the castes continue to marry earlier than the minimum ages fixed by the Hindu Marriage Act of 1955, which is 15 for girls and 18 for boys. Obviously, the legislation relating to the age at marriage has had little impact, if any, on the marital practices of the people. (Gupta 1974:65-66)

Note in the quotation above Gupta's statement that "A girl married before puberty becomes an economic partner in her conjugal family much earlier." What both Gupta and Mehta suggest is that in some communities and places in Rajasthan, the bride actually does take up residence with her husband's family before age 14, and possibly before first menstruation. Needless to say, among illiterate people who do not keep exact records, the exact age of a bride upon joining her husband's household may not be known, but it seems safe to say that brides by age sixteen have joined their mothers-in-law. In the case of such early marriages, the joint-family functions to support very young couples not mature enough to manage a household economic enterprise alone. The Rajasthani joint-family can thus be understood to be a reversal of the pre-industrial nuclear family in western Europe, a family founded by an adult male in his mid- or late twenties, trained and ready to support a wife and children, the wife also being in her twenties at marriage (Laslett 1972:85; 1984:99–101). Instead of postponing marriage and child bearing as the English pre-industrial family required, the Rajasthani family supports marriage for even physically immature adolescents, and child-bearing for sexually mature adolescent wives, by having the family unit joint, composed of at least one adult couple and possibly one or more pre-adult couples (couples under age 20).

Prakash Tandon made this contrast between British and Punjabi assumptions about the age of marriage:

> . . . it was in accordance with father's own ideas that uncle preferred to wait for his marriage till he was settled in life. To the old way of thinking this was irrelevant. You married when you came of age and not when you began to earn. Marriage and earning were two separate things. Marriage was a social, familial and religious obligation, while earning was a matter of circumstance. (Tandon 1961:124)

This Punjabi view is quite in line with the Rajasthani view. The joint-familism of the north Indian family can be understood, at least for much of Rajasthan, as more a matter of an adult male and his wife in their thirties or forties taking the lead, with inexperienced married teen-agers following their directions, than as a matter of an elderly patriarch in his fifties or sixties ordering about fully adult sons who are men in their twenties to forties.

These findings strongly suggest a kind of joint family composed of a head couple plus a young teen-age couple living together until either the members of the older couple die or the young couple mature and have so many children that they need more living space. The question would then be whether all joint-families in Rajasthan, and in India as a whole, are 'protective joint-families' of this type.

Of course, the strategy for establishing a couple at a young age may involve a belief that young adolescents are more malleable than older ones, that once a bride has adjusted to her husband's joint-family she is less likely to be discontented that she does not have a home of her own. (See Kolenda 1987:104-105)

The Well-Team Joint-Family

The high correlation between young adolescent marriage and the two measures of joint family (Married Sons and Other Married Relatives) is partly an artifact of the data, since married males aged 10-14 are included in the proportion of married sons in the household sample. Similarly, males and females aged 10-14 who are represented as married are included in the proportion of other married relatives in the sample. What the high correlations between the two measures of joint-family and adolescent marriage measure, then, is the correlation between the whole variable (the married sons or other married relatives of all ages) and part of it (the Married Sons or Other Married Relatives aged 10-14). Thus, the high correlations appear to be a matter of a variable relating to part of itself. Only if the couples in which one spouse was aged 10-14 lived separately in their own households, separate from the Other Married Relatives, would the previous statement be untrue. The ethnographic evidence, however, does not suggest that neolocal residence for such young couples occurs.

One way to find out whether there are other kinds of joint-family besides the 'protective joint-family' is to remove from the household samples the effects of the presence of married 10-14 year olds. This was done[11], and a third measure of family structure was developed, called 'Revised Family Structure'. How then does Rajasthan appear in comparison with the rest of India when joint-family living is measured by Revised Family Structure?

Map 10 shows the seven Rajasthan districts which fall in the top quintile of all the 326 districts in India on Revised Family Structure. The number, of course, is considerably less than the 15 districts in the first quintile on Married Sons (see Map 3 above) or the 11 districts in the first quintile on Other Married Relatives (see Map 4 above). We may presume that the decline in the ranking of other districts in Quintile 1 on Married Sons and Other Married Relatives is due to the considerable prevalence in them of 'protective joint-families'. Indeed, all of these districts fall in the second quintile on the Revised Family Structure measure, indicating that the frequency of joint-families that are not just protecting adolescent brides and grooms is still above average for India as a whole.

How are we to understand the seven districts that are in the first quintile on joint-families once the effect of adolescent brides and groom is factored out? Here I would like to return to the village of Maharajapur-Kishanpur and the third factor contributing to the occurrence of joint-families: the need for the family to function as a work team and, more specifically, a well-team.

To help analyze this factor, I would like to introduce the mapping of Rajasthan into ecological zones by A.K. Sen of the Central Arid Zone Research Institute (CAZRI) in Jodhpur. In the

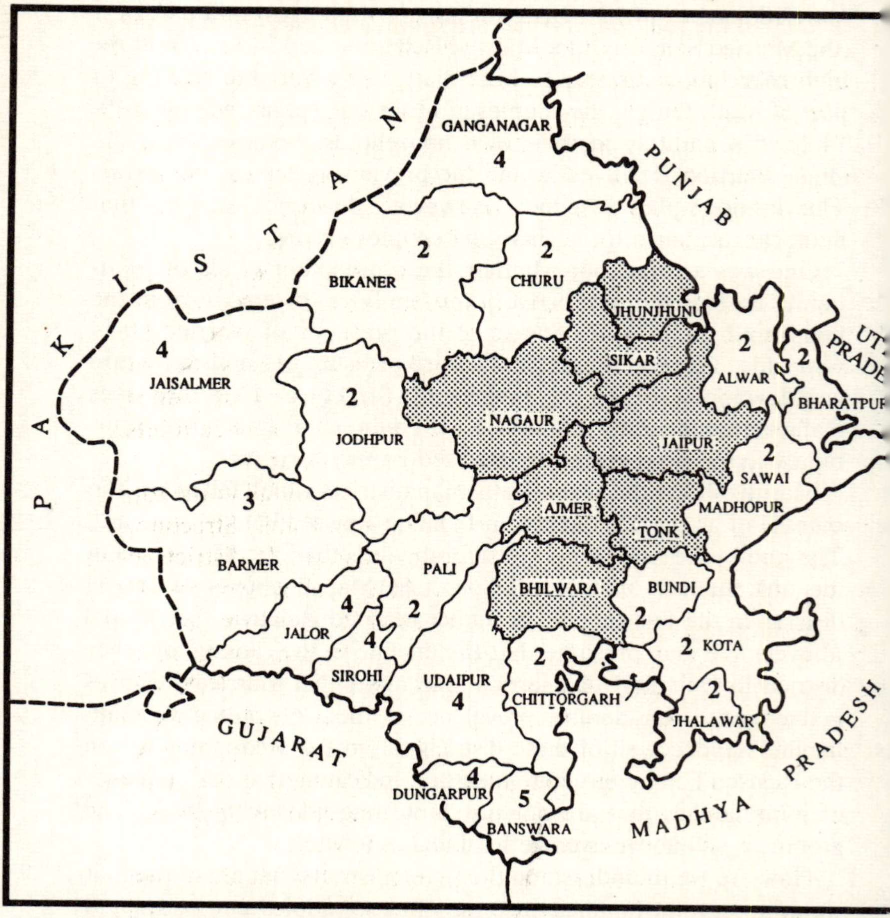

Map 10: **Seven Districts in Rajasthan in First Quintile on Revised Family Structure (Census of India 1961)**

Agricultural Atlas of Rajasthan (1972), he divided Rajasthan into four major ecological zones: the Hot Desert, the Steppe Desert, the Semi-Arid Region, and the Humid Region. With Sen's permission, an adapatation of that map appears below as Map 11. Each of the four major zones are subdivided into three or four sub-zones, yielding a total of 13 ecological sub-zones.

When the seven districts in the first quintile on Revised Family Structure (see Map 10) are superimposed on the ecological map, they fall almost entirely into three sub-zones (see Map 12). Two sub-zones (2-c and 2-d) are in the Steppe Desert, and one (3-b) is in the Semi-Arid Region. Small portions of the seven districts fall into three other sub-zones (1-b, 2-b and 3-a). With the exception of a small portion of Nagaur District, which falls into sub-zone 1-b of the Hot Desert, all seven districts fall into the Steppe Desert and Semi-Arid Region. What this suggests is that, in Rajasthan, the joint-family is a more important adaptation in these two zones than it is in either the Hot Desert or in the Humid Region.

Map 10 shows the quintile rankings of all the districts of Rajasthan on Revised Family Structure. When compared to the map of ecological sub-zones (Map 11), a pattern emerges. In two sub-zones of the Humid Region of southern Rajasthan and Gujarat (4-a and 4-b), all four districts are well below average on Revised Family Structure, falling into either the fourth quintile (Sirohi, Udaipur and Dungarpur) or the fifth (Banswara). The 4a and 4b sub-zones of the Humid Region are distinguished from the 4c sub-zone (composed of Jhalawar, Kota and parts of Bundi and Sawai Madhopur districts) by the considerably greater agricultural activity in the latter called by V.C. Misra the Southeastern Agricultural Region (1967:176-177), due to its closeness to the Chambal River waters and its flatter and better soil.

Conversely, in the Hot Desert, three of the districts (Jodhpur, Churu, Bikaner) are average to low (second quintile) on Revised Family Structure. Barmer, in the third quintile, is average in an all-India ranking, while Jaisalmer and Ganganagar are well below average.

The strength of the joint-family in the Steppe Desert and the Semi-Arid Region suggests that the joint-family is most adapted to areas where there is water for irrigation, but not so little that agriculture is impossible (as in Jaisalmer in the Hot Desert), or enough so that it is not a serious problem as in the Humid Region. The joint-

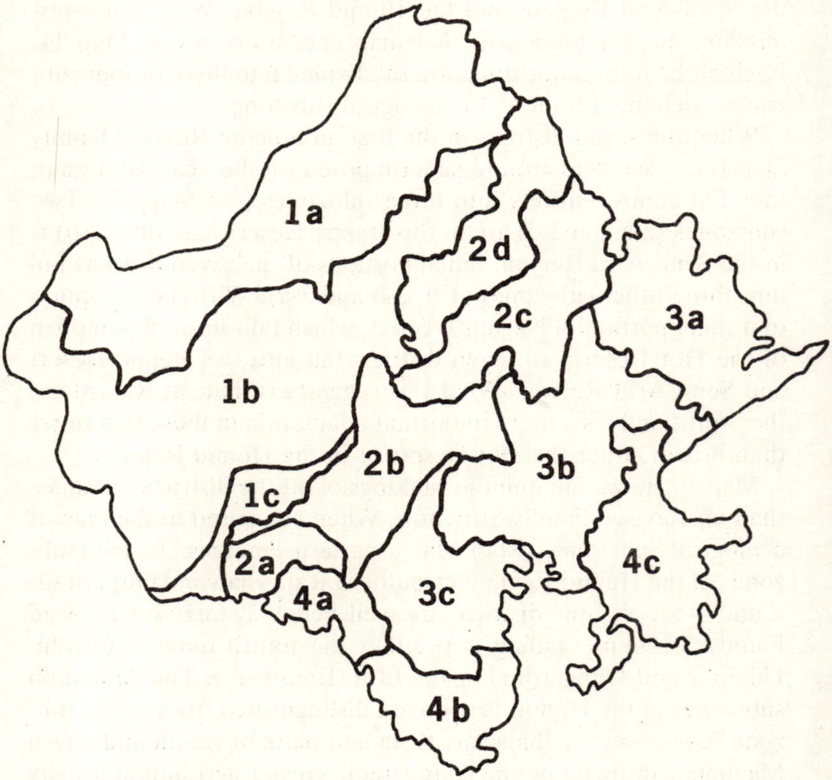

Map 11: Adaptations on "Geographical Regions of Rajasthan Based on Natural Regions" (Source: A. K. Sen Cartography Laboratory, Central Arid Zone Research Institute, Jodhpur, Rajasthan 1967. *1 Hot Desert*: 1a Ganganagar-Jaisalmer Region (Rajasthan Canal Area); 1b Jodhpur Region (Dry Desert); 1c Luni Region (Central and Lower Luni Basins). *2 Steppe Desert*: 2a Jalor Region (Jawai Basin); 2b Ajmer-Pali Region (Upper Luni Basin); 2c Sikar-Didwana Region (Kantli and Didwana-Sambhar Salt Basin); 2d Churu Region (Dry Steppe). *3 Semi Arid Region*: 3a Alwar-Bharatpur Region (Sota Sahibi and Barh Basins); 3b Jaipur Region (Lower Bansi and Morel Basins of the Chambal Catchment); 3c Udaipur-Chittorgarh Region (Chambal-Mahi Waterparting Zone). *4 Humid Region*: 4a Sirohi Region (Upper Sabarmati-Banas Basins); 4b Dungarpur Region (Upper Mahi Basin); 4c Kota Region (Chambal Project Area).

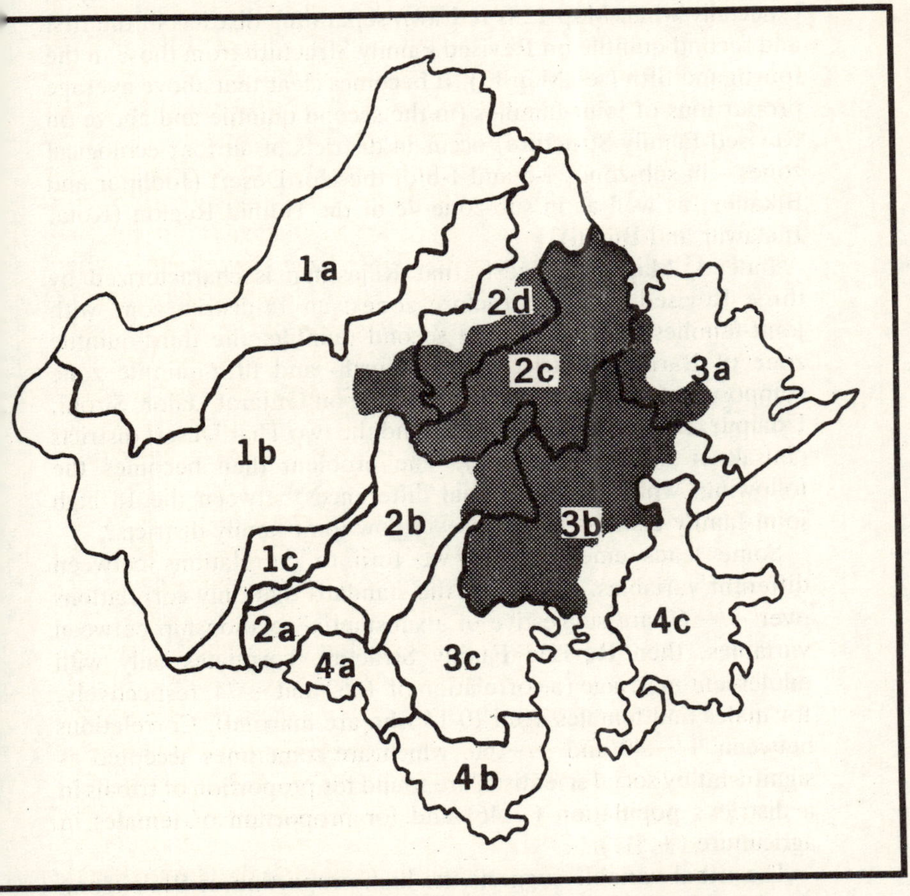

Map 12: **Seven Districts in Rajasthan in First Quintile on Revised Family Structure by Geographical Regions (Census of India 1961)**

family as a well-team thus appears to be one effective strategy for coping with the irrigation problems of the Steppe Desert and Semi-Arid Region.[12]

There are, however, a number of problems with such an analysis, especially when Map 12 is redrawn separating districts in the first and second quintile on Revised Family Structure from those in the fourth and fifth (see Map 13). It becomes clear that above average proportions of joint-families (in the second quintile and above on Revised Family Structure) occur in districts of all four ecological zones – in sub-zones 1-a and 1-b of the Hot Desert (Jodhpur and Bikaner) as well as in sub-zone 4c of the Humid Region (Kota, Jhalawar and Bundi).

Indeed, Map 13 suggests that Rajasthan is characterized by three Revised Family Structure zones: an 18-district zone with joint-families in the first and second quintile, the third-quintile zone of Barmer District, and a fourth- and fifth-quintile zone composed of the five districts bordering on Gujarat (Jalor, Sirohi, Udaipur, Dungarpur, Banswara) and the two Thar Desert districts (Jaisalmer and Ganganagar). The problem then becomes the following: what are the crucial differences between the 18 high joint-family districts and the seven low joint-family districts?

Some leads emerge when we turn to correlations between different variables. If we take the standard that only correlations over +/−.60 are suggestive of a substantial relationship between variables, then Revised Family Structure correlates only with adolescent marriage (a correlation of +.62 and +.74, respectively, for males and females aged 10-14 who are married). Correlations between +/−.40 and +/−.60, which are sometimes accepted as significant by social scientists, are found for proportion of tribals in a district's population (−.46) and for proportion of females in agriculture (+.511).

The tribal variable suggests the high proportion of Bhils along the Gujarat border, especially in the districts of Dungarpur and Banswara, where over half the population are Bhils. However, as we saw above in the discussion of Table 8, the village surveys suggest that Bhils sometimes have low proportions of joint-families and sometimes do not. The variable of females in agriculture suggests joint-family work-teams or well-teams. However, as shown in Map 14, the districts of Dungarpur and Banswara fall into Quintile 1 on females in agriculture but in the fourth and fifth

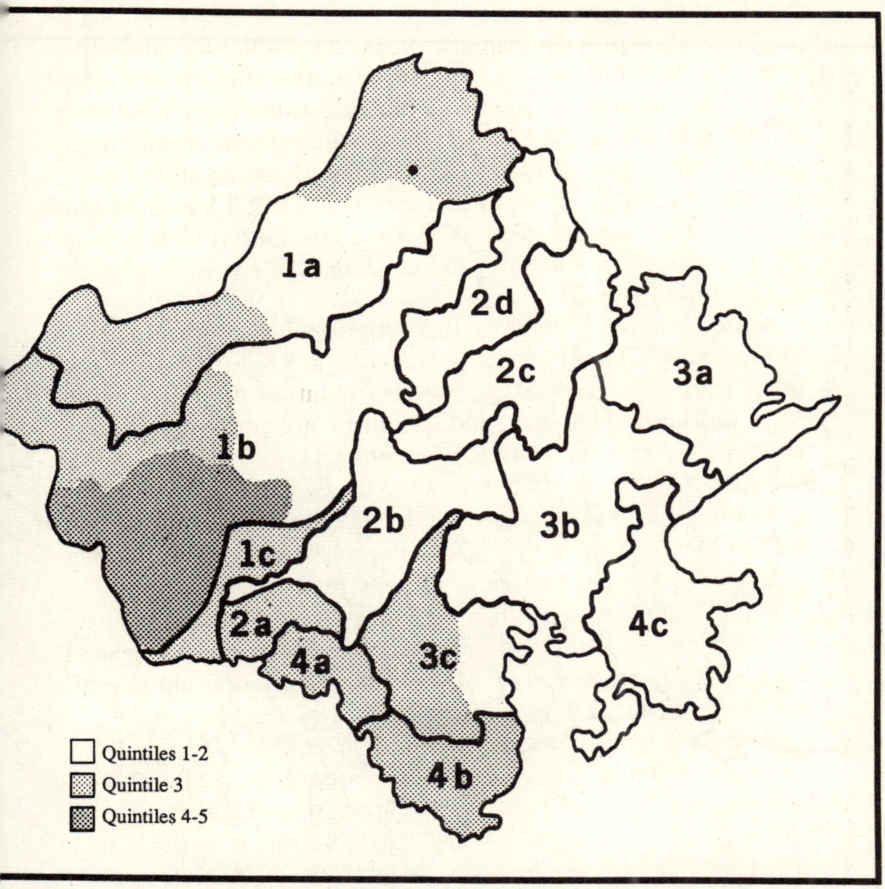

Map 13: **Proportions of Joint-Families in Rajasthan by Quintile Rankings on Revised Family Structure by Geographical Regions (Census of India 1961)**

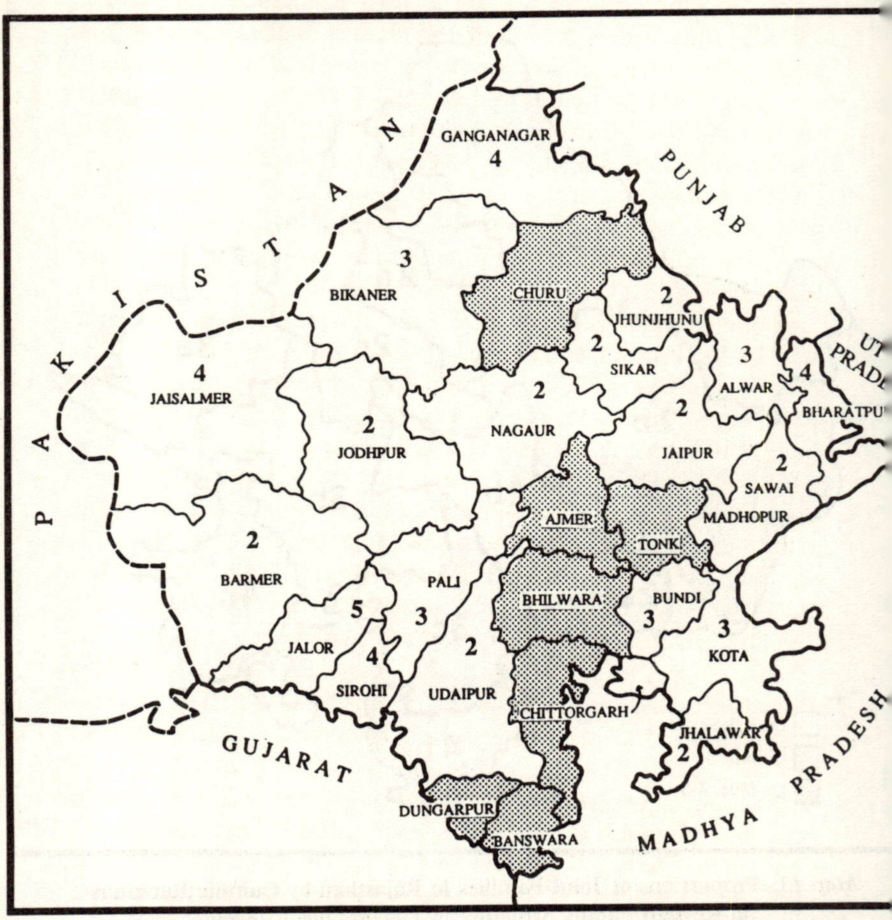

Map 14: **Rajasthan Districts in First Quintile on Proportions of Females in Agriculture (Census of India 1961)**

quintile on Revised Family Structure, thus actually lowering the correlation between these two variables.

The factor that seems to be common to all seven districts in the fourth and fifth quintiles seems to be a paucity of wells. Let us consider the districts first along the Gujarat border, moving from west to east. The 1961 Census District Gazetteer for Jalor reports that only 9% of the land is irrigated (Sehgal 1973a:61). What V.C. Misra calls the Aravalli Region (composed of all of Udaipur, southeast Pali, Sirohi and western Dungarpur) makes up much of the Gujarat border area. "The area being hilly, it is only a small part of the land where irrigation is possible. In Udaipur nearly two-thirds of the land is barren and is not suitable for agricultural use" (1967:173).

At the east end of the Aravalli Region is Dungarpur, characterized in its District Gazetteer as "stony hills covered with low jungle" (Sehgal 1974:2), with its cultivated area "confined to valleys and low ground between the hills" (*ibid.*, 3). Its well irrigation is by the pole-rope system (*ḍhenklī*) or Persian wheel (*ibid.*, 79), both methods requiring only one person rather than a team (Michael 1978:198). Most of the Banswara district is also hills and forest. Thus the mountains and hills on the Gujarat border seem to prevent much well-team irrigation. Jaisalmer District, likewise, which is almost entirely pastoral in its adaptation to the Thar desert, has "hardly any good wells which can be the sources of irrigation" (Sehgal 1973b:7) and extremely deep water tables. Ganganagar too, irrigated since 1927 by the Gang Canal, is characterized by "no well irrigation nor tanks and lakes" (Sehgal 1972:7).

This more refined analysis of well irrigation suggests that the first- and second-quintile districts on Revised Family Structure are districts in which, along with the practice of adolescent marriage, well-team irrigation is important, while the fourth- and fifth-quintile districts tend to be bereft of wells and hence irrigation methods do not require a team. Some of the Gujarat border districts (see Maps 7 and 8) are high on the variable of young adolescent marriage (all of them are in the first and second quintiles on male adolescent mariage, while on female adolescent marriage, Udaipur and Sirohi are in the second quintile, and Jalor, Dungarpur and Banswara in the third). The Gujarat border districts thus seem to be districts in which more 'protective joint-families' occur than well-team joint-families.

The Census figures I have examined thus suggest that the joint-family structure in Rajasthan is associated with an agrarian economic-ecological adaptation which results in adult responsibilities that are incompatible if a single person has to carry them all out. My fieldwork in Maharajapur-Kishanpur likewise suggested that the joint-family in Rajasthan is a work-team, associated especially with well-irrigation in semi-arid regions. While the Persian wheel, counterpoise-bucket lift or *ḍhenklī* are appropriate for water on the surface or close to the surface, and can be operated by a single person (Michael 1978:198), the rope-and-bucket lift (*charas*) method of irrigation appropriate for deeper water requires the cooperation of at least two people. It is the *charas* and deeper water that are characteristic of the wells of the Steppe Desert and Semi-Arid Regions of Rajasthan where Quintile 1 districts on Revised Family Structure are located. The *charas*-teams often consist of brothers, or of a father and son, and may also include a wife or unmarried daughter guiding water into the patches of crop-plants. This need for females to help in the field work in a demographic situation characterized by a general shortage of women in Rajasthan may be responded to by an eagerness to "reserve" wives for sons through the *shādī* ceremony of marriage as early as possible, and thus results in early marriage for females and resultant 'protective joint families'.

Fertility, Sex-Preference and the Joint-Family in Rajasthan

A final question to be examined is whether the data for Rajasthan show any correlation between the joint-family, fertility, and preference for male children. Looking first at fertility, are districts high in proportions of joint-families also high in size of family, average number of children per family, and child/woman fertility rates? High correlations between measures of joint-family living and these variables would suggest that joint-families tend to stimulate fertility more than nuclear families.

Table 12 presents the correlation coefficients for the relationships between these measures and proportion of Married Sons, proportion of Other Married Relatives, and Revised Family Structure. For all three measures, the correlation coefficients are very small, and mostly negative in direction. Thus, no relationship between family structure and these measures (see Table 13)

Table 12: **Rajasthan: Correlations Between Family Size, Number of Children, Child/Woman Fertility, and Measures of Joint-Families and Early Adolescent Marriages (Based on Census of India-1961)**

	Married Sons	Married Relatives	Revised Family Structure	Married Females 10–14	Married Males 10–14
Family size	−.167	.014	.152	−.377	−.433
Average no. of children	−.402	−.245	−.12	−.587	−.556
Child/woman fertility	−.636	−.561	−.49	−.720	−.571

Table 13: **Rajasthan and All-India Compared on Family Size, Number of Children and Child/Woman Fertility (Based on Census of India-1961)**

	Rajasthan			All-India		
	mean	median	range	mean	median	range
Family Size	5.42	5.48	4.81 – 6.08	5.26	5.24	2.91 – 6.59
Average no. of children	2.33	2.32	1.91 – 2.73	2.19	2.18	1.54 – 3.00
Child/woman fertility	.795	.797	.675 – .949	.739	.743	.0793 – .9942

appears of any importance. The list of means and medians shows something else, however: that the average values on the variables of family size, number of children, and child/woman fertility ratios are higher for Rajasthan than the national averages. On all three of these values, Rajasthan lies in the second quintile nationwide. Thus it seems that Rajasthani families tend to be larger and have more children than the average for all of India, and that a woman in her child-bearing years has more children under the age of five than the national average.

The correlation coefficients nevertheless indicate that the higher values on these measures in Rajasthan tend not to be in districts with higher proportions of joint-families (see Map 15 for districts of Rajasthan with high child/woman fertility ratios). This negative relationship is suggested by the fact that the seven districts high in proportion of joint-families on Revised Family Structure fall into the second, third and fourth quintiles on child/woman fertility ratios. When a bilinear analysis between measures of joint-family and child-woman fertility was run, it was found that above 40% of the variance in joint-family values overlapped with (negative) variance in child/woman fertility. This value is much lower than the 70% and higher (positive) variances for the measures of adolescent marriage. It does, nevertheless, suggest a notable negative relationship between the prevalence of joint-families and fertility in women.

The hypothesis that joint-families encourage high fertility is thus incorrect. A striking demonstration of this are the figures for Bhilwara District. Bhilwara was the district in Rajasthan with the highest proportion of married sons in the population of household sample (8.98%), the third highest proportion of married relatives (24.28%), the highest proportion of married females aged 10-14 (63.92%), and the highest proportion of married males aged 10-14 (32.48%). It was also found to have the third lowest average family size (4.88 persons), the third lowest average number of children (1.91), and the lowest child/woman fertility ratio (.67451) of all the districts in Rajasthan. Similar results could be shown for Chittorgarh District, which had the smallest average family size (4.81), the second lowest child/woman fertility ratio (.6965), and the second lowest average number of children (1.93).

The expectation that joint-families encourage high fertility may be based on various assumptions – that a general ideology of

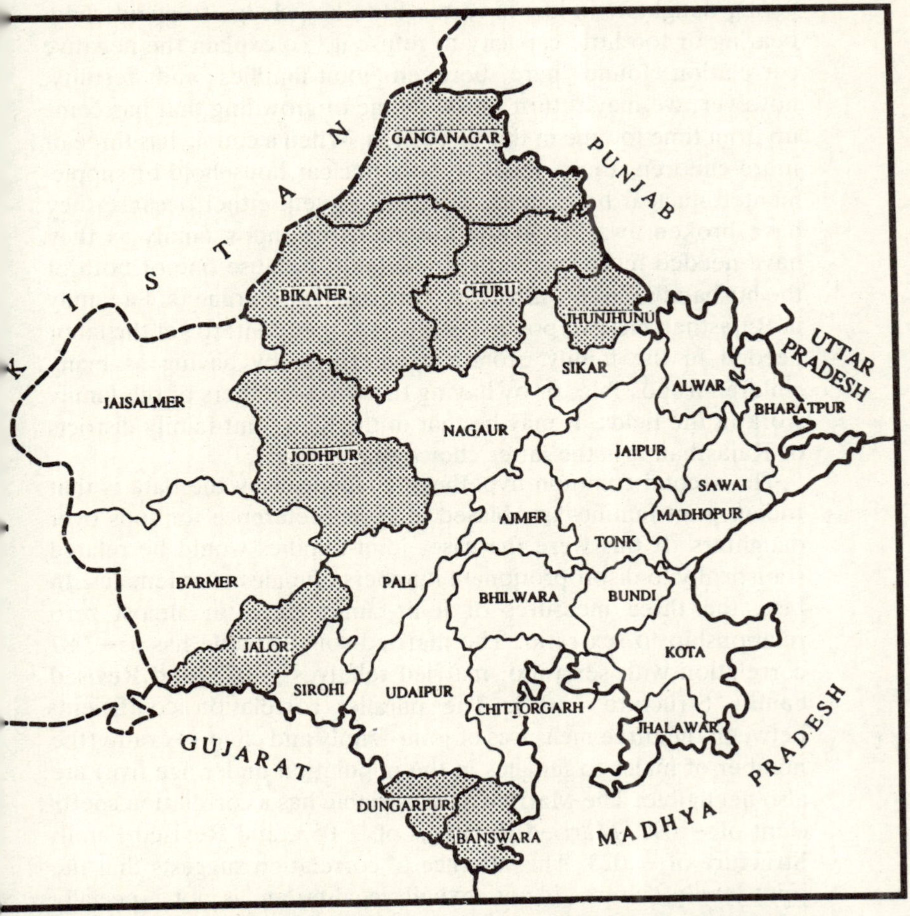

Map 15: **Rajasthan Districts in First Quintile on Child/Woman Fertility Ratio (Census of India 1961)**

'familism' prevails with joint-families, one that encourages wives to reproduce; or that patrilineal joint-families partake of a 'patriarchalism' that includes producing sons for the patriline; or that young daughters-in-law have too little knowledge to avoid childbearing or too little capacity to refuse it. To explain the negative correlation found here between joint-families and fertility, however, we may return to the theme of crowding that has come up from time to time in this discussion. When a couple has three or more children, theirs tends to be a nuclear household or supplemented nuclear household, it can be argued, either because they have broken away from the husband's brother's family as they have needed more space, or, by default, because one or both of the husband's parents are dead. One could also argue that a family in Rajasthan has two possible strategies open to it: to get the labor needed in the family economic enterprise by having as many children as possible, or by having the wives-mothers of the family work in the fields. It may be that in the high joint-family districts of Rajasthan it is the latter choice that is made.

The second common hypothesis challenged by the data is that Indian joint-families are biased in their preference for sons over daughters. If this were the case, joint-families would be related statistically to disproprotionate numbers of males over females. In fact, the three measures of joint-family have an almost zero relationship to sex ratio. The married sons variable has a −.087 correlation with sex ratio, married relatives −.072, and Revised Family Structure −.043. The parallel correlation coefficients between the three measures of joint-family and child-sex ratio (the number of males to females in the population under age five) are also negligible. The Married Sons variable has a correlation coefficient of −.097, Married Relatives of −.053, and Revised Family Structure of −.023. This absence of correlation suggests that the joint-family culture, if not sexually egalitarian, is not especially male-preferential.

Conclusion

This paper has raised the question: why has there traditionally been a higher proportion of joint-family households in Rajasthan than in other states of India? While this question cannot be said to have been finally answered, what this exploration of ethnographic materials and statistical data from the 1961 Census has suggested is that there are interrelated factors contributing to this high proportion of joint-families in the population. Chief among these factors are the tradition of early marriage, leading to the need for the joint-family to function as protector and guide of young couples, and dependence on the joint-family as a work-team. In some parts of Rajasthan, particularly the Semi-Arid Region and the Steppe Desert this work-team is often a well-team as well. Related to and reinforcing early marriage and the 'protective joint-family' are the customs of sibling-set and collateral-set marriage, and multiple weddings on very few auspicious wedding days as a means of curtailing expenses.

Several commonly held hypotheses concerning joint-family living have also been tested in the course of this study, and proven erroneous. Among them is the idea that there are clear caste or tribal preferences for joint-family living, especially on the part of higher castes, as well as the belief that joint-families encourage high-fertility and show a marked preference for male children. A surprising finding was the high proportions of joint-families found among untouchable Chamars, possibly due to their very limited housing. Data from some of the village surveys suggested that one of the effects of land reform has been to encourage land-holding joint-families to fragment themselves into their nuclear components.

The most important finding, one important for understanding the joint-family in many parts of India, is the correlation between young adolescent marriage and joint-families. This suggests a model family structure quite the reverse of that found in much of pre-industrial Europe (Laslett 1984:99-101), in which a man was required to be trained in an occupation and able to support a wife and children before he married, and the newly married couple set up its own household from the start. In the Rajasthani model of the family, young people are expected to be married and ready to reproduce when their bodies are mature enough to do so, and the adolescent husband is not expected to be able to support himself and his wife and children on his own; instead, his parents and/or older brothers expect to both support and supervise the young married couple as long as it is either necessary or desired by the couple themselves. A further contrast between the European pre-industrial family and the Rajasthani joint-family is that the former existed in a demographic context in which many adult men and women remained unmarried all their lives, while the latter exists in a context in which virtually all females and almost all males marry.

In one of his essays Laslett raises the question of whether there is a polar family type to the western famiy:

> an 'Eastern' familial category, where all mothers were young when their children were born, and much younger than their husbands with whom they lived in multiple family households having no servants (1977:15).

Possibly a prime candidate for such a polar type 'Eastern' familial category would be the joint-family household of Rajasthan.

ENDNOTES

A brief version of this paper was read at the Annual Conference on South Asia at the University of Wisconsin-Madison, November 8, 1986. It is also appearing in John N. Gray and David. J. Mearns, eds., *Society From Inside Out: Anthropological Perspectives on the South Asian Household* (New Delhi: Sage Publications, 1989), pp. 55-106. Field work in Rajasthan was supported by Faculty Research Fellowships of the American Institute of Indian Studies, and by grants from the National Science Foundation and the University of Houston. Statistical analysis of the data was supported by the University of Houston through computer time and two Grants-in-Aid.

This study would not have been possible without the work of Lorraine Haddon, who calculated measures of over 60 variables for 326 districts and territories of India from the statistics in the 1961 Census, and Indira Sapru, who served as research assistant on the project in Rajasthan. Others who contributed to the statistical research and analysis were Albert Ballinger, Diane Ballinger, Nancy Bernard, Pam Brown, David Cohen, Gary Dworkin, Christopher Kolenda, Carolyn Lewis, Kevin Olive, Leslie Pinter, Moniker Reuter-Echols, and Rebecca Story. I am also grateful to Joseph E. Schwartzberg for having called my attention in 1965 to the C-I tables of the 1961 Census of India.

Help in obtaining the scores of Census volumes used in the study was given by a number of individuals at several libraries: Gene Jackson, Helen Tatman and Michael Biggs at the University of Houston Library; T. Tsuchiyama and Merry Burlingham at the University of Texas Library; Richard Martin at the University of Virginia Asia Library; and anonymous but helpful librarians at the Louisiana State University Asia Library and the Library of the University of Texas at Arlington.

Thanks are hereby extended to Karine Schomer and the other editors of this volume, and to Thomas Rosin, all of whom made significant suggestions for improving earlier versions of this paper. Ved Vatuk helped me with a calendrical reference. William Skinner's unpublished papers on Chinese demography, which he kindly made accessible to me, gave me courage to apply ethnographic evidence directly to demographic evidence for Rajasthan. Molly Block prepared Maps 1 and 2, Shelby Hall Maps 3 through 15.

1. While these tables are consistently labeled 'C-1', the title for the C-1 Table varies among states.
2. Not all the districts and territories of India as it was in 1961 are included in the study. Excluded are Daman, Diu, Goa, the Yenam portion of Pondicherry, and the divisions of the Northeast Frontier Agency for which data were not available to us. The three divisions of Nagaland are merged and treated as one unit, as are the Laccadive, Amindivi and Minicoy Islands. The protectorate of Sikkim is included. Note that in 1961, the state of Haryana did not yet exist, nor did a number of subsequently designated districts (Rupar, Punjab; Jind, Haryana; Bulsar, Gujarat; or Rajura, Maharastra), and that some districts now in Himachal Pradesh were in the Punjab (Simla, Lahaul and Spiti, Kangra, and Kulu). Finally, since these data are only for rural populations, entirely urban districts (Bombay, Madras, Calcutta, and Bangalore) have been omitted.
3. Regional differences in family structure in various European countries both in the present and the past are beginning to be recognized by social historians (Wall 1983:52-60; Laslett 1977:16-27).
4. One of the founding fathers of modern cultural anthropology, Lewis Henry Morgan, did conceive of sibling-set joint-families. According to Morgan, the second in a series of five successive forms of marriage throughout human evolution was the Punuluan. He described it as follows:

   > It was founded upon the intermarriage of several sisters, own and collateral, with each others' husbands in a group; the joint husbands not being necessarily kinsmen of each other. Also, on the intermarriage of several brothers, own and collateral, with each others' wives, in a group; these wives not being necessarily of kin to each other, *although often the case in both instances* (italics mine). (Morgan 1964:325-326).

   My thanks to the anthropologist Edward Norbeck who mentioned this old reference to me.
5. In this paper, I do not have space to discuss the subject of brideprice or dowry in Rajasthan. Careful examination of the 24 Census village surveys treated below as well as other ethnographic evidence indicates that brideprice is much more prevalent in Rajasthan than is dowry. Neither seems to influence in any obvious way the timing of weddings.
6. Czap (1983:122) noted that large complex households – joint-family households, in the Indian term – were also reported for Latvia and Hungary in the 18th and 19th centuries.
7. At the beginning of each village survey report, the titles of all 36 done in Rajasthan are listed. Unfortunately, despite all the efforts of inter-library loan librarians, I was unable to acquire 12 of these.

8. We are dealing here only with Hindu Rajputs; Gagron also had a large population of Muslim Rajputs (see Table 4).
9. The issue of unbalanced sex ratios in India as a whole and in the districts of Rajasthan more specifically is one I do not have the space to discuss here. The reader may wish to refer to Miller 1981 on this topic. That measures of joint-family do not correlate highly with district sex-ratios or child sex-ratios in Rajasthan is shown in the last section of this paper.
10. Statisticians hold that correlations of from +/−.60 to 1.00 are worth interpreting. Sometimes this criterion is relaxed to allow for interpretation of correlations as low as +/−.40.
11. The effects of married 10-14 year olds upon the indices of joint family was removed by finding in the CII Tables of the Census ("Age and Marital Status") for each district the number of males aged 10-14 who were reported as married, dividing this number by 5 to correspond to the 20% household sample, and subtracting this dividend from the number of Other Married Relatives. The same thing was done for the figures on females aged 10-14 who were married. The resulting remainder was then divided by the total population of the 20% household sample and that proportion was the measure of Revised Family Structure.
12. It is not claimed here that the joint-family is the only organization on which Rajasthan agriculturalists base a work-team. R. Thomas Rosin (1978:469) describes a standard work team for Undhyala village, Nagaur, as follows:

> The organization of labor crucial to the irrigation of a second crop was provided by a four-man team, each member of which was an equal partner, usually from separate families which could contribute kinsmen and affines as needed to augment the labor force at the well. (See also *ibid.*, 475, 487 for other details of this work-team.)

Rosin promises to report in the near future on a survey of irrigation work-teams in Rajasthan that he made in 1982-83.

REFERENCES CITED

Twenty-four Rajasthan village surveys compared and drawn upon in this paper follow. All are in *Census of India 1961* Volume XIV, Part VI-A.

Agarwal, G.D. and G.R. Gupta
1964 *Malar* (Palodi Tehsil, Jodhpur District).
1965 *Nangal Sooswatan* (Amber Tehsil, Jaipur District).
1969 *Aghapur* (Bharatpur Tehsil, Bharatpur District).

Agarwal, G.D. and L.R. Pendharker
1965 *Abhaneri* (Baswa Tehsil, Jaipur District).

Bhargava, R.C. and G.R. Gupta
1965a *Mudh* (Kolayat Tehsil, Bikaner District).
1965b *Mukam* (Nokha Tehsil, Bikaner District).
1965c *Rangmahal* (Suratgarh Tehsil, Ganganagar District).
1966 *Bhadwasi* (Nagaur Tehsil, Nagaur District).

Bhargava, R.C. and L.R. Pendharker
1968 *Bagor* (Mandal Tehsil, Bhilwara District).
Gulati, G.R. Gupta
1966 *Goriya*, (Pali Tehsil, Pali District).
Gulati, B.R. and L.R. Pendharker
1965a *Sanwara* (Shahbad Tehsil, Kota District).
1965b *Panarwa* (Phalasia Tehsil, Udaipur District).
1965c *Bhangarh* (Rajgarh Tehsil, Alwar District).
Gupta, B.R. and L.R. Pendharker
1969 *Gagron* (Kanwas Tehsil, Kota District).
Sharma, B.L. and G.R. Gupta 1967
1967a *Ramnagar Kanjar Colony* (Bundi Tehsil, Bundi District).
1967b *Kailashpuri* (Girwa Tehsil, Udaipur District).
Sharma, B.L. and L.R. Pendharker
1969 *Hasanpur* (Tijara Tehsil, Alwar District).
Singh, Shamsher and G.R. Gupta
1964 *Khajoora* (Kushalgarh Tehsil, Banswara District).
1965a *Kyasara* (Dag Tehsil, Jhalawar District).
1965b *Peepal Khoont* (Ghatol Tehsil, Banswara District).
1966a *Bujawa* (Jodhpur Tehsil, Jodhpur District).
1966b *Janvi* (Sanchore Tehsil, Jalor District).
1967 *Bujawa* (Udaipurwati Tehsil, Jhunjhunu District).
Singh, Shamsher and L.R. Pendharker
1967 *Kalijal* (Jodhpur Tehsil, Jodhpur District).

Buhler, George, transl.
1886 *The Laws of Manu*. Oxford: Clarendon Press.
Chauhan, Brij Raj
1967 *A Rajasthan Village*. New Delhi: Vir Publishing House.
Czap, Peter, Jr.
1983 "'A Large Family: The Peasant's Greatest Wealth': Serf Households in Mishino, Russia, 1814-1858." In *Family Forms in Historic Europe*. Richard Wall, Jean Robin and Peter Laslett, eds. pp. 105-151. New York: Cambridge University Press.
Dandekar, Hemalata C.
1986 "Men to Bombay, Women at Home: Urban Influence on Sugao Village, Deccan Maharashtra, India, 1942-1982." *Michigan Papers on South and Southeast Asia*. University of Michigan: Center for South and Southeast Asian Studies.
Gupta, Giri Raj
1974 *Marriage, Religion and Society: Pattern of Change in an Indian Village*. Delhi: Vikas.
Hajnal, J.
1983 "Two kinds of Pre-Industrial Household Formation Systems." In *Family Forms in Historic Europe*. Richard Wall, Jean Robin and Peter Laslett, eds. pp. 65-104. New York: Cambridge University Press.

Johnson, Erwin

1964 "The Stem Family and Its Extension in Present Day Japan." *American Anthropologist* 66:839-851.

Kane, P.V.

1941 *History of Dharmaśāstra*. Vol. 2, Part 1. Poona: Bhandarkar Oriental Research Institute.

1958 *History of Dharmaśāstra*. Vol. 5, Part 1. Poona: Bhandarkar Oriental Research Institute.

Kolenda, Pauline

1967 "Regional Differences in Indian Family Structure." In *Regions and Regionalism in South Asian Studies*. Robert Crane, ed. pp. 147-225. Durham, North Carolina: Duke University Program in Comparative Studies on Southern Asia Monograph Series. Monograph No. 5. (also in Kolenda 1987)

1968 "Region, Caste, and Family Structure: A Comparative Study of the Indian 'Joint' Family." In *Structure and Change in Indian Society*. Milton Singer and Bernard Cohn, eds. pp. 339-396. Chicago: Aldine Publishing Company. (also in Kolenda 1987)

1969 "Minas of Maharajapur-Kishanpur." Unpublished manuscript.

1978a "Sibling-Set Marriage Alliances and the Structure of the Joint-Family among the Annana Jats of Jaipur, Rajasthan." Unpublished paper read at the 30th annual meeting of the Association for Asian Studies.

1978b "Sibling-Set Marriage, Collateral-Set Marriage, and Deflected Alliance among Jats of Jaipur District, Rajasthan." In *American Studies in the Anthropology of India*. Sylvia Vatuk, ed. pp. 242-277. Delhi: Manohar. (also in Kolenda 1987)

1987 *Regional Differences in Family Structure in India*. Jaipur: Rawat.

Kolenda, Pauline and Lorraine Haddon

1987 "Marked Regional Differences in Family Structure in India." In *Regional Differences in Family Structure in India*, by Pauline Kolenda, pp. 214-288.

Laslett, Peter

1972 "Introduction: The History of the Family." In *Household and the Family in Past Time*. Peter Laslett and Richard Wall, eds. pp. 2-89. London: Cambridge University Press.

1977 "Characteristics of the Western Family Considered over Time." In *Family Life and Illicit Love in Earlier Generations*, by Peter Laslett, pp. 12-49. Cambridge: Cambridge University Press.

1984 *The World We Have Lost Further Explored*. New York: Charles Scribner's Sons.

Lushington, C.S.

1833 "On the Marriage Rites and Usages of the Jats of Bharatpur." *Journal of the Asiatic Society* 18:273-297.

Mehta, Ram

1982 "Purdah among the Oswals of Mewar." In *Separate Worlds: Studies of Purdah in South Asia*. Hanna Papanek and Gail Minault, eds. pp. 139-163. Columbia, Missouri: South Asia Books.

Michael, A.M.

1978 *Irrigation: Theory and Practice*. New Delhi: Vikas.

Miller, Barbara Diane

1981 *The Endangered Sex*. Ithaca, New York: Cornell University Press.

Misra, V.C.

1967 *Geography of Rajasthan*. New Delhi: National Book Trust of India.

Morgan, Lewis H.

1964 *Ancient Society*. Cambridge: Belknap Press of Harvard University Press.

Nakane, Chie

1967 *Kinship and Economic Organization in Rural Japan*. New York: Humanities Press.

Pasternak, Burton, Carol R. Ember and Melvin Ember

1976 "On the Conditions Favoring Extended Family Households." *Journal of Anthropological Research* 32:109–123.

Rosin, R. Thomas

1968 "Changing Land Tenure and Village Polity in Rajasthan, India: An Interactional Perspective." Ph.D. Anthropology Department, University of California at Berkeley.

1978 "Peasant Adaptation as Process in Land Reform: A Case Study." In *American Studies in the Anthropology of India*. Sylvia Vatuk, ed., pp. 460-495. Delhi: Manohar Publications.

1987 "Set Marriage and the Continuity of the Joint Family in Rajasthan." Paper read at the Conference on Conservation of the Environment and Culture in Rajasthan, Jaipur, December 1987.

Sehgal, K.

1972 *Ganganagar*. Rajasthan District Gazetteers. Jaipur: Central Government Press.

1973a *Jalor*. Rajasthan District Gazetteers. Jaipur: Central Government Press.

1973b *Jaisalmer*. Rajasthan District Gazetteers. Jaipur: Central Government Press.

1974 *Dungarpur*. Rajasthan District Gazetteers. Jaipur: Central Government Press.

Sen, A.K.

1972 *Agricultural Atlas of Rajasthan*. Jodhpur: Central Arid Zone Research Institute.

Tandon, Prakash

1961 *Punjabi Century, 1857-1947*. Berkeley: University of California Press, 1968. (1st ed. 1961)

Wall, Richard

1983 Introduction to *Family Forms in Historic Europe*. Richard Wall, Jean Robin and Peter Laslett, eds. pp. 1-63. New York: Cambridge University Press.

PANCHAYATI RAJ IN RAJASTHAN: THE PENALTIES OF SUCCESS

JAMES WARNER BJÖRKMAN AND HET RAM CHATURVEDI

Panchayati Raj, the scheme proposed in 1957 by the Balwantray Mehta Report to India's National Development Council,[1] was a bold experiment in democratic decentralization whose adoption was expected to affect the entire system of local self-government in India. The scheme was launched on Mahatma Gandhi's birth anniversary in 1959 when two states, Rajasthan and Andhra Pradesh, legislatively enacted the recommendations of the Report. While other states later adopted various alternative schemes for democratic decentralization, only Rajasthan and Andhra Pradesh closely followed the framework recommended by the Report.

Rajasthan was created after independence by the merger of princely states which had "acceded" to the Government of India. Its people had played a rather minor role in India's independence movement, and its princely states had not experienced the growth of local and provincial representative government brought about elsewhere by the Government of India Acts of 1909, 1919 and 1935. Most people therefore thought Rajasthan to be the state least prepared for an experiment in democratic decentralization.

But a few saw the absence of fixed ways and vested interests as an advantage. These latter were convinced that social and political reconstruction of the sort envisioned by the Mehta Report *could* be achieved in a society that had only recently ceased being ruled by princes and *jāgīrdārs* (feudal landed aristocrats) and that only recently had acquired a statewide political leadership and a unified civil administration. If the new social order had to confront institutional legacies that militated against it, it had unique opportunities created by the very fact that previous structures of local rule had been displaced and discredited by the termination of princely rule. Furthermore, Rajasthan had the advantage of a strong sense of historical continuity shared by its former princely status.

This paper draws on the extensive literature on Panchayati Raj and on post-independence politics in Rajasthan, and on the authors' own field work during 1970-72, 1979-80, 1986-87 and periodic brief visits in between. It presents an overview of Panchayati Raj in Rajasthan from its inception in 1959 to the situation in the late 1980s. It looks at the dynamics of the institution and its fate over time – initial success followed by gradual erosion – and seeks to identify factors that contributed to both. In analyzing the problem, the paper considers Panchayati Raj from four different, though often interwined perspectives: (1) the ideological perspective – Panchayati Raj as a government policy grounded in Gandhian principles but implemented in a post-Gandhian era; (2) the developmental perspective – Panchayati Raj as a developmental strategy, later by-passed in favor of others; (3) the political perspective – Panchayati Raj as both a force and a pawn in the struggle among different political levels and interests in Rajasthan; and (4) the administrative perspective – Panchayati Raj as a new administrative entity that challenged the existing framework, but whose transformative potential was eventually neutralized.

Our central thesis is that Panchayati Raj got off to a fast start in Rajasthan because of the discredited nature of the old order and its local institutions. Panchayati Raj then became so successful, however, that it threatened both the recently arrived state-level political class and the newly established state administrative agencies. Ultimately Panchayati Raj was undermined by these competing interests.

Panchayati Raj: An Overview

Gandhi's belief in the intrinsic strength and moral value of Indian village life (its capacity for community, self-reliance and self-government) was the source of India's post-independence efforts to create viable institutions for local self-government and rural development. Gandhi's own experimental programs in rural reconstruction had begun at Sevagram in 1920 and after 1938 had been expanded at Wardha. These programs aimed at the reconstruction of rural society through local-level initiatives and voluntary associations of dedicated workers. Gandhi assumed that village self-governance through the traditional institution of the *panchāyat* would provide an important foundation for India's nascent democracy. This goal is now enshrined in Article 40 of the Constitution of India, which states that "the state shall take steps to organize village panchayats and endow them with such powers and authority as may be necessary to enable them to function as units of self-government" (Basu 1983:110).

From the beginning, the government expected *panchāyats* to go beyond mere administration and even beyond the dispensing of justice to a level of active responsible participation in the Community Development Program. Initiated during the first Five-Year Plan (Government of India 1952), the Community Development Program was conceived as a well-rounded scheme for comprehensive community uplift which simultaneously set goals in health, education, social welfare, agriculture, animal husbandry, co-operation, cottage industries and small-scale industries. One of its basic tasks was to reorganize localities in order to render them capable of action on these diverse fronts. Traditionally, Indian government administration had been geared toward maintaining law and order and collecting revenue. In contrast a new role was envisioned for local government which would be based on broad social and political participation. Since the Mughal era, districts (*zilās*) had been the lowest level of effective state administration. While the district remained important for planning, coordination and supervising of government activities in the post-independence period, the Planning Commission judged it too large a unit for effective development programs. At the same time, however, the Planning Commission considered the villages themselves too numerous and too diverse to serve as primary units for development schemes. Gandhi's vision of the villages notwithstanding, they were thought by almost everyone else to be weak in resources, prone to divisive factors of caste and faction, dominated by the few, accustomed to a *mā-bāp* ('mother-and-father') tradition of government from above, and lacking in a sense of energetic self-help (Tinker 1954:94-133).

Administrative units called development blocks were therefore proposed, each to include about 100 villages with a total population of about 100,000. These units paralleled but did not always overlap the sub-district revenue units (*tehsīls*). Each block had to provide "an area large enough for functions which the village *panchayat* (council) cannot perform and yet small enough to attract the interest and service of its residents" (Government of

India 1957:I, 9). These blocks were to be not only administrative devices, but centers of political participation, decision and implementation.

Some five thousands blocks were needed to cover all of India. From a modest beginning of 155 units in 1952, almost 1500 blocks had been established by 1957; by 1963 the country was blanketed by 5182 of them (Maddick 1970:48). Located at block headquarters were the extension staff of various government departments, specialized cooperatives and, in some states, the primary land development banks. This administrative reform was designed to produce convenient middle-range units for the organizing and implementing of development programs, and to provide the kind of face to face contacts between cultivators and change agents that would not have been possible if the programs had been administered at the district level (Beer and Ensminger 1959:135-152; Mehta 1962).

The government's high expectations of the Community Development Program were not entirely fulfilled. Unlike districts or villages, the blocks lacked established identities as territorial units. Furthermore, as the scheme unfolded, the original Community Development Program did not elicit the level of popular participation anticipated but rather bogged down in bureaucratic rules. While the stated goal was to encourage popular participation in the development process, Community Development officials tended to patronize the villagers just as colonial magistrates had done before. The people did not become as involved as the government had hoped nor were development goals set by the Plans attained (Potter 1964:45-47). Evaluation reports from that period also indicate that the Community Development activities failed to help economically disadvantaged classes; those who succeeded in improving their economic and social conditions usually belonged to sections of village society already better off than others.

In 1957, in order to examine the problems faced by the scheme, the Committee on Plan Projects of the National Development Council commissioned a special team, chaired by Balwantray Mehta, an experienced administrator and politician as well as a committed Gandhian.[2] The Report issued by the Mehta team (Government of India 1957), recommended that development efforts be expedited through a system of government designed to decentralize administrative functions, elicit local participation in development planning, and bring about joint implementation of development programs by officials and local leaders. The name given to this scheme was Panchayati Raj.

Panchayati Raj was a system of three distinct tiers below the state government. At the grass-roots level were the Gaon Panchayats or village councils. *Panchas* (members of the Panchayat) were elected on the basis of universal adult franchise, while the *sarpanch* (Panchayat chairman) could be elected either directly by the villagers or indirectly by the other *panchas*. At the block level were the Panchayat Samitis or Block Councils whose members were the *sarpanchas* of the constituent villages and other co-opted and *ex officio* members – women, representatives of scheduled castes and tribes, and leaders of cooperative societies. From among the Samiti membership, a chairman or *pradhān* was indirectly elected. The chairmen of all the Panchayat Samitis in any single district then constituted a Zila Parishad or district association. Additional members were co-opted to this district-level unit to represent women, scheduled castes and tribes. Furthermore, all local Members of the Legislative Assembly (MLAs) and Members of Parliament (MPs) were automatically members of the Zila Parishad. This augmented body elected its own presiding officer, the *pramukh*.

The political fulcrum of the Panchayati Raj system was its middle tier, the Panchayat Samitis. These block level units were responsible for development functions, especially preliminary plans and implementation of community development schemes. The Samitis also were to control most of the physical resources for development, including tax monies and material inputs, their allocation and use. The Zila Parishads were coordinating and advisory bodies. Few administrative activities were assigned to the village Panchayats.

As will be seen in the case of Rajasthan, Panchayati Raj, though expected to operate in a non-partisan fashion, soon became another battleground for political parties (Brass 1965:225). At least during the 1960s, local leaders found it politically advantageous to control Panchayat Samitis and their resources. As the same time, owing to successive reorganizations of activities and boundaries, confusion grew about duties at the block level. Revenue and development functions had been separated, so their potential complementarity was obscured. As long as government funds were made available to the blocks, they remained salient social institutions, but when authority over investment funds was shifted to other agencies, their importance diminished. The decline of block level administration marked a crisis in Panchayati Raj in Rajasthan from which it has not to this day recovered.[3]

The Rajasthan Context for Panchayati Raj: Environment and History

Rajasthan posed certain special problems for the Panchayati Raj experiment. Not only was the state very poor, but it had extreme internal variation in ecology and a very diverse social composition. Perhaps most important of all, it had only recently replaced princely rule with a democratic system of government. All four of these factors influenced the fate of Panchayati Raj in Rajasthan.

Rajasthan's geography presented particular problems in terms of communications networks and possibilities of logistical support for government programs. First of all, with a total area of 342,239 square kilometers, Rajasthan is India's second largest state. Secondly, the Aravalli range, diagonally bisecting Rajasthan from southwest to northeast, and separating the more arable eastern and southern zones from the sands of the Thar Desert, forms a natural barrier to communication between the two parts of the state. Finally, one-third of Rajasthan's administrative districts fall in the Dry Zone, which experiences chronic drought conditions. Thus, because of differences in natural resources and variations in climatic conditions, there is considerable disparity in economic development among the various regions of Rajasthan.

Economically, Rajasthan was and still is one of the poorest regions of India. With four-fifths of its population rural, agriculture is singularly important. Yet in terms of both per acre production and per person engaged, productivity in Rajasthan was for some time far lower than elsewhere in India. Because rainfall is low, and because barely a quarter of the total area under cultivation has irrigation facilities, the supply of water through tube-wells and/or canals as well as the supply of electricity for pumping sets become critical political issues. As it turned out, neither of these fell under the jurisdiction of Panchayati Raj institutions. Thus although agricultural production had to be increased, Panchayat administration had no control over these critical resources.

Rajasthan's social composition also presented special problems for Panchayati Raj. Though the population of Rajasthan has doubled since independence, it was then and has remained the most sparsely populated of the major states of India. Great internal variation in population density has also been a continuing pattern.[4] Moreover Rajasthan's population was and is still predominantly rural. While the overwhelming majority (89%) is Hindu, more than a quarter are from scheduled castes and tribes.[5]

The upper and middle castes also present a segmented picture. Rajputs, constituting a mere 6% of the population, are historically the dominant social group which ruled all the erstwhile princely states except Bharatpur, Dholpur and Tonk. Numerically less than the Rajputs, the Hindu and Jain merchant castes have been very influential as entrepreneurs and financiers. Brahmins (5% of the population) played a leading role in the States Peoples Freedom Movements in the various princely states and, since independence, have held impfotant political positions in the state. The largest single caste in the state, the Jats, account for 9% of the total population. As an economically prosperous agricultural middle caste, the Jats have periodically but thus far unsuccessfully challenged Brahmins and Rajputs for leadership of the Congress and other parties.[6] Thus the social composition of Rajasthan, in which no group or community accounts for even 10% of the population, presented Panchayati Raj with the problem of segmentation.

The most crucial factor in both the early success and the later problems of Panchayati Raj in Rajasthan was the state's political background. Until 1947 the whole region had been almost entirely under princely rule, with only Ajmer District, once directly ruled by the Mughals, being part of British India.[7] Like most of the other princely territories that became integrated into the Indian Union, the states of Rajputana had experienced very little of the political organization and mass participation in the independence movement characteristic of areas directly ruled by the British. Even the Indian National Congress had not organized directly in princely India but had worked through the Praja Mandals,[8] also called States Peoples Freedom Movements, which were popular organizations and committees sponsored by the Congress (Sisson 1972:50-72). Although by the late 1930s and early 1940s, a number of British Residents at princely courts were urging rudimentary experiments in local self-government, few states even gave such experiments a try, especially in Rajasthan. Thus princely India had less direct exposure to 20th century politics than did the territories of British India (Saksena 1972). Likewise its infrastructure for mass markets, communications, transportation, administration, education and other intangible technologies was much less developed. There was, of course, some variation among the princely states themselves. Jaipur, for example, was regarded as relatively "advanced" whereas Udaipur was more "backward."

Despite these inhibiting factors, the early 20th century witnessed political unrest in Rajasthan just as in other parts of India. Its genesis lay in the repressive policies of the rulers and their *jāgīrdārs*, the mass upsurge against colonial rule elsewhere, and the freedom movement which was spreading throughout India. Organized protests took place on an accelerating basis from the 1920s onward in the various princely states of Rajputana.

Led by Jai Narayan Vyas (Jodhpur), Manik Lal Verma (Udaipur), Hiralal Shastri and Gokulbhai Bhatt (Jaipur), Hari Bhau Upadhyaya (Ajmer) and others,[9] these movements challenged princely rule. They were largely urban-based and led by upper-caste Hindus, but some mobilization of the rural masses took place as well. Jat leaders like Khumbha Ram Arya in Bikaner and Baldev Ram Mirdha in Jodhpur organized Kisan Sabhas (farmers' associations). Because they were directed by the landed peasantry against their Rajput rulers, these movements had a rather different character and support base; their primary goal was to acquire secure land ownership and tenancy rights. This gave rise to agitation in some of the states and, at least in one case, in Sikar, led to open confrontation.

Despite these sporadic movements and revolts, political action oriented to challenging princely rule in the various states remained uncoordinated and largely ineffective. The Indian National Congress, working through the Praja Mandals, was unable to organize the people around a common cause. While there were a number of able leaders in various princely states, their efforts were directed at grievances and reforms in particular states. No political unit or entity came into being which could serve as a focus for common action. Thus the political legacy with which the new state of Rajasthan had to contend was one of fragmented leadership and a relatively low level of popular participation. This legacy had important implications for the Panchayati Raj experiment.

Meanwhile, outside the urban centers and areas affected by

Kisan Sabhas, control over the countryside and its cultivators remained largely in the hands of the *jāgīrdārs*. In exchange for collecting revenue from their *jāgīrs* (estates), they exercised ruler-like authority over their domains, enjoying considerable power and autonomy.[10] The princely rulers had direct control only over their own *khālsā* lands – lands directly administered through their administrative staffs. When the modern state of Rajasthan came into existence, two-thirds of its area was under the *jāgīrdārī* system.

In some ways, the *jāgīrdārs* and their agents did provide rudimentary government services at the local level. Records from some of the *ṭhikānās* (estates) indicate that the *jāgīrdārs* provided basic services such as security, law and order, support for religious institutions and, to an extent, education and welfare.[11] In Kanota, one such estate in Jaipur state, the *jāgīrdārs* acted as capitalist bankers by lending money to merchants and agriculturalists for constructing local development projects (Rudolph and Rudolph 1975). In another, Bedla in Udaipur, they lent money for agricultural development projects. On *khālsā* lands, princely states occasionally engaged in settlement operations that gave cultivators land rights and a lower fixed revenue demand. And in Jaipur, Sir Swinton Jacob, under Maharjas Ram Singh and Madho Singh, built dams and hospitals and provided cultural amenities. Thus, while limited in both the range and quality of the services provided, some kind of local government did exist in pre-independence Rajputana.

All these activities, however, were in the hands of maharajas' administrators and the Rajput lineages allied with the ruling princely houses. The bulk of the local population consisted of cultivators who had limited rights to the land they tilled, and certainly no control over their local government. In such a situation, Panchayati Raj came not only as a revolutionary idea but also as a way to meet development needs that were only rudimentarily met by the princes and *jāgīrdārs*. The relative backwardness of the newly formed state of Rajasthan may partly account for the early success of Panchayati Raj there.

Panchayati Raj and Post-Independence Politics in Rajasthan

Panchayati Raj was adopted by the Congress government of

Rajasthan, and its fate was intertwined with that party's strength in state electoral politics. Designed to encourage village-level participation in the political process, Panchayati Raj depended on the Congress party having well-developed grass-roots. As will be demonstrated, Congress was able to maintain its hold on Rajasthan primarily because the political opposition was fragmented, but its own organizational base was never strong. As a result, Panchayati Raj never received the benefit of a strong Congress presence that would create stability and continuity at the grass-roots level.

At the time of independence, no political party had a secure base in Rajasthan and no leader was acceptable to all groups and factions. Before independence, no political leader had operated in more than one region of the state, and consequently each had a very narrow base of political support. As a result, the initial political leadership of Rajasthan was unstable. Slowly, however, Mohan Lal Sukhadia, a protege of Udaipur's Praja Mandal leader Manik Lal Verma, emerged as the dominant political figure in Rajasthan. By successfully managing competing factions and groups from his base in Udaipur he gradually consolidated his position as leader of the Congress party in the state. Starting in 1954, Sukhadia held the Chief Ministership for 17 consecutive years, the only Chief Minister anywhere in India to remain in power for such an extended period of time. For 12 of those years he was assisted by Bhagwat Simha Mehta, scion of an important Udaipur bureaucratic lineage and an early enthusiast for Panchayati Raj.

Despite Sukhadia's hold on the Chief Ministership, however, the Congress party itself was never very strong. As can be seen from Table 1, voter support for Congress from 1952 to 1984 in both state assembly (Vidhan Sabha) and national (Lok Sabha) elections remained at less than half of the electorate. At times it fell below one-third.[12] In other words, even though almost continuously in power for over three decades, the party failed to consolidate its electoral base.

While Congress was always able, by hook or by crook,[13] to obtain enough legislative seats in Vidhan Sabha elections to form majority governments (except for the brief two-year interregnum between 1977 and 1979 when the Janata party was in power), this long spell of Congress rule must be largely attributed to Sukhadia's personal political skill. By accomodating and co-opting various

Table 1: **Party Position in Rajasthan Elections**

Election Year	Assembly Elections*				Lok Sabha Elections**			
	Valid votes and seats	Percentages of votes and actual seats			Valid votes and seats	Percentages of votes and actual seats		
		Congress	All other parties	Independents		Congress	All other parties	Independents
1952	3,261,442 N=100	39.5% 82	33.0% 43	27.5% 35	3,526,957 N=20	41.4% 9	29.5% 5	29.2% 6
1957	4,746,398 N=176	45.1% 119	20.8% 25	34.1% 32	3,649,083 N=22	53.6% 19	18.8% 0	27.5% 3
1962	5,132,963 N=176	40.0% 88	39.1% 67	20.9% 21	5,192,952 N=22	37.6% 14	38.0% 5	24.4% 3
1967	6,756,264 N=184	41.4% 89	42.3% 79	16.3% 16	6,814,419 N=23	40.4% 10	43.0% 11	17.1% 2
1971	–	–	–	–	6,924,879 N=23	50.4% 14	35.6% 7	12.3% 2
1972	7,775,814 N=184	51.1% 145	31.5% 28	17.4% 11	–	–	–	–
1977	8,525,664 N=200	31.5% 41	52.6% 153	16.0% 6	8,404,427 =25	30.6% 1	66.5% 24	2.9% 0
1980	9,252,664 N=200	43.0% 133	44.0% 55	13.1% 12	9,474,979 N=25	42.6% 18	50.6% 7	6.8% 0
1984	14,473,975 N=200	46.4% 113	41.5% 77	11.9% 10	11,187,715 N=25	52.7% 25	40.4% 0	6.8% 0

Note: These data have been compiled on the basis of the source books prepared by the Data Unit of the Centre for the Study of Developing Societies. The data have been published in separate volumes, and the full citations for relevant volumes are as follows:

* V.B. Singh and Shankar Bose, *State Elections in India: Data Handbook on Vidhan Sabha Elections 1952–1985*, Vol. 1 (New Delhi: Sage Publications, 1987).

** V.B. Singh and Shankar Bose, *Elections in India: Data Handbook on Lok Sabha Elections 1952–1985*, 2nd ed. (New Delhi: Sage Publications, 1986).

contending groups and factions both within Congress and outside, he steered the party through difficult times and kept it in power. Sukhadia's successors have been less successful; during the 16 years since he stepped down as Chief Minister in 1971, the office has been held by six different people. Such turnover in high office has naturally contributed to factionalism and internal instability in the party.

The opposition to Congress in Rajasthan has always been fragmented. Over the period from 1952 to 1984, it came from 19 different political parties[14] as well as from a relatively large number of independents. Often, opposition parties received active support from former princely rulers. During the 1950s the main force behind the Ram Rajya Parishad in Rajasthan, for example, was Thakur Madan Singh of Danta. Similarly, the Swantantra party during the 1960s was led by Maharani Gayatri Devi of Jaipur and Maharawal Laxman Singh of Dungarpur. Independents likewise tended to be former rulers or *jāgīrdārs*, who had a popular personal base but did not wish to commit themselves to any political party or, especially later on, failed to secure party tickets to contest elections.[15] If elected, they could then join the ruling party with considerable personal advantage – especially if their support was essential to secure a majority coalition. Their number gradually declined over successive assembly elections, and they won no Lok Sabha seat after 1971.

Leftist political parties like the Praja Socialist Party, the Samyukta Socialist Party, the Communist Party of India and the Communist Party of India (Marxist) never posed any serious threat to the Congress party in Rajasthan. They never elected a single representative to the Lok Sabha from the state and, after holding a relatively stable position for some 20 years, their support base of about 6% has steadily eroded since 1970.

By the 1972 assembly elections, the opposition in Rajasthan had become more fragmented than ever. Congress, on the other hand, despite its 1969 split,[16] had strengthened its position. At the national level it won the 1971 Lok Sabha elections by riding the "Indira Wave,"[17] and in 1972, for the first time, the Congress-I won an absolute majority of seats in the Rajasthan state assembly. Yet five years later the united opposition under the Janata banner won a thumping victory in Rajasthan and reduced the Congress-I party to its poorest showing ever in both the popular vote and seats won. Thus, while Congress was able to rule in Rajasthan for many years thanks to Sukhadia's adroit leadership and a divided opposition, the party's organizational base remained insecure. As demonstrated most dramatically by the 1977 Janata victory, but also by other elections in which the Congress lost significant numbers of seats, a coalition of opposition parties or even a small challenge from princely rulers could easily cripple its majority control.[18]

This erratic record on the part of the Congress party can be attributed to its feeble local organization. The same has been true of the opposition. In addition, however, the opposition has suffered from its own fragmentation. Though a temporary consolidation took place in 1977 under the Janata Chief Minister Bhairon Singh Shekhawat, it was a temporary phenomenon and did not last long. In the 1984 elections, the fragmentation of the opposition parties was greater than ever, with an average of twelve candidates filing nomination papers for each of the 25 Lok Sabha seats. Even for the assembly election of 1985, there were 1305 opposition candidates for 200 seats, an average of more than 6 candidates per seat.

This instability and grass-roots weakness of the political party system hampered the development of Panchayati Raj because the local government institutions could not assert their rights or exercise their capacities. The lower level was thus subjected to manipulation by state-level action. Because the "ideology" of Panchayati Raj was intentionally non-partisan, in order that *local* interests be properly represented, the ill-developed political parties were unable to penetrate and control Panchayati Raj. Indeed the success of Panchayati Raj actually *threatened* party MLAs.

The non-electoral inter-group power conflicts of the post-independence period also weakened Panchayati Raj institutions. This is especially true of the conflicts created by land reform, which was unusually far-reaching in Rajasthan (Narain and Mathur 1985:24). Thanks to the 1955 tenancy reforms, 90% of rural households are now owner-cultivators, with less than 10% of the population in the 1981 Census classified as landless agricultural laborers (*ibid.*, 28-29).

However, at the time of the land reform legislation, the Rajput community split into virtually warring factions over this issue. Though some Rajputs owned large amounts of land while others owned only small parcels that they cultivated themselves, abolition of *jāgīrdārī* entailed the expropriation of *all* Rajput land owners. As a result, the larger land-owning Rajputs benefited because of the lump sum compensation they received, equivalent to ten times their annual revenue. The small cultivators, on the other hand, while they received higher multiples of net value, lost their land but received only small absolute sums in compensation. Generally, their compensation was too little to engage in the income generating investments many large *jāgīrdārs* were able to make. Only after massive mobilization among the lesser Rajputs, which included *hartāls* (strikes), sieges and actual battles with the Jats – the chief beneficiaries being allowed to take over Rajput lands – did the Congress leaders revise the land reform law to exempt landholders below a certain size.

The bitterness over this explosive issue – pitting Rajputs against Jats and small land-holder Rajputs against large land-owning Rajputs – created a very factionalized environment at the village level. This further bedeviled the workings of Panchayati Raj, which required for its functioning either cooperation among contending groups or the ability of one, or a coalition, to establish hegemonic domination over the others. In fact, both of the latter occurred often enough to make Panchayati Raj a relative success – a success which threatened state level MLAs and ministers or potential ministers.

The degree to which Panchayati Raj in Rajasthan succeeded in bringing about mass participation in the political process and effective local government and development is thus debatable. The first round of Panchayati Raj elections was held in 1962, and the 1964-65 elections were held on schedule. Congress did poorly in 1962, but claimed to have recovered its position in 1964-65. Then came the two years of drought and near famine conditions, and the Congress party's nation-wide setback in the 1967 general elections. The number of Congress MPs from Rajasthan declined, and continued Congress control over the Rajasthan state government in Jaipur fell into doubt because the party had won only 89 of the 184 state legislative assembly seats. The issue of a proper governing majority was endlessly debated, with defections and counter-defections rampant. Finally, the state governor invoked President's Rule until Sukhadia could shore up his lines of support. Even after his eventual success, the political balance remained delicate and the Congress majority precarious.

As a result of the 1967 debacle, the Congress leadership in Rajasthan became convinced that it was futile to try to develop the institutions of Panchayati Raj as vote banks. To avoid the risk of yet another Congress defeat, Panchayati Raj elections were repeatedly postponed by extending and re-extending the statutory three-year term of office specified in the 1959 act. In addition, the training of Panchayati Raj leaders was dramatically curtailed.[19] During the decade after 1967, the Congress governments of Rajasthan manipulated and controlled the Panchayati Raj leadership in order to retain control over resources and patronage. Though the promise – or threat – of local elections hovered in the political air, it never materialized as a palpable event until 1978 after the Janata coalition had secured control of the state government. Thus for over a decade the Panchayati Raj electoral system remained dormant.

After the fall of the Janata government, a fourth Panchayati Raj poll was held in December 1981 and January 1982. The fifth round scheduled for December 1986 and January 1987 has been indefinitely postponed due to severe drought conditions in the state. Though the electoral dimension of Panchayati Raj has somewhat revived, however, there has been little turnover in the elected officials; and even when there has been some turnover the new incumbents share the same relatively high socio-economic status as the people being replaced. Furthermore, since Panchayati Raj elections are technically contested on a non-partisan basis, the relative success of political parties in securing control of Panchayats, Panchayat Samitis or Zila Parishads is a disputed matter – or at least subject to self-interest or self-serving reinterpretations.

Some people expected Panchayati Raj leaders to have a direct as well as an indirect voice at the state government level. After 1962 a number of *pradhāns* (heads of Panchayat Samitis) sought election to the Vidhan Sabha. But the limits of Panchayati Raj as a launching pad for rural leaders can be judged by the fact that out of the 232 *pradhāns* elected in 1965 (and who continued in office until the Janata government terminated their tenure in 1978), only one, Hiralal Deopura, rose to occupy a seat in the state cabinet and later served as Chief Minister for a brief period in 1984. And although 17 of 35 *pradhāns* who contested the Vidhan Sabha elections in 1967 were successful – at a time when they still controlled considerable local resources – few *pradhāns* contested subsequent elections. Some have argued that *pradhāns* preferred to be king-makers rather than kings, i.e. they preferred to control who could be nominated and elected in order to extract a price for their support. This argument constitutes a partial explanation of why Congress state-level politicians turned against Panchayati Raj. Simply stated they feared and rejected the competion for local influence and control.

The introduction of elected power holders at the village Panchayat and Panchayat Samiti levels thus did not disturb the contours of Rajasthan state-level politics. Indeed, many of the *pramukhs* of Zila Parishads have been urban-based leaders. Some of them, like B.N. Bhargava of Ajmer, became Lok Sabha members, while others, like Gulab Singh Shaktawat from Udaipur and Shiv Charan Mathur from Banswara, became members of the Rajasthan cabinet; Shiv Charan Mathur also served as Chief Minister for two and a half years in the early 1980s. Despite the Gandhian ideology of Panchayati Raj, rural Rajasthan has thus remained under-represented at the state level.

The problems of Panchayati Raj were analyzed by committee after committee, all with little effect. At the state level, the Rajasthan government appointed the Sadiq Ali Committee in 1964, and then in 1973 a high-powered Committee on Panchayati Raj chaired by Girdhari Lal Vyas. The latter committee recommended that the Zila Parishad should be strengthened by devolving upon it additional power, resources and personnel on the model of Maharashtra but this report was not taken seriously by the state cabinet.[20] The declaration of the Emergency in June 1975 further deflected attention from the devolution of power to Panchayati Raj or any other local institution. When the Janata party came into power after the Emergency, the central government appointed a national-level committee, headed by Asoka Mehta. This committee submitted its report in August 1978, but before any action could be initiated, the Janata governments collapsed. Thus despite many official committees and reports the problems of Panchayati Raj as a mechanism for encouraging local political participation have not been seriously addressed by either state or central government (Jain 1985).

Administrative Structure of Panchayati Raj: The Thwarted Revolution

In the decade following independence, the new state government now responsible for people and territory formerly under princely rule saw its primary tasks as those of institution building, i.e., transforming both political ideas and practice. Boundaries had to be redrawn and a new identity forged among the once diverse but now formally amalgamated units; political organization and procedures had to be devised and nurtured to draw the population into the democratic process; and an integrated bureaucracy had to be established for the administration of the state.

The Mehta report provided Rajasthan with what appeared to be an ideal structure through which to accomplish all three of these tasks, as well as an ideological justification for decentralizing government. In 1959, the Panchayat Samiti Act and the Zila Parishads Act established Panchayati Raj institutions and cooperative societies as autonomous bodies and Panchayati Raj began to function in 1962. But while Panchayati Raj was intended to decentralize government and emphasize local political institutions, the administrative decisions of the Panchayati Raj units remained subject to centralized control. An awkward dyarchy ensued.

While the development block – the unit most often selected to implement government programs to stimulate development – was in theory subject to guidance by political leaders from the Panchayat Samitis, it was administratively controlled by the appointed district officials. Any village, block or district official could object to any Panchayat, Samiti or Parishad proposal with which he did not agree. If a contrary decision was still taken by the majority in a particular Panchayati Raj unit, the official could forward a note of dissent to the District Collector and suspend the decision for a month while waiting for instructions from above. If the Collector (who was also the District Development Officer) deemed the decision to be against the public interest, he could cancel it and forward the whole matter to the state capital for final disposal by the Development Commissioner. Likewise, an Assistant Registrar of Cooperatives, acting on behalf of the Minister of Cooperation, had the power to supersede local cooperative institutions and dissolve their governing boards. "Officials always have their way," a Zila *pramukh* from Kota ruefully remarked to us in 1971 when commenting on these overriding powers of state officials. "There is therefore 'Adhikari' (official) Raj and no Panchayati Raj."

Over time, patterns of funding and staffing further increased the degree of state control over local units. At their inception, the Panchayati Raj units in Rajasthan were variously empowered to impose taxes that would supplement and eventually replace grants from the state governments and the local share of the land revenue. Panchayat Samitis were specifically authorized to levy taxes and surcharges. However, the Panchayati Raj units never really used this authority, and local institutions remained dependent on state coffers for their operating costs and investment resources. In their first decade of existence, Panchayati Raj institutions in Rajasthan did not mobilize any significant local resources. Instead, their funds were mainly Community Development grants supplied by the central government – a source of money that eventually tapered off as the central government's development strategies shifted from overall rural development to a more narrow focus on agricultural growth based on new inputs and technologies.

The reasons most often given by elected members of Panchayati Raj units for this unwillingness to impose local taxes are the constraint of poverty and the need for votes in future elections. A familiar observation repeated again and again is that the people were too poor to be taxed any more. That there is a shortage of rural resources in Rajasthan is a fact, but the rural sector is not as totally resourceless as this observation suggests. As the history of *jāgīrdārī* rule indicates, there were and are rural assets that can be tapped and taxed. The problem was that no one – and certainly no political leaders – wanted to extract resources from neighbors and potential voters. Thus local taxes were almost never imposed and, in the few exceptional cases where they were, they were not collected. In short, while Panchayati Raj in Rajasthan developed a high distributive capacity, political constraints drastically curtailed its extractive capabilites.

A dramatic example from Udaipur District illustrates the problem. Limited local taxation had actually been tried in 1969-70 in the form of an educational cess levied on households to raise construction funds for school buildings. Shortly thereafter, in 1971, the Congress party suffered a defeat in the Udaipur parliamentary constituency. The reversal was particularly embarassing because that constituency included Sukhadia's legislative district, which had always been in the Congress fold. In the aftermath of the defeat, local and district Congress politicians blamed the educational cess for their party's reversal at the polls, making it a convenient scapegoat for this serious political setback. The irony of the situation, and indeed of the general claim that the need for votes made levying and collecting taxes impossible, was that no Panchayati Raj elections were held in Rajasthan for 12 years.

Even more significant in crippling Panchayati Raj in Rajasthan than its inability to muster revenue was the resistance to its success that developed among state-level politicians and the administrators of line agencies (i.e. public works departments, agriculture departments, electricity boards, transport offices, etc.). In the initial phase of Panchayati Raj, Block Development Officers (BDOs) were drawn from the Rajasthan cadre of the central government's Indian Administrative Service (IAS) in order to better carry out the scheme's development mandate (Mathur 1977:19). Previously, the lowest rung on the career ladder of IAS officers had been to head the district-level administration. To assign them to the block level was a revolutionary administrative innovation. Not only did local governments thereby obtain central government resources, but their elected officials could have direct access to the highest levels of administration – not only state headquarters but the central government in New Delhi as well. If an IAS officer at the block level wanted to do his job well and thereby advance his career, he would make sure that the Rajasthan Administrative Service (RAS) officials from the state line agencies did their jobs well too. This innovation, setting up direct avenues of communication to the state secretariat and even the central government administration, gave local Panchayati Raj bodies an unprecedented amount of power.

However, within a decade, this administrative revolution came to an end. A counter-revolution launched by an alliance of line agency administrators and state-level politicians (especially MLAs) persuaded – some analysts would say forced – Sukhadia to withdraw the IAS officers from the block level and replace them with RAS (Rajasthan Administrative Service) personnel. In 1969, Finance Minister Mathur Das Mathur declared in his budget speech to the Vidhan Sabha that Rajasthan could no longer afford to squander its IAS officers on Panchayati Raj institutions – especially since, as will be seen below, most development funds were now flowing through other channels. In 1970 the IAS role in Panchayati Raj was officially terminated, a change that symbolically and practically ended the role of Panchayati Raj as the jewel in the crown of Rajasthan's new identity as the state that had come the furthest the fastest.

Although billed as an economy measure in state government, the real motive for this decision was to remove the double threat which the success of Panchayati Raj had become – a threat to the RAS-staffed line agencies from IAS administrators, and a threat to state-level politicians from local political leaders. The line agency administrators, caught in the classic "pincer" situation of mid-level bureaucrats,[21] wanted freedom from interference by superiors (i.e. IAS officers) but control over subordinates (i.e. local Panchayati Raj officials). As has been more or less true of the entire Indian bureaucracy,[22] increased political participation was a distinct threat to the power and social standing of state-level politicians and administrators. It was therefore to their advantage to see the Panchayati Raj program sabotaged.

The second major adversaries of Panchayati Raj, the state-level politicians, were ironically the very people who had established it in the first place. Initially speaking eloquently about grass-roots democracy, they soon came to recognize that Panchayati Raj leaders were becoming their competitors in local arenas by developing bases of power rather than remaining dependent on politicial superiors for authority and resources. When the state leaders did not or could not sustain the flow of state resources into their constituencies, the Panchayati Raj leaders strongly criticized them. And indeed, through the annual allotments and grants to development programs under Panchayati Raj jurisdiction, local leaders obtained resources they could allocate independently. As a result, it was no longer essential for them to support the sitting MLAs, ministers or other state leaders automatically. Instead, the Panchayati Raj leaders became king makers or king breakers, a force with which to reckon and bargain at election time and subsequently.

An indication of this political "clout" of the Panchayati Raj leaders is the fact that the Congress party's share of the electoral vote decline between 1957 (the last poll before Panchayati Raj took effect) and 1962. The Congress vote remained low in 1962 and only revived in 1972 after the resources which the state leadership had at its disposal were re-routed through other non-Panchayati Raj channels (rural banks, cooperatives and a rash of special projects and "crash programs"). These shifts clearly indicate that Congress had not managed to benefit as a party from Panchayati Raj.

A third force that worked against Panchayati Raj as an administrative structure was the shifting basis of government development goals or, perhaps more accurately, their clear articulation. If one follow's Nayar's argument (1974), the Indian government's development and welfare goals of social uplift, education and increased food production were always secondary to its defense goals: the "modernization imperative" has not been national welfare but national security. As a result, the central government was not inclined to invest its limited resources in local development programs, and hence Panchayati Raj was starved of financial resources. But even if this is an overstatement of the case, shifts occurred in development strategy that undermined the rationale for Panchayati Raj. Specifically, when the "green revolution" strategy of focusing narrowly on agricultural growth was adopted in the mid-1960s, it was at the expense of the Community Development programs that had been channeled through the Panchayati Raj units. As part of this reorientation from rural development to agricultural production, both central and state government authorities gradually scaled down the activities of Panchayati Raj, by concentrating economic resources for development in a variety of production-oriented cooperative bodies instead. As a result, the Panchayati Raj units lost resources proportionally as well as absolutely.

Conclusion: Panchayati Raj in Rajasthan as a "Failure of Success"

The evidence this paper has surveyed leads us to the conclusion that the erosion of Panchayati Raj in Rajasthan is not attributable to a single cause, but to a cluster of five interconnected factors.

First, local Panchayati Raj leaders chose a political strategy of avoiding risk by almost uniformly failing to extract and deploy local resources for development. All resources continued to come from the central government via the state government. While the tax base of rural Rajasthan was, and remains, neither high nor elastic, the history of Panchayati Raj has been marked by a tenacious reluctance to raise even voluntary resources in kind or in labor. The cash value of "people's participation" under Panchayati Raj has been for all intents and purposes nil.

Second, the defeat of the Congress party in the 1967 general elections weakened the commitment of its political elite to develop decentralized institutions of decision making and administrative control. The party regarded its 1967 debacle as a continuation of its poor showing in 1962, even though the 1964-65 Panchayati Raj elections had been hailed as a Congress victory. Congress came to regard Panchayati Raj as a hindrance rather than a help to its electoral prospects. The restoration of Congress dominance triggered by Mrs. Gandhi's victory in the 1971 Lok Sabha poll further sidelined Panchayati Raj institutions.

Third, Panchayati Raj never had its "own" administrative cadre, but was managed by officers drawn from various line departments of the state government who were seconded to community development and Panchayati Raj posts. With moorings in their parent departments, these officials had few incentives, much less compulsion, to develop new ways of working or shift their loyalties to the new structure. Thus Panchayati Raj was run by a bureaucracy with little commitment to its success.

Fourth, the IAS administration of Block Development Officer posts – an administrative innovation that greatly strengthened Panchayati Raj – was terminated in 1970 by a decision of the state government. This seriously undermined Panchayati Raj because local officials now had to struggle for influence and effectiveness against the entrenched power of both state-level politicians and state-level bureaucrats, and without the prestige and authority of IAS leadership backing them.

Finally, the central government launched a series of new development schemes that ignored or by-passed the three-tiered structure of Panchayati Raj. Among these were the Intensive Agricultural District Program (IADP) later changed to Intensive Agricultural Area Program (IAAP), the Small Farmers Development Agency (SFDA) and Marginal Farmers and Agricultural Laborers Agency (MFAL), the Rural Works Program (RWP), the Drought Prone Areas Program (DPAP), and Food For Work (FFW). Most of these programs were aimed at specific areas, target groups and problems. A number of new agencies and special-purpose organizations were created to implement these programs, quite independent of Panchayati Raj. In the process, Panchayati Raj lost its original monopoly over integrated development through all-purpose local government.

To sum up the performance of Panchayati Raj institutions in Rajasthan, their strong initial promise gradually but progressively weakened. In its first phase, Panchayati Raj seemed ideally suited for administrative penetration of the rural areas during the years immediately after the abolition of *jāgīrdārī* and the implementation of land reforms. Its institutions acquired considerable legitimacy during the first half-decade of their existence, a period of time which included not only the inauguration of the scheme but also two rounds of elections to fill Panchayati Raj posts.

However, in the mid-1960s, the attitudes of both central government and state policy makers shifted in favor of a new development strategy focused specifically on agricultural productivity. The Community Development approach – which emphasized all-purpose institutions of local government, the general quality of life, and improving human capital as a means to also increase production – was displaced by focused programs featuring new agencies and target groups. Elections to Panchayati Raj institutions were repeatedly postponed on the somewhat specious excuses that famine-relief work took precedence over organizing local elections, that administrative officers were already overworked, and that people were unlikely to engage in thoughtful politics anyway. Thus the popular mandate initially earned at the 1962 and 1964 polls steadily eroded as no Panchayati Raj elections were held for 13 years. At the same time, several new agencies were created to channel development funds toward local areas. Since Panchayati Raj institutions had systematically neglected the mobilization of their own local resources, the re-channeling to central development funds significantly diminished the power and relevance of Panchayati Raj.

Despite periodic fanfare about the revival of local government – such as the Sammelan or get-together held in Bikaner in 1982, where Prime Minister Rajiv Gandhi was the chief guest – the purpose of such pronouncements appears to be markedly prophylactic. This is to say, there have been lots of suggestive movements but no embarrassing consequences. In the politics of the late 1980s, Panchayati Raj institutions in Rajasthan lie in limbo.

ENDNOTES

1. The National Development Council (NDC) is an apex body consisting of the Council of Ministers, all State Chief Ministers and leaders of the opposition parties in Parliament. Presided over by the Prime Minister, it reviews development plans, the progress thereof, plan allocations and plan priorities.
2. The Mehta Report was the product of a committee chaired by Balwantray Mehta to study Community Projects and National Extension Services. Published in three volumes by the Government of India (1957), this report became the basis for the Panchayati Raj system. Balwantray Mehta was the second Chief Minister of Gujarat, a Gandhian by disposition and an ardent supporter of Panchayati Raj.
3. For further general reading on the intended goals and the practical implementation of Panchayati Raj, see Björkman 1979, Chaturvedi 1977, Darda 1973, Dey 1969, Haldipur 1971, Maddik 1970, Mathur 1977, Mehta 1961, and Narain *et al.* 1970.
4. The total population of Rajasthan recorded by the 1981 census was 35 million. The average population density was approximately 100 persons per square kilometer, compared to a national average density of 215 persons per square kilometer, but varied from six persons per square kilometer in Jaisalmer District to 242 in Jaipur District (Government of Rajasthan 1982:35-38).
5. The breakdown for religious minorities in the 1981 census is: Muslims (7%), Jains (2%), Sikhs (1%), and others (1%). The Scheduled Castes are most heavily concentrated in the districts of Jaipur, Ganganagar, Bharatpur and Sawai Madhopur, while the tribals live primarily in Udaipur, Banswara, and Dungarpur districts (Government of India 1982:14).
6. Four of the nine Chief Ministers of Rajasthan have been Brahmins. The other five Chief Ministers since the 1956 States Reorganisation included one Baniya, one Muslim, one Scheduled Caste, one Kayastha and one Rajput. There has never been a Jat Chief Minister; some argue that it is unlikely there will be one in the near future.
7. The present state of Rajasthan is a conglomeration of 19 erstwhile princely states and 3 chieftainships.
8. Praja Mandal literally means "people's group" or "people's organization." In the context of Rajasthan these Praja Mandals were formed as part of the freedom struggle in the erstwhile princely states.
9. Jai Narayan Vyas (Jodhpur) organized the Marwar Hitkari Sabha (organization to protect the interests of Marwar region) in 1938, while Manik Lal Verma formed the Praja Mandal in Udaipur at about the same time; a little later Hiralal Shastri and Gokulbhai Bhatt organized the Charkha Sangh (union of those using the spinning wheel) in Jaipur State. In 1938 the Indian National Congress decided at its Haripura session to extend the national struggle to princely India (Wood 1984:72). Others active in the movement were Arjunlal Sethi, who was the founder of the Congress Party in Rajasthan, and Vijay Singh Pathik who led the Bijolan Satyagraha. The Bijolan agitation, popularly known as Bijolan Satyagraha, was the first major political event in Rajputana intended to overthrow the unpopular feudal regime. All these agitations began in the 1920s when Mahatma Gandhi appeared on the national scene.

10. For a more in-depth treatment of this subject see Narain and Mathur 1985.
11. See Rudolph and Rudolph (1975), reprinted in Rudolph and Rudolph (1984), pp. 81-140.
12. It should be noted that there was little difference in terms of electoral performance between "linked" and "delinked" polls (i.e. whether or not state-level and national elections were held simultaneously).
13. In 1952 and 1967 the Congress lost the elections but, with help from Delhi, managed nevertheless to form the government.
14. In 1952 and 1957, the principal opposition party was the Ram Rajya Parishad, while in 1962 and 1967 it was mainly the Jana Sangh and Swatantra parties. Over the next three decades of electoral politics in Rajasthan, the following political parties appeared and sometimes disappeared: Akhil Bharatiya Ram Rajya Parishad (1952, 1957, 1962, 1977, 1980); Hindu Maha Sabha (1952, 1962); Communist Party of India (all elections); Kisan Mazdoor Praja Party (1952); All India Scheduled Caste Federation (1952); Krishikar Lok Party (1952); Kisan Janata Samyukta Party (1952); Praja Socialist Party (1957, 1967); Communist Party of India - Marxist (1967, 1971, 1977, 1980, 1984); Samyukta Socialist Party (1967, 1971); Republican Party of India (1967); Vishal Haryana Party (1971); Socialist Party - Splinter Group (1971); Muslim League (1977); Bharatiya Socialist Party (1980); Janata National Party – Secular (1980); and Indian National Congress – Jagjivan Ram (1984).
15. Outstanding examples were Karni Singh and Brajendra Pratap Singh.
16. 1969 marked a major split in the Congress Party. One faction led by Mrs. Indira Gandhi was called Congress (R) [ruling] which later became Congress (I) [Indira]. The other faction was Congress (O) [Organization].
17. After the 1969 split of the Congress party, Mrs. Gandhi fought the 1971 election on the slogan of "Garibi Hatao" (remove poverty). This slogan, among other factors, brought Mrs. Gandhi a massive mandate.
18. Thus, for example, in the 1971 Lok Sabha poll, Maharana Bhagwat Singh of Udaipur, who had never before participated actively in electoral politics, openly lent his support to the opposition party. Even though it was the year of the "Indira Wave" and even though Udaipur had been Sukhadia's legislative constituency, the Congress Party suffered a serious setback there that year.
19. By 1967, five of the ten Panchayati Raj training centers had been closed; another two were closed by 1969; today the remaining two centers display scant activity.
20. The Committee headed by Girdhari Lal Vyas recommended strengthening the Zila Parishad and making it a more executive body rather than an advisory body as had been the case. In both Maharasthra and Gujarat, the Zila Parishad has executive powers and functions; therefore it becomes the main center of power.
21. In his classic work on bureaucracy, Crozier (1964) demonstrates how officials in France sought to limit the political authority of subordinates and yet demand maximum autonomy for themselves from superiors.
22. For further analysis of this pattern , see Taub 1969 and Chaturvedi 1977.

REFERENCES CITED

Basu, Durga Das
1983 *Constitutional Law of India*. 3rd ed. New Delhi: Prentice Hall of India.

Beer, Howard W. and Douglas Ensminger
1959 "The Development Block as a Social System." *Indian Journal of Public Administration* 5:135-152.

Björkman, James Warner
1979 *Politics of Administrative Alienation in India's Rural Development Programs*. Delhi: Ajanta Publications.

Brass, Paul R.
1965 *Factional Politics in an Indian State: The Congress Party in Uttar Pradesh*. Berkeley: University of California Press.

Chaturvedi, Het Ram
1977 *Bureaucracy and Local Community: Dynamics of Rural Development*. Bombay: Allied Publishers.

Crozier, Michel
1964 *The Bureaucratic Phenomenon*. Chicago: University of Chicago Press.

Darda, R.S.
1973 "Panchayat Samitis in Rajasthan: A Study in Supervision and Control." *Journal of the Society for Study of State Governments* 7:240-248.

Dey, S.K.
1969 *Power to the People*. Bombay: Orient Longmans, Ltd.

Government of India
1952 *First Five Year Plan*, New Delhi: Planning Commission.
1957 *Report of the Team for the Study of Community Projects and National Extension Service*. 3 vols. New Delhi: Planning Commission.
1982 *Census of India 1981*. Series I. Paper I. New Delhi: Registrar General and Census Commissioner.

Government of Rajasthan
1982 *Basic Statistics*. Jaipur: Director of Economics and Statistics.

Haldipur, R.N.
1971 "On Remodelling Panchayati Raj." *Indian Journal of Public Administration*. 17:527-538.

Jain, L.C.
1985 *Grass without Roots*. New Delhi: Sage Publications.

Maddick, Henry
1970 *Panchayati Raj: A Study of Rural Local Government in India*. London: Longman Group Ltd.

Mathur, Prakash Chand
1977 "Performance of Panchayati Raj Institutions in Rajasthan 1959-1974: A Critical Survey." *Social Change: Journal of the Centre for Social Development* (New Delhi) 7:16-30.

Mehta, Balvantray
1961 "Some Aspects of Relationship in Panchayati Raj." *Indian Journal of Public Administration* 7:297-305.

1962 "The Panchayat Samiti at the Block Level as the Basic Unit of Panchayati Raj." *Indian Journal of Public Administration* 8:471-477.

Narain, Iqbal *et al.*

1970 *Panchayat Raj Administration*. New Delhi: Indian Institute of Public Administration.

Narain, Iqbal and P.C. Mathur

1985 "Regional Segmentation, Ritual Secularization and Elite Pluralism: Continuities and Change in the Princely States of Rajasthan Before and After 1947." Jaipur: Draft Typescript.

Nayar, Baldev Raj

1974 "Political Mainsprings of Economic Planning in the New Nations: The Modernization Imperative Versus Social Mobilization." *Comparative Politics* 6:341-366.

Potter, David C.

1964 *Government in Rural India: An Introduction to Contemporary District Administration*. London: G. Bell and Sons.

Rudolph, Lloyd I. and Susanne Hoeber Rudolph

1975 "A Bureaucratic Lineage in Princely India: Elite Formation and Conflict in a Patrimonial System." *Journal of Asian Studies* 34 (3):717-753.

1984 *Essays on Rajputana: Reflections on History, Culture and Administration*. New Delhi: Concept Publishing Company.

Saksena, K.S.

1972 *Political Awakening in Rajasthan*. Delhi: S. Chand and Company.

Singh, V.B. and Shankar Bose

1986 *Elections in India: Data Handbook on Lok Sabha Elections 1952-1985*. 2nd ed. New Delhi: Sage Publications.

1987 *State Elections in India: Data Handbook on Vidhan Sabha Elections 1952-1985*. Vol. 1. New Delhi: Sage Publications.

Sisson, John Richard

1972 *The Congress Party in Rajasthan: Political Integration and Institution Building in an Indian State*. Berkeley: University of California Press.

Taub, Richard P.

1969 *Bureaucrats under Stress: Administrators and Administration in an Indian State*. Berkeley: University of California Press.

Tinker, Hugh

1954 *Foundations of Local Self-Government in India, Pakistan and Burma*. London: Pall Mall Press.

Wood, John R.

1984 "British versus Princely Legacies and the Political Integration of Gujarat." *Journal of the Asian Studies* 44:65-99.

POWER AND HEGEMONY

THE EMERGENCE OF THE RAJPUTS AS HISTORICAL PROCESS IN EARLY MEDIEVAL RAJASTHAN

B. D. CHATTOPADHYAYA

The origin of the Rajputs is a red herring that has been much dragged about in historical writings on early medieval and medieval India. These writings reveal an extreme polarity of opinions, which extends in range from attempts to trace the Rajputs to foreign immigrant stocks of the post-Gupta period – explaining in the process a later origin myth, namely the *agnikula* ('origin from sacrificial fire') myth, as a purification myth – to contrived justifications for viewing the Rajputs as of pure Kshatriya origin.[1] The question of the indigenous origin of the Rajputs assumed symbolic overtones in the heyday of nationalist historiography and, in the historical and purely literary writings of various genres, the military and chivalrous qualities of the Rajputs were repeatedly projected. At the level of historical writing, C.V. Vaidya may be cited as epitomizing an extreme stand in this viewpoint. He states:

> The Rajputs who now came to the front and who by their heroism diffuse such glory on the period of Medieval Indian history *cannot but have been* the descendants of Vedic Aryans. *None but Vedic Aryans* could have fought so valiantly in defence of the ancestral faith (1924:7). (Emphasis added)

Another facet of this viewpoint is revealed by the suggestion – repeated in recent writings – that the Rajputs rose to prominence in the process of resisting foreign invasions and that they "shouldered willingly the Kṣatriyas' duty of fighting for the land as well as its people and culture" (D. Sharma 1966:I, 106).

At the level of narrative political history, the reconstruction of the early history of the Rajputs follows a pattern which has recently been characterized as a tendency to "dynasticize." This tendency is evident in most attempts to deal with genealogies found in epigraphs, and what such attempts manifest is " . . . the practice of rationalizing the inscriptions of a number of rulers of uncertain date and lineage into dynastic superstructures, thereby conferring both temporal and genetic relationships on them where the data provide neither," and further, the "even more wide practice of juxtaposing and concatenating short genealogies and grafting them into an impressive whole which is truly greater than the sum of its parts" (Henige 1975:526).

The most recent writings on the early history of the Rajputs have not substantially deviated from these assumptions and methods. As a result, even in detailed studies on Rajasthan, the origin of the Rajputs in the early medieval period has hardly been examined as a process which may have had parallels or otherwise in early medieval developments outside the region. The study of the Rajputs in isolation, therefore, seldom refers to the factors, except in the form of facile generalizations, which are known now to have been in operation in early medieval India.[2] Admittedly, the pattern of the emergence of the Rajputs may show substantial deviations from developments outside western India, but the plea that the phenomenon should be examined as a total process still holds good. What is attempted in this paper, which is only an outline of an intended fuller study, is to view this process and to trace the early stages of the history of such clans as came to be recognized as Rajput.[3]

The general framework for this paper is provided by the recent analyses of claims to traditional Kshatriya status, which became widespread in the early medieval period.[4] Such claims were attempts to get away from, rather than reveal, the original ancestry, and they underline the nature of a polity in which new social groups continued to seek various symbols for the legitimization of their newly acquired power. Furthermore, 'Rajput', like the traditional *varṇa* categories (the traditional division of society into four orders), is known to have been assimilative in space and time and has, until recent times, been a recognizable channel of transition from tribal to state polity.[5] The processes of Rajputization, thus at work in different periods and different areas, may have been dissimilar, and the concept of Rajputization, which also has some bearing on the present problem, is taken here to be relevant only to the extent that it points to the necessity of viewing the Rajput phenomenon in the early medieval period in terms of a process, rather than in terms of the ancestry, genuine or concocted, of individual dynasties.

A preliminary idea of the processes involved may be formed by trying to define the term "Rajput." As in other periods, so in the early medieval period too, it may not be at all easy to distinguish the Rajputs from the non-Rajputs, despite the clear evidence regarding certain recognizable clans and frequent references to the *rājaputras* (sons of kings) in inscriptions and literature. One way of recognizing the early Rajputs may be by extrapolating evidence from later literature. Statements regarding the lists of Rajput clans, traditionally numbering 36, are available in relatively early works such as the *Kumārapālacarita* and the *Varṇaratnākara*.[6] The *Rājataranginī* too (VII. 1617-1618) refers to the number 36. An analysis of the composition of various lists – for the lists never tally with one another[7] – suggests that the composition was not such as could be considered immutable by the contemporary compilers. If the early medieval and medieval references to the *rājaputras* in general are taken into account, they represented a "mixed caste" (Yadava 1973:34) and "constituted a fairly large section of petty chiefs holding estates."[8] The criterion for inclusion in the list of Rajput clans was provided by the contemporary status of a clan, at least in the early stages of the crystallization of Rajput power. However, the names of certain clans – such as the Chahamanas and Pratiharas – occur regularly in the lists, possibly due to their political dominance. Sources relating to them are also voluminous, and as such referecnes to these clans will be more frequent throughout this paper than to others.

Territorial Expansion and the Transition from Tribalism

There are two important pointers to the processes of the emergence of the Rajputs in the early medieval records. As these records suggest, at one level the process may have to be juxtaposed with a spate of colonization of new areas. The evidence of such colonization has to be traced not only in the significant expansion of the number of settlements but also in some epigraphic references, suggesting an expansion of agrarian economy. Any assertion about an increase in the number of settlements is, in the absence of any detailed historical-geographical study, only impressionistic. But in view of the widespread distribution of archaeological remains[9] and epigraphs of the period as well as the appearance of numerous new place names, there cannot be any doubt about the validity of the assumption.

A brief reference to the names of several places and territorial divisions may be meaningful in this context. The term *sapādalakṣa* (125,000), which was used to denote the territory of the Chahamanas (D. Sharma 1966:I, 18), may indicate, like the territorial divisions of the Deccan suffixed with numbers, an expansion of village settlements.[10] In fact, some of the territorial divisions with suffixed numbers mentioned in the *Skanda Purāṇa* such as Vaguri 80,000 or Viratà 36,000, have been located in Rajasthan (*ibid*.:I, 19). The Nadol Chahamana kingdom was known as *saptaśata* (700) and an inscription from Nanana, relating to this family, claims that it was made into a *saptasāhasrika* (7,000) by a Chahamana king who killed *sīmādhipas* (chiefs of the boundaries of his kingdom) and annexed their villages.[11] In records of about the 12th century, the Abu area was known as *aṣṭādaśaśata* (118) (*ibid*.:I, 18-19). If all this cumulatively suggests a proliferation of settlements, then the relationship of this process, through an expansion of agrarian economy, may be postulated with the emergence of the early Rajputs from about the 7th century.

Apart from the inscriptions of the Guhilas of Kishkindha (Sircar 1965:74-75) and of Dhavagarta (*EI* 20:122-125), which refer to irrigation-based agriculture,[12] a more specific connection is suggested by a few records of the Mandor Pratiharas. A Ghatiyala inscription of Kakkuka, of A.D. 861 (*JRAS* 1895: 519-520), credits him with cattle raids and the destruction by fire of villages in the inaccessible Vatananaka. Kakkuka made the land "fragrant with the leaves of blue lotuses and pleasant with groves of mango and madhuka trees, and covered it with leaves of excellent sugarcane." Another Ghatiyala record, also of his time and dated A.D. 861 (*EI* 9:280), mentions the resettlement of a place characterized as *Ābhīrajanadāruṇaḥ*, "terrible because of being inhabited by the Abhiras." The place was not only conquered, but a village, Rohinsakupa, as well as Maddodara (identified as Mandor) were provided with markets. Kakkuka is repeatedly mentioned in the Ghatiyala inscriptions as having installed *haṭṭa* (markets) and *mahājana* (merchants) in the area which, apparently uninhabitable by good people (*asevyaḥ sādhujanānām*), came now to be crowded by Brahmans, soldiers and merchants.

When seen in the light of some other inscriptions of western and central India, which also speak of the suppression of the Shabaras, Bhillas and Pulindas (*EI* 1:337, v. 22), this evidence from Rajasthan may reveal two important aspects of a process. First, the territorial expansion of what came to be known as Rajput power was achieved, at least in certain areas, at the expense of the erstwhile tribal settlements. Similar movements for expansion are found in the cases of the Guhilas and Chahamanas as well. Though the Guhila settlements in various parts of Rajasthan are found as early as the 7th century A.D., slightly later traditions recorded in the inscriptions of the Nagda-Ahar Guhilas trace their movement from Gujarat (*IA* 39:186ff.; *EI* 31:237ff.). There is also a voluminous bardic tradition which suggests that the Guhila kingdoms in south Rajasthan succeeded the earlier tribal chiefdoms of the Bhils (Sircar 1965:3-4). The Guhila connection with the Bhils, implied in the part that the latter played in the coronation ceremony of the Guhila kings (Tod 1971:262), is also suggested in an Ekalingaji temple inscription of A.D. 1282:

> The enemies of king Allaṭa being impotent to show their contempt (towards him) in battlefield treat the Bhílla women disrespectfully who describe his actions with pleasures in each of the mountains. (Bhavnagar Archaeological Department n.d.: 74ff.)

The movement of the Chahamanas, according to the tradition mentioned in their inscriptions, was from Ahicchatrapura to Sakambhari or Jangaladesa, which, one would assume from the name and topography of Jangaladesa,[13] led to the colonization of a generally uncharted area. The Nadol branch of the Chahamana family was founded in the Godwar region by Lakshmana, whose military adventurism, according to tradition recorded in the *Purātanaprabandhasaṃgraha* and Nainsi's *Khyāt*,[14] led to the formation of a kingdom at the expense of the Medas of that area. Another example of the same process is available in the bardic legends of *Pallival Chand*, which narrate how the Rathor Siha was brought in to keep away the Medas and the Minas (*IA* 40:183). Secondly, as already mentioned in connection with the reference to Pratihara Kakkuka's inscriptions, the colonization of new areas appears to have been accompanied by what may be loosely termed a more advanced economy. In other words, Rajasthan, in the period when Rajput polity was beginning to emerge, was, in its various areas, undergoing a process of change from tribalism. Some facets of change that such transition presented elsewhere in India may thus be expected to have been present in early medieval Rajasthan as well.

As the second point suggests, to conceive of the emergence of the Rajputs only in terms of colonization would be to take a wrong view of the total process involved, and here we come to the second pointer provided by the records. The fact that the mobility to Kshatriya status was in operation elsewhere in the same period prompts one to look for its incidence also in Rajasthan. The cases of two groups who are included in the list of Rajput clans are significant in this context. One is that of the Medas, who are considered to have reached Rajput status from a tribal background (Yadava 1973:34). The other is that of the Hunas (*ibid.*). The inclusion of these two groups in the Rajput clan structure is sufficient to belie any assumption that the structure could be composed only of such groups as were initially closely linked by descent, "foreign" or "indigenous."

Political Ascendancy and Genealogical Claims

Apart from the fact that the *rājaputras* are mentioned in certain sources as of mixed caste, the evidence relating to the Medas and the Hunas cited above thus leads one to search not for the original ancestry of the clans but for the historical stages in which the Rajput clan structure came to be developod. This can initially be done with reference to some major clans which played a politically dominant role in early medieval Rajasthan. For the purpose of this paper, these clans are the Pratiharas, the Guhilas and the Chahamanas.

To start with the Pratiharas, despite some labored attempts to dissociate them from the Gurjaras on the plea that the Gurjara, in the "Gurjara-Pratihara" combine, represented the country and not the people (D. Sharma 1966:I, 472ff.), it would appear that the Pratiharas who rose to prominence some time in the 8th century were really from the Gurjara stock. In early India, *janapada* (country, kingdom) names were commonly interchangeable with tribal names (Raychaudhuri 1960). Secondly, the argument that the Pratiharas could not have emerged from the pastoral Gurjara stock is misplaced, because as early as the 7th century, the Gurjaras of Nandipuri represented a ruling family (*IA* 13:70ff.; *EI* 23:147ff.). Thirdly, a branch of the Pratiharas in the Alwar area is taken to represent the Bad Gujars (Jain 1972:195).

Documents dating from the 7th century suggest a wide distribution of the Gurjaras as a political power in western India, and references to Gurjara commoners may indicate that the political dominance of certain families reflected a process of stratification that had developed within the stock. The *Panchatantra* evidence which mentions the Gurjara country as providing camels for sale[15] may suggest, though inadequately, pastoralism. The Gurjaras are mentioned as cultivators also in an inscription of a Gurjara-Pratihara king Mathana from Rajogarh in Alwar.[16] It would seem that the Pratiharas, like several other Gurjara lineages, branched off the Gurjara stock through the channel of political power, and the case probably offers a parallel to that of the Kushanas who, originally a sept of the Yüeh-chih, rose to political eminence and integrated five different *jabgous* (septs).[17] Further, the fact that some Pratiharas also became Brahmans will find parallel in developments among the Abhiras, out of whom emerged Abhira Brahmans, Abhira Kshatriyas, Abhira Shudras and so on (Suryavansi 1962:39-40).

Admittedly, all this reconstruction is tenuous and, in the absence of evidence, even such reconstruction is not possible in the case of the Chahamanas and the Guhilas. But a definite correlation did exist between the achievement of political eminence and a movement towards a corresponding social status. The pattern of this correlation may be indicated by Tables 1, 2 and 3, prepared mostly on the basis of epigraphs of the various Pratihara, Guhila and Chahamana families.[18]

The three tables given here seem to demonstrate a close correspondence between the different stages in the assumption of political power and the stages in which various claims to ancestral respectability were made, although the genealogies, having been drafted by different hands, did not always follow a uniform pattern. It would appear that feudatory status[19] was incompatible with the stage when detailed and fabricated references to a respectable ancestry could be made. Apart from the evidence already cited, one further point should make this clear. In a period when detailed genealogies with a respectable ancestry were being put forward on behalf of sovereign families of a clan, another section of the same clan, placed in a feudatory position, did not advance any such claim at all. Thus a Guhila record of A.D. 1145 from Mangrol in south Gujarat (Bhavnagar Archaeological Department n.d.: 157ff.) speaks of three generations of Guhila rulers of Mangalapụra, feudatories of the Chalukyas, simply as Shri Guhila, although in the same period claims to respectable ancestry were being made by the Guhilas elsewhere.

When one looks at the different stages in which the genealogies were being formulated, it further appears that for the majority of the new emerging royal lines, *brahmakṣatra* (Brahman Kshatriya) was a transitional status, which once acquired was not, however, entirely given up, and explanations continued to be given for the supposedly authentic transition from Brahman to Kshatriya status. If it be accepted, on the strength of their relatively later records, that both the Guhilas and the Chahamanas were originally of Brahmanical descent – although no claims to such descent have been made in their early records – then the status was being projected in order to legitimize their new Kshatriya role. It may also well be that *brahmakṣatra* was a relatively open status, as can be gathered from its wide currency in India in this period (Sircar 1969:6-11; Bhandarkar 1911:85-86), which was seized upon by the new royal families before they could formulate a claim to pure Kshatriya origin.

This gradual change is perhaps illustrated by a comparison between two Pratihara inscriptions of the 9th century from the Jodhpur area. While one, dated A.D. 837 (*EI* 18:97-98), explains the origin of the Pratihara Brahmans and Pratihara Kshatriyas in terms of two wives (one Kshatriya and another Brahman) of Brahman Harichandra, in the second, dated A.D. 861 (*JRAS* 1985:519-520), the Brahman wife is dropped from the genealogical list. The continuation of reference to Brahmanical origin was as much related to a concern for pure descent as the need for finding a respectable source from which Kshatriya status was derived. The genealogy of the Jodhpur Pratiharas starts with Harichandra who is described in one record as *Pratihāravaṃśaguru* (guru of the Pratihara lineage) (*EI* 9:279), but an elaborate statement of connection with such a source is provided by a Guhila inscription of A.D. 1285 from Achaleshwar (Mt. Abu):

Table 1: **Gurjara-Pratiharas: Correlation Between Political Status and Genealogical Claims**

Locality	Date	Family Name	Political Status	Nature of claims about the origin of the family
Gurjaras of Nandipuri	7th century[a]	Gurjara-Nrpati-vamsha	Feudatory, suggested by such titles as *mahāsāmanta*, etc., but special position suggested by the claim that they gave protection to the overlord.	In some records, claim made about descent from Maharaja Karna, which substitutes the family name.
Pratiharas of Mandor	837 AD[b]	Pratiharavamsha		Descent traced from the Kshatriya wife of a Brahman, implying *brahmakṣatra* status. Links established with Lakshmana, who acted as the *pratihāra* (door-keeper) of Rama.
	861 AD[c]	Pratihara		Similar, but name of the Brahman wife, mentioned in earlier record, dropped

Pratiharas of Rajasthan and Kanauj	9th century[d]	Pratihara	Sovereign power	Descent traced from the Sun, suggesting claims to solar origin through Lakshmana, who served as *pratihāra* (door-keeper) of Rama.
	10th Century[e]	Indirectly referred to in the inscription of their Chahamana feudatories.	Mentioned as the overlords of the Chahamanas.	Mentioned as the family of Raghu.
Gurjara-Pratiharas of Rajor	960 AD[f]	Gurjara-Pratihara-vamsha	Feudatories of the Pratiharas of Rajasthan and Kanauj	

Notes

[a] *IA* 13:70ff.; *EI* 23:147ff.
[b] *EI* 18:97–98.
[c] *JRAS* 1985:519–520.
[d] *EI* 18:110.
[e] *IA* 42:58. A contemporary text, Rajashekhara's *Karpūramanjarī*, also refers to Mahendrapala and Mahipala as *Raghukulatilaka* (ornament of the Raghu Family). Cited in Bhandarkar 1911:83*n*80.
[f] *EI* 3:263–267.

Table 2: **Guhilas: Correlation Between Political Status and Genealogical Claims**

Locality	Date	Family Name	Political Status	Nature of Claims about the origin of the family
Guhilas of Kishkindha	Second quarter of 7th century	Guhila-putranvaya	Feudatory, suggested by such titles as *sāmanta*, *samadhigata-panchamahā śabda*, *mahārāja*, etc.	
Guhilas of Chatsu	Middle of the 10th century[b]	Guhilavamsha	Originally, feudatories of the Mauryas and Pratiharas.	*brahma-kṣatrānvita* ('connecting Brahman and Kshatriya')
Guhilas of Mewar	661 AD[c]	Guhilanvaya		
	Late 10th to late 11th century tradition[d]			Originator of the family described as *ānandapura vinirgataviprakulānandaḥ mahīdevaḥ* ('lord of the earth, joy of a Brahman Family issued from Anandapura'), implying descent from a Brahman family.
	1285 AD[e]	Guhilavamsha		Record implies claim to *brahmakṣatra* status
	1540 AD[f]	Shiladityavamsha		*sūryavaṃśa*, implying claim to ṣolar origin

Notes

[a] Sircar 1965: 71–76.
[b] *EI* 12:10ff.
[c] *EI* 4:29ff.
[d] *AI* 39:191; *EI* 31:237ff.
[e] Bhavnagar Archaeological Depạrtment n.d.:89.
[f] *Ibid.*, 141.

Table 3: **Chahamanas: Correlation Between Political Status and Genealogical Claims**

Locality	Date	Family Name	Political Status	Nature of claims about the origin of the family
Early Chahamanas of Gujarat	Middle of the 8th century[a]	Chahamana	Feudatory, as suggested by such titles as *mahāsāmantadhipati*, *samadhigatapanchamāśabda*, etc.	
Chahamanas of Dholpur	827 AD[b]	Chahamana	Possibly feudatories of the Pratiharas	
Chahamanas of Nadol	1119 AD[c]	Chahamana	—	Ancestry traced to Indra through a person who came out of Indra's eyes.
Chahamanas of Shakambhari	946 AD[d]	Chahamana	Feudatories of the Pratiharas	
	1169 AD[e]	Chahamana Kshitiraja-vamsha	Independent power	Viprashri Vatsagotra, implying claim to Brahmanical descent.
	12th century[f]	Chahamana	Independent power	Ancestry traced to Sun-god, described as the right eye of Vishnu.

	1191–1193[g]	Chahamana	Independent power	Origin traced to the Sun and the family related with the Ikshavakus of the Krita Age.
Chahamanas of Mt. Abu	1320 AD[h]	Chahamana		Origin traced to the holy sage Vaccha who created the Chahamanas as a new race of warriors when the solar and lunar races became extinct.

Notes

[a] *EI* 12: 197ff.
[b] *ZDMG* 40:38ff.
[c] *EI* 11:304.
[d] *IA* 42: 57ff.
[e] *EI* 26:84ff.
[f] *EI* 29:179.
[g] *Pṛthvīrājavijaya* of Jayanaka. The evidence of this text as also that of other sources bearing on the changing claims regarding their ancestry made by the Chahamanas has been extensively analyzed in Pathak 1966:136.
[h] *EH* 9:75ff.

> Assuredly from Brahmalike Hārīta (Hāritarāśi-sage) Bappaka obtained, in the shape of an anklet, the lustre of a Kṣatriya and gave the sage, his own devotion, his own brāhmaṇical lustre. Thus even till now, the descendants of that line shine on this earth, like Kṣatriyahood in human form. (Bhavnagar Archaeological Department, n.d.:89)

Though not exactly identical, but in a largely similar way, the Cheros of Bihar, some of whom claimed Rajput status, claimed their descent from Chyavanarishi (Singh 1974).

All this suggests that detailed genealogies of ruling clans, which came to be formulated only in the period of change from feudatory to independent status, can hardly be extrapolated for an assessment of actual origin, although some parts of such genealogies may have been based on genuine tradition. The different stages in the formulation of genealogical claims thus also reveal a political process, that of upward mobility from an initial feudatory position. The Gujarat Gurjaras, both in their titles and in the declaration of their allegiance to the Valabhi king, are stated to be feudatories. The early Guhilas of Kishkindha and those of Dhavagarta were feudatories too, and Bappa Rawal, the traditional founder of the Guhila line of Mewar, appears to have started with a feudatory status, as the title *rāvala* (identical with *rājakula*, which was sometimes associated with a subordinate position) suggests. The Chahamanas, both of Gujarat and Rajasthan, were clearly feudatories of the Gurjara-Pratiharas, and it may be significant that the second name in the Chahamana genealogy is *sāmanta* (lord, vassal), which suggests a feudatory status, in contrast with the next name, *nṛpa* or *naradeva* (both meaning 'king').[20] The transition from feudatory to independent status was clearly through the growth of military strength. The Nandipuri Gurjaras boast of the protection they gave to the lord of Valabhi, who had been overpowered by Harsha (*EI* 23:147ff.). The Hansot plates of the Chahamanas begin with the invocation, "Victorious be the Cāhamāna family excelled with a large army" (*EI* 12:197ff). Similarly, inscriptions of the Chahamana and Pratihara feudatory families from Rajasthan highlight the part played by them in the military expeditions of their Gurjara-Pratihara overlords (*IA* 42:58).

The point just made should be interesting inasmuch as it shows that the emergence of the early Rajput clans took place within the existing hierarchical political structure. This point is often missed in efforts to build an image of the Rajputs as making a sudden and brilliant debut on the North Indian political scene. An understanding of this initial political stage is important on more than one count. It provides us with a vantage point from which to examine further processes, namely, how from their initial feudatory position, the Rajput clans, in their bid for political ascendancy, moved towards creating economic and social bases for their interlocking interests.

Territorial System and Clan Networks

The process of the emergence of the early Rajputs is associated, at the level of economy, with certain new features of land distribution and territorial system, which were perhaps present both in the large empires of the Pratiharas and the Chahamanas as well as in localized kingdoms such as those of the Guhilas. Such features have often been discussed before (R.S. Sharma 1965:176ff.; Gopal 1963-64:75-103), but in view of their continued association with the Rajputs, in some form or other, till later times, we shall only examine them in relation to the consolidation of clan networks among the early Rajputs. One feature, the incidence of which in this period appears to have been higher in Rajasthan than elsewhere, was the distribution of land among the royal kinsmen.[21] It must, however, be underlined – because it is not usually so done – that this feature appears to have represented a process which developed gradually and was associated in particular with the spread of one clan, the Chahamanas. The Pratihara empire being of a rather vast dimension, the composition of the assignees in the empire was varied (Puri 1957:109ff.), although such expressions as *vaṃśapotakabhoga* (estate to be enjoyed by the descendants of the lineage) occurring in the Rajorgarh inscription of Gurjara-Pratihara Mathana of Alwar (*EI* 3:266ff.; Gopal 1963-64:91), have been understood in the sense of clan patrimony.

A certain measure of clan exclusiveness, which could not have been very rigid in the system of land distribution, appeared in a nebulous form in Rajasthan in a slightly later context, and was, as mentioned earlier, associated in particular with the Chahamanas. The Harsha inscription of A.D. 973 from the Jaipur area (*EI* 2: 116-130) gives perhaps the earliest evidence of such distribution. Here are mentioned the *svabhogas* (personal estates) of king Simharaja, his two brothers Vatsaraja and Vigraharaja, and his two sons Chandaraja and Govindaraja. The inscription also mentions another assignee, perhaps of the Guhila clan, holding a *bhoga* (estate). A *duḥsādhya* (official) had his own estate too within this kingdom, but his rights were obviously limited inasmuch as his authority to grant land depended on the approval of the king, whereas others needed no such sanction and made grants on their own. The process seems to have gone through further development till the 12th century when, in the areas held by the Nadol Chahamanas, the assignments, termed variously as *grāsa*, *grāsabhūmi* or *bhukti*, came to be held by the king, the *kumāra* (crown prince), the *rājaputras* (sons of the king), the queens and, in one case, the maternal uncle of the king, who obviously was not a member of the same clan (*EI* 11:32-33; Gopal 1963-64:92-94).

To some extent tied up with this feature, but in operation separate from it also, was a new land unit which appears to have consisted of six villages and the multiples thereof (Ghosal 1929:260). The use of this land unit was by no means limited to Rajasthan; even so the incidence of its use in this period appears to have been higher in western India than elsewhere. The units were in many cases parts of such administrative divisions as *maṇḍala*, *bhukti* or *viṣaya* (*EI* 9:2-6; 3:116-130), but the statements in inscriptions that villages were attached (*pratibaddha*) to such units may suggest that the units became the nuclei of some kind of local control. The earliest references to units of 84 villages seem to be available in Saurashtra (*EI* 9:2-6), which was held by the Gurjara-Pratiharas towards the close of the 9th century, and its spread to Rajasthan was perhaps intended to facilitate the distribution of land and political control among the ruling elites. The Harsha inscription of A.D. 973, cited earlier, mentions the Trinakupaka group of 12 villages as having been held by Chahamana Simharaja. In the 11th century, a unit of 12 villages (. . . *radrahadvādaśa*) located within Chacchurini *maṇḍala*, was held by the Paramaras of Kota (*EI* 23:135), and in A.D. 1160, 12 villages attached to Naddulai (*Naḍḍulai-pratibaddhadvādaśagrāmāṇi*) were assigned by Chahamana Alhana and his eldest son to Kirttipala, a younger son (*EI* 9:62-63). By the later part of the 14th century, the *chaurāsia* (holders of 84 villages) had become, as the evidence of the *Visaladeva Rāso* suggests, "a well-known class of chiefs"[22] and, if the pieces of evidence cited above are any indication, such big holdings emanated from the process of land distribution among the members of the ruling clans. The *chaurāsia* arrangement was not always strictly adhered to in the territorial system of the Rajputs, but it did provide a "theoretical frame" to that system in which the hierarchy of units and linkages between clan members and units could be worked out fairly well (Wills 1919:199). Obviously, the details for identifying such linkages are absent in our records, but it is significant that, despite inadequate inscriptional evidence, the rudiments of the *chaurāsia* arrangement and its connection with the distribution of land can be traced to the early phases of the crystallization of Rajput polity.

The early phase of Rajput ascendancy also coincided with the construction of fortresses, numerically on a large scale – a feature which appears to have been absent in the earlier kingdoms of Rajasthan,[23] but which came to be very much a part of the Rajput territorial system later on. Early medieval inscriptions suggest their location in different parts of Rajasthan: Kamyakiyakotta in the Bharatpur area (*EI* 24:329ff.), Rajayapura at Rajor in Alwar (*EI* 3:263), Mandavyapuradurga at Mandor near Jodhpur (*EI* 17:98), Chitrakutamahadurga at Chitor (Ray 1973:1191), Koshavardhanadurga at Shergarh in Kota (*EI* 23:132), Suvarnagiridurga at Jalor (*EI* 1:54-55),[24] Shrimaliyakotta at Bhinmal (*EI* 22:196-198), Takshakagarha (Jain 1972:256-258) and other places. The fortresses served not only defense purposes but had, as the composition of population in some of them will show, wider functions (*EI* 24:329ff; 23:137-141; *IA* 40:175-176). They represented the numerous foci of power of the ascendant ruling families and appear to have had close links with landholdings in the neighbouring areas. The Ropi plates of Paramara Devaraja, dated A.D. 1052, mention the grant of a piece of land in the *svabhujyamānaviṣaya* (personal domain) of Devaraja, the land having been located to the south of Shrimaliyakotta (*EI* 22:196-198). Among its boundaries are mentioned lands belonging to two Brahmans and a *mahāsāmantādhipati* (chief vassal). Another inscription, of the time of Paramara Udayaditya, from Shergarh in Kota district, mentions the village Vilapadraka as belonging to a temple in the Koshavardhanadurga (*EI* 23:131-136).

References to *durgas* (forts) in the context of lands donated obviously suggests that the forts were foci of control for their rural surroundings – a point which may be further substantiated by a reference to the Gopagiri inscriptions of the time of the Gurjara-Pratiharas (*EI* 1:154ff), which also suggest the same kind of control wielded by an early medieval fortress. Thus along with the assignment of land, occasionally in terms of units which could be made into administrative units as well, the construction of fortified settlements in large numbers could be seen as part of a process of consolidation of their position by the ruling clans.

At the level of social relations, the obvious pointer to this process would be the marriage network among the clans. The information available from inscriptions is unfortunately rather limited, so when in the genealogical lists in a few cases of marriage are mentioned, it may be assumed with certainty that they have been recorded because of their significant political implications for the family. Proceeding onward chronologically from the Pratihara family, one can see a change in the marriage network patterns in which not only the supposed origin of a family plays an unimportant part, but there is also a development towards an understandable pattern of interclan relationship. As mentioned earlier, in an inscription of A.D. 837 of the Pratihara family from the Jodhpur area, the originator of the family is mentioned as having married a Brahman and a Kshatriya wife. In another inscription, of A.D. 861, the Brahman wife is dropped from the account of the ancestry. Towards the end of the genealogy, Kakka, who is very close to the last and the current ruler in the genealogical list, is mentioned as having married Padmini of the Bhatti clan, considered by some to be identical with the Bhattis of the Jaisalmer area (*EI* 18:87-99; D. Sharma 1966:I, 124, *n*2).

Records of other families suggest a similar development towards a network which involved mostly the ruling Rajput clans. In the inscriptions of the Chahamanas there seems to have been a distinct preference for the Rashtrakutas, Ratraudhas or Rathors. A *rāṇaka* Tribhuvanesvara of this family was married to Rashtrakuta Lakshmidevi (*EI* 37:155-158). Alhana of the Chahamana family of Nadol also married Annalladevi of the Rashtrakuta family (*EI* 9:66ff). Among the Paramaras of Rajasthan, the marriages known to have been contracted were with the Chahamanas. Paramara Dharavarsha of Mt. Abu married the daughter of Chahamana Kelhanadeva (*EI* 32:135-138). Paramara Satyaraja of the Vagada family married Rajashri, apparently of another Chahamana family

(*EI* 21:42-50). The network was, however, more varied and widespread with the Guhilas. Two records, respectively of A.D. 1000 and A.D. 1008 (*ARRM* 1936:2), mention two wives of the Guhila *mahāsāmantādhipati* of Nagahrada: *mahārājñī* (queen) Sarvadevi, daughter of a *mahāsāmantādhipati* of the solar family, and *mahārājñī* Jajuka, daughter of a *mahāsāmantādhipati* of the solar family of Bharukaccha. Alhanadevi, from a Guhila royal family, was married to Gayakarna of the Chedi family (*IA* 16:345-355). Marriage relations contracted by the Guhilas with specifically Rajput clans extended to the Chalukyas (*PRASWC* 1905-06:61), the Paramaras and Rashtrakutas (*EI* 31:237-248), the Chahamanas (*IA* 39:188-189), and the Hunas (*ibid.*).

Interclan relationship through marriages could, at a certain point of time, be limited to two clans, and any consistency in the pattern may have been due to the nature of political relations between such clans or, as in the case of the Guhilas, it could be quite expansive. But the network operated mostly among such clans as came to constitute the Rajput category. The choice was essentially political, because the families cited here constituted the ruling elites of early medieval Rajasthan.

Interclan relationship through marriage seems to have had wider social implications as well. It could provide social legitimacy to such groups as the Hunas, who had acquired sufficient political power in western India by this period,[25] leading finally to their inclusion in the Rajput clan list. Secondly, interclan marriage relationships may have led to collaboration in wider areas of social and political activity. Thus Guhila Allata, who was married to a Huna princess, had a Huna member in a *goṣṭhī* (assembly) in the kingdom of his son Naravahana (*IA* 58:161ff.) Similarly, Ana, belonging to the family of the Hastikundi Rashtrakutas, was involved in activities concerning a religious institution in the kingdom of Paramara Dharavarsha, who had entered into matrimonial relations with the Hastikundi family (*IA* 56:50-51). In an inscription of A.D. 1168 from Hansi, in Hissar district, there is a reference to one Guhilauta Kilhana, who was the maternal uncle of Prithviraja Chahamana and put in charge of the Asika fort of the Chahamanas (*IA* 41:17-19). These examples are obviously inadequate, but interclan relationship offers a key to understanding the processes through which Rajput polity evolved it the early medieval period.

Proliferation of Clans and the Structure of Rajput Political Dominance

In our discussion of the processes leading to the emergence of the Rajputs in the early medieval period, we have focused so far on a few major ruling families. Although the term *rājaputra*, along with *mahārājakumara*, continued to denote 'son of a king', as in the inscriptions of the Nadol Chahamanas (*EI* 11:49-51), the term gradually came to denote descent groups and not necessarily a particularly exalted political status. A Chitor inscription of A.D. 1301 (Asopa 1976:9-10) mentions three generations of *rājaputras*, perhaps suggesting that by the close of the 13th century the term *rājaputra* conveyed not merely a political status, but an element of heredity as well.

The proliferation of the Rajputs in the early medieval period is suggested by a variety of sources. Hemachandra's *Triṣaṣṭiśalākāpuruṣacarita* refers to *rājaputrākaḥ* or numerous persons of *rājaputra* descent (*ibid.*); a Mt. Abu inscription of the late 11th century speaks of "all the *rājaputras* of the illustrious *Rājaputra* clan" (*ibid.*). Merutunga in his *Prabandhacintāmaṇi* mentions a hundred *rājaputras* of the Paramara clan (*ibid.*). It is understandable then that among the ruling elites, *rājaputra* covered a wide range, from the "actual son of a king to the lowest ranking landholder" (Habib 1974:285). In terms of the actual clans recognized as Rajputs, it is clear from the evidence in the *Kumārapālacarita* and the *Rājataranginī* that the number had become substantial, as mentioned earlier. However, the number given by these texts suggests not so much a rigid set of 36 clans as the idea of descent as marking out the *rājaputras* from the others. To quote a relevant passage from the *Rājataranginī*, "Even those Rājaputras Anantapāla and the rest, who claim descent from the thirty-six families and who in their pride would not concede a higher position to the sun himself . . . " (*Rājataranginī* 1961:593).

From about the 12th century onward, one comes across a variety of expressions which are applied to the ruling elites and which are different from such ranks as *sāmanta* (lord) and *mahāsāmanta* (great lord), the use of which appears to have become less frequent now. The most common terms are *rājaputra*, *rāutta* or *rāuta*, *rājakula* or *rāvala*, *mahārājakula* or *mahārāvala*, *rāṇaka*, and so on, and to these are sometimes tagged official titles like *sāmanta* (lord) or *mahāmaṇḍaleśvara* (*PRASWC* 1910-11:38-39) and *mahāmāṇḍalika* (*ibid*., 35) (chief, official of a large territorial administrative division), indicating the ranks that the *rājaputras* and such others may have attained in the administrative arrangement. What is common to all such terms as *rājakula, rājaputra* or *rāṇaka* is suggested affiliation to royalty. Although it is not always possible to trace a direct lineal connection between a *rājaputra* or *rāṇaka* and a royal family, an explanation for the use of such terms may be sought in the high incidence of their connection with the clans and families which constituted the royalty in early medieval Rajasthan. Indeed, references to the *rājakula* (A.D. 1208), *mahārājakula* (A.D. 1186, 1292, 1302), *mahārāvata* (A.D. 1302), *rāṇā śrī rājakula* (A.D. 1167), *ṭhakkura rāuta* (A.D. 1138), etc., of Guhila families, and the *rāṇaka* (son of a *māṇḍalika*) or *rājaputra* (A.D. 1287), etc. of Chahamana families, and so on, become frequent from the 12th century onward.[26] This evidence should certainly not be construed to mean that *rājaputra* and such other distinguished epithets were confined to a few select clans. In the inscriptions one comes across *śrīvaṃśagottiya rāuta* ('*rāuta* of the Shri lineage') (A.D. 1156), *gurjarajātiya ṭhakkura* ('lord of the Gurjara caste') (A.D. 1283), or "a *rāṇaka* from the Karnata country" (A.D. 1143).[27] These are a measure of the flexibility of the system, in which new groups could be accommodated by virtue of their political initiative and power.

The proliferation of the Rajputs in the early medieval period, both among the established clans and those outside them, is a key indicator for an analysis of the structure of Rajput political dominance. There is no direct evidence regarding the changing status of the traditional "Kshatriya" groups or ruling elites of Rajasthan, and one can even assume their incorporation into the Rajput structure if they survived in power, but the evidence of two inscriptions from the 10th century may suggest the possibility that some among the traditional "Kshatriyas" were going through a process of change. A record of A.D. 956 from Mandkila Tal, near Jodhpur (*EI* 34:77ff.), mentions the son of a learned Kshatriya who engraved a *praśasti* (eulogistic inscription) and was a *sūtradhāra* (artisan) by profession. Another 10th century inscription, of the Gurjara-Pratiharas from the Doab area in U.P. (*EI* 19:52-54, no. 6), refers to a Kshatriya *vaṇik* (merchant). Though obviously inadequate, these examples may nevertheless be taken to indicate that the proliferation of the Rajputs contributed towards an undermining of the political status of the early Kshatriya groups, who were taking to less potent occupations, and also that the preferred term for the ruling stratum was now not so much "Kshartiya" as "Rajput."

As a hypothesis, the substitution of the traditional "Kshatriya" groups by the Rajputs and the consolidation of the Rajput structure may be viewed as a result of collaboration between the emerging clans, not only in terms of interclan marriage relationship but also in terms of participation at various levels of polity and the circulation of clan members in different kingdoms and courts. While the beginning of this process may be traced to the feudatory-overlord relationship between the Pratiharas, Chahamanas and others, a wider network of relationship appears to have spread to other levels of polity only gradually.

One may start here by pointing to the changing typology of Rajasthan inscriptions. Whereas the royal commands conveyed through epigraphs from about the 7th to the 10th century – and in some cases to the 12th century as well – were addressed to various categories of officials,[28] in later inscriptions lists of such officials are generally absent. The change is perhaps best shown in the form of address in a Nadol Chahamana inscription of A.D. 1161: *deśānto rājaputrān janapadagaṇān bodhayatyeva* ('he informs the Rajputs and the groups of common people of the kingdom') (*EI* 9:62-66). Here the *rājaputras*, who are distinguished from the *janapadagaṇa* (common people) seem to stand for all the categories of officials mentioned in the earlier inscriptions. This is not to say that the earlier ranks had completely disappeared. In fact, according to traditions relating to the 12th century (D. Sharma 1966:I, 359), there were 100 *sāmantas* in the Chahamana court. But from the study of the inscriptions one is strongly tempted to assume that such ranks mostly circulated among those groups who were claiming to be *rājaputras* as well. Although there is an early reference to a Pratihara member of a *goṣṭhī* in the 7th century Vasantgarh inscription of Varmalata (*EI* 9:187-192), it is only in a much later period that the *rājaputras*, or more generally the members of various clans, are found placed at various positions in the Rajput socio-political structure.

It is in this period that the inscriptional evidence relating to the composition of elites suggests a distinct trend towards what we have earlier called collaboration between the clans. Thus in the Ahada inscription of Guhila Allata (A.D. 942) (*IA* 58:161ff.), a

Huna and a Pratihara are mentioned as members of a *goṣṭhī*; again, in the Paldi inscription of Guhila Arisimha (A.D. 1059) (*EI* 30:8-12), a *saulaṃkivaṃśiya rājaputra* (*rājaputra* of the Solanki lineage) figures as a member of a *goṣṭhika*. In the Mala plates of Virasimha (A.D. 1287) (*EI* 22:192-196), a *rāuta* is among various witnesses mentioned. The Hansi stone inscription of Prithviraja Chahamana (*IA* 41:17-19) contains some relevant information in this connection: (i) Asikadurga, a fort, was given to a Guhilautanvaya or person belonging to the Guhila clan; (ii) a Dodanvaya or person belonging to the Doda subclan was a subordinate to Prithviraja's maternal uncle. Both these references, showing the inclusion of Guhila and Doda elements in the Chahamana polity, are by no means exceptional, because in the same kingdom one comes across references to *mahāmāṇḍalikas* (chiefs) of Bodana origin (*IA* 41:202-203) and other categories of feudatories of Dadhicha origin (*EI* 12:56-61). The presence of Guhila landowning elites in the Chahamana kingdom is revealed by the Bijholi inscription of A.D. 1169 (*EI* 26:84ff), which refers to grants of land made to a Jain temple by Guhilaputra Ravala Dhadhara and Guhilaputra Ravala Vyaharu. In the Delhi-Siwalik pillar inscription of A.D. 1163 (*IA* 19:215-219), a *rājaputra* named Shri Sallakshanapala is mentioned as the *mahāmantri* (chief minister) of Vigraharaja, of the same line. In A.D. 1164, in the Nadol Chahamana kingdom, a Rashtrakuta or member of the Rathor clan probably figures as a *talāra* (military official) in A.D. 1164 (*EI* 11:46-47).

This kind of information is available from other kingdoms as well. An inscription of A.D. 1287 (*IA* 45:77ff.) mentions a Guhilaputra and also a member of the Devara subclan as important landholders in the kingdom of the Sirohi Paramaras. Between the middle of the 12th and the early part of the 13th century the Chalukya feudatories in southern Rajasthan were Paramaras (*IA* 61:135-136) and Chahamanas (*PRASWC* 1907-08:49; *IA* 62:42). These few examples are likely to represent a wide range of similar information and may show that apart from kinship ties within a clan, shown earlier to have at least partly influenced the distribution of land, the interclan relationships governing the distribution of power helped consolidate the structure of Rajput polity in the early medieval period.

An extension of this argument would be to examine the nature and incidence of participation, among the ascendant clans, in the military exploits of the period. There is practically no direct and detailed evidence on the composition of the warriors of various levels, but one can make use here of the evidence of a particular type of sculptured stone which, though originating elsewhere much earlier, became widespread in Rajasthan from the early medieval period onward.[29] These stones are memorial relics, usually known and referred to in inscriptions as *govardhana dhvaja (ARIE* 1964-65:102), *paliya*, and *devali, deuli* or *devakulikā (PRASWC* 1911-12:53). They were installed to commemorate death, including death on the battlefield. The range of social groups which the memorial stones generally cover is quite extensive, but the memorials to violent deaths relate mostly to such groups as came to be recognized as Rajputs , and the incidence of memorial stones in general among them, at least in the early medieval period, seems to be higher than among others.[30] The names of clans found on memorial stones include Pratihara, Chahamana, Guhila, Paramara, Solanki, Rathor, Chandela, Mahavaraha, Mangaliya, Bodana, Mohila, Devara, Doda, Dahiya, Pavara, Dohara, Bhichi, Ghamgala, and Dharkata.[31] Furthermore, in a number of cases, titles indicative of the political and social status of the commemorated (*rājā, mahāsāmanta, rāṇā, rāuta, rājaputra* etc.) occur in the same records.[32] The memorial stones may have been a borrowed concept, but the way they were fashioned and the contexts many of them represent in early medieval Rajasthan relate largely to the new "Kshatriya" groups which together made up the political order of Rajasthan.

"Localism" and Clan Segmentation

It should be clear from some references made in the preceding section that an important aspect of the proliferation of the Rajputs in the early medieval period was the emergence of various minor clans and subdivisions of the major clans. Mention has been made earlier of the *Prabandhacintāmaṇi* evidence which refers to 100 *rājaputras* of the Paramara clan. Speaking of the Guhila family, the Achaleshwar (Mt. Abu) inscription of A.D. 1285 (Bhavnagar Archaeological Department n.d.:88) describes it as full of branches and sub-branches which consist of good members (*suparvāḥ patravibhūṣitāṃśāḥ*). This development seems to apply to all the major clans. Furthermore, the continuing process of the formation of Rajput clans, presumably through the acquisition of political power, is attested by a few inscriptions. A record of A.D. 1156 (*IA* 41:202-203) mentions a *mahārāja* who was a Bodana. Mahavaraha, another clan, appears in a record of A.D. 1011 (*PRASWC* 1911-12:53). The subdivisions of the major clans had become fairly numerous at this time, as will be clear from the following list: Doda, subdivision of Paramara; Pipadia (*PRASWC* 1911-12:52) and Mangalya, subdivisions of Guhila; Devara, Mohila and Soni or Sonigara (*EI* 11:60-62), subdivisions of Chahamana; Dadhicha, subdivision of Rathor. That the new clans and what came to be recognized as subdivisions of earlier clans were being drawn into the Rajput network is suggested by a few cases of marriage of which records are available. In a record of A.D. 1180 (*PRASWC* 1911-12:53), a *rāṇā* of the Guhila family is mentioned as having married a Bodani, that is, a girl of the Bodana family. Another record, of A.D. 1191 (*ibid.*), refers to a Guhila who married a girl from the Mohila subdivision of the Chahamanas.

How did these subclans emerge? The process expected to explain this phenomenon would be the segmentation of clans, which sometimes resulted from their movements to new areas. But there is no actual evidence in our period of such segmentation leading to the formation of subclans. For example, the Chahamanas of the Shakambhari line segmented to form the Chahamana family at Nadol, a splinter group from which again established itself at Jalor (D. Sharma 1966:I, 546-547). No subclan seems to have emerged from this process. Similar events also took place in the royal family of the Paramaras, which resulted in the starting up of new lines at Vagada and Mt. Abu, which nevertheless continued as Paramara (*ibid.*:I, 549-552).

What may be useful to invoke in this context is the phenomenon of caste formation in the early medieval period in which the element of "localism" was substantially involved (R.S. Sharma 1969). In Rajasthan the working of "localism" may be seen in the rise of the Shrimala or Bhillamala Brahmans (D. Sharma 1966:I, 442-444), and the process may be further extended to analyze such groups as the Dahiya Brahmans and the Dahiya Rajputs who, having originated in the same locality, had strong "affinities" with each other (*EI* 12:56-61; *IA* 41:85-88). Secondly, as has been already indicated, Rajputization was a process of social mobility which, in the wake of its formation into a structure, drew in such disparate groups as the Medas and the Hunas. From these perspectives, the formation of various subclans was not necessarily a result of direct segmentation of clans, but perhaps a product of the mechanism of absorption of local elements, when such elements came into contact with some already established clans. This element of "localism" in the formation of Rajput subclans is suggested in the early medieval period by the Pipadia Guhilas and the Sonigara Chahamanas, Pipadia having been derived from the place name Pippalapada and Sonigara from Suvarnagiri (Jalor). That one of the channels for rising to the status of a recognized clan was through marriage relationships is suggested by the cases of such relationships between the Guhilas on the one hand and the Bodanas and Mohilas (subdivision of the Chahamanas) on the other.

Summary and Conclusions

From what has been written above, two chronological stages of the emergence of the Rajputs in the early medieval period may be envisaged. In the first stage it was essentially a political process in which disparate groups seeking political power conformed to such norms as permeated the contemporary political ideology. As entry into the Rajput fold continued basically to be through political power, the traditional norms or the need for legitimization remained.

In this respect, the emergence of the Rajputs was similar to a pan-Indian phenomenon, namely the formation of dynasties, many of which sought legitimization through zealously claimed linkages with Kshatriya lines of the mythical past. But in the second stage, which we would roughly date from the 11th-12th centuries, the rise of the Rajputs became a comprehensive social phenomenon as well.

As such, the multiplication of the *rājaputras* should not be viewed as merely reflecting the consolidation of a political power structure; its implications should be extended also to explain the growing phenomenon of minor clans and subclans. And, to venture a final hypothesis, it may well be in this expansion of mere "dynastic" relations towards a wider arena of social relations that the seeds of the future growth of the Rajput network in space and time are to be found.

ENDNOTES

This paper originally appeared as "Origin of the Rajputs: The Political, Economic and Social Processes in Early Medieval Rajasthan" in the *Indian Historical Review* 3(1):59-80. Reprinted here by permission of the author and the Director of the Indian Council of Historical Research.

1. Theories about the origins of the Rajputs constitute a voluminous literature. Relevant bibliographical references are, however, available in some recent works on Rajasthan (D. Sharma 1959, 1966; Asopa 1976).
2. What we have in mind here are such factors as the formation of numerous new castes, the emergence of dynasties seeking Kshatriya status, the accent on locality in social relations, and so on. For a brief statement of some of the factors, see R.S. Sharma 1969.
3. The existence of the Rajputs in the 10th-12th centuries has often been doubted; see Ziegler 1976:242. The doubt is, however, unfounded, since by the 12th century the term *rājaputra* had come to acquire the later connotation of the term "Rajput." See below for details.
4. For relevant details regarding such claims, see Sircar 1965:1-23; also Thapar 1971:427-429. For a few examples of how a standard *gotra* (exogamous section of a clan) provided legitimacy, see Nandi 1970:118-122. The *gotras* of the Rajput clans also require a fresh analysis.
5. See Sinha 1962:35-80; also Singh 1974:317-336.
6. Cited in Yadava 1973:37.
7. Compare the lists given in *ibid.*, 36-37.
8. *Aparājitapṛcchā*, a text of the 12th century, cited in *ibid.*, 34.
9. Compare the lists of early historical sites with those of the early medieval period in Jain 1972. Archaeological reports covering sites, monuments ad epigraphs of Rajasthan convey the same impression.
10. See Diksit 1964:24-28; also Venkateswara Rao 1974:53-58.
11. *hatvā sīmādhipān saṃkhye teṣāṃ grāmān pragṛhya ca, deśaḥ saptaśato yena saptasāhasrika kṛtaḥ* ('having killed numerous chiefs of the boundaries of his kingdom and having taken their villages, he made his kingdom of 700 [villages] into one of 7000'). Nadol fragmentary grant (V. 14), in D. Sharma 1959:189.
12. For an idea of the methods and spread of irrigation in early medieval Rajasthan see Chattopadhyaya 1973.
13. D. Sharma (1966:I, 12) cites *Śabdārthacintāmaṇi* to show the following characteristics of the region: "the sky is generally clear, trees and water are scarce, and the land abounds in *śamī* (propis spicigena) *karira* (capprisaphylla), *pilu* (cereya arborea) and *karkandhu* (ziziphus jujula) trees."
14. Cited in D. Sharma 1959: 121-122.
15. *mayā gurjaradeśe gantavyaṃ karabhagrahaṇāya . . . tataśca gurjaradeśe gatvā uṣṭrīṃ gṛhītvā svagṛhamāgataḥ* ('I went to the Gurjara country to get elephants, and having gone there I returned home having gotten a she-camel'). Cited in Asopa 1976:81n1.
16. *Śrīgurjaravāhitasamastakṣetra* ('the entire land cultivated by the Gurjars') (*EI* 3:263-267).

17. See the evidence of the *Hou Han-shu* cited in Nilakanta Sastri 1957:226.
18. The inscriptional references from which these tables are drawn up are selective but not arbitrary. The column indicating "political status" has often been left blank, as such status, not always defined in the records, has to be reconstructed. The status is mentioned in the column only when definite indications are available about it.
19. The term "feudatory" is being used here, in the absence of a better alternative, simply to imply a subordinate position. For a recent critique of the indiscriminate use of this and such other terms, see Stein 1975:83-84.
20. The evidence is that of the Bijholi inscription of A.D. 1169 (*EI* 26:84ff.).
21. For a general review of the evidence, see Gopal 1963-64.
22. Cited in *ibid.*, 96.
23. See, for example, the early historical material in Jain 1972:80-154.
24. Also mentioned as Kanchanagirigarha.
25. For the pockets of Huna power in this period, see Sircar 1969:83-87.
26. Sources for these references are: *ARRM* 1927:3; *PRASWC* 1914-15:35; *PRASWC* 1911-12:52; *EI* 11:36-37; *EI* 37:157-158; *IA* 45:77ff.
27. Sources for these references are Nahar 1918-27:I, 218; II, 25; *PRASWC* 1908-09:45.
28. In the Dungarpur inscription of A.D. 689, for example, the list included *nṛpa* (king), *nṛpasuta* (prince), *sandhivigrahādhikṛta* ('peace and war, i.e. foreign affairs, secretary), *senādhyakṣa* (commander of the army), *purodhā* (royal chaplain), *pramātṛ* (superintendent of measures), *mantrī* (minister), *pratihāra* (doorkeeper), *rājasthānīya* (viceroy), *uparkia* (governor), *kumārāmātya* (minister attached to the crown prince), *viṣayabhogapati* (administrator of lands), *chauroddhoraṇika* (official in charge of apprehending thiefs), *śaulkika* (superintendent of taxes), *vyāpṛtaka* (superintendent of trade), *daṇḍapāśika* (superintendent of police), *chata* (superintendent of forced labor), *bhata* (panegyrist), *pratisaraka* (superintendent of servants), *grāmādhipati* (village chief), *drāngika* (?) (*EI* 34:173-176). See also the Rajor inscription of A.D. 960 (*EI* 3:263-267), the A.D. 1019 Bamnera plate of Paramara Bhoja (*IA* 41: 201-202), and the Nadol inscription of A.D. 1119 (*EI* 11:304ff.)
29. For useful details on the memorial stones of early medieval Rajasthan, see Goetz 1960:61ff. and Agrawal 1963.
30. I have discussed this elsewhere in a paper prepared on the occasion of a seminar on Memorial Stones held at Dharwar in December 1974.
31. Sources: *IAR* 1959-60:60; *IAR* 1962-63:54; *PRASWC* 1909-10:61; *PRASWC* 1911-12:52; *PRASWC* 1916-17:70; *IA* 40:181-183; *ARRM* 1935:3-5; *PRASWC* 1911-12:53; *ARRM* 1909:10, Appendix D; *ARRM* 1922-23:2; *IA* 42:267-269; *ARIE* 1964-65:102; *ARIE* 1959-60:113; *JPASB* 1916:104-106. For the Devaras, see also *IA* 45:77ff. and *EI* 9:79.
32. Sources: *PRASWC* 1909-10:51; *ARIE* 1961-62:115; *PRASWC* 1911-12:53; *ARIE* 1954-55:59.

REFERENCES CITED

Abbreviations

ARIE	*Annual Report on Indian Epigraphy*
ARRM	*Annual Report of the Rajputana Museum* (Ajmer)
BSOAS	*Bulletin of the School of Oriental and African Studies*
EI	*Epigraphia Indica*
IA	*Indian Antiquary*
IAR	*Indian Archaeology – A Review*
IESHR	*Indian Economic and Social History Review*
JESHO	*Journal of the Economic and Social History of the Orient*
JPASB	*Journal and Proceedings of the Asiatic Society of Bengal*
JRAS	*Journal of the Royal Asiatic Society of Great Britain and Ireland*
PIHC	*Proceedings of the Indian History Congress*
PRASWC	*Progress Report of the Archaeological Survey, Western Circle*
ZDMG	*Zeitschrift der Deutschen Morgendlaendischen Gesellschaft*

Agrawal, R.C.
1963 "*Paścimī Rājasthān ke kuch prārambhik smṛtistambha*". *Vāradā*, April issue.

Asopa, Jai Narain
1976 *Origin of the Rajputs*. Delhi: Bharatiya.

Bhandarkar, D.R.
1911 "Foreign Elements in the Hindu Population." *IA*.

Bhavnagar Achaeological Department
n.d. *A Collection of Prakrit and Sanskrit Inscriptions*. Bhavnagar: Bhavnagar Archaeological Department.

Chattopadhyaya, B.D.
1973 "Irrigation in Early Medieval Rajasthan." *JESHO* 16(2-3):298-316.

Dikshit, G.S.
1964 *Local Self-Government in Medieval Karnataka*. Dharwar.

Ghosal, U.N.
1929 *Contribution to the History of the Hindu Revenue System*. Calcutta: University of Calcutta.

Goetz, Hermann
1960 *The Art and Architecture of Bikaner State*. Oxford: B. Cassirer.

Gopal, K.K.
1963-64 "Assignment to Officers and Royal Kinsmen in Early Medieval India (c. 700-1200 A.D.)." *University of Allahabad Studies*, Ancient History Section, pp. 75-103.

Habib, Irfan
1974 "The Social Distribution of Landed Property in Pre-British Indian (A Historical Survey)." In *Indian Society: Historical Probings (In Memory of D.D. Kosambi)*. R.S. Sharma and V. Jha, eds.

Henige, David P.
1975 "Some Phantom Dynasties of Early and Medieval India: Epigraphic Evidence and the Abhorrence of a Vacuum." *BSOAS* 38(3).

Jain, Kailash Chand

1972 *Ancient Cities and Towns of Rajasthan: A Study of Culture and Civilization*. Delhi: Motilal Banarsidass.

Nahar, P.C.

1918-27 *Jaina lekha saṃgraha*. 2 vols. Calcutta.

Nandi, R.N.

1970 "*Gotra* and Social Mobility in the Deccan." *PIHC*, 32nd session: 118-122.

Nilakanta Shastri, K.A.

1957 *A Comprehensive History of India*. Vol. II. *The Mauryas and Sātavāhanas*. Bombay.

Pathak, Vishwambhar Sharan

1966 *Ancient History of India: A Study in Historical Biographies*. Bombay: Asia.

Puri, Baij Nath

1957 *The History of the Gurjara-Pratiharas*. Bombay.

Rājataranginī

1961 *Kalhaṇa's Rājataranginī: A Chronicle of the Kings of Kashmir*. Edited and translated by Mark Aurel Stein. Vol. I. Reprint ed. Delhi: Motilal Banarsidass.

Ray, Hem Chandra

1973 *The Dynastic History of Northern India (Early Medieval Period)*. Vol. II. 2nd ed. Reprint ed. New Delhi: Munshiram Manoharlal.

Raychaudhuri, H.C.

1960 In *The Early History of the Deccan*. Ghulam Yazdani, ed., chap. 1. London: Oxford University Press.

Sharma, Dasharatha

1959 Early Chauhan Dynasties (A Study of Chauhan Political History, Chauhan Political Institutions and Life in the Chauhan Dominions from c. 800 to 1316 A.D.). Delhi: Motilal Banarsidass.

1966 (ed.) *Rajasthan Through the Ages*. 2 vols. Bikaner: Rajasthan State Archives.

Sharma, Ram Sharan

1965 *Indian Feudalism, c. 300-1200*. Calcutta: University of Calcutta.

1969 *Social Changes in the Early Medieval India (circa A.D. 500-1200)*. Delhi.

Singh, K. Suresh

1974 "A Study in State-Formation among Tribal Communities." In *Indian Society: Historical Probings (In Memory of D.D. Kosambi)*. R.S. Sharma and V. Jha, eds. pp. 317-336.

Sinha, Surajit

1962 "State Formation and Rajput Myth in Tribal Central India." *Man in India* 42(1):35-80.

Sircar, Dinesh Chandra

1965 *The Guhilas of Kiṣkindhā*. Calcutta.

1969 *Some Problems of Kuṣāna and Rajput History*. Calcutta: University of Calcutta.

Stein, Burton

1975 "The State and Agrarian Order in South India." In *Essays on South India*. Burton Stein, ed. Honolulu: University of Hawaii Press.

Suryavanshi, Bhagwansingh

1962 *The Abhiras: Their History and Culture*. Baroda: Maharaja Sayajirao University of Baroda.

Thapar, Romila
1971 "The Image of the Barbarian in Early India." *Comparative Studies in Society and History* 13(4).

Tod, James
1971 *Annals and Antiquities of the Rajasthan*. Vol I. Reprint ed. Delhi: Motilal Banarsidass.

Vaidya, Chintaman Vinayak
1924 *History of Medieaval Hindu India*. Vol. II *Early History of the Rajputs (750 to 1000 A.D.)*. Poona.

Venkateswara Rao, T.
1974 "Numerical Figures Affixed to the Names of Territorial Divisions in Medieval Andhra." *Itihas*, Journal of the Andhra Pradesh Archives 2(1):53-58.

Wills, C.U.
1919 "The Territorial System of the Rajput Kingdoms of Medieval Chattisgarh." *Journal and Proceedings of the Asiatic Society of Bengal*. New Series 15.

Yadava, B.N.S.
1973 *Society and Culture in Northern India in the Twelfth Century*. Allahabad.

Ziegler, Norman P.
1976 "Marvari Historical Chronicles: Sources for the Social and Cultural History of Rajasthan." *IESHR* 13(2).

EVOLUTION OF THE RATHOR STATE OF MARVAR: HORSES, STRUCTURAL CHANGE AND WARFARE

NORMAN P. ZIEGLER

The 15th and early 16th centuries were a formative period for many of the Rajput kingdoms of what is now Rajasthan. These were years of diminished Muslim power over North India[1] that witnessed a shift toward increasingly centralized rule within the Rajput kingdoms and, ultimately, the emergence of state systems. The centralization of authority around local rulers and their ability both to regulate access to land in their kingdoms and greatly to increase scale in the deployment of military force contributed significantly to the growth in importance of several kingdoms. Mevar, for instance, rose to assume a position of regional dominance under Sisodiyo Rano Kumbho[2] (*ca.* 1433-1468) in the mid-15th century. The most dramatic example of the emergence of a Rajput kingdom to regional supremacy, however, is that of Marvar in the early 16th century under Rathor Rav Malde Gangavat (1532-1562). By the 1540s, Rav Malde of Jodhpur controlled not only Marvar, but also Ajmer, Nagaur, Sivano, Bikaner, Didvano and Sambhar; he also raided wide areas of southern and central Rajasthan as far east as Chatsu (south of Amber), and in 1544 was powerful enough to challenge the Afghan Sher Shah Sur's supremacy over North India.

This paper examines the evolution of the Rathor kingdom of Marvar, focusing specifically on changes that culminated in its rise to regional prominence under the rulership of Rav Malde. It first considers horses as a central military supply, and demonstrates their introduction into Marvar in increasing numbers during the late 15th and early 16th centuries. It then discusses the impact of horses on the structure and organization of the kingdom. Finally, it assesses the extent to which the use of greater numbers of horses and related organizational changes influenced Rajput military behavior and the technology of warfare – which, despite the evolving political order of Marvar, remained rooted in the ideologies and equipment of past centuries. The paper concludes by relating the changes that transformed Marvar into a dominant regional power to the broader context of evolving Rajput kingdoms in late 15th- and early 16th-century Rajasthan.

Emerging Role of Horses in Marvar Politics

> Asapuri Devi [tutelary deity of the Sonagaro Chauhans] . . . was pleased with Rav Lakhan. [She] gave him [a] kingdom . . . Then [the Rav] entreated the goddess, "I have no horses." Then the goddess said, "On such and such a day, the horses [from] a caravan will get loose and will come [to you] of their own accord." Afterwards, 13,000 horses were allowed to wander off [to graze], and [they] came [to the Rav] . . . (Sakariya 1960-67:I, 202)

Horses have played an important role in Rajput history, and local sources often relate the rise to prominence of different clans to their possession and use in campaigns. The types of horses, their supply and availability, and the specific use to which they were put are, however, difficult questions to answer. Much of the secondary literature about Rajputs clouds these issues by always portraying Rajputs as horse-mounted warriors (Banerjee 1962:109-135; Bhargava 1966:1-43; Crooke 1920; Sharma 1977:1-18). In contrast to this timeless image, the bulk of evidence from local texts indicates that the Rajput association with horses evolved over a period of centuries, and that prior to the 16th century, Rajputs generally functioned without horses, because they were in very short supply and those available were of poor quality, unfit for use in battle.

Stories from the *Khyāt* of Nainsi[3] about 14th- and 15th-century Rathor rulers speak about local armies comprised solely of contingents of warriors on foot (Sakariya 1960-67:II, 276-279, 338), and about horse stealing from caravans moving along the high roads from Gujarat to Agra and Delhi because of short local supplies (Bhati 1968-74:I, 16, 18, 22-23; Sakariya 1960-67:II, 299, 302, 307-308, 318; III, 8, 123). One story even describes the unsuccessful attempt *ca*. 1438 by Rathor Jodho Rinmalot (Rav of Mandor and

Jodhpur, *ca*. 1453-1489) to find horses on which to mount his Rajputs when he sought to reassert his family's authority in Marvar following the murder of his father at Chitor and the subsequent Sisodiyo occupation of Marvar (Bhati 1968-74:I, 33-34; Sakariya 1960-67:III, 7). *Ca*. 1453, Jodho Rinmalot finally met Sisodiyo Rano Kumbho of Mevar near Pali (36 miles southeast of Jodhpur) in battle. The *Vigat* of Nainsi records this confrontation:

> One time later, Rano Kumbho gathered together all the contingents of Mevar and came and halted at Pali. News [of the arrival of the Sisodiyos] reached Rav Jodho. *At this time, Rav Jodho had very few horses*. Then 10,000 Rathors [seated in] 2,000 carts resolved to die. And Rav Jodho went and encamped above Pali. The news reached the Rano: "*Jodho has come sitting in a cart*." (Bhati 1968-74:I, 35; emphasis mine)

Additional evidence about the relative unavailability of horses and their poor quality comes from textual references to horses themselves. The chronicles refer to local horses by the single term *ghoṛo* ('horse'), while they use specific names to describe the few special horses that appeared in Marvar, and characterize them as faster and stronger than local horses. These special horses were rare possessions distinguished by their origin in Kutch or Umarkot, areas known for breeds of fine horses (Sakariya 1960-67:I, 349; II, 294; III, 64, 97, 109-111, 257, 259, 280-282). Into the 16th century, fine horses remained symbols of prestige and position, suitable only for the few. The following passage from a story about Rathor Rav Viramde Vaghavat of Sojhat, brother of Rav Gango of Jodhpur (1515-1532), illustrates this situation:

> Then one day a battle occurred [between the Rajputs of Rav Viramde and those of Rav Gango]. So [the stable keeper] had given [the Uhar Rathor][4] Hardas [Rav] Viramdeji's fine horse to ride, [the horse] that was used on ceremonial occasions; thus, Hardas and the horse were both wounded . . . [Then] Hardas came to Sojhat. [His] wounds were bound. Then [Rav] Viramde said, "Be off, Hardas! You caused injury to my horse [worth] five thousand [rupees]." Then Hardas said, "Worthless Rajput! I caused injury to my own body [as well]." Then Hardas, being offended, set off without [his] wounds being healed. (*ibid*.:III, 88)

With the exception of a few such special horses, local horses appear to have been Indian country-bred nags or poines, suitable primarily for riding or transporting goods, not for use in battle. Texts describe these horses as weak, slow-footed and of poor quality. Fine horses were to be found at Umarkot (*ibid.*:III, 110-111, 163).

Simon Digby provides some perspective on the availability of horses in his recent study of military supplies under the Delhi Sultanate (late 12th through 14th centuries). He argues that the Muslim rulers of North India were able to maintain power during these centuries primarily because they controlled the supplies of horses (and elephants). He writes: "Once the Delhi Sultanate had been established, the surviving land-based chieftains of northern India were probably very ill-provided with horses" (1971:49). This control extended into the late 14th century. The only horses that escaped rigid control during the period of Sultanate supremacy were the Indian country-bred nags or ponies (*ibid.*, 28). With specific reference to Rajputs, Digby notes that they were not worse horsemen than the Muslims. They simply had less access to horses suitable for fighting (*ibid.*, 21-22).

By the early 15th century, political control in northern India had become divided among a number of rival kingdoms including Delhi, Jaunpur, Mandu and Gujarat. Sultanate armies that had once ranged in numbers from 300,000 to 500,000 horsemen now dwindled to 50,000 and then to 10,000 (*ibid.*, 23-26, 41), because adequate supplies of horses no longer reached Delhi. During this period, it is probable that horses became more available in Rajasthan as a whole. Based upon his study of early Rathor rulers of Marvar, Richard Saran has commented that supplies of horses (and camels) moved regularly from Gujarat to the Indus Valley region and then on into northern India and Multan, and that some supplies reached Marvar by way of Jaisalmer (personal communication). Despite this fact, horses appear to have remained in relatively short supply.

In the early 16th century, the situation changed markedly. It was at this time that Rathor Rav Gango Vaghavat of Jodhpur (1515-1532) established a stable of horses at an outpost on the eastern borders of his kingdom to protect his capital against his brother, Rav Viramde of Sojhat. The *Khyāt* of Nainsi includes the following passage about this stable:

> Then [Rav Gango's leading Rajput, Rathor Kumpo Mahirajot], brought [horses] to Dhaulharo [village near Sojhat] and established a stable. [He] stationed four thousand of Rav Gango's household warriors at [this] outpost . . . [and he] stationed [four of the Rav's] nobles with [these men] and the horses. (Sakariya 1960-67:III, 84)

This is the first such reference to a stable in the local texts. Its importance lies both in the mention of the stable and in the stable's size.

Deployment of warriors at outposts has earlier precedents in Marvar. However, these outposts were small-scale operations. For example, in the latter part of the 15th century, Sujo Jodhavat (Rav of Jodhpur, *ca*. 1492-1515) organized the conquest of Phalodhi in northern Marvar. Following the conquest, he transferred authority in this area to his son, Naro. With his son he stationed five hundred horsemen, whom Naro in turn dispersed among several different outposts in the area (Bhati 1968-74:I, 10-11, 22; Sakariya 1960-67:III, 105, 112; see also II:307-308).

This small scale of deployment is far surpassed in the first half of the 16th century. Rav Gango's successor, Rav Malde Gangavat (1532-1562), initiated an aggressive campaign of expansion of the borders of his kingdom. Much of his success was based on greater availability of horses and the mobility they provided. Central to his strategy was the deployment of his warriors at strategic outposts along the borders of Jodhpur. Initially, these outposts included Rarod village on the border of Merto and Nagaur, Sojhat on the eastern edge of Marvar facing Ajmer, and selected other sites along the western edge of the Aravallis fronting Mevar. With these mobile strike forces at his command, Rav Malde was able to conquer much of central and northern Rajasthan during the first eleven years of his rule (1532-1543).

Rav Malde's expansion from Jodhpur occurred during a time of changing political fortunes in northern and western India. In the north, the fledgling empire of the Mughals under Humayun fell to the Afghan Sher Shah Sur. And in the west, Malva came under the control of the Sultan of Gujarat. These developments and the unrest they generated undoubtedly contributed both to the increased flow of horses into Marvar and other areas of Rajasthan, and to the successful conduct of Rav Malde's campaigns. Rav

Malde also established important marriage alliances with the Sultan of Gujarat, the ruler of Nagaur (Mohammad Daulat Khan) and the Sodho Rajputs of Umarkot (Bhati 1968-74:I, 52-53, 55-56; Murardan n.d.:137-139; Svami 1956:18-20), which may have helped sustain the movement of this central military supply into Marvar. In turn, the greater availability of horses influenced in significant ways the emerging political order of the Rathor kingdom.

Structural Change in the Rathor Kingdom of Marvar

Prior to the late 15th century, political organization in Marvar was centered on the "little kingdoms"[5] of important landed Rajputs and their retinues of household warriors. These little kingdoms had developed from within the egalitarian brotherhoods of Rajput society and were stratified and hierarchically ordered rulerships differentiated on the basis of descent. Sons of ruling houses received larger shares of land in inheritance than other Rajputs of the brotherhood, and one among the sons, usually a favorite, was chosen successor and received the largest share.[6]

Differential control over lands and access to strategic resources facilitated the development of patronage around the households of these important Rajputs. Texts refer to these Rajputs as *vaḍā ghar rā chhoru* ('sons of great houses'), *ṭhākurs* ('gods, lords, rulers, masters') and *dhaṇīs* ('masters, rulers, husbands') (Bhati 1968-74:I, 10, 38; Sakariya 1960-67:I, 70, 77; II, 121, 268; III, 23, 239). Kher in western Marvar in the 14th century, and Mandor, Jodhpur and Merto in central and eastern Marvar in the 15th century, are kingdoms that emerged under prominent Rathors. A passage from the *Vigat* of Nainsi about Rathor Rav Chundo Viramot, the ruler of Mandor (*d. ca.* 1423), describes the emerging kingdom:

> Day by day, circumstances became [more] favorable. Rav Chundo performed exceedingly great devotions to Chanvda Deviji [the tutelary deity of the Marvar Rathors]. Ten times more [traffic] began to pass along the roads. [Rav] Chundo continued to acquire wealth. A gathering of warriors and horses continued around him. Chundo adopted the behavior [of a ruler]. He had [large amounts of] cooked food prepared. And he had offerings given [to the Charans and the Brahmans]. (Bhati 1968-74:I, 22)

Important to the rise of these kingdoms were personal retinues of warriors maintained by a local ruler as part of his household. These warriors were "bound" to him by obligations of service in return for his patronage and support. In the local idiom, they had eaten the *ṭhākur*'s "grain" or "salt," and were indebted to him for this sustenance (Sakariya 1960-67:II, 273, 296).[7] They formed part of his *vasī* (lit. '[those] of the household, residence, dwelling').[8] But while they were bound to the *ṭhākur*, they did not constitute a permanent body or force. Their attachment remained tied to his patronage. Thus, warriors attached to the household of Rav Chundo Viramot of Mandor left the Rav when, as an economy measure, one of the Rav's wives arbitrarily reduced the amount of clarified butter (*ghī*) supplied to them. As a result of their departure, Rav Chundo's "rulership grew weak" (*ibid.*: II, 313). Thus in a system where service was exchange for sustenance, both the idiom and the substance of food were central.

During the later 15th and early 16th centuries, the structure of these small kingdoms began to change in fundamental ways. This change involved the emergence of prebendal domain alongside prior patrimonial domain in the ordering of relationships among Rajputs on the land. Patrimonial domain is exercised by those who inherit control over land through membership in kinship groups. Such control implies the right to receive tribute from inhabitants of the land in return for their rights of occupancy. Prebendal domain is not inheritable, but is granted by a ruler to his officials in return for service to the state. Such officials draw tribute from the land in their capacity as state servants, and their lands are therefore grants of income, or prebends, in return for this service (Wolf 1966:50-51).

The shift away from households of important landed Rajputs and their personal retinues of warriors, and toward a form of organization based on links between a ruler and Rajputs who received land in return for loyalty and military service to the throne coincided with the more extensive use of horses in Marvar. Given the restricted production of this semi-arid land and the inherent difficulties in overland movement of supplies, the most practical way to provision large numbers of horses (and men) was to disperse them throughout the countryside on assigned lands. This necessity profoundly influenced the emerging political order of Marvar.[9]

The exercise of prebendal domain is seen in the introduction of *paṭo* land grants. The term *paṭo* means both 'written title or deed' and 'land granted under such a title or deed' (Lalas 1967-73:III-A, 2318-2319). A *paṭo* designated lands and villages, and the produce thereof, that a ruler granted to a Rajput in return for obligations of military service. References to these grants appear in local texts with relation to the rule of Rav Gango Vaghavat of Jodhpur (1515-1532), and then increase markedly for his son, Rav Malde Gangavat (1532-1562).[10] *Paṭos* are also mentioned in material pertaining to the late 15th century. However, these references are relatively few in number and their contexts difficult to interpret. In addition, because the texts in which they appear date from the 17th century, these references are possibly anachronistic (Bhati 1968-74:II, 43; Sakariya 1960-67:II, 192; III:24, 129). In general, evidence points to the early 16th century as the period when *paṭo* grants tied specifically to military service became widely current. And while in the later 17th century. such grants held specific valuations (*rekh*) and supply quotas of horses and warriors based on these valuations, the original *paṭos* appear to have been simple grants of land and its produce for maintenance in return for a generalized obligation of military service. These original grants were also movable grants of land, in the sense that they were transferable from one area to another at the whim or design of the ruler.

Local texts do not speak directly about the relation between maintenance needs for horses and grants of land to Rajputs. Rather, they deal with questions of authority at the center and fulfillment of service obligations. It is clear from the texts that once prebendal domain was established, it quickly became a tool for the creation of a much more expansive form of organization than previously known. Examples of *paṭo* grants during the time of Rav Gango indicate that such grants were used both to enforce obligations of service to the ruler and to recruit new Rajputs into military service. In one situation, the Rav's son, Kunvar Malde, took villages from one Uhar Rathor in his father's service and gave them to another because the Uhar had failed to provide expected services and pay court to the Rav at the time of the Dassehra festival at Jodhpur. The Uhar who failed to perform services was eventually forced to leave his land (Sakariya 1960-67:III, 85, 87). In another situation, Rav Gango openly recruited an important Rajput warrior who was in the service of his brother, Rav Viramde of Sojhat, and brought him to Jodhpur with the offer of a large grant of villages. Recruitment of this warrior was an important factor in Rav Gango's eventual success in hostilities against his brother (*ibid.*: III, 83).

Following Rav Gango, Rav Malde used *paṭos* extensively to recruit warriors, reward peformance in battle and strengthen his authority at Jodhpur. In many cases, lands the Rav granted to his Rajputs were lands these Rajputs had previously occupied under patrimonial tenure. He merely confirmed them in their holdings. But he also granted new lands and recruited Rajputs from Rathor and other clans who had been outside his service before that time (Bhati 1968-74:I, 43-49, 60; II, 61-63). In addition, he used his authority to station his Rajputs at outposts away from lands they held in grant and placed them with other Rajputs of different clans and brotherhoods. These actions facilitated the breakup of the close association Rajputs held with particular family or lineage territories in Marvar and focused attention on initiatives from the center.[11] During Rav Malde's rule, Marvar emerged as a true state with a defined and institutionalized locus of authority in the person of the ruler, who controlled the issuing of sanctions and the enforcement of regulations.[12]

The new control exercised from the center at Jodhur raised the level of Rajput involvement in the affairs of the kingdom as a whole and greatly increased the scale of force. It is estimated that on the eve of the battle of Samel in January 1544, when Rav Malde met his first major defeat at the hands of Sher Shar Sur, the size of his army was 80,000 warriors (Bhargava 1966:29; Bhati 1961:42; Ohja 1927-41:IV-A, 302*n*2; Reu 1938:I, 218; Shyamaldas 1886:II, 810, Svami 1956: 12). Personal retinues of warriors recruited and maintained as part of a ruler's household would never have allowed this scale. And while this number, like all numbers derived from local texts of the period, is undoubtedly an exaggeration, it dwarfs anything previously mentioned in such texts.

This evolution can be traced through changes in the meaning of terms used to designate categories of Rajput warriors. For example, before the 16th century, the term *chīṅdhaṛ* was employed to denote warriors attached to households of the rulers of little kingdoms. Derived from *chīṅdh* ('a small flag or bunting, a banner, a pennant'), its earlier meaning was 'chosen warrior; one who was capable of holding up or placing his personal standard [in battle]' (Lalas 1967-73:II-A, 920). A story from the *Khyāt* of Nainsi about Rathor Raval Maloji, a 14th-century ruler of Kher in western Marvar, speaks of "500 men, *chīṅdhaṛs*, wearing weapons" who were seated in his *darbār* as his personal warriors (Sakariya 1960-67:I, 249). Into the early 16th century, the term still held this meaning of household warrior. Rav Gango of Jodhpur had 4,000 of his *chīṅdhaṛs* stationed at his outpost near Sojhat to protect his borders (*ibid.*: III, 84).

A century later, this term had acquired new meanings indicating that *chīṅdhaṛs* now occupied an inferior rank among Rajput warriors. The 17th-century Bikaner chronicle, *Dalpat vilās*, for example, speaks of *chīṅdhaṛs* as "inferior or subordinate soldiers" (Sarasvat 1960:30, 53, 63-64). And elsewhere, the *Jodhpur Hukūmat rī Bahī* mentions *chīṅdhaṛs* as a general category of inferior soldier along with *bārgīr rajpūts* ('soldiers hired for wage')[13] and *tobchīs* ('gunners') in its detail of the armies of Maharaja Jasvantsingh Gajsinghot of Jodhpur (1638-1678) (Chandra et al. 1976:19, 69-70). This inferior ranking and position is consistent with the gloss of the term *chīṅdhaṛiyo* by the editor of *Dalpat Vilās*, Ravat Sarasvat: "inferior Rajput soldiers (those Rajputs who, only after taking grain, clothing and opium, perform military service and fight when the time comes)" (1960: *Śabdakoś*, p. 5).[14] During this same period, other terms become significant. The two most prominent were *ṭhākur* and *chākar*. *Ṭhākur* came to designate Rajput warriors who held lands in *paṭo* directly from the ruler of the kingdom and served as his leading warriors. *Chākar* was a more general term meaning 'military servant', and designated a Rajput who held lands in grant, but from either a ruler or a *ṭhākur*.

By the early to mid-16th century, then, a series of fundamental changes had occurred in the structure of the Rathor kingdom of Marvar which marked its emergence as a state. The impetus for these changes lay in the greater availability and use of horses, a crucial military supply. The need to feed and maintain these horses initiated the development of prebendal tenure, or land granted to Rajputs in return for military service. The ability of the local rulers to regulate access to land quickly became a primary tool for the control of men, arms and loyalties.

The Conduct of Warfare

Rav Malde's armies achieved an impressive series of conquests over the first 11 years of his rule, from 1532 to 1543. These victories were based on the Rav's ability to mass forces and to exploit the mobility that adequate supplies of horses allowed. In other respects, however, the conduct of warfare remained unaltered from earlier periods. Rathor military technology consisted, for the most part, in weapons and equipment drawn from the 14th and 15th centuries. In addition, the ideology of combat remained an archaic form rooted in concepts of duty to one's master, individual honor, and a view of the Rajput himself as a "shame-fortress" (Bhati 1968-74:II, 45; Sakariya 1960-67:II, 269-273; III, 127).[15]

Basic military equipment for Rajputs of Marvar consisted of the following:

1. Swords known as *tarvār* and *khaṇḍo*. The *tarvār* was a sabre, a cutting weapon with a one-edged blade that was curved and pointed at the end. The *khaṇḍo* was a double-edged weapon with a heavy, straight blade that gradually tapered to a point (Bhati 1968-74:I, 90, 122; Pant 1970:Pls. IX, XVI, XL; Sakariya 1960-67:III, 11, 83, 85, 113; Verma 1973:83-84).
2. Bows (*kabāṇ*) with bow cases (*kūrbāṇ*), quivers (*tarkas*) and arrows (*tīr*) (Bhati 1967-74:I, 16, 120, 122; Sakariya 1960-67:II, 336; III, 60, 65-66, 72, 120, 130, 203, 260-262; Verma 1973:92-94). The specific type of bow in use during the 15th century and early 16th century is unknown. Simon Digby notes that the Rajput bows and bowstrings in use during the Sultanate period were made of cane fibre, and that the archer's thumb ring may not have been known or in use at that time (1971:15-16). Specific mention of the thumb ring has not been found in local texts under review for the 16th century.
3. Spears called *bhālo* and *barchhī*. The *bhālo* was a long spear like a lance with a narrow, arrowhead-shaped point. The *barchhī* was a short spear with a broad-bladed point. Shafts for both were made of bamboo (Bhati 1968-74:I, 29, 80; Sakariya 1960-67:II, 339; III, 1-2, 90, 96, 111, 113, 119, 125, 138, 196-197, 261, 263; Verma 1973:88-89).

4. Round shields of hide referred to as *ḍhāl*. These were the same for both horsemen and footmen (Bhati 1968-74:I, 90; Sakariya 1960-67:III, 11, 40, 127; Verma 1973:85-86).
5. A variety of daggers. The *kaṭārī* and the *jandhār* were long-bladed daggers with broad hilts that tapered sharply to a point. Their hilts were embellished with handles consisting of two flat projections that extended up from either side of the blade and were joined in the middle with a crossbar which acted as a grip. When held, these daggers extended straight out from the fist. The *chhurī* was a small dagger styled like a knife. The blade could be straight or curved (Bhati 1968-74:I, 30, Sakariya 1960-67:II, 335, 341; III, 96, 101, 198, 292; Verma 1973:86-87).
6. Two types of armor, both made of cloth. The *jīṇsāl* or *jīṇsāliyo* (derived from *jīṇ*, 'a type of thick cotton cloth') was a quilted armor made in the form of long coats of thick cotton padding covered with coarse cloth. The *gātī* was a length of heavy cotton cloth wrapped over the shoulders and under the arms, then pulled around the back and tied in front of the chest (Bhati 1968-74:I, 122; Lalas 1962:I, 717; Platts 1968:891; Sakariya 1960-67:III, 47, 269). From the texts, it is unclear what type of garment Rajputs wore underneath their cloth armor. Heavy, raw silk cloth was used in Central Asia. This cloth was remarkable in that arrowheads generally would not pierce it, but carried the fabric into the wound, permitting easier extraction of the arrowhead from a wound and lessening infection (Hurley 1975:26). But it is not known if this practice was current among Rajputs.
7. Helmets called *ṭop*. The helmets of this period were of several types. The most common were dome-shaped head covers with a pinnacle or knob on the top. Side plates may also have extended down over the ears in addition to a front piece down over the nose (Sakariya 1960-67:II, 296; Verma 1973:96-97).
8. Equipment for horses included the bridle, a saddle of cloth without a tree, and the stirrup (which had been known in India since the 12th century, if not earlier). Horseshoes may also have been in use, but local texts make no specific mention of them (Bhati 1968-74:I, 9, 31, 34; Digby 1971:12-14; Lalas 1962:I, 406; Sakariya 1960-67:II, 331; III, 109, 129, 161, 194, 255, 258, 263; White 1968:14-27).

The only new weapons that came into use in Marvar during the first half of the 16th century were matchlocks. Mention of these guns occurs in a description of the battle of Merto (1554) between Rav Malde of Jodhpur and Rathor Rav Jaimal Viramdevot of Merto. The *Khyāt* of Nainsi records that in Rav Malde's camp prior to this battle, "sharp edges were being applied to swords. [And] several Rajputs were [test] firing guns" (Sakariya 1960-67:III, 117; translation by Richard Saran). Later, in 1562, Rathor Devidas Jaitavat, Rav Malde's commander of the fort of Merto, had a personal gun of the Rav's with him when Merto came under siege from the Mughals (Bhati 1961:55; 1968-74:II, 64). Matchlockmen were also present at the fort with Devidas. But they appear to have been inexpert and uncoordinated in their actions. The *Akbar-Nāmā* records in a description of the battle at Merto that the Rajputs in the fort "made the battlement their shields and discharged confusedly bricks, stones, arrows and bullets, and also boiling pitch" (Beveridge 1972:II, 248). Matchlocks used in India at that time were rather crude, heavy weapons consisting of a long barrel fitted on a one-piece wooden rest that was almost cylindrical near the butt. In general, these guns were simply smaller versions of cannon, quite unwieldy and cumbersome to use (Verma 1973:111-112). Into the mid-17th century, guns continued to play only a minor role in Rajput warfare.

Cannon are not mentioned in local texts from Marvar for periods prior to the 17th century. This absence is significant, for the Sisodiyos of Mevar had small cannon at Chitor and used them against the Mughals in 1568 (Bussagli 1969:P1. XXII; Srivastava 1972:106-108). None of the forts constructed by Rav Malde during his rule were supplied with cannon, nor were they built as prime defensive sites capable of withstanding siege. In the case of Merto, for example, Rav Malde built his fort of Malgarh on the open plain, in direct opposition to the counsel of the Rathor warrior he placed in command (Bhati 1961:53). Sites the Rav selected for his forts and their design appear to have been based less on military considerations than on the Rav's desire to express his power, prestige and wealth. Their main features were tall, massive walls and towers. And while defense was a consideration, it was only one among others (Toy 1957:1). Rajputs stationed at these forts used them primarily as headquarters from which to emerge and fight on the open plains (Beveridge 1972:II, 248-249; Bhati 1968-74:I, 68).

The warriors of Marvar embodied an ideology of combat that emphasized honor and death in battle in fulfillment of duty to one's master. Honor was acquired by acts of bravery, such as touching the body of an opposing warrior of renown with a sword or lance without doing him harm, and by death (Bhati 1961:47; 1968-74:II, 53). To die in battle meant to fulfill one's appointed duty (Ziegler 1973:67-68). During conflicts, Rajputs often appeared armed with swords, shields, and spears or bows and arrows, and dressed in saffron robes, with turmeric paste applied to their hands and foreheads – symbolic of dedication to death in battle (Bernier 1979:52*n*1; Bhati 1968-74:I, 35; II, 52; Crooke 1920:I, 226*n*5; Sarasvat 1960:68, 106, *Śabdakoś*, p. 5). Prior to the battle of Reyan village (near Merto) *ca.* 1536, for example, a Mertiyo Rathor in the service of Rav Malde of Jodhpur donned saffron robes and led 500 warriors outside the gates of the village. There they spread cloths on the ground and sat down to await the arrival of their opponent, resolved to die defending the village and their lands (Bhati 1968-74:II, 53).

The classic battle, however, was contest between champions or chosen warriors, where fighting itself was hedged about with great formality and deference. The following example is illustrative:

> Then Kumbho got down [from his horse] . . . , went into the camp and bowed to Hemo. Hemo said, "Very fine, Kumbho!" Then Hemo said, "Kumbho! You inflict a wound." Kumbho said, "Hemoji! You inflict a wound." Hemo said, "Kumbho! You are a boy. I have had *nīm* leaves bandaged on many [a wound]." Then Kumbho was saying, "Hemoji! You inflict a wound." Hemo said, "Kumbho! Your body has yet felt no sword; you are a boy. You inflict a wound. I am an elder; why should I inflict the [first] wound?" Kumbho said, "Hemoji! In years you are elder, but in rank I am senior. You have taken my grain in the hem of your clothes; you are my military servant, [and] therefore, I am senior; you inflict [the first] wound." Then Hemo said, "What should I do? You allow me no choice." Then Hemo wounded Kumbho. The blow [of his sword] severed Kumbho's helmet, split [his] skull [as though smashing] a clay

> bowl, sliced between his eyebrows and lodged [itself] at the tip of [his] ear. Kumbho inflicted a wound; [he] cut Hemo in two parts. Hemo fell down. Then Kumbho drew his dagger and stabbed [it] into Hemo's chest. (Sakariya 1960-67:II, 296; translation by Richard Saran)

Techniques of combat also did not change during the 16th and early 17th centuries. Despite the greater availability of horses and the deployment of warriors at outposts, an arena that might have provided opportunity for the training and disciplining of horse-mounted warriors, nothing resembling cavalry warfare developed among the Rajputs of Marvar. This situation may have been due, in part, to the fact that horses of the quality necessary for use in battle were still insufficiently available. More important, however, is the fact that in Marvar during this period, horses were used for riding, not for fighting. Rajputs fought on foot.[16]

Actual descriptions of Rajputs in battle come from a number of sources. The *Khyāt* of Nainsi records an account of the battle of Sevaki village (near Jodhpur) which took place in December 1529. This battle was fought between Rav Gango of Jodhpur and his father's brother, Rathor Sekho Sujavat, over control of land in Marvar. The *Khyāt* notes that Sekho Sujavat enlisted the support of the Khanzada Khan ruler of Nagaur, who appeared before Sevaki with 80 elephants armored with iron-plate and arranged on either flank of his men. Sekho himself and Rav Gango each came with their own Rajputs. Both sides cleared the field of battle before the engagement, removing brush and other obstacles that might impede the movement of men. When the fighting began, Rav Gango's Rajputs concentrated their attack on the Khan's elephants, loosing a shower of arrows and scattering the elephants. The Khan's warriors then fled the field, leaving Rav Gango and Sekho Sujavat to face each other. When the two armies joined, Sekho "dismounted [from his horse] along with seven hundred men" and died fighting on foot alongside his son (Sakariya 1960-67:III, 90-92).

The *Muntakhabu-T-Tawārīkh* of Al-Badaoni contains an important account of the battle of Samel (January 1544) between Rav Malde Gangavat of Jodhpur and Sher Shah Sur. This account also mentions fighting on foot. In addition, it describes a more extreme form of combat that Rajputs adopted in defense of their homelands, namely binding themselves together with sashes and joining hands during battle to form a defensive wall of men:

> After striving to the utmost of their powers, when they had abandoned all hope of life, at the very moment when the army of Shīr Shāh came in sight, as a result of their own stupidity, by the good luck of Shīr Shāh or by the superior fortune of Islam, the *infidels in a body dismounted from their horses*, and renewing their vows and singleness of purpose and mutual assistance, *binding their sashes together and joining hand to hand*, attacked the army of the Afghans with their short spears, which they call *Barchha*, and with their swords . . . [Shīr Shāh then] ordered the elephant troops to advance and trample them down. In the rear of the elephants, the artillery and archers gave them a taste of the bowstring . . . (Ranking 1973:I, 368-369; emphasis mine)

Accounts concerning other areas of Rajasthan support these two descriptions of 16th-century Rajput combat in Marvar. The Jesuit priest, Monserrate, who visited Akbar's court between 1580 and 1582, provides a more generalized view of Rajput combat in his *Commentary*. He also notes the type of horses the Rajputs used, and his comments substantiate earlier remarks about Rajput horses and their use in battle:

> The methods of warfare employed by the Persians, Mongols, Chacattaei [Chaghtā'ī], Osbechii [Uzbegs], and the Turquimanni [Turkomans] differ very greatly from those of the Gedrosii [people of Gujarāt and part of Rajpūtānā], or again from those of the Balochii [Baluchīs], or from those of the Indians. For *the cavalry of the Gedrosii, who are called Rasputi* [Rājpūts], . . . *all ride on little ponies hardly as big as donkeys. Arriving in this manner in the place of battle, they dismount and await the attack of the enemy armed with short spears* (or rather javelins) *and light shields:* The Musalmans say that these Rasputi . . . know how to die, but not how to fight. (Holland 1922:83-84; emphasis mine)

Two early 17th-century chronicles of Sindh, the *Beg-Lār-Nāmā* and the *Ta'rikh-i Sind*, corroborate Monserrate's observations. In a description of battle between Sodho Rajputs of Umarkot and

Rathors of Nilma (located midway between Umarkot and Jaisalmer), for example, the *Beg-Lār-Nāmā* notes that "it was an old established custom amongst [opposing Rajput forces] that both parties should alight from their horses and engage on foot" (Elliot and Dowson 1867-77:292-293). The text records this custom among Rajputs as widely separated as the Jarecos of Gujarat and the Sisodiyos of Mevar (*ibid.*, appendix, p. 535). The *Akbar-Nāmā* makes the same observation about Jhalo Rajputs of Gujarat (Beveridge 1972:III, 700, 905). In addition, the *Ta'rikh-i Sind* records that Rajputs formed shield walls in battle by locking their shields together after they had dismounted from their horses and binding themselves together with their mantles (Siddiqi 1972:27, 45, 72). These shield walls could offer a very effective deterrent both to missile attacks and to the charge of horsemen.[17]

Although this style of combat continued into the late 16th and 17th centuries, it did change in some respects with the incorpora tion of Marvar and other areas of Rajasthan within the Mughal empire. Under Mughal tutelage, Rajputs adopted a broader and more sophisticated use of the cannon and the matchlock. However, even with the Mughal example of horse-mounted warfare, cavalry tactics and the intimate use of the horse in battle appear to have been limited. Two short excerpts from eyewitness accounts of Rathor actions in Marvar in the mid-17th century are illustrative.

First, a description of joint Marvar Rathor and Jaisalmer Bhati actions against Mughal Khan Baloch in 1637 near Phalodhi in northern Marvar;

> [After] 4 *gharīs* [approximately one and a half hours] of the night had passed, [the Rathor contingents] arrived within 1 *kos* of [the Baloch] camp. Then they refreshed [themselves]. The [men of the] contingents went to relieve themselves and ate opium. There was quilted armor; they did not put [it] on. They put on *gātīs* . . . The Ravalji [of Jaisalmer] reached there at this time, the time of the gong, [when] shadows departed and the sun was up. The *shahnāīs* of the Baloch were playing. From there they drew their swords and began. The swords were flashing from the rays of the sun . . . The Raval formed [his army into] 3 wings. Positioning the contingent of the Rajaji [of Jodhpur] on the right side, in the middle of his own contingent, and on the left side the contingent of Rav [Manohardas], [he]

> had [them] ride out. The Baloch also charged straight toward them; 3 volleys of arrows were fired . . . 120 men took up the reins and killed Mughal Khan and 4 [of his] chiefs; [they] carried the field. The Baloch fled. The contingents rode after them and within 1/2 *kos* struck down 50-60 men of the Baloch (Bhati 1968-74:I, 122-123).

Second, an account of Rathor actions against Bhati Rajputs in 1649 at the fort of Pokaran in northern Marvar:

> . . . the contingent of [Maharaja Jasvantsingh] attacked the fort of Pokaran. Cannon were fired not only from this side, but also from that side. For 1 *pohar* [approximately three hours], Rathors Gopaldasji, Vithaldasji and Naharkhanji, these *ṭhākurs* launched the attack and stood their ground. Afterwards, these *ṭhākurs* went to [their] camps and Munhato Nainsi took [over command of] the contingent of Naharkhan and remained beside the cannon . . . When the 4th *ghaṛī* of the day had passed, then [other] *ṭhākurs* attacked the town [of Pokaran]. Having taken the town under their authority, they rode before the fort and had entrenchments constructed. There were these *ṭhākurs* and 200 horsemen, so they tethered their horses in the stalls and bazaar of Pokaran. And [the *ṭhākurs*] had [the contingent] take up a position in the [Jain] temple, while [other] contingents [and those] inside the fort maintained a steady fire of bullets and arrows. (*ibid.*:II, 302)

These accounts of Rajputs in battle clearly show that, despite the greater availability of horses and the mobility they accorded, and despite the structural and organizational changes brought about in Marvar by increased reliance on this important military supply, the concepts, strategies and weapons of warfare remained essentially those of the 14th and 15th centuries.

Summary

The first half of the 16th century was an important period of transition for the Rathor kingdom of Marvar. During this time, a strong central authority emerged at Jodhpur based on the exercise of prebendal domain. The ability of the Jodhpur rulers to regulate other Rajputs' access to land provided them with a powerful mechanism for reordering the structure of the state. This development of centralized rule and prebendal domain followed in large part from the availability and use of greater numbers of horses. In turn, horses quickly became a pivotal military supply that allowed increased mobility. The rulers of Jodhpur used this mobility to station military servants at strategic outposts along the borders of the kingdom and then to mass forces in campaigns of conquest. Broadening of parochial loyalties and closer identification with the center were outgrowths of the increased political involvement among Rathor and other Rajput military servants in the affairs of the kingdom as a whole. However, despite the profound nature of these changes, local rulers of Marvar did not incorporate any new technology or new styles of combat. Horse-mounted cavalry warfare did not develop, and combat remained tied to the traditions and values of earlier centuries.

Placed in broader perspective, these same processes can be seen in varying degrees during this period in all the kingdoms that comprised the area that is now Rajasthan. Amber, Mevar, Bikaner, Jaisalmer and others displayed increasing centralization and exercise of prebendal domain, as well as greater use of horses. The process of evolution was differential, however, beginning first in Mevar in the mid-15th century because of Mevar's close proximity to Malva and Gujarat and its involvement in the affairs of these areas. Change spread from there with the movement and supply of horses, and culminated with Marvar's dramatic rise in the mid-16th century.

In all areas, the processes of structural change and associated reorientation of values and ideology were incomplete. Local loyalties and identifications still remained strongly entrenched, and the values and assumptions associated with patrimonial domain continued within Rajput brotherhoods in spite of the assertion of hierarchy and the issuing of sanctions from the center. But by the time of Akbar's accession to the Mughal throne in 1556, and the ushering in of a different era of political involvement in North India, most of the new patterns of authority and control had become established norms in Rajasthan and did much to shape the Rajput response to and eventual incorporation into the Mughal empire.

ENDNOTES

Research for this paper was done, in part, under grants from the Social Science Research Council (1981-82) and the American Philosophical Society (1981). I would like to express my appreciation to Simon Digby and Richard Saran for their helpful comments about this paper, and to Richard Saran for his review of several of my translations from Marvari texts. My primary source for definitions of Marvari terms has been Sitaram Lalas's *Rājasthānī Sabdakoś*.

1. The period being referred to is roughly that between the end of the Tughluq dynasty (1388) and the accession of the Mughal emperor Akbar to the throne (1556).
2. Throughout this paper, I have used the Rajasthani *o* ending for personal and place names: hence, 'Rano' instead of Rana, 'Kumbho' instead of Kumbha, and 'Merto' instead of Merta, etc. The *o* ending is consistent with the spelling and pronunciation of names in Middle Marvari, the language of the primary sources upon which this paper is based, whereas the *ā* ending is a later interpolation derived from the influence of Hindi. I felt it important to be consistent with indigenous materials rather than capitulate to a norm imposed from outside.
3. Munhato Nainsi Jaimmalot was an Osval Jain *mutsaddi* (clerk) in the service of Jodhpur under Maharajas Gajsingh Surajsinghot (1619-1638) and Jasvantsingh Gajsinghot (1638-1678). During Maharaja Jasvantsing's reign, he was appointed Chief Revenue Minister, and it was during his tenure as Revenue Minister between 1658 and 1666 that two of the major chronicles of Marvar, *Nainsī rī Khyāt* and *Mārvāṛ rā Parganāṅ rī Vigat* were compiled under his direction. The *Khyāt* is essentially a collection of tales or stories and genealogies dealing with the history of all the major Rajput clans of Rajasthan. The *Vigat* is a detailed survey of the seven *parganos* granted to Maharaja Jasvantsingh by Shah Jahan within two years of his accession to the Jodhpur throne in 1638. It is written in the form of a clan history of the Rathors of Marvar, with lists of rulers and their descendants and descriptive stories about important events relating to each of the seven different *parganos*. The *Vigat* also contains an exhaustive listing of all villages belonging to each *pargano* along with details of revenue associated with each village. For more information about these texts, see Ziegler 1976a and 1976b:219-235, 245-248.
4. The Uhars are a subdivision of the Rathor clan of Marvar. In local terminology, Uhar is a *khāṅp* (twig) of the Kanaujiyo *sākh* (branch) of the Rathor *kul* (clan) of Marvar.
5. For the original use of the term "little kingdom," see Cohn 1962:312-320.
6. For a more detailed discussion of early Rajput political organization, see Ziegler 1973:36-66.
7. For a more complete discussion of the obligations inherent in these systems of patronage, see Ziegler 1973:85-106; 1978:224-225. H.M. Fried has noted in his essay on the evolution of the state that one of the characteristics of a 'ranked society' is a supra-familial network of redistribution in which a leader or big man assumes the role of one who collects goods from and redistributes them to his clients or followers (1960:718)

8. Richard Sâran presents an excellent discussion of the *vasī* and its place in Rajput society. He offers two possible derivations for the term: 1) from the Sanskrit root *vas-* ('to dwell, to settle'), and 2) from the Sanskrit root *vaś-* ('to declare for, desire, wish, aver'). From *vaś* comes the word *vaśani* ('performing the will of another, subject, vassal of') (1978:56, 78*n*3).
9. There are a number of interesting parallels to these developments in Marvar in other areas of the world. For example, when horse-mounted warfare with heavy cavalry developed in the Carolingian empire under Charles Martel, it led directly to the dispersement of land holdings among lords subordinate to the king. A primary reason for decentralization was the need to feed and maintain large numbers of horses. In contrast to Marvar, these developments in France coincided with the introduction of the stirrup, the key to heavy cavalry warfare, and the appearance in northern Gaul of a new, heavy plow capable of handling deep, wet soils. This plow allowed the production of food necessary to feed an unprecedented number of cavalry mounts (Fox 1971:43-44).
10. In a prior article (1978:227), I stated that *paṭo* grants did not gain wide usage in Marvar until the late 16th century. Based on further research, this judgement now appears premature.
11. An interesting parallel with Rav Malde's activities emerges in the literature on the Zulu kingdom in South Africa. Max Gluckman writes that when Shaka, the Zulu chief, set his nation on a war footing, he ordered all young men to serve in military barracks for one year according to age grades. The regiments that comprised these barracks were the king's alone, and Shaka's dispersement of young men to distant parts of the country did much to break up the Zulu clans and their close association with particular territories. These actions focused attention on the center and the king, and the talk of the country became the talk of the king's exploits and campaigns (1950:25-55).
12. For a useful definition and discussion of the state, see Service 1975:14-15, 71-102. See also Ziegler 1978:223-231 for further remarks about this issue with regard to Marvar and Rajasthan.
13. *Bārgīr* is a Mughal term used in Marvar to designate Rajputs who had no horses of their own and who were hired and equipped for specific campaigns by the state. Abdul Aziz defines *bārgīr* as "a soldier who rode a horse furnished by someone else" (1972:183; see also Platts 1968:120).
14. Into the 19th century, the term *chīṅdhaṛ* continued to be applied to Rajputs who were members of households of prominent men. It is probable that the Rajputs of whom Ravat Sarasvat writes were household retainers dependent upon their patrons for food, clothing and military supplies, and responsible for the more menial tasks of supply and transport in Rajput armies. During the 18th and 19th centuries in Marvar, *chīṅdhaṛ* designated members of older Rajput clans, such as the Sankhlo Chauhans, the Indo Parihars, and the Dhandhal and Pethar Rathors, who were attached to local courts and performed guard duties in the women's quarters. Their jurisdiction covered the last line of male guards immediately preceding the area for which women attendants were responsible. Into the 20th century, these Rajputs held villages from local rulers called *chīṅdhaṛāṅ rā gāṅv* ('villages of the *chīṅdhaṛs*'). Thanks go to Shri Kailash Danji Ujval of Jodhpur for the above information.

15. Among Rajputs, shame was a tangible quality that a man kept and stored. He could lose it with improper actions, and once it was lost, he could not regain it. Julian Pitt-Rivers has written that as a basis for repute, honor and shame are synonymous. To be without shame is also to be without honor, or dishonorable (1974:41-43).
16. Leslie White has written the following about the development of horse-mounted warfare in Europe:

> . . . quite apart from the cost of arms and horses, the new mode of fighting necessarily destroyed the old Germanic idea that every freeman was a soldier. Mounted shock combat was not a business for part-time warriors; one had to be a skilled professional, the product of long technical training, and in excellent physical health (1968:31).

These same tenets apply to the development of cavalry warfare among the Rajputs. While the necessary organization began to emerge under Rav Malde in Marvar, there is no evidence of trainers or of adequate supplies of good war horses and equipment. In addition, development of cavalry warfare would have entailed overcoming the individualistic code of the Rajput warrior.
17. For some studies of comparative interest, see Glover 1952:1-18; Howarth 1982:166-184; White 1968:37.

REFERENCES CITED

Aziz, Abdul
1972 *The Mansabdārī System of the Mughal Army*. Delhi: Idarah-i-Abadiyat-i-Delli.

Banerjee, A.C.
1962 *Medieval Rajput Policy*. Calcutta: Firma K.L. Mukhopadhyay.

Bernier, Francois
1979 *Travels in the Mogul Empire, A.D. 1656-1668*. Archibald Constable, transl. Reprinted. New Delhi: S. Chand & Company, Ltd.

Beveridge, H., transl.
1972 *The Akbar Nāmā of Abu-l-Fazl*. 3 vols. Reprint ed. Delhi: Rare Books.

Bhargava, V.S.
1966 *Marwar and the Mughal Emperors*. Delhi: Munshiram Manoharlal.

Bhati, Narain Singh, ed.
1961 "*Aitihāsik Bātāṅ*." *Paramparā* 11:17-109. Chaupasni: Rajasthani Shodh Sansthan.
1968-74 Nainsi. *Mārvār rā Parganāṅ rī Vigat*. 3 vols. Jodhpur: Rajasthan Prachyavidya Pratishthan.

Bussagli, Mario
1969 *Indian Miniatures*. London, New York, Sidney & Toronto: Paul Hamlyn.

Chandra, Satish, et al., eds
1976 *Marwar under Jaswant Singh (1658-1678): Jodhpur Hukumat ri Bahi*. Meerut: Meenakshi Prakashan.

Cohn, Bernard S.
1962 "Political Systems in Eighteenth Century India: The Benares Region." *Journal of the American Oriental Society* 82(3):312-320.

Crooke, William, ed.
1920 James Tod. *Annals and Antiquities of Rajasthan*. 3 vols. London: Oxford University Press.

Digby, Simon
1971 *War-Horse and Elephant in the Delhi Sultanate: A Study in Military Supplies*. Oxford: Oxford University Press.

Elliot, H.M. and J. Dowson, eds.
1867-77 *Beg-Lār-Nāmā*. In *The History of India as Told by Its Own Historians*, I:289-299. Reprint ed. Allahabad: Kitab Mahal Pvt., Ltd.

Fox, Edward W.
1971 *History in Geographic Perspective: The Other France*. New York: W.W. Norton & Co., Inc.

Fried, H.M.
1960 "On the Evolution of Social Stratification and the State." In *Culture in History: Essays in Honor of Paul Radin*. S. Diamond, ed. pp. 713-731. New York: Columbia University Press.

Glover, Richard
1952 "English Warfare in 1066." *English Historical Review* 68(262):1-18.

Gluckman, Max
1950 "The Kingdom of the Zulu in South Africa." In *African Political Systems*. M. Fortes and E.E. Evans-Pritchard, eds. pp. 25-55. New York & London: Oxford University Press.

Holland, J.S., transl.
1922 *The Commentary of Father Monserrate, S.J., on his Journey to the Court of Akbar*. Oxford: Oxford University Press.

Howarth, David
1982 *1066, The Year of the Conquest*. Reprint ed. Penguin Books.

Hurley, V.
1975 *Arrows against Steel: The History of the Bow*. New York: Mason/Charter.

Lalas, Sitaram
Rājasthānī Sabdakos.
1962 Vol. 1. Jodhpur: Rajasthani Shodh Sansthan.
1967-73 Vols. 2-3, Vol. 4-A. Jodhpur: Upasamati Rajasthani Sabdakos.
1976-78 Vols. 4-B, 4-C. Jodhpur: Chaupasni Shiksha Samiti.

Murardan, Kaviraj
n.d. *Rāṭhoroṇ kī Khyāt Purāṇī Kavirājjī Murārdānjī ke Yahāṇ se Likhī Gaī*. MS n. 15672, no. 2. Jodhpur: Rajasthan Prachyavidya Pratishthan.

Ojha, G.H.
1927-41 *Rājpūtāne kā Itihās*. 5 vols. in 9 parts. Ajmer: Vedic Yantralaya.

Pant, G.N.
1970 *Studies in Indian Weapons and Warfare*. New Delhi: Army Educational Stores.

Pitt-Rivers, Julian
1974 "Honour and Social Status." In *Honour and Shame: The Values of Mediterranean Society*. J.G. Peristiany, ed. pp. 19-77. Midway reprint ed. Chicago and London: University of Chicago Press.

Platts, John T.
1968 *A Dictionary of Urdū, Classical Hindī, and English*. 5th ed. (1930 reprint). London: Oxford University Press.

Ranking, G.S.A., ed. & transl.
1973 Al-Badaoni. *Muntakhabu-T-Tawārīkh*. Reprint ed. Delhi: Īdarah-i-Adabiyat-i-Delli.

Reu, B.N.
1938 *Mārvāṛ ka Itihās*. 2 vols. Jodhpur: Archaeological Department.

Sakariya, Badri Prasad, ed.
1960-67 Nainsi. *Naiṇsī rī Khyāt*. 4 vols. Jodhpur: Rajasthan Prachyavidya Pratishthan.

Saran, Richard
1978 "Conquest and Colonization: Rajputs and Vasis in Middle Period Marvar." Ph.D. dissertation, Department of History, University of Michigan.

Sarasvat, Ravat, ed.
1960 *Dalpat Vilās*. Bikaner: Sadul Rajasthani Research Institute.

Service, Elman R.
1975 *Origins of the State and Civilization: The Process of Cultural Evolution*. New York: W.W. Norton & Co., Inc.

Sharma, G.D.
1977 *Rajput Polity*. New Delhi: Manohar Book Service.

Shyamaldas, Kaviraja
1886 *Vīr Vinod*. 2 vols. Udaipur: Rajyantralaya.

Siddiqi, Mahmudul Hasan, transl.
1972 *History of the Arghans and Tarkhans of Sind (1507-1593)*. An annotated translation of the relevant portions of Mir Ma'sum's *Ta'rikh-i Sind*. Pakistan: Institute of Sindology, University of Sind.

Srivastava, A.L.
1972 *Akbar the Great*. Vol. I: *Political History, 1542-1605 A.D.* Agra: Shiva Lal Agarwala & Co.

Svami, Narottamdasji
1956 *Bāṅkīdās rī Khyāt*. Jaipur: Rajasthan Puratattvanveshan Mandir.

Toy, Sidney
1957 *The Strongholds of India*. Melbourne, London and Toronto: William Heinemann, Ltd.

Verma, S.P.
1973 *Art and Material Culture in the Paintings of Akbar's Court*. New Delhi: Vikas Publishing House Pvt., Ltd.

White, Leslie
1968 *Medieval Technology and Social Change*. Reprint ed. London, Oxford and New York: Oxford University Press.

Wolf, Eric
1966 *Peasants*. Englewood Cliffs, N.J.: Prentice-Hall, Inc.

Ziegler, Norman P.
1973 "Action, Power and Service in Rajasthani Culture: A Social History of the Rajputs of Middle Period Rajasthan." Ph.D. dissertation, Department of History, University of Chicago.

1976a "The Seventeenth Century Chronicles of Marvar: A Study in the Evolution and Use of Oral Tradition in Western India." In *History in Africa: A Journal of Method, III*. D.P. Henige, ed. pp. 127-153.

1976b "Marvari Historical Chronicles: Sources for the Social and Cultural History of Rajasthan." *Indian Economic and Social History Review* 13 (2):219-250.

1978 "Some Notes on Rajput Loyalties during the Mughal Period." In *Kingship and Authority in South Asia*. J.F. Richards, ed. pp. 215-251. University of Wisconsin-Madison: South Asian Studies Publication Series.

HONOR AND ALLIANCE: RECONSIDERING MUGHAL-RAJPUT MARRIAGES

FRANCES H. TAFT

Some four hundred years ago, in 1585, the Mughal emperor Akbar celebrated with splendid festivities the first marriage of his young heir Prince Salim to the daughter of the raja of Amber (Jaipur). And in the following year, the Persian histories tell us, daughters of the rajas of Bikaner and Jodhpur were married to Salim no less magnificently. The rajas' descendants, however, did not mark the anniversaries, for by and large Rajputs have come to regard the marriage of Rajput daughters to the Mughals as shameful deeds that to this day reflect on their own honor.[1]

Prince Salim's Rajput marriages in 1585 and 1586 were only the most brilliant in a series of Mughal-Rajput marriage alliances begun by Akbar and continuing through the reign of Farukhsiyar. The literature concerning them is not large since, as a result of Rajput prejudices, Mughal-Rajput marriages have been virtually ignored in the *khyāts* (traditional histories) and in modern histories from Rajasthan as well. Only in recent years have historians begun to fill the gap by systematically documenting the marriages and exploring their significance.[2] New information from unpublished Jodhpur genealogical sources (Ziegler and Saran 1984), as well as from Persian sources,[3] now indicates that these marriages were more extensive than had been realized. Table 1 lists 27 documented Mughal-Rajput marriages over the period 1562-1715, and it is quite likely that additional marriages have yet to be traced.

How and why have Rajput attitudes toward Mughal marriage alliances changed so drastically between the 16th and the 20th centuries? To address this question, it is necessary to examine the origins of these marriages and their role in Mughal-Rajput relations, from both Mughal and Rajput perspectives. From the Mughal

Table 1:Mughal-Rajput Marriage Alliances

Father of Girl Married	Father's Clan	Father's Place	Date	Source
AKBAR'S REIGN (1556-1605)				
To Akbar:				
1 Bharmal Prithirajot	Kachhvaha	Amber	1562	*AN*: II, 242–244
2 Jagmal Viramdevot	Mertiya	(Merta)	*ca.* 1563	*MD*: II, 520–521
3 Isardas Viramdevot[a]	Mertiya	(Merta)	*ca.* 1569	*MD*: II, 512–513
4 Kanha Jaitsiot (b/o Raja Kalyanmal)[b]	Rathor	Bikaner	1570	*AN*: II, 518; *DV*: 14–15
5 Bhimvaraj Jaitsiot (b/o Raja Kalyanmal)[b]	Rathor	Bikaner	1570	*DV*: 14–15
6 Harraj Maldevot	Bhati	Jaisalmer	1570	*AN*: II, 518–519
7 Askaran Prithirajot	Ahar Gehlot	Dungarpur	1577	*AN*: III, 278; 295
8 Maldev Gangavat[c]	Rathor	Jodhpur	?	*MD*: II, 145–150; *BK*: 20
9 Chandrasen Maldevot[c]	Rathor	(Jodhpur)	?	*MD*: II, 164, *BK* 22
10 ?[d]	Tanvar	(Gwalior)	?	*ZK*: I, 104
11 ?[d]	Baghela	?	?	*ZK*: I, 104
To Jahangir (Salim):				
12 Bhagvantdas Bharmalot	Kachhvaha	Amber	1585	*AN*: III, 678
13 Raysingh Kalyanmalot	Rathor	Bikaner	1586	*AN*: III, 748–749
14 Mota Raja Udaisingh Maldevot	Rathor	Jodhpur	1586	*MJ*: 13
15 Keshavdas Jaimalot	Mertiya Rathor	(Merta)	(1585–89)	*AN*: III, 880; *TJ*: I, 19
16 Bhim Harrajot	Bhati	Jaisalmer	?	*TJ*: I, 326
To Daniyal (s/o Akbar):				
17 Raymal Maldevot[e]	Rathor	?	1595	*AN*: III, 1040

JAHANGIR'S REIGN (1605-1627)				
To Jahangir:				
18 Jagatsingh Mansinghot	Kachhvaha	Amber	1608	*TJ*: I, 144–145
19 Ramchand Madhukariyot	Bundela	(Bandhu)	1609	*TJ*: I, 160
To Shahjahan (Khurram):				
20 Sakatsingh Udaisinghot	Rathor	?	Prior to 1627	*NV*: I, 111; *RV*: f. 78
To Parvez (s/o Jahangir):				
21 Gajsingh Sursinghot[f]	Rathor	Jodhpur	1623	*NV*: I, 108; *TJ*: II, 295
To Dawar Baksh (s/o Khusrau s/o Jahangir):				
22 Mirza Raja Jaisingh Mahasinghot	Kachhvaha	Amber	1625/26	Akhbarat, 20th RY, Sarkar Collection, cited in Zaidi, Appendix C
SHAHJAHAN'S REIGN (1627-1658)				
To Sulaiman Shikoh (s/o Dara Shikoh s/o Shahjahan):				
23 Amarsingh Gajsinghot[g]	Rathor	Nagaur	1654	Qanungo 163–165
AURANGZEB'S REIGN (1627-1658)				
To Mu'azzam (Bahadur Shah):				
24 Mansingh Rupsinghot[h]	Rathor	Kishangarh	1661	*MA*: 22
To Azim-ush-Shan (s/o Bahadur Shah):				
25 Kiratsingh Jaisinghot (b/o Raja Ramsingh)	Kachhvaha	Amber	1678	*MA*: 103

To Kam Baksh (s/o Aurangzeb):				
26 Amarchand[i]	Shekhavat Kachhvaha	Manoharpur	1681	*MA*: 129
AFTER AURANGZEB				
To Farukhsiyar:				
27 Ajitsingh Jasvantsinghot	Rathor	Jodhpur	1715	Irvine 1921-22:I, 303-305

Notes

[a] Married by her brother Narhardas Isardasot.

[b] Married by her father's brother Raja Kalyanmal of Bikaner.

[c] See endnote 15.

[d] The source says only that Akbar made marriage alliances with the Kachhvahas, Rathors, Tanvars, Bhatis, and Baghelas; not is it certain that the marriages were with Akbar rather than one of his sons.

[e] Raymal Maldevot died in *ca*. 1581, and his son Kalyanmal (Kalla) was killed by Mota Raja Udaisingh in a battle at Sivana in 1589 (*NV* I, 120–121; II, 219). It is unclear by whom this girl was subsequently married.

[f] Married by her brother Raja Gajsingh of Jodhpur.

[g] Married by her mother's brother Mirza Raja Jaisingh of Amber.

[h] Married by her brother Raja Mansingh of Kishangarh; see endnote 7.

[i] Married by her brother Jagatsingh Amarchandot.

point of view, Akbar's conception of the Rajput role in his expanding empire was responsible for a majority of the marriages, and after his death their number and importance declined. On the Rajput side, a substantial number of the Rajput rajas and chiefs, capitulating to the demands and/or rewards of Mughal suzerainty, married daughters to the Mughals. However, there was always Rajput opposition, fostered by the Mevar *darbār*, to Mughal marriages. The discussion then traces the intriguing series of circumstances that ultimately resulted in general acceptance of the Mevar viewpoint. The keys to the evolution of Rajput attitudes, it will be argued, lie in the intense rivalries among the Rajput clans and kingdoms in combination with the traditional force of caste endogamy, which left those who violated it vulnerable to attack in the name of *dharma*. With Mughal decline and the consequent disappearance of the counterweight that the imperial system had provided, the predominance of the Mevar perspective became almost inevitable.

Mughal Perspectives

Babur's Timurid dynasty brought to India marriage traditions that included both Muslim cousin marriage and politically inspired marriage alliances. Political marriages soon came to play a significant role in the establishment of Mughal rule. A story has it that during his exile in Persia, Babur's son Humayun was counseled by Shah Tahmasp that he had lost India because he had neglected to strengthen his position by making marriage alliances with locally powerful men (*VV*:II, 132). Humayun seems to have heeded the advice, since after his return to Delhi in 1555 "in order to soothe the minds of the *zamīndārs* [local ruling families]" he promptly married a niece of the powerful Hasan Khan of Mewat and married her sister to his chief general Bairam Khan (*AN*:II, 76).

Humayun's heir Akbar absorbed the lesson as well. With an acute sense of the difficulties inherent in establishing the rule of a foreign dynasty over large and diverse territories, the young emperor made an early decision to use political marriage alliances as an important means of building and consolidating local support. In pursuit of this strategy, Akbar did not hesitate to ignore the Muslim canon that would have limited him to four wives. Between 1562, when he was 19, and his death in 1605, Akbar made at least

40 political marriages for himself, his three sons and his eldest grandson, with both court and *zamīndār* families.[4]

In geographical terms, the *zamīndār* families (both Muslim and Hindu) with whom Akbar made marriage alliances covered much of his empire, from Jaisalmer to Bihar and from Kashmir to the Deccan. However, these political marriages were dominated by Rajput alliances: of the known *zamīndār* marriages during Akbar's reign almost half were with Rajputs. Ultimately the emperor made marriage alliances for himself or his sons with all the major Rajput *zamīndārs* (or rajas) of Rajasthan and Central India, with the exception of Mevar and Bundi. These extensive marriage ties were at the heart of what has come to be known as Akbar's "Rajput policy." The emperor perceived that if Rajput *zamīndārs* were brought into his imperial framework on the basis of alliance rather than subjugation, not only would he be able to secure the territories they controlled without extended and costly campaigns, but the substantial military strength the Rajputs represented would be available to serve the purposes of imperial expansion and rule elsewhere in India. Furthermore, Rajput support directly linked to the emperor provided a vital counterweight to the factional interests of the Irani and Turani groups that dominated the Mughal *darbār*. It is also clear that the emperor came to desire personal ties as well as political alliances with the Rajput rajas in furtherance of his efforts to create a joint Islamic-Hindu court culture that could bridge the religious, cultural and social gulfs perennially threatening the unity of his expanding empire.

The importance Akbar placed on Rajput alliances is underlined by the early marriages he arranged for his heir Salim (Jahangir). In 1585, when Salim was in his 16th year, he was married first, with great eclat, to the daughter of Raja Bhagvantdas (and sister of Kunvar Mansingh) of Amber. The marriage was celebrated with a mixture of Muslim and Hindu ceremonies, a practice that appears to have been retained subsequently (*MT*:II, 352; *ML*:135; Bhargava 1966:193-194). In the following year Salim was married as well to daughters of the rajas of Bikaner and Jodhpur. Salim's Amber and Bikaner marriages, and a Jaisalmer marriage, the date of which is not known, represented marriage ties over a second generation, since his father had previously taken wives from all these houses. The presence of Hindu wives and their entourages in the harems of Akbar and his sons had a significant impact. The women were allowed to maintain their own customs and religious observances (S.R. Sharma 1972:33; Rizvi 1975:179), and the conservative Muslim historian Badaoni complained bitterly of the role that the emperor's numerous Hindu wives played in leading him astray – that is, away from orthodox Islam (*MT*:II, 312).

Mughal-Rajput marriages were not reciprocal, since no Mughal princess was ever married to a Rajput house.[5] Akbar, however, further strengthened his Rajput ties by "adopting" the daughters of Rajputs who were his personal courtiers and giving them in marriages that in effect functioned as Mughal alliances. The most notable of these marriages took place *ca.* 1587, when Akbar married the daughter of Shekhavat Durjansal Karamsiyot to Suratsingh, the heir of Mota Raja Udaisingh of Jodhpur.[6]

With Jahangir's accession in 1605, Mughal marriages took on a different character. Jahangir continued to make political marriages (at least two additional Rajput marriages and a court marriage) prior to his final marriage to Nur Jahan in 1611. However, in marrying his sons he abandoned his father's unorthodox practices, arranging only two marriages each for his sons Parvez and Khurram (Shahjahan). Subsequently no Mughal ruler made more than the four prescribed marriages for himself or his sons, thus ending the possibility of marriage alliances on the scale utilized by Akbar. In fact, with Akbar's death the impetus for making such alliances appears to have waned. The secure establishment of the empire undoubtedly was responsible in part, but Akbar's conception of the role such marriages could play faded as well. By Aurangzeb's time Hindu wives were formally converted to Islam (*MA*:22), an unmistakable indication of the transition that had taken place.

Akbar's successors did not altogether abandon Rajput alliances. The assertion that Shahjahan had no Rajput wives (S.R. Sharma 1972:104) is incorrect, since Rajasthani sources indicate his marriage, prior to his accession in 1627, to a daughter of his maternal uncle Rathor Sakatsingh Udaisinghot, evidently for personal rather than overtly political reasons (*RV*:f. 78; *NV*:I, 111). Both Jodhpur and Amber marriages were arranged during the struggle for succession that clouded the latter years of Jahangir's reign. In the following generation, as part of the maneuvering that preceded the succession war among Shahjahan's sons, Dara Shikoh arranged a marriage for his eldest Sulaiman Shikoh with the niece of Mirza

Raja Jaisingh of Amber (her father, Rao Amarsingh Rathor of Nagaur, was dead), while Dara's brother and rival Aurangzeb betrothed his eldest son Mu'azzam (Bahadur Shah) to a daughter of Raja Rupsingh Rathor of Kishangarh.[7] A generation after his accession to the throne, Aurangzeb, most probably prompted by his break with Jodhpur after the death of Raja Jasvantsingh in 1678, married a son of Mua'zzam to a niece of Raja Ramsingh of Amber. In 1681, he married his own youngest son Kam Baksh to a daughter of the Shekhavat *ṭhākur* of Manoharpur.

The last Mughal-Rajput marriage took place in 1715 when the emperor Farukhsiyar demanded a daughter from Maharaja Ajitsingh of Jodhpur, and Ajit, to avoid a Mughal attack, was forced to agree. Mughal power, however, was declining: after Farukhsiyar's deposition in 1718 and subsequent assassination (in which Ajit played a large role), the Jodhpur ruler was allowed to reclaim his widowed daughter and all her wealth, which, as noted by a contemporary historian (*E&D*:VII, 483), would have been inconceivable in a previous era.[8]

Rajput Perspectives

In contrast to Muslim practices, the restrictions of caste endogamy and clan exogamy limited the geographical and social scope of Rajput marriage.[9] Within these limits, however, unrestricted polygyny meant that marriages played a key role in the formation and reinforcement of alliances and were also instrumental in the settlement of feuds (*vair*) (Plunkett 1973; Ziegler 1976:240; 1978:224). Elite Rajput houses made marriage alliances of two sorts: (1) hypergamous, and (2) equal status or exchange (i.e., with families to whom daughters, at least potentially, could be given as well as from whom wives could be taken). Hypergamous marriages were frequently associated with patron-client (*dhāṇ-chākar*) relationships.[10] Exchange marriages linked houses of roughly equivalent status, and despite the restriction of cousin marriage, polygyny made possible links over successive generations.

The fairly complete genealogical information available for the ruling Rathor family of Jodhpur and its collaterals for the 16th and 17th centuries (Ziegler and Saran 1984) provides useful illustrations of the extent and functions of elite Rajput marriage networks. A total of 24 marriages is known for Rav Maldev (1532-62), who expanded his Jodhpur inheritance into a powerful kingdom. At least 9 of them can be considered as marriages of the exchange type, another 4 involved families powerful in western Marvar, and 3 are specifically identified as marriages to daughters of *chākars*. Marriages for 14 daughters of Maldev are also known. In 6 instances Maldev gave daughters to ruling houses from which he had taken wives, 2 daughters were married in settlement of feuds, and another 4 were given to Muslims (the rulers of Nagaur and Gujarat, Haji Khan of Mewat and Sher Shah Sur).[11]

The marriages of Maldev's son Mota Raja Udaisingh (1583-95) show a basically similar pattern. However, Udaisingh was not Maldev's heir and did not become ruler of Jodhpur until late in his life. Between 1562 and 1574 his authority was centered at Phalodi, northwest of Jodhpur, and this is reflected in the marriages he made: of 19 known marriages 9 were "local," that is, with the daughters of western Marvar families, 3 were of the exchange type, and 2 were in settlement of feuds. The Mota Raja gave daughters to 4 ruling houses to which his father had also given daughters, married others in Kathiavar, Saurashtra and Central India, and gave 2 to Muslims (the Khan of Nagaur and Prince Salim).[12]

The marriages of daughters to Muslims by Rao Maldev and Mota Raja Udaisingh, for the sake of political alliances though in violation of caste endogamy, were not isolated incidents. For more than four centuries prior to the advent of the Mughals, Rajput rule in northern India had been contested by Muslims. Muslim dynasties had ruled in Delhi since the 12th century, established kingdoms in Gujarat and Malwa, and controlled local areas (for example, Nagaur and Jalaur in Marvar) as well. Rajput daughters were given to Muslim rulers from early on: there are references to marriages involving the 13th- and 14th-century Ghuri and Tughluq rulers of Delhi (Bhargava 1966:197). The relatively complete genealogical records available for the Jodhpur Rathors and their collaterals make it clear that from Rao Jodha (1453-89) onwards they did not hesitate to make Muslim marriages when it seemed politically advantageous to do so; in fact, obtaining a Muslim alliance by giving a daughter appears to have been an accepted tactic.[13] Other available records are less complete, but there are references to pre-Mughal Muslim marriages by Jaisalmer, Mevar and Amber as well (*ibid.*, 197; *Tod*:I, 233; Khan 1976:7).

Prior to the Mughal era, then, Muslim-Rajput marriages were by no means unknown, although there was no precedent for the extensive network of alliances that Akbar promoted. Without dates it is not possible to interpret the significance of some of the earlier marriages listed in Table 1, and the list is almost certainly incomplete,[14] but the general patterns are clear. As in previous eras, the first Rajputs to make marriage alliances with the newly emergent Muslim (i.e. Mughal) dynasty were seeking support for their efforts to gain or retain lands. Raja Bharmal Kachhvaha, involved in a long and bitter contest with a brother for control of Amber, and Mertiya Rathor Jagmal Viramdevot, similarly struggling with his brother Jaimal for Merta, both married daughters to the young emperor, *ca.* 1562 and 1563 respectively.

By 1570, however, the situation had changed. Akbar had firmly established his position in Rajasthan, having taken eastern Marvar as well as the major Rajput fortresses (Ajmer and Nagaur in 1558, Jodhpur in 1565, Chitor in 1568, Ranthambhor in 1569). In that year, after a pilgrimage to the Ajmer *dargāh*, Akbar continued on to Nagaur "for political reasons" (*AN*:II, 517), that is, to order the affairs of Rajasthan and to bring additional Rajput *zamīndārs* into his service. (Service under Akbar offered very lucrative prospects that proved irresistible to most of them, although it meant acceptance of Mughal suzerainty and service away from their homes for extended periods.) At the time of the *darbār* two prominent Rajput rajas, the rulers of Bikaner and Jaisalmer, also married daughters or nieces to the emperor. The ruler of Dungarpur made a marriage alliance somewhat later, in 1577.

In the following generation, Akbar's decision to marry his young heir Prince Salim (Jahangir) first to the daughter of Raja Bhagvantdas of Amber must have been a great coup for the Amber *darbār*. Under the circumstances, it is not difficult to understand why the Amber raja's Rajput rivals in the Mughal *darbār*, the rajas of Jodhpur and Bikaner, would have wanted to marry their own daughters to Salim, which both of them did in the year following the Amber marriage. (A Jaisalmer girl was also married to Salim, although the year is not known.) From the perspective of the rajas, though, the significance of the marriage alliances appears to have remained straightforwardly political; there is no suggestion that any of them adopted Akbar's wider outlook.

Not all of the Rajput rajas, however, accepted Akbar's overlordship. Neither Rao Chandrasen of Jodhpur nor Rana Pratapsingh of Mevar ever came to terms with the emperor. Their opposition to Akbar is traditionally ascribed to their desire to preserve the independence of their kingdoms and, in the case of Rana Pratap, to his unwillingness to suffer the degradation of sending a daughter to the imperial harem (e.g., *Tod*:I, 265; II, 22). In fact, their attitudes may be better understood in somewhat different terms, involving their sense of personal honor as well as traditional Rajput rivalries.

Rao Chandrasen, who had fled when the Mughals took the Jodhpur fort in 1565, attended Akbar's Nagaur *darbār* in 1570 in the obvious hope of regaining his patrimony. He was welcomed by the emperor (*AN*:II, 518; *NV*:I, 69), but for reasons that are not clear they did not reach an understanding. Chandrasen was evidently an overbearing individual, and he may well have found the prospect of accepting Mughal suzerainty insupportable, even in exchange for Jodhpur. Although even after Nagaur Akbar persevered in his effort to persuade Maldev's heir to accept his terms (*AN*:III, 113), by 1574 Chandrasen had begun a campaign of organized opposition to the Mughals that he pursued until his death in 1581. However, whatever the reasons for Chandrasen's unwillingness to accept Akbar's service, he nevertheless recognized that the future lay with the Mughals and at Nagaur left two young sons in the emperor's charge (*NV*:I, 72). At some point he also gave a daughter to Akbar, but since the date is not known, the significance of this marriage is not clear.[5] Not until 1583, after Chandrasen's death, did Akbar finally grant Jodhpur to a son of Maldev, Mota Raja Udaisingh, who in the mid-1580s, along with other prominent rajas of Rajasthan, married a daughter to the young Prince Salim.

The one prominent Rajput house that was able to resist successfully both Akbar's diplomacy and his armies was Mevar. Following the death of Rana Udansingh in 1572, Akbar made a concerted effort to bring his son and successor, Rana Pratapsingh, into his evolving imperial system. Initially Pratap procrastinated and even sent his heir to the Mughal darbar "to pay hommage" as he brooded over his predicament (*AN*:III, 92-93). The reasons for his decision are not explicitly recorded, but evidently Pratap possessed in full measure the proverbial stiff-necked Rajput temperament, and given Mevar's standing among the Rajput kingdoms he would scarcely have welcomed the prospect, no matter how lucrative, of becoming a Mughal servant. What is more, at the time he was considering his position, he would have been aware of the growing prominence at the Mughal court of the rulers of Amber and Bikaner; the rise of Raja Bhagvantdas of Amber and his son Mansingh must have been particularly galling, since the ranas of Mevar considered Amber a dependency. It may well have been factors such as these, rather than an unwillingness to marry a daughter to the emperor, which influenced Pratap. It is not at all clear that Akbar, who was anxious to avoid a struggle, would have insisted on a marriage alliance; after Rao Surjan Hara of Bundi surrendered Ranthambhor and became a Mughal servant in 1569, he had not married a daughter to the emperor.[16]

Ultimately Pratap did not agree to enter Mughal service, and by 1576 he, like Rao Chandrasen, had embarked on a lifelong course of armed resistance to Mughal hegemony. However, not all of Pratap's collaterals or allies supported his anti-Mughal stance. A number of his numerous younger brothers left Mevar to become Mughal *mansabdārs* (*NK*:I, 21-26). And even more revealing are the careers of the heirs of Mertiya Rathor Jaimal Viramdevot, one of the heroes of Rajput legend, who died leading the defense of Chitor against Akbar. Jaimal had recovered Merta, the family patrimony, with Mughal assistance in 1562 but lost it to his brother Jagmal in the following year when Akbar, suspecting Jaimal of disloyalty, threw his support to Jagmal (*AN*:II, 247-250, 305). Jaimal and a brother then took service with the rana of Mevar, to whom they were related by marriage. After Jaimal's death, the overriding concern of his sons and nephews was to regain Merta. Within a year or two of the Mughal victory at Chitor, a nephew had joined the Mughal service and married a sister to the emperor. At least two of Jaimal's sons followed their cousin's lead in accepting service under Akbar, and one of them later married a daughter to Salim in the (ultimately successful) effort to persuade the emperor to grant Merta to them (*NV*:II, 69-72; Ziegler and Saran 1984).[17]

Akbar's death in 1605 marked a turning point. Although Abul Fazl's rhetoric in the *Akbarnāmā*, which always attributes the proposal for a marriage alliance to the bride's side (e.g., *AN*:II, 242, 518; III:678, 749), may be taken as conventional, in fact the initiative for at least some of the early Mughal alliances, including those made by Raja Bharmal of Amber, Rathor Jagmal Viramdevot and Rathor Narhardas Isardasot, as well as some of the marriages to Salim and Parvez (Table 1), almost certainly came from the Rajput side. However, the more orthodox attitudes of Akbar's successors, in particular their abandonment of extensive marriage alliances, diminished both the opportunity and the motivation for the Rajput houses to give daughters to the Mughals. With the possible exception of the Bundela marriage of 1609, which the rebel Ramchand of Bandhu made as a gesture of submission to Jahangir (*TJ*:I, 160), the impetus for the post-Akbar marriages appears to have come from the Mughal side. Only Amber, the house whose fortunes were most closely linked to Mughal patronage, maintained consistant Mughal marriage ties. Of the six Amber rajas from Raja Bharmal to Maharaja Ramsingh (1547 to 1688), five married either a sister, daughter or niece to the Mughals.[18]

By the end of Akbar's reign, Raja Mansingh of Amber as perhaps the single most powerful figure in the empire after the emperor himself, and the rajas of Bikaner and Jodhpur had become prominent as well. Mughal historians of the 17th and 18th centuries laid stress on the importance of their Mughal marriage connections in the rise of these rajas. For example, the *Ma'āsir-ul-Umarā* (an 18th-century biographical compilation) recorded the following:

> The Mota Raja put the ring of servitude in his ear and gave his daughter [Manbhavati, i.e. Jodh Bai] in marriage to Sultan Salim; Sultan Khurram [Shahjahan] was her child. After that Udai Singh was greatly in royal favour, and was exalted by the grant as *jāgīr* of his homeland, the territory of Jodhpur (*MU*:II, 915).

(Chronologically, this is not strictly accurate, since Akbar granted Jodhpur to Udaisingh in 1583 and his daughter was not married to Salim until 1586, but this does not necessarily invalidate the association made between the two events.)

Despite the curtailment of Mughal-Rajput marriage alliances after Akbar's time, when Khurram became his grandfather's favorite and ultimately his father's successor the Jodhpur Rathors continued to benefit from their Mughal ties. The *Ma'āsir-ul-Umarā* accounts for the rise of Kishansingh, one of the Mota Raja's younger sons and the founder of Kishangarh, to the fact that "He was . . . the full brother of the mother of Shah Jahan. By virtue of this great relationship he, in the time of Jahangir, became an intimate courtier and rose to a great position" (*MU*:I, 829-830). Others of the Mota Raja's numerous sons profited handsomely as well. Shahjahan also favored his Jodhpur relatives: the *Ma'āsir-i-'Ālamgiri* recounts that Jasvantsingh (1638-78), the Mota Raja's great grandson and the heir to Jodhpur "being related to Shah Jahan's mother was greatly trusted and given the title of Maharaja . . . . " (*MA*:1).[19]

The Mevar Interpretation

Through the *mansabdārī* system, the Rajputs became an integral part of the Mughal empire. Given Mughal domination of the Rajput kingdoms and the subordinate status of Rajput rulers as Mughal servants, two opposite "ideological" reactions were possible and perhaps inevitable: one stressing an identity between Mughals and Rajputs, the other viewing the association as an unavoidable but essentially degrading necessity. It is hardly surprising that the first view appears in the Jodhpur chronicles (Ziegler 1976:239), while the second is associated with Mevar.

The question of Mughal marriages was a natural focus for these opposing perspectives. While even in Akbar's time sentiment against such marriages was never limited to Mevar,[20] it was clearly centered there. Jahangir had reached a political settlement with Rana Amarsingh in 1614 that called for the attendance of the Mevar heir (although not the rana himself) at the Mughal *darbār* and the provision of a Mevar contingent to the Mughal army. Nevertheless, Mevar never became as closely linked to the Mughal system as were other Mughal houses, particularly Jodhpur and Amber. During the reign of Rana Rajsingh (1652-80), the gulf widened. Rajsingh consciously cultivated Mevar's reputation as the defender of Rajput tradition and Hindu *dharma*. The image he sought is well reflected in the account of a dispute over precedence that occurred when Maharaja Jasvantsingh of Jodhpur and Rajsingh both went to Bundi to marry daughters of the rao. The rao supported the claims of Mevar on the grounds that "since ancient times the ranas have been called 'the sun of the Hindus,' and because of them our [i.e., Rajput] *dharm* has been preserved in the time of the Muslim emperors" (*VV*:II, 243).

Significantly, it was during Rajsingh's time that the heroic legend associated with Rana Pratap took shape and was incorporated into the Mevar *khyāt* literature. There appears, for instance, the story that when Kunvar Mansingh of Amber came to Udaipur in 1573 in an effort to persuade Pratap to come to an accommodation with Akbar, Pratap had refused to eat with his guest on the grounds that Mansingh's aunt (i.e., the daughter of Raja Bharmal) had been married to the emperor. Critical examination of the evidence, however, indicates that this incident, and much of the rest of the Pratap legend as well, are not authentic (G.N. Sharma 1962:79-80).

Mughal-Rajput relations were torn apart by the conflict between Aurangzeb and Jodhpur that followed Raja Jasvantsingh's death in 1678 and were never fully restored. Then, as Mughal power declined in the course of the 18th century, the perennially bitter Rajput clan and state rivalries, masked to some extent since Akbar's time by larger imperial involvements, once more came to dominate the affairs of Rajasthan. In the struggle for pre-eminence among the Rajput houses, the ranas of Mevar were in a position to capitalize on Mevar's history of opposition to the Mughals and the claim, as evidenced by the fact that Mevar had never made a Mughal marriage alliance, that Mevar was the defender of Hindu *dharma*.

From Pratapsingh to Rajsingh (1572 to 1680), no Mevar rana had himself married, or arranged marriages in his immediate family, with either the Amber or the Jodhpur houses.[21] Rana Jaisingh (1680-98) supported Jodhpur's resistance to Aurangzeb among other means by declaring his willingness once again to enter into a marriage alliance with Jodhpur and married a niece to Maharaja Ajitsingh, Jasvantsingh's son, in 1694. Rana Amarsingh (1698-1710) used the renewal of marriage ties with Amber in 1708, arranged as part of an effort to forge a united Rajput front against Aurangzeb's succesor Bahadur Shah, to attempt a major assertion of the political primacy and social superiority of Mevar. The marriage was hedged with conditions, to which Raja Savai Jaisingh of Amber, whose state had been confiscated by Bahadur Shah, assented. Although this was not Jaisingh's first marriage, he agreed to grant to the Mevar rani the position of senior (*paṭ*) rani as well as various related privileges; a son born to her was to be Jaisingh's heir in preference to any other sons, and daughters were never to be married to Muslims (Bhatnagar 1974:54-55).

James Tod, the first British agent appointed to Mevar, to which he was devoted, is known as the chronicler of Rajput history, but it is the Mevar interpretation of Rajput-Mughal relationships that is reflected in his monumental *Annals and Antiquities of Rajast'han*. Tod's account of the legend of Rana Pratap reflects the literary sources and oral traditions current in Mevar in the early 19th century. The *Annals* contain stinging denunciations of those Rajputs who bartered their daughters, and thus their honor, for Mughal wealth and power; Rana Pratap, by contrast, is glorified for his refusal, in the face of either adversity or temptation, to sacrifice the independence of Mevar or to submit to the "degradation of uniting his family by marriage to the Tartar" (*Tod*:I, 264-265; II, 26-27). The intensity of moral feeling in Mevar that had come to be associated with the issue of Mughal-Rajput marriages is well reflected in Tod's gloating account of Mevar's renewal of marriage alliances with Jodhpur and Amber:

> When Hindu prejudice was thus violated [by Mughal marriages] by every prince in Rajasthan (that of Bundi alone excepted), the Rana denounced all alliance with those who were thus degraded . . . . It is a proud triumph of virtue to record that [the rulers of Jodhpur and Amber, who] had risen to greatness from the surrender of principle, as Mevar had decayed from her adherence to it, should solicit, and that humbly, to be re-admitted to the honour of matrimonial intercourse – 'to be purified,' 'to be regenerated,' 'to be made Rajpoots' . . . . (I, 267).

The Mevar tradition also shapes Shymaldas's *Vīr Vinod* (1886), often termed the first modern history of Rajasthan for its use of contemporary documents. However, Shymaldas, the court poet of Mevar, also drew heavily (and uncritically) on literary sources and incorporated the legend of Rana Pratap and similar material wholesale into his volumes. Shymaldas's discussion of Mughal-Rajput marriages is defensive and not entirely consistent. He first claims that behind the political facade the emperors' real motive was to collect beautiful girls for their harems, then argues that since such alliances diminished the honor of the Rajputs, they would never have been made willingly, as the *Akbarnāmā* has it, but only "from necessity" in response to the demands of the emperors (*VV*:II, 437).

It is ironic that ever since their publication in 1829-32, Tod's *Annals*, which were translated into Hindi in 1925 and are very widely known in Rajasthan, have been regarded as a primary source concerning questions of Rajput history and tradition. However, the pervasive inaccuracy of Tod's historical accounts usually is not recognized, nor is the Mevar orientation of the *Annals* generally perceived as such. As inquirer soon discovers that Marvar Rajputs, no less than those from Mevar or any other part of Rajasthan, refer to the *Annals* as definitive. The continuing influence of the *Annals* is clearly a major factor shaping 20th-century Rajput attitudes towards the Mughal-Rajput marriage alliances.

So long as the Rajputs, and those who identify with them, consider events of the 16th century to have a direct bearing on their own standing, and so long as the marriage of Rajput daughters to Muslims is seen as dishonorable, the successful diplomacy of the Amber, Bikaner or Jodhpur rajas who were Akbar's contemporaries is likely to have few modern Rajput defenders, even among the rajas' direct descendants. In such circumstances, a dispassionate examination and interpretation of the historical record is impossible. The facts are grounded too firmly to be denied entirely, but no matter how extensive the documentation, there still will be many who regard the Mughal-Rajput marriage alliances as shameful skeletons in the closet of Rajput history, to be shut away and forgotten.

ENDNOTES

This paper could not have been written without the encouragement and assistance of Norman Ziegler, who unstintingly shared unpublished materials as well as his extensive knowledge of medieval Marvar. Walter Andersen, G.S.L. Devra, B.S. Rathore, Richard Saran, and the editors of this volume made valuable comments on earlier versions. Thanks are also due to S.I.A. Zaidi, who made available the unpublished appendices to his 1974 paper.

1. It is said in Rajasthan that Gangasingh (1887-1940), the prominent maharaja of Bikaner, would gladly have paid any sum to a historian able to prove that no Mughal-Bikaner marriages had ever occurred. There were evidently no takers, since the facts of the matter are incontrovertibly documented, as the maharaja was surely aware.
2. Dasaratha Sharma (1962:7) notes that "later *khyāts*, generally, omit all references to such marriages." The avoidance of the subject in modern works is striking. In his Bikaner and Dungarpur volumes, Ojha does not mention the Mughal marriages involving those states listed in Table 1, and he gives one sentence to the marriage of the daughter of Mota Raja Udaisingh of Jodhpur to Prince Salim. Reu does not mention this marriage in his history of Jodhpur (1938-40), nor in his history of Jaipur does M.L. Sharma (1969) take any note of the marriage alliances which had such important consequences for the rise of Amber in the Mughal era. Mughal marriages are also ignored in Raghubir Sinh's summary of relations between the Mughals and Jodhpur in his account of Durgadas (1975), and by G.D. Sharma in his study of the Jodhpur *rāj* in the Mughal era (1977). Bhargava does devote an appendix to the subject in his book on Jodhpur and the Mughals (1966), the defensive tone of which is typical of Rajasthan historians. An interesting exception is an article on Mughal-Rajput marriage alliances by Rani Lakshmi Chundavat (1967), in which she characterizes attempts by some historians to ignore these marriages as silly. Useful discussions are those by Zaidi (1974) and Khan (1976:Appendix I). Goetz's piece (1958) on the Rajput queens of Akbar and Jahangir is, like so much of his writing, stimulating if at times extravagant, but unfortunately the facts are often incorrect.
3. The marriages of a daughter of Jagmal Vikramdevot (no. 2 in Table 1) and a sister of Narhardas Isardasot (no. 3) were previously unknown, and the marriage of a daughter of Sakatsingh Udaisinghot to Shahjahan (no. 20), listed by Zaidi (1974) on the basis of an ambiguous reference in Nainsi's *Khyāt*, can now be confirmed. Zaidi mentions a number of marriages that previously had not been noted, but because the appendices to his paper were never published, the references were not available.
4. Khan (1976:Appendix I) contains a list of 38 marriages during Akbar's reign, of which he classifies 3 as personal, 3 as family (i.e. with close relatives), and 32 as political (8 with court families and 24 with *zamīndārs*). Table 1 gives 7 Rajput marriages that do not appear in Khan's list. In addition, Khan appears to have missed one court and one *zamīndār* marriage by Akbar mentioned in the *Akbarnāmā* (III, 52, 167) as well as a Qaimkhani marriage (Zaidi 1974:Appendix C), for a total of 42 known political marriages. The documentation is obviously incomplete; for example, many of the wives of Jahangir known from the *Akbarnāmā* are mentioned on the occasion of the births of children rather than their marriages. Akbar's multiple marriages involved him in a famous controversy with the religious establishment concerning their legality; see the account by the historian Badaoni (*MT*:II, 211–213), who was involved. Badaoni obligingly provided the emperor with a justification in law, and the emperor then appointed a compliant *qāzī* who promptly declared the marriages to be legal.
5. Because Shahjahan did not permit any of his four surviving daughters to marry, the impression has grown up that this was true of all the Mughal emperors. In

fact, of Akbar's three surviving daughters, two were married to Timurid collaterals, as was one of Jahangir's two surviving daughters (*AN*:III, 990; *TJ*:I, 19). Aurangzeb was persuaded to abandon his father's prohibition and married his two younger daughters to cousins (*MA*:323).

6. Other known instances include Akbar's marriage of a daughter of Kachhvaha Ramdas Darbari Udavat to Raja Shyamsingh Tanvar in 1601 (*AN*:III, 1197), and perhaps the marriage of a granddaughter of Ramdas Darbari to Raja Surajsingh of Jodhpur c. 1614 (*MD*:II, 208).
7. This betrothal led to the preservation of the name of Charumati, the eldest daughter of Raja Rupsingh Rathor of Kishangarh, in a well-known Rajput tale. Rajasthani sources indicate that the betrothal was arranged by Rupsingh without his daughter's knowledge (G.N. Sharma 1962:139–140). According to the account in *Vīr Vinod* (*VV*:II, 437–443), when, after Rupsingh's death, Aurangzeb requested that the marriage take place, Charumati refused to marry a Muslim and was rescued by Rana Rajsingh of Mevar, who married her himself. To avoid offense to Aurangzeb, the Kishangarh *darbār* substituted a younger sister, who was married to Aurangzeb's eldest son Mu'azzam in 1662 (*MA*:22). It is extremely unlikely that, as stated in *Vīr Vinod*, the original betrothal involved Aurangzeb himself rather than his son.
8. In addition to the Rajput marriages mentioned here and listed in Table 1, Shahjahan married his sons Shuja and Aurangzeb to daughters of the hill rajas of Kishtvar and Rajauri respectively (*AS*:II, 445; Sarkar 1924–30:I, 37); Aurangzeb also married his son Muhammad Sultan to a Kishtvar girl (*MA*:91).
9. In elite Rajput kinship, marriage between members of the same (patrilineal) clan is prohibited, as in marriage between first cousins of any kind. There is a prejudice against a man's marrying any woman of his mother's clan, but such marriages were made when they were advantageous (Plunkett 1973:69–70). The marriage of second cousins is unusual, although the 16th and 17th-century Jodhpur genealogical sources (Ziegler and Saran 1984) list instances of such alliances.
10. Whether a given marriage alliance indicates a hypergamous or exchange relationship between the bride-givers and the bride-takers of course depends on circumstances that may well change over time as the relative status of the parties changes. For instance, Rao Rinmal Rathor and his son Rao Jodha (1453-89) married granddaughters or daughters to Sonagara and Mohil Chauhan families as well as taking wives from them, but later Jodhpur rulers no longer gave daughters to such families.
11.

Marriages of Rao Maldev		*Marriages of Rao Maldev's Daughters*	
Ruling Houses	9	Ruling Houses	7
Amber		Amber	
Amarkot		Amarkot	
Bundi		Bundi	
Dungarpur		Dungarpur	
Jaisalmer (2)		Gvalior	
Karauli		Jaisalmer (2)	

Navanagar		Settlement of Feuds	2
Rampura		Other	1
Western Marvar families	4	Muslims	4
Bhati (2)		Sher Shah Sur	
Sonagara Chauhan (2)		Khanzada of Nagaur	
Chākars	3	Shah of Gujarat	
Other	8	Haji Khan of Mewat	
Total	24	Total	14

In addition to Maldev's Rajput daughters, the sources cited in Table 1 list a daughter by a *pātar* (concubine) sent in *ḍolā* to Akbar. (A *ḍolā* – lit. 'palanquin'-marriage is one where, contrary to the usual practice, the bride is sent to the bridegroom, indicating a concession of lower status on the part of her family.) See also endnote 15.

12\.

Marriages of Mota Raja		*Marriage of Mota Raja's Daughters*	
Ruling Houses	3	Ruling Houses	7
Gvalior		Amber	
Jaisalmer		Bhuj	
Mevar		Dungarpur	
Western Marvar Families	9	Gvalior	
Bhati (5)		Halvad	
Sanchora Chauhan (3)		Jaisalmer	
Sonigara Chauhan		Mau	
Chākars	1	Other	4
Settlement of Feuds	2	Muslims	2
Other	4	Khan of Nagaur	
Total	19	Prince Salim	
		Total	13

All three of the Mota Raja's successors in the Mughal era – Surajsingh (1595-1619), Gajsingh (1619-38), and Javantsingh (1638-78) – had only 5 or fewer surviving children in contrast to their predecessors' two dozen or so offspring, while both Gajsingh and Jasvantsingh had significantly fewer wives as well. The reduction in the number of marriages is largely accounted to by fewer "local" marriage alliances, presumably because the rajas' prominent Mughal positions diminished the need for such alliances. There is no immediate explanation, however, for the drastic reduction in the number of children. In Amber as well, many fewer children were born to 17th-century rulers after Raja Mansingh.

13\. A daughter of Rao Jodha (1453-89) was married to the Khan of Nagaur (*NV*:I, 40). Nainsi also mentions that *ca*. 1540 Mertiya Rathor Viramdev Dudavat betrothed a daughter to the son of Sher Shah's governor at Ranthambhor in an effort to gain Sher Shah's assistance against Rao Maldev (*NV*:II, 54-56). The general attitude is indicated by a humorous anecdote in Nainsi's *Khyāt* concerning a *chākar* who incurred the displeasure of Rao Maldev. The *chākar* proposes to a supporter that they obtain the assistance of the Khanzada rulers of Nagaur by marrying daughters to them. The supporter objects that neither of them has a daughter; the *chākar* replies that if they win they can always marry off the daughters of some Rathor or other, and if they lose, they won't be marrying anyone anyway (*NK*:III, 90; Ziegler and Saran 1984).

14. The mention in the *Zakhīrat-ul- Khawānīn* of Farid Bhakkari (*ZK*:I, 104) that Akbar made Baghela and Tanvar marriage alliances is valuable because, although it is reasonable to expect that Akbar took wives for himself and/or his sons from these clans, they do not appear to be mentioned in other Persian sources. (It is quite possible that references to these and other marriages may eventually be located in local sources.) Curiously, there is no mention of any marriages with Shekhavat families; such alliances would also have been logical, but the lack of documentation up to the present is not sufficient grounds for concluding that they did not occur.
15. The Rajasthani sources cited in Table 1 state that Rao Maldev sent to Akbar in *ḍolā* a daughter by a *pātar* (concubine) and that Rao Chandrasen also sent a daughter, by his Naruki rani, to the emperor in *ḍolā*, but no date is given for either marriage. If Rao Maldev's daughter was married by her father (who died late in 1562), the marriage would have taken place early in Akbar's reign, although not necessarily prior to Akbar's marriage to the daughter of Raja Bharmal early in 1562. However, *Vīr Vinod* (*VV*:II, 174) states that this girl was married to Akbar at Nagaur in 1570 (by Chandrasen?). Without dates it is not possible to know whether Chandrasen used the marriage of a sister and/or daughter in an effort to establish ties with Akbar before the Nagaur *darbār* in 1570 or whether, even after his unsuccessful meeting with the emperor, he attempted to use a marriage alliance as a means of appeasement. It is also possible that Chandrasen's daughter was married after her father's death in 1581.
16. In his *Annals* (*Tod*:II, 382-383) Tod gives the text of a ten-point "treaty" between Akbar and Rao Surjan, supplied to him by the Bundi *darbār*, representing the conditions under which the rao surrendered the Ranthambhor fort to Akbar. The first of the points stipulates that the Bundi rulers would not be obliged to marry a daughter to the emperor. However, while both the *Akbarnāmā* (*AN*:II, 494) and Nainsi's *Khyāt* (*NK*:I, 111-112) mention that an agreement was reached, there is no reference to a written document or to the marriage of daughters. The "treaty" given to Tod is almost certainly a later fabrication.
17. The chronology of these passages in Nainsi's *Vigat* is garbled, and the statement (*NV*:II, 70) that Keshavdas Jaimalot married a daughter to the emperor (i.e., Akbar) is incorrect. It is clear from the Persian sources that it was Salim, not Akbar, to whom Keshavdas married a daughter. No date is given, but since Salim's first marriage took place in 1585 and a daughter was born to Keshavdas's daughter late in 1589 (*AN*:III, 880), the marriage must have taken place between those years.
18. Tod (II, 392) refers to a betrothal between a sister of Savai Jaisingh and Bahadur Shah, but there does not appear to be any mention of this in other sources.
19. The benefits that the Jodhpur Rathors derived from their relationship to Shahjahan raises the still unsettled question as to whether Jahangir's mother

was the daughter of Raja Bharmal of Amber, accounting for the early rise of the Amber Kachhvahas. No contemporary source gives the name of Jahangir's mother, and there is a good deal of evidence, although almost entirely negative, to indicate that she could not have been Bharmal's daughter (see Khan 1976:Appendix II). The *Ma'āsir-ul-Umarā*, for instance, does not speak of any relationships between the Kachhvahas and the Mughals through Jahangir's mother.

20. Indications of Rajput sentiment against Mughal marriage alliances in the 16th and early 17th centuries include the verses attributed to Prithviraj Rathor, a brother of Raja Raisingh of Bikaner (Ojha 1939-40:I, 157-161; *Tod*:I, 273-274); Rathor Kalyandas Raymalot's defiance of Akbar (*MD*:I, 605; II, 188-191, 199); and the objections of Rao Bhoj Hara of Bundi to a marriage between his granddaughter and Jahangir (*MU*:I, 409; Gahlot 1960:II, 65-66).
21. Zaidi's claim (1974:142-143) that this was not the case will not bear examination. Marriages between collaterals of the ranas who became Mughal servants and the Jodhpur house are not relevant, nor is the marriage between Rao Amarsingh Rathor of Nagaur and the daughter of Rana Karansingh in 1622, since Amarsingh had been disinherited by his father, Raja Sursingh of Jodhpur. However, it is not true that over this period Mevar made no marriages with any house that had given daughters to the Mughals, since there were both Bikaner and Jaisalmer marriages.

REFERENCES CITED

Abbreviations

AN Abul Fazl, *Akbar Nāmā*
AS Mhd. Salih Kanbu, *Amal-i-Salih*
BK Bankida, *Khyāt*
DV *Dalpat Vilās*
E&D Elliot and Dowson, *The History of India as Told by its own Historians*

Historians

MA Saqi Must'ad Khan, *Maāsir-i-' Ālamgīrī*
MD Murardan, *Rāṭhoroṅ kī Khyāt*
MJ Kamgar Husaini, *Ma'āsir-i Jahāngīrī*
ML Khafi Khan, *Muntakhab al-Lubāb*
MT Badaoni, *Muntakhab ut-Tawārikh*
MU Shah Nawaz Khan, *Maāsir-ul-Umarā*
NK Nainsi, *Khyāt*
NV Nainsi, *Vigat*
RV *Raṭhoṛāṅ rī Vanśāvalī*
TJ Tūzuk-i-Jahāngīrī
Tod Tod, *Annals and Antiquities of Rajast'han*
VV Shyamaldas, *Vīr Vinod*
ZK Farid Bhakkari, *Zakhīrat ul-Khawānīn*

Abul Fazl
1976 *Akbar Nāmā*. 3 vols. H. Beveridge, transl. 2nd reprint ed. Delhi: Ess Ess Publications.

Badaoni
1973 *Muntakhab ut-Tawārikh*. 3 vols. G. Ranking, W.H. Lowe, W. Haig, transls. Reprint ed. Delhi: Idarah-i Abadiyat-i Delli.

Bankidas
1956 *Khyāt*. P.J. Muni, ed. Jaipur: Rajasthan Oriental Research institute.

Bhatnagar, V.S.
1974 *Life and Times of Sawai Jai Singh*. Delhi: Impex India.

Bhargava, Visheshwaṛ Sarup
1966 *Marvar and the Mughal Emperors*. Delhi: Munshiram Manoharlal.

Chundavat, Rani Lakshmi Kumari
1967 "*Rājpūt aur Musalmānoṇ ke bīch Vivāh-sambandh*." *Mārū Bhāratī* 18 (2):96-100.

Elliot, Henry and John Dowson
1964 *The History of India as Told by its Own Historians*. 8 vols. Reprint ed. Allahabad: Kitab Mahal.

Farid Bhakkari, Sheikh
1961-74 *Zakhīrat ul-Khawānīn*. 3 vols. Syed Moinul Haq, ed. Karachi: Pakistan Historical Society.

Gahlot, Jagdish Singh
1960 *Rājputāne kā Itihās*. 5 vols. Jodhpur: Hindi Sahitya Mandir.

Goetz, Hermann
1958 "The Rajput Empresses of Akbar and Jahangir." In *Jadunath Sarkar Commemorative Volume*. Vol. II. Hari Ram Gupta, ed. pp. 125-134. Hoshiarpur: Punjab University.

Jahangir
1968 *Tūzuk-i-Jahāngīrī*. 2 vols. H. Beveridge, ed. A. Rogers, transl. Delhi: Munshiram Manoharlal.

Irvine, William
1921-22 *Later Mughals*. 2 vols. Jadunath Sarkar, ed. Calcutta: M.C. Sarkar & Sons.

Khafi Khan
1975 *Muntakhab al-Lubāb*. S. Moinul Haq, transl. Karachi: Pakistan Historical Society.

Khan, Refaqat Ali
1976 *The Kachhwahas under Akbaṛ and Jahangir*. Delhi: Kitab Publishing House.

Kamgar Husaini, Khwaja
1978 *Ma'āsiri-i Jahāngīrī*. Azra Alavi, ed. Bombay: Asia Publishing House Pvt Ltd.

Muhammad Salih Kanbu
1923-46 *Amal-i-Salih*. 2 vols. G. Yazdani, ed. Calcutta: Asiatic Society.

Murardan
n.d. *Rāṭhoṛoṅ kī Khyāt No. 1*, Ms. no. 25658; *Rāṭhoṛoṅ kī Khyāt No. 2*, Ms. no. 156672. Jodhpur: Rajasthan Oriental Research Institute.

Nainsi, Munhata

1960-67 *Naiṇsī rī Khyāt*. 4 vols. B. Sakariya, ed. Jodhpur: Rajasthan Oriental Research Institute.

1968 *Mārvār rā Parganāṅ rī Vigat*. 2 vols. N.S. Bhati, ed. Jodhpur: Rajasthan Oriental Research Institute.

Ojha, Gaurishankar Hirachand

1939-40 *Bikāner Rājya kā Itihas*. 2 vols. Ajmer: By the Author.

Plunkett, Frances Taft

1973 "Royal Marriages in Rajasthan." *Contributions to Indian Sociology* 7:64-80.

Qanungo, Kalika Ranjan

1935 *Dara Shikoh*. Calcutta: M.C. Sarkar & Sons.

Rāṭhoṛāṅ rī Vanśāvalī

n.d. *Rāṭhoṛāṅ rī Vanśāvalī*. Ms. no. 20130. Jodhpur: Rajasthan Oriental Research Institute.

Reu, Vishveshvarnath

1938-40 *Mārvāṛ kā Itihās*. 2 vols. Jodhpur: Archeological Department.

Rizvi, Saiyid Athar Abbas

1975 *Religious and Intellectual History of the Muslims in Akbar's Reign*. Delhi: Munshiram Manoharlal.

Saqi Mast'ad Khan

1981 *Maāsir-i-'Ālamgīrī*. Jadunath Sarkar, transl. Reprint ed. Lahore: Suhail Academy.

Sarasvat, Ravat, ed.

1960 *Dalpat Vilās*. Bikaner: Sadul Rajasthani Research Institute.

Sarkar, Jadunath

1924-30 *History of Aurangzeb*. 5 vols. Calcutta. M.C. Sarkar & Sons.

Shah Nawaz Khan

1941-64 *Maāsir-ul-Umarā*. 3 vols. H. Beveridge and B. Prashad, transls. Calcutta, Asiatic Society.

Sharma, Dasharatha

1962 "The Bhuteshvara Temple Inscription of Parvati, a Foster-Sister of Akbar's Jaisalmer queen Sri Nathibai, V. 1634." *The Researcher* (Jaipur) 2:7-8.

Sharma, Ghanshyam Datt

1977 *Rajput Polity*. Delhi: Manohar Book Service.

Sharma, Gopi Nath

1962 *Mewar and the Mughal Emperors*. 2nd ed. Agra: S.L. Agarwala

Sharma, Mathura Lal

1969 *History of the Jaipur State*. Jaipur: Rajasthan Institute of Historical Research.

Sharma, Sri Ram

1972 *The Religious Policy of the Mughal Emperors*. 3rd ed. London: Asia Publishing House.

Shyamaldas, Kaviraj

1886 *Vīr Vinod*. 2 vols. Udaipur.

Sinh, Raghubir

1975 *Durga Das Rathor*. New Delhi: National Book Trust.

Tod, James
1971 *Annals and Antiquities of Rajast'han*. 3 vols. Reprint ed. Delhi: K.M.N. Publishers.

Zaidi, S. Inayat Ali
1974 "The Pattern of Matrimonial Ties Between the Kachawaha Clan and the Mughal Ruling Family." *Proceedings of the India History Congress* I:131-145.

Ziegler, Norman
1976 "Marvari Historical Chronicles: Sources for the Social and Cultural History of Rajasthan." *Journal of Indian Economic and Social History* 13:219-250.
1978 "Some Notes on Rajput Loyalties During the Mughal Period." In *Kingship and Authority in South Asia*. J.F. Richards, ed. pp. 215-251. University of Wisconsin-Madison: South Asian Studies Publication Series.

Ziegler, Norman and Richard Saran
1984 "Merto, Rajasthan, and Its Rulers, the Mertiya Rathors, 1462-1665." 2 vols. Manuscript.

THE DADU-*PANTH*: A RELIGIOUS ORDER IN ITS RAJASTHAN CONTEXT

DANIEL GOLD

Rajput institutions and ideals of martial valor are known throughout North India, but seem to have developed with particular strength in Rajasthan. Sometimes obviously, sometimes less so, their influence is visible far beyond the courts. How pervasive *is* this impact of Rajput institutions on the regional culture? Does it extend even to religious traditions that have developed in Rajasthan?

To explore these questions, I propose looking at the history and institutional structures of the Dadu-*panth*, the sectarian tradition (*panth*, 'path') stemming from the 16th century Rajasthani poet-saint or *sant* Dadu Dayal (1544-1603). The Dadu-*panth*, which flourished particularly during the 18th and 19th centuries, produced both scholars and warrior ascetics and found special favor with the ruling house of Jaipur. The Dadu-*panthī* warriors or Nagas,[1] in fact, served the Jaipur state as soldiers and tax collectors from 1797 until they were disbanded in 1938.

This martial evolution of the Dadu-*panth* and its integration into the Rajput political order presents a unique development in the larger North Indian *sant* tradition within which Dadu stands. Why did this particular kind of evolution take place? Was the Dadu-*panth* significantly shaped by the Rajput environment in which it developed? This paper, an exploratory essay designed to raise suggestive comparative questions, will first look at the figure of Dadu as a regional *sant* and the Dadu-*panth* as a variant of the North Indian *sant* tradition. Next, it will trace the rise and fall of the Dadu-*panth*, stressing especially aspects of its history connecting it to Rajput values, Rajput institutions and the Jaipur state. Finally, it will suggest some overall contrasts between the Dadu-*panth* and *sant panths* that did *not* evolve within the context of princely patronage in Rajasthan.

Like many exploratory papers, this one is indebted to the work of specialists, particularly scholars of literature and religion who have studied the texts of the tradition.[2] Archival and other primary historical sources have not been accessible, and should definitely be examined in any future research along the lines suggested here. The main primary source that has been used is the three-volume sectarian history of the Dadu-*panth* published in 1978-79 by the octogenarian Dadu-*panthī* scholar Narayandas, *Śrī Dādū Panth Parichay*. Using his access to unpublished manuscripts and long years of memories, Narayandas presents the lore of his tradition in thousands of pages of Hindi prose. He places Dadu clearly within the aniconic and unorthodox style of *sant* piety heralded by the great Kabir and Nanak, the first Guru of the Sikhs, but distinguishes Dadu as a *sant* for and of Rajasthan.

Though Narayandas's work includes an extended biography of Dadu himself, it is for the most part comprised of stories about later figures in the *panth*, from Dadu's death to the present. Narayandas begins with a long history of the gurus at the main Dadu-*panthī* shrine at Naraina but, aiming to be comprehensive, eventually covers all the *panth*'s notable figures, the centers founded by them, and the evolution of the centers. He thus orders his narrative according to the sublineages of the *panth*, presenting stories of gurus and disciples in succession. However accurate his depiction of the Dadu-*panthī* sublineages may be as history, his text derives its importance largely as a mine of sectarian narrative. Most of the stories he tells are thus properly treated by the scholar as legend, meaningful as a construction of reality from within the tradition. As such, however, they are richly suggestive, especially for the historian of religions concerned with the interpretation of legendary texts. Indeed, it is exegesis of Narayandas's text which has stimulated the kinds of questions being explored here.[3]

Dadu as Regional *Sant*

Legend, as recorded by Narayandas, paints Dadu in the same brilliant colors used to depict Indian holy men in general – but in a characteristically Rajasthani setting. Like Kabir, Nanak and other *sants*, Dadu displays charity, chastity and magical power. But to a greater extent and in a different way than Kabir and Nanak, Dadu is shown interacting with figures from the royal court. Unlike Kabir and Nanak, moreover, he is never said to have ventured far beyond his immediate cultural region.

Though there is little we can know for certain about Dadu's life (see Callewaert 1978:21-56; 1987), the legends surrounding him do seem to derive from a historical kernel. Mahipati's *Bhaktivijaya*, a Marathi hagiographical collection, refers to Dadu as a *pinjārī*, a cotton carder (Abbott 1982:II, 384). Other references, both within the Dadu-*panthī* tradition and elsewhere, lead us to believe this was probably his hereditary occupation (Orr 1947:49-52; Callewaert 1988:3-15). Like Kabir, then, Dadu may have come from one of the many low artisan castes that had converted to Islam (Vaudeville 1974:83-89).

According to tradition, Dadu was born in Ahmedabad, but as a young man had settled in Rajasthan. First at Sambhar, then at Amber – both in the general region of present-day Jaipur – Dadu practiced his craft and, it is said, raised a family. Two sons are mentioned, who were to play notable roles in the *panth* after his death; reference is also sometimes made to two daughters. Along with raising a family, Dadu is said to have attracted numerous disciples. Toward the end of his life, according to tradition, he spent several years travelling around Rajasthan, finally settling at the village of Naraina, between Jaipur and Ajmer, where his tomb and the headquarters of the *panth* are located to this day.

In the legends, Dadu appears as a *sant*, with all the characteristics Indians expect to find in pious holy men. For example, he is portrayed as not having been a coarse creature of the flesh. Thus his sons and daughters were not conceived in the usual way, but from two cloves and two peppercorns which he gave his wife to eat when he saw her desire for offspring. Dadu is not only shown as having managed to remain chaste within family life, but also as selfless within domestic poverty. Jan Gopal, the most important early biographer of Dadu, tells us for instance that when a thief entered Dadu's house and banged against some cotton-carding instruments, the *sant* exhorted him to leave quickly so as to avoid capture (Orr 1947:29, 47, Callewaert 1988:39-40, 94). Later traditon makes Dadu learned too, the clatter of cotton-carding instruments eventually replaced by the rustling pages of books (*ibid.*, 47; Callewaert 1988:19). From an illiterate householder *sant* plying a humble trade, then, Dadu is gradually turned into a detached, saintly scholar.

The traditional biographies on which Narayandas' account is based (Callewaert 1987) present him in frequent contact with royalty – a situation that may reflect something of the political world in which the *sant* lived. That Dadu impressed the Raja of Amber during his stay there and made disciples of some local rajas during his wanderings (Orr 1947:39-41) are both plausible. He may also have had the audience with Akbar that is described by Jan Gopal (*ibid.*, 31-36; Callewaert 1988:46-55; 98-104). It seems entirely within what we know of Akbar's character to have wanted to meet Dadu – a holy man who might have been mentioned by the emperor's Rajput nobles but was also probably known as a Muslim saint. Yet the extravagant description of the audience found in later Dadu-*panthī* hagiographical tradition (Narayandas 1978-79:II, 1-63; Orr 1947:56-58; Callewaert 1988:21-22) greatly outshines the meetings with royalty found in the biographies of Kabir, Nanak and other *sants*.

Though Kabir and the Sikh Gurus are also said to have met with royalty, their relationships with rulers differ from Dadu's. Kabir's meetings with kings, though they do appear in later Kabir-*panthī* literature, are not an important part of the common lore about him. Furthermore, they generally show the fearless *sant* challenging monarchs with novel and striking religious truth; the emphasis throughout Kabir-*panthī* literature is on Kabir's cosmic role as a great being offering a new religious dispensation.[4] Later Sikh Gurus, on the other hand, though certainly shown as embodying spiritual virtues, also appear as ruling monarchs, regional political and military leaders in the Punjab. Thus, confronting the Mughal emperors as political rivals, Guru Arjan and Guru Tegh Bahadur faced situations leading to martyrdom. Kabir and the Sikh Gurus, then, stand in tension against the power of princes – Kabir with renunciatory aims that mock all worldly authority, the Sikh Gurus as insubordinate rival secular powers. Dadu's relationship to royal authority, by contrast, seems to reflect the Rajput political ideals of the Mughal period. Within Rajasthan, Dadu is shown as enjoying the patronage of local rulers and nobles, while outside, he is recognized with due respect at the Mughal court.

Dadu also contrasts sharply with Kabir and Nanak in that he is said to have travelled outside his home region only as far as Akbar's court at Fatehpur Sikri. Kabir, on the other hand, is believed to have travelled all over India (Tapaswi 1976:284-405), while Nanak, according to Sikh sources, reached even Baghdad, Mecca and Medina (McLeod 1968:122-152). But Dadu's later wanderings are shown as entirely confined to Rajasthan, where, mixing with high and low in villages of the different states, he crossed boundaries of locality and social status to achieve recognition within large segments of Rajasthani society.

The Dadu-*Panth* and the *Sant* Tradition

The unorthodox poet-saints referred to as *sants* appeared in North India from the end of the 14th century, singing popular verses of yoga and devotion.[5] Though heirs to an earlier tradition of Vaishnava *sants* to the south, in Maharashtra, the North Indian *sants* came more directly under the impact of Islam than did their prececessors. Recognizing a divinity beyond the established forms of both Hinduism and Islam, the *sants* characteristically sang of a Lord without qualities, in the image of no Hindu deity. Invoked by both Hindu and Islamic honorifics, the Lord of whom the *sants* sang was also often referred to as the guru, and the mystery of the guru – at once a formless being beyond and a living person at hand – is a recurrent theme in *sant* verse.

This importance given in *sant* verse to the idea of the guru adds weight to the role of a great *sant*'s successors – gurus in the lineage stemming from the original *sant*, the propagators of the *sant*'s *panth*. Some of these successors wrote verses of their own which became part of the *panth*'s cumulative heritage. Others wrote no verses, but through the example of their practice kept alive the traditions of past gurus.

Following teachings that were syncretic to begin with and reinterpreted in different ways by idiosyncratic holy men, *sant panths* developed in highly divergent ways. The most important *panths* contemporaneous with that of Dadu were those deriving from Kabir and Nanak, the two best known *sants* of North India. For Kabir-*panthī* sectarian tradition, Kabir as incarnation of the divine left an image that has taken on mythic proportions.[6] For later North Indian *sants*, Kabir set an iconoclastic tone adopted by most, though to greater or lesser degrees. Nanak (1469-1539), about a century later than Kabir, composed verses that are frequently less abrasive in tone than those of his predecessor but still stand clearly within the iconoclastic sensibility of *sant* tradition.

Yet the sectarian movement that grew out of Nanak's teachings, the Sikhs, came to distinguish itself from the rest of the *sant* tradition. Spread widely throughout the Punjab and far beyond, Sikhs nowadays consider themselves to be adherents of a separate religion – with a codified scripture (the *Gurū Granth Sāhib*) and customs that recall the days of their early military struggles as a community.[7]

Despite their diversity, most *sant panths* share common social origins, having drawn their membership mostly from low and middle castes dissatisfied with religious orthodoxies.[8] Many *panths*, too, as they became established, underwent familiar processes of routinization and Sanskritization – so much so that several have been finally reabsorbed into conventional Hinduism, leaving only the memory of a past local *sant*.[9] This easy assimilation of *sant panths* into conventional Hinduism is indicative of the ambiguous role *sants* have played in the complex interaction between India's Great Tradition and its regional Little Traditions.[10] Like many of the regional Little Tradition figures, the *sants* were largely illiterate and used profane vernacular speech to express sacred religious truth. But as vernacular poets, they differed from the bards of regional epics and even from the vernacular poets of Krishna *bhakti*. Unlike these poets, who used regional literary dialects, the *sants* used a more workaday language based on the Hindustani understood all over North India. In contrast to the Krishna poets, moreover, they usually sang of stark renunciation from the world – a theme which is more characteristic of the Great Tradition. Thus, *sant panths* that have continued to flourish, like the Kabir-*panthīs* and the Sikhs, tend to present middle-caste, low-caste and outcaste Indians with alternatives – sometimes radical alternatives – to the Great Tradition of Hinduism. In this context, the success of the Dadu-*panth* – with its orientation toward the worldly values and royal power sometimes associated with the Little Tradition – appears as an exception and invites explanation.

Clearly, the Dadu-*panth* presents some sharp socio-religious contrasts to both the Kabir-*panth* and the Sikh tradition. Both the Kabir-*panthīs* and the Sikhs developed important institutions through which they challenged religious and political establishments. However, their institutions did not give equal importance to scholarship and military skills, while both were well cultivated in the Dadu-*panth*. Kabir-*panthīs*, if not characteristically scholars, produced a profusion of metaphysical writings in Hindi, with deities and cosmologies diverging widely from those of classical Hinduism. The Sikhs, on the other hand, produced powerful military institutions and several noted warrior-gurus, and have fought repeatedly in their own defense against outside political interference. The institutions of the Dadu-*panth*, by contrast, did not evolve as a challenge to either a great religious establishment or outside political power. Focused on no single, overriding socio-religious end, the *panth* could grow in diverse ways and come to include both scholarly and military traditions.

Moreover, both the scholars and the soldiers of the Dadu-*panth* existed ideally as celibate orders. Like most other Indian religious traditions, the Dadu-*panthīs* had both ascetic and lay divisions: renunciates, and the householders who supported them. As in other traditions, members frequently joined the celibate orders as children – sometimes in fulfillment of a parent's vow, sometimes as orphans with nowhere else to go, and sometimes, it is said, through their own attraction to a particular guru.[11] In its recruitment of children to celibate orders, the *panth* of Dadu is similar to that of Kabir, though the Kabir-*panthīs* had a wider range of lay devotees from which to draw, and in some Kabir-*panthī* lineages gurus have traditionally married. The Sikhs diverge even further from celibate ideals, with marriage among gurus the norm and no important ascetic branch. Relative to these traditions, the predominance of the celibate soldiers and scholars in the Dadu-*panth* appears striking.

The predominant place occupied by the celibate soldiers and scholars of the Dadu-*panth*, it may be argued, derives from the *panth*'s development in a circumscribed regional tradition with particular local needs. Thus, while Dadu is the most highly regarded *sant* after Kabir and Nanak, and his *panth* the next best known after the Kabir-*panth* and the Sikhs, the Dadu-*panth* is much more limited in both numbers and regional spread. According to the 1981 census, there are about ten million Sikhs in India (Government of India 1986:14) and the current population of Kabir-*panthīs* has been estimated at over two and a half million (Lorenzen 1987:291-292). The number of Dadu-*panthīs*, on the other hand, was judged to be about fifteen thousand in 1947 (Orr 1947:216-217).[12] Thus it seems that by 1947, the *panth*, particularly its military branch, had gone into a steep decline, its membership but a remnant of a tradition that had known its period of glory a century earlier. Nevertheless, the Dadu-*panth* probably always existed on a scale much smaller than either the Kabir-*panth* or the Sikhs.

While reflecting the large proportion of celibates in the *panth*, this relatively smaller size of the Dadu-*panth* also coincides with its more exclusive regional scope. To be sure, both the Sikhs and the Kabir-*panthīs* have distinct regional centers, the former in the Punjab and the latter in the eastern Gangetic plain and the Chhattisgarh region of Madhya Pradesh (Lorenzen 1987). But Sikhs are visible throughout India, and the Kabir-*panth* has spread well beyond the Hindi-speaking areas, with many establishments in Gujarat (Bhatt 1975) and outposts as far south as Bangalore.[13] The Dadu-*panthīs*, on the other hand, are clearly centered in Rajasthan, spreading outward only into the neighboring regions of Gujarat and the Punjab (Ghurye 1964:196), and with just a few individuals in cities elsewhere in North India. The limited geographical spread of the *panth* thus presents a parallel to the image of Dadu as a distinctly regional *sant*.

Rajput Identity in the Dadu-*Panth*

It took about 90 years from Dadu's death in 1603 for his *panth* to emerge as a distinct sectarian institution. Dadu's disciples in the meantime had scattered throughout the towns and villages of Rajasthan, preserving his verses, publicly reciting them, and sometimes composing new ones of their own. Sites founded by disciples became focal points for new lines of succession, but Dadu's tomb at Naraina remained the central Dadu-*panthī* shrine. In its early stages, the shrine at Naraina seems to have been treated in much the same way as the tombs of many Indian holy men are today, particularly in Islamic tradition. It was seen as a continuing source of grace for the holy man's devotees – and of both income and dissension for his descendants. We read of members of Dadu's family quarelling among themselves over control of the shrine, and of the important role played in these early disputes by some of the women of the family. Dadu's descendants are also shown as having had to meet challenges to their authority from disciples outside the family (Narayandas 1978-79:I, 31-44; Orr 1947:191-192).

One of these challenges was finally successful. In 1693, through a series of events that have become legend in the *panth*, the control of Dadu's tomb passed decisively from his descendants to a devotee named Jait Ram, who remained in authority for nearly 40 years. Jait Ram was a charismatic leader with good political skills, and was able to bring the many groups of Dadu's followers together into a coherent institution. He is thus remembered as the real founder of the Dadu-*panth*, divinely appointed to the task during a time of rivalry and confusion in the order. The junior of two devotees with the same name, Jait Ram is said to have been chosen and given an honorific title by the voice of Dadu coming down from the sky: "Accept the younger Jait Sahib, head and shoulder of all the *sants*" (Narayandas 1978-79:I, 53).

The tradition over which Jait Sahib came to wield authority included not only contemplative monks following in Dadu's footsteps, but also warrior-ascetics who took Dadu's name in battle. Warrior-ascetics, collectively called Nagas, have a long history in Hindu tradition. The image of the fighting *sādhū* is preserved in sectarian religious texts,[14] and by the 16th century we hear of ascetic military orders organized both to protect the interest of monasteries and to rebel against political authority (Lorenzen 1978:63). These ascetic armies seem to have been recruited from middle and lower castes during times of crisis, but once formed were not easily disbanded (Orr 1940:82-83). The collapse of Mughal rule in the 18th century not only allowed great ascetic leaders to rise to prominence (Sarkar 1958), but also made it common for bands of armed ascetics to make demands on the populace (Orr 1940:88). Eventually, groups of militant *sādhūs* became part of the armies of the princely states. Under Jait Sahib's authority, the Dadu-*panthī* Nagas were made a separate branch of the order, and the annual festivals of the *panth* at Naraina were used as occasions at which he gave them specific instructions about the deployment of troops (Orr 1947:200).

As might be expected in Rajasthan, some Dadu-*panthī* Nagas are remembered as having come from Rajput backgrounds – though the caste origins of *panth* members through most of its history cannot readily be determined. Many of Dadu's first followers probably came from the humble, minimally Islamicized castes from which Dadu himself probably emerged. But several of the *sant*'s important disciples are traditionally given origins in respectable Hindu castes. Thus, of Dadu's two disciples named Sundar Das, the younger, a gifted poet, is matter-of-factly termed a Khandelwal *baniyā* (Shastri 1978:53), while the elder is remembered more glamorously as a Rajput prince from Bikaner. Higher caste Hindu models eventually became formative in the *panth*, which developed along the lines of a Hindu monastic organization.[15] At the same time, with its unorthodox, syncretic origins, the *panth* was able to assimilate forms of non-Brahmanical culture in ways less easily adopted by conventional Hindu monastic institutions. It could thus be attractive to Rajputs, who both joined it and left their mark on it.

An anecdote narrated by Narayandas (1978-79:I, 74-76) illustrates the fact that the Dadu-*panth* had to make some specific concessions to Rajput custom in order to bring the Nagas into the order. At one of the annual Dadu-*panthī* festivals at Naraina, there was a suggestion that all celibate members of the order shave off their mustaches and wear the garb of the Hindu ascetic. Dadu was clean-shaven and wore mendicant's robes, some of the monks said, so why shouldn't the Dadu-*panthī sādhūs* follow his example? It would provide a modicum of outward uniformity in a sectarian tradition seeking to establish itself. Opposed to the idea were Keval Das and Hirday Ram, Naga heroes in the spiritual lineage of Dadu's bold Rajput disciple, Sundar Das the elder. Most of the *sādhūs* in their branch of the order were of Rajput background, where mustaches, a sign of virility, were the norm. Sundar Das had worn mustaches, so why shouldn't those in his lineage be allowed to keep theirs? The two sides could reach no immediate agreement, and Keval Das led his men away to hold their festival at another place. Only after five years was Jait Sahib able to bring them back into the fold with a polite, diplomatic letter.

Through compromise and concession, then, Jait Sahib was able to let the Dadu-*panthī* Nagas preserve their Rajput ways. Thus visible forms of Rajput culture began to penetrate into the Dadu-*panthī* ascetic order – the type of institution that in conventional Hinduism either adopts Brahmanical norms or else features the wild, casteless *sādhū* (Ghurye 1964). Nagas in Shaivism and Vaishnavism usually took on the dress and grooming of other Hindu ascetics – that is, when they were groomed and dressed at all. But while many of the fighting *sādhūs* of India often did present a fierce visage, with little or no clothes and unkempt hair and beard, in the Dadu-*panth* Keval Das's men were able to be militant ascetics as well as fully clothed and mustachioed Rajputs.

Hereditary rulers as well as soldiers, Rajputs as recruits and patrons seem to have been able to introduce their ideas of political lineage even among the contemplative Dadu-*panthīs*. For example, Narayandas (1978-79:I, 416-423) tells of a meditative monk named Hapaji who was born a prince and left a spiritual lineage recognized at court. Said to have been the youngest son of Raja Bhagwant Das of Amber (the old Jaipur capital), Hapaji was of grave countenance even as a child. Meeting his guru and renouncing the world, he eventually became established in sainthood. Following Hindu custom, Hapaji returned 12 years after his initiation for a visit to his native place. When the new raja heard that his brother was camped outside the city with his disciples, he invited Hapaji to come to court. There Hapaji impressed the members of the twelve noble houses of Amber to such an extent that they declared him to be the founder of a "thirteenth noble house" (*ibid.*, 418). Though beseeched by all to stay, Hapaji was firm in his renunciation and abandoned Amber, though not without leaving behind a few disciples to carry on the "thirteenth house" he had founded.

With flexibility derived from the unorthodox *sant* tradition, the Dadu-*panth* thus offered means for individual Rajputs to maintain important aspects of their social identity while still being part of an ascetic religious order. Thus, in the anecdotes related by Narayandas, Hapaji and his followers see Dadu-*panthī* spiritual authority treated on a par with temporal authority in their local court, while Keval Das's men are allowed to keep both their mustaches and their fierce devotion to Dadu's name. More crucial yet to the vitality of the Dadu-*panth* in its heyday than this internalization of certain Rajput cultural norms, however, were the various roles it played in the socio-religious world of princely Rajasthan.

The Dadu-*Panth* and Princely Power

In their relationship to religio-political authority, the scholars and soldiers of the Dadu-*panth* differed both from each other and from their Sikh and Kabir-*panthī* counterparts. The scholars of the Dadu-*panth*, I would argue, in addition to serving princes as Ayurvedic physicians, were able to offer the regional elite a version of the Brahmanical Great Tradition that might have been more to their taste than that presented by court Brahmans. Drawing on certain areas of Sanskrit learning, they presented congenial aspects of the Great Tradition to interested laymen in the vernacular. Kabir-*panthī* scholars, by contrast, presented the Great Tradition in a radically altered form, and Sikhs divorced themselves from it altogether. Moreover, the soldier-ascetics of the Dadu-*panth*, like the Sikhs belonging to the Khalsa, and in contrast to most Vaishnava and Shaiva Nagas, maintained a loyalty to their sovereign. But unlike the Sikhs during the formation of their military tradition, the Dadu-*panthīs* found their temporal ruler not at the camp of the guru, but at the court of a prince.

The scholars of the Dadu-*panth*, though perhaps most accomplished in practical Ayurvedic learning, also took interest in classical Hindu philosophy. With their spiritual roots in the *sants*' worship of the Lord without qualities, the Dadu-*panthīs* were led especially to Hindu traditions of non-dualism. The most polished of the early Dadu-*panthī* poets, Sundar Das the younger, is said to have gone to Kashi to learn the four Vedas, six Shastras and eighteen Puranas (Raghav Das 1969:737). "He was a second Shankaracharya," says the 18th century Dadu-*panthī* hagiographer Raghav Das, "Dadu's Sundar . . . put the dualistic attitude aside, and sang of non-duality alone" (*ibid.*, 736). Yet Sundar Das's verse, however erudite, remained within the tradition of *sant* piety. Later, learned Dadu-*panthīs* left the tradition of *sant* verse to express themselves in modern Hindi prose. Nischal Das, for example, the most prolific Dadu-*panthī* scholar of the 19th century, was famous for his philosophical works in Hindi, some of which were particularly abstruse.[16] Indeed, part of his success among the princely elite may have derived from the prestige accorded to the very difficulty of his work: he remained for a time under the patronage of the raja of Bundi, "who thought there should be some high-level philosophical books in Hindi" (Narayandas 1978-79:II, 842).

With its scholars, then, the Dadu-*panth* emerged as a respectable religious community that could offer regional rulers some prestigious knowledge from the Great Tradition. Yet it did this without Sanskrit and without Brahmans. Perhaps the unorthodox origins of the Dadu-*panth* – according to which an individual's caste was seen as having little bearing on his spiritual qualifications

– equalized the religious potential of Brahmans and Rajputs in the tradition.

The new relationships that became possible in the *panth* are well illustrated in the story of Sundar Das the elder, the Rajput prince, and his family priest, the Brahman Prahlad Das (*ibid.*:I, 378-386). Thought to have been killed in battle, Sundar Das accidentally met Prahlad Das as the latter was returning from Gaya, where he had performed his patron's death rites. Since Sundar Das had thus effectively lost his throne, he renounced the world, and Prahlad Das followed him. Both eventually came to Dadu. At the same time Sundar Das became Dadu's disciple, we are told, Prahlad Das became the disciple of Sundar Das (*ibid.*:I, 396). If a Rajput could prostrate himself before a Muslim cotton-carder, then a Brahman could certainly humble himself spiritually before his former Rajput patron. The double submission narrated here suggests the socio-religious value a non-Brahmanical tradition could have for members of the Rajput princely elite. If Rajputs could thus command in spiritual matters as they did in temporal affairs, Brahmans as such were in a sense superfluous.

Eventually, moreover, Rajput rulers were able to command Dadu-*panthī* soldiers in battle. With the death of Jait Sahib in 1732, the authority of the guru at Naraina over the Nagas waned, and power was exercised instead by individual Naga chiefs. Often fighting side-by-side with militant Vaishnavas (Vairagis), Dadu-*panthī* Nagas began both to work as mercenaries and also to do some plundering of their own. They also started their career as tax collectors – an occupation that demanded at least the threat of military force. In 1779, an important Naga leader named Santokh Das was able to amass a large force of Dadu-*panthīs* and help repel a Mughal invasion of Jaipur (Orr 1947:202). Eighteen years later, a large force of Dadu-*panthī* Nagas, recognizing Santokh Das as chief, formally entered the service of Jaipur state. When Santokh Das died in 1825, however, his successor was unable to maintain command over rival chiefs. As had happened after the death of Jait Sahib, the Nagas became organized into separate divisions. But now, being officially connected to the Jaipur state, these divisions became more formalized, each group demanding its share of the state grant (*ibid.*, 200-06).[17]

Whatever their internal divisions, the Dadu-*panthīs* always remained loyal to Jaipur. During the end of the 18th and the beginning of the 19th centuries, an era of constantly shifting princely fortunes when Vaishnava and Shaiva Nagas switched masters as easily as did other mercenaries, the Dadu-*panthī* Nagas remained firm in their allegiance to the Jaipur throne (*ibid.*, 205). Even during the 1857 rebellion, which invoked Indian religious sentiment against the British, the Dadu-*panthī* Nagas maintained their loyalty to the Jaipur state and through Jaipur to the British crown.[18]

What might be some reasons for this steadfast allegiance of the Dadu-*panthī* Nagas to the Jaipur state? It could have derived in part from historical causes. The Dadu-*panthīs* developed as a vital military force during a period when Nagas from many traditions had already begun to serve rajas in large numbers. The fact that the Dadu-*panthī* Nagas emerged later than other Naga groups might be one reason why their traditions as fighting men were informed at least as much by state service as by independent marauding. But another possible reason for the Dadu-*panthīs*' unswerving loyalty to the Jaipur court might have to do with what happens when the *sant* tradition evolves in a region that idealizes royal authority.

The rise of guru devotion in most post-classical Indian traditions – Vaishnava, Shaiva and *sant* – coincided historically with the fragmentation of Hindu political power in the medieval period. Like temporal power, spiritual power came to be seen as residing less in distant sovereigns that in specific individuals at hand. Gurus, I have argued elsewhere (Gold 1987b), came to be seen in the image of feudal lords, and feudal lords were of course military men. The guru as military chief thus did not appear as an extraordinary religious phenomenon. At best, these chiefs could be powerful, charismatic individuals, initiating young men into the order and training them in military practice. The loyalty soldiers often feel toward strong, nurturing leaders could then be assimilated to the bonds that traditionally tie a disciple to a powerful guru. Indian ideals of devoted service to a spiritual master thus became transmuted into those of dedicated military service to a warrior chief. As objects of veneration, however, the Naga chiefs of the Dadu-*panth* differed from those found in Vaishnava and Shaiva traditions. The latter were ideally understood as incarnations of Vishnu or Shiva, their authority thus strengthened by the full weight of powerful myth from the Great Tradition. The Nagas of the Dadu-*panth*, which rejects the iconic imagery of the Great Tradition, had to seek other sources of symbolic power. It was to this end, I would suggest, that they turned to the Jaipur throne.

Of the many vehicles of the immanent divine found in the Little Traditions of India, perhaps the one most crucial to the workings of princely rule is the royal throne, the *gaddī* – in fact as well as literal meaning an elaborately covered "cushion." Not only a symbol of the state's legitimacy, the *gaddī* also has a power of its own, a *śakti*, which it gives to the ruler. According to the former Maharaja of Dewas, people's duty to the raja entails both "loyalty to the person sitting on the *gaddi and* to the *gaddi* itself" (Mayer 1982:144). And of the *gaddī* and the raja as objects of loyalty, the *gaddī*, representing the state, is the more real – in the Hindu religious sense of having an unchanging, permanent basis. Thus the *gaddī* "since its foundation has been, is, and shall be whether there is a Ruler or no Ruler. The *gaddi is*" (*ibid.*, 145). So even when nobles fall out with their raja and do not go to the palace to visit him personally, they still attend court ceremonies exalting the *gaddī* (*ibid.*, 144). The symbolic power of the *gaddī*, then, together with the elaborate pageantry of the court, were resources from the princely regional tradition that could enhance the authority of a military leader.

Brought into the Jaipur establishment with state grants and as recognized divisions of the Jaipur military, the Dadu-*panthī* Nagas had evident material incentives for loyalty to the state. But the authority they derived from the Jaipur court made them less flexible in their political allegiance than were the Shaiva and Vaishnava Nagas. The Shaiva and Vaishnava gurus, considered to be icons of the great Hindu gods, could move from state to state for short-term profit without any loss of symbolic power. The gurus of the Dadu-*panthī* Nagas, by contrast, had established their position and glory in the Jaipur court, and it was for the Jaipur *gaddī* that their men learned to fight.

By the 19th century, the Dadu-*panthīs* had thus developed traditions that drew on the elevation of princely power found in Rajput culture. Not only were the Dadu-*panthī* soldiers able to harmonize religious devotion and political loyalty, but Dadu-*panthī* scholars were likewise able to combine scholarship with aristocratic privilege and open-handedness. On the one hand, Dadu-*panthī* Nagas worked as tax men for the rajas, while on the other,

Dadu-*panthī* gentlemen-scholars enjoyed state patronage and could avoid taxes as mendicants. These complementary niches found by Dadu-*panthī* soldiers and scholars in the Jaipur state structure are brought out in a story Narayandas tells about Maniramji, a disciple of the great 19th century scholar Nishchal Das (1978-79:II, 856-857). As a physician, Maniramji is said to have kept on amassing wealth and, emulating the Kshatriya model, distributing it to a large circle of dependents. When a Jaipur tax officer, hearing of Maniramji's great wealth, came to make an assessment, he found nothing of value stored away, but saw Maniramji feeding a long line of beggars. The tax man questioned Maniramji: "If you give everything away to the poor, then you'll have nothing left for yourself!" "If it turns out like that," Maniramji replied, "then I'll join the line of beggars myself" (*ibid.*:II,. 857). Pleased with this answer, the tax man left empty-handed.

The Dadu-*Panth* and the Decline of Princely Power in Rajasthan

As a religious sect that was closely tied to the Jaipur court, the Dadu-*panth* had a firm institutional base within the princely political structure of Rajasthan. In this, it differed from religious communities with a strong presence in Rajasthan, but grounded in the Sanskritic tradition and including many adherents outside the region. And while these communities (e.g. the Vallabha *sampradāy*)[19] continue to thrive in modern India, neither the soldiers nor the scholars of the Dadu-*panth* have successfully withstood the collapse of princely power in Rajasthan.

With the establishment of British paramountcy over the princely states in the 19th century, the Dadu-*panthī* Nagas lost much of their value as military troops. Yet by then they had become a traditional fixture of the Jaipur court. Long after their military usefulness had ended, the Nagas remained as honor guards for the Jaipur raja, and were not formally disbanded until 1938.[20] For ordinary members of the *panth* today, Naga institutions remain as cherished memories. Evoking nostalgia for most, Naga traditions are still carried on as sport by a few. Even today, Dadu-*panthīs* around Jaipur continue to study the martial arts, and give public performances at the *panth*'s major festivals.

The scholars of the Dadu-*panth* have also declined as a specifically Dadu-*panthī* community. This decline may be related to the role they played in pre-Independence Rajputana, where they may be said to have mediated the Great Tradition to the regional elite. In this role, the Dadu-*panthī* scholars naturally experienced conflicts of loyalty and identity. In a story related by Narayandas about Nishchal Das (1978-79:II, 836-837), the distress created by these conflicts is shown as having lead to actual physical symptoms. A Jat who had to pose as a Brahman in order to study the Vedas with a pandit in Banaras, Nishchal Das is said to have revealed his true identity to avoid a marriage – only to be cursed to a daily fever by the angry father of the girl. The only way he was able to stop this fever, the story goes, was by returning to his guru's place and reading Dadu's verses daily. When Dadu-*panthī* scholars today experience conflicts similar to those of Nishchal Das, many make the opposite choice, opting for the Brahmanical Great Tradition instead of the Dadu-*panthī* identity. Not only has the power of the regional elite they had served as mediators diminished in modern India, but the secrets of the Great Tradition itself are more publicly available. A few Dadu-*panthī* scholars have as a result achieved scholarly recognition far outside the parochial confines of the *panth* – e.g. teaching Pali at the Sanskrit University of Banaras, or presiding over an All-India Ayurvedic Conference in Calcutta (Jain and Jain 1935:20-21).

The tendency among educated Dadu-*panthīs* to identify closely with Hindu, particularly Vaishnava, tradition was already evident by the 18th century in the *Bhaktamāl* of Raghav Das, which includes short biographies of Dadu-*panthīs* and other *sants* alongside those of Vaishnava devotees. Today, both educated and uneducated Dadu-*panthīs* around Jaipur usually refer to themselves flatly as Vaishnavas.[21] They tend to think of themselves, and are often recognized by others, as one of many Hindu Vaishnava sects.[22]

This Vaishnava identity assumed by Dadu-*panthīs* today differs from stances taken toward the Great Tradition of Hinduism by both the Kabir-*panthīs* and the Sikhs. Kabir-*panthīs* often identify themselves as Vaishnavas – though not as a mere Vaishnava sect. Instead, they boast that they are "*param* Vaishnavas," the highest Vaishnavas of all, clearly different from others.[23] The Sikhs, of course, are not Vaishnavas by anyone's standards. Though most of them have Hindu origins, and some families in the Punjab include both Sikh and Hindu members, Sikhs in the last decades of the

20th century have increasingly stressed their own distinct identity. Indeed the Sikh cause has now become equated by many with Punjabi regional autonomy.

Thus all three of the *sant panths* discussed here have dealt differently with the conflicting aims of the renunciatory Sanskritic tradition, regional identity, and royal authority. The Kabir-*panthīs*, with the least regional identity of the three, began as a renunciatory alternative to Brahmanical tradition and now stand as a distinct adjunct to it. The Sikhs have long had a stronger regional identity, probably important in making the Guru a political as well as a religious leader. In Sikh nationalism today, the great renunciatory strain that Sikhism shares with much Indian religion appears subordinated to the political imperatives of Punjabi regionalism. In the Dadu-*panth* too, the renunciatory tradition historically has served regional political imperatives. In contrast to the Sikhs, however, the Dadu-*panthī* military leaders, while carrying religious authority for those under their command, ceded political authority to the state. As much as the support of the Jaipur state and the dominant role of Rajputs in the *panth* may have nurtured Dadu-*panthī* institutions, it may also have limited the *panth*'s scope – both numerically and religiously. Never having developed the strong, independent traditions one finds among the Kabir-*panthīs* and the Sikhs, Dadu-*panthīs* today find themselves becoming increasingly absorbed into conventional Hinduism.

The Dadu-*panth*, then, grew up within the Rajput state system and collapsed with its decline. Developing celibate orders that often drew more support from the princely elite than from a large popular following, it displays the transitory nature of any religious institution that has become dependent on impermanent temporal authority. Yet at the same time, the vitality of the *panth* during its heyday attests to the power of the authority that nurtured it, thus confirming the crucial role of princely power in pre-modern Rajasthan.

ENDNOTES

1. Armed ascetics known as Nagas – a word that refers literally to their nearly "naked" state in battle (Orr 1940:94) – have been identified in many Indian

religious orders from the 16th century onward, and were highly visible in the wars accompanying the final collapse of the Mughal empire. On the Nagas, see Orr 1940 and Lorenzen 1978.

2. In 1947, W.G. Orr, a Scottish missionary who had long worked in Jaipur, published a study of Dadu and his tradition. It still contains the fullest scholarly English translation of Dadu's verses, and some of the only accessible information on the Dadu-*panthī* Nagas. In works devoted largely to the religious and literary import of Dadu's verses, Sharma (1969) and Singh (1971) have little new information to offer on the *panth*. More recently, fresh material has been brought to light by Callewaert, who has explored the Dadu-*panthī* texts (1973, 1974b, 1977a) and translated two of the more interesting of them (1974a, 1977b, 1988). His monograph on Dadu's disciple Rajjab (1978) provides a critical review of the scholarship on Dadu. Thiel-Horstmann (1983) has recently undertaken field studies on the Dadu-*panth*.
3. In January, 1988, I was able to meet Narayandas in Ajmer, where he is revered as a scholar and religious teacher. Sitting on the floor of his small fourth-story room, pen in hand and surrounded by old manuscripts, he presented a striking image of an urban scholarly *sādhū*. When asked about the sources for his history, Narayandas indicated that in this book more than in many of his others, he relied on lore he was able to remember personally or draw out from his wide circle of Dadu-*panthī* acquaintances. The ways in which Narayandas's reliance on personal resources have structured his work is suggested by his treatment of the military branch of the Dadu-*panth*. A scholar himself, Narayandas has given the Naga lineages only limited attention: one chapter (ch. 11), out of a total of 18 (1978-79:III, 1-224). He notes there, moreover, that he was hampered in his efforts at further research by the enmity of a Naga guru who kept slandering him (*ibid*., III, 70-71). As if to make up for this lack, though, Narayandas is able to offer a lyrical account of Naga customs recalled from his lengthy childhood visits to their settlements during the early decades of the present century (*ibid*., III, 60-68).
4. In Tapaswi's contemporary Kabir-*panthī* work, a thousand-page verse tome recounting legends of Kabir, conversations with ascetics from orthodox traditions are found scattered throughout the section treating the *sant*'s encounters with Hindu and Muslim royalty (1976:333-472). On the one side, then, we have the combined forces of religious orthodoxy and political authority; on the other, the challenge of Kabir.
5. On the Hindi *sant* tradition, see Schomer and McLeod 1987, which contains essays presenting different perspectives, and Gold 1987a, which focuses on guru devotion among the *sants*.
6. For example, Kabir is said to have incarnated in all the four ages of the Hindu cycle. The *Anurāg Sāgar*, an important Kabir-*panthī* manuscript where this and other esoteric doctrines are articulated, is accessible in English as *The Ocean of Love* (Bagga 1982).
7. The most important critical work on the Sikhs has been done by W.H. McLeod. His 1968 volume treats the life and traditions of Guru Nanak; his 1976 volume covers the development of the Sikh *panth*.
8. On the caste background of the Sikhs, see McLeod 1976:92-104. For the Kabir-*panthīs*, see Lorenzen 1987:292-303.

PATRONAGE FOR THE ARTS AND THE RISE OF THE ALWAR STATE

EDWARD S. HAYNES

During the 18th century the Rajput states of northern India achieved a new level of autonomous political power under the faltering Mughal imperial umbrella. As the central authority of the empire declined, local Rajput chieftains gained increasing independence and sovereignty. Centralized stability gave way to a more fluid system in which emergent local rulers were relieved of the external sanctions that had maintained the political equilibrium in north India since at least the reign of Akbar. This new regional political dynamic – especially in the eastern areas of Rajasthan - led to a resurgence of tensions inherent in Rajput political and kinship systems, and resulted in the establishment of new regionally based states. Without the overarching presence of a paramount power with both the will and strength to maintain stability, the newly independent ruling lineages and states could secure political and economic independence only through careful use of their intricate kinship networks and prevailing norms of rulership and power.

Patronage of the arts was one important way for these newly independent rulers to enhance their status and legitimacy. This paper examines the ways it was used by the Rajput rulers of Alwar State (or, as it was known at the time, Macheri *rāj*) in order to first secure and then maintain their position of power. It will examine in particular the changing relationship between arts patronage and the requirements of the state and its ruling lineage, showing how both patronage patterns and the environment in which the state existed changed from the 18th to 20th centuries.

Alwar State emerged in the 1770s when Pratap Singh Naruka, head of a cadet branch (*tār*) of Jaipur's ruling Kachhwaha clan (*kul*), was able to declare, obtain, and sustain his independence from the Jaipur state (Haynes 1978a). In a period when Jaipur's internal stability was weakened by a regency administration which he himself dominated, Pratap Singh founded a new independent political entity in Jaipur's mountainous northeastern territory between the centers of power of Jaipur and Delhi,[1] basing his claim to rule on the support of his kindred Naruka Rajputs. Like other rulers in the area (including Jaipur), Pratap Singh and his successors saw patronage of the arts as a means of validating, symbolizing and supporting their dynasty. Each raja used this patronage in different ways. As this paper will show, both the role and the patterns of patronage changed as the state and its rulers became more firmly established or had to look in different directions for their external political sanction.

Kinship, Patronage and Power in the Rajput State

The Rajput state system within which Pratap Singh Naruka (*r.* 1775-91) and his successors had to function was based on the theoretically coequal right of all major families within the ruling lineage to participate in the management of the lineage territories comprising their corporate state. Moreover, within these areas, there were often preexisting chieftains who by no means accepted the primacy of the new rulers and, therefore, had to be subdued. The survival of the *rāj* (state and ruling lineage conjoined) demanded that the ruler find means to establish stability and to balance the external challenges of his foes on the battlefield with the internal dynamics of a kinship system that made all kinsmen potential challengers. The maintenance of such a conquest state – often characterized as "feudal" – required a careful balancing of centrifugal and centripetal forces within the segmentary lineages of the state's ruling elite.[2] Challengers from both within and without the ruling lineage often posed major threats to the raja's position; at best, the ruler's status was that of "first among equals." Commonly, the military force needed to establish and defend the state was provided solely by the ruler's senior landholding kinsmen, the *jāgīrdārs*, and was therefore inadequate for securing and maintaining the primacy of the lineage head. To achieve these aims, the ruler had to distinguish himself from his kinsmen and potential rivals by embracing the entire arsenal of traditional emblems associated with power and rule.

These emblems of power were of greater utility in establishing

Pratap Singh's indepedence from his nearer kinsmen – including those in Jaipur – than in suppressing preexisting non-Naruka chiefs. His ability to award, augment or revoke *jāgīr* and durbar honors, for example, went beyond simple economic considerations. Status, "face," and *'izat* (honor) were all extremely important in the Rajput system. Alliances could be made or positions strengthened by the award of titles or a more prestigious place in formal durbar. The ceremonials of the durbar served as open confirmation of the primacy of the raja, and as an opportunity to act out the relationships that supported the organic structure of the state.[3]

The new Alwar regime's need for legitimizing symbols extended beyond its territory. Pratap Singh sought and obtained such legitimacy from the Mughal empire as well. In 1778, he received a *sanad* to hold his territories in technical *jāgīr* from Emperor Shah Alam II; in addition, he was confirmed officially in his presumptive title of "Rao Raja" and was awarded other insignia of honor, including the prestigious *`Māhī-o-Marātib*.[4] Although the political and military power of the Mughal empire was much reduced by this time, its value as a source of sovereignty was still important. Imperial sanction alone could no longer sustain a new conquest state, but the remnants of Delhi's symbolic authority were still sought by local rulers such as Pratap Singh. Mughal titles served as an additional buttress to whatever legitimacy the Alwar ruler had obtained independently.[5] Pratap Singh Naruka also experimented with alliances with the Marathas. His successor, Bakhtawar Singh (*r.* 1791-1815), further secured the state and lineage with an 1803 *sanad* and engagement from the East India Company.

As useful as such external recognition of legitimacy may have been in the formation and maintenance of Alwar State, internal symbol management was more necessary. To mark his emergence as something more than a mere lineage head and local chieftain, it was necessary for Pratap Singh to adopt the accepted trappings of the Rajput raja as they had developed in eastern Rajputana in a blending of Hindu and Perso-Turkish ideologies of statecraft (Fox 1971:58-127; Haynes 1984). To a greater degree than ordinary Rajput chieftains, a ruler was expected to be not only a leader on the battlefield and the dispenser of largess to his followers and kinsmen, but also an active patron of culture and the arts. In accordance with the traditional Brahman-Kshatriya relationship of ancient Aryan society, the raja was expected to grant revenue-producing lands to religious institutions and indigent *paṇḍits*. In the eclectic Rajput style, however, this state patronage of religion was extended to Islamic institutions as well as Hindu. In contrast to the situation in southern India, however, the Rajput raja's involvement as a direct patron of organized religion was not a necessary precondition to or determinant of his royal power and authority.[6] While in both regions symbols of the divine clustered about the raja, the Rajput ruler was not in the same close relationship to temples and religious leaders as were southern rulers. He depended instead on support by secular elements, particularly his kinsmen, the landholding *jāgīrdārs* of the state. Yet this very support structure could hinder the emergence of the ruler as anything more than seniormost *jāgīrdār*. To place more distance between the ruler and his kinsmen, other symbols of power were desirable, one of which was patronage of the arts.

A raja was traditionally expected to be a patron of the arts, an activity which came to be seen as both the responsibility of a ruler and an emblem of his status. All too frequently, the arts in Rajasthan have been examined piecemeal, in isolation from the political culture which has traditionally supported them, with more attention devoted to their artistic quality than to their larger social and political function. By viewing the arts as an integral part of the state system, our appreciation of the Rajput state and Rajput art alike can be placed in context.

The expectation that a king should support the arts is implicit in both Hindu and Persian theories of kingship (Kangle 1960; Jahangir 1968:I, 7-8). One of the strongest statements of this expectation is found in the *Arthaśāstra* (2.27.28), which advises the prince to

> provide maintenance from the king's exchequer to the (teacher) who imparts . . . the knowledge of the arts of singing, playing on musical instruments, reciting, dancing, acting, writing, painting, playing on the lute, the flute, and the drum, reading the thoughts of others, preparing perfumes and garlands, entertaining in conversation, shampooing and the courtesan's art. (Kangle 1960; Basham 1954:90)

Moreover, arts patronage was seen in both traditions as a visible indicator of the ruler's good taste and, presumably, of his worthiness to rule. Royal patronage of religious institutions might placate a faction whose sanction was necessary for the raja's accession and reassure them of his religious fervor. However, the feeding of *paṇḍits* or cows was hardly an act likely to inspire awe or occasion great public note of the ruler's presence on the throne.[7] If managed on a proper scale, patronage of the arts could serve as a powerful reenforcement of the raja's right to rule, a sign that his status was greater than that of his kinsmen. This concern was reflected in a popular Dhuṅdhari proverb of Pratap Singh Naruka's time, "*Kaī nāṅv gītarāṅ kaī bhīṅtaṛāṅ*," which can be roughly translated as "One's name can be perpetuated either in ballads or by buildings" (Bahura 1976:77-78). For the rulers of Alwar, a sensitivity for and large-scale patronage of the arts could thus become a powerful legitimizing and advertising factor for state, dynasty, and ruler. For the rajas of Alwar, this was especially true in light of the Kachhwaha tradition of arts patronage.

Arts Patronage in Alwar's Formative Years, 1775-1826

Although issues of personal and dynastic survival dominated the decisions of Pratap Singh Naruka at the time he achieved his independence from Jaipur, he also managed to bring to Alwar several artists, notably Daluram, Dalchand and Shivkumar – all well-known but hardly prominent painters at the Jaipur court. As was typical, given the shifting patterns of allegiance in Alwar at the time, Shivkumar, who was a specialist in miniature painting, remained with Pratap Singh only briefly before returning to Jaipur; Dalchand then moved to prominence in this specialization (Neeraj 1969: 150; Gupta 1969:1).

The artistic achievements of Alwar were directly linked to broader political and patronage patterns. There was a long and well established tradition of fresco wall painting in eastern Rajasthan (Agarwal 1969, Khandalavala 1974:1-4; Wacziarg and Nath 1982; Aggarwala 1977). The earliest reference to it is an account of Sultan Jalaluddin Khilji's conquests (*ca*. 1290-96) where "exquisite paintings on the walls of the palace" at Jhain are described. More to the point for Pratap Singh, however, were the elaborate murals in Raja Bharmal's *chhatrī* at Amber, which probably dates from the period 1590-1614.[8] Other examples from Jaipur State must have been known to Pratap Singh Naruka, for the fresco tradition was well established and included such important sites as Bairat, Bhaopura, and Mozamabad. In the early years of state formation in Rajasthan, it was not surprising that such public art forms should receive more patronage than the more private artistic forms – miniature painting, calligraphy, book binding, dance, music, or poetry. As in Renaissance Italy, a politically sensitive mural tradition could be used to increase the public image of a ruler and the overall impact of court ceremonial.

This was the pattern followed in Alwar. Even before Pratap Singh's open break with Jaipur in 1778, he had attempted to express a degree of independence when he laid out plans for the expanded city of Rajgarh in 1770. He saw this new city as a mark of his independence and ordered the construction of a new fort and street system which, while drawing from the Jaipur tradition of politicized public architecture and urban planning, also incorporated elements from Mughal architecture. Even after his seizure of the city of Alwar in 1775 and the gradual transfer of his seat of administration to this older Pathan city (some 20 km to the north), Pratap Singh's base of ceremonial power remained in "his" fort and city at Rajgarh (Neeraj 1969:150).

Under Daḷuram's direction (and perhaps in his own hand), frescoes were added to the Shish Mahal (or "Palace of Mirrors") in the Rajgarh fort which dominated the core region of Naruka Kachhwaha power in Alwar. The Shish Mahal, which functioned as a ceremonial center within the fort (serving as a hall of public audience, as we can reconstruct its 18th-century structure and function today), was a more accessible area than most within the fort and thus appears to have been designed to impress both close kinsmen (all potential rivals) and the wider populace. While there is some evidence that the present frescoes were completed (or refurbished) during the reign of Pratap Singh's successor, Bakhtawar Singh, it is obvious that such an artistic venture served political as well as aesthetic purposes (Neeraj 1972:39-42; 1969:150-151).

In October 1866, when the French traveler Louis Rousselet passed through Rajgarh, the buildings still had tattered draperies hanging and the Shish Mahal paintings were still very bright.

> The principal hall is inlaid with pieces of glass of different colours, amongst which are placed beautiful golden arabesques; and the panels are ornamented with curious frescoes representing the principal Raos of Matchery [Macheri] and are mytho-

> logical and other scenes. These frescoes are executed with great delicacy, and most of them contain thousands of figures. There is a verandah in front of this hall, supported by fine marble pillars, the dome of which, worked in stucco, is made to resemble a golden curtain embroidered with flowers and animals. On the right-hand side of the verandah hangs a superb picture, representing the descent of King Pertab Singh into the Elysian fields where Krishna reigns; on the other side there is a fresco of the same dimensions, representing the enthronement of Pertab Singh, presided over by Krishna. (Rousselet 1876:250-251)

While the metaphors drawn by Rousselet are (at best) mixed, his identification of Krishna somewhat suspect, and his "Elysian fields" not visible in the surviving frescoes, the political statement of the paintings is clear: the rebel chieftain of Macheri has been transformed into the raja of Alwar, and he is under divine sponsorship. Indeed, it cannot be coincidental that this message is delivered in the entryway, one of the most public areas of the Shish Mahal. Whether portrayed in armed procession – mounted on an elephant with his troops and retainers clustered on the ground about him – or in formal durbar with courtiers and dancers, Pratap Singh Naruka was shown with all the proper characteristics of a ruler, and any who doubted his status had only to look around the Rajgarh Shish Mahal. It was, in fact, to the courtyard in front of the Rajgarh Shish Mahal that Pratap Singh brought his most potent rivals for conferences and, frequently, for their subsequent executions.

Pratap Singh's successor, Bakhtawar Singh, continued the development of the school of art that had emerged under the patronage of the state's founder. The more urgent military and political concerns which had faced Pratap Singh during the early years of Alwar's existence had precluded his wide-ranging patronage of the arts. The more public arts had suited his political needs more directly and had therefore received his patronage, while the private arts had been ignored. Bakhtawar Singh, by contrast, was a poet (writing unremarkable verse under the pen names "Chandrasakhi" and "Bakhtesh") and this artistic sensitivity, combined with the more settled conditions in the state, encouraged the development of an independent and self-conscious school of art which drew from both Rajput and Mughal traditions (Neeraj 1969:151-152).

The growth of the Alwar school of miniature painting under Bakhtawar Singh's patronage has often been attributed simply to his good taste or some ethereal desire to support the arts, but the simple availability of trained artists from other areas of northern India was equally important. By the late 18th century, the ability of the Mughal court, its satellite courts and many of the major Rajput courts to maintain large numbers of painters was waning. As artists such as Baldev and Saligram came to Alwar for employment in the early years of the 19th century, the older Rajput heritage of Dalchand was broadened by contact with the more cosmopolitan Mughal style and a composite Alwar school of painting began to emerge (Neeraj 1972:152; Gupta 1969:1-2).

This new Alwar artistic tradition became important under Bakhtawar Singh not only as a means to impress potential rivals or coequal kinsmen with the sophistication and grandeur of Alwar state, but also because the very act of patronizing the arts was seen as appropriate for an independent Rajput raja. Patronage for private artistic expression increased along with the stability and financial base of the state. Bakhtawar Singh's requirements of art were not those of his predecessor, and the directions of his patronage make this clear.

Perhaps because the Alwar school of painting is comparatively late and regionally limited, it has not received the attention that has been directed by art historians to other Rajput schools and to Mughal painting. Ananda Coomaraswamy's classic work on Rajput painting avoids any mention of an Alwar school beyond indicating the location of Alwar city on his map (1977:11-12). Furthermore, the Alwar school of artistic expression is only incompletely represented by miniature painting. A full appreciation of the intertwined Alwar traditions requires attention to frescoes, as well as screen painting and carving, calligraphy and book binding, armory, poetry and other literary forms, architecture and the performing arts (although these last mentioned are especially difficult to document). Few specimens of Alwar painting or other art are present in the major museums of Indian art, and even these tend to be dismissed by most art historians as less professional and less attractive than other works of the last 18th century (Neeraj 1969:150).

Arts patronage under the rulers of Alwar went hand-in-hand with the importation of a new state bureaucracy which added administrative substance to the state and demonstrated the growing political and symbolic distance between the ruler and his *jāgīrdārs* (Haynes 1975:21-28). As was the case with the imported artists, the bureaucrats came from many areas and backgrounds. Among these early imported administrators were a number of Muslims of Transoxanian Seljuk origin. Several related families came to Alwar in the first years of the 19th century. The progenitors of the two major families to take service in Alwar were Qasim Jah (whose son, Ahmad Baksh Khan, was granted the independent state of Loharu by Lord Lake in 1803 for his services during the Second Maratha War) and the father of Abdulla Beg Khan Bahadur. Abdulla Beg's father (whose name is not known) had held a position with Nawab Asaf-ud-Daula of Oudh since 1775. In 1802, after a few intervening years in the service of Nawab Nizam Ali Khan of Hyderabad, Abdulla Beg entered Alwar service. Soon after his arrival in Alwar, however, he was killed in battle while in state service. This left his five-year-old son, Mirza Asadullah Khan (later to be better known by his pen name of 'Ghalib') under the care of Abdulla Beg's brother Nasrulla Beg, who was also the brother-in-law of the new ruler of Loharu, Ahmad Baksh Khan (Ghalib 1969:23, 44-45, 370; Russell 1972). As will be seen, it is of more than coincidental interest that Ghalib, perhaps the most famous Persian and Urdu poet of his age, had Alwar connections. Ghalib and the artist-patron (or bureaucrat-patron) tradition that he and his family represented were characteristic of values of reciprocal loyalty and patronage that survived in states such as Alwar even as they were passing in the wider north Indian world. Beyond adding complexity to the state system of Alwar, such intertwining bureaucratic lineages and linkages also represent the integration of cultural (as well as political) affairs in Alwar into a larger network of north Indian, Delhi-centered, events.

The Alwar-Tijara School of Art, 1826-1845

At the time of Bakhtawar Singh's death in 1815, there was no clear successor and the right to the Alwar *gaddī* was contested by his nephew Banni Singh and his son by a Muslim "concubine," Balwant Singh (Haynes 1978a:441-451). To resolve this rivalry, the state was partitioned by the British in 1826, with Banni Singh receiving power in Alwar (and the southern and western parts of the state) and Balwant Singh taking power as the semi-independent raja of Tijara (in the predominantly Muslim north-north-eastern corner). In addition to the political and administrative partition, this resolution of the disputed succession led to a split in the Alwar school of art, yet the artistic tradition now shared between Alwar and Tijara grew substantially during the first half of the 19th century. As the power and wealth of the Mughals continued to decline during the reigns of Emperors Muhammad Akbar II (*r.* 1806-37) and Bahadur Shah II 'Zafar' (*r.* 1837-58), so did their ability to act as patrons of the arts. Scholars, craftsmen, artists and musicians came to Alwar and Tijara from posts in Delhi and, to a lesser extent, from Agra. Many of these new artists were drawn to Alwar and Tijara not only by proximity and the available patronage, but also through ties of kinship with members of the Alwar and Tijara bureaucracies.[9]

The painter Baldev, who had come to Alwar in Bakhtawar Singh's time, remained at Alwar as chief artist, obtained a position of ceremonial prominence in Banni Singh's durbar, and personally taught painting to the ruler. Other painters such as Gulam Ali Khan, Kari Adb-al-Rahman and Gangasivhan came to Alwar from Delhi at this time and further enriched Alwar's artistic tradition by bringing new techniques and new influences from the declining Mughal workshops. Under Banni Singh's patronage, the manufacture of swords, sword fittings and armor rose to a position of prominence in Alwar. As in Renaissance Europe and Tokugawa Japan, when weapons and armor ceased to be tools of warfare and became pieces of artistry to publicly display the warrior virtue of the rulers and nobility, the armorer moved from craftsman to artist. The sword makers Mohammed Sheikh and Haji Nuru Mohammed, the damascer Sheikh Rahimullah, and the hilt maker Ahmed Baksh all rose to prominence in Banni Singh's court (Gupta 1973). Patronage was also extended to musicians during Banni Singh's reign, and was dominated by the *dhrupad* singer Behram Khan Dagar, who came to Alwar from Bahadur Shah's court in Delhi after prior service with Maharaja Ranjit Singh at Lahore. Behram Khan was related to Allah Bande Khan and his son Hussain Uddin, also musicians at Alwar who appear to have been instrumental in drawing Behram Khan into Alwar service (Erdman 1985:103; Neuman 1980:119). In addition, other skilled artists came to Banni Singh's court, notably the calligrapher Agha Mirza Dehalavi and the book binders Nattha Khan Darvesh and

Abdul Rahman. Unlike most artists who came to Alwar at this time, Abdul Rahman came from Lahore, where he had learned his art at the court of Ranjit Singh (Hendley 1888:ch. 9).

Combining forces, Baldev, Gulam Ali, Agha Mirza, and Nattha Khan produced many beautiful volumes for Banni Singh, most importantly a copy of Sheikh Muslih-ud-din Sa'di's *Gulistān* which was completed in 1856, after twelve years of work, and is reported to have cost over a lakh of rupees to prepare (Neeraj 1972:152-53; Gupta 1973:1-2; Government of Rajasthan 1961:97; Hendley 1888:ch. 9). The *Gulistān* had been a classic focus for Persian royal patronage, as it stressed the fruits of royal justice, the joys of a prosperous domain and the impact of the good ruler in securing the welfare of state and subjects alike (Hodgson 1974:306). Therefore, it was not surprising that the Persian classic became a frequent subject for Banni Singh's artists. Five elaborate copies survive in the Alwar Museum today (Government of Rajasthan 1961). But to what ends would the production of costly copies of the *Gulistān* have been directed? There would certainly have been little or no circulation of the books outside the court, and literacy among the Alwar *jāgīrdārs* was, at best, rare. What is more likely is that the production of these treatises on kingly virtue was directed at the imported administrative classes of Alwar and may have been an attempt to reinforce the raja's status in their eyes by the use of a cultural idiom and symbol familiar to the north Indian administrative elite.

In Tijara, the Alwar school of art – or, rather, the sibling Tijara school – was also able to draw skilled artists from Delhi. The largest number of surviving works in Tijara were probably produced in this prolific satellite school under the patronage of raja Balwant Singh. When Tijara State was formed, the painter Saligram moved there from Alwar, leaving the shadow of Baldev to become the central personality in the art of the new state. In addition, the painter Chotelal came to Tijara from Jaipur and introduced the technique of stippling into the Alwar-Tijara artistic tradition. Other artists who availed themselves of Balwant Singh's patronage included Jaman Das, Baksh Ram, Valesh Ram and Nand Ram. While the Rajput and Mughal artistic traditions (and the patronage patterns that had supported them) were declining in their customary seats of patronage, new schools of art were springing up as localized patrons in areas such as Alwar and Tijara were able to fill their durbars with skilled artists seeking patrons. In addition to individuals, the Tijara and (to a lesser extent) Alwar durbars were able to obtain paintings, books and other works of art sold by prominent families in Delhi and Agra. In fact, it appears that large portions of the Mughal imperial library were acquired by the rulers of Alwar and Tijara (Neeraj 1969:153; Gupta 1973:2; Government of Rajasthan 1961:98). After Balwant Singh's death without heir in 1845, both the limited territories and the surviving artists in Tijara reverted to Banni Singh and Alwar.

During the period of Tijara's separation from Alwar, the rivalry between Banni Singh and Balwant Singh introduced new stresses into an already uncertain state system. Pratap Singh's foundation of the state had been secured by a combination of internal subjugation of rivals, external sanctions and symbolic display. Bakhtawar Singh had been able to maintain the state by continuing these practices and, in addition, had attempted to magnify the distinctions between himself as raja and the *jāgīrdārs*. One of the ways he had done this was by increasing his patronage of the arts. Not only had he come to view this patronage as part of his *rājadharma* (royal duty), but it was also very much a part of his *'izat*.

By extension, the political role of arts patronage in Alwar came to affect the life style of state servants brought in to aid in the management of Banni Singh's state. To remove daily administration of lineage territories from succession disputes, and to create a bureaucratic elite responsible only to the raja, Banni Singh, starting in the 1820s, had introduced a new generation of administrators into Alwar. To survive in office, these new, non-*jāgīrdārī* state servants had to link themselves to the raja and adopt some of his emblems of authority (Haynes 1978a:447-450). Around 1828, Banni Singh had brought in a new minister (diwan) from Jaipur, Surput Ram, whose father seems to have served Bakhtawar Singh for a short period of time. With Banni Singh's support, Surput Ram had achieved considerable power in the state and was pressing an aggressive set of reforms (Lockett 1831:31-33). Aiding Surput Ram in this process was another diwan from Jaipur, Balmukand. Shortly after arriving in Alwar around 1830, Balmukand built a *havelī* (mansion) near the central well in the Munshi Bagh neighborhood of Alwar city. As a part of this *havelī*, Balmukand had a Shish Mahal constructed, presumably to be used for entertainments and public audiences. To decorate his Shish Mahal, Balmukand ordered extensive ornamentation, including inlaid mirrors and frescoes covering all the walls. The names of the artists responsible for this work are unknown, but the decorative work, durbar scenes, *rāgamālā* paintings, portraits and other fresco works are well executed and almost certainly the work of artists employed at Banni Singh's court. While generally similar in both theme and execution to the earlier fresco tradition of the Rajgarh Shish Mahal, the frescoes of what is now called "Dewanji ki Haveli" are still impressively fresh and represent a far more sophisticated technical artistry than the wall paintings of Pratap Singh's time (Neeraj 1969:154; 1972).

Arts patronage was assuming greater political significance than simply a personalized indication of royal power. As other members of the raja's administrative elite began to participate in arts patronage, they acquired a portion of the ruler's status and thus were able to associate themselves more closely with the emblems of power in Alwar.

By contrast, there is little evidence of large-scale patronage of the arts by the Alwar *jāgīrdārī* elite. The only significant example of *jāgīrdārī* architecture is the *chhatrī* of the Thana *jāgīrdār*, Hanuwant Singh, constructed about 1860. This *chhatrī* is quite similar to the one prepared for Banni Singh – Hanuwant Singh's brother – after his death in 1857. Located in the *jāgīr* town of Thana, only a few kilometers west of the lineage fort at Rajgarh, the *chhatrī* is today in very good condition and maintained in both artistic and ritual terms. Constructed of white marble and profusely decorated with blue-and-white paintings, Hanuwant Singh's *chhatrī* features the traditional durbar and elephant procession themes, but often depicts the Alwar ruler as well, thereby enhancing the deceased *ṭhikānedār*'s tie to the ruling house (Neeraj 1969:155).

Why did the Alwar *jāgīrdārs* not on the whole adopt wider patronage of the arts to legitimize their power, when the new state servants (non-*jāgīrdārs* and outside the ruling lineage) had been constructing such impressive edifices? A simple answer would be that they did not have the funds at hand for such expenditure. By the early 1850s, the continuing demand that the *jāgīrdārs* maintain horsemen for state service was creating a considerable drain on their resources. Only a senior *jāgīrdārī* lineage such as that of Hanuwant Singh could afford such an expense. New bureaucratic structures had begun to replace older kinship structures as sustainers of the ruler's administration and power. In addition, the Alwar *jāgīrdārs* were (and remained through the early part of this century) fairly "backward" in cultural terms. There may have been patronage of "folk" arts (*khayāl*, popular dance, wrestling etc.), but documentation of this must await closer examination of mid-19th century *jāgīrdārī* records, where such exist. In any case, the Alwar *jāgīrdārs* never appear to have participated in large-scale patronage of the "high" arts, and remained more isolated and on the fringes of cultural trends than their counterparts in other states.

Even the political involvement of Alwar's *jāgīrdārs* was gradually eroding as a result of the raja's importing new bureaucratic classes into the state. Indeed, much of the surviving "royal" architecture that dates from the reign of Banni Singh represents an effort to adopt new idioms of public ceremonial display that would place additional distance between the raja and his kinsmen. The new city palace in Alwar, for example, was constructed not in the fort (on a hill overlooking the town), but at the foot of the hill, in the town, accessible to those outside the kinship elite, whether Indian or British.[10] Thomas Hendley, a scholar of Rajput art who also served as agency surgeon at Alwar, commented on the overall patronage situation as he saw it in 1888:

> The art work is all done for the Court by State Servants, who have been attracted to Ulwar by the munificence of the present [Mungul Singh] or former chiefs. In fact, there are no wealthy persons in the State, and few who may be termed even rich; the Maharaja is really the only person who is in a position to employ artists of any note. (Hendley 1888:ch.5)

The Years of Decline, 1857-1947

After the death of Maharao Raja Banni Singh in 1857, arts patronage in Alwar entered a new era under his son and successor, Sheodan Singh. The new ruler was a minor at the time of his accession and his rule was dominated first by his diwans and after 1858 by British political agents. One of the first priorities of the British officials when they came to Alwar to direct a *jāgīrdār*-dominated Regency Council was to balance the state budget by dismissing what were viewed as wasteful retainers. Beyond the expected reduction in concubines, wrestlers, eunuchs, dancing girls and jugglers, British budget cutting also reduced Alwar's patronage of painters, poets and musicians (Haynes 1975:58-170). Among the prominent artists who found themselves without patronage were the sword makers Mohammed Ibrahim and Panna Lal (although the latter managed to stay on in Alwar), the embroiderers Buland Baksh and Ahmed Khan, the gold and silver worker Lala Nand Kishore (who went to Jaipur), and the musician Behram Khan Dagar (who also chose this moment to seek richer patronage in Jaipur) (Hendley 1888:chs. 7-8, 10; Erdman 1985). Only at this stage is there any sense of a downward filtration, of any increase in *jāgīrdārī* patronage of the arts. Many of the senior Alwar *jāgīrdārs* engaged the now patronless artists, though their taste ran more to dancing girls and eunuchs than to painters or musicians. During this period of intense British intervention in what they saw as the feudal society of Rajasthan, the power of the Alwar *jāgīrdārs* increased, and it was at that very time that they finally began to adopt traditional emblems such as arts patronage.

Sheodan Singh's patronage of the arts extended only slightly beyond his desire to maintain a few of his dancers, musicians and wrestlers. Paintings produced under his limited patronage were mostly within the rich tradition of Indian erotic art. Many of these paintings, difficult to study, partially because they remain uncatalogued, seem to represent the raja's frustrations with the political changes in his state: there are several noteworthy depictions of especially despised political agents engaged in gymnastic sexual activities with concubines and, occasionally, with animals.

Nevertheless, in the years after the "Mutiny" of 1857, many dispossessed artists from Delhi and Agra sought refuge with and patronage from the Rajputana princes. Alwar, with its proximity to the imperial cities and a long tradition of personal bureaucratic and artistic linkages with Delhi and Agra, received many political, military and cultural fugitives. Other artists, even if settled elsewhere, strove to gain contacts and patronage from the princes. One of these was Ghalib, who attempted to gain a place in the Alwar durbar by reference to his father's death in Alwar state service and with the support of friends from Delhi who had entered service under Sheodan Singh. Yet as long as Alwar remained under strict British administrative and financial management (1858-64), Ghalib could find no place there and had to seek patronage from Rampur and other states instead. In September 1862, Ghalib had written to a friend at Alwar: "I hear that in November the Maharaja of Alwar's powers are to be restored, but it will be the same sort of power as God has given to all creatures – all power is in His mighty hand, we mortals are disgraced" (Ghalib 1969:277).[11] Despite his fears regarding the full scope of Sheodan Singh's powers (and, correspondingly, of his ability to extend patronage), Ghalib petitioned another friend in Alwar in January 1864:

> The moment I was weaned of my mother's milk I began eating Alwar's bread . . . . I am sixty-nine years old. I have gone deaf. I cannot walk without a staff or sit up without a pillow or a wall to support my back. I am not a wordly man, but a darwesh. I seek ample honour, and a little wealth. God preserve His Highness! He will both give me honour and bestow wealth upon me. And leaving that aside, I long to look upon his High Highness' splendour. I wrote a poem hailing his accession to the throne with a chronogram, and sent it along with a petition. Why has His Highness not replied to my petition and why has he not sent for me? . . . I ask you as a particular favour to keep this my letter to you carefully and that when His Highness comes you will show it to him. (*Ibid.*, 296)

Despite hints of impending patronage, Ghalib was still without a link with Alwar when he wrote in mid-July 1865:

> I asked . . . [my friend], 'Have you heard from Alwar?' He said, 'No, not this week.' How shall I describe to you the state I am in? I used to chant this verse of mine to myself:
>
> Back! Thronging hosts of black despair lest
> you reduce to dust as well
> The one joy left to me – the joy that
> unavailing struggle brings.
>
> But now this is a song I can no longer sing, because the joy of unavailing struggle has turned to dust. (*Ibid.*, 318-319)

Despite obvious disappointment and failing health, Ghalib

never gave up his quest for patronage in Alwar. In December 1868, two months before his death and four years after Sheodan Singh's return to full power, Ghalib wrote to his contacts in Alwar:

> Last month I had a copy of *Sabad i Chin* [a collection of his later Persian verse] along with a petition, sent to Alwar . . . . Accordingly, this week, I received . . . a letter from His Highness . . . the Raja, in which he . . . has addressed me with titles of great honour and written many kind and gracious things about me. You are on the spot. Did you know of this or not? And if you did, why didn't you write to me? Now I want to ask you whether anyone ever speaks of me in durbar or not, and if they do, in what forms; and when I am mentioned, what does His Highness say? (*Ibid*., 367)[12]

Ghalib received no answer, and died unsummoned by his prospective patron, Maharao Raja Sheodan Singh of Alwar. The real anguish and confusion Ghalib felt must have been shared with other poets, painters, dancers, wrestlers and musicians of the time. The old standards and patterns of patron-artist interaction had changed, and few artists or patrons understood what was taking place. Traditional bonds of loyalty and surrogate kinship had been broken – as much for the *jāgīrdārs* as for the jugglers – and a new system was rising to take their place. Instead of the older linkages, there was a rationalized, utilitarian mode of state administration, one which left no room for traditional arts patronage and, perhaps, none for the patterns of state organization which the older patronage structures and arts had represented and supported. The traditional patronage that might have been extended not only to a famous poet but to the son of an ex-state servant no longer existed in the years after 1857. The older patterns, structures and loyalties had begun to be swallowed up in the change in state system that the extension of an activist British paramountcy into Rajputana implied.

For Sheodan Singh, as for his heir Mungul Singh (*r*. 1874-92), patronage of the traditional fine arts held little interest and less political reward, and the camera increasingly replaced the painter's brush as the recorder of the raja's life style. In fact, there was frequent concern over the passing of the old arts, as the old artistic families died out, literally as well as financially, in the absence of state patronage. In 1888, Thomas Hendley expressed concern that, with the death of the book binder Abdul Rahman (who had come to Alwar in Banni Singh's time), this art form, so advanced in Alwar, was threatened with extinction. Although Abdul Rahman's son had succeeded him, Hendley feared that book binding in Alwar would degenerate into a mere trade.

It is surprising that Hendley, who seems to have grasped so well both Rajput art and Rajput statecraft, could accurately diagnose the problem of decline in the arts but, like so many other British administrators of his day, could not see beyond "Indian character" as an all-purpose explanation to the deeper historical processes at work.

Having fallen on hard times, the old gold and silver workers of Alwar, descendants of Lala Nand Kishore Khati (who had moved to Jaipur where more patronage existed), joined with Panna Lal, one of the last of Alwar's surviving armorers, to produce what must be one of the prime examples of late-19th century Rajput "kitsch": a mammoth silver dining table with glass tubes down each side, through which running water passed to nourish the goldfish swimming beside the diners' plates (Hendley 1888:ch 10; Government of Rajasthan 1961:47).

In what may have represented a Hendley-inspired effort to preserve the old art forms of Alwar, an art school was established in 1888, under the directorship of an Englishman, George Wyatt. However, the school came to assume the nature of a trade school and focused more on modern crafts than on the traditional art forms of Alwar (Hendley 1888:ch. 10).[13]

The standards and expectations of appropriate arts for Rajput patronage had changed. No longer were Rajput rulers expected to patronize the arts of their own culture, the art forms which had long met their specific dynastic, societal or personal needs. The Paramount Power had preferences and peculiar modes and symbols of rule, and if the political agent liked (or was imagined to like) goldfish swimming in his dining table, then state resources would be diverted to assure that he got them. Moreover, the problem extended even beyond British officials. In Alwar especially, the lower and middle levels of the administration had been dominated since the 1880s by professional Indian bureaucrats, migratory ministers who, under British sponsorship, had "improved" the administration of any princely state where the British had gained enough influence to have them placed. With this class in power in Alwar, the wishes of the British rulers of India were anticipated and met without even the necessity of a direct imperial suggestion (Haynes 1978b).[14]

There were also changes in the artistic and architectural preferences of the Indian rulers themselves. Educated in schools such as Mayo College, they had began to adopt values and artistic tastes that made the new arts more appropriate to their perceived status as modern rulers and encouraged them to allow older directions of patronage to atrophy in favor of new pastimes (Gütman 1982). Despite attempts by Maharaja Jai Singh (*r.* 1892-1933) to revive the Alwar school of art by combining it (often uncomfortably) with European styles, the Alwar raja's role as a patron of the arts declined steadily.[15] What support he did extend went to individuals, not to schools, groups or traditions. As often as not, such patronage supported education rather than traditional artistic endeavors. For example, the education of the famous historian K.M. Ashraf (an Alwar native) was paid for – at Jai Singh's inspiration – from Alwar State funds (Ashraf 1969:396-398). Even well into the 20th century, however, the idea of the raja as patron of the arts persisted as part of the ruler's proper responsibility or *dharma*, inclucated both by past tradition and by the instruction given at Mayo College (Haynes 1978b; Sherring 1897; McGreal 1971). In 1925, Jai Singh (already gaining an India-wide reputation for misrule and debauchery), approached the famous Urdu and Hindi author Premchand with unproductive offers of employment – not, perhaps, patronage in the old sense (Premchand 1956:71; Swan 1969:29). This was a last gasp of the old modes of patronage, part of the last Alwar raja's tragic effort at fulfilling his role as he had been taught to understand it.

Conclusion

For the new Rajput states of the 18th and 19th centuries, the problems of state and dynasty maintenance were severe. Trapped by the rival paramount forces of the Mughal empire, the Marathas and the East India Company, as well as threatened by internal tensions in his kinship-based political system, the raja of a state such as Alwar had to secure both the authority and emblems of rule. Lavish patronage of the arts was something that could help set the Alwar rajas apart from their kinsmen, providing a public image to impress and awe potential and actual rivals alike.

The geographic location of Alwar made the acquisition of artists – especially painters – easy, for the patronage of the Naruka Rajputs rulers of Alwar was being extended at the same time as Shah Alam, Muhammad Akbar, and Bahadur Shah were retrenching the artists and artisans of the Mughal empire. Ultimately, for Bakhtawar Singh, Banni Singh and Balwant Singh, patronage of artists became an important emblem of their status as rajas.

Whatever its value in purely artistic terms, the late and short-lived Alwar school of art came to occupy an important niche in the cultural and political life of northeastern Rajputana in the 18th and 19th centuries. From an emblem of the new state's independence, patronage under Bakhtawar Singh, Banni Singh and Balwant Singh changed into a means of validating and acting out the proper role of a ruler – a role challenged by Jaipur, local non-kindred chiefs and the Alwar rajas' own kinsmen. As the new imperial power of the British empire came to dominate politics in Rajasthan, Rajput patronage of the arts was first undercut by fiscal "reforms" and then redirected into channels that would (or were expected to) appeal to the Paramount Power and its representatives, the new source of legitimacy. Sheodan Singh, Mungul Singh and Jai Singh accodingly used patronage to further their interactions with the new imperial representatives. Miniature painting gave way to photography, architecture was formulated to isolate and placate Europeans rather than to emulate relations with kinsmen, and armory turned into the making of trinkets and curiosities to impress (or amuse?) the Crown's representatives.

As Bakhtawar Singh's political requirements had departed from those of Pratap Singh, the forms and patterns of arts patronage were modified by him to mirror changes in the nature of the state. Thus the public artistic advertising of Pratap Singh gave way to a wider range of "cultured" artistic expressions, which continued under Bakhtawar Singh, Banni Singh and Balwant Singh. Architecture and cultural display moved from the placation and domination of rivals to a celebration of the unequal interaction between ruler and subordinates. Arts patronage shifted from the preserve of the ruler to a symbol of association with the ruling house, whether for non-Rajput bureaucrats or for landholding *jāgīrdārs*. Likewise, in the late 19th and early 20th centuries, Sheodan Singh,

Mungul Singh and Jai Singh were forced – by changing political circumstances as much as by overt imperial policies or any independently shifting aesthetic – to redirect the focus of their own patronage for the arts. The camera and modern architectural influences on palace design replaced older modes of artistic and political expression and interaction. Like so many other facts and symbols of Rajputana's nominal independence, the arts and patronage norms of Alwar withered as a result of the growing imposition of British political and cultural paramountcy.

ENDNOTES

The research presented in this paper has been supported by grants from the American Institute of Indian Studies, the National Endowment for the Humanities, and the Shell Companies Foundation. A much earlier version was presented in November 1970 at the annual meeting of the Southwest Conference of the Association for Asian Studies, in Arlington, Texas. Without forcing on them any responsibility for my conclusions, I must acknowledge the encouragement, assistance, advice and toleration of Cathy Asher, John C. Hume, Jr., Jeysingh 'Neeraj', Brijen Goswamy, Joseph Arlinghaus, Thakur Mohan Singhji of Kanota, Gavin Hambly, John F. Richards and – of course – the editorial team for this volume.

1. The youth of the Jaipur ruler presented Pratap Singh Naruka with his opportunity to break away. The independence and legitimacy of Alwar, obtained through what was viewed in Jaipur as circumstances of disloyalty, was not accepted by the "parental lineage" until the 1930s, and some deny it even today.
2. On the general topic of segmentary lineages and Indian feudal polity, see Thorner 1965; Lyall 1876; Haynes 1979a, 1979b; Vyas 1969; Sharma 1977; Ziegler 1973; Perlin and Stein 1985; Stein 1977, 1980.
3. The general issue of ceremonial relations as a mirror of state structure is suggested by Cohn 1977.
4. Literally, "The Insignia of the Fish." It was a large gilded image of a fish, and was intended to be carried in processions. The entire range of Mughal decorations of rank and honor has been little studied.
5. In his study of Banares, Cohn (1959:113) suggests a similar pattern.
6. Comparative studies on South India have been done by Price (1979) and Stein (1980).
7. A contrary example, in a rather different political context, is found in Lodrick 1981:23, 68-80.
8. The latest possible date for this structure is 1621. There is some question whether it is Bharmal's or Man Singh's *chhatrī*.
9. See Bahura 1976:70-85.

10. Similar trends have been examined in the Gangetic Plain by Metcalf (1984).
11. See also Ghalib 1969:160, 227, 257-258, 261.
12. See also Ghalib 1969:254-255, 324, 364.
13. This was a favorite subject for Hendley, who promoted many schools and exhibits in order to encourage a new industrial artistic mode in Jaipur and elsewhere.
14. Consider also the Umaid Bhavan Palace in Jodhpur, begun in 1928 and completed in 1943, as a classic late art deco work and as an employment-providing public works project (Ivory 1975:91-100).
15. Jai Singh is a complex and controversial figure. He is most frequently condemned as a communalist sadist (and worse), but this is an incomplete view of his considerable abilities. A full examination of his life and times is far beyond the scope of this paper.

REFERENCES CITED

Aggarwala, R.A.
1977 *Marwar Murals*. Delhi: Agam Publishers.

Agrawal, O.P.
1969 "A Study of the Techniques of Indian Wall Paintings." *Journal of Indian Museums* 25-26:99-118.

Ashraf, K.M.
1969 "K.M. Ashraf on Himself." In *Kunwar Mohammed Ashraf: An Indian Scholar and Revolutionary 1903-1962*. Horst Kruger, ed., pp. 389-398. Delhi: People's Publishing House.

Bahura, Gopal Narayan
1976 *Literary Heritage of the Rulers of Amber and Jaipur*. Jaipur: Maharaja Sawai Man Singh II Museum.

Basham, A.L.
1954 *The Wonder That Was India*. New York: Grove.

Cohn, Bernard S.
1959 "Political Systems in Eighteenth Century India: The Banaras Region." *Journal of the American Oriental Society* 82:312-320.
1977 "The Mughal, Court Rituals, and the Theory of Authority in the 16th and 17th Centuries." Manuscript.

Coomaraswamy, Ananda
1977 *Rajput Painting*. Vol. 1, Text. Reprint ed. Delhi: Motilal Banarsidass.

Erdman, Joan
1985 *Patrons and Performers in Rajasthan: The Subtle Tradition*. New Delhi: Chanakya Publications.

Fox, Richard G.
1971 *Kin, Clan, Raja, and Rule: State-Hinterland Relations in Preindustrial India*. Berkeley: University of California Press.

Government of Rajasthan
1961 *Catalogue and Guide to Government Museum, Alwar*. Part I. Jaipur: Department of Archaeology and Museums.

Ghalib (Mirza Asadullah Khan)

1969 *Ghalib, Life and Letters*. Vol 1. Edited by Ralph Russell and Kurshidul Islam. Cambridge: Harvard University Press.

Gupta, Mohanlal

1969 *Alwar Sangrahālay ke Chitra*. Alwar: Sarvodaya Press.

1973 *Arms from the Alwar Museum*. Jaipur: Shyam Litho Offest Press.

Gutman, Judith Mara

1982 *Through Indian Eyes*. New York: Oxford University Press.

Haynes, Edward S.

1975 "Jagirdars and Government: The Political Role of the Kinship Elite in Alwar (Rajputana, India), 1858-1910." Ph.D. dissertation, History Department, Duke University.

1978a "Imperial Impact on Rajputana: The Case of Alwar, 1775-1850." *Modern Asian Studies* 12:419-453.

1978b "Alwar: Bureaucracy versus Traditional Rulership: Raja, *Jagirdars*, and New Administrators, 1892-1910." In *People, Princes and Paramount Power*. Robin Jeffrey, ed., pp. 32-64. Delhi: Oxford University Press.

1979a "The Political System of Alwar: Patrimonialism and the *Jagir* System." Paper Presented at the 31st Annual Meeting of the Association for Asian Studies.

1979b "A Corinthian Capital on a Column of Ellora: The Transfer of the Concept of Feudalism to the Rajput States of North India." *Journal of Indian History* 57:152-187.

1984 "Land Use and Land-Use Ethic in Rajasthan, 1850-1980." Paper Presented at the 13th Wisconsin Conference on South Asia.

Hendley, Thomas Holbein

1888 *Ulwar And Its Art Treasures*. London: W. Griggs.

Hodgson, Marshall G.S.

1974 *The Venture of Islam*. Vol. II. *The Expansion of Islam in the Middle Period*. Chicago: University of Chicago Press.

Ivory, James, comp.

1975 *Autobiography of a Princess, Also Being the Adventures of an American Film Director in the Land of the Maharajas*. New York: Harper & Row.

Jahangir

1968 *The Tūzuk-i-Jahāngīrī; or, Memoirs of Jahangir*. Translated by A. Rogers, edited by H. Beveridge. 2nd ed. 2 vols. in 1. Delhi: Munshiram. (1st ed. 1904-14)

Kangle, R.P., transl.

1960 *The Kauṭilīya Arthaśāstra*. 3 vols. Bombay: University of Bombay.

Khandalavala, Karl

1974 *Wall Paintings from Amber*. Delhi: Lalit Kala Akademi.

Lockett, A.

1831 *Bhanswar to Ajmere: Lt. Col. A. Lockett's Narrative of a Journey from Bhuswar in Bhurtpore Territory to a Part of the North-West State (Ajmere), April-June 1831*. Foreign Department Miscellaneous Series, No. 273. New Delhi: National Archives of India.

Lodrick, Deryck O.

1981 *Sacred Cows, Sacred Places: Origins and Survivals of Animal Homes in India*. Berkeley: University of California Press.

Lyall, Alfred C.
1876 "The Rajput States of India." *Edinburgh Review* 144:169-203.
McGreal, Shirley
1971 "A History of Mayo College, Ajmere, India, 1875-1971." Ed. D. dissertation, University of Cincinnati.
Metcalf, Thomas R.
1984 "Princes, Artisans, and Architects: Colonial Building in Princely India, 1850-1930." Paper presented at the 13th Wisconsin Conference on South Asia.
Neeraj, Jeysingh
1969 (ed.) *Vinay: Alwar Ank*. Alwar: Raj Rishi College.
1972 *"Alwar ke Bhiṭṭī-chitra." The Researcher* 12-13:39-42.
Neuman, Daniel M.
1980 *The Life of Music in North India: The Organization of Artistic Tradition*. Detroit: Wayne State University Press.
Perlin, Frank, and Burton Stein
1985 "The Character of Old Regime Societies: State Formation and Economy Reconsidered." *Modern Asian Studies*.
Premchand, Shivrani Devi
1956 *Premchand Ghar meṅ*. Delhi: Atmaram.
Price, Pamela G.
1979 "Raja-dharma in 19th Century South India: Land, Litigation, and Largess in Ramnad Zamindari." *Contributions to Indian Sociology* 13:207-239.
Rousselet, Louis
1876 *India and Its Native Princes: Travels in Central India and the Presidencies of Bombay and Bengal*. Revised and edited by Lt. Col. Buckle. London: Chapman and Hall.
Russell, Ralph
1972 "Ghalib: A Self-Portrait." In *Ghalib: The Poet and His Age*. Ralph Russell, ed. London: George Allen & Unwin, Ltd.
Sharma, G.D.
1977 *Rajput Polity: A Study of Politics and Administration of the State of Marwar, 1638-1749*. Delhi: Manohar Publications.
Sherring, Herbert
1897 *The Mayo College, "The Eton of India": A Record of Twenty Years, 1875-1895*. 2 vols. Calcutta: Thacker, Spink, & Co.
Stein, Burton
1977 "The Segmentary State in South Indian History." In *Realm and Region in Traditional India*. Richard G. Fox, ed. Durham, N.C.: Duke University Program in Comparative Studies on Southern Asia.
1980 *Peasant State and Society in Medieval South India*. Delhi: Oxford University Press.
Swan, Robert O.
1969 *Muṇshi Premchand of Lamhi Village*. Durham: Duke University Press.
Thorner, Daniel
1965 "Feudalism in India." In *Feudalism in History*. Rushton Coulborn, ed. Hamden: Archon Books.

Vyas, R.P.
1969 *Role of Nobility in Marwar (1800-1873)*. New Delhi: Jain Brothers.
Wacziarg, Francis and Aman Nath
1982 *Rajasthan: The Painted Walls of Shekhavati*. New Delhi: Vikas.
Ziegler, Norman P.
1973 "Action, Power, and Service in Rajasthani Culture: A Social History of the Rajputs of Middle Period Rajasthan." Ph.D. dissertation, University of Chicago.

APPENDIX

CONTENTS OF VOLUME II

IDENTITY AS PROCESS

ART AS COMMUNICATION

NOTES ON CONTRIBUTORS

JAMES WARNER BJÖRKMAN, Ph.D. (Yale University), formerly Director of the American Studies Research Centre in Hyderabad, is now Professor of Public Policy and Administration at the Institute of Social Studies, The Hague, Netherlands. He has published extensively on Indian politics and comparative health policy. (Vol. II)

B.D. CHATTOPADHYAYA, M.A. (Calcutta University), Ph.D. (Cambridge University), is Professor of Ancient Indian History at the Centre for Historical Studies at Jawaharlal Nehru University. He is the author of *Coins and Currency Systems in South India* (1977, awarded the Prix Duchalais by the Institut de France in 1978), *A Survey of Historical Geography of Ancient India* (1984) and *Aspects of Rural Settlements and Rural Society in Early Medieval India* (1990), and the editor of D.D. Kosambi's *Indian Numismatics* (1981), *Essays on Early Indian Economic History* (1987), and (with B.M. Pande) *Archaeology and History: Essays in Memory of A. Ghosh* (1987). His current research focuses on the state and society in early medieval India. (Vol. II)

HET RAM CHATURVEDI (1932-1988), Ph.D. (Poona University), was Senior Fellow at the Centre for the Study of Developing Societies, Delhi, at the time of his demise. After graduating from Delhi University in 1952, he earned a Master of Social Work degree in 1955 at Baroda University and then an M.A. in Sociology in 1963 at Poona University. In 1966 he joined CSDS and in 1973 received his Ph.D. for a doctoral thesis published as *Bureaucracy and Local Community: Dynamics of Development*. A prolific writer of field reports and articles, he has also authored and/or edited three other books on citizen participation, rural development and Panchayati Raj. Known to his friends as 'Panditji', Chaturvedi was also a classical scholar of *Rāmāyaṇa* and *Mahābhārata*. (Vol. II)

VISHAKHA N. DESAI, Ph.D. (University of Michigan), is Director of the Asia Society Galleries in New York and Associate Professor of Asian Art at the University of Massachusetts, Boston. She has worked extensively on the political and literary context of Rajasthani painting and on the nature of Rajput-Mughal interactions as seen in the visual arts. She was principal organizer and author of the catalogue for the exhibition *Life at Court: Art for India's Rulers, 16th-19th Centuries* (1985). Her recent research projects include an exhibition of Asian portraits from the collection of the Museum of Fine Arts, Boston (1989-90), and an international exhibition of sculptures from the temples of North India which will take place in 1993. (Vol. I)

JOHN EMIGH, M.F.A., Ph.D. (Tulane University), is a director, playwright and performer, and Chair of the Theatre, Speech and Dance Department of Brown University. He has written on the masked theatre of New Guinea, Bali and Eastern India, as well as on contemporary Western theatre. Among his publications are *Masking and Playing: Studies in Mask Performance* (in press). He is currently involved in documenting the Bhand Pather theatre of Kashmir and the Prahlada Nataka of Orissa. He has served as Chairperson of the Asian Theatre Program of the American Theatre Association and of the Association for Asian Performance. (Vol. I)

ULRIKE EMIGH, M.A. (Brown University), was born in Stuttgart, Germany. She studied Classics and English at Heidelberg University and came to Brown University in 1982 on a Fulbright Fellowship. She has directed medieval and contemporary Western dramas and acted the role of Padmini in Girish Karnad's *Hayavadana*. In 1982-83 she worked with John Emigh on the research and documentation of theatrical traditions on Orissa and Rajasthan. (Vol. I)

JOAN L. ERDMAN, Ph.D. (University of Chicago), is Research Associate in the Committee on Southern Asian Studies at the University of Chicago and Professor of Anthropology in the Department of Liberal Education, Columbia College Chicago. Her research has focused on the social organization of Indian performing arts, arts patronage, and cultural policy in India. She is the author of *Patrons and Performers in Rajasthan: The Subtle Tradition* (1985), and the editor of and a contributor to *Arts*

Patronage in India: Methods, Motives and Markets (1991). She is currently working on a co-authored autobiography of actress Zohra Segal, and a book on the life and artistic achievement of dance choreographer Uday Shankar. (Vol. I)

HENRI-PAUL FRANCFORT, Docteur-ès-Lettres in Archaeology, is Directeur de Recherches at France's Centre National de la Recherche Scientifique, and Director of the Research Team on Irrigation and Settlement in Central Asia. His publications based on research in Afghanistan include *Les Fortifications en Asie Centrade de l'Age du Bornze à l'Èpoque Kouchane* (1979), *Fouilles d'Ai Khanoum III* (1984), *Les Palettes du Gandhara* (1979), and *Fouilles de Shortughai* (1989). In 1982, he founded the Indo-French Archaeological Mission, which worked for six years on the archaeology of the Ghaggar basin. He edited the Mission's first report, *Prospections Achéologiques au Nord-Ouest de l'Inde* (1985), and is currently preparing the final publication. (Vol. I)

ANNE-MARIE GASTON, D.Phil. (Oxford University), is a professional performer of the Bharata Natyam, Odissi and Kuchipudi styles of classical Indian dance. Under the stage name Anjali, she regularly performs in Canada, India, the United States and Europe. She is the author of *Śiva in Dance, Myth and Iconography* (1982). Her doctoral research centered on the sociology of Indian performing arts, and is being considered for two publications by Oxford University Press: *The Makers of Modern Bharata Natyam* and *Drumming for the Child God Kṛishna: Guru Purushottam Das and the Nathdvara Pakhavaj Tradition*. (Vol. I)

ANN GRODZINS GOLD, Ph.D. (University of Chicago), has done anthropological field work on Hindu pilgrimage, women's songs and stories, and Nath oral epics in Rajasthan's Ajmer District. Her first book, *Fruitful Journeys: The Ways of Rajasthani Pilgrims* (1988) received the Hans Rosenhaupt Memorial Book Award from the Woodrow Wilson Fellowship Foundation. A second book, *A Carnival of Parting* (forthcoming), is an annotated translation and interpretation of two related oral epics performed by a Rajasthani bard. She is currently completing a coauthored volume on women's lore and lives in rural North India and beginning a comparative research project on farmers and the environment in New York and Rajasthan. (Vol. I)

DANIEL GOLD, Ph.D. (University of Chicago), is Director of the South Asian Program and Associate Professor of South Asian Religions in the Department of Asian Studies at Cornell University. He has written *The Lord as Guru: Hindi Sants in North Indian Tradition* (1987) and *Comprehending the Guru: Toward a Grammar of Religious Perception* (1988). His current research interests include the relationships between religious imagination and literary form in India and the development of Nath tradition in Rajasthan. (Vol. II)

EDWARD S. HAYNES, M. Phil. (Jawaharlal Nehru University), Ph.D. (Duke University), is Associate Professor of History at Winthrop College, Rock Hill, South Carolina. He has served in teaching and research positions at Kansas State University, Skidmore College, the University of Northern Iowa, and Duke University. He is the author of a number of articles on the modern history of India, especially on Rajasthan and the Indian princely states. He is completing a manuscript entitled "Jagirdars and Government: Rajput Kingship and Kinship Polity in Alwar State Under British Paramountacy. 1775-1947." (Vol. II)

CAROL HENDERSON, Ph.D. (Columbia University), has taught Anthropology at Columbia University and Emory University. She had done field research in the Jodhpur district of Rajasthan. Her doctoral dissertation was entitled "Life in the Land of Death: Famines and Droughts in Arid Western Rajasthan." Forthcoming publications focus on desertification and human response to natural disasters. Her current research is on wool production in Rajasthan. (Vol. II)

PAULINE KOLENDA, Ph.D. (Cornell University), is Professor of Anthropology at the University of Houston. She has done ethnographic field work in Indian villages in Uttar Pradesh, Rajasthan and Tamil Nadu, and has written *Caste in Contemporary India* (1985). Many of her papers appear in *Regional Caste, Cult and Hierarchy* (1981) and *Regional Differences in Family Structure in India* (1987). (Vol. II)

KOMAL KOTHARI, M.A. (Calcutta University), was co-founde and is Director of Rupayan Sansthan (Rajasthan Institute of Folk lore), established in 1960 in the village of Borunda to collect, preserve and disseminate the oral traditions of Rajasthan. He has investigated and documented numerous Rajasthani folk traditions, given expert guidance to film makers, ethnomusicologists and other scholars, and has become known in international folklore study circles as a key source for the understanding of Indian folklore. Among his interests are folk professional musician communities, the relation between ecology and folk customs, and changes in patronage patterns since Indian independence. He has travelled abroad extensively to present Rajasthani folk artists and to deliver papers at scholarly conferences. He has received from the Government of India the honor of Padma Shri. He is the author of *Monograph on Langas* (1972) and a variety of articles on the folk arts, religion and literature of Rajasthan. For many years, he co-edited with Vijay Dan Detha the journal *Lok Sanskriti* (Folk Culture). (Vol. I)

DERYCK O. LODRICK, Ph.D. (University of California, Davis), was born in Ajmer, Rajasthan, and spent his early childhood in India. He was educated in England (Reading and St. Andrews) before completing graduate studies in Geography in the United States. His publications include *Sacred Cows, Sacred Places: Origins and Survivals of Animal Homes in India* (1981) and articles in geographical and anthropological journals focusing on the relations between religious values, behavior and the environment in South Asia. Ongoing research includes studies of animals and culture in South Asia, the cultural ecology of cattle-keeping in Rajasthan, and fairs and festivals of India. He is currently visiting Lecturer in the Department of Geography at the University of California, Davis, and a Research Associate of the Center for South Asia Studies at the University of California, Berkeley. (Vol.I)

MICHAEL W. MEISTER, Ph.D. (Harvard), is Professor of the History of Art and South Asia Regional Studies and Chair of the Graduate Group in Art History at the University of Pennsylvania. His research and publications have largely been on the symbolic morphology of the Indian temple. He has done field research in western and central India as well as in the Deccan and the south. He is general editor of the *Encyclopaedia of Indian Temple Architecture* (1983, 1986, 1988) and Curator of the South Asia Art

Archive at the University of Pennsylvania. Other edited volumes include *Discourses on Śiva* (1984) and *Making Things in South Asia: The Role of Artist and Craftsman* (1988). (Vol. I)

WILLIAM A. NOBLE, Ph.D. (Louisiana State University), was born in Nagarcoil, South India, and received his early education in Ootacamund. He is Associate Professor of Geography at the University of Missouri. His research has been in the prehistory and traditional peoples of the Nilgiri Hills of Tamil Nadu, the symbolic dimensions of sacred and folk architecture in India, and the memorialization and worship of *satīs*. His publications have appeared in geographical and anthropological journals, and in several edited volumes. He is currently working on a monograph on the momentous economic and technological changes which the Todas of the Nilgiri Hills have undergone since their first contact with the British in the early 1800s. (Vol. I)

R. THOMAS ROSIN, Ph.D. (University of California, Berkeley), is Professor of Anthropology at Sonoma State University in northern California. He has been researching the adaptive capabilities of the rural peoples of Rajasthan for the past 25 years. His major work is *Land Reform and Agrarian Change: Study of a Marwar Village from Raj to Swaraj* (1987). Other writings have appeared in anthropological journals and collections on India such as *American Studies in the Anthropology of India* (1979) and *Dimensions of Social Life* (1983). With photographer Gail Wread, he has presented several exhibits, which they plan to develop into an illustrated volume on the peoples of rural Rajasthan. (Vol. II)

LLOYD I. RUDOLPH, Ph.D. (Harvard), is Professor of Political Science and the Social Sciences at the University of Chicago. With his wife, Susanne Hoeber Rudolph, he is the author of *The Modernity of Tradition* (1967), *Education and Politics in India* (1972), *The Regional Imperative* (1980), *Gandhi* (1983), and *In Pursuit of Lakshmi: The Political Economy of the Indian State* (1987). He has edited and contributed to a book on cultural policy in India, and has contributed many articles on a wide range of subjects to scholarly journals and books in the United States, Britain and India. The Rudolphs have spent seven of their nine research years in India in Rajasthan, and they are the authors of

Essays on Rajputana: Reflections on History, Culture and Administration (1984).

AD RAM SANKHYAN, M.A. (School of Urban Planning, Punjab University), is completing a Ph.D. in the Department of Geography of Guru Nanak Dev University. He is currently Assistant Town Planner in the Town and Planning Organization for Himachal Pradesh, General Secretary of the Himachal Town Planners Association, and an Associate of India's Institute of Town Planners. He has been involved in the preparation of numerous development master plans for urban centers in Himachal Pradesh, and has contributed to the Uttar Pradesh Town and Country Planning Department's volume *Growth Centers in Jhansi-Lalitpur-Jalaun Region*. (Vol. I)

KARINE SCHOMER, Ph.D. (University of Chicago), formerly on the faculty of the Department of South and Southeast Asian Studies of the University of California at Berkeley, is now Dean of the School of Arts and Sciences at Golden Gate University, San Francisco. She has done field research on the *Ālhā* epic of North India, Rajasthani language and literature, and the modern Hindi literary community. She is the author of *Mahadevi Varma and the Chhayavad Age of Modern Hindi Poetry* (1983), and senior editor of *The Sants: Studies in a Devotional Tradition of India* (1987), and has contributed articles on the medieval, modern and folk literatures of the Hindi area and Rajasthan to scholarly journals and books. She was the founder and first president of the Rajasthan Studies Group of the Association for Asian Studies. Her current research interests include the preservation of Rajasthani culture among expatriates. (Vol. I)

FRANCES R. TAFT, M.A. (University of California, Berkeley), M.A. (Georgetown University), has research interests in the Rajput states during the Mughal and British periods. Her publications include an article on royal marriages in Rajasthan and forthcoming articles on rajas and *ṭhākurs* in Bikaner, the Shekhawati *ṭhikānās* of Jaipur, and the history of Mayo College, Ajmer. She is currently a Project Officer at the India Department of the World Bank. (Vol. II)

NORMAN P. ZIEGLER. Ph.D. (University of Chicago), has taught South Asian History at the University of Denver. He currently resides in Denver, where he works in a hospital while attending Nursing School. His doctoral research focused on the social and cultural history of the Rathor Rajputs of Marvar. His publications include articles in journals and in collected volumes such as *Kingship and Authority in South Asia* (1978). In collaboration with Richard Saran, he is the author of *Merto, Rajasthan, and Its Rulers, the Mertiyo Rathors* (forthcoming), a book of translations from 17th-century Marvari historical material, linguistic and historical annotations and biographical notes. (Vol. II)

INDEX

(Combined index for Vols. I and II)